THEORIES
OF
INTERNATIONAL RELATIONS

THE CENTURY POLITICAL SCIENCE SERIES

EDITED BY FREDERIC A. OGG, *University of Wisconsin*

VOLUMES PUBLISHED

Frederic A. Ogg and P. Orman Ray, INTRODUCTION TO AMERICAN GOVERNMENT and ESSENTIALS OF AMERICAN GOVERNMENT; Walter F. Dodd, STATE GOVERNMENT IN THE UNITED STATES; John M. Mathews, AMERICAN FOREIGN RELATIONS: CONDUCT AND POLICIES; Herbert Adams Gibbons, INTRODUCTION TO WORLD POLITICS; Pitman B. Potter, INTRODUCTION TO THE STUDY OF INTERNATIONAL ORGANIZATION; Graham H. Stuart, LATIN AMERICA AND THE UNITED STATES; Charles G. Fenwick, INTERNATIONAL LAW; Raymond G. Gettell, HISTORY OF POLITICAL THOUGHT and HISTORY OF AMERICAN POLITICAL THOUGHT; Thomas H. Reed, MUNICIPAL GOVERNMENT IN THE UNITED STATES; Lent D. Upson, THE PRACTICE OF MUNICIPAL ADMINISTRATION; Edward M. Sait, AMERICAN PARTIES AND ELECTIONS; John A. Fairlie and C. M. Kneier, COUNTY GOVERNMENT AND ADMINISTRATION; Harold S. Quigley, JAPANESE GOVERNMENT AND POLITICS; J. Mark Jacobson, THE DEVELOPMENT OF AMERICAN POLITICAL THOUGHT; Francis W. Coker, RECENT POLITICAL THOUGHT; Andrew C. McLaughlin, CONSTITUTIONAL HISTORY OF THE UNITED STATES; Frank M. Russell, THEORIES OF INTERNATIONAL RELATIONS.

VOLUMES IN PREPARATION

Edward S. Corwin, CONSTITUTIONAL LAW OF THE UNITED STATES; Edward M. Sait, OUTLINES OF POLITICS; William Y. Elliott, PRINCIPLES OF POLITICAL SCIENCE; William S. Carpenter, COMPARATIVE GOVERNMENT; James K. Pollock, COMPARATIVE PARTY POLITICS; Joseph P. Chamberlain, LEGISLATIVE PROCESSES: NATIONAL AND STATE; Thomas H. Reed, MUNICIPAL GOVERNMENT IN EUROPE; Charles Seymour, EUROPEAN DIPLOMACY SINCE 1914; Edwin M. Borchard, HISTORY OF AMERICAN DIPLOMACY; J. R. Hayden, COLONIAL GOVERNMENT AND ADMINISTRATION; Stanley K. Hornbeck, AMERICAN INTERESTS AND POLITICS IN THE FAR EAST; Denys P. Myers, INTERNATIONAL RELATIONS; Charles G. Fenwick, THE FOREIGN POLICY OF THE UNITED STATES.

OTHER VOLUMES TO BE ARRANGED

THEORIES
OF
INTERNATIONAL RELATIONS

By

FRANK M. RUSSELL

PROFESSOR OF POLITICAL SCIENCE
UNIVERSITY OF CALIFORNIA

D. APPLETON-CENTURY COMPANY
INCORPORATED

NEW YORK LONDON

PRINTED IN THE UNITED STATES OF AMERICA.

PREFACE

The literature of international relations has expanded greatly within recent years. Many stout volumes, as well as innumerable monographs and articles dealing with various aspects of international law and relations, have served to open up this *terra incognita* to students and scholars if not to the man in the street. Several excellent surveys intended to acquaint the general reader or the less advanced student with the elements of international politics and with the current problems of international relations have appeared since the World War. Moreover, there have been a number of treatises on international law, volumes dealing with diplomacy and foreign policy, and studies of nationalism, imperialism, international organization, and international administration.

The present volume represents a new approach. It is designed to do for the field of international relations what historical surveys of political theory have done for the entire field of political thought. Up to the present there has been no survey of the development of man's ideas concerning the relationship of independent political communities. Works embracing the field of political theory in general have either ignored or treated inadequately this important area of political and social relationships. It is true that certain writers in the field of international relations, as well as many in international law, have made valuable contributions to various phases of international political thought. For example, Christian Lange, in his *Histoire de l'Internationalisme* (Christiania, 1919) and in his *Histoire de la Doctrine Pacifique* (Paris, 1927), has made a signal contribution to pacifist and internationalist thought. And as regards the development of ideas of international organization, Jacob ter Meulen's two volumes, *Der Gedanke der Internationalen Organisation in Seiner Entwicklung* (The Hague, 1917-1929) are likewise excellent. Others, as well, might be mentioned, such as F. Laurent's *Histoire du Droit des Gens et des Relations Internationales: Études sur l'Histoire de l'Humanité*, 18 vols. (Brussels, 1861-1870); A. C. F. Beale's *The History of Peace* (London and New York, 1931); and F. M. Stawell's suggestive little volume in the Home University Library series, *The Growth of International Thought* (New York and London, 1930). However, there is no book in any language, as far as I know, that attempts to present from the earliest times, and in the light of environmental influences, the more significant ideas, whatever their character or implications may be, that men have entertained concerning international relations. The author, although painfully aware of the shortcomings of his own effort in this direction, and cognizant of the fact that others in the field who might have set their hand to this task could have done it better than he, hopes that his own venture may be regarded as not altogether unworthy. Moreover, he dares to believe that, for the thoughtful reader, it may contribute toward the attainment of a better perspective in the field of international relations.

It is a pleasure to record my gratitude to those who have aided me in one way or another in bringing this work to completion. My wife has stood by at all times to render needed assistance. Professor Frederic A. Ogg, general editor of the Century Political Science Series, has gone over the manuscript and made many valuable suggestions to improve the style. He and the officials of the D. Appleton-Century Company with whom I have dealt have been most courteous and helpful at all times. Eleanor van Horn, Assistant in the Bureau of International Relations at the University of California, has, in the midst of numerous and exacting duties, labored hard and long to save me from as many errors as humanly possible in connection with the preparation of the manuscript for publication, and has given me invaluable assistance throughout. Mr. A. Manell, one of my graduate students, has done me a great service in checking the page proofs and in preparing the index.

FRANK MARION RUSSELL

BERKELEY, CALIFORNIA.

CONTENTS

Appendix I

Appendix II

Appendix III

Appendix IV

THEORIES OF INTERNATIONAL RELATIONS

CHAPTER I

INTRODUCTION: PRIMITIVE MAN AND INTER-GROUP RELATIONSHIPS

UNTIL recently, political philosophers and theorists have, with few important exceptions, dealt with the subject of international relationships only incidentally. Their attention has been focused chiefly upon questions concerning the origin, nature, and justification of the state, the source of political authority, and the organization and functions of government. That this has been true need occasion no surprise. Until the nineteenth century, conditions were not conducive, except at particular periods in limited areas, to the elaboration of a theory of international relations. A world made up of relatively isolated and, for the most part, largely self-contained states, with vast cultural if not racial differences, did not furnish the physical foundation, at any rate, upon which to build a realistic theory of international solidarity. With the industrial revolution, however, forces were set in motion which were to broaden and multiply the contacts of sovereign states and provide the conditions for continuous and fruitful international intercourse and likewise for harmful collision. The industrial revolution led to an enormous increase in economic productivity and, along with the development of rapid transportation on land and water and eventually instantaneous communication over great areas, to the development of a world-wide commerce. On the other hand, the invention of new weapons of tremendous destructive power, for use on land and sea and in the air, revolutionized warfare and made it increasingly costly and devastating. These developments, and a world war that shook the foundations of the civilized world, have finally pushed problems of international relations to the front and compelled attention to them.

It is also to be noted that, almost up to the present time, theories of international relations have been concerned to a very considerable extent with the most disturbing element in the relationship of organized independent communities, i.e., war. Even among primitive peoples, as we shall see, notions were developed as to its justification, as to the manner in which it should be conducted, and the circumstances under which it should be terminated. Today war brings in its train such evil consequences to victors and vanquished alike that less thought is being given to the formulation of "rules of war" than formerly, and more attention to the building of an organized world community. Nevertheless, until states perfect alternative methods of adjusting their differences, abandon the principle of self-help, and "outlaw" violence as they have done within their borders, international political thought must continue to concern itself with war as the central problem, and be conditioned by the necessity of devising institutions to control it.

International political thought in the strict sense may be regarded as including the reflections, speculations, ideas, and conclusions of men concerning the interrelations of the national states composing the modern international community. Broadly speaking, however, international political thought is as old as the existence of separate independent political communities, whether primitive tribes or ancient city-states and empires. Many of the institutions, practices, and ideas bearing on present-day international relations, commonly regarded as originating in the early modern period in Western Europe, were known to the ancients and were to be found in rudimentary form even among primitive peoples.[1] Anyone attempting, therefore, to deal with the development of international political thought for purposes of orientation and perspective cannot afford to neglect altogether the thought of primitive and ancient peoples as revealed chiefly, in their customs, practices, and institutions.

The life of prehistoric man is, and is likely to remain, a closed book, or at best a matter of speculation. The earliest humans did not chronicle their adventures, nor did they fashion tools or weapons. The guesses that scientists make today as to what they were like and what they did, are based, in part, upon scattered and fragmentary remains

[1] S. A. Korff, "An Introduction to the History of International Law," *American Journal of International Law,* XVIII (1924), 246-247. Paul Vinogradoff, *Outlines of Historical Jurisprudence,* 2 vols. (London, 1920-22), Vol. I, Ch. X. Some writers deny that international law was known to the ancient world. For example, see F. Laurent, *Histoire de Droit des Gens et des Relations Internationales: Études Sur l'Histoire de l'Humanité,* 18 vols. (Brussels, 1861-70), Vol. I, Ch. I.

left not by them but by their distant descendants, and upon a study of the habits of animals supposed to be nearest to man in the scale of life. More extensive studies have likewise been made of present-day primitives, who, though they are much farther advanced than prehistoric man, may afford some clue to the nature and social characteristics of our early ancestors.

Despite the poverty of evidence concerning prehistoric man, the majority of writers who have speculated on the subject do not paint a flattering portrait of him. Lagorgette, after remarking that primitive man was unacquainted with labor, knew no society, and had no moral code, says further that to these defects "he added a ferocity and aggressiveness, a lust for violence, which led him to commit the most useless cruelties, and to appeal to arms to settle the slightest quarrel."[2] Another writer also asserts quite positively that in all savage races the rule of force existed unadulterated, and that only after the advent of civilization was primitive violence somewhat mitigated.[3] Still others, without necessarily sharing completely this view of man's innate human pugnacity, subscribe to the opinion that frequent conflict was in the nature of things more or less characteristic of the early stages of human development. Ratzenhofer, for example, points out that in the early stages of culture, before inter-tribal trade developed, war was almost the only form of contact between alien groups.[4]

Other writers have emphasized fear rather than ferocity as an important factor making for conflict between early primitive groups, asserting that when hordes came into contact they fell into a frenzy of fear and terror from which bloodshed was likely to result.[5] The view that primitive man in any case was predisposed toward violence has also received support from psychologists on the basis of observation of his civilized descendants. The wars of civilized societies, for example, are from this point of view reversions to a primordial animal-human type of behavior. They furnish a desired relaxation from the restraints of civilization, for, as expressed by Nietzsche, "men have always wanted

[2] *Le Rôle de la Guerre* (Paris, 1906), p. 53.

[3] Raoul de la Grasserie, "The Evolution of Civil Law," in Kocourek and Wigmore, comps., *Formative Influences of Legal Development* (Boston, 1918), p. 649.

[4] *Wesen und Zweck der Politik* (Leipzig, 1893), p. 9.

[5] A. W. Small, "Types of Conflict Situations," in Park and Burgess, *Introduction to the Science of Sociology* (Chicago, 1921), p. 586. See also L. R. Aldrich, *The Primitive Mind and Modern Civilization* (London, 1931), Ch. XII.

not peace but battle." [6] Whenever the restraints of civilization are removed, the fighting instinct breaks out with slight stimulus.[7]

These views have been challenged vigorously within recent years on several grounds. How, it is asked, can it be known with such certainty and precision what man was like several hundred thousand years ago, in view of the fact that no actual evidence is available? [8] On the other hand, it is asserted that there is indirect and circumstantial evidence sufficient to refute the claim that man was at first dominated by a fighting instinct and only gradually and imperfectly brought it under control with the growth of civilization. Man is not "an animal with a musket." His nearest animal relatives, the anthropoid apes, are not combative by nature. Vacher de Lapouge points out that neither collective violence nor individual murder are found among them, and that the criminal instinct "appears to be developed in a measure as our species has disengaged itself from the rest of the animal kingdom. Murder and war . . . are human acts and not the atavistic legacies of far distant ancestors." [9]

That violent human behavior and war came with the development of civilization rather than in the earlier stages of man's life on the planet, is asserted also by the English scientist, W. J. Perry,[10] who remarks: "The prehistoric food-gatherers of Europe—the men of the Old Stone Age—do not seem to have been concerned with combat. They do not appear to have made weapons of stone. They may, of course, have made them of wood; but it is hardly likely that, since they were masters of stone-working, they would have failed to make serviceable weapons for combat if they needed them. . ." Perry also cites the apparent absence of special weapons for fighting among other early peoples, and draws the conclusion that the "bloody savage" view cannot be sustained: "Are we thus to look back into a Golden Age of peace, when violence was practically absent from human relations? I see no other interpretation of the facts. It may be admitted that occasional violence was present, but it

[6] G. T. W. Patrick, "The Psychology of War," *Popular Science Monthly*, LXXXVII (1915), 166-168.

[7] H. R. Marshall, *War and the Ideal of Peace* (New York, 1915), pp. 96-110.

[8] G. Nasmyth, *Social Progress and the Darwinian Theory* (New York, 1916), p. 157.

[9] *Les Sélections Sociales* (Paris, 1896), p. 209. See also G. Ratzenhofer, *Die Sociologische Erkenntniss* (Leipzig, 1898), p. 133; Nasmyth, *op. cit.*, p. 164; G. M. Stratton, *Social Psychology of International Conduct* (New York, 1929), p. 231.

[10] *The Growth of Civilization* (London, 1924), pp. 191-197.

certainly was not enough to cause men to make special weapons for the purpose of fighting as they did later on." According to the same writer's view, war arose along with the development of the institution of private property, and the rise of ruling groups seeking greater power. It increased in frequency once it became established in human society due to a variety of causes associated with the fears and ambitions and rivalries of ruling aristocracies.[11]

Another adherent of this view holds, in language reminiscent of Rousseau, that although "all men will fight in defence of their lives and for the safeguarding of their families," the necessity for doing so has arisen as a result of a "departure from the original Arcadian manner of living." Man is innately peaceful, but civilization has brought strains and stresses which prevent the true expression of his nature. "Most of the friction and discords of our lives are obviously the result of such exasperations and conflicts as civilization itself creates."[12]

Other writers taking a similar position base their contentions on the actual observations that have been made of behavior of primitive peoples in different parts of the world. The testimony of the Norwegian explorer, Dr. Nansen, is cited to show that ferocity is not ingrained in man and that violence is no necessary characteristic of human existence. Fighting and brutality, according to Nansen, are unknown, and murder is very rare, among the Greenlanders. To them war is "incomprehensible and repulsive, a thing for which their language has no word. . ."[13] Westermarck,[14] and Davie,[15] although taking the position that the number of primitive peoples living in a continual state of war outnumber those which are peaceful, give a number of instances of tribes which maintain amicable relations with their neighbors, and a few which carry their pacifism to the length of non-resistance when injured.

Nevertheless, it seems to be true that most of the primitive peoples whose manners and customs have been observed or studied, know war

[11] *Ibid.* See also Havelock Ellis, *The Philosophy of Conflict* (Boston, 1919), p. 42, and R. M. MacIver, *The Modern State* (Oxford, 1926), pp. 241-242, for substantially the same view.

[12] G. Elliott Smith, *Human History* (New York, 1929), p. 174.

[13] *Eskimo Life* (London, 1893), p. 162.

[14] *The Origin and Development of the Moral Ideas,* 2 vols. (New York, 1906-1908), I, 334-336.

[15] *The Evolution of War* (New Haven, Conn., 1929), pp. 48-49. See R. Holsti, *The Relation of War to the Origin of the State* (Helsingfors, 1913), pp. 70-75, for collected testimony of numerous authorities as to the peaceable character of many primitive communities.

and evince a disposition not infrequently to employ it. How is this to be explained? The upholders of the "gentle savage" thesis reply that in many instances these peoples have been corrupted by unhappy contacts with civilized peoples, that they have developed a militant character as a result of the aggressive actions of civilized visitors, the introduction of firearms, and the resultant disruption of their life.[16]

The character of warfare as observed among various primitive communities, and the expedients used to overcome the reluctance of those expected to engage in it, have also been advanced as evidence that there is no natural urge in men to fight and that the asserted ferocity of primitive tribes is the exception rather than the rule. It is pointed out, for example, that in many cases savages have to be prodded and stimulated in one way or another before they can work up the necessary enthusiasm for combat.[17] Thus they are abused or ridiculed by their women who call them cowards if they do not exhibit a belligerent spirit, and in some instances their women folk accompany them to the battlefield in order to spur them on by visible evidence of continued moral support. Before the battle, oratorical appeals are usually made to the perhaps not altogether happy warriors, reminding them of the bravery of their ancestors, telling them they are fighting for their wives and children, for the honor of the tribe, and suggesting also that cowardice will result in punishment.[18] On the other hand, marks of distinction and rewards will be bestowed upon them if they are brave—perhaps the right to wear an ostrich feather, or to marry.[19]

Religious superstition, it is pointed out, also often plays a part in the attainment of martial ardor. Perhaps it is believed that some deity

[16] R. Holsti, *op. cit.*, pp. 94-102, cites a number of authorities who offer various explanations for the development of war among these peoples, none of which have their foundations in a fighting instinct.

[17] The war dance, found among nearly all savage peoples, is for the purpose of getting the support of the gods in the coming struggle with the enemy, and to work the dancers up to such a frenzy that they will rush into battle and show no mercy. L. Havemeyer, *The Drama of Savage Peoples* (New Haven, Conn., 1916), pp. 157-158.

[18] R. H. Lowie, *Primitive Society* (New York, 1920), p. 356, says that "the Plains Indian fought not for territorial aggrandizement nor for the victor's spoils, but above all because fighting was a game worth while because of the social recognition it brought when played according to the rules." This writer also makes the following interesting generalization (p. 357): "Primitive man is not a miser nor a sage nor a beast of prey, but, in Tarde's happy phrase, a peacock."

[19] R. Holsti, *op. cit.*, p. 58, quotes from the declamation of a chief who suggested to the young warriors that it would be "far better to die in war than to live to be assassinated at home or to die of a lingering disease."

can be propitiated only by the slaughter of tribal enemies, and will support the warriors in the undertaking. The latter also are taught that the souls of brave warriors will spend an eternity in dancing, feasting, and experiencing all kinds of bliss; the souls of cowards, on the other hand, will be doomed to wander about in regions of darkness and encounter all manner of hardships.[20]

Although the use of such stimuli is common where fighting is more deadly, primitive warfare in general consists chiefly in shouting and attempting to terrify the enemy rather than in serious fighting. In some cases, in fact, there is no bloodshed at all, the opposing groups satisfying their martial ardor with threats and vociferations, and speeches of defiance. In others, the fighting is confined to individuals selected from the opposing tribes. In instances in which actual fighting is started, it often ceases when some one on either side is wounded or killed.[21] As a matter of fact, there is much testimony to the effect that the warfare of simple societies is often largely ceremonious in character, and therefore relatively innocuous.[22] Altogether there is considerable evidence of this character to sustain the position of those who contend that uncivilized man was essentially peaceful, or at least to cast considerable doubt on the opposite and more generally accepted thesis that he was by nature predisposed to slaughter. As one writer [23] reminds us, if men were wholly unsocial, war, which requires group cooperation and individual sacrifice on behalf of the community, could never have arisen. Men could have engaged in single combat only.

Nevertheless it is not to be denied that certain characteristics of human nature, working under the environmental influences that in general seem to have obtained among primitive groups, furnished the conditions under which war might, and did, grow. As Stratton [24] has pointed out, man is a creature with innate desires and is also endowed with impulses to action to achieve these desires, whether for food or drink or glory. He is also subject to the passions of anger and fear when these desires are thwarted or their realization endangered, and

[20] *Ibid.*, pp. 48-52, 57.
[21] Deniker, *Les Races et Peuples de la Terre* (Paris, 1900), pp. 305 *ff.*, cited in Holsti, *op. cit.*, p. 39. See also M. R. Davie, *op. cit.*, Appendix C, for a number of instances of mild warfare among primitive peoples, gathered from different parts of the world.
[22] W. H. R. Rivers, ed., *Psychology and Ethnology* (London, 1926), pp. 295-296.
[23] G. M. Stratton, *op. cit.*, p. 243.
[24] *Ibid.*, pp. 237-241.

capable of developing hatred toward the object of his anger. But he is also a gregarious creature, endowed with strong cooperative instincts which may become dominant under environmental conditions, such as obtained among the Greenlanders.[25] Nature may lay a hand upon human nature, stifle violent impulses, and prevent the development of war altogether. But such conditions were doubtless rather exceptional in primitive communities. Hobhouse[26] is probably not far wrong when he says: "To represent primitive man as in a state of perpetual warfare with his fellows is, indeed, a gross exaggeration. . . The actual frequency and seriousness of warfare, of course, vary very greatly, according to the more or less martial character of the people, their geographical conditions, and economic circumstances."

It is also to be observed that, contrary to the popular notion, warfare among primitive peoples is frequently carried on under certain rules and with certain restrictions which, in some instances, bear a striking resemblance to the laws of war supposed to obtain among civilized peoples in modern times. Observations of the customs of primitive peoples in different parts of the world reveal that many tribes do not attack one another without first making a declaration of war through a messenger or in some conspicuous manner. In some instances, several days must elapse between the quarrel and the opening of warfare. Grievances may be stated and an ultimatum delivered which, if complied with, may result in the maintenance of peace. In east equatorial Africa, for example, the chief of a tribe, deciding the time has come for war or a composition of differences with a neighboring tribe, sends an ambassador bearing a leaden bullet and a hoe to the chief of the latter. If the chief selects the bullet, war ensues; if he chooses the hoe, he thereby signifies his desire to enter into peace negotiations.[27]

Some of the more advanced primitive peoples not only follow the chivalrous practice of notifying the enemy before beginning hostilities,

[25] The population of Greenland was scattered, small, and altogether engrossed in the difficult task of winning a livelihood from an inhospitable environment. Cooperation in the struggle for existence was indispensable to survival; wrangling and warfare would have been fatal.

[26] *Morals in Evolution* (New York, 1906), p. 234.

[27] M. R. Davie, *op. cit.*, pp. 292-296. Among many interesting ceremonies cited by Davie in connection with the declaration of war is that followed by certain South African tribes. The members of different tribes have special kinds of hair coiffures designed to distinguish the members of one tribe from those of another. If trouble develops, and a messenger is sent home with his hair cut, it is taken as a declaration of war.

but have rules tending to mitigate the harshness and cruelty of war. In many instances, as has already been pointed out, warfare is more of a ceremony than a deadly armed contest. In addition, certain rules of the game are observed by various tribes that take their warfare seriously. Some follow the practice of sparing women and children. In other instances, the use of poisoned weapons is forbidden. In still others, the starving out of an enemy is not allowed. The custom is widespread, among primitive peoples, of holding the persons of messengers and ambassadors of enemy tribes inviolate while they are performing their duties, and of respecting flags of truce. It is the practice in some tribes, also, to differentiate between combatants and non-combatants or neutrals and to grant the latter immunity from attack. In some cases this practice is extended to cultivators of the soil. Agreements between primitive tribes are also known, in which certain territory is marked off as neutral and within which no fighting may take place. Treaties following the suspension of hostilities are usually surrounded by solemn ceremonies and followed with feasting, dancing, and public games. Such testimony as we have indicates that in general such treaties of peace are faithfully kept.[28] Altogether, as Hobhouse remarks, in war savages and barbaric men at their best are better than civilized men at their worst.[29]

Certain additional observations concerning inter-group relationships, in primitive society, may be offered. With the attainment of group consciousness and solidarity, and a settled abode, the sentiment of patriotism arises. It is made up of a deep attachment for the individual's own group, a love of his native place, and the mores of his group which he associates with this place.[30] In fact, there is reason to suppose that the sentiment is likely to be purer and more spontaneous in such a group than it normally is in modern national states. In the latter, the individual citizens have various economic interests, some of which even lie far beyond the borders of the state. They profess different religious faiths, and, in peace times, have a number of competing loyalties of one kind or another. Furthermore, as a result of relatively easy communication and travel, an awareness and appreciation of other peoples is possible. In primitive communities, the individual is merged in the group,

[28] *Ibid.*, pp. 176-195. L. T. Hobhouse, *op. cit.*, Ch. VI.
[29] *Op. cit.*, p. 243.
[30] E. A. Westermarck, *op. cit.*, II, 167-168.

with rights and duties only as a member of his group,[31] and with no interests beyond it. The relatively small size and homogeneous character of these communities made for greater intimacy and cohesion, and their social isolation from one another helped to deepen the attachment of the members of each group to it, and to aggravate their fear and distrust or, at any rate, ignorance of foreigners, and feeling of superiority to them.[32]

The notion of the superiority of one's own group, so prevalent among the citizens of modern civilized nations, was naturally common, perhaps universal, among uncivilized peoples. It has even been observed that latter-day primitives often show astonishment at the manner of white visitors. They regard the latter as distinctly inferior to themselves, and do not always hesitate to say so. The Eskimos, for example, are said to entertain the belief that God made a failure of his first attempt to create a man. He therefore rejected it and called it a white man. The next day he tried again and succeeded in making a perfect man—an Eskimo! [33]

One would hardly expect anything in the nature of an international law of peace over any considerable area to grow up, considering the relatively unimportant and infrequent contacts of most uncivilized peoples, and the rigid exclusiveness that characterizes most primitive communities. Nevertheless there are many instances of peaceful inter-group intercourse, of practices designed to further that intercourse, and even of well-developed institutions of cooperation among certain advanced primitives. The growth of the practice of marriage outside the group under treaties of *connubium* helped to bind separate groups together and enable them to live in peace, cooperate in the struggle for existence, and overmatch the strength of intramarrying groups.[34] Likewise, treaties

[31] If he wrongs some one in another group, his own must assume a collective responsibility for his act; if he is wronged by a member of another group, the entire group is held accountable for the misdeeds of its member and a blood feud may result. Lowie, *op. cit.*, p. 399.

[32] It must not be supposed that no amicable intercourse occurred between primitive communities. The institution of guest friendship is found among practically all primitive peoples. It required a visiting stranger to be treated with kindness, given food, shelter, and protection during the period of his stay. See Westermarck, *op. cit.*, I, 570-576, and E. E. Hoyt, *Primitive Trade, Its Psychology and Economics* (London, 1926), pp. 126-130. For other forms of peaceful intercourse, see *ibid.*, pp. 13-14.

[33] Westermarck, *op. cit.*, II, 171.

[34] This reminds one of the common practice of matrimonial alliances between the ruling houses of civilized European states. Davie, *op. cit.*, p. 197, notes, among other specific instances of the practice of endogamy between primitive clans and

of *commercium* or trade, providing for mutually beneficial inter-group exchange, were entered into as primitive tribes came to realize its advantages as an alternative to the costs and hazards of plundering expeditions and war. Instances are even on record showing that tribes possessing stone quarries or other natural deposits freely accorded outsiders the privilege of entering the area of the deposits and taking what they needed [35] without molestation. Finally, instances of treaties between semi-primitive and ancient peoples, for the mutual extradition of criminals or deserters, have been recorded.[36] Perhaps the farthest advance made politically by any primitive people was that of the Iroquois Indians in the seventeenth century, when five tribes, still in the hunter stage, formed a confederacy for the purpose of securing peace among themselves and enabling them to control or absorb surrounding tribes and build up an Indian empire.[37] The government of the League was organized and administered on the same principles that obtained in the case of each nation. The League did not destroy the autonomy of the several tribes, but provided for a central control of external relations. Once a year, or oftener, sachems from the different tribes met in council to legislate for the confederacy. They sent and received embassies, arranged alliances with outside tribes, admitted new members, and decided questions of peace and war. This inter-tribal confederacy operated with remarkable success over a long period, finally succumbing before the advance of the white men.[38]

The observations that have been made concerning the external relations and ideas of primitive groups are not intended as generalizations from which deductions can be drawn of validity for all primitive peoples. Different primitives, under the necessity of adapting themselves to varying environments, show marked differences in social customs and group reactions. Whatever may have been true of the habits and proclivities of our prehistoric ancestors, the relatively advanced primitives of the historic period, whose lives have been reconstructed or observed,

tribes, the following passage from the history of the Israelites: "Then will we give our daughters unto you, and we will take your daughters to us, and we will dwell with you, and we will become one people."

[35] Davie, *op cit.*, Ch. XV.

[36] For example, the Pharaoh Rameses II entered into a treaty with the Hittites about 1272 B.C., providing for the mutual extradition of deserters to their original home unharmed. J. H. Breasted, *History of Egypt* (New York, 1905), pp. 437-438.

[37] Lewis H. Morgan, *League of the Iroquois* (New York, 1904), pp. 54, 57.

[38] *Ibid.*, pp. 62-63, 72-73.

have been found in some cases to be highly competitive and militant, and, in others, of a cooperative and pacific disposition. Among some a spirit of group individualism and independence is pronounced, and peaceful contacts with other groups relatively rare. In others, a less exclusive and more tolerant temper, or a more progressive spirit, leads to the development of commercial relationships of some importance and even to the voluntary formation of political unions.

The international political thought of primitives must, for the most part, be gleaned from their inter-group practices and institutions rather than from their discourses. The ancient peoples, however, with whom the following chapters will deal, speak not only through their institutions, but also in the recorded utterances and the disquisitions of their wise men.

REFERENCES

Aldrich, C. R., *The Primitive Mind and Modern Civilization* (London, 1931), Ch. XII, esp. pp. 103-107, 189-199.

Boas, F., Article on "Anthropology," *Encyclopaedia of the Social Sciences,* II, 73-110, and bibliography.

Davie, M. R., *The Evolution of War* (New Haven, Conn., 1929).

Ellis, Havelock, *The Philosophy of Conflict* (Boston, 1919), Ch. VI.

Fairchild, H. P., *Foundations of Social Life* (New York, 1927).

Ferrero, G., *Militarism* (Boston, 1903), Ch. II.

Havemeyer, L., *The Drama of Savage Peoples* (New Haven, Conn., 1916), Ch. VI.

Hobhouse, L. T., *Morals in Evolution* (New York, 1906), Ch. VI.

————, Wheeler, C. C., and Ginsberg, M., *The Material Culture and Social Institutions of the Simpler Peoples* (London, 1915).

Holsti, R., *The Relation of War to the Origin of the State* (Helsingfors, 1913), Chs. II-V.

Hoyt, E. E., *Primitive Trade; Its Psychology and Economics* (London, 1926), pp. 125-136.

James, E. O., *Primitive Ritual and Belief* (London, 1917), Ch. VI.

Kanter, E., *The Evolution of War* (Chicago, 1927).

Korff, S. A., "An Introduction to the History of International Law," *American Journal of International Law,* XVIII (1924), 246-259.

Kropotkin, P., *Mutual Aid a Factor of Evolution* (London, 1904), Ch. III.

Lagorgette, J., *Le Rôle de la Guerre* (Paris, 1906).

Letourneau, C., *La Guerre dans les Diverses Races Humaines* (Paris, 1895).

Lowie, R. H., *Primitive Society* (New York, 1920).

Massingham, H. J., *Downland Man* (New York, 1926), Chs. I, XI.
Macklin, J. M., *An Introduction to Social Ethics* (New York, 1920), Chs. VII-X.
Morgan, L. H., *The League of the Iroquois* (New York, 1904).
———, *Ancient Society* (New York, 1907), Ch. V.
Myers, P. V. N., *History as Past Ethics* (Boston, 1913), Ch. XVIII *et passim.*
Nansen, F., *Eskimo Life* (London, 1893).
Nasmyth, G. W., *Social Progress and the Darwinian Theory* (London, 1916), Chs. I-V.
Nicolai, G. F., *The Biology of War* (New York, 1918), Ch. I.
Novicow, J., *La Critique du Darwinisme Social* (Paris, 1910)
———, *Les Luttes Entre Sociétés* (Paris, 1904).
Perry, W. J., "An Ethnological Study of Warfare," *Memoirs and Proceedings, Manchester Literary and Philosophical Society,* 1917.
———, *The Children of the Sun* (London, 1923), Ch. XI.
———, *The Growth of Civilization* (London, 1924).
Radin, P., *Primitive Man as Philosopher* (New York, 1927).
Reclus, E., *Primitive Folk* (London, 1891).
Smith, G. Elliott, *Human History* (New York, 1929), Chs. V-VII.
Sorokin, P. A., *Contemporary Sociological Theories* (London, 1928).
Steinmetz, R., *Die Philosophie des Krieges* (Leipzig, 1907).
Stratton, G. M., *Social Psychology of International Conduct* (New York, 1929), Chs. XVIII-XXI.
Sumner, W. G., *War and Other Essays* (New Haven, Conn., 1911).
Todd, A. J., *Theories of Social Progress* (New York, 1918), pp. 294-298.
Vaccaro, M., *Les Bases Sociologiques* (Paris, 1898).
Westermarck, E. A., *The Origin and Development of the Moral Ideas,* 2 vols. (New York, 1906-1908), I, 331-370; II, 167-185.
Wingfield-Stratford, Esmé, *They That Take the Sword* (New York, 1931), Ch. III.

CHAPTER II

ANCIENT CHINA

PERHAPS the outstanding fact in the history of ancient China, from the point of view of the growth of interstate ideas and relationships, was the development of a great empire in virtually complete isolation from other civilized states. For a long period China had no contact with other great civilizations. Even India seems to have been for centuries unknown to her. Her contacts were exclusively with the "barbarians" on her borders, peoples obviously far inferior to her in culture, and whom she fought off, absorbed, or reduced to vassalage. Thus, although there were, of course, actual limits to their control, it was natural for the Chinese to regard the emperor as ruling the entire world by the decree of Heaven. For the same reason, foreign affairs were not considered of much importance and were given slight attention in the organization of the administrative services of the empire.[1]

The attitude of the rulers of the Chou dynasty toward the border peoples and, in fact, toward all foreigners, was frankly different from that shown toward Chinese and those who had become assimilated to Chinese ways. Confucius is said to have lent the weight of his authority to this attitude, and to have remarked: "It is advisable to treat in a barbarous way those feudal lords who perform barbarous rites and ceremonies; and to treat in a Chinese way those barbarians who have become Chinese."[2] Apparently, if one may judge from this quotation, the Chinese did not take the attitude that once a barbarian, always a barbarian. A barbarian people, in their view, seems to have been one which had not developed a high culture such as the Chinese possessed, rather than a people innately and therefore permanently inferior.[3]

[1] F. Hirth, *The Ancient History of China* (New York, 1911), pp. 111-112. The theories of interstate conduct which arose during the period of the Chou dynasty (about 1122 B.C.-249 B.C.) had their origin in the struggles and adjustments among the Chinese states, especially during the period of the decline and eventual impotence of the central authority.

[2] H. F. McNair, "Some Observations on China's International Relations," *Journal of the North China Branch of the Royal Asiatic Society*, LVI (1925), 8.

[3] It is also to be noted that the Chinese did not always assume an attitude

What was meant by the "barbarous way" in which these backward peoples were to be treated? As one might expect, the restraints and amenities existing between the great vassals of the empire in their dealings with one another, were not observed toward the barbarians except as policy might dictate forbearance or leniency in particular cases. Thus, when the Tartars on one occasion sought a treaty of peace and amity and asked to be accepted as vassals of the Duke of Ch'in, he is said to have replied that they were barbarous savages and natural enemies and that war should be their portion. They were later accepted as vassals on the advice of the Duke's minister, apparently as a matter of policy.[4] A common device, also used effectively by Imperial Rome, was to divide the barbarians, and, wherever possible, play one against another. This policy of "divide and rule" took the form of granting temporary concessions to certain tribes and proceeding vigorously against others. Whatever lenient treatment was accorded, however, was a means to an end—that of keeping the surrounding world of barbarism in a state of subjection and impotence, wherever assimilation was not possible.[5]

No systematic and comprehensive theory of interstate relations was developed in ancient China. However, during the Golden Age of Chinese philosophy from about 530 B.C. to 23 B.C., when the various Chinese states within the empire flouted the central authority, assumed an attitude of virtual independence, and struggled with one another for mastery, certain fundamental precepts and many rules for interstate intercourse were laid down by the philosophers. It may also be remarked that the gap between theory and practice in public affairs was not likely to be so great in ancient China as has usually been true in the Western world. In the first place, the philosophers were not given to pure speculation. Chinese philosophy was essentially practical in that it was designed to further the art of social adjustment rather than to inquire into the whence and whither of man. The sage came to occupy

of haughty disdain toward all non-Chinese, regardless of the degree of culture of the latter. During the Han dynasty, about the beginning of the Christian era, after the Chinese had received accounts of the civilization of Rome, their attitude seems to have become one of friendliness and respect; and envoys bringing presents from Rome are reported to have been received as ambassadors rather than as tribute bearers. Perhaps the fact that the Romans were described as "tall, well-proportioned, and like Chinese" earned them the consideration. (McNair, *loc. cit.*)

[4] W. A. P. Martin, *The Lore of Cathay* (New York, 1901), p. 436.

[5] In the third century B.C., the Great Wall, fifteen hundred miles long, was built to ward off intruders.

a place of influence and importance in affairs of state probably never duplicated elsewhere.[6] The prince not only sought, but also frequently followed, the advice of the philosopher both in internal and external affairs. Furthermore, the holding of high public office was regarded as the natural and proper function of the scholar. Mencius expressed the popular view when he said that some labor with their minds and others with their strength; and that those who labor with their minds govern others, while those who labor with their strength are governed by others.[7]

In order fully to understand the underlying reasons for many of the precepts for interstate intercourse laid down by individual philosophers, some aspects of the orthodox Chinese conception of life and human relationships must be kept in mind. Fundamental in Chinese thought was the conception of Nature, man's place in it, and his relation to it. The Western peoples in the Christian era have looked upon nature as an enemy to be conquered and subdued. Man wins his way to material freedom by battling, controlling, and harnessing natural forces. The same view, perhaps even more pronounced, is taken of human nature. Man's original nature is sinful, according to the Christian conception, and he must wage a perpetual, albeit a never entirely successful, fight against it, for this is the only way in which he can achieve a measure of spiritual freedom. The orthodox view of the ancient Chinese was quite the opposite. Nature is kindly rather than cruel. Man cooperates with, he does not struggle against, natural forces, and is in fact looked upon as one among them. There is, therefore, no point in speaking of mastering these forces. It is merely a question of fitting into the natural scheme of things. Heaven produces the seasons, the sun, and the rains; the earth, its many substances; man, by conforming to heaven and earth, produces the things necessary to sustain life. Nature is always good; human nature is likewise good. If evil appears, it is a result of man's disregard of the natural conditions of living. War and strife, there-

[6] The fact is not overlooked that the "Enlightened Despots" of eighteenth-century Europe frequently sought the opinions and occasionally the active help of the philosophers of the period—Voltaire, Rousseau, Turgot, Beccaria and others—in connection with governmental affairs. Bearing in mind the unusual interest at that time manifested by the West, especially France, in the civilization of the Chinese, this rather infrequent practice, in the West, of kings consulting and employing philosophers is interesting and possibly significant.

[7] H. H. Dubs, *Hsüntze, The Moulder of Ancient Confucianism* (London, 1927), p. 12.

fore, are not to be attributed to the original nature of man, but rather to an unwise departure from the principles of nature herself.[8]

Bearing in mind this general assumption, and remembering that the only politically significant world the Chinese knew for many centuries was a Chinese world, that the only culture with which they were familiar was a Chinese culture, one is prepared to understand why they also held as a fundamental conception the essential unity of the human race, and why their political thinking was in terms of mankind and a world order rather than in terms of separate and warring political units. In this world order the proper relationship of the component states was one of peace. There were rules of propriety governing individual, family, and intrastate relations in general. The same idea was carried into the field of interstate relationships, and it is to be observed that a separate standard of morality for states was not taught. Thus *raison d'état,* invoked by rulers of the West as justification for conduct condemned in private relationships, had no standing in China.[9] Interstate relations were viewed as an extension of other relations calling for the use of the same principles of conduct followed in all other social relationships.

In ancient China, four principal systems of philosophy were evolved. Representing these systems were the Confucian, Taoist, Mo Ti, and Legalist schools of thought. The first three differed less fundamentally among themselves than they did with the Legalist school. In fact, the ethical system of the ancient Chinese was fused from the teachings of Confucius, Lao Tzŭ (the founder of Taoism), and Mo Ti.[10] The Legalists were not without influence, but are not to be regarded as most representative of Chinese thought. The views of the principal representatives of these schools, in so far as they have a bearing on interstate relations, may now be examined.

Confucius (552-479 B.C.) applied the rules of propriety to the relationship of states as well as to the relationship of individuals. He and his followers taught that states in their dealings with one another

[8] J. W. Slaughter, "East and West in China," *Rice Institute Pamphlet,* Vol. XIV (April, 1927), No. 2, pp. 159-161; W. S. A. Pott, *Chinese Political Philosophy* (New *York,* 1925), pp. 37-40; A. Forke, *World Conception of the Chinese* (London, 1925), p. 74.

[9] Liang Chi-Chao, *History of Chinese Political Thought During the Early Tsin Period* (London, 1930), *passim;* Yuan Chaucer, *La Philosophie Morale et Politique de Mencius* (Paris, 1927), pp. 242-3.

[10] Liang Chi-Chao, *op. cit.,* p. 33; K. C. Wu, *Ancient Chinese Political Theories* (Shanghai, 1928), p. 70.

should observe good faith, be trustworthy, and practice moderation. As to good faith, he is reported to have said: "Of the three essentials, the greatest is good faith. Without a revenue and without an army, a state may still exist; but it cannot exist without good faith."[11] Intemperate expressions of friendship, or extravagant promises, later to be broken, should not be made by the envoys of one state to another; strong expressions of hostility should likewise be avoided. States should so speak and act that reliance may be placed upon their friendliness and trustworthiness. Envoys on a diplomatic mission must not depart from their instructions, and must not resort to coercive tactics to bring their business to a successful issue.[12]

It was perhaps natural that Mencius, who lived nearly two hundred years later, should direct more of his attention to interstate affairs than did his master.[13] Conditions had changed. The times were out of joint. A number of feeble men had succeeded to the imperial throne, a struggle for power among the princes took place, wars of elimination were waged, leagues were formed to resist the encroachments of the most powerful, and these in turn were destroyed by internal rivalries and jealousies. Mencius greatly deplored the prevailing anarchy and confusion and pleaded for a return to the principles of Confucius.[14] He did not attribute the turmoil and strife and general demoralization to the evil nature of man, as some of his contemporaries were wont to do, but to man's lack of understanding of the true principles of conduct, causing him to follow a false course. "The tendency of man's nature to good is like the tendency of water to flow downwards. There are none but have this tendency to good, just as all water flows downwards."[15]

Mencius was anti-imperialistic in his thinking. He observed that men

[11] Martin, *op. cit.*, p. 443. Confucius was a transmitter rather than an originator. He sought to preserve and teach the best thought of the ancients. He was likewise a moral reformer rather than a philosopher.

[12] Chuang Tsze, *The Divine Classic of Nan-Hua*, tr. by F. H. Balfour (1881), pp. 47-48. Apparently an envoy must rely exclusively on the justice or reasonableness of his case to win his point. He is not to suggest that if his views are not accepted, force will be used to have them complied with.

[13] Legge's assertion that "Confucius makes no provision for the intercourse of his country with other and independent nations," is correct, for there were no civilized states at the time nor in the time of Mencius, either, with whom China had contacts. (*The Chinese Classics;* 7 vols. [Hongkong-London, 1861-1872], Vol. I [2nd ed. rev., 1893], p. 107.) His principles applied to intercourse (1) between Chinese states within the empire, and (2) between China and the border peoples.

[14] Legge, *op. cit.*, II, 22-24.

[15] *Ibid.*, p. 61. See also Yuan Chaucer, *op. cit.*, Ch. V.

were constantly "struggling over gains, making gains the basis of all their relationships, unsatisfied till they have usurped all," and he attacked their acquisitiveness.[16] Carrying this idea over into the field of interstate relations, Mencius was an opponent of wars of conquest and imperialistic gain. They injured the people who, in the opinion of Mencius, hated war, and were interested in peaceful pursuits. The widespread warfare of his day, he asserted, was due to the inordinate ambitions and cupidity of princes, aided and abetted by selfish ministers and false counsellors. He counselled princes to beware of men who would advise them to go to war, and remarked that those who boasted of their skill in marshalling troops and conducting battles were "great criminals."[17] States following an imperialistic policy will find sooner or later that their own territories will be annexed. In any case, he warned, the addition of territory will be a burden rather than otherwise.

The political views of Mencius were democratic in the sense that the interests of the people should be the sole consideration of rulers. In his discussion of the place of the prince, the ministers, and the people in a state, he asserted that the people were the most noble element of the state, and the prince the least essential. Government is set up for the welfare of the people, and the wise ruler will guide his policy by their wishes, and govern so as to win their support. With that support all things are possible.[18] It is thus not surprising that Mencius was also an exponent of self-determination for peoples. When the ruler of a certain state told Mencius that he had completely conquered a neighboring state, whose ruler had been tyrannizing over the people, and expressed the conviction that Heaven willed that he should annex it, the sage answered that the decision should rest with the people of the conquered state; if they were opposed, the state should not be annexed. The conqueror was then advised to restore booty carried out of the conquered country, and after consulting its people, appoint a new ruler, if they wished, and withdraw from the country.[19]

It was apparently not unusual for a prince to attack another state on the ground that its ruler needed to be punished for oppressing the people, or for some other reason. Mencius denied the right of one state to intervene in the affairs of another and inflict punishment upon it,

[16] Liang Chi-Chao, *op. cit.*, pp. 54-58; Yuan, *op. cit.*, pp. 265-269.
[17] E. Faber, *The Mind of Mencius* (London, 1882), pp. 293-294.
[18] Yuan, *op. cit.*, pp. 269-272.
[19] E. D. Thomas, *Chinese Political Thought* (New York, 1927), p. 244.

pointing out that only a minister of the son of Heaven, who represented all of the states, was entitled to punish any of them for misconduct. "'Correction' is when the supreme authority punishes its subjects by force of arms. Hostile states do not correct one another."[20] In the absence of any strong federal authority capable of "correcting" the member states, however, it must have been quite difficult, if not impossible, to convince these solicitous princes that a hands-off policy should be followed, leaving each state to "correct" itself.

Mencius, though strongly opposed to war in principle, and outspoken in his condemnation of interference of one state in the affairs of another which so frequently involved war, did not counsel non-resistance to attack. During those troubled times a state could not depend upon the protection of the central authority and could not be certain of the aid of other states. It must, therefore, look primarily to its own defense or risk being overrun and perhaps absorbed. In any case, Mencius seems to have advised that states should rely upon themselves rather than trust to alliances for protection. When the ruler of a small state put to him the question whether an alliance should be contracted with one or the other of two powerful states, Mencius is said to have remarked: "If you will have me counsel you, there is one thing I can suggest. Dig deeper your moats; build higher your walls; guard them along with your people. In case of attack, be prepared to die in your defense, and have the people so that they will not leave you: this is the proper course."[21] This advice was doubtless based on a conviction frequently expressed by Mencius—that the real strength of a state lies in the morale of its people. The strongest forts, he said, may very well be lost through a lack of moral union in the defenders. Proper military preparations are no guarantee against deceit, treachery, and neglect. They may be necessary, but most important of all is a happy, contented, loyal, united, benevolently governed people.[22]

It has been observed that in the Confucian system the rules of propriety, whereby individual and social conduct is regulated, were regarded as the foundation of human intercourse, whether between individuals or between states. In the Chou period, the states varied greatly in size. Some were large and powerful, others small and weak. Were

[20] Mencius, *op. cit.,* Bk. II, Pt. II, Ch. VIII; Bk. VII, Pt. II, Ch. 2, as cited by Thomas, p. 250.

[21] *Ibid.,* Bk. I, Part II, Ch. XIII, as cited by Thomas, pp. 246-247.

[22] E. Faber, *op. cit.,* pp. 287-288; Thomas, *op. cit.,* p. 246.

they, nevertheless, to be regarded as political and social equals, or were size and power to be regarded as entitling the possessor to a special position? It seems to have been the Confucian doctrine, though not necessarily formulated by the sage himself, that all states great and small, should keep good faith with one another, and that great states should exercise restraint in their dealings with weaker states. On the other hand, the small state was expected to look up to, respect, and obey the large state somewhat as a big brother, in accordance with the rules of propriety. This is illustrated in the following passage from Tso's *Commentary* [23]: "When a great state goes to a small one it rears a high structure. When a small state goes to a great one, it should construct a booth. I have heard this: When a great state visits a small one, it should do five good things: be indulgent to its offenses, pardon its errors and failures, relieve its calamities, reward it for its virtues and laws, and teach it where it is deficient. There is thus no pressure on the small state. It cherishes (the great) state's virtue, and submits to it, fondly as one goes home. On this account a high structure is reared, to display the merit (of the great state), and to make it known to posterity, that they may not be idle in the cultivation of virtue. When a small state goes to a great one, it has five bad things to do. It must explain its trespasses, beg forgiveness for its deficiencies, perform governmental services, and contribute its proper dues, and attend to its seasonal commands. And not (only so):—it has to double its various offerings, to felicitate (the great state) on its happiness, and show its condolence with it in its misfortunes. Now all these things are the sad fate of a small state." [24]

This passage seems to indicate that the author took the position that a great state can do no wrong: for which, at any rate, a small one can properly call it to account. It is instructed to be virtuous, but is seemingly to be the judge of its own rectitude. A small state, on the other hand, must adopt an attitude of humility and, although it is not clear how far a large state is entitled to "correct" (punish) a small one, it certainly has the right to instruct and admonish, and to demand tribute from it. Thus the actual physical inequality of the states seems to have been reflected to a considerable extent in the rules of intercourse prescribed by the Confucian philosophers.

[23] Supposed to be the work of one of Confucius' disciples, Tso Chin-ming.
[24] As quoted in Thomas, *op. cit.*, p. 251.

Confucianism found another able expounder in Hsün Tzŭ (320-235 B.C.?), who was born toward the end of Mencius' life. He does not seem to have given much attention to interstate affairs, but such views as have come down to us are in accord with those of Confucius and Mencius. For example, his general attitude toward war is similar. He is represented as discussing military affairs with a general on one occasion, and denying the importance of strategy in warfare. What is important, said Hsün Tzŭ, is that a ruler should be so benevolent and righteous that his people will unite behind him, and his soldiers will be so inspired with loyalty and devotion that they will be irresistible. His virtue will have a like effect on the soldiers of the enemy, who will transfer their love to him. Thus the ideal king will make a peaceful conquest. Such a conquest of hearts was much to be preferred to a conquest of arms. For one thing, it would be more durable. War, said Hsün Tzŭ, destroys the warrior. In the first place, the victorious prince injures his own people, and their affection for him is weakened. His conquests breed hatred in the conquered, and the latter will resume the struggle at the first opportunity. The result, then, is that conquest weakens the conqueror and strengthens the conquered. As soon as the victorious prince gets into difficulties, his enemies will combine against him. This does not mean that the philosopher is against war under all circumstances. If it is for the benevolent purpose of "stopping tyranny and getting rid of injury," Hsün Tzŭ holds with most of the other philosophers of the period that it is justified.[25]

The views of the Confucianists in general and of Hsün Tzŭ in particular, on the subject of interstate and foreign trade were liberal. The sage lived toward the end of the period of "the Warring States" when, as a result of conquest and absorption, the number of states had been reduced from fifty-five to ten, with seven of the more powerful fighting for mastery. The diminution in the number of states does not seem, however, to have reduced the number of customs barriers. Within every great state, as well as between them, there were a number of such trade restrictions which, in the view of Mencius and other Confucian teachers, worked considerable economic injury. Hsün Tzŭ was among the leading thinkers of the day who advocated free trade, not only within China, but with the outside world. His enumeration [26] of the articles that came

[25] H. H. Dubs, *op. cit.*, pp. 266-270.

[26] Included in the enumeration were: feathers, ivory, rhinoceros hides, copper,

from each of the four quarters testifies that the trade of China with her neighbors must have been extensive, and the position of the philosophers that it should not be restricted is what one might expect from men who bespoke the value of peaceful pursuits for the people and pacific intercourse between states.

The philosopher Mo Ti, who lived about the middle of the fifth century B.C. or possibly somewhat later, taught a doctrine of universal love different in conception from that of the followers of Confucius. Love, in the Confucian view, starts with self, but should extend to others; love for one's family comes first, but should extend to love for other families; likewise, love for one's own country precedes, but should extend to, love for other countries. There is thus a natural discrimination between "self" and "other." In the view of Mo Ti, this notion led to a conflict of interests and inevitable sacrifice of "other" to "self." The conception of partiality must therefore be replaced by impartiality. Elaborating this idea, the philosopher asks: "When the other man's house is looked upon as one's own house, who will steal? When the other man's interest is looked upon as one's own interest, who will offend? When the other man's home is looked upon as one's own home, who will violate it? When the other man's country is looked upon as one's own country, who will attack it?"[27] Mo Ti concluded that a cure for the troubles of society lay in the substitution of universal love and mutual aid for partiality and selfishness, and that the people would "tend toward universal love and mutual aid like fire tending upward and water downwards" if stimulated by a suitable system of rewards and punishments.[28]

It is obvious that in Mo Ti's system there is no place for war in interstate relations, and one is prepared for the indictment he brings against those who undertake it. It is recorded that on one occasion when he learned that a certain ruler intended to attack a smaller neighboring state, he engaged in argument with the ambitious prince by asking: "Suppose that the large cities of your kingdom were to attack the small ones, and the powerful families were to attack the more humble families, what would you say?" The ruler is said to have replied that all were

cinnabar, cornelian, purple, linen, fish, salt, felt, rugs, furs, yak tail, horses, and dogs. See Dubs, *op. cit.*, pp. 19, 263-264.

[27] Liang Chi-Chao, *op. cit.*, p. 95; Y. P. Mei, *The Ethical and Political Works of Mo-tze* (London, 1929), pp. 79-82.

[28] Mei, *op. cit.*, p. 97.

his subjects and that he would punish the aggressors. Mo Ti then replied that Heaven possessed the entire universe as the king possessed his kingdom, and said: "If you attack the people of your neighbor state will not Heaven punish you?" The ruler, however, rationalized his proposed action after a fashion that is even now not unknown among imperialist statesmen. He said that in attacking the neighboring state he was really carrying out the will of Heaven, because for three generations the people of this state had been guilty of crimes including the killing of their sovereigns. In chastising them, therefore, he was aiding Heaven. Mo Ti, aware of the speciousness of this argument, and apparently thinking that Heaven would punish where punishment was necessary, said: "Imagine that a father having a bad son punishes him and that all the fathers of the vicinity, arming themselves with sticks set upon him also, saying—in beating him we are doing the will of the father. Would this be reasonable? This is what you pretend to do." [29]

Mo Ti was opposed to the double standard of morality which entitled states to plunder their neighbors and to kill them in warfare, although forbidding individuals to commit theft and murder. In his opinion, robbery on a large scale, such as the seizure of territory, should be regarded as a more serious offense than simple theft, and the killing of many people in war a much more grievous crime than an individual murder. "Killing one man constitutes a crime and is punishable by death. Applying the same principle, the killing of ten men makes the crime ten times greater and ten times as punishable; similarly, the killing of a hundred men increases the crime a hundred fold, and makes it that many times as punishable. All this the gentlemen of the world unanimously condemn and pronounce to be wrong. But when they come to judge the greatest of all wrongs—the invasion of one state by another—(which is a hundred thousand times more criminal than the killing of one innocent man) they cannot see that they should condemn it. On the contrary, they praise it and call it 'right'." [30] This reminds one of a similar observation by the western philosopher, Voltaire, about 2000 years later: "War is the greatest of all crimes. . . It is

[29] A. David, *Le Philosophe Meh-te et l'Idée de Solidarité* (London, 1907), pp. 116-127.

[30] Chi Fung Lui, "The Ethical Implications of Moh Tih's Philosophy," *International Journal of Ethics,* XXXV, 77.

forbidden to kill; therefore all murderers are punished unless they kill in large numbers and to the sound of trumpets."[31]

Mo Ti also attacked aggressive war on various economic grounds. In the first place, he pointed out, if a war is undertaken in the spring or autumn, it will take people away from planting or harvesting the crops, disrupt economic life in many ways, and thereby cause hunger and want. It will also result in the destruction of materials used in war, and the loss of many lives. The philosopher observed further that the states most disposed toward war for the extension of their territories were the very ones having a surplus of land. Their true need is a larger population, yet they aggravate the situation by pursuing a policy which results in death to a great many in order to obtain more territory, which is already too abundant.[32] War, then, stands condemned as an uneconomic enterprise. "The invader gets no profit, neither does the invaded. War does not profit anybody."[33]

Standing farthest to the left among the philosophers of ancient China is Lao Tzŭ. There is considerable difference of opinion even as to the century in which he lived, some writers making him an older contemporary of Confucius. However that may be, Taoism constituted essentially an attack on Confucianism,[34] Taoism represented a return-to-nature movement. The problem of human relations is to eliminate or reduce desire which was the source of crime, war, and other evils. This may be accomplished by returning to the ways of primitive times when men desired little and were therefore practically free from covetousness and dishonesty. The Tao, or "way" of life, then, is to attain harmony with nature. The realization of this harmony comes through quietude, and the absence of striving, rather than effort and active pursuit of desires.[35] The latter involves human strife and conflict.

[31] See article "Guerre" in his *Dictionnaire Philosophique;* 3 vols. (Éditions de Cluny, Paris, 1930). Chinese philosophy had quite a vogue in France in Voltaire's day. It is not impossible that the inspiration for this statement came from Mo Ti.

[32] Mei, *op. cit.*, pp. 101-103.

[33] Liang Chi-Chao, *op. cit.*, p. 98.

[34] Liang Chi-Chao, *op. cit.*, p. 35. During the Han dynasty (202 B.C.-A.D. 263), Taoism seems to have had considerable vogue, the emperors themselves expressing their sympathy and lending their patronage. During the second century B.C., it was ordered that Taoism should be studied at Court. (Lao Tzŭ, *The Simple Way,* tr. by W. G. Old (London, 1913), Introduction.)

[35] Confucius had not taught against having desires, but merely against satisfying them in the wrong way (Dubs, *op. cit.*, p. 169). Harmony was to be attained by the deliberate regulation of human relationships so that maladjustments and conflicts would be eliminated. It is to be observed, however, that both Confucius

Taoism, however, except perhaps in the case of its more extreme representatives, did not mean complete apathy, and inaction. Its founder advocated, rather, "production without possession, action without self-assertion, development without domination."

The views concerning interstate relations attributed to Laotze fit nicely into this philosophy. For him, wars and victories had no romantic aspects. He saw "prickly briars and thorns flourishing" where battalions had been quartered, and bad times following in the wake of marching armies. "Victory is no cause for exultation if it is purchased with human blood, rather is it a cause for sorrow. If men would recognize and follow the doctrine of Original Simplicity they could make an end of war."

The Old Philosopher regarded imperialism as futile and mischievous. The building up of empires and principalities was getting far away from the simplicity of early times. It represented human interference with the maker of all things, a process of pulling down in one place to set up in another. Furthermore, the establishment of empire could be gained only at the sacrifice of the unity of the human race. The contender for empire may gain it temporarily, but sooner or later he will lose it. Men should accordingly have regard for their limitations and mortality, "regard God and nature as already in possession," and give up their unworthy and bootless strivings.

Despite the fact that the weight of the philosophers of the most influential schools of thought in ancient China was thrown against violence in interstate relations, as well as in other relationships, the Chinese, as we have seen, were by no means total abstainers from war. That diverting pastime of princes was indulged in quite freely, in fact, in certain periods, although the common people apparently never had much stomach for it.[36] It is not to be supposed that the acquisition of tributaries such as Korea, Burma, and Indo-China was the result of the use of peaceful methods alone, although diplomacy was probably the chief reliance in establishing and maintaining the relationship. In any case, war was used against the barbarians pressing on the frontiers,

and Lao Tzŭ had the same aim—the avoidance of conflict and the attainment of harmony.

[36] It is significant that the character for "male" is in two parts meaning "strength" and "field." Thus the distinctive characteristic of man is not strength-for-combat (war) but strength-in-field (agriculture). See H. H. Dubs, *op. cit.*, pp. 270-271; also H. F. Rudd, *Chinese Social Origins* (Chicago, 1928), pp. 201-210, for pacific character of the Chinese people.

the Chinese on occasion even sending armies beyond their borders and carrying on offensive warfare in order to render the uncivilized tribes impotent. On the other hand, after the eighth century B.C. the empire began to disintegrate and warfare became common among the rebellious and self-seeking feudal states. It was not brought to an end until the third century B.C., when Ch'in Shih Huang Ti, the warlike ruler of a principality on the remote frontier of China, conquered the contending states and imposed upon them a forced unity and a new empire.

Warfare was indeed so common that rules for its conduct were evolved and theories regarding its justification and necessity grew up. It seems that it was a general practice to respect the persons and property of non-combatants. It was also regarded as improper to attack an enemy without first beating the drum and giving him an opportunity to prepare for his defense. This chivalrous attitude seems to have been carried even further on one occasion when a virtuous prince ordered his forces not to attack hostile forces while the latter were crossing a stream, and waited until they had formed in order of battle before giving the signal to advance. It is said, however, that the prince was reproached by his generals for such forbearance, and that the military men of his staff laughed at his simplicity.[37] It seems, however, that the business of fighting was considerably diluted, as among many primitive peoples, with ceremonial. There was much emphasis on grand equipment and glittering array, and in the Odes expressing military sentiments the overawing of the enemy rather than his destruction was the chief objective. In short, the Chinese seemed to glory more in their appearance than in fighting.[38]

At times, religion was called into the service of the sword, just war being regarded as an enterprise sanctioned by supernatural forces. Thus when war was undertaken, each side would call upon the divine Powers to bless its cause and aid in subduing the enemy, because it was fighting for justice and righteousness.[39] This doubtless did a great deal to stimulate a martial spirit. Soldiers feeling themselves to be divine instruments for the destruction of evil, and believing the spirits

[37] Martin, *op. cit.*, pp. 443-444.

[38] Rudd, *op. cit.*, pp. 201-208. This author adds that the Odes do not glory in bloodshed and conquest, but rather in the dignity, wisdom, and skillful tactics of the commanders.

[39] R. F. Johnston, "The Cult of Military Heroes in China," *New China Review*, Vol. II, No. 1, pp. 41-42.

to be on their side, could usually be depended upon to bring to the business at hand considerable enthusiasm. When the Duke of Chou and his army were engaged in overthrowing the Chang dynasty they were encouraged by being reminded, "God is with you, set your heart at rest." [40] The following address to an army about to engage the enemy is in the same spirit and, incidentally, does not sound altogether strange to modern ears: "You are acting in accordance with the clear will of heaven, and in obedience to your ruler's commands. It is for you, in this engagement, to vindicate the supremacy of virtue and righteousness." [41] Reliance upon the divine Power, however, seems to have been tempered by the practical attitude that Heaven is more likely to help those who help themselves. Thus a prince who addressed his army before engaging in battle expressed his belief that God had condemned the enemy, and then added that the chariots, horses, bows and arrows and weapons of war should be gotten ready.[42] Defeat of the enemy was regarded, of course, as an evidence of his iniquity and of the divine wrath.[43]

The Chinese evidently paid some attention to the imponderables in warfare. War was not to be undertaken without a decent pretext, the Chinese maxim being: "For war you must have a cause that may be named." Wars were justified by most philosophers under certain circumstances. The preservation of the balance of power was upheld by some as a just cause of war even though a state might not be immediately threatened by the action of the state disturbing the equilibrium. During the Chou period, the right of existence, at least for the greater states holding in fief from the imperial throne, was held sacred, so that it may be inferred that war for the preservation of the existence of a state was regarded as justified. On the other hand, the right to maintain a neutral position amidst warring neighbors was admitted. Thus a state desiring to remain at peace might refuse to allow belligerents to pass over its territory.[44] The extent to which neutral as well as belligerent rights were respected in practice is not so clear. It may be surmised, however, that calculations of expediency and considerations of "military necessity" weighed heavily when the stakes were high and the prospect of punishment for transgression remote.[45]

[40] Legge, *op. cit.* Vol. IV, Pt. II, p. 436.
[41] Legge, *op. cit.,* Vol. V, Pt. II, p. 799.
[42] H. A. Giles, *Confucianism and Its Rivals* (London, 1915), p. 75.
[43] Legge, *op. cit.,* Vol. III, Pt. II, pp. 281-288.
[44] Martin, *op. cit.,* pp. 445-449.
[45] Martin asserts that military leaders were disposed to hold that laws were

Ancient China was not altogether without defenders of war and conquest among the intellectuals. Various representatives of the Legalist school accepted, and in one or two instances even extolled, the use of violence in interstate relations. For the most part, the outstanding exponents of the legalist philosophy were practical men of affairs, and several were statesmen of distinction. They exerted an influence, therefore, perhaps out of proportion to their numbers. Their political thinking was based on their view of the evil propensities of human nature, which contrasts strongly with the view of Mencius and most of the Confucian scholars, and reminds us of the conception of Hobbes and Machiavelli.

The earliest representative of the Legalist school was Kuang Chung, who lived in the seventh century B.C. He believed that law and order, established by force among men, who were in general predisposed toward violence, had replaced the early state of nature, which was a state of war. "In ancient times the people . . . lived promiscuously like beasts, they attacked one another by force. Consequently the intelligent took advantage of the ignorant, the strong oppressed the weak, and no one took care of the aged, the weak, the young or the fatherless. In later times the intelligent people prohibited cruelty and oppression, and by means of united efforts they stopped violence."[46] Thus, government was established for an ethical purpose, and rulers should themselves be virtuous and observe moderation in order to set a correct standard for the people governed; but they should exact prompt obedience to their commands.

Starting with this assumption of the evil nature of man, and concluding that his predatory instincts can be kept within bounds only by stern repression, what prospect would such a philosopher see for orderly and peaceful interstate relations? One would expect Kuang Chung to assume the necessity for some strong central authority able to coerce and subordinate individual states, or, if there were no such authority, for each state, recognizing the likelihood of attack, to keep itself in a position to resist. He seems to have taken the latter position, and may be set down as one of the earliest advocates of military preparedness of which we know. His advice to rulers was to refuse to listen to disarmament proposals or "general love all round," for though able to depend on

not made for them and rules of war were doubtless often disregarded. *Op. cit.*, pp. 443-444.

[46] Liang Chi-Chao, *op. cit.*, pp. 123-124.

their own self-restraint, they could not be certain that others would not attack *them*.[47] War was usually to be deplored in that it dissipated wealth, impoverished the people, and was dangerous to the state. War for war's sake could not be justified. Yet, said Kuang Chung, in fatalistic vein, wars have always gone on and always will. Apparently he favored a judicious mixture of war and diplomacy as the best means of advancing the external interests of a country, holding that under certain circumstances two-thirds of the revenue of a state might well be devoted to diplomatic activity and the achievement of a peaceful conquest.

A prince, before raising an army for purposes of armed conquest, should put his own domain in order and secure his popularity, said the philosopher. The cultivators of the soil must be protected and a fair share of their produce left to them; otherwise they will have no interest in repelling an invading enemy, and will be without the stimulus necessary to produce the grain upon which the soldiers must be sustained. As for the soldiers, "the joy of battle lies in a full belly and the prospect of reward." Kuang Chung found "the prospect of reward" to be the main incentive in the field as well as at court. Having put his own house in order, the prince should then insure the good will of petty neighboring states by making slight concessions of territory to them. Finally, having conquered the enemy, the wise prince will treat him with courtesy and generosity, but at the same time spy out his secrets and keep the upper hand by "artful trickery."[48]

A more extreme representative of the Legalist school was Shang Yang (Kung-sun Yang), who lived in the fourth century B.C., and was therefore a contemporary of Mencius, with whom he stands in sharp contrast.[49] Shang seems to have been thoroughly ruthless and unscrupulous. If the accounts are trustworthy, his system enabled one of the Chinese states to rise rapidly to a temporary ascendancy over the other states, and he himself seems to have enjoyed a brief period of power, and then to have met a tragic end. The period, as will be re-

[47] Mencius, on the other hand, was later to anticipate some modern critics of preparedness by holding that for a prince to assemble materials of war was to stimulate other princes to take similar action.

[48] E. H. Parker, "Kwan-Tsz on the Theory of War," *New China Review*, Vol. III (Dec., 1921), No. 6, pp. 405-411.

[49] *The Book of Lord Shang*, tr. by J. J. L. Duyvendak (London, 1928), upon which this account is based, was probably his only in small part. It seems to have been written by different individuals. See discussion by Duyvendak, p. 143-159.

membered, was one which would appeal to the ambitious adventurer. The old imperial power had been so weakened that there was no prospect of its being revived. A new imperial authority was the only alternative to continued strife among the states. In these circumstances, Mencius took the position that a feudal lord should succeed to the imperial throne who could win it by moral virtue.[50] Shang, on the other hand, worked out a system whereby a prince might attain mastery of the empire without reference to any system of ethics. Entering the service of the Duke of Ch'in about 350 B.C., he fired the latter with ambition to possess the imperial throne and advised him how it was to be accomplished.

In the first place, the system called for the organization of the state for the conquest of the empire, and for no other purpose. To this end it must be made rich and strong. On the other hand, the people must be kept weak and poor, and in complete subjection and dependence. In order to insure this dependence, a system of rewards and punishments was worked out. The old traditional virtues, including filial piety, brotherly duty, sincerity, and faith, were to be discarded, since they would make the people quite useless to accomplish the task set. The real virtues of the people, from the point of view of the business in hand, were simplicity and ignorance. They must therefore be kept poor, be forbidden education, and denied all opportunities to develop culture. They were to be allowed only two kinds of employment, only two avenues to rewards: agriculture and war! [51] Agriculture is necessary, Shang pointed out, because without it there will be no food, without food there will be no people, and without people there could be no army for conquest. Furthermore, people engaged in agriculture will be simple and easy to correct; scattered as they will be, they will be easy to command; and fixed to the soil, they will value their lands and may be depended upon to fight for their country.[52]

Shang assumes, however, that people will have a natural aversion to both occupations on account of the toil and hardships associated with them. For this reason, a judicious system of rewards and punishments must be contrived in order to stimulate them. They should be employed constantly in either one or the other, but inasmuch as they will hate war

[50] *Ibid.*, p. 76.
[51] *Ibid.*, pp. 82-85.
[52] Wu, *op. cit.*, pp. 176-177.

even more than farming, they must be made to toil, so hard that they will welcome war as a release from toil and as an opportunity to earn rewards. The people must be made to enjoy war in order that the state may use them. "When its people look at war as if they were hungry wolves looking at a piece of meat, then it is able to use its people." [53] This happy condition of wolfish energy is essential if conquests are to be made. On the other hand, this energy will constitute a danger to the state if not so utilized. If it is not given a vent, people will fall back upon their selfish desires and weaken the state. They will grow strong and active on their own behalf, and perhaps imbibe the "poison" of cultural pursuits. The wise ruler will be vigilant and prevent this by absorbing their energies in more warfare.[54] Here is the complete antithesis of everything taught by Mencius and the adherents of the other two schools of thought, and probably few representatives of the Legalist school subscribed to the program of ruthless exploitation of human beings which the "system" required. Doubtless its author prided himself on being a realist, but he was much less realistic than his idealistic contemporary, Mencius. It seems that his system, after a brief period of fictitious success, involved the state undertaking it, as well as himself, in irretrievable disaster and ruin.[55]

The frank glorification of wars of conquest, however, is rarely to be found even among military men in ancient China. In early treatises on the art of war, compiled by famous Chinese generals, and used in the examination of aspirants for the military service, are to be found certain maxims that might be regarded today in some military circles as endangering the morale of the military novice. Thus it was held that "war is in respect to people what a violent sickness is to the body." As one would take precautions against bodily illness, so should an effort be made to avoid war. Even victory was not to be regarded with unqualified satisfaction, for "combats of whatever nature always have something baleful for the conquerors themselves." Emphasis was laid on the admonition that war was never to be made except in the general interest, that it was to be undertaken only as a last resort, and that

[53] Wu, *op. cit.*, pp. 182-183.
[54] *The Book of Lord Shang*, p. 86.
[55] The system reminds us, especially in its complete disregard of all ethical considerations, of that of the "Indian Machiavelli" (*infra*, pp. 44-45), of the "Prince" by the Florentine Machiavelli (*infra*, pp. 119-124) and in its subordination of all interests and activities to war, of ancient Sparta (*infra*, pp. 52-54).

before engaging in it one "must be sure to have humanity for a principle, justice for the object, honesty for the rule." [56] It may be that many of the military men of ancient China would not have subscribed to all of these admonitions—they sound very much like the disquisitions of the pacifist philosophers. It is even likely that enterprising officers "interpreted" them in such a way that their activities would not be unduly circumscribed. Nevertheless, one would not expect to find some of these statements in military manuals at the present time. Probably they could not be duplicated outside ancient China.

REFERENCES

Carus, Paul, *Lao Tze's Tao-Teh-King* (Chicago, 1898).

Chavannes, E., *Les Mémoires Histoirques de Se-ma Ts'ien;* 5 vols. (Paris, 1895-1905).

Cholet, E., *L'Art Militaire dans l'Antiquité Chinoise: Une Doctrine de Guerre Bi-millenaire* (1922).

Chuang Tsze, *The Divine Classic of Nan-Hua,* translated by F. H. Balfour (1881).

Creel, H. G., *Sinism—A Study of the Chinese World View* (Chicago, 1929).

David, A., *Le Philosophe Meh-ti et l'Idée de Solidarité* (London, 1907), Ch. IV, pp. 116-127.

Dubs, H. H., *Hsüntze, the Moulder of Ancient Confucianism* (London, 1927), Chs. I-IV, pp. 263, 266-271.

Forke, A., *The World-Conception of the Chinese* (London, 1925).

Giles, H. A., *Gems of Chinese Literature* (Shanghai, 1923).

Grousset, R., *Histoire de la Philosophie Orientale* (Paris, 1923).

Hirth, F., *China and the Roman Orient* (Shanghai, 1885).

Hirth, F., *The Ancient History of China to the End of the Chóu Dynasty* (New York, 1911).

Hu, Shih, *The Development of the Logical Method in Ancient China* (Shanghai, 1922), pp. 69-71.

Hobhouse, L. T., *Morals in Evolution* (New York, 1924), pp. 253-256.

Hsü, Z. S., *The Political Philosophy of Confucianism* (London, 1932), pp. 119-120; 212-213 *et passim.*

Hummel, A. W., "The Case Against Force in Chinese Philosophy," *Chinese Social and Political Science Review,* April, 1925, pp. 334-350.

Kung-sun Yang, *The Book of Lord Shang,* tr. by J. J. L. Duyvendak (London, 1928).

[56] Lieut. Col. E. Cholet, *L'Art Militaire dans l'Antiquité Chinoise: Une Doctrine de Guerre Bi-millenaire* (1922), p. 6 ff.

Lao, Tzŭ, *The Simple Way,* tr. by W. G. Old (London, 1913).
Legge, Jas., *The Chinese Classics;* 7 vols. (Hongkong-London, 1861-1872). (Vols. I and II, 2nd ed., rev., Oxford, 1893-1895.)
Letourneau, C., *La Guerre dans les Diverses Races Humaines* (Paris, 1895), pp. 232-242.
Li, Chi. *The Formation of the Chinese People* (Cambridge, Mass., 1928).
Liang, Chi-Chao, *History of Chinese Political Thought During the Early Tsin Period* (London, 1930).
Lui, Chi Fung, "The Ethical Implications of Moh Tih's Philosophy," *International Journal of Ethics,* XXXV, 72-81.
Maeterlinck and others, *What Is Civilization?* (New York, 1926), Ch. V.
Martin, W. A. P., *The Lore of Cathay* (New York, 1912).
————, "Diplomacy in Ancient China," *Journal of the Peking Oriental Society,* III and IV, 241-263.
Mei, Y. P., *The Ethical and Political Works of Mo-Tse* (London, 1929), Books IV, V.
Morgan, Evan, *A Guide to Wenli Styles and Chinese Ideals* (Shanghai, 1912).
Parker, E. H., "Kwan-Tsz on the Theory of War," *New China Review,* Vol. III (Dec., 1921), No. 6, pp. 405-411.
Pott, W. S. A., *Chinese Political Philosophy* (New York, 1925).
Rudd, H. F., *Chinese Social Origins* (Chicago, 1928).
Siu Tchoan-Pao, Sim, *Le Droit des Gens et la Chine Antique* (Paris, 1926).
Suzuki, D. T., *A Brief History of Early Chinese Philosophy* (London, 1914).
Thomas, E. D., *Chinese Political Thought* (New York, 1927), Ch. XV.
Yuan, Chaucer, *La Philosophie Morale et Politique de Mencius* (Paris, 1927), esp. Chs. V, IX, XV.
Wu, K. C., *Ancient Chinese Political Theories* (Shanghai, 1928).

CHAPTER III

ANCIENT INDIA

CHINA excepted, the most continuous and unbroken civilization of ancient times was that of India. The earliest inhabitants of this great sub-continent of whom we have any definite knowledge were the Indo-Aryans, who seem to have invaded and settled India, after conquering its earlier inhabitants, at least as early as 2000 B.C., possibly much earlier.[1] We get glimpses of the political institutions and ideas of these people from the *Rigvedas,* collections of hymns and prayers composed by the seers and sages of the period, and addressed to the gods. Another source of information for these early times, as well as for the later ancient period, is the *Mahâbhârata,* a great epic narrative composed by many different authors separated by centuries of time. As a result of the laborious work of some unknown person who synthesized and edited it, we have a fairly complete account of Hindu political thought in northern India in the ancient period. Southern India, it may be noted, does not appear to have made any significant contribution to political ideas such as we find in northern India with its more fertile contacts and more stirring life. As Smith points out, "India primarily is a Hindu country, the land of the Brahmans, who have succeeded by means of peaceful penetration, not by the sword, in carrying their ideas into every corner of India." [2]

It is not to be inferred, however, that ancient India was free from strife. Far from it. There is sufficient evidence to show that from the time of the early invasions, at any rate, war played a far more important part in the life of ancient India than it did among the Chinese.[3] This may doubtless be accounted for in part by the fact that there were few natural frontiers between the Indian states behind which a success-

[1] V. A. Smith, *The Oxford History of India* (2nd ed., Oxford, 1923), pp. 7-8.
[2] *Ibid.*
[3] P. Chakravarti, "Philosophy of War among the Ancient Hindus," *Journal of Indian History,* VII (1928), pp. 157-158.

ful defense of territory might be made and an aggressor discouraged. Except possibly during brief periods, there were a large number of separate states. Megasthenes, Greek envoy to Emperor Chandragupta in the fourth century B.C., mentions 118 kingdoms. Their inhabitants were sprung from the same stock, they appear to have been on the same general level of culture, and thus it was perhaps natural for aspiring rulers to think imperially and to nurse ambitions to rule over the entire Indian continent. Such ambitions were not likely to be realized, however, by diplomacy alone. The thirst for power was probably too widespread among the strong, and the love of independence too pronounced among the weak, for imperial ambitions to be realized without resort to the sword.

We have already seen that, although the Chinese, especially at certain periods, resorted to armed force more frequently than is commonly thought,[4] they never raised war to the rank of an institution, and no separate warrior class, devoted to the profession of arms, grew up. In India, on the other hand, conditions were such that a distinct fighting class emerged as one among four orders of society which early came to be recognized. The first order in point of rank, it is true, was that of the Brahmans, a learned, priestly class. However, second only in rank and influence was the Kṣatriya class, which was depended upon to do the fighting and to furnish rulers. Third in rank was the Vaiśyas, an agricultural and trading class; and fourth, the Sûdras, a proletariat class of humble folk. In the *Râmâyana,* which may be classed with the *Mahâbhârata* as a great epic, the relative position of these classes is indicated in the statement that Brahmans were honored by the Kṣatriyas, both were honored and obeyed by Vaiśyas, and Sûdras obeyed them all.[5]

The Brahmans, it seems, were at one time kings as well as philosophers, exercising the supreme governing authority. According to the *Mahâbhârata,* the experiment of Brahman rule was tried in early times, but resulted in disaster, so that henceforth sovereignty was vested in the Kṣatriyas. In any event, the theory came to be held that no Brahman was eligible to the kingship.[6] Rulers were to come from the Kṣatriyas alone. On the other hand, the Brahmans were the repositories

[4] *Supra,* pp. 28-34.

[5] B. Prasad, *Theory of Government in Ancient India* (Allahabad, 1927), pp. 67-68.

[6] *Ibid.,* pp. 23-26.

of wisdom, the interpreters and teachers of social rights and obligations, were counsellors to the kings, and often held high offices of state as well. Virtuous kings were expected to yield them precedence and rule by their aid. They were to be protected like sons and worshipped like fathers. Thus although we observe a specialization of function between the two orders, it is apparent that they supplemented each other and were expected to cooperate and work in harmony. In fact, it was taught that alliance between the Brahman and the Kṣatriyas was necessary to the state. "As the fire helped by the wind can burn down entire forests, so the union of the energies of the priest and the warrior can destroy all enemies."[7]

The existence of this warrior class, and the fact that it held the supreme governing authority, would seem to indicate, even if there were no other evidence, that war as an institution was rather firmly fixed in Indian society. By contrast with ancient China, where war was regarded as unnatural and undesirable, in India it seems to have been accepted as part of the eternal scheme of things, if we except the Buddist teachings, and sanctioned to some extent by religious authority. For example, a Kṣatriya was required to engage in battle in order to acquire religious merit. If he should flee from the field, he was not only socially ostracized as a cowardly deserter, but when he died he was doomed to go to hell. On the other hand, should he die in battle, he would earn a higher reward even than the Brahman would attain by the performance of sacrifices.[8] As an ancient writer, quoted by Banerjae,[9] pointed out, "People should not regret the death of the brave man who is killed in battle. He is purged of all sins and for him is the Kingdom of Heaven. The fairies in the world above vie with each other for espousing the dead hero as their husband in the next life." Thus war seems to have been envisioned as something ordained from on high as the exclusive function of a particular class which must engage in it as faithfully as the other orders of Indian society were expected to function in their respective spheres.

War, however, was not only in theory restricted to a professional class, and therefore limits set to its destruction, but rules designed to mitigate its severity likewise had the sanction of religious authority.

[7] N. K. Sidhanta, *The Heroic Age of India* (New York, 1920), p. 133; Prasad, *op. cit.*, pp. 33-35, 42-43.
[8] S. V. Viswanatha, *International Law in Ancient India* (London, 1925), p. 115.
[9] *International Law and Custom in Ancient India* (Calcutta, 1920), p. 101.

Unfair, unchivalrous, and inhumane practices in war were positively prohibited.[10] A king must not kill his foes, for example, if they throw away their arms, beg for mercy, or eat grass and behave like priests. Thus there was no unqualified right to kill even in war.[11] It must also be added that with the rise and spread of Buddhism, a faith so strongly opposed to all killing, religious influence came to be more unqualifiedly opposed to violence between states. Asoka (274-236 B.C.), whose vast empire extended from Afghanistan to Mysore, including the Deccan and most of southern India, indulged in but one war of conquest. It involved so much suffering and loss of life that he determined never to repeat it, and under the influence of Buddhism adopted the creed of non-violence. Declaring that "the chiefest conquest is the conquest of Right and not of Might," he is said to have scrupulously respected the independence of other states whether large or small, and even to have sent missions to them because of his solicitude for their spiritual welfare. He hoped thus to win them by "a conquest full of delight" to the Buddhist way of life. It is said, however, that if the peoples bordering his empire refused this peaceful conquest and did not conform to Asoka's moral code, they might expect to have their freedom taken away.[12]

Although it is obvious that during twenty centuries the theory and practice of interstate relations must have shown great variation, and although materials are often quite scanty, it is possible to discern certain notions concerning the relationship of states that seem to have had the weight of considerable authority in the last few centuries before the Christian era. For example, fairly well-settled principles concerning the treatment of foreigners were accepted, and from them one deduces that Indian thought favored the maintenance of a sphere of pacific inter-

[10] See *The Ordinances of Manu,* ed. by E. W. Hopkins (London, 1884), Lecture VIII, par. 90-92, for a number of prohibitions, including the use of poisoned weapons, the killing of a prostrate, sleeping, or defenseless enemy, etc.

[11] E. W. Hopkins, *Ethics of India* (New Haven, Conn., 1924), pp. 101-102, 104. We find even in the rules of statecraft, compiled by secular writers and dictated by considerations of expediency rather than by a concern to inculcate obedience to religious precepts, such passages as these: "Having captured the fort or having returned to the camp after its capture, he (the conqueror) should give quarter to those of the enemy's army who, whether as lying prostrate in the field or as standing with their back turned to the conqueror, or with their hair disheveled, with their weapons thrown down or with their body disfigured and shivering under fear, surrender themselves." (*Arthasâstra,* R. Shamasastry, translation [Mysore, 1923], p. 471.)

[12] R. Mookerji, *Men and Thought in Ancient India* (London, 1924), pp. 99-110.

course between different peoples. During the Maurya Empire (322-185 B.C.), a board or commission for foreigners was set up. Its duties were similar to those of modern consuls. The members were responsible for finding housing for foreign visitors, were required to keep them under surveillance during their stay to guard against spying, and to escort them to the frontier when their visit was concluded. The duties of the board also included the supplying of medical service or burial in case a foreigner suffered illness or died, and of protecting and accounting for his property.[13] If a foreigner should be guilty of espionage and intrigue, however, he would forfeit the right to protection and could be put to death.[14]

Intercourse between states in ancient India had not reached such a point or attained such a character that the conception of permanent embassies, to establish continuous official relationships, developed. On the other hand, diplomatic missions to foreign states were of enough importance and frequency in the latter period that rules regulating the appointment, qualifications, duties, and immunities of ambassadors are to be found in the works of the various religious and secular writers. As in the Middle Ages in Western Europe, envoys were charged with the fulfillment of particular missions and were often entrusted with tasks of great delicacy and high import. They were regarded as the mouthpiece of the sovereign in these enterprises, and his eyes and ears as well, for they were expected to inform themselves as thoroughly as possible of the strength and weakness of the country to which they were sent, and to spy out as many secrets as possible.

It is evident from all of the dissertations on polity in ancient India that espionage reached a high development as an art for the conduct of both internal and external relations. Some writers simply divided foreign spies into two classes, open spies and secret spies. The latter traveled in a foreign country disguised as traders, ascetics, or to represent some other occupation, and were charged with obtaining information of military value for their own state. An open spy was an ambassador. In view of the detailed instructions as to espionage laid down in the *Arthasâstras* for the information of ambassadors, the characterization was probably accurate. Whatever special mission might be entrusted to

[13] Smith, *op. cit.*, pp. 87-88; Viswanatha, *op. cit.*, p. 53.
[14] Banerjea, *op. cit.*, p. 53.

them, it was understood that they should constantly employ themselves by fair means or foul to worm out the secrets of the state to which they were sent in order that it might later be overreached by their king.[15] The practice reveals that war in one guise or another was tacitly assumed, and that good faith and fair dealing were not relied upon in the relationship of states.

Nevertheless ambassadors seem to have enjoyed, as in modern times, a high degree of immunity. An envoy was regarded as the mouthpiece of his sovereign and as such his person was inviolable, for he advocated not his own cause but that of his master. Therefore, although he might do some serious wrong, he must not be killed. The *Mahâbhârata* even prescribes a penalty for a violation of this rule. "That king who slays an envoy sinks into hell with all his ministers." An offending envoy was nevertheless subject to dismissal and even severe punishment for a serious offense.[16]

Among the specific and avowed purposes for which ambassadors were sent to foreign courts were the contracting of alliances and the negotiation of treaties. In any society of independent states, it is to be expected that alliances will be formed for the purpose of uniting two or more states against another or others in self-defense or for purposes of aggression, or for the purpose of maintaining an equilibrium or balance of power among them. Alliances for the attainment of one or another of these objects, or as part of a general plan of a state for the ultimate domination of allies as well as enemies and the attainment of empire, were well-known in ancient India, and, by many writers, were treated at length as a separate department of statecraft.[17]

In general, alliances among the Indian states were for purposes of war rather than for securing peace, and the breaking out of war between two or more states was likely to draw in others as allies on one side or the other. Neutrality seems to have been rather rare, although a state which regarded itself as strong enough might temporarily remain aloof from a war in order to maintain and perhaps increase its strength while its enemy was being weakened. The writers of the *Arthasâstras*, however, seem to have advised non-participation in certain circum-

[15] Viswanatha, *op. cit.*, pp. 64-78; *Arthasâstra* (Shamasastry translation, 1923), pp. 31-34.
[16] Viswanatha, *op. cit.*, pp. 86, 88.
[17] *Ibid.*, pp. 90-96.

stances merely as a matter of strategy to be followed only as occasion seemed to justify in the course of the struggle for power.

Alliances between states unequal in power, and need for outside aid, put the weaker state in a subordinate position in the relationship, for the aid it could give was presumably less than the benefit and protection it would receive. To compensate for this inequality of service and benefit, the weaker power was expected to recognize the superiority of its ally, and to give such help as it could in men, money, and supplies whenever called upon, but to leave to its superior the conduct of affairs for which the alliance was contracted. If it should violate the terms of the alliance, it likewise had to suffer heavier penalties than the dominant power.[18]

Treaties of alliance, as well as those for the termination of wars and for the securing of peace, were recognized as solemn agreements not lightly to be broken. They might be negotiated by ambassadors or other accredited ministers, but their ratification was exclusively the prerogative of the sovereigns of the contracting states and bound them in faith to each other. In some instances, treaties were unsupported by anything other than the word of honor of the contracting parties. In other cases, when there was fear that a treaty might be broken, it was customary for the parties to swear by fire, water, plough, the brick of a fort wall, the shoulder of an elephant, the hips of a horse, the front of a chariot, a weapon, seeds, scents, juice, wrought gold or bullion gold, and to declare that he who violated his oath would be destroyed or deserted by these things. Any breach of faith might therefore bring calamity on the violator. Furthermore, as a violator of the Dharma (the law or custom), an offender risked arousing a combination of states against him for the purpose of holding him to account. There was thus a double sanction for the faithful observance of agreements.[19]

In many instances, however, substantial guarantees for the faithful observance of treaty obligations seem to have been demanded as well. Thus, ascetics engaged in penance, or nobles, might be given as security. In other cases, children might be given as hostages. In the *Arthasâstra*, it is pointed out, however, that a shrewd king may actually turn the

[18] *Ibid.*, pp. 102-106, 108. See *Arthasâstra*, pp. 320-322, 331-332, 340-343, for discussions of the ways in which to utilize alliances for the advancement of a state's power; and N. N. Law, *Interstate Relations in Ancient India* (London, 1920), pp. 69-85.

[19] Viswanatha, pp. 107, 166-167; *Arthasâstra*, p. 369.

whole matter to his advantage by the selection and dispatch of hostages who will prove an embarrassment and danger to the other party to the agreement. Thus, it is asserted, whoever gives a princess as a hostage gains an advantage for she will cause trouble to the receiver! On the other hand, to give a prince as hostage is to lose an advantage, apparently on the theory that the prince is more valuable to the state. On the same theory, it is better to give a stupid or base-born son as a hostage than to hand over a high-born son endowed with intelligence and other virtues.[20]

Although Viswanatha [21] asserts that treaties seem rarely to have been violated in ancient India, it is to be observed that the question is put on the plane of pure expediency in the *Arthasâstra.* "Whoever is rising in power may break the agreement of peace." Instructions are also laid down in much detail in this treatise as to ways and means of effecting the escape of hostages held by the other party to a treaty of peace when a "rising" king has decided to break it. Espionage, which occupies such a large place as a fine art in Indian statecraft, is always advocated. It is to be supplemented, however, by bribery, arson, and the liberal use of poison, if necessary.[22]

In the *Arthasâstras,* or treatises on government and politics, which were written in the latter part of the ancient period, may be found the most detailed treatment of interstate relations. In 1904, one of these treatises, based on previous *Arthasâstras* composed by ancient teachers, according to its author, was discovered in southern India. The treatise has been traditionally attributed to Kautilya (Chânakya), the prime minister of the Emperor Chandragupta (326-298 B.C.), although authorities are not agreed either as to the author or date of composition, and some recent scholars are more inclined to think it was not written prior to the first or second century A.D.[23] The question of time and authorship is not as important for our purpose as the fact that this treatise on statecraft, divorcing politics from religion and ethics almost as completely as did Machiavelli in his *Prince* [24] (which it resembles in many ways) seems to have embodied and systematized the thought

[20] *Arthasâstra,* pp. 369-370, for detailed advice on this subject.
[21] *Op. cit.,* p. 169.
[22] *Arthasâstra,* pp. 371-372.
[23] See Prasad, *op. cit.,* pp. 91-92, for discussion of this point, and citation of authorities.
[24] *Infra,* pp. 119-124.

of a number of secular writers in India more than a thousand years before the Florentine was born.

The *Arthasâstra* to which reference has been made is primarily concerned with the internal affairs of a state, but it contains, nevertheless, an elaborate and detailed treatment of interstate relationships in which a complete system of tactics for the advancement of state interests is delineated. As in the case of other Hindu writers on the subject, the author imagines a circle of states forming a kind of political solar system and tending to gravitate toward one another as friends or come into collision as enemies according to their respective positions in the circle. Thus, states adjacent to each other, and therefore in the nature of things bound to have a greater number of points of friction, are to be regarded as natural enemies.[25]

This assumption rests in turn upon the conception that human nature is essentially warlike and aggressive, and that a ceaseless "upward striving" characterizes life on the earth. According to Indian legend, men in their original state of nature followed the Logic of the Fish—they pursued and devoured one another, and had a very active but uncertain existence. In time their situation became unbearable, and they selected Manu to be their king and establish a government over them.[26] In the absence of a similar restraining authority between states, the Hindu theorists taught that rulers in general would likewise be motivated by predatory ambitions. Furthermore, they regarded the state as an organism which must grow or decay like any other organism. It was, therefore, taken for granted that every state would seek to expand at the expense of the others.

This dynamic conception underlies the whole scheme of interstate relationships as developed in the *Arthasâstras*.[27] Visions of empire and world dominion naturally followed. As one ancient Hindu text puts it, "Monarchy at its highest should have empire extending right up to

[25] Prasad, *op. cit.*, p. 144; N. N. Law, *op. cit.*, pp. 7-9.

[26] Prasad, *op. cit.*, pp. 28-30, 149-150. Kalidas Nag, "The Diplomatic Theories of Ancient India and the Arthosâstra," *Journal of Indian History,* V, 333. The English philosopher, Thomas Hobbes (1588-1679), advanced an almost identical theory based on the same view of the anti-social nature of man. It should be mentioned, however, that in India as well as among other ancient peoples, theories of an original "golden age" of peace and happiness are to be found in Buddhist and other works. See Ghoshal, *History of Hindu Political Theory* (London, 1923), p. 275, and Prasad, *op. cit.*, p. 27.

[27] B. K. Sarkar, *The Political Institutions and Theories of the Hindus* (Leipzig, 1922), pp. 215-219.

natural boundaries, it should be territorially all-embracing, up to very ends uninterrupted, and should constitute and establish one state and administration up to the seas." [28] The writers of the *Arthasâstras*, however, do not seem to have had in mind that the aspirants for empire should seek to extend their dominion beyond the borders of India. India, to them, was doubtless identical with the politically significant world just as China was "all under Heaven" to most Chinese, and the medieval conception of an empire embracing all Christendom was "universal" to western writers. In any case the vision of an all-Indian empire was an ideal not necessarily unattainable. The conquest and political control of the entire earth, considering that most of it was largely unknown to ancient India and in any event could not be reached by armies, was beyond the conception of the ancients.

The doctrine of Mandala, or circle of states, to which reference has already been made, starts with a given state, A, in the center of a circle of eleven surrounding states. The ruler of this central state (Vijigīsha, or aspirant bent on conquest) must base his foreign policy on an understanding of the attitude of the different states toward it and toward one another. The attitude of these states will vary, according to their geographical location, with respect to one another. Thus B, the immediate neighbor of A, is to be regarded as a natural enemy, and hostility between the two is normally to be expected. The same assumption holds with respect to any other state adjacent to A; the latter must regard all of them as natural enemies. In the same way, state C in the next zone and adjacent to B but not to A, will be the enemy of B but will be friendly to A. The same principle holds as additional states in zones eventually reaching to the circumference of the circle, are taken into account. Thus D, adjacent to C, will be the friend of B, the enemy; E will be C's friend, i.e., the friend's friend, and F will be D's friend, i.e., the friend of the enemy's friend.

There are, however, two types of states not so definitely classified as friend or enemy, the Madhyama and Udāsīna. The former, a state of medium strength, apparently, lies within the first zone of both the central state and its enemy, and is therefore, according to location, to be reckoned as an enemy of both of them. If it expresses hostility toward one, however, it thereby evidences friendliness toward the other. Until by word or act it crystallizes its position, it cannot be classified either

[28] As quoted in Sarkar, *op. cit.*, p. 222.

as friend or foe. Should the central state by any chance be allied with its natural enemy, the Madhyama's policy should be to help both, for it will not be strong enough to offend both of them. If they are not allied, however, it is capable of resisting or destroying each of them, and therefore has a choice of policy. The Udāsīna also lies within the first zone. It is stronger than any of them, but not able to cope with all three. Should they form an alliance, therefore, it should adopt a friendly attitude toward them. If they are not combined, however, it can decide freely whether to help or destroy them individually.[29]

A second doctrine of the *Arthasâstra* writers held that each state was made up of seven elements, and that the strength of any state depended upon the individual excellence of each of these constituents. They were (1) the king; (2) the ministers; (3) the territory; (4) the fortresses; (5) the treasury; (6) the army; and (7) the allies. The king, according to the *Arthasâstra,* is the center of the whole system. He has great responsibilities and must possess exceptional qualities of mind, high moral virtues, and outstanding personal qualities. He must discipline himself before all others. Then if he acts in conformity with the advice of the treatises on polity, he will be able to make much of the other six elements, secure greater and greater power and perhaps ultimately rule the entire earth. On the other hand, a ruler with an empire and great resources will come to grief if he exhibits the reverse of these qualities.[30] Nevertheless, it is recognized that even a perfect king will be unable to govern alone. He needs advice and counsel, and must have ministers and assistants, even though he is versed in all the sciences and is an expert in diplomacy. The third element—the country or kingdom—to be ideal should be large, self-sustaining, able to defend itself against enemies, with great natural wealth, and with a loyal, honest, and intelligent population. Among the other elements it may be noted that the army should be hereditary and permanent, composed mostly of Kṣatriyas, well disciplined and skilled, and faithful in adversity as in prosperity. An ally's friendship should endure generation after generation, its devotion unchanging.[31]

[29] Law, *op. cit.,* pp. 1-13. Viswanatha (*op. cit.,* pp. 32-33) and other writers render Madhyama as mediatory, and Udāsīna as neutral or indifferent. Law's interpretation, however, seems well sustained.

[30] C. Nag, *Les Théories Diplomatiques de l'Inde Ancienne et Arthaśastra* (Paris, 1923), p. 69; Law, *op. cit.,* pp. 14, 18-20, 27.

[31] Nag, *op. cit.,* pp. 69-73; Law, *op. cit.,* pp. 20-22. For full discussion of the

These seven elements form the bases of diplomacy, and it becomes the task of the aspiring king to utilize them to the best advantage in improving his situation in the circle of states and enhancing his prosperity. The central state might or might not be powerful. If it were not and yet aspired to world power, an appropriate line of policy was mapped out for it in the *Arthasâstra*. Its first step, which was, of course, likely to be difficult and take much time and maneuvering, was to subdue the adjacent state, or enemy, then attempt to conquer the medium state, and, if successful, try conclusions with the Udāsīna, or most powerful state. If this first step should be accomplished, the conqueror should endeavor to subdue the other states within the first zone, and then proceed against the states within the other zones in the same way. When all of the states in the circle shall have been brought into subjection, the conquering state will then face from the circumference of the circle other states friendly and hostile, which must be dealt with according to further directions which need not be discussed here.[32]

Certain observations seem to be called for at this point to correct any impression gathered from the foregoing that unceasing and ruthless conquest and absorption of other states was the single objective of sovereigns, to be achieved at any cost, and by any means. Treacherous and unprovoked attacks on other friendly or weak states merely to satisfy hunger for territory, seem not to have been sanctioned by the *Arthasâstra*, and ruthless exploitation of conquered territories and annihilation of peoples were likewise not approved. In the *Arthasâstra*, conquerors were divided into three classes: (1) just, (2) greedy, and (3) demon-like. The just conqueror required only allegiance; the greedy conqueror was interested only in exploiting the vanquished state for gain; and the demon-like conqueror was cruel and bloodthirsty. Whether the author considered a more humane attitude was preferable principally because it was in accord with religious teachings, or on grounds of expediency, he urged a conquering king to treat his new subjects with kindness and consideration, and to have respect for their established customs as far as possible. Expediency probably was the chief, if not the sole, consideration, for the author points out that the conqueror can only win the loyalty of the vanquished by being just and

seven elements, see Nag, *op. cit.*, or his article on "The Diplomatic Theories of Ancient India and the 'Arthosastra,'" *Journal of Indian History,* V (1926), 331-340.

[32] Law, *op. cit.*, pp. 31-32.

following a policy of reconciliation. In furtherance of this object of attaching his new subjects to him, a king is advised even to adopt their dress, language, and customs and, in general, their mode of life. It was also regarded as expedient for the conqueror to maintain the ruler of a conquered kingdom on his throne as long as he should be well-behaved; for should he be deposed without cause, an appeal to the circle of states might be made against the decision and trouble ensue. In short, a conquering king should immediately adopt a most liberal policy of conciliation, and work for the improvement and prosperity of his new subjects.[33]

Conquest was, of course, not always feasible, and the *Arthasâstra* writers laid down six measures of policy to fit the different circumstances with which a king might have to contend. These six courses of action, which might be employed in various combinations were: (1) peace, (2) war, (3), equilibrium, (4) attack, (5) resigning oneself to the protection of another, and (6) making alliance with one and fighting with another.[34] Although the detailed discussion, concerning the employment under different circumstances of this sextuple policy, is too detailed and intricate to be dealt with here, an important principle of diplomacy, which seems to have been widely supported, is to be observed. As far as possible, a king should seek to attain his objectives without war. In any case he should (1) consolidate his own kingdom before undertaking war. When that is done he should (2) calculate the advantages to be derived from peace and war. If they seem to be equal, he should prefer peace, "for disadvantages such as the loss of power and wealth, sojourning, and sin, are ever attending upon war."[35] Thus war, in ancient India, as a means of realizing the objectives of a state, was recognized as costly and unsatisfactory, and was apparently never extolled as a good in itself.[36]

[33] Viswanatha, *op. cit.*, pp. 119-120, 173-184. Ghoshal, *op. cit.*, pp. 145-147. Conquests in ancient India do not seem to have affected the position of the peasants. Taxes and tribute were exacted of them but they were not despoiled of their proprietary rights and reduced to slavery or serfdom as often happened in the case of people conquered by the Greeks and Romans.

[34] Based on Law, *op. cit.*, p. 24, and Nag, *op. cit.*, pp. 78-81. Prasad, *op. cit.*, p. 365, gives the six measures of policy as alliance, war, marching, halting, dividing the army, and seeking protection. In *The Ordinance of Manu*, Lecture VII, as translated by A. C. Burwell and edited by E. W. Hopkins, they are set down as alliance, war, marching, encampments, stratagems, and recourse to protection.

[35] *Arthasâstra*, p. 320; Prasad, *op. cit.*, p. 61; Viswanatha, *op. cit.*, pp. 118-119.

[36] Nag, *op. cit.*, p. 82, in discussing *Kautilya's Arthasâstra*, asserts that "l'entente occupe la plus grande place dans son système."

REFERENCES

Banerjea, P., *International Law and Custom in Ancient India* (Calcutta, 1920).

Benerjee, G., *India as Known to the Ancient World* (London and Bombay 1921).

Bhandarker, D. R., *Ancient History of India* (Calcutta, 1919).

Chakravarti, P., "Philosophy of War Among the Ancient Hindus," *Journal of Indian History,* VII (1928), 157-184.

Courtillier, G., *Les Anciennes Civilisations de l'Inde* (Paris, 1930).

Ghoshal, A., *History of Hindu Political Theory* (London, 1923).

Gowen, H. H., "Indian Machiavelli; Political Theory in India 2000 Years Ago," *Political Science Quarterly,* LXIV (June, 1929), 173-192.

Hopkins, E. W., ed., *The Ordinances of Manu,* translated from the Sanskrit by A. C. Burwell (London, 1884), Lecture VII, par. 155-210.

————, *The Ethics of India* (New Haven, Conn., 1924), pp. 101-106.

————, *The Social and Military Position of the Ruling Caste in Ancient India* (New Haven, Conn., 1889).

Jayaswal, K. P., *Hindu Polity* (Calcutta, 1924).

Laurent, F., *Histoire du Droit des Gens et des Relations Internationales,* 18 vols. (2nd ed., Brussels, 1861-1870), I, *L'Orient* (1861), 160-259.

Law, N. N., *Inter-state Relations in Ancient India* (London, 1920).

Letourneau, C., *La Guerre dans les Diverses Races Humaines* (Paris, 1895).

Mookerji, R., *Nationalism in Hindu Culture* (London, 1921).

————, *Men and Thought in Ancient India* (London, 1924), pp. 99-110.

Muller, Max, ed., *Sacred Books of the East,* 50 vols. (Oxford, 1879-1926), Vol. I for index.

Nag, K., *Les Théories Diplomatiques de l'Inde Ancienne et Arthaśâstra* (Paris, 1923). ————, "The Diplomatic Theories of Ancient India and the Arthosastra," *Journal of Indian History,* V, 331-358; VI, 15-35.

Prasad, B., *Theory of Government in Ancient India* (Allahabad, 1927), pp. 144-150.

Rapson, E. J., *The Cambridge History of India,* 6 vols. (Cambridge, Eng., 1922-1932), Vol. I, *Ancient India.*

Shamasastry, R., tr., *Kautilya's Arthasâstra* (2nd ed., Mysore, 1923).

Sidhanta, N. K., *The Heroic Age of India* (New York, 1930), pp. 126-234, 175-192.

Smith, V. A., *Oxford History of India* (2nd ed., Oxford, 1923), Introduction and Bks. I and II.

Vinaya-Sarkar, B. K., *Chinese Religion through Hindu Eyes* (Shanghai, 1916). ————, *The Political Institutions and Theories of the Hindus* (Leipzig, 1922), pp. 186-188, and Ch. IX.

Viswanatha, S. V., *International Law in Ancient India* (London, 1925).

CHAPTER IV

ANCIENT GREECE

We now turn to the West, and to a physical environment quite different from that in which the institutions and ideas of the Chinese and Hindus developed. The latter peoples occupied and extended political control over large continental areas; the Greeks established their communities and achieved their intellectual triumphs principally in the islands of the Aegean area. The stimulating environment doubtless made a strong contribution to the exceptional vigor of mind and speculative activity which led to the great achievements of the fifth and fourth centuries. On account of their location in the eastern half of the Mediterranean sea, and their possession of many excellent harbors in the innumerable islands of the Aegean, the Greeks were splendidly situated not only to develop trade and intercourse among themselves, but to make invigorating and enlightening contacts with other peoples to the east. In time, this operated to modify their ideas of other races and break down their exclusiveness.

The Greeks were a warlike people, and in the Homeric age, when they had ceased their wanderings and had begun to have a settled life, the picture of inter-tribal relations is not edifying. Piracy was recognized as an honorable occupation, and tribal forays for the seizure of cattle, the burning of crops, and enslavement of the owners seem to have been normal in the relations of the Greek communities.[1]

The joy of battle, and the glory and fame of heroes, constitute the main theme of the *Iliad* and the *Odyssey,* in which war was pictured as the chief occupation of men. The gods themselves not only sanctioned the carnage indulged in by the happy warriors, but were regarded as active partisans in the warfare of communities, and often as direct participants. They were considered capable of taking terrible

[1] T. D. Seymour, *Life in the Homeric Age* (New York and London, 1907), pp. 270-271 *et passim.*

revenge on those mortals who displeased them, but if properly cultivated and propitiated would lend invaluable aid against the enemy.[2] The Greek states, therefore, were careful to do them honor by means of festivals, processions, and sacrifices.

Yet there is one outstanding representative of Greek thought in this early period who glorified the common man rather than the fighting chieftains. Hesiod, in his *Works and Days,* depicts the hard life of the farmer to whom war brought hardship and ruin rather than honor and fame. War and discord, he avers, result from an evil form of rivalry among men. But Zeus has taken care to implant good rivalry in the very order of things, and this form of rivalry urges man on to work and not to conflict. War does not plague those who are just to others, and Zeus rewards justice with well-being. "Peace, which nurtures youth, dwells in the land and never does far-seeing Zeus bring fearful war upon the inhabitants." [3]

The strife which Homer glorified and Hesiod deplored was not quite continuous and not altogether unrestrained even in those far off days. No formal treaties were known and foreigners had no rights. On the other hand, strangers were not always regarded *ipso facto* as enemies, might even be welcomed permanently, and were under the special care of Zeus. The distinction between "Greeks and barbarians" was not as yet known, and such restraints or chivalry in warfare as might be observed seem not to have been based on racial or cultural grounds.[4]

Throughout Greek history, conflict occupies a large place in the relations of the various states, although special circumstances caused it to play a larger rôle in the case of some than of others. Such was true of Sparta in the sixth century B.C. In Sparta we find the embodiment of the ideal of the militant closed state. Its government was that of a camp, ancient critics said, rather than that of a state. Its educational system, its laws, its institutions, its arts were all utilized and in fact

[2] Aristides, an early Christian writer and philosopher of Athens, attributed the continual warfare among the Greeks to what he regarded as their erroneous belief that the gods waged war. See C. J. Cadoux, *The Early Christian Attitude toward War* (London, 1919), p. 50.

[3] C. H. Moore, *The Religious Thought of the Greeks* (Cambridge, Mass., 1916), pp. 28-33; W. E. Caldwell, *Hellenic Conceptions of Peace* (New York, 1919), pp. 36-37. Hesiod was born in Boeotia during a time of invasion when war had exhausted the land and bore heavily on the farmer. He wrote out of the bitterness of his experience.

[4] Seymour, *op. cit.*, pp. 112-114.

made a means to one end—the breeding of warriors and the development of the warrior mind. The thoroughness with which she did this made Sparta unique among the Greek states. "In the story of Hellas, Sparta stands alone among the peoples as yielding no foothold to the life of the mind, bare of nearly all memory of beauty, indigent of all that belongs to the spirit, morally sterile as steel." [5]

This unhealthy and one-sided development may doubtless be related to the peculiar Spartan environment rather than to any theory of interstate relationships. Sparta was physically isolated from other states to an unusual degree. It was described by one of the ancients as "hollow, surrounded by mountains, rugged, and difficult of access to an enemy." [6] The militarization of Sparta is also to be attributed to the fact that the hostility of the Achaeans whom the Spartans dispossessed when they came into the Peloponnesus did not die out as elsewhere, and that the Spartans lived in a state of constant apprehension of risings of the oppressed helots amongst whom they were numerically insignificant.

Spartan citizens were debarred from engaging in trade or manufacture, and were put through a course of rigorous military training from the age of seven when the state took over their education. When they reached the age of twelve, their heads were closely cropped and they were required to go barefoot and play in the nude. In order further to test and harden them the young men, when they had reached a certain age, were required to undergo terrible whippings, which they were expected to bear with stoicism. All their exercises and games were designed to give them warlike skill. The cultural side was altogether eliminated.[7] Thus along with the hardening of their bodies went an ossification of their minds that was eventually to handicap them against more alert, imaginative, and resourceful rivals in the business of war itself.[8]

The development of pacific intercourse with other states was, of

[5] J. M. Robertson, *The Evolution of States* (New York and London, 1913), p. 130.

[6] As quoted in Robertson, *op. cit.*, pp. 130-131.

[7] G. Gilbert, *The Constitutional Antiquities of Sparta and Athens* (New York, 1895), pp. 63-64.

[8] In the wars of the Greek allied states against Persia in the fifth century, B C., Athens rather than Sparta won renown and leadership because of her superior energy and brilliance. See A. J. Grant, *Greece in the Age of Pericles* (New York, 1897), p. 94.

course, not consonant with this ideal, and Sparta under Lycurgus, at any rate, was consistent. Commercial intercourse with citizens of other states was forbidden, foreigners were expelled, and Spartans were not allowed to travel in other countries.[9] This, it is to be observed, was not for the purpose of allowing Sparta to develop her institutions and live her own life free from outside interference. It was to enable her to dominate other states and impose her will upon them. The Spartan system, therefore, embodied an idea foreign to most Greek thought, and was criticized by Plato, Aristotle, and other Greek thinkers.

During the greater part of the ancient period the Greeks remained divided politically into hundreds of small independent states, being unable or unwilling to develop any single all-embracing political organization of any permanence. Here, too, their physical environment contributed powerfully toward the maintenance of political separatism. Physically, there was not the unity that an unbroken land area gives. Island communities such as the Greeks established were not isolated from one another and the rest of the world, but the Greek states were sufficiently insulated by sea and mountain to enable them to develop an individual character and spirit of independence, and to make their forceful subjugation to a common political authority a difficult matter. The Greek ideal of the city-state was a natural outgrowth of this environment. As conceived by the philosophers, it should not be so large that the citizens would be unable to assemble for the performance of their duties, or that its unity would be endangered. It was regarded as a complete, self-sufficient, and politically independent entity. To it the citizens owed supreme loyalty and devotion, and within it they would find full scope for their energies and the full realization of their aspirations. And no Hellenic interstate citizenship was recognized. To the citizens of one state the citizens of all other Greek states were aliens in the political sense, and thus subject to the disabilities of travel, residence, and intercourse attaching to foreigners except as these were modified by the custom of "guest-friendship."

Among these communities, however, there did develop a certain consciousness of Greek kind which bound them all together in one cultural unity and made them feel and act differently toward non-Greek peoples. Even so, this Pan Hellenic cultural consciousness never

[9] C. Phillipson, *The International Law and Custom of Ancient Greece and Rome*, 2 vols. (London, 1911), I, 39.

resulted in a desire or willingness on the part of the Greek states to submerge their identity politically in a Greek nation. In fact they quarreled and bickered and fought among themselves frequently, and were often only constrained to cooperate by threat of danger from outside the Hellenic world. Then the Pan Hellenic spirit would usually be shown as illustrated in the reply of Aristides on behalf of Athens to an offer of alliance by Persia: "There is not enough gold on the earth, no land fine or rich enough, nothing whatever can induce us to take the part of the Medes to reduce Greece to slavery. . . The Hellenic race being of one blood, speaking the same language, having the same gods, temples, sacrifices, customs, and usages, it would be shameful of Athenians to betray it."[10]

From the Greek point of view Hellas constituted "a small oasis of intelligence and culture ringed round by a wide and indefinite expanse of barbarism."[11] Thus the Medes, and in fact all other non-Hellenic, peoples were not only different from, but were regarded as inferior to, the Hellenes. They were barbarians, and as such to be considered as natural enemies. To conquer and enslave them, therefore, was a natural right arising out of their inferiority, and any means, no matter how cruel or perfidious, of accomplishing this object was regarded as justifiable in the eyes of the gods. There was no question of right and justice between Greeks and non-Greeks. The latter were outside the pale. The Greek attitude, it will be observed, was essentially the same as that of the Chinese, although actual contact with cultured "barbarians" eventually modified the attitude of the good people of Hellas.[12]

[10] As a matter of fact, there were many more or less important religious, social, economic, and political differences that often made for dissension or lack of understanding among the Greek states. See Phillipson, *op. cit.*, Vol. I, Ch. I. It must also be remarked that the idealism expressed in the quotation from Aristides was not always realized in practice, Greek states on occasion allying themselves with the "Barbarian" against other Greek states.

[11] R. W. Livingstone, ed., *The Legacy of Greece* (Oxford, 1922), p. 327.

[12] As early as the fifth century B.C., Antiphon of Rhamnus (in Attica) anticipated later cosmopolitan thought by attacking the distinction between Greek and barbarian, pointing out that the physical attributes and natural endowment of both were the same. (See E. Barker, *Greek Political Theory* [London, 1918], pp. 69, 85.) Aristotle, on the other hand, held the orthodox view as to Hellenic superiority. In cold countries such as those in northern Europe the people were distinguished for their courage, but were deficient in understanding; the Asiatics had quick understandings, but were deficient in courage; the Greeks alone had both sets of virtues. (*Politics*, tr. by Jowett (Oxford, 1885), p. 1327b.)

The different attitude of the Greek peoples towards one another is seen in their theory as to the proper conduct of war between Greek states; for although some of the more advanced spirits deplored all war between the states of Hellas, the latter were all organized to a greater or less degree on a military basis and warfare among them was generally accepted as a constant. It was not regarded as proper, however, for a Greek state to wage war on another without alleging a definite cause. To do so was irregular, and forbidden by law and religion. This was quite superfluous when the war was against a barbarian state. Greek thought also condemned certain inhumane and brutal practices that were held justified as against non-Hellenic enemies. For example, Socrates is said to have drawn a distinction between inter-Hellenic war and war against the barbarians. The former should be carried on solely for the purpose of correction and reconciliation, not for destruction or enslavement: "And as they are Hellenes themselves they will not devastate Hellas, nor will they burn houses, nor ever suppose that the whole population of a city—men, women, and children—are equally their enemies for they know that the guilt of war is always confined to a few persons and that the many are their friends. . . Their enmity to them will only last until the many innocent sufferers have compelled the guilty to give satisfaction." [13]

The view that warfare among Greek states should be held within certain limits received concrete expression in the Delphic Amphictyony. The representatives of the member states of this organization took an oath that they would not destroy any city of the Amphictyony or cut it off from running water either in war or in peace. It was also agreed that any member violating the agreement would be attacked by the others, who would destroy its cities.[14]

The idea of preventing wars between Greek states whenever possible by substituting arbitration of differences was not only supported by the best Greek thought, but also the conception was more fully developed, and the principle of arbitration came to be more extensively

[13] Phillipson, *op. cit.*, II, 192-193. The view that "the few" rather than "the many" are responsible for war reminds us of the teachings of Mencius, and will be met with often among later thinkers as well.

[14] See article by William Linn Westerman on "Greek Culture and Thought," *Encyclopaedia of the Social Sciences*, I, 14. The Delphic Amphictyony was one among a half dozen amphictyonies which developed rather early in Greek history among neighboring cities, for religious purposes of one kind or another.

applied among the Greek states than among any other ancient people.[15] The significance of resort to arbitration lies in the fact that parties to a dispute agree to dispense with self-help and the hazardous decision of force, and allow a presumably disinterested third party to render a decision after hearing the disputants and examining the evidence. It is quite understandable why this conception took firm hold in ancient Greece. There were a large number of rather evenly-balanced states and the resort to war for settlement of the differences of any two of them was often likely to be inexpedient from the point of view of both.[16] If two evenly-matched states with a grievance against each other arrived at a stalemate after a long war, neither side could expect to reap any benefit. If, however, they could bring themselves to submit the matter at issue to arbitration in the first place, any decision likely to be made would probably be more satisfactory to both parties than to fight an inconclusive war.

It is also to be observed that another set of conditions in the Greek world suggested the practicality of interstate arbitration. There were a sufficient number of points of cultural contact in this relatively homogeneous society, a sufficient like-mindedness, and enough likeness of institutions that resort to arbitration within the Greek community could be made with more confidence and with a better prospect of success than with peoples on quite different levels of culture and with strange institutions. It is significant that the Greeks, for a considerable time at least, do not seem to have thought of its use in their relations with other peoples.

From the seventh century to the second century B.C., interstate arbitration seems to have been resorted to in various parts of Greece and by large as well as small states in the settlement of various types of disputes.[17] In many instances it was employed to end wars rather than to prevent their occurrence.[18] By the middle of the fifth century, however, the idea of forestalling wars by a system of arbitration, as contrasted with sporadic and occasional resorts to arbitration, was

[15] M. N. Tod, *Greek International Arbitration* (Oxford, 1913), p. 169; Phillipson, *op. cit.*, II, 129.

[16] A. H. Raeder, *L'Arbitrage International Chez les Hellènes* (New York, 1912), p. 145.

[17] H. Ralston, *International Arbitration from Athens to Locarno* (Stanford University, Cal., 1929), p. 156.

[18] Caldwell, *op. cit.*, p. 50.

conceived. For example, treaties would often contain clauses requiring arbitration of all disputes that might arise concerning the obligations of the parties under them, and of all other disputes as well.[19] This idea of insuring the peaceful settlement of future controversies by undertaking in advance to arbitrate them when they arise rather than leave the matter to chance and the disposition of the parties at the moment, is still too advanced for some modern statesmen who are reluctant to bind their governments to the use of the arbitral process in unforeseen contingencies.

Although the Greeks did not, apparently, think it necessary to exclude any particular categories of disputes from arbitration, leaving the formula of "national honor" and "vital interests" to be worked out in modern times, it appears that most of the questions submitted to arbitration concerned the occupation of territory, the ownership of which was disputed, and questions involving the delimitation of boundaries.[20]

In the later period, arbitrators were required to take an oath that they would judge the question at issue fairly, and that they had no financial stake of any kind in the outcome. If they could secure a settlement of the controversy by bringing the parties themselves together and trying to get them to reach an agreement, they would often do so. If this failed, they would then pronounce judgment. Thus in the Greek conception arbitration might take on the character of conciliation, with the judge in the rôle of conciliator.[21]

It remains to observe that the various leagues and confederacies which arose in Greece at different times to meet external dangers considered it necessary in their own interests to prevent their members from resorting to war when disputes arose among them. Internal warfare would have made such unions weak and futile. Thus arbitration came to be practically mandatory on the member states of a league for the settlement of all quarrels among themselves.[22] They do not, however, seem to have conceived of a general arbitration tribunal before which all cases should be taken. On the contrary, disputant states seem to have been left free in most instances to select by special agreement the particular arbiter and determine the particular procedure to be followed. This was true in the case of the Cretan Union, a league of

[19] Tod, *op. cit.*, p. 169; Phillipson, *op. cit.*, II, 136.
[20] Tod, *op. cit.*, p. 69; Phillipson, *op. cit.*, II, 131.
[21] Ralston, *op. cit.*, p. 161.
[22] *Ibid.*, p. 156.

thirty-one states (183 B.C.) on the island of Crete. These states were obligated in the articles of union to employ arbitration for the settlement of all disputes arising among them, but no particular court was designated to hear cases. The omission was cared for by the negotiation of arbitration treaties by the several states. In some instances, these treaties specified the tribunal and laid down the procedure for the settlement of future disputes between them.[23]

In the foregoing practices and institutions, whatever breaches in their observance or inconsistencies in their application may be recorded,[24] inheres the notion of a Greek society of states the members of which have certain common interests and objectives not shared with states of the non-Greek world. This conception was voiced many times by the outstanding Greek thinkers. Aristophanes (445-385 B.C.), comic poet of Athens sought to develop an anti-war spirit among the Greek states in his plays. He deplored the Peloponnesian War in which the rivals, Athens and Sparta, were the chief antagonists. Although an Athenian, he did not blame the Spartan people and felt they should not suffer because of the intrigues of the rulers and those groups that utilized war to advance their own interests or satisfy their desire for glory and profit. He makes Lysistrata rebuke both the Spartans and Athenians for their fratricidal strife:

> And now, dear friends, I wish to chide you both,
> That ye, all of one blood, all brethren sprinkling
> The selfsame altars from the selfsame laver,
> At Pylae, Pytho, and Olympia, ay
> And many others which 'twere long to name,
> That ye, Hellenes—with barbarian foes
> Armed, looking on—fight and destroy Hellenes![25]

Plato likewise regarded war between Greek states as fratricidal. It should be called discord and disorder, or civil strife, rather than war. Within Greek society, peace should normally rule. Occasionally it might be abandoned where a state found it necessary to do so in order to

[23] M. van der Mijnsbrugge, *The Cretan Koinon* (New York, 1931), pp. 13, 26, 73.

[24] At times, it is true, warfare among the Greeks was carried on with the greatest savagery. It is likewise true that arbitration agreements were not always respected, although it seems that repudiation of agreements to arbitrate, or refusal to accept awards were exceptional. (See Tod, *op. cit.*, pp. 69, 176 ff.)

[25] From the play *Lysistrata*, as quoted in Caldwell, *op. cit.*, p. 100.

maintain its freedom, but in such a case war should be conducted with humanity and restraint and the door to reconciliation should always be kept open. Accordingly Greek cities should never reduce other Greeks to slavery or burn their houses or crops. Greek states should preserve their strength, on the other hand, in order to wage war and maintain their freedom against the barbarians who were regarded as their natural enemies.[26] Thus Plato thought of the Greek world not as a political unit, to be sure, in which war would automatically be ruled out, but as constituting a single society of politically independent states living under and recognizing certain rules of comity. It is for this reason that Barker calls him "the first thinker who stood for the rule of international law."[27]

Yet the picture would not be complete without sketching certain views, as well as practices, not in harmony with those so far mentioned. The doctrine of expediency was not infrequently advanced as absolving a state from adherence to principles of conduct which, though generally accepted in theory as right and proper as between Greek states, might prove injurious to its immediate interests. In fact occasionally it was asserted that justice had no place in human affairs except in cases where might was checkmated. Thucydides gives us some instances in which this theory was expressed with the most brutal frankness. One of them occurred in 416 B.C., when Athens determined to subjugate Melos, a colony of Sparta, because it had refused to submit to Athenian authority. Replying to the protests of the Melians, the representative of Athens said: "Well, then, we Athenians will use no fine words; we will not go out of our way to prove at length that we have a right to rule, because we overthrew the Persians, or that we attack you now because we are suffering any injury at your hands. We should not convince you if we did; nor must you expect to convince us by arguing that, although a colony of the Lacedaemonians, you have taken no part in their expeditions, or that you have never done us any wrong. But you and we should say what we really think, and aim only at what is possible, for we both alike know that into the discussion of human affairs the question of justice only enters where the pressure of

[26] E. Barker, *op. cit.*, pp. 266-267. See "The Republic," in *The Works of Plato*, English translation by Henry Davis (London, 1916), Vol. II, Book V, Chs. 15-16, pp. 154-157.

[27] *Op. cit.*, pp. 265-268.

necessity is equal, and that the powerful exact what they can, and the weak grant what they must." [28]

It may be remarked that this cynical theory of force as the only determinant in human affairs provided no foundation upon which a system of Hellenic interstate law could be built, for it took into account state interest alone and it ruled out considerations of justice and good faith. For the same reason it presented an insuperable obstacle to the growth of a deep-rooted system of interstate arbitration, although it did not prevent its use by leagues and confederacies as long as they held together, or its employment on occasions when it was calculated that the use of force would be too costly or of no avail. It was, of course, a handy doctrine for a powerful state with imperial ambitions. Athens, as we have observed, and other Greek states as well, came to nourish such ambitions, and so

> For them the Ancient rule sufficed,
> The well-tried, simple plan
> That they should take who have the power
> And they should keep who can.

Consistent with this theory of interstate irresponsibility, and in part a deduction from it, was the maxim, not originating with the Greeks but familiar to other ancient peoples as well, that a state to be safe must constantly strive to keep the balance of power in its own hands, or at least on its own side. Thus when Athens sought to dominate the Greek world, a league of states was formed to thwart her ambitions, and ranged itself against her in the Peloponnesian War. When Athens declined in power, Thebes and Sparta became rivals for a place of dominance in Hellas, and Athens in turn threw herself into the lighter scale in order to maintain a balance of power and prevent either from realizing its ambitions. Throughout Greek history up to the time of the successful Roman conquest, the Greek states habitually resorted to temporary and shifting alliances, coalitions, and combinations as a method of checking power with power when reason and justice proved of no avail.

Although there were many bids not merely for leadership but for dominion by one or another of the Greek states, especially Athens, no

[28] See Phillipson, *op. cit.*, Vol. II, Ch. XVIII, "State Interest and Balance of Power."

general theory of imperialism was developed by the Greek philosophers. The Athenian historian Thucydides, in his history of the Peloponnesian War, has Pericles and other spokesmen for Athens explain and interpret the motives and ideals animating that state in her imperialistic enterprises, but he presents at the most a theory of Athenian imperialism.

The foundations for an aggressive expansionist Athenian policy were perhaps unwittingly laid in the time of Solon, about 594 B.C., when the latter decided to make Athens a manufacturing center, to foster trade, encourage immigration as a part of his plan of economic development, and repair the damage done to her prosperity by incessant war and strife. This policy resulted in Athens' population outgrowing her means of subsistence, and in her having to depend upon outside sources for much of her food supply. The Greek ideal of the self-sufficient state was no longer possible for Athens. Nor could she treat her relations with other states as incidental. She must safeguard her food supply, and in order to do so she must pay more attention to her external relations, and build a navy adequate to the new situation. "Her strength lay no longer in quietness and confidence. She needed to look abroad for her safety, to be active as well as vigilant, and daring as well as prudent. She had entered upon the path, so dangerous to ambitious nations, of Defence through Offence." [29]

The threatened Persian invasion of Greece in 493 B.C. brought Athens into a campaign against Persia three years later in which she won such renown that she was given the presidency of the Delian league. For a time, her policy was "peace at home and the complete humiliation of Persia." But, due perhaps to fear as well as ambition, Athenian power under Pericles was pushed vigorously in all directions —in the Levant and Sicily as well as in Greece proper. To other states Athenian conquests often looked like wanton acts of aggression and were roundly condemned. One example was the Athenian expedition to compel the submission of Sicily. To Athens these things were rather acts of far-sighted defense, as the following excerpt from Thucydides makes plain: "We make no fine professions of having a right to our Empire because we risked our existence for the sake of our dependents and of civilization. States, like men, cannot be blamed for providing for their proper safety. If we are now here in Sicily, it is in the interest of our own security. . . It is Fear that forces us to cling to our

[29] A. Zimmern, *Greek Commonwealth* (4th ed., Oxford, 1924), p. 353.

Empire in Greece, and it is Fear that drives us hither, with the help of our friends, to order matters safely in Sicily."[30]

But mere security was not sufficient to explain other things. The Allies of Athens in the Delian league were gradually reduced to subjection. Matters relating to the Confederacy were no longer taken before the Delian Congress but were settled in the Athenian Assembly. The Empire was divided into tribute districts, and assessments were periodically levied to swell the Athenian treasury and make Athens the city beautiful. Legal cases of major importance were taken to Athenian courts for trial, incidentally another source of revenue. Soldiers of the allies were likewise drawn into the army of Athens at half the rate of pay earned by Athenians, and the Athenian navy, supported by tribute money, was used to coerce the rivals of Athens into granting her a monopoly of the shipping and markets of the Aegean.[31]

Now what did all this represent but an arrogant irresponsible parasitism, and the negation of city-state ideals? To Pericles, if Thucydides reflects his views, these things are, however, but the means to an end—that incomparable Athens may lead and guide the world to the highest attainments of the good life, and thereby serve mankind:

> We are the leaders of civilization, the pioneers of the human race. Our society and intercourse is the highest blessing man can confer. To be within the circle of our influence is not dependence but a privilege. Not all the wealth of the East can repay the riches we bestow. So we can work on cheerfully, using the means and money that flow in to us, confident that, try as they will, we shall still be creditors. For through effort and suffering and on many a stricken field we have found out the secret of human power, which is the secret of happiness. Men have guessed at it under many names; but we alone have learnt to know it and to make it at home in our city. And the name we know it by is Freedom, for it has taught us that to serve is to be free. Do you wonder why it is that "alone among mankind" (will there ever be another nation which can understand what we mean?) we confer our benefits, not on calculations of self-interest, but in the fearless confidence of Freedom? [32]

From the middle of the 8th century to the middle of the 6th century, different Greek states planted colonies, but the theory of their

[30] As quoted in Zimmern, *op. cit.*, p. 355.
[31] Caldwell, *op. cit.*, p. 83. A. Zimmern, *Solon and Croesus* (London, 1928), pp. 87-88.
[32] Zimmern, *op. cit.*, pp. 104-105 for quotation.

relationship with the mother country was quite different from that which determined the relationship of Athens to her colonies, and the actual relationship was in most instances different. In time, if not in the beginning, they became independent political units or city-states, reproducing the parent state, and bound to the latter only by ties of sentiment and perhaps interest rather than by political obligation.

The procedure for the establishment of a colony was usually to consult the oracle at Delhi and get the god's consent. The colonizing state then drew up a charter of incorporation setting forth the character of the relationship between it and the colony. The relationship was in theory like that of parent and child. It was the duty of the mother country to educate and protect, the duty of the colony to preserve the religion and gods of the parent, though it might supplement them with gods of its own, and to show filial devotion in other ways. If the mother country was at war, the colony was expected to render such assistance as was in its power, and it was a serious religious breach for either to make war on the other. The colony was to be free to order its own internal life, and any interference by the mother country was regarded as automatically releasing it from the connection. On the other hand, it was to extend hospitality to the parent state, and inter-marriage between the inhabitants of the two states was allowed. The tendency toward eventual separation from the mother country was, of course, rather strong. Frequently the colony was located at a considerable distance, communications were difficult, and local conditions made even the slight political and religious obligations onerous. As the child matured and felt the need of the parent no longer, it was natural that a more or less complete separation should take place. Moreover, such a development did no violence to the fundamental assumption of the Greeks that the city-state is the highest and most efficient political unit.[33]

In any discussion of interstate ideas among the Greeks, Plato and Aristotle deserve more than incidental attention. Plato (427-347 B.C.), in the wide range of his thought, included a number of reflections on interstate relations which are to be found principally in the *Republic* and the *Laws*. Orthodox in his thinking, his greatest interest, of course, is directed toward the character and internal organization of the city-state as furnishing the conditions under which the individual may realize the good life. It was not possible, however for any state to live quite

[33] Phillipson, *op. cit.*, II, 116-123.

to itself alone, and that fact had to be recognized in the discussion of its internal structure, as well as in the field of its external policy.

The philosopher, in his later life at any rate, clearly reveals the conviction that war between states interfered with the good life, and was to be deplored. In the *Laws,* written toward the end of his life and thus embodying his most mature reflections, he voiced the opinion that war furnished neither amusement nor instruction in any degree worth considering.[34] Picturing conditions as he imagined them in human society when population was sparse, before men had become skilled in the arts, and when their wants were few and easily satisfied—the far-off Golden Age—he saw no civil strife and no war. Men were simple-minded and good. In time conditions changed; mankind multiplied; cities were founded; ambitions and rivalries grew up, encroachments on one another's land followed, and war as well as civil strife resulted.[35]

Given the conditions which Plato observed in the age in which he lived, when men had learned to love luxury and had become greedy, one can understand why he regarded war as something that had become inevitable and a contingency for which provision must be made by the wise legislator. The one condition under which it could be eliminated, in his view, was the attainment by states of that original goodness which had characterized people in the Golden Age. As perfect goodness in the individual is his only insurance against injury from others, so goodness in the state would enable it to live a life of peace.[36] But is there hope that such goodness can be attained? The extended treatment Plato gives to the matter of military preparedness, both in the *Republic* and in the *Laws,* seem to provide his answer.[37]

In the *Republic,* Plato concerns himself throughout with the noncommercial or military class. He seems to have been considerably influenced, when he wrote it, by the extreme military institutions of Sparta and, in fact, modeled the *Republic* to some extent on the Spartan state.[38] Men are not content, he writes in effect, to fill their stomachs; they have need for things of the spirit—music, poetry, pic-

[34] *Laws,* p. 803.

[35] *Laws,* pp. 677-679.

[36] "And until philosophers are Kings, or the rulers are imbued with the spirit of philosophy, there will be no deliverance either of cities or the human race." (*Republic,* p. 473.)

[37] *Laws,* pp. 625-628; 829.

[38] G. L. Dickinson, *The Greek View of Life* (London, 1914), p. 74. E. Barker, *op. cit.,* p. 167.

tures. In order that these refinements of life may be realized, a larger population is necessary. This in turn leads to the necessity of acquiring a larger territory. To acquire and defend this territory, it will be necessary to wage war. The element of spirit, which inspires men to battle, now appears, and finds expression in the organization within the state of a military force of guardians whose business it is to protect the state. In Plato's state, however, there is another class of guardians whose characteristic is reason. These philosophic guardians are the rulers, reason being placed above spirit. It is at this point that Plato parts company with the Spartan conception. In Sparta, the element of spirit dominated everything else. Military skill was the passport to office, the soldier ruled in place of the philosopher, and thus the ideal state was corrupted.[39]

In the *Laws,* Plato was more critical of the military state, possibly because he observed that Sparta, in spite of (or because of?) concentrating all her thoughts and energies on the enterprise of war, had gone down before Thebes at the battle of Mantinea in 362 B.C. Thus the war-state had become discredited. The attempt to base the Spartan state exclusively on the virtue of courage had failed. It must be remembered, after all, says the Athenian in the Platonic dialogue, that glorious as courage is, it comes after the virtues of wisdom, prudence, and justice in order of excellence.[40] A genuine statesman, therefore, will never direct his attention exclusively to the needs of foreign warfare, and he will design his war legislation for peace rather than his peace legislation for war.[41]

It is of interest to observe, in the light of certain medieval and modern views of war as a supreme test of rightness or fitness,[42] that Plato did not regard war as furnishing a decisive and ultimate test of the strength and merits of the institutions of states. He observed that larger states seemed to emerge victorious over smaller ones (anticipating Napoleon's "big battalions" dictum), and that well-governed states were often subjugated by states with inferior institutions. He concludes, therefore, that the test of the goodness or badness of the institutions of states must be made in some other way.[43]

[39] *Republic,* pp. 372-376, 414. Barker, *op. cit.,* pp. 167-168, 251-252.
[40] *Laws,* p. 630.
[41] *Laws,* p. 629.
[42] *Infra,* p. 102, and Ch. XII.
[43] *Laws,* p. 638.

The essence of Plato's philosophy, in so far as it touched on interstate life, was that states must look inward rather than outward, seek goodness and perfection and harmony within, rather than dissipate their energies in fruitless struggles without. Nevertheless, this did not lead him to neglect or ignore the outward relationship. In the *Laws,* his conception of the ideal state was one more or less isolated and self-contained. It was not to be on the sea-coast, with good harbors, and therefore in an advantageous position for commerce and interstate intercourse; it was to be located inland, and was to be economically independent of other states as far as possible. Otherwise it would be exposed to the development of luxurious and depraved habits. Trade and commerce were regarded as harmful in that they fostered greed and sharp practices, thus tending to render a city faithless to itself and the rest of the world.[44]

It is clear that such conditions were scarcely to be found in the Greek world, and Plato was careful to work out a system of defense from attack by neighboring states whose ambitions might go beyond mere trading. The question of defense was not to be left to chance, and certainly there was no thought of a policy of non-resistance. In the *Republic,* Plato argued the necessity of a trained and specialized soldiery whose business it should be to devote themselves exclusively to war.[45] Recruits were to be selected on the basis of their special aptitude, their possession of the element of spirit. They were then to go through a course of special training.[46]

In the *Laws,* there is likewise much attention to military defense. Although Plato opposed the idea of building walls about the city, he did so principally because he felt the protection would tend to make the inhabitants soft. Instead of repelling an enemy, they would be inclined to seek refuge within the walls. Moreover, they would not be as watchful and energetic, thinking their safety ensured. On the other hand, Plato advocated marching of all the inhabitants—men, women, and children—for at least one day in each month, and the holding of games and contests that simulated war as closely as possible. Sham

[44] *Laws,* pp. 704-705.

[45] Men train for athletic contests, says Plato, and should they be less prepared for the greatest of all contests in which the goods and lives of the people of the state are at stake? (p. 830.)

[46] See *Republic,* pp. 376-412, for detailed treatment.

battles in which real, though blunted, weapons were to be used was also advocated.[47]

Plato has been characterized as a deductive, idealistic thinker as contrasted with Aristotle and others. Whatever may be true of other matters, his deductions and reflections in the sphere of interstate relations are based on observation and experience, and, so far from being visionary, are quite orthodox for the most part. On the whole, he is not an iconoclast or a pioneer here—he reflects the current thought of his race and his time.

Aristotle (384-322 B.C.), the pupil of Plato, had the same general outlook on interstate relations. Concentrating most of his attention on the problem of the development of justice and goodness within the state, at the same time he was compelled to recognize that the character of the state and the life of its citizens were of necessity in some measure related to, if not conditioned by, the co-existence of other states.

From a theoretical standpoint, the prevailing Greek view was that the state was complete in itself. It was in accordance with this view that Aristotle contended that a well-governed city with a good system of laws, and situated so that it would have no intercourse with other states, might be very happy without providing in its constitution for the contingency of war and conquest; for under these conditions there would be no occasion for either. Recognizing, however, the improbability of a state's realizing such a happy situation, he held it to be the duty of the legislator of a city to work out a policy toward other states suitable in each case to the needs of the situation.[48]

In his discussion of the most advantageous location of a state he parts company with Plato and, moreover, seems to recognize the desirability of some commercial intercourse between states. Looking at the question from the point of view of the city's ability to defend itself, he concludes that it should be near the sea. It can then prepare its defense by sea as well as by land. Such a location is advantageous also from the point of view of a state's exchanging commodities, of which it has a surplus, for foreign products in which it is deficient. Under the circumstances, it will probably be necessary for the state to become, to some extent, a naval power; for not only must it defend

[47] *Laws*, pp. 760-761, 778, 829.
[48] *Politics*, p. 1325a.

itself, but it may be necessary to assist neighboring states against a common enemy by sea as well as by land. From which one may conclude that Aristotle did not quite believe a state could be economically self-sufficient, whatever he might think of its political and cultural self-sufficiency, and that he did think a temperate and regulated intercourse with other states might be salutary. Yet it is evident that he thought of such intercourse as incidental in the life of the well-regulated state.

The relative place that war should occupy in the life of a state, from Aristotle's point of view, may be gathered from certain of his remarks on the proper education of youth. The education of children should be so directed that they will be fitted both for labor and war, but more particularly for leisure and peace. Likewise, although they should be taught to do what is necessary and useful, the emphasis in this training should be on what is fair and noble. Yet, says Aristotle, legislators seem not to have framed their legal and educational systems with the best end in mind. In Sparta, for example, the legislator makes war and victory the end of his government. The people are trained for it only, and know not how to use leisure or employ themselves in anything else. What have they gained? They have had to endure a despotic government, and even so they have not been able to win supremacy over the other states. The legislator, concludes Aristotle, should not train people for war in order that they may reduce their inferiors to slavery, but only in order that they themselves may not be enslaved by others.[49]

If he had said nothing else on the subject, one might reasonably conclude that Aristotle believed only in wars of self-defense, even against inferior peoples. The matter, however, is not so clear. He shared the generally accepted opinion of his day that some men are slaves by nature and are therefore intended to be used as such by a highly endowed master class. Should they refuse to submit, force may be used to compel them. By the same token, in at least one of the passages of his *Politics,* Aristotle seems to take the position that if any people intended by nature for slavery is unwilling to submit to it, a war waged against them is justified.[50]

There is no ground for inferring, however, that Aristotle had any definite convictions of the necessity or desirability of a state's expand-

[49] *Politics,* pp. 1271, 1333, 1334a.
[50] *Ibid.,* p. 1256b. See also p. 1255.

ing at the expense of other states or peoples.[51] He recognized, as Barker[52] points out, that in principle a state has two alternatives. It may pursue an active vigorous policy in contact with other states, which will correspond somewhat to a life of action for the individual, or it may forego this outer activity and concentrate on a life of virtuous activity within, which will bear a resemblance to the life philosophic of the individual. Anticipating the objection that if a state renounces intercourse with others it will stagnate, he points out that there will still be intercourse and activity within, and between parts of, the state. It can therefore lead a life of virtuous activity just as the individual philosopher who maps the way for others to follow may lead an active virtuous existence. This is the better choice, he concludes, for the state as well as for the individual.[53]

Quite consistent with the foregoing are Aristotle's remarks about the proper size of a city. To those who feel that a city should be large to be happy, he points out that the difficulties of government and the maintenance of order increase with size, and the conditions necessary for the good life with its resultant happiness are impaired. On the other hand, it must not be so small as to be incapable of self-defense.[54] From all this it would seem to be clear that Aristotle's city was not designed for a career of expansion and militant happiness, but rather for the realization of happiness within.

By the third century B.C., the federation became the normal type of polity in Greece, marking an advance beyond the conception of the city-state. More or less loose unions of states are to be found as early as the sixth century and in the fourth century federations played a not inconspicuous part in the politics of the time. But the Aetolian and Achaean leagues of the third century represented in their constitutions an approach to a representative system in that the real power in both of them was exercised by a federal council composed of representatives of each of the member states. This development came after imperial Athens had fallen from her high estate, and after the passing of the Macedonian Empire. Its significance lies in the fact that it was "the

[51] Although he was later to support the imperialistic enterprise of his pupil Alexander because, apparently, he felt order, security, and peace in the distracted Greek world of his day could be secured only by a unified political control.

[52] *Op. cit.*, pp. 287-288.

[53] *Politics*, p. 1325b.

[54] *Ibid.*, p. 1326.

first attempt on a large scale to reconcile local independence with national strength" and that it gave "to a larger portion of Greece than any previous age had seen, a measure of freedom, unity, and general good government. . ."[55]

Toward the end of the Greek period of independence, a new conception of cosmopolitanism began to gain ground among the Cynic and Stoic philosophers. Conditions of the time favored the development. The conquests of Alexander of Macedon played an important part. Alexander did not share the racial prejudices of his tutor, Aristotle, who advised him to preserve the distinction between Greeks and barbarians in his state policy. He sought rather to unite the peoples of the East and West on a basis of equality, and to fuse the two cultures.[56] To that end, he encouraged the intermarriage of Greeks and Persians, absorbed Persians into his army, and even adopted certain of their customs and institutions. The closer and friendlier contacts of the Greeks with other peoples, brought about with the establishment of the empire, doubtless contributed to the dissipation of ancient prejudices and paved the way for a new political outlook. A new orientation for the individual was indicated, for the center of authority and interest had shifted from the city-state to the distant capital of an empire.[57]

The term cosmopolitanism seems to have been used as far back as the fourth or fifth century B.C. by Antisthenes (450-366 B.C.), the pupil of Socrates and founder of the Cynic school of philosophy.[58] The idea for which it stands is undoubtedly much older. The more sensitive and refined spirits of every age, shocked by human strife and turmoil, have turned their gaze in the direction of a world order in which unity and peace might be attained. And the legends and myths of all peoples testify that there have always been those who have held the conviction of the fundamental unity of the human species. Even in the Old Testa-

[55] E. A. Freeman, *History of Federal Government in Greece and Italy* (2nd ed., London, 1893), pp. 553-554. But this effort toward unity soon failed for, as H. G. Wells expresses it, ". . . the Greeks, with all their aptitude for political speculation, were blind to the insecurities of their civilization from without and from within, to the necessity for effective unification, to the swift rush of events that was to end for long ages these first brief freedoms of the human mind." *The Outline of History* (Garden City, N. Y., 1921), p. 308.

[56] It must be noted that there is a difference of opinion as to Alexander's motives and intentions. He may not have had the grand conceptions attributed to him, but he was certainly no provincial in his policies or in his thinking.

[57] C. Bailey, ed., *The Legacy of Rome* (Oxford, 1923), pp. 47-48.

[58] See article on "Cosmopolitanism" by Max Boehm in *Encyclopaedia of the Social Sciences*, IV, 460.

ment, which displays so strongly the exclusiveness and martial ardor of the Chosen People, there are aspirations toward spears being beaten into pruning-hooks, and swords being turned into plough-shares.[59]

The cosmopolitan outlook of the Cynics was negative rather than positive. They attacked all of the institutions of their day, not as reformers but as revolutionaries who desired to see them completely scrapped. As they saw it, society and its institutions—social classes, property, the family, the city—obstructed the development of the individual, held him in shackles and chains. The city-state was too small in area for these wandering philosophers, too restricted in outlook. They were the anti-patriots of Greek antiquity. Not only did they consider one man as good as another, but one place was as good as another. A cynic could ask in all seriousness, "Why should I be proud of belonging to the soil of Attica with the worms and slugs?" They were no better than the worms and slugs of other places. The individual had no need of the state. Citizenship meant nothing to the Cynics unless it was citizenship of the world. Diogenes alone seems to have recognized the necessity of the intermediate government of the state.[60] "For the several sections of the Earth give different men different countries, yet this world in its whole circumference gives all men one country, all the earth, and one home, the world."

In all this we see the antithesis of orthodox Greek thought and to a large extent the reflection of changing political conditions in which ultimately the Greek states lost their independence to Rome. The Roman state, as we shall see when these ideas are further developed in the next chapter, was to take over the conceptions of the Cynics and Stoics and give them a positive expression.

REFERENCES

Aristotle, *Politics,* tr. by Jowett, 2 vols. (Oxford, 1885).

Barker, E., *Greek Political Theory* (London, 1918), pp. 166-169; 264, 268, 298-330.

———, *The Political Thought of Plato and Aristotle* (New York, 1906).

Bonner, R. J., *Aspects of Athenian Democracy* (Berkeley, Cal., 1933), Ch. VIII.

[59] C. Lange, *Histoire de l'Internationalisme* (New York, 1919), p. 27.
[60] E. Barker, *op. cit.,* pp. 105-107.

Botsford, G. W., "Amphictyony," *Encyclopedia Britannica* (11th ed., 1910).

——————, *Hellenic History* (New York, 1922).

Bury, J. G., ed., *The Hellenistic Age* (Cambridge, Eng., 1923), pp. 79-107.

Caldwell, W. E., *Hellenic Conceptions of Peace* (New York, 1919).

Chadwick, H. M., *The Heroic Age* (Cambridge, Eng., 1912). (Cambridge Archeological and Ethnological Series.)

Croiset, M., *Aristophanes and Political Parties at Athens,* tr. by J. Loeb (London, 1909).

Darby, W. E., *International Arbitration* (4th ed., London, 1900), pp. 1-10.

Dawson, M. M., *The Ethics of Socrates* (New York and London, 1924), Ch. XIV, pp. 246-250.

Dickinson, G. L., *The Greek View of Life* (London, 1914).

Ferguson, W. S., *Greek Imperialism* (Boston and New York, 1913).

Fitzgerald, A., *Peace and War in Antiquity* (London, 1931).

Freeman, E. A., *History of Federal Government in Greece and Italy,* ed. by J. B. Bury (2nd ed., London, 1893).

Fuller, B. A. G., *History of Greek Philosophy,* 3 vols. (New York, 1923).

Gilbert, G., *The Constitutional Antiquities of Sparta and Athens* (New York, 1895), pp. 230-235.

Greenidge, A. H. J., *A Handbook of Greek Constitutional History* (London and New York, 1896), Ch. VII.

Grundy, G. B., *Thucydides and the History of His Age* (London, 1911).

Gwynn, A., *The Character of Greek Colonization.* Johns Hopkins University Studies in History and Political Science, XXXVIII, 88-123.

Harris, H., "The Greek Origin of the Idea of Cosmopolitanism," *International Journal of Ethics,* XXXVIII (Oct., 1927), 1-10.

Hershey, A. S., *The Essentials of International Public Law and Organization* (rev. ed., New York, 1927), pp. 41-47.

Hesiod, Extracts from "Works and Days" and "Theogony," with critical note. In *Warner's Library of the World's Best Literature, Ancient and Modern* (New York, 1902), XII, 7329-7332.

——————, *Works and Days,* ed. by T. A. Sinclair (London, 1932).

Holtzendorff, F. von, and Rivier, A., *Introduction au Droit des Gens* (Paris, 1889), pp. 49-56.

Hume, D., *Essays and Treatises on Several Subjects,* 2 vols. (London, 1772), Vol. I, Pt. II, Essay VII.

Lang, A., *Homer and His Age* (London, 1906).

Lange, C., *Histoire de l'Internationalisme* (New York, 1919).

Laurent, F., *Histoire du Droit des Gens et des Relations Internationales,* 18 vols. (Brussels, 1861-1870), Vol. II.

Lord, L. E., *Aristophanes, His Plays and Influence* (Boston, 1925).

Marvin, F. S., ed., *Evolution of World Peace* (London, 1921), Chs. II-III.
Mühl, Max, *Die Antike Menscheitsidee* (Leipzig, 1928).
Myers, P. V. N., *History as Past Ethics* (New York, 1913).
Myres, J. L., *The Political Ideas of the Greeks* (New York, 1927).
Olphe-Galliard, G., *La Morale des Nations* (Paris, 1920), Ch. II.
Phillipson, C., *The International Law and Custom of Ancient Greece and Rome;* 2 vols. (London, 1911).
Plato, *Republic,* tr. by Davies and Vaughan (London, 1929).
———, *Laws,* tr. by R. G. Bury; 2 vols. (London, 1926).
Plutarch, *The Writings of Plutarch,* 10 vols. (New York, 1905).
Raeder, A. H., *L'Arbitrage International Chez les Hellènes* (New York, 1912).
Ralston, J. H., *International Arbitration from Athens to Locarno* (Stanford University, Cal., 1929).
Redslob, R., *Histoire des Grands Principes du Droit des Gens* (Paris, 1923), pp. 43-109.
Robertson, J. M., *The Evolution of States* (London, 1912), Ch. III.
Sabine, G. H., and Smith, S. B., *Cicero on the Commonwealth* (Columbus, Ohio, 1929), pp. 11 ff., 217 *et passim.*
Seymour, T. D., *Life in the Heroic Age* (New York and London, 1907), Ch. XVIII.
Stawell, F. M., *Growth of International Thought* (London, 1930), Ch. I.
Thucydides, *History of the Peloponnesian War,* tr. by William Smith (London, 1831).
Tod, M. N., *International Arbitration Among the Greeks* (Oxford, 1913).
Walker, T. A., *A History of the Law of Nations* (Cambridge, Eng., 1899), pp. 38-43.
Walsh, E., ed., *History and Nature of International Relations* (New York, 1922), pp. 31-60.
Wheaton, H. A., *History of the Law of Nations* (New York, 1845), pp. 16 ff.
Willoughby, W. W., *Political Theories of the Ancient World* (New York, 1903).
York, E., *Leagues of Nations* (London, 1919), Ch. I.
Zimmern, A., *Greek Commonwealth* (4th ed., Oxford, 1924).
———, *Solon and Croesus* (Oxford, 1928), Ch. III.

CHAPTER V

ROME

It has often been pointed out that the Romans, as contrasted with the Greeks, were little given to speculative thought, and that their particular genius lay in the selection and application of ideas for the solution of the problems confronting them in their march toward political supremacy. Hardheaded and practical in their outlook on the world, their ideas as to the nature of the state and their views of interstate relations are seldom expressed directly and as philosophic concepts, but must be extracted from their institutions, their practices, and their policies.

Rome originally was a city-state along with a number of other independent Italian communities. The selection of the region of the seven hills, in contact with the sea, yet relatively secure against attack and favorable to expansion, laid a physical foundation for the career which was to carry her to a position of complete political ascendancy in the western civilized world. All this seems to have been appreciated by Camillus, soldier and statesman of the fifth and fourth century B.C., who is described by Mommsen as the one who first opened up to his fellow-countrymen the brilliant and perilous career of foreign conquest. "Not without cause did gods and men select this place for establishing our city—with its healthful hills, its convenient river, by which crops may be floated down from the midland regions and foreign commodities brought up its sea, near enough for use, yet not exposing us, by too great propinquity, to peril from foreign fleets, a situation in the heart of Italy—a spot, in short, of a nature uniquely adapted for the expansion of a city."[1]

It may be, as the poet Vergil suggests, that the early Romans, like Cincinnatus, preferred the plough to the sword, and that they turned reluctantly to the latter in self-defense when menaced by their neigh-

[1] Quotation from Livy, Vol. V, Sec. LIV, p. 4, as given in E. D. Wilsey, *Roman World Philosophy* (New York, 1930), p. 7.

bors and by the incursions of more distant tribes. In any event, they handled the sword with such effectiveness and consolidated their gains with such skill that by the beginning of the third century B.C. Rome had become mistress of the Italian peninsula. By the middle of the second century she had extended her hegemony over the Mediterranean littoral, after finally defeating and destroying her rival, Carthage. Under Pompey and Caesar, toward the end of the pre-Christian era, the Roman frontiers were pushed eastward to the Euphrates and westward to the Atlantic.

In the earlier period before Rome was able to dominate the Mediterranean world, she quite generally showed a disposition to recognize certain rules of international conduct as applicable in her relations with other peoples, and to accept the principles of reciprocity and juridical equality in her political and commercial dealings with other states. For example, the Romans entered into treaties with their neighbors on terms of equality, and seem to have lived up to them in most instances. Foreigners enjoyed hospitality, were often admitted to Roman civic rights, and when sojourning in Rome were assured the protection of their legal rights through the system of the *ius gentium.*[2]

Although the earlier wars of the Romans were perhaps more frequently characterized by an unrestrained ferocity, this was due to the fact that they were often vital defensive struggles for Rome's very existence, whereas later the object was the advancement and extension of the rule of a power sure of itself and certain of its success.[3] From very early times, however, the system of the *ius fetiale* operated as a restraint in the conduct of war, as well as regularizing the conduct of peace-time relations. The college of fetials was a semi-political priestly board invested with the supervision of the formalities requisite for the declaration of war and the swearing of treaties, and also having the

[2] It was applied by the praetors and was based upon practices that were found prevalent in a large number of Italian cities and among Mediterranean peoples. These practices were considered to have inherent elements of justice on account of their widespread existence. T. A. Walker, *A History of the Law of Nations* (Cambridge, Eng., 1899), pp. 44-47. C. Phillipson, *The International Law and Custom of Ancient Greece and Rome,* 2 vols. (London, 1911), I, 103, 411. The *ius gentium* consisted of a body of rules for the settlement of disputes arising between aliens, and between Roman citizens and aliens. (The *ius civile* was applied only to Roman citizens.)

[3] Phillipson, *op. cit.,* II, 224. In the later wars under the Empire there are also instances of inhuman butcheries and disregard of all legal and religious restraints.

authority of a court of first instance in the settlement of various international disputes.[4] The fetials also acted as ambassadors of the Senate and the Roman people to other states when Rome had complaints to lodge or matters to adjust.

The Romans were outstanding among the peoples of antiquity in their emphasis upon the meticulous observance of certain formalities of interstate intercourse.[5] The rules were laid down and interpreted by the Romans themselves, it is true, but in theory they were to be applied to Rome and other states alike. Only "just wars" were regarded as permissible. Justice required that certain formalities be complied with in connection with the commencement and prosecution of a war. Should it be alleged that a neighboring people had committed some act justifying war, the fetial board was expected to make an investigation for the Senate. If the charge was substantiated, a formal demand for redress was made, and a period of thirty-three days was allowed within which restitution must be made, or war would be declared.[6] Among the offenses which were regarded as justifying war were the violation of a treaty, the desertion or ill-treatment of an ally, refusal to receive embassies or failure to observe the sanctity of ambassadors, rendering aid to an enemy, infringement of territorial rights, desecration of sacred places, and refusal to give up a person or persons guilty of serious offenses.[7] Cicero in his *Commonwealth* adds his testimony to that of many others that Roman thought regarded war not as a normal relation of peoples, although admittedly of frequent occurrence. If undertaken without a reason, he said, it is unlawful. An injury must first be shown for which redress has been refused, and finally a public declaration must be made before hostilities are commenced.[8] In general, the Romans considered that they were entitled to dispense with this procedure only in case they were suddenly attacked or subject to acts of hostility and when they were dealing with peoples lacking the requisite political organization.[9]

[4] T. Frank, *Roman Imperialism* (New York, 1914), p. 8. Walker, *op. cit.*, p. 47.
[5] The various ceremonials were not necessarily Roman in their origin, however.
[6] Phillipson, *op. cit.*, II, 329-343, for interesting details of the procedure.
[7] *Ibid.*, II, 182.
[8] G. H. Sabine and S. B. Smith, *Cicero on the Commonwealth* (Columbus, Ohio, 1929), p. 217. The position of Cicero may be contrasted with that of Aristotle in so far as the latter seems to regard war as justified when waged against a people intended by nature for slavery. (*Politics*, p. 1256b.)
[9] Phillipson, *op. cit.*, II, 199. Rome recognized no obligations to the barbarians, who were, in the Roman view, those peoples living outside Roman jurisdiction, who did not recognize Roman law and authority, and with whom Rome had no

When war had been declared, there were certain rules of the game which Rome acknowledged as normally binding upon all belligerents, and which she sought to have respected. "There are laws of war as well as of peace; and we have learned to enforce them not less justly than bravely." [10] In theory, the reason for which the war was begun in the first place was regarded as indicating the object for which it was pursued, and therefore as setting limits to its prosecution. If, for example, it resulted in redress of an injury or proper restitution by the enemy, it should not be carried further in order to accomplish his destruction. Likewise, truces for the burial of the dead, for the carrying on of peace negotiations, or for other purposes were to be respected. Phillipson says: "The methods of Roman warfare indicate a distinct advance on that of the Greeks, and of all other ancient nations. On the whole, we perceive further mitigations, and more deliberate attempts to regularize belligerent proceedings, and a greater disposition to insist on and appeal to the sanctions of positive law, apart from those of sacred law." [11]

The Romans, like the Greeks and other ancient peoples, regarded treaties as sacred contracts under the special guardianship of the gods, and their infraction an offense against the gods as well as against the law of nations. Various formulae were used at one time or another to invoke the attestation of the deities when a treaty was entered into, so that these divine witnesses might punish the party breaking it. As a more mundane guarantee, it was also frequently provided, as in ancient India and Greece, that hostages should be exchanged.[12]

Yet a state which embarks upon a career of expansion and absorption of other peoples, and is habituated to the use of force in its dealings with other states, is inclined to be cautious about accepting obligations that will restrict its freedom of action too much. Hence interstate arbitration was not employed by Rome as it was by the states of Greece. Before her goal of empire was attained, she gave it practically no recognition. To have resorted to it would have handicapped her in the realization of her ambitions.[13] After she was recognized as imperial

regular relationships. In theory they were in the position of enemies. See R. Redslob, *Histoire des Grands Principes du Droit des Gens* (Paris, 1923), p. 63; and Phillipson, *op. cit.*, I, 230-231.

[10] Attributed by Livy to Camillus. See Walker, *op. cit.*, pp. 48-49.

[11] Phillipson, *op. cit.*, II, 223.

[12] *Ibid.*, II, 389-390, 398-406.

[13] *Ibid.*, II, 152-153. Redslob, *op. cit.*, p. 87.

mistress of the Western world, and desired to maintain the *Pax Romana,* her attitude changed. She favored the peaceful settlement of interstate disputes between the peoples under her suzerainty, and she herself acted as arbitrator. "Hast thou appealed unto Caesar? To Caesar shalt thou go." Those who have arrived and find power sweet, favor law and order, the maintenance of the *status quo.*

Rome, for somewhat the same reason, never was interested, as were the Greek states, in preserving a balance of power. A balance of power system is essentially a device for keeping the power of different states within limits by a system of checks and balances. Rome certainly was not interested in a balance of power for the very reason that she was interested in a monopoly of power. And on the other hand her advance was too steady, her setbacks too few, and her subtlety in dealing with other states too great to afford an opportunity to her foes to form effective coalitions against her. The Roman policy of divide and rule kept her enemies apart and helped her realize a monopoly of power which was her aim.[14]

The Roman view of neutrality presents still another contrast with Greek thought,[15] and another illustration of the attitude to be expected of a state with far-reaching political ambitions. To recognize that a state may be free to elect to remain at peace and to have its peacetime freedom of intercourse respected, is likely to prove an impediment to a state seeking to have all states in definite subjection to it. Hence Rome regarded other states as falling into but two classes—friends and enemies. Those who were not for her were regarded as against her. To be for her meant to be an active ally. An intermediate position was not admitted, although in practice it might be thought expedient to tolerate neutrality in certain circumstances.[16]

Early in their history the Romans made alliances with other peoples, at first for protection, later as a means of advancing their power. In general the rights and obligations contracted were, in the earlier period at least, similar to those to be found in treaties of alliance among other ancient peoples substantially equal in power. Adequate assistance

[14] Phillipson, *op. cit.,* II, 110-112.

[15] The Greeks held that it was the duty of a state at peace with, and in friendly relationship with, two belligerent states not actively to assist either and not to allow one combatant, without granting permission to the other, to use its territory in any way for war purposes. It was also regarded as a violation of the rights of neutral states for a belligerent to interfere with its peaceful commerce.

[16] See Philippson, *op. cit.,* II, 311-313.

in war, for which the alliance was primarily contracted, was required in the treaties of Rome with her allies. No treaties might be concluded with the common enemy. Plunder taken in war was to be shared equally. Allies were debarred from enslaving one another's citizens, and in certain instances citizens of the allied states were privileged to settle anywhere within the territories of the confederates.[17]

Strategic considerations influenced the founding and character of Roman colonies. It has already been seen [18] that the relations between mother country and colony in Hellas was normally that of separate though allied states. Rome established colonies principally in order to consolidate her position, keep her gains, and augment her power. They never attained or approximated separate statehood, and therefore their relations with Rome need not be discussed.[19]

In the later period of her history there was a perceptible decline in the willingness of Rome to acknowledge in practice principles of fair play and progressive rules of international conduct in her relations with other peoples. As time went on, she became more and more imperious and less and less scrupulous. The older practices and formalities were dispensed with, legal fictions to give the color of legality to her conduct were invented, and flimsy pretexts for attacking other peoples were resorted to whenever legal obstacles to the realization of her ambitions needed to be removed. By the fourth century A.D. the fetial procedure had been abandoned, and the rules of war were not observed. State interest and expediency tended to reign supreme.[20] As regards treaties, they were recognized in earlier times as in the nature of agreements voluntarily made between legally equal states to serve their interests. In the later period, on the other hand, Rome tended to regard them largely as embodying obligations owed by a dependent to a sovereign, obligations which the sovereign dictated.[21] In the case of treaties of alliance, the same tendency is to be observed. Rome gradually came to assume the position of an overlord among her allies, and to arrogate to herself the right to decide vital issues.[22]

The small city-state on the Tiber became Imperial Rome, undisputed mistress of the Western world. It would be a mistake, nevertheless, to

[17] Phillipson, *op. cit.*, II, 33-42.
[18] *Supra*, pp. 63-64.
[19] Phillipson, *op. cit.*, II, 124-126.
[20] *Ibid.*, II, 345-348. Walker, *op. cit.*, pp. 55-58.
[21] Phillipson, *op. cit.*, I, 411.
[22] *Ibid.*, II, 43.

think that the Romans had a Grand Design from the start, and moved forward deliberately and relentlessly toward its realization. Chance and "an extraordinary conjunction of circumstances" played a large part.[23] The Romans, endowed with a practical common sense, met the problems arising from their contact and struggle with other peoples in a pragmatic fashion, though certainly not in a fit of absent-mindedness, and gradually became conscious, as their dominion grew, that Rome was destined for greatness and that she had an historical mission to fulfill.[24] In the meantime, however, and even before her arms and diplomacy had carried her far, a philosophic basis for the eventual political development was being laid by certain thinkers in the later days of Greece.[25]

The Stoics, like the Greek Cynics, were unfavorably impressed by the city-states and their institutions, representing, as they did, divisions among mankind. For the Stoics could not subscribe to the nationalist pride and prejudice of orthodox Greek thought, and its racial distinctions. Nor could they accept the notion of philosophers such as Aristotle that some people, by reason of superior intelligence, are intended by nature to rule and that others are fitted only to obey.[26] Their emphasis was on the underlying kinship and brotherhood of all peoples rather than on race, caste, and class distinctions. But the Stoics were not merely negative critics; they had a certain positive conception of human society. They conceived of the Cosmos as a single whole pervaded by reason. On the political side, this conception leads to the World-State, an organization of human society held together not by force and statecraft but by the good-will which grows up naturally

[23] L. Homo, *Primitive Italy and the Beginnings of Roman Imperialism* (London, and New York, 1927), p. 349.

[24] Ernest Barker says: "The type and the genius of the absolute monarchies of the East became familiar to ambitious Romans; and when they received the shadow of divine consecration, they could not but covet the substance of absolute power which cast the shadow. The foundations of imperialism are being laid when the great leaders of the standing armies of the West begin to meet in the East the type of institution and the temper of spirit which can give a concrete body to their dreams and a definite goal to their ambitions. A Roman development meets a Greek conception. That is the genesis of the conception of the Roman Empire." (*The Legacy of Rome,* ed. by C. Bailey [London, 1923], p. 60.)

[25] *Supra,* pp. 71-72.

[26] The Stoic position on the relationship of master and slave was perhaps stated by Chrysippus (280-206 B.C.), who defined a slave as a laborer hired for life. This makes the relationship one of contract rather than that of inherent status. The Stoics, however, were inclined to hold that all men who did not acquire the wisdom to direct their own actions were slaves.

among men who bring themselves into harmony with universal reason. "One universal society, one state of the whole world; one law of nature, with which all its members must live in conformity—these are the two great tenets of Stoicism." [27]

Although Stoicism had its origin in Greece, the early Stoics were not Greeks by birth, but came from the East and had no preconceived notions about superior and inferior peoples and no prepossessions for the City-State to close the vista of a world view. On the other hand, they had seen and must have pondered, as did Zeno, the possibilities of such an enterprise as was undertaken by Alexander of Macedon.[28] Zeno (345-265 B.C.), a Phoenician from Cyprus, was the founder of the Stoic School. He taught that all human beings were fundamentally equal for they all possessed the faculty of reason, and that men should not live in separate cities each with its special rules of justice, but that there should be a single world order. His ideal state, therefore, would embrace the entire earth, and a man would no longer say, 'I am of Athens,' or 'of Sidon,' but 'I am a citizen of the world.' [29] Nor would the World-State need such institutions as courts or money, for it would be composed of wise men capable of living in a state of nature.[30]

Stoicism found ready acceptance at Rome. It was well adapted to the Roman type of mind, which was stern, serious, practical, seeking a "way of life," and at its best disposed to "scorn delights and live laborious days." The Stoics' approach was essentially different from that of the Greeks in that they did not regard philosophy as properly the gratification of intellectual curiosity quite apart from any practical results that might flow from it. They did not divorce theory from practice. Knowledge was to be sought in order to free the individual from feverish restlessness and indecision, and that he might learn virtue—an even, steady course of action. Stoicism, therefore, was welcomed by the Romans, who cared nothing for abstract discussion and subtle reasoning as ends in themselves but were interested in doctrines from the point of view of their serviceableness. And it was possible for

[27] E. Barker, "The Conception of Empire," in *The Legacy of Rome,* ed. by Cyril Bailey, p. 51. Cf. E. F. Arnold, *Roman Stoicism* (London, 1911), pp. 274-275.

[28] Barker, *loc. cit.,* p. 51.

[29] E. V. Arnold, *op. cit.,* p. 66. In reply to the frequent question, "Of what city are you?," Socrates and Diogenes are said always to have replied, "Of the Universe."

[30] G. H. Sabine and S. B. Smith, *op. cit.,* pp. 19, 22-23.

Stoicism to furnish a strong moral support for empire as well as to lead the individual into the paths of virtue.[31]

Cicero (106-43 B.C.), who was to have a brilliant career at the bar and afterwards in high public office at Rome, was much attracted to certain of the ideas of the Stoics, and we find them occupying a prominent place in his eclectic philosophy.[32] The conditions of the time also favored the adoption by thoughtful men of the larger outlook of Stoicism. Rome as a Republican City-State was no longer able to handle the responsibilities of empire, and the theory back of the City-State was no longer followed in practice. The Roman citizen did not function, at least in a real and effective sense. Cicero followed the Stoics in envisaging a law of right reason which was not to be found here or there at certain times, and as the property of certain peoples, but was universal in scope and unchangeable in character. The substance, if not the exact wording, of his thought on this subject is found in the following passage from his *De Republica* as handed down by Lactantius. "True law is right reason conformable to nature, universal, unchangeable, eternal, whose commands urge us to duty, and whose prohibitions restrain us from evil. . . This law cannot be contracted by any other law, and is not liable either to derogation or abrogation. Neither the senate nor the people can give us any dispensation for not obeying this universal law of justice. It needs no other expositor and interpreter than our own conscience. It is not one thing at Rome, and another at Athens; one thing today, and another tomorrow, but in all times and nations this universal law must for ever reign, eternal and imperishable. It is the sovereign master and emperor of all beings. God himself is its author, its promulgator, its enforcer. . ."[33] In this formulation of the idea of natural law is a conception essentially Stoic in character. It was to provide a foundation for the *ius naturale* of the Roman jurists, who were to have the task of working out a legal system for diverse peoples, was to be passed on through them to enter

[31] Arnold, speaking of the Gracchan period, says: "The Greeks had taught their Roman pupils to see in the nascent Roman empire . . . at least an approximation to the ideal Cosmopolis: and many Romans so far responded to this suggestion as to be not unfriendly toward plans for extending their citizenship and equalizing the privileges of those who enjoyed it." (*Op. cit.*, p. 382.)

[32] After being driven from political life during the tempestuous period that was finally to bring the fall of the Roman Republic, he turned to the consolations of philosophy and devoted his time to writing.

[33] *De Republica*, III, 22, as translated in Cicero's *Nature of the Gods, On the Republic, etc.*, ed. by C. D. Yonge (London, 1878), p. 360.

prominently into mediaeval thought, and was later to furnish the chief support for the great work of Grotius.[34]

Cicero's cosmopolitanism did not lead him to ignore the state in which a man lives, or to place it in a subordinate place. "The love of humanity, which has its beginnings in the love of parents for their offspring, binds together first the members of the family, then gradually reaching out beyond the domestic circle, embraces successively relatives, friends, neighbors, fellow citizens; next broadens to include allied nations; and finally comes to embrace the whole human race." [35] The duty one owes his family and country, with which he is more intimately associated, apparently takes precedence of that which he owes to the broader circle.[36]

Among the Roman Stoics, Seneca (4 B.C.-65 A.D.) is an outstanding representative. He was born nearly half a century after the death of Cicero, and saw the complete fulfillment of Rome's aspiration for empire and world unity measurably realized. He was also an active participant in the public life of Imperial Rome. Doubtless he, as well as the other intellectuals of his day were impressed by the conscientious efforts of the Roman emperors to equalize conditions between the different provinces and make a world empire based on justice for all alike. In any event he was strongly imbued with the world view, holding that the value of a man was to be measured by the width of the circle in which he was able to be useful, and that his superior duty was to the world society rather than to his birthplace. His service to this society, whose limits are to be measured only by the reach of the sun's rays, lies in the realm of the intellect, by contemplation and philosophical thought. His active life must be reserved to the service of the state to which he belongs by birth. The work for the establishment of a universal political society had already been accomplished by the organization of the Roman Empire, so that form of service for humanity was naturally not dwelt upon. Like the other Stoics, he held to the fundamental tenet that men are by nature essentially equal, whether of the slave or master class. The slave can possess the virtues of bravery, magnanimity, and a sense of justice as well as another. Men differ from one another only

[34] *Infra*, p. 150-158.

[35] Quoted from *De Finibus*, in P. V. N. Myers, *History as Past Ethics* (Boston, 1913), pp. 238-239.

[36] Lange, *op. cit.*, p. 28. Here Cicero seems to stand with Confucius. Nevertheless there seems to be the conception of a citizenship of the world, in addition to the citizenship of a particular state, implicit in his writings.

in that the temper of some is more upright, and their capacities are better developed.[37] Holding this belief, Seneca could not approve war for the subjection of peoples on the ground, advanced by the Greeks, that they were fit only for slavery. His Stoic philosophy caused him to express admiration for military leaders who bravely faced privation and suffering in perilous enterprises, and to contrast them with those men of soft fiber who preferred lives of ignoble ease. But he condemned military captains like Philip and Alexander who waged wars of conquest and exploitation. Their work was as great a misfortune to humanity as destructive conflagrations, or the floods that submerged fertile plains. He much preferred to honor the works of the gods.[38]

Marcus Aurelius (A.D. 121-180), "the philosopher upon the throne," early took to philosophy, attached himself to the Stoic School, and led an austere life, eventually bearing the heavy responsibility of emperor. He did not accept all of the Stoic beliefs, but he followed Seneca and the others in the doctrine that the world in which man lives is not a meaningless chaos, but an ordered cosmos. "The world is either a welter of alternate combination and dispersion, or a unity of order and providence. If the former, why crave to linger on in such a random medley and confusion? why take thought for anything except the eventual 'dust to dust'? why vex myself? do what I will, dispersion will overtake me. But on the other alternative I reverence, I stand steadfast, I find heart in the power that disposes all." [39]

But Aurelius was both a man and an emperor. Might not the loyalty he owed the Empire conflict with his duty to humanity? He does not quite answer the question when he says that as Emperor his city and country is Rome, but that as a man his country is the world; and that only that which is good for both Rome and the world could be good for him.[40]

If Stoicism furnished a certain philosophical basis for a world-embracing Empire, primitive Christianity supplied it with a theological foundation. As a matter of fact, Christianity derived considerable inspiration from the ethical tenets of Stoicism. Paul of Tarsus, zealous Christian propagandist, was reared in a city which was a center of

[37] R. W. and A. J. Carlyle, *History of Medieval Political Theory in the West;* 5 vols. (London, 1903-1928), I, 20-21; Lange, *op. cit.*, pp. 29-30; Wilsey, *op. cit.*, p. 43.
[38] Lange, *op. cit.*, p. 30.
[39] "To Himself," as quoted in Arnold, *op. cit.*, pp. 123-124.
[40] P. V. N. Myers, *op. cit.*, p. 239; Lange, *op. cit.*, p. 33.

Stoic philosophy, and his teaching shows that he was strongly though unconsciously influenced by Stoic conceptions.[41] The fundamental dogma of Christianity that there is but one God, that He is the Universal Father, that all humans are His children and brothers one to another, leads to the same conclusion reached by the Stoics, that the human race is a unity. Moreover, as the offspring of one God, all men, regardless of race or social status, are invested with a sacred character. Paganism, on the other hand, was polytheistic. Different peoples had different gods; some were the children of Mars, others the offspring of Zeus.[42] At the best, this usually meant a religious barrier between peoples; at the worst, a narrow racialism often leading to war by one Chosen People upon another. Some of the pre-Christian philosophers, it is true, rejected polytheism, and certainly the Stoic philosophers thought in terms of a Supreme Being, although not in the sense of a personal deity as did the Christians.[43]

Early Christian teachings were against all violence, and therefore against war, even of a defensive character, being waged by the children of God against one another. Meekness, humility, and non-resistance to evil were preached.[44] As a result, many Christians apparently refused to enter the Roman armies, and were attacked by Celsus, an opponent of Christianity, as remiss in their duty to the Emperor. If all did as they, he pointed out, the Empire would be at the mercy of savage and lawless barbarians. Origines, outstanding exponent of Christian doctrine of the third century A.D., replied that if all men were to follow the example of the Christians the world would not fall a prey to the barbarians, for they would likewise come to the word of God and become law-abiding. The Romans should overcome their enemies by prayer and not by the use of violence, which God abhors. Christians, although not taking part in government or serving in the armies, serve the Emperor and the powers that be more effectively by prayers, supplications, and thanksgivings. Lactantius, an aggressive Christian critic of the early fourth century A.D., indulged in a scathing denunciation of the Romans who seemed, he said, to think that the only road to immortality was the road of war and slaughter, and the enslavement of peoples. In almost

[41] Arnold, *op. cit.*, pp. 414-415.
[42] Myers, *op. cit.*, pp. 256-257.
[43] Arnold, *op. cit.*, pp. 18-19.
[44] Lange, *op. cit.*, pp. 35-36.

the identical expression of the ancient Chinese sage,[45] he bitterly pointed out that anyone who slays a single man is denounced as sinful and contaminated, but that he who kills thousands is highly applauded. War, which cuts the human race asunder, cannot result in justice, for "how can he be just who injures, hates, despoils, kills?"[46]

In the first centuries of the Christian era the new cult made for division within the Roman Empire rather than unity. Christianity was exclusive, obdurate when it came to recognizing other cults. Moreover, as worshipers of the One God, Christians felt the urge to make proselytes from other religions, and eliminate all false gods from men's thoughts. At first the Roman government was indifferent to the new sect as it was toward the many other cults within it, but the non-cooperation of the Christians in certain matters regarded by the state as essential led soon to savage persecution. The deification and worship of the Emperor, regarded by the Roman authorities as important in completing Roman unity by uniting in the Emperor the religious as well as the political headship of the world, met with stout and sustained resistance by the Christians. But emperor-worship could in any case not survive. What was it but, in the final analysis, the worship of the State? And the state is mundane, and fallible, unsatisfying to the religious aspirations of the time. By the end of the third century emperor-worship had ceased, and Christianity was ready to take its place. "It offered itself as a world-religion to hold together on the ground of religious unity an empire which was doomed to dissolution if it sought to remain on the ground of political unity. The emperors accepted the offer. They became the powers ordained of God for the guidance of things temporal in a new Empire now conceived as a Christian society."[47]

The realization of the Roman Empire meant for the moment the end of theorizing concerning the relationship of states, for now there was but one State. There remained, nevertheless, many peoples whose rela-

[45] *Supra*, p. 26.

[46] C. J. Cadoux, *The Early Christian Attitude to War* (London, 1919), pp. 245-256. On the other hand it must be remembered that Paul of Tarsus advised his followers: "Submit yourselves to every ordinance of man for the Lord's sake; whether it be to the King, as supreme; or unto governors, as unto them that are sent by him for the punishment of evil-doers and for the praise of them that do well." This might well be interpreted as a command to cooperate with the Roman government in war as well as in other ways.

[47] E. Barker, "The Conception of Empire," *loc. cit.*, p. 80.

tionships must be regulated and whose interests must be cared for by the central authority. The problems presented by this situation tested the skill of the Roman jurists who, however, developed a jurisprudence upon which free states in later centuries could build an international law.

REFERENCES

Abbott, F. F., *Roman Politics* (Boston, 1923), pp. 115-137.

Arnold, E. V., *Roman Stoicism* (Cambridge, Eng., 1911).

Bailey, C., ed., *The Legacy of Rome* (Oxford, 1923), pp. 45-89.

Carlyle, R. W. and A. J., *A History of Medieval Political Theory in the West;* 5 vols. (London, 1903-1928), Vol. I.

Declareuil, J., *Rome et l'Organisation du Droit* (Paris, 1924), tr. by E. A. Parker as *Rome the Lawgiver* (London, 1927).

Dickinson, Edwin D., *The Equality of States in International Law* (Cambridge, Mass., 1920), pp. 8-20.

Dunning, W. A., *A History of Political Theories, Ancient and Medieval* (New York, 1902).

Frank, T., *Roman Imperialism* (New York, 1914).

Fenn, P. T., "Justinian and the Freedom of the Seas," *American Journal of International Law,* Vol. XIX (Oct., 1925), No. 4, pp. 716-727.

———, *An Economic History of Rome* (2nd ed., Baltimore, 1927).

Freeman, E. A., *History of Federal Government in Greece and Italy* (London and New York, 1893).

Gettell, R. G., *History of Political Thought* (New York, 1924), pp. 76-77 and select references, pp. 79-80.

Gibbon, E., *Decline and Fall of the Roman Empire* (London, 1897-1900).

Greenidge, A. H. J., *Roman Public Life* (London and New York, 1901).

Hershey, A. S., *Essentials of International Public Laws and Organization* (New York, 1927), pp. 47-50.

Hill, D. J., *History of Diplomacy in the Development of Europe,* 3 vols. (New York, 1905-1914), I, 8-11.

Holtzendorff, von F. and Rivier, A., *Introduction au Droit des Gens* (Paris, 1889), pp. 57-64.

Homo, L., *Primitive Italy and the Beginnings of Roman Imperialism* (London and New York, 1927).

———, *L'Empire Romain* (Paris, 1925).

Kamarowsky, L., *Le Tribunal International,* tr. by S. de Westman from the Russian (Paris, 1887), especially pp. 111-123.

Marvin, F. S., ed., *The Evolution of World Peace* (London, 1921), Ch. III.

McIlwain, C. H., *The Growth of Political Thought in the West* (New York, 1932), Ch. IV.

Merignhac, A., *L'Arbitrage International* (Paris, 1895), pp. 22-30.

Myers, P. V. N., *History as Past Ethics* (Boston, 1913), Chs. XI-XII.

Olphe-Galliard, G., *La Morale des Nations* (Paris, 1920), Chs. III, IV.

Phillipson, C., *The International Law and Custom of Ancient Greece and Rome;* 2 vols. (London, 1911).

Pollock, F., *Essays in Jurisprudence and Ethics* (London, 1882), Ch. XII.

Redslob, A., *Histoire des Grandes Principes du Droit des Gens* (Paris, 1923), pp. 43-109 for treatment of Greek and Roman antiquity.

Reinaud, J. T., *Relations Politiques et Commerciales de l'Empire Romain avec l'Asie Orientale* (Paris, 1863).

Rostovtzeff, M., *Social and Economic History of the Roman Empire* (Oxford, 1926).

Stawell, F. M., *Growth of International Thought* (London, 1930), Ch. II.

Walker, T. A., *A History of the Law of Nations* (Cambridge, Eng., 1899), pp. 43-64.

Walsh, E. A., ed., *History and Nature of International Relations* (New York, 1922), pp. 61-65.

Watson, J., *The State in Peace and War* (Glasgow, 1919), pp. 53-60.

Wheaton, H. A., *History of the Law of Nations in Europe and America* (1st ed., New York, 1845), pp. 20-24.

Willems, P., *Le Droit Public Romain* (Louvain, 1888).

CHAPTER VI

MEDIEVAL EUROPE

In the fifth century, after a long period of internal decay and successive waves of barbarian invasions, Rome succumbed and her western Empire fell to pieces.[1] The succeeding centuries may, from the point of view of international relationships at least, be called the Dark Ages. Law gave way to lawlessness and government to anarchy. The *ius gentium,* never a truly international law, in the sense in which we use the term today, nevertheless had been a universal law unilaterally applied for the peoples of the Empire. With the break-down of the Roman administration and the general chaos that followed, there was no chance for it generally to survive. There was not only no State; there were no settled states. There were disorganized peoples, roving and warring tribes, and barbaric chieftains who, for a time, under the spell and glamour of the Roman name and the influence of the Roman Church, were induced to accept commissions from the Eastern emperor and carry on the imperial tradition. But by the sixth century they no longer recognized the imperial authority.[2]

The taming of the barbarians in the first instance was, in fact, left largely to the Church. The lowly and despised Christian sect, once persecuted by the emperors, finally saw Christianity become the religion of the Empire. It then gradually built up a strong, disciplined ecclesiastical hierarchy under the headship of the Bishop of Rome, and was able to step into the breach when the Empire crumbled under the successive onslaughts of the barbarians, and save Rome to some extent from their fury.

On the other hand, the development of feudalism, although anarchical in so far as it represented a devolution and confusion of authority, contributed to the same end. With the break-up in the ninth century

[1] The Byzantine Emperor still asserted and maintained the imperial power in the eastern Mediterranean and succeeded in fighting off all attacks until the fifteenth century.

[2] T. A. Walker, *A History of the Law of Nations* (Cambridge, Eng., 1899), pp. 63-64.

of the short-lived empire of Charlemagne, which had for a time brought a semblance of order to part of the Western world, some means of defense against a new series of barbarian attacks had to be found. Feudalism grew out of the conditions and needs of the times. "The leading features of feudalism in its fully developed form are the system of vassalage and the institution of the fief. As early as the Frankish and Lombard periods, a great number of freemen of all ranks felt the need of seeking protection of someone more powerful than themselves or of securing a decent livelihood by offering their military services to a superior. . . Exalted persons, on the other hand, sought to surround themselves with loyal people who should be attached to them by solid bonds. Thus arose the contract of dependence most characteristic of the feudal system." [3]

Feudalism thus represented a substitute for the state to the extent that it was a cohesive agency, and with its walled castles and armored knights provided "islands of secure refuge amid the floods of invasion" sweeping over Europe during this period. On the other hand, the practice of sub-infeudation, and the confused relationships often arising from the fact that most nobles were both lords and vassals, furnished many occasions, eagerly seized by the ambitious and war-loving, for private warfare. Lords and vassals constantly quarreled over the terms of their relationship, and sought by the sword to enlarge their fiefs.

War in medieval Europe arose out of other conditions as well. Independent cities grew up and warred on each other; rulers of the various barbarian peoples sought to extend their power and carried on war against one another; others with ambitions to wear the imperial crown made incursions into Italy on numerous occasions and embroiled themselves with the Popes, to add to the anarchy of the times. Nor were these "rosewater wars." The Teuton peoples were ferocious in combat, seldom recognizing any rules of the game, but slaying, pillaging, and burning without mercy. Life was of no consequence, for Valhalla (heaven) was to be won only by death in battle. Conversion to Christianity did not immediately convert them to peaceful ways or more humane practices. They infused their fighting spirit and brought their old practices into the new creed.[4]

[3] *Encyclopaedia of the Social Sciences,* Vol. VI, article on "Feudalism" by Marc Bloch.

[4] Walker, *op. cit.,* pp. 64-65. The remark attributed to the barbarian convert, Clovis, when the latter was told of the Crucifixion shows that the pagan lion

The prevalence of warfare compelled the Church to adopt an attitude toward it, and eventually to formulate philosophical concepts of war and peace. Long before the final break-up of the Roman Empire, the Christian attitude toward service in the imperial armies had changed, and the secularized Church, growing in power and influence, and perhaps forced to think more of the kingdoms of this world [5] than formerly, came to adapt itself to the war-like state with which it had, as it were, become allied. In the time of Constantine the sign of the cross was used as a military emblem and carried in the forefront of the Roman armies; and although at one time no arms might be admitted into a church, later the Church provided that in the course of the religious ceremony necessary to the conferring of knighthood, the candidate must keep watch over his arms in a church the night before the investiture.[6]

The position of the Church fathers on the subject of war was based mainly on the writings of St. Augustine (354-430), who viewed the matter in practical fashion and concluded that under certain conditions war was a necessity.[7] Reasoning from the accepted fact that it was lawful for princes to defend the state with the sword against internal peace breakers, he concluded that they were likewise justified in using it to defend the state from attack by alien enemies. The safety of the state must be preserved, otherwise many would die violent deaths and innumerable evils, both of a temporal and a spiritual nature, would result. The influence of Roman ideas and practices is clearly evident in his further position that wars are just when declared by the state for the purpose of avenging unredressed injuries. But, contrary to the tendency of the Roman conception, the mere observance of formalities in the declaration of war was not enough. A war must be intrinsically just. St. Augustine was against wars of conquest, but regarded it as better for the righteous to conquer a bad neighbor than to be conquered by him. In any case, war was only to be declared by the ruler of the state. This legalized war for his subjects, although they ought not to

had not become the Christian lamb: "Oh, if only I could have been there with my trusty warriors." Myers, *History as Past Ethics* (Boston, 1913), p. 303.

[5] Jesus had said, "My Kingdom is not of this world." In other words, for Christians, political problems did not exist. They were completely disinterested.

[6] W. E. Lecky, *History of European Morals from Augustus to Charlemagne;* 2 vols. (New York, 1910), II, 248-256; L. Thorndike, *History of Medieval Europe* (rev. ed., Boston, 1928), p. 252.

[7] Tertullian (155-222), outstanding early church writer, took the position of many early churchmen that war and Christianity were incompatible.

do what was clearly contrary to the commandments of God. If they entertained a doubt, however, they should follow the orders of the ruler, who must take the responsibility before God.[8]

In the thirteenth century the great medieval schoolman, Thomas Aquinas, basing his position mainly on that of St. Augustine and Gratian,[9] formulated authoritatively the doctrine of the Church on the subject of peace and war. His philosophical concept of peace reveals that he does not regard it merely as the absence of armed strife. "Two separate concepts are discoverable under the word peace—namely, first, that two or more things or persons should be united, and that, secondly, they should agree." But even agreement, he points out, is not sufficient to attain peace. "If a man agrees with another, and yet not freely but under compulsion of some threatened evil, such agreement cannot be called peace." It is only when men are in agreement, and "desire to coincide in agreement" that true peace is realized.[10]

As regards armed conflict Aquinas clearly deplored it, and preached its avoidance as far as possible. "It produces little good and it wastes much more than it produces. . . Moreover it is inhuman that a Christian should make war on a Christian."[11] And in the following reflection there appears to be the germ of a constructive suggestion for the avoidance of war: "The distance indeed between peace and war is so great, than in every difficulty there must be some shorter cut to

[8] B. Jarrett, *Social Theories of the Middle Ages* (London, 1926), pp. 187-188; C. Lange, *Histoire de l'Internationalisme* (New York, 1919), pp. 43-44. In principle, it would appear that the right of private judgment as to the legitimacy of a war was recognized by the Church Fathers in the Middle Ages in cases in which individuals or associations felt that the war was clearly unjust. Sturzo even says: "In the Middle Ages the estimation of the justice of a war was not merely reserved to the Sovereign, but was vested in all the various orders of society—vassals, in virtue of their semi-autonomous position, and Free Cities, Guilds, Universities, Churches, Monasteries, in virtue of their immunities, might judge a war unjust or inopportune, and, even in the heart of the warring kingdom, remain aloof from it." (*The International Community and the Right of War* [London, 1929], p. 180.)

[9] Monk and professor at the University of Padua in the twelfth century. In his *Decretum* on the Christian theory of war, he confirmed the position of St. Augustine. See R. F. Wright, *Medieval Internationalism* (London, 1930), pp. 137-138.

[10] Jarrett, *op. cit.*, p. 183. This seems to have a bearing on so-called treaties of peace forced upon the vanquished by the victor, and regarded by the defeated power with resentment and a sense of injustice.

[11] This seems to leave the door open to religious crusades of the cross against the crescent. Elsewhere Aquinas seems to have taken the position that Christians might not make war on pagans "in order to compel them to believe" but only "in order to compel them not to obstruct the exercise of the Christian faith." See Jarrett, *op. cit.*, p. 190.

peace than going all the way round by war to reach it. It is reached more surely by giving than by taking."[12]

Yet Aquinas upholds the morality of war on the grounds advanced by St. Augustine. In general, his position was that war could be justified only when it was for the defense of peace. "All who make war seek through war to arrive at a peace more perfect than existed before war." He found it justified under three conditions. First, it is essential that it be declared by the public authority of the state. Believing as he did in the monarchical form of government, this meant the rightful prince. The prince held in his hands the supreme power, and was even able to dispense with the law when he saw fit.[13] It was quite consistent with such a theory that the prince should have the exclusive power to declare and wage war. In the second place, the war must be declared in a just cause,[14] and finally with a good intention. Although in the final analysis this seems to do nothing more than lay down certain principles for the guidance of rulers, who are then responsible only before God for observing these principles, it is to be observed that it does close the door to private warfare altogether. And private wars had by no means become unimportant in Aquinas's time.[15]

Recognizing public war, under certain circumstances and for certain purposes, the Churchmen found it necessary to go into the question of its proper conduct. In passing, it may be noted that the Canon Law absolutely prohibited those in Holy Orders from engaging in it on pain of excommunication.[16] It also insisted on the distinction between belligerents and non-combatants. At the Council of Clermont in 1095, at

[12] Varrett, *op. cit.*, pp. 185-186.

[13] R. W. and A. J. Carlyle, *A History of Medieval Political Theory in the West;* 5 vols. (London, 1903-1908), Vol. I, p. 230. The ruler in a legal sense was irresponsible, but he was answerable to God for his stewardship according to Aquinas.

[14] Thus, a war can be just only for one side. St. Augustine said that the justice of one side was created by the iniquity of the other. The prince declaring a "just war," says Aquinas, is in the position of a judge punishing a malefactor. See L. Sturzo, *op. cit.*, pp. 177-178.

[15] In fact, in the later medieval period during the development of national states, private warfare of one kind or another seems to have been quite prevalent. See Jarrett, *op. cit.*, pp. 191-192, for some amusing examples of challenges and feuds.

[16] Wright, *op. cit.*, pp. 140-141. The practice of the clergy in bearing arms and carrying on war was sufficiently prevalent that the Council of Westminster in 1268, confirming preceding Councils, denounced it and provided penalties. But the Church did not prohibit clergymen from exhorting others to bear arms in defence of the weak and oppressed and against God's enemies. (*Ibid.*, p. 209.)

the time of the First Crusade, it was decreed that women, priests, and unarmed agriculturists were to be regarded as non-combatants and were to enjoy immunity from attack. An obligation was laid on the counts and bishops to punish offenders, and if they were derelict in their duty, were themselves to be excommunicated and interdicted.[17] The question as to the lawfulness of deceiving the enemy was taken up by Aquinas and most of the other writers, who seem to have agreed that deception of the enemy by failure to reveal one's purpose or plans is legitimate, but that to deceive him by direct false statement or by failure to carry out a promise is illegitimate. When the warrior pledges his faith to the enemy, he must not violate such a pledge.[18]

There is no question but that the Church attempted in various ways to soften the rigors of war and banish it altogether as far as possible. The Church fathers, however, could hardly regard its complete eradication possible in a world doomed to sinfulness. For war, like slavery and other forms of control, was regarded as the consequence of sin, which originated with the Fall and the passing of the original primitive condition of innocence. It was fixed in society as a punishment for sin, and as a remedy for wrongs. This theory did not prevent Churchmen from seeking by positive measures to prevent particular wars. In 990 Church synods in France started a movement designed completely to abolish private warfare. Proclaiming the Peace of God, they announced that every act of private warfare proscribed would be punished by excommunication.[19] But it was impossible to get many of the powerful feudal lords to desist from fighting even with the threat of hell-fire. Prohibition having failed, the Church next sought to enforce temperance. Toward the middle of the eleventh century, leading Churchmen in France instituted the Truce of God. An edict was issued forbidding all private war and violence during four days of every week. Every man was required to take an oath, renewed every three years, that he would obey the injunction; and henceforth boys reaching the age of twelve years were likewise required to swear that they would observe the Truce. The movement spread to other parts of Europe, and various consecrated periods such as Easter and Christmas came to be included among the warless days.[20] These breathing spells doubtless provided

[17] *Ibid.*, pp. 150-152.
[18] *Ibid.*, pp. 207, 212. Jarrett, *op. cit.*, pp. 201-203.
[19] Wright, *op. cit.*, p. 162; Myers, *op. cit.*, pp. 312-313.
[20] Walker, *op. cit.*, pp. 85-86; Wright, *op. cit.*, pp. 163-164.

brief opportunities, at least, for the Church to divert the attention of medieval warriors to the ideals of the Prince of Peace, but they were not sufficient to cause many spears to be beaten into pruning hooks.

In such a warlike age the relinquishment of war for the settlement of disputes, and the employment of arbitration were, in the earlier medieval period at least, quite rare. In fact, arbitration does not seem to have been employed in medieval Europe prior to the twelfth century. With the development of commercial cities as semi-independent states and of a new social class more interested in the exchange of goods than in the exchange of blows, arbitration came to have an appeal as a convenient and economical substitute for war, for the latter is a form of competition which is not ultimately "the life of trade." And when the time came, the Church was at hand to offer its services. Accordingly, when Venice and Genoa made an agreement to arbitrate their future differences, they selected the Pope as arbiter; and the same was true of the cities of the Hanseatic Confederation.[21] The Pope as God's vicar, and presumably above partisanship, was, in fact, often selected as an arbitrator of the disputes of princes and cities. The prestige and importance of the head of the universal Church, on the other hand, made an arbitral decision by him the judgment of an authority superior to the parties and independent of the procedure customarily followed in later times. As expressed by Ralston: ". . . the Papacy . . . could not conceive of the idea of arbitration as we understand it. All notion of equality between states, and consequently of common rights and duties, was absent from its politics. Thus it was that the arbitration of the Popes was not the final sentence of a judicial suit freely engaged in, legally conducted, subject to certain rules of international procedure, and determined according to the principles of an overruling law of nations."[22]

In another respect the conception of arbitration in the Middle Ages was at variance with the modern conception, for in general no opposition was seen between war and arbitration from the point of view of law.[23] Particular conflicts, at any rate, were regarded, as Dante[24]

[21] J. H. Ralston, *International Arbitration from Athens to Locarno* (Stanford University, Cal., 1929), p. 188.
[22] *Ibid.*, p. 175.
[23] Lange, *op. cit.*
[24] *Supra*, p. 102.

interpreted the wars of the Romans, as means of discovering the judgment of God on the merits of a controversy between two peoples. And so the tendency was to look upon war as a form of judicial trial rather than as the abandonment of judicial means and the substitution of force, as we are more inclined to do today.[25] If the Middle Ages resorted to arbitration, therefore, it was not so much on principle as it was to avoid the hardships and ravages of war. And it must have occurred to rival cities, more interested in trade than in trouble, that the judgment of God through His Vicar, the Pope, was available in a less costly form than war.[26]

The picture of strife and disintegration and diversity, presented especially in the earlier medieval period by the peoples of Western Europe, hardly justifies one in referring to them as constituting a society. Yet all medieval thought ran in the direction of universalism quite as strongly as Stoic thought and Christian doctrine in the beginning of the Christian era. In that earlier period, theory squared with the facts, doctrine gave them a religious significance. In medieval Europe, the society is shattered, but the ideal lives on. But now it is more completely a theological conception, for a second universal authority, the Church, stands alongside the State.

St. Augustine and the later Church fathers formulated the conception on the basis of the Bible, by occasional recourse to profane history, and by drawing at times upon Greek and Roman philosophy. Inquiring into the end of human existence, they taught that man has a two-fold destiny. He has a temporal life on earth, which is brief and intended by God as a period of preparation for the ultimate divine destiny in the life beyond. In his earthly existence, man lives in a universal Christian society; and as sin has entered into the world, his actions need to be controlled by government. Coextensive, therefore, with the universal society there must be a universal temporal authority. This authority, in the medieval view, was a restored Roman Empire. But man has need of spiritual guidance in order that the divine pur-

[25] F. S. Marvin, ed., *The Unity of Western Civilization* (London, 1915), p. 104. Even now in time of war the older idea lingers on. Each nation calls upon God to "bless our arms" and give victory to the right; and the victorious side is likely to ascribe its success to the justice of its cause, and to thank God for his perspicacity.

[26] It should be pointed out that the ordeal and the conception behind it did not receive the sanction of the Church. Likewise, the extension of the idea of individual trial by battle to nations was given no encouragement by the Church except perhaps in such definitely religious enterprises as the Crusades.

pose of his ultimate redemption may be realized. The indispensable agency for the satisfaction of this need is the universal Church. There are thus two earthly authorities paralleling, supporting, and supplementing each other throughout the single universal society. In the temporal sphere the emperor is supreme; in the spiritual sphere, the Pope. In theory, each respects the other's prerogatives, the ecclesiastical authority rendering unto Caesar the things that are Caesar's, the lay authority rendering unto Peter the things that are Peter's.[27] Such was the theory of the fifth century.

But the conception of a harmonious, divinely-appointed functional partnership of Church and State, in which each had its sphere of complete competence and independence, presented difficulties. Both sets of authorities at times harbored ambitions to dominate in both spheres. And as the Church, under strong Popes, grew in wealth and in temporal possessions concurrently with the weakening of the revived Empire, the line of demarcation could not well be maintained. Alleged encroachments led to assertions and counter-assertions of supremacy, bringing a conflict between Church and State, and the development of a new supporting theory on each side.

The position of the supporters of ecclesiastical supremacy was in general that the King of the universe and, therefore, of all humanity, was Christ, and that his viceroy on earth was the Pope. The Pope, as the direct representative of God, delegated temporal power to kings and even to emperors. They were thus subordinate to him and he might withdraw their power in his discretion. As worked out by John of Salisbury in the twelfth century, God gave two swords to St. Peter: a temporal sword and a spiritual sword. St. Peter and his successors gave the temporal sword to the temporal prince or ruler of Christendom, subject to its being used properly. This gives the Pope the supreme voice in both spiritual and temporal affairs, but still recognizes distinct spheres of activity for Church and State. By the time of Thomas Aquinas in the thirteenth century, the Church was actually at the height of her power, and was less disposed to separate temporal from spiritual authority. Aquinas, therefore, abandoned the attempt to sepa-

[27] M. De Wulf, *Philosophy and Civilization in the Middle Ages* (Princeton, N. J., 1922), pp. 114-116. F. J. C. Hearnshaw, ed., *The Social and Political Ideas of Some Great Medieval Thinkers* (London, 1923), p. 12. Carlyle, *op. cit.*, I, 184-193.

rate the two and asserted Church jurisdiction over temporal as well as spiritual matters.[28]

In Dante Alighieri (1265-1321) the secular viewpoint received its completest expression, and in his *De Monarchia* we have a remarkable treatise on the necessity of a Christian world organized, for the sake of peace and unity, on an imperial basis. In its approach, in its method, and for the most part in its thought, it is definitely medieval. It is the last eloquent expression of the medieval ideal. Dante lived after the chief struggles for supremacy between Church and Empire had apparently resulted in the victory of the Church. But the power of the Church itself had been weakened through internal as well as external troubles, and neither institution was able to bring peace or unity to Christendom. On the other hand, newly-formed European states were becoming stronger and more self-conscious, and inclined to throw off all outside authority. Italy, Dante's home-land, long the victim of the ambitions of rival claimants beyond the Alps, was torn by the strife of parties and factions—"a ship without a pilot," as Dante says in the *Divine Comedy*.[29] In view of these conditions, and inspired with the vision of imperial Rome, the spell of which men of the medieval age had never been quite able to shake off, Dante wrote what Lord Bryce has called "an epitaph rather than a prophecy," *De Monarchia*.[30]

Much has been said of the tendency of men of action of the medieval period to appeal to the sword. Men of reflection were quite as prone to appeal to the syllogism. It tended to dominate medieval thought. Dante's approach was accordingly by the deductive method. He started his work with the major premise that God, working through Nature, creates nothing that is superfluous.[31] Everything is created to serve some divine purpose. The minor premise which follows is that God has created man. The conclusion logically follows that man is created for some end. His life is not meaningless. It is also asserted,

[28] See R. G. Gettell, *History of Political Thought* (New York, 1924), Ch. VI, for good discussion of the theory of both parties in the conflict between Church and State.

[29] The lack of a pilot was brought directly home to Dante in the struggle, for mastery, of the Guelphs and Ghibellines in his native city of Florence.

[30] See R. W. Church, *Dante: An Essay* (London, 1878), which contains translation by F. J. Church. Another English translation is by A. Henry (Boston and New York, 1904). *De Monarchia* was an epitaph in the sense that empire as a way of international life was already dead.

[31] Compare with Aristotle, *Politics,* p. 1256b.

in agreement with Aristotle, upon whom Dante relies frequently, that man is by nature gregarious, fitted to live in communion with his fellowmen. It is, therefore, not the individual man but humanity whose end is to be considered. What is the goal toward which mankind moves? This raises the question as to what distinguishes men from plants and the brutes, and the answer is that God has bestowed on man alone the power of "apprehension by means of the potential intellect," an intellect capable of understanding and achieving more than it actually achieves at any given moment. This distinguishing characteristic of man furnishes the key to an understanding of his particular function on earth, which is to develop and realize the full powers of the potential intellect, primarily for contemplation and speculation, secondarily for action.

The indispensable condition for the attainment of this purpose of human existence is universal peace, just as a man's peace with himself is the necessary condition of his personal happiness. International peace, in Dante's conception, is to be regarded as a good in itself, because without it mankind cannot realize what Aristotle, having in mind the individual, called the "good life." But how is universal peace to be secured? The answer is universal empire. Turning again to the authority of Aristotle, Dante argues that when several things are tending toward the same end, one should rule and direct the rest. This is found to be necessary in the family, village, and individual kingdom, and is equally necessary for the whole human race which in its totality, has a single end and therefore needs a single directing authority. The medieval method of reasoning was always to start from the whole and then consider the parts with reference to each other and to the whole. For it was assumed that the parts, themselves wholes for certain purposes, exist above all else for the sake of the larger whole. Were it not so, there would be no greater whole but merely a number of inarticulated, and therefore ultimately meaningless, fragments.[32] So the various institutions within a kingdom must be ordered with reference to that kingdom of which they form a part; and the various kingdoms within the world kingdom must, in like manner, be directed with ref-

[32] In medieval thought the universe was looked upon as "one articulated Whole and every Being—whether a Joint-Being (Community) or a Single-Being—as both a Part and a Whole: a Part determined by the final cause of the Universe, and a Whole with a final cause of its own." O. Gierke, *Political Theories of the Middle Age* (Cambridge, Eng., 1927), p. 7.

erence to the whole of which they form a part. Yet mankind itself is a part with reference to the universe over which presides the universal Monarch who is God. As the universe is under one supreme ruler, it is likewise best for mankind to be under a single directing authority.

As illustrative of the practical necessity of having a single supreme authority at the head of the world state, Dante instanced the controversies that arise between the princes of various states. Now inasmuch as a dispute between two independent princes is between equals neither of which has jurisdiction over the other, it is necessary to have recourse to the judgment of a third whose jurisdiction extends over both of them. This must be the universal Monarch, for any lesser prince might be involved in a controversy with another with whom he was on a plane of equality. Another alternative, the submission of disputes between princes to a jury of their peers, organized as an arbitration tribunal, either did not occur to Dante or was regarded as not feasible. In any event, he makes it clear that he regards the world Monarch as best fitted to dispense justice because, having all that he desires and possessing the supreme power, he is free from cupidity and above all concern as to the effect of his decisions on his own fortunes. He has both the desire and the effective will to do justice.

Yet Dante's conception did not involve the obliteration of the various kingdoms within the world empire,[33] nor did it mean that the supreme power was to reach down and minutely regulate them. Dante clearly understood that no single system of law could be applied to all states; that their varying situations as regards climate and culture and tradition made uniformity impossible, and that therefore the retention of their own particular laws and customs was necessary. On the other hand, there must be a general law applicable to all, regulating their common life. This law must come from the top—the various princes "receive" it from the emperor. For it is the function of the emperor to coordinate and direct in order to attain the unity sought. The relation between the emperor and the princes is further explained by a simile. The princes receive the rule of life or law from the emperor as the practical intellect gets its major premise from the speculative intellect. Then each prince, by reference to the conditions in his own kingdom, supplies the minor premise, and in accordance therewith proceeds to

[33] To destroy them would be inconsistent with the view, shared by Dante, that as creations of God they have a purpose, and with the medieval conception that they constitute wholes, having an intrinsic value of their own.

the practical conclusion. It may be remarked that Dante seems to look in the direction of world federation in so far as he contemplates the preservation of the legal systems of various states and admits in principle that they are entitled to a sphere of political autonomy. But after all the emperor may presumably interpose his authority at any time and in any way in order to maintain justice, and preserve peace and order. And in so far as the law common to all is concerned, it does not have its origin in agreement of the several princes but originates with the world Monarch. Any remaining doubt about the matter is resolved by Dante's discussion of the instrument best fitted to direct the destiny of mankind.

Looking backward over human history, Dante found but one period in which universal peace had reigned over the world. That was in the reign of Augustus, when there was a perfect monarchy. And the great empire had been built up, according to Dante's interpretation, not for any sordid or unworthy purpose and not by chance, but because the Romans had been chosen of God to bring law and order and justice to mankind, just as the Jews had been divinely appointed to reveal the gospel to all men. In carrying out their mission, the Romans had been compelled to resort to conquest, to be sure, but these conquests had always been undertaken in a spirit of justice and were consciously directed toward a noble end. How different all this from the caustic remark of Tacitus about the conquering Romans: "They make a solitude and call it peace."

Dante is so intent on making out a strong case for the legality of the Roman Empire that he is led to justify war as a form of judicial trial between nations and peoples, in which God gives victory to the righteous cause. The early Germans brought with them in their migrations an institution for deciding the guilt or innocence of accused persons, known as the ordeal by combat.[34] Accused and accuser engaged in a wager of battle, God awarding victory to the innocent. This conception found some lodgment in the common body of Christian beliefs, and there was a tendency to regard it as applicable in the disputes of nations as well. It is, in fact, this idea which Dante extends to the international field. The Romans with pure hearts appealed to the wager of battle, when other pacific means had failed against those opposing

[34] There was also the ordeal by fire, and by water. The ordeal was not peculiar to the Germans, many primitive peoples following a similar custom. Myers, *op. cit.*, p. 304.

them, and, God having given them success over all enemies, the unmistakable conclusion is that their cause was just, and that the Empire they built up was ordained of God. It is this Empire, or its successor, the Holy Roman Empire, which Dante regarded as the necessary instrument through which the world's shattered unity might be restored. But though Voltaire's oft-quoted remark that the Holy Roman Empire was neither Holy nor Roman nor an Empire should be qualified—if one is thinking of the thirteenth century—it was, nevertheless, but a feeble instrument for the accomplishment of such a great design, and other thinkers were already beginning to look in another direction for a solution of the prevailing anarchy among states.[35]

When Dante wrote his *De Monarchia,* the Church was not only theoretically but also actually the great international institution of western Christendom and at the height of its power, universal and all inclusive in the sweep of its authority. The mandates of the Holy Roman Empire, whatever might be the theory, never ran beyond the Germanies and Italy, and at times were challenged even there. Such unity of Christendom as was to be found was due to the ubiquity of Church officials and Church law, and to the fostering by the Church of Latin as the universal language. The great hierarchical Church organization, with the Pope at the apex of the pyramid and the priest at the base, spread a unified system of administration throughout Western Europe. Its canon law [36] was not confined to ecclesiastical matters, but dealt with such subjects as oaths, usury, contracts, and international relations, in instances displacing the secular laws of Europe, and touching not only the lives of individuals but reaching into the affairs of states. It was "the legal weapon which held the centrifugal tendencies (in medieval Europe) at bay." And in order that it might be enforced, ecclesiastical courts were established throughout Europe, from which appeals might be taken to the Roman *curia,* presided over by the Pope.

[35] See article by E. Sherwood Smith on "Dante and World-Empire," in F. J. C. Hearnshaw, ed., *Social and Political Ideas of Some Great Medieval Thinkers* (London, 1923), for Dante's argument concerning the position of the Pope in the world-state. Briefly it amounts to this. Man needs not only a temporal guide, the emperor, but also a spiritual guide, the Pope. They are chosen for their respective tasks directly by God, and although the emperor owes the Pope a certain reverence, the latter has no share in the imperial authority.

[36] The canon law was based not only on the scriptures and ecclesiastical customs, but also on Roman law, Germanic law, and custom, medieval city law, and feudal custom. See article by H. D. Hazeltine on "Canon Law," *Encyclopaedia of the Social Sciences,* III, 179-185.

Moreover, the Sacraments of the Church from baptism to extreme unction were regarded as absolutely indispensable for the salvation of the individual, whether prince or peasant. Nor did the Church rule by precept alone. Its most drastic punishments for wrong-doing were more far-reaching than anything princes could devise. The excommunication of a prince deprived him, temporarily at the very least, of the ministrations of the Church, which were regarded as essential to his salvation. Therefore, unless he should receive absolution before death, he was a damned soul. If the Pope should lay a kingdom under interdict because of the recalcitrance of the ruler, all of the inhabitants were deprived of the vital services of the Church, and their very salvation imperiled. This was a very serious matter in medieval Christendom, and more than one recreant son of the Church had to make his journey to Canossa [37] to have the blight removed from him and his subjects. In short, the Church came to assume and, as far as possible, to exact throughout the Western world submission and obedience to its authority in the realm of religion, morals, politics, and economics; and this enveloping control extended to princes and kingdoms as well as to private individuals.

The first vigorous and effective challenge to all this came at about the beginning of the fourteenth century, and, in its most pronounced form, from the most outstanding of the developing nation-states, France. The occasion was the ambition of Pope Boniface VIII to follow up the Church victory over the Empire and place himself at the head of the confederation of the states of Europe. At the great jubilee of 1300, legend makes him boast, "I am Caesar, I am Emperor." At any rate he sought to assert his authority over Philip the Fair of France, who had begun to extend the jurisdiction of his courts over matters formerly handled by the Church; a quarrel ensued, the Pope was taken prisoner, and shortly afterward the Babylonian Captivity began. Thenceforth for seventy-three years the Popes were to have their headquarters at Avignon rather than at Rome. What the empire had never been able to do was accomplished without hesitation and with great despatch by a new political entity, the nation-state.[38]

[37] The castle in Italy made famous as the spot to which Emperor Henry IV journeyed in 1077 to do penance before Pope Gregory VII.

[38] It is, of course, understood that the temporary removal to Avignon (from 1309 to 1377) did not bring the Church down to irretrievable ruin or put an end to its influence as an international power.

In the meantime, a theoretical basis for the new *de facto* situation was being laid. John of Paris, philosopher and theologian, conceded that the spiritual organization of Christendom under one head, the Pope, was proper, for the faith necessary to salvation was one and the same everywhere, and a unified ecclesiastical organization was therefore necessary. But on the non-spiritual side, he contended, Christians were most diverse, and needed correspondingly different kinds of political leadership. Moreover, one man may rule the entire world on the spiritual side, for this type of government operates through words, which may be sent everywhere. But when it comes to temporal government, force is necessary, and it is difficult to exercise force at great distances. This was designed to dispose of the lay empire. As for the claims of the Papacy to exercise temporal power, it was asserted that the temporal power was bestowed directly by God on princes, and was in no sense derived from the head of the Church. On the other hand, the Pope and the Catholic clergy do have a certain power in temporal matters, but it results from a grant or concession of princes.

It was also necessary, in order to establish the freedom of kings from outside authority, whether that of Pope or Emperor, to abandon the medieval notion of law. That notion was that law comes solely from ancient custom. It was not something a king could "make." A king, St. Augustine had said, is "not to judge of the law but to judge according to the law." Thus the king is not the author of the law, and certainly he is not above the law. Rather is he limited and controlled by the law, which it is his duty to observe and apply. This view was now attacked, and eventually it came to be displaced by the conception that law is derived from the definite human will of the sovereign prince of a state. This view, as will be seen later, has important implications in the field of international law and relations. In the fourteenth century, however, the newer conceptions had not always taken as definite and uncompromising a form as they were to take in the following century. This will perhaps appear in the consideration of certain of the views of the most original of the thinkers of the later medieval period.

Pierre Dubois (1250?-1322?), French lawyer of Constance in Normandy, and a counsellor of Philip the Fair, wrote the first outstanding contribution to a solution of the problem of international organization during the age of transition from the old ideas of universal Church and universal Empire on the one hand, and feudal decentralization on the other. His most important work was the *De Recuperatione Terre Sancte,* written between 1305 and 1307.[39] Although this was not a systematic work—it was repetitious and full of digressions—it is noteworthy because of its frank break with much of medieval thought and methods, and its more realistic approach to the question of the attainment of peace and unity in Christendom. It took the form of a circular addressed to Edward I of England, of which a copy was sent to the Pope, and another, with additional considerations that might not have been too reassuring to other ears, to Philip the Fair of France. The author hoped they would approve it and transmit it to other princes of Europe for their consideration.[40]

Like Dante, his contemporary, Dubois' great concern, at least ostensibly, is that peace shall be realized in Christendom. Internal peace, everyone recognizes, is important, but it is even more important, in his opinion, to work for perpetual peace, temporal and spiritual, between Catholics throughout Christendom. On the other hand, possibly because he realizes that there is a good deal of fighting energy among Christians that must be absorbed in some direct way, and that a common enemy will serve to unite them, he takes the position that war with the Eastern infidels is not only permissible but is a positive duty. They are natural enemies of the Christian community, and it is necessary to combat and expel them from Christian territory in the same way that any community deals with the malefactors within it. He therefore maps out a plan for the recovery of the Holy Land.[41] But the success of this project, he argues, will depend upon the maintenance of peace in Europe. And future peace in Europe, he is keen enough to realize and point out, will depend upon the immediate establishment of a régime of

[39] English translation of the *De Recuperatione* by Ruth Hardy (Berkeley, Cal., 1920). See interesting commentaries on Dubois by Eileen E. Power in *Social and Political Ideas of Some Great Medieval Thinkers,* ed. by F. J. C. Hearnshaw (London, 1923); W. J. Brandt, "Pierre Dubois: Modern or Medieval?," *American Historical Review,* XXX (1929-1930), 507-521; and especially Lange, *op. cit.,* pp. 90-108.

[40] Edward I was the only king living at the time who had undertaken a crusade to the Holy Land. Both he and Philip could be depended upon to be especially interested in such projects, France having taken a very prominent part in crusading activities. As Dubois' scheme involved new expeditions to the Holy Land, it was perhaps natural that he should first seek support in these quarters. Both monarchs, likewise, had power and influence.

[41] Dubois was only one of a number of writers who had plans for a crusade against the power of Islam in the early years of the fourteenth century. In former crusades, contacts had been made with the Tartars in the Near and Middle East, and dreams were entertained of converting them and using them against the Moslems.

peace, for each war contains the germs of new wars rather than leading to lasting solutions of international controversies. Lasting hates, rather, are engendered between peoples, and the hunger for revenge is constantly fed by the sting of defeats suffered.

But how is peace between Christians to be secured? Certainly not, says Dubois, by exhortation. Neither the Holy Scriptures, which abhor war, nor all the preachers who have fulminated against it, have had any important influence in checking it. If that has been true in the past, there is no more reason to expect the solution to come through the Church in the future. Nor can peace be brought about by the revival of a Roman empire. This seems to him, if anything, even more absurd. " . . . no sane man could really believe that at this period of the world's history one individual could rule the whole world as a temporal monarch, with all men obeying him as their superior. If a tendency in this direction did appear, there would be wars and revolutions without end. No man could put them down because of the huge populations involved, the distance and diversity of the countries, and the natural propensity of human beings to quarrel." [42]

Now the peace of Europe must be organized, but along different lines, if it is to be lasting. Dubois had in mind a Christian republic, apparently uniting the various kingdoms and princes in a kind of permanent confederate bond in which the different Christian nations would retain their independence, but would give up their right to wage war against one another. The Holy Roman Empire was to be regarded as one state along with the others, the leadership in the enterprise already being reserved for France. This was perhaps quite natural, for after all there must be a Chosen People to take the place of the Roman Empire and provide leadership, and Dubois was a Frenchman. As such he was aware of the peculiar fitness of the French, by reason of their statesmanlike qualities and trustworthiness, to direct the destinies of other peoples. France, for example, was "not liable to gusts of passion and, unlike other nations, [was] always accessible to reason." [43]

[42] As translated and quoted in F. M. Stawell, *Growth of International Thought* (London, 1929), p. 63. See also Lange, *op. cit.*, p. 98. Dubois concedes that in purely spiritual matters it is possible to have a single governing and directing authority. But he makes it quite clear that this authority, the Pope, except as a court of appeal in arbitration cases, is not to meddle in politics but is to confine himself to saving souls.

[43] Quoted in Stawell, *op. cit.*, p. 64. Similar discoveries of like qualities as the exclusive possession of their respective countrymen have since been made by the spokesmen of many other nationalities.

The plan of Dubois called for the reformation and strengthening of the Church as a moral and spiritual power, after which the Pope would be asked to take the initiative in convoking at Toulouse, it is suggested, a general Council of the princes and prelates of Christendom. This Council was to launch the plan of peace. France had already (1305) "pocketed the Papacy" by requiring that the Popes should be elected and reside at Avignon, so that there was every guarantee that the Pope would not unduly exalt his position in the scheme envisaged by Dubois. In fact, it was an essential part of the plan of Dubois that the temporal power of the Papacy should be transferred to France because its exercise by the Pope interfered with his spiritual functioning. "Wars therefore are stirred up, numbers of princes are condemned by the Church, together with their adherents, and thus die more men than can be counted, whose souls probably go down to hell and whom nevertheless it is the Pope's duty to save. . . Because of his sanctity the Pope should aspire only to the glory of pardoning, praying, giving judgment in the name of the Church, preserving peace among Catholic princes, so as to bring souls safe to God." [44]

Dubois, as one would expect from his profession, pays most attention to the judicial aspect of his plan of international organization, and it is just here, incidentally, that his conception of the true function of the Papacy is revealed. The plan calls for a rather complete system of arbitration of all disputes arising between Christian princes. The general Council, of which mention has been made, would have the duty of enacting that a body of arbitrators, prudent, experienced, and reliable men, should be appointed.[45] These, after taking the oath, would in turn be empowered for any particular dispute to select three judges among the prelates, and three lay judges for each party. These would constitute an arbitration tribunal, and care must be taken to see that they are men incapable of being corrupted or influenced by love, hate, fear, greed, or anything else. Dubois also lays down minute instructions as to the procedure that shall be followed by the members of the

[44] As quoted by Eileen Power, "Pierre Du Bois and the Domination of France," in F. J. C. Hearnshaw, ed., *The Social and Political Ideas of Some Great Medieval Thinkers* (London, 1923), p. 154. Dubois also pointed out that the Popes were unfitted for the strenuous life on account of their advanced age. They were usually old men when they reached the Papacy.

[45] Dubois is not clear as to how large this body or college of arbitration is to be, or just how it is to be selected, and he says nothing as to the term of office of the members.

arbitration board. They are to come together in a suitable place, they are to be strictly sworn, are to be presented with the case of both sides, and are to follow a prescribed procedure, designed to assure fairness, in the examination of witnesses. If necessary they are to have assessors, skilled in divine, canon, and civil law, to assist them. He also anticipates dissatisfaction on the part of one or another of the litigants by providing that an appeal may be taken from the arbitral decision to the Pope, who may confirm, alter, or amend the decision as seems best to him.

The realism of Dubois is perhaps nowhere better shown than in his observations on the need for physical sanctions to keep princes from going to war, and to encourage those to whom an arbitral decision might be distasteful to yield obedience to it nevertheless. Considering the character of the times, and the cheerfulness with which princes—and sometimes prelates—reached for the sword when a controversy arose, Dubois was probably right in his contention that immediate and drastic penalties were necessary. His proposals were that those making war against their Catholic brothers should have all their goods confiscated; and a similar penalty was to be meted out to those aiding them with counsel, with arms, food, supplies, or in any other way. Finally, after the guilty were vanquished, by cutting them off from food supplies and starving them out, if possible, or by war if necessary, the survivors, young and old, were to be packed off to the Holy Land. So much fighting energy would thereby be drained out of Europe, one infers, and used where it would do the most good instead of the most harm. Dubois also had far-reaching plans of colonization in the Holy Land and the promotion of trade between East and West, so the exiles might serve a purpose in this direction as well. But however hard Dubois would be on the transgressors, as far as their life on earth was concerned, he drew the line at damning them eternally. They were not to be excommunicated and no anathema was to be pronounced against them. This was "in order to avoid the danger to their souls and an increase in the numbers of the damned. . ."

Dubois was, in many respects, ahead of his time, and his plans aroused no interest among his contemporaries. If he dreamed of a world-empire for France as the outcome of all his planning, he was, in a sense, pursuing a medieval ideal, but even here he "wears his medievalism with a difference." The new empire was to have a national basis, it was to exalt the monarch, and keep Peter in his place and at his task of saving souls. On the other hand, his arbitration proposals were definitely forward-looking in character and, if they could have been developed, might have been of distinct service in quickening the slow movement toward the substitution of law for violence in international relations.

Dubois, in providing sanctions for the execution of arbitration agreements, was reflecting medieval thought. It was not customary to entrust the carrying out of an award to the good faith of the parties. In general, the preliminary agreement to arbitrate defined the point at issue, laid down the procedure, and prescribed the penalty for failure to respect the award. But in some cases the arbitrator himself, and it is to be noted that arbitral *commissions* were unusual, decided what the penalty of non-observance of his decision should be. In any case, a party who had taken an oath to abide by an award and failed to do so, was regarded as guilty of perjury, and was liable to be prosecuted in the ecclesiastical and secular courts. In addition, large payments of money were often stipulated, and not infrequently excommunication was employed as a sanction. As in modern times, the decision, even when it was rendered by a lesser person than the Pope, was normally regarded as final and without appeal.[46]

In the century following Dubois' contribution to the organization of Christendom, another remarkable plan was put forward by George of Poděbrad (1420-1471), King of Bohemia.[47] Like the earlier project, it was immediately motivated by a desire to unite the nations of Western Europe in a crusade against the infidel. For the Terrible Turk had taken Constantinople, the seat of the Eastern Empire, and all Christendom was aroused by the humiliation and the oppression of its Turkish conquerors. But neither the Holy Roman Empire nor the Roman Catholic Church was able to supply the leadership and resources necessary to oust the invaders. The Empire had grown steadily

[46] Ralston, *op. cit.*, pp. 187-188. See also, on entire question of arbitration in the Middle Ages, A. Merignhac, *L'Arbitrage International* (Paris, 1895), pp. 31-42, and Novacovitch, *Les Compromis et les Arbitrages Internationaux du XIIe au XVe Siècle* (Paris, 1905).

[47] For an analysis of the plan in English, see W. E. Darby, "Some European Leagues of Peace," *Transactions of the Grotius Society* (London), IV (1919), 170-179. A good discussion of the project is also to be found in Lange, *op. cit.*, pp. 108-118, and J. ter Meulen, *Der Gedanke der Internationalen Organisation in Seiner Entwicklung* (1300-1870), 2 vols. (The Hague, 1917-1929), I (1300-1800), 108-119.

weaker, and the Church had been unable to recover the proud and influential position it had occupied in the days of Gregory VII. If the task was to be accomplished, it would have to be under the leadership of one of the new monarchies, or as a collective effort of the states of Europe under a well-conceived plan. Such a plan, ultimately envisaging a perpetual political union of all Europe, was advanced by George of Bohemia through his able minister, Marini, in 1462, and dispatched to the Courts of France, Poland, Hungary, and Venice.

It is significant that the Pope was to play a relatively minor part in the scheme. The latter had made an unsuccessful attempt a few years earlier to organize the Christian world against the Turks, and doubtless regarded such an enterprise, as had his predecessors, as one in which the Church should play a prominent if not a leading part. But George was a Protestant heretic and was quite as distasteful to the Pope as the latter was to him.[48] It was also no part of Poděbrad's plan to allow the Empire to assume a prominent part in the scheme. But the latter had sunk so low in prestige that he could ignore it altogether.

The plan did not call for the immediate union of all European states, but conceived of an alliance and confederation of certain states such as France, Poland, Hungary, and Venice. In principle, nevertheless, it was European rather than designed to serve the ends of the group which was to be the nucleus, for it was to be open to other states, who apparently might join by a simple declaration of adhesion to the articles of confederation.

Poděbrad and his adviser, Marini, foresaw that the essential condition for the successful pursuit of Turks was the maintenance of peace and a united front in Europe. Until the Confederation should include all of the European states, therefore, it was necessary to provide some means for keeping peace outside as well as within the Confederation. Within the alliance, the members pledge themselves to friendship and to render assistance to one another in case of attack from outside. Should a quarrel arise between a member and an outsider, the Confederation should attempt to effect a peaceful settlement by inducing the non-member state to agree to the selection of arbiters by leaving the matter to the decision of a competent judge, or by having it settled by

[48] In 1466 Pope Paul II excommunicated Poděbrad and pronounced his deposition from the throne.

the Court (Parlamentum) of the Confederation.[49] The Confederation would thus attempt to mediate between the parties and avoid war. If, nevertheless, war should break out as a result of the fault of the state outside the Confederation, the members of the latter are obligated to come to its aid. The project also anticipates war between states both of which are outside the alliance, by providing that the Confederation shall attempt a peaceful settlement along the lines of the previous case.[50] Finally, whoever shall trouble the peace thus instituted shall be regarded as an outlaw to whom no one shall give protection or aid. And anyone failing to observe this obligation shall himself be punished as a malefactor.

As regards the organization and machinery of the Confederation, there is, first of all, emphasis upon the necessity of the establishment of a *Parlamentum,* or Federal Court, on the theory that a durable peace can be founded only upon justice. This Court, as has been indicated, not only was to constitute a "fountain of justice" for the states of the Confederation, but also might be called upon to give decisions in cases in which outside states were involved. Ultimate control of the Court, as well as of the other agencies of the Confederation, was in the primary general assembly of representatives of the union. The *Collegium,* in turn, established the Court, had the power to declare war, to determine the financial contribution of the members of the Confederation, and to decide other matters of a like nature. In order, apparently, that no single state should seem to have undue power or influence, it was provided that meetings of the *Collegium* should be held in one country of the Confederation for a period of five years, for a second five-year period in another, and so on.

It is worthy of attention that the voting in the *Collegium* was to be by nations, the king of France together with the other Gallic princes having one vote, the king and princes of Germany another, and the doge of Venice together with the princes and communes of Italy, a third. It is also of interest that not only was the court to be empowered to hand down judgments by a majority vote, but that apparently the *Collegium* also operated under the majority rule.[51] The

[49] The Court before which the princes of the Confederation were obligated to take their disputes.

[50] The framers of the Covenant of the League of Nations were faced with the same problem and dealt with it in much the same way in Article XVII. See text of the Covenant in Appendix.

[51] See Lange, *op. cit.*, p. 114.

matter of procedure in the *Collegium* is perhaps not entirely clear, but if a majority vote was sufficient to reach important decisions involving finances, and peace and war, the plan envisaged an organization more far-reaching in its power than is true of the ordinary confederate union.

Poděbrad's plan was short-circuited by the Pope before it was put into operation. In any event, it is probably doubtful whether the ambitious monarchs of the new nations would have been willing to surrender to a new authority, even of which they were a part, the freedom of action which they were vigorously asserting as against the Empire and the Church.

REFERENCES

Augustinus, Aurelius, St., *Works,* ed. by Marcus Dods; 14 vols. (Edinburgh, 1872-1882). English translation.

Battifol, Pierre, and others, *L'Église et le Droit de Guerre* (Paris, 1920).

Bryce, J., *The Holy Roman Empire* (rev. ed., New York, 1904), Chs. III-IV.

Cadoux, C. J., *Early Christian Attitude to War* (London, 1919).

Chossat, M., *La Guerre et la Paix d'Après le Droit Naturel Chrétien* (Paris, 1918).

Dante Alighieri, "De Monarchia," tr. by F. J. Church, in R. W. Church, *Dante: An Essay* (London, 1878). See also, for another English translation, *De Monarchia,* ed. by Aurelia Henry (New York, 1904).

De Wulf, H., "The Society of Nations in the 13th Century," *International Journal of Ethics,* XXIX, 210-229.

Dunning, W. A., *History of Political Theories, Ancient and Medieval* (New York, 1902, Chs. V-IX.

Forsyth, P. T., *The Christian Ethic of War* (London and New York, 1916).

Gettell, R. G., *History of Political Thought* (New York, 1924), Ch. V and references.

Gierke, O., *Political Theories of the Middle Age* (Cambridge, Eng., 1927).

Hastings, James, *Encyclopedia of Religion and Ethics* (Edinburgh and New York, 1908-1922).

Hearnshaw, F. J. C., ed., *Medieval Contributions to Modern Civilization* (New York, 1922).

————, *The Social and Political Ideas of Some Great Medieval Thinkers* (London, 1923).

Hershey, A., *Essentials of International Public Law and Organization* (rev. ed., New York, 1927), pp. 51-56.

Hill, D. J., *A History of Diplomacy in the International Development of Europe,* 3 vols. (New York, 1905-1914).

Jarrett, B., *Social Theories of the Middle Ages, 1200-1500* (London, 1926), pp. 181-212.

Korff, S. A., "An Introduction to the History of International Law," *American Journal of International Law,* Vol. XVIII (April, 1924), No. 2, pp. 255-258.

Krey, A. C., "The International State of the Middle Ages, Some Reasons for Its Failure," *American Historical Review,* Vol. XVIII (Oct., 1922), No. 1, pp. 3-4.

Lange, C., *Histoire de l'Internationalisme* (Christiania, 1919), Chs. II-IV.

McIlwain, C. H., *The Growth of Political Thought in the West* (New York, 1932), Ch. V.

Marvin, F. S., ed., *The Unity of Western Civilization* (London, 1915), Ch. IV.

Merignhac, A., *Traité Théorique et Pratique de l'Arbitrage International* (Paris, 1895), pp. 31-42.

Meulen, J. ter, *Der Gedanke der Internationalen Organisation in Seiner Entwicklung* (1300-1889); 2 vols. (The Hague, 1917-1929), I (1300-1800), 3-32.

Murray, R. H., *The History of Political Science from Plato to the Present* (Cambridge, Eng., 1926), pp. 74-81.

Myers, P. V. N., *History as Past Ethics* (Boston, 1913), Ch. XV.

Novacovitch, M., *Les Compromis et les Arbitrages Internationaux du XIIe au XVe Siècle* (Paris, 1905).

————, *Études de Droit International et de Droit Politique* (Brussels, 1896).

Nys, E., *Les Origines du Droit International* (Brussels and Paris, 1894).

Olphe-Galliard, G., *La Morale des Nations* (Paris, 1920), Ch. V.

Pardessus, J. M., *Us et Coutumes de la Mer,* 2 vols. (Paris, 1847).

Potter, P. B., *Introduction to the Study of International Organization* (New York, 1922), Ch. III.

Ralston, J. H., *International Arbitration from Athens to Locarno* (Stanford University, Cal., 1929).

Redslob, R., *Histoire des Grands Principes du Droit des Gens* (Paris, 1923), Ch. II.

Rolbiecki, J. J., *The Political Philosophy of Dante Alighieri* (Washington, 1921), Ch. XI.

Ryan, J. K., *Modern War and Basic Ethics* (Washington, 1933), Chs. II, III.

Salvioli, G., *Le Concept de Guerre Juste* (Paris, 1918).

Stawell, F. M., *Growth of International Thought* (London, 1929), pp. 40-75.

Sturzo, L., *The International Community and the Right of War* (London, 1929), pp. 170-180.

Vanderpol, A., *La Doctrine Scolastique du Droit de Guerre* (Paris, 1919).
Walker, T. A., *A History of the Law of Nations* (Cambridge, Eng., 1899), pp. 64-137.
Walsh, E. A., ed., *History and Nature of International Relations* (New York, 1922), article by C. J. H. Hayes on "Medieval Diplomacy."
Watson, J., *The State in Peace and War* (Glasgow, 1919).
Wright, R. F., *Medieval Internationalism* (London, 1930).

CHAPTER VII

RENAISSANCE AND REFORMATION

THE renaissance of the fifteenth century was many-sided, but we are concerned only with those aspects that affected politics and international relations. The central fact is, of course, that a revolution took place in men's thinking about the world in which they lived and the institutions which they had hitherto accepted. For a thousand years, men had been held in a sort of intellectual bondage. They were expected to submit to the authority of the Church in all matters of faith and morals, and to accept without question its divinely-inspired revelation of the nature and meaning of all things in the universe.

Every society generates its own heretics, and the Christian society of the Middle Ages was no exception. But the Church took appropriate and effective measures against heretics within. The damage was unconsciously done by unsealing Europe to the ideas and influences of the East at the time of the Crusades. For the Crusaders came in contact with a civilization much higher and finer in many respects than their own, and learned of religious and political institutions of which they had previously had no knowledge. Moreover, in the thirteenth century the great Genghis Khan and his successors pushed their vast empire west to the shores of the Black Sea. This fresh contact of Europe with the East had far-reaching results. It is sufficient to recall that, as a consequence, the West learned of the printing press, the mariner's compass, and gunpowder; for their development and utilization worked a revolution in the material and social side of Western life. The development of nautical instruments alone made possible the sailing of uncharted seas and the discovery of new continents, and furnished visible proof of the fallacy of the geographical notions which the Church had taught for centuries.[1] Thus in many respects were discoveries made that were eventually to cause men to reject revelation, and discard supernatural

[1] The astronomical discoveries of the Renaissance also dealt a blow at Church teachings. Copernicus (1473-1543) destroyed the notion that the earth is the center of the universe by discovering that the sun is the center of a planetary system, and that the earth moves around it.

explanations of natural phenomena in favor of the rational approach. Skepticism replaced belief; individualism and the spirit of venturing on new paths displaced uniformity and the dead hand of tradition.

The Renaissance began in Italy. The individualism which was manifested in art, philosophy, and science was likewise carried into the field of politics and international relations. The new ideal state was conceived not as a harmonious though partial construction, intended by God to fit into a larger whole and so make its contribution to the unity of a Christian society, but as the conscious creation of a prince. And it was organized exclusively with reference to its own individual needs and the desires of the prince rather than to serve universal ends. It must therefore emancipate itself from all outside authority, whether of Church or Empire, and look to war and diplomacy for its maintenance. To that end it must perfect its internal organization and make the most of its resources, and the tyrants in the various Italian states were assiduous in their attention to these matters. From an international point of view, this self-reliant individualism made for anarchy in international relationships. Strong states, conscious of their power, are normally inclined to seek the maximum realization of their objectives by means of force rather than to content themselves with the slower and possibly less fruitful processes of peaceful adjustment and accommodation. Thus the influence of the Italian Renaissance was in the direction of furthering international disorganization and a régime of *laissez faire*.[2] This may all be very well for the stronger, but smaller and weaker states, necessarily dependent for their security upon other means than self-help, are driven to alliances and the pooling of their resources against the strong and ambitious. Thus we find the principle of equilibrium, employed in ancient times by the Greeks,[3] reappearing in Europe at the beginning of the modern period. Says Hill: "The conception of 'equilibrium,' developed as a necessity of defence, was soon reduced to a science, and served to secure to the Italian commonwealths many of the advantages which might have been afforded by confederation. Always changing, requiring the utmost vigilance and sagacity, the system of transitory alliance, as tested and applied by the princes and republics of Italy, was a prototype and epitome of what all Europe was soon to become on a grander scale."[4]

[2] Lange, *op. cit.*, pp. 132-133.
[3] *Supra*, p. 61.
[4] *A History of European Diplomacy*, 3 vols. (New York, 1921-1925), I, 361.

During this period diplomacy was developed as a fine art in the Italian states. It was conceived as a means alternative to war for the attainment of the objectives of rulers, and as in the nature of war. A diplomat must be full of guile and willing to stick at nothing. Certain laws of Venice as early as the thirteenth century are eloquent testimony as to the sweet atmosphere in which the game was played. For example, an ambassador was forbidden to take his wife with him on his mission lest she disclose his secrets, but he was required to take his own cook to avoid the risk of being poisoned. Thus peace had its hazards as well as war, if one were a diplomat, and it is not surprising that other laws had to be passed to overcome the reluctance of gentlemen who seem to have been indisposed in many instances to serve their state abroad in a diplomatic capacity.[5]

The practice of sending resident ambassadors to foreign courts, and the establishment of permanent legations also arose in the Italian city-states in the fourteenth century. It will be recalled that the nations of antiquity never developed beyond the stage of despatching envoys for the discharge of special missions, withdrawing them when the particular business for which they were sent had been completed. In the Middle Ages the Pope sent his legates to various countries not only on special missions, but apparently to reside and often represent the supreme pontiff in a diplomatic capacity.[6] But it seems clear that the Italian city-states of the renaissance period were the first lay states to establish the practice which was to systematize international intercourse and furnish continuous contacts between governments in time of peace.[7] In the fifteenth century the institution of permanent embassies spread to the states of northern Europe and laid the foundation of the system of diplomacy which is now common to the entire world.

The geographical discoveries must also be noted because of their far-reaching effects on international relationships and international theory as well. In the first place, they greatly enlarged the stage upon which the drama of national states was to be enacted, and raised fresh questions of property and power and privilege on new seas and continents. The major problems of international relations henceforth were to be, increasingly, problems of world politics [8] rather than problems

[5] Hill, *A History of European Diplomacy*, pp. 360-361.

[6] R. F. Wright, *op. cit.*, pp. 93-106, for contention that the institution of the resident ambassador originated with the Church.

[7] Lange, *op. cit.*, pp. 134-135. P. B. Potter, *Introduction to the Study of International Organization* (New York, 1922), pp. 88-89.

[8] The "world empire" of Rome was, after all, insignificant from the point

exclusively concerned with Mediterranean or European or Asiatic politics. The immediate effects of the discoveries of new lands and riches was to stimulate rivalry and wars between the stronger, more fully developed national states for the possession of overseas colonial domains. These wars were to last with slight breathing spells into the nineteenth century. And during this epoch the individualism of the Renaissance was expressed in the domain of international relations by an unwillingness of states to be fettered by rules of international conduct.

The Reformation likewise caused repercussions in the field of international relations. In the first place, it split the theoretically single Christian society of the Middle Ages into two societies, one secular, the other sacred. Henceforth, in the countries which broke with the Church, at any rate, Church and State stood forth not as partners in the common enterprise, but as antagonists. The break with Rome increased the political power and prestige of national monarchs by adding to their economic resources, in states where Church property was taken over, and by the establishment of subservient state churches organized on a national rather than on an international basis. And finally the Reformation ushered in the era of religious wars which were to last for a century and to have devastating effects especially in Central Europe.

The thought most typical of the period of the Italian Renaissance in the field of politics, is to be found in the writings of the Florentine, Nicolo Machiavelli (1469-1527), who was born just two hundred years after Dante. The latter's dream of a politically united Christendom was no longer possible of realization even at the time he wrote, although his world was still thinking for the most part in medieval terms. But the world of Machiavelli was vastly different from that of Dante, and Machiavelli took his Europe as he found it, and sought to adjust his statecraft to it rather than to alter it. The picture of his day is not a pretty one, but a recent writer [9] has faithfully portrayed it in the following: "Unchecked by either papal or imperial authority, regardless of both canon and civil law, emancipated alike from the restraints of religion and of ethics, the 'new monarchs' of the political jungle were

of view of its extent; and the universalism of the medieval world on the religious as well as the political side was in practice co-extensive with Western Europe and little more.

[9] F. J. G. Hearnshaw, *Social and Political Ideas of the Renaissance and Reformation* (London, 1925), pp. 90-91.

displaying in a desperate struggle for existence those qualities of the lion and the fox which, in the earlier ages of the cosmic process of biological evolution, had enabled the animal possessors of these qualities to survive and prevail. The weapons in this fierce political struggle for existence were war and diplomacy. On the one hand, new armies, new means of offence and defence, new tactics and strategy, and, above all, a new ferocity, completely changed the military art from what it had been during the Middle Ages. On the other hand, missions, embassies, royal visits, supplemented by dispatches, memoranda, and reports, instituted a new science of diplomacy in which craft and guile found a limitless field for exercise. The princes who had to defend themselves in arms against a circle of powerful, alert, and merciless foes, and to protect themselves diplomatically against the conspiracies and intrigues of countless malignant rivals, both within and without their states, had no use for the lofty speculations of Aquinas or Dante respecting the two powers, the two lights, the two swords, and the general duality of things. What they required was not a *Mappa Mundi* giving them sanctified information respecting the imaginary situation of the Garden of Eden, the Tower of Babel, and the Kingdom of Prester John; it was a *portolano* providing, in the form of a precise chart, the data indispensable for the navigation of the stormy and rock-infested seas on which their frail barques were tossing. It was such a *portolano* that Machiavelli professed to provide."

The political treatises of Machiavelli were inspired above all by a desire to see matters righted in Italy. The Italy of his day was sadly divided and torn by internal dissensions and schisms, and demoralized by foreign invasions. Italy had indeed become a battleground for French, Germans, Spanish, and Swiss who poured their armies into it and sought to realize selfish claims of one kind or another and dominate the peninsula. In Florence, the native city of Machiavelli, the French gained control in 1494 and, although aiding the Florentines against their enemies and rivals, dominated the city and treated it with contempt. These things aroused a passionate resentment in Machiavelli and a desire to see these predatory foreigners driven from Italy, and a unified Italian state replace the innumerable struggling political atoms which were so completely impotent before the more unified invaders. To that end he hoped to see such internal reforms in Florence as would strengthen and enable her to dominate Tuscany and then push on to the consolidation of all Italy.

Machiavelli was not a speculative thinker interested in the construction of ideal systems of politics, but he was a keen observer of men and his frequent employment on diplomatic missions and in other high public capacities on behalf of Florence gave him opportunity to study the men and methods of his time. He came to the conclusion, as *The Prince*[10] and *The Discourses on Livy* testify, that to accomplish one's aims in politics one must set aside all considerations of religion and ethics, which are well enough in private relationships, and employ fraud and force as needed. He saw Savonarola, with passionate eloquence, seek by exhortation to lead the Florentines to internal reform and political unity, and he noted his failure and death by fire. Why had Savonarola failed, he asks. Because behind his eloquence, which for a brief moment aroused the fickle populace, there was no physical force to coerce and compel. Eloquence and exhortation were not enough. On a diplomatic mission to Caesar Borgia, son of Pope Alexander VI and duke of Romagna, who was threatening Florence, Machiavelli came into close contact for a number of months with one of the most remorseless and unconscionable scoundrels of history. Machiavelli scrutinized his methods, observed his ability to manipulate men, and his dazzling success.[11] Ten years later many of the rules of successful statecraft, which began to take form in the mind of Machiavelli in the course of that visit, were set down in *The Prince*. The axioms and principles of statecraft presented in this work and in the *Discourses* were intended to apply to the intercourse of states quite as much as to internal politics. Moreover, certain chapters in both works dealt exclusively with problems arising in connection with defensive war and external conquests.

Some one has said that certain chapters of *The Prince* should have been headed, "The circumstances under which it is right for a prince to be a scoundrel." It may be added that the observations of Machiavelli

[10] Both of these works breathe the same spirit; their difference is one of form and purpose. The *Discourses*, which were never finished, were intended to educate the public mind to the need for the establishment of a unified Italian state on the ancient Roman model and to prepare it to accept the necessary means of accomplishment. *The Prince* was intended only for the eyes of the ruler, Lorenzo the Magnificent, to whom it was dedicated, and for whom it was to serve as a manual of statecraft. It was not published until 1532, five years after Machiavelli's death. See *Encyclopaedia of the Social Sciences*, I, 91-92.

[11] Borgia, after a brief period of power, was hounded out of Italy.

under this heading constitute the vital essence of the treatise, and that they have such implications in the field of international relations as to deserve special notice. In the first place Machiavelli's observations of men had given him a very poor opinion of human nature. Men in general are ungrateful, inconstant, deceitful, cowardly in the face of danger, greedy and avaricious.[12] The prince must bear this in mind and act accordingly or he will come to grief. And so, although one would feel it praiseworthy for a prince to keep his word and avoid artifice in his public dealings, it is evident that great things have been accomplished by those who have had no such scruples, and it has been observed that they have triumphed over those who have followed the practice of keeping faith. In fact a prince, to succeed, must be as ferocious as the lion and as cunning as the fox. If he is only a lion he will not see the snares set for him; if only the fox, he will not be able to defend himself against wolves. He needs to be both. And when it would be hurtful to fulfil a promise, a prince should not do so. Nor should he keep a promise if the conditions under which it was made no longer exist. If all men were good, a prince could afford to be good; but as they are wicked and faithless, why should a prince be held to his word? Besides, asks Machiavelli, can a prince fail to find legitimate reasons for not executing his promises? As a matter of fact, history abounds in instances of those who have prospered by breaking treaties of peace. But a prince must know how to give the appearance of being frank and open at the same time that he is practicing deceit. Pope Alexander VI, for example, was one who always cheated, but he was such an artist in convincing others of his straightforwardness that he always did it successfully. Thus it is not necessary, though it may be desirable, for a prince to possess good qualities, but it is highly essential that he should *seem* to have them. After all, men and especially princes are judged by results. Let the prince keep in mind the preservation of his life and that of the state, and all means that he finds necessary to employ will be judged by the world as honorable.[13]

In neither of the works cited does Machiavelli consider the standards of conduct that should be followed by private individuals. He is dis-

[12] *The Prince,* Ch. XVII.

[13] *Ibid.,* Ch. XVIII, also Ch. XV. The same point of view is expressed in the *Discourses,* Bk. II, Ch. XIII, when Machiavelli expresses the conviction that men seldom rise from low condition to high rank without employing either force or fraud unless they attain it by gift or inheritance.

cussing princes and principalities,[14] and he makes it clear that in public relationships morals are not to enter at all; that the only question that need trouble a prince is whether the means he employs—and if necessary they may include assassination—are best adapted to the great end, the preservation and advancement of the state. In the *Discourses* [15] he says that where the safety and liberty of the state are involved no considerations of justice or injustice, humanity or cruelty, glory or ignominy should be taken into account in the means used to avert the danger. Thus he seems to advance the principle that in the last analysis principle has no place in politics!

Although Machiavelli wanted to see Italy attain unity and regain its freedom from foreign interference, he did not look forward to a state organized for peace rather than conquest. The Greek ideal of the small state free from preoccupation with external affairs, absorbing its energies within itself, he did not regard as practicable, whatever its theoretical merits might be. He held that nothing is permanent in human affairs, that things cannot remain stable but rise or fall. So it is with states. If organized only to live, with no thought of foreign conquest, necessity may nevertheless drive them to it and, being unprepared, to their ruin. It is therefore the part of wisdom to organize the state along Roman lines so that in case a policy of aggrandizement is necessary, conquests can be undertaken with success.[16] That the necessity is almost certain to arise, and that in any case the only concern need be that the conquest shall be successful, Machiavelli points out in another place.[17] It is natural, he says, for a state to desire the territory of another, and when it has the means to acquire territory by conquest the world will praise rather than blame it. But if it has not the power to execute its plans and realize its ambitions, it will incur blame and commit an error.

Machiavelli next addresses himself to the question of the best policy for the successful conqueror. If the people of a conquered state have been accustomed to live under their own laws, one of three different ways of dealing with them are open to the conqueror. He can destroy

[14] Machiavelli, as was common in his day, thought of the state in terms of the person concretely representing it. It was therefore natural that he should call his book *The Prince* rather than give it the title of *On Principalities,* although in referring to it, on one or two occasions, he used the latter designation.

[15] Bk. III, Ch. XLI.

[16] *Ibid.,* Bk. I, Ch. VI.

[17] *The Prince,* Ch. III.

the conquered state, he can take up his residence in it and rule it directly, or he can allow the people to retain their own laws and government, contenting himself with the exaction of tribute. These different possibilities are discussed dispassionately and the conclusion reached that, when a people have been accustomed to liberty and are therefore inclined to seize every opportunity to regain their freedom, the conquered state will either have to be destroyed as Carthage was by Rome, or colonized.[18] Once more Machiavelli turns to imperial Rome for his inspiration.

It is an interesting fact that Machiavelli's *Prince* made such a favorable impression on Pope Clement VII that he caused its publication in 1513. Within a short time it was translated into all the languages of Europe and was eagerly devoured by rulers throughout Christendom who desired to perfect their technique of domination. Needless to say, it appealed to strong men of action, ambitious to rule successfully over others, and desirous of being a law unto themselves. And many others, even today, are inclined to praise it, as well as his other political treatises, "for facing stern realities" in realistic fashion. From the point of view of international relations, nevertheless, it offered a confirmation of the worst practices of statesmen rather than a contribution toward a better international order. It carried likewise an assumption that there is a necessary and natural hostility between states, and that the advancement of the interests of one must necessarily be at the expense of the others. Limited in imagination, Machiavelli's work shows an insufficient appreciation of the imponderables. Abandoning good faith as an essential of public intercourse, and elevating *raison d'état* above every other consideration, it afforded no foundation upon which a system of international law might be built. And finally, in any long time view, many believe that the Machiavellian recipe can only produce failure. Says Lord Morley:[19] "The effect was fatal even for his own purpose, for what he put aside, whether for the sake of argument or because he thought them in substance irrelevant, were nothing less than the living forces by which societies subsist and governments are strong."

Among the admirers of Machiavelli in the sixteenth century was the great English philosopher and political adviser of Queen Elizabeth and King James I of England, Francis Bacon (1561-1626). In the

[18] *The Prince,* Ch. V.
[19] *Machiavelli* (London, 1897), Romanes Lecture.

writings of Bacon in the field of politics the influence of the Florentine is quite manifest, and the English statesman pays the latter explicit or implicit tribute in several of the Essays that deal with social relationships.[20] Both men were animated by ambitions to acquire high political station and the preferment of "the great," and both studied their fellows with cool detachment from the point of view of understanding how they may be used by those interested in the pursuit of power. The following excerpt from one of Bacon's essays might have been written by the author of the *Prince:* "If you would work any man, you must either know his nature and fashions, and so lead him; or his ends, and so persuade him; or his weakness and disadvantages, and so awe him; or those that have interest in him, and so govern him." [21] The employment of dissimulation and the practice of deceit as a general rule were not encouraged by Bacon, principally because such practices are not well calculated to advance one's interests in the long run. Deceit is "culpable, and less politic, except it be in great and rare matters." [22]

Bacon was, like Machiavelli, an imperialist. He seems to have looked upon life as essentially a struggle for power and domination. Individuals compete with one another for preferment and power, states struggle for the high stakes of empire, mankind struggles to increase its dominion over nature.[23] In the struggle of states for imperial dominion, the building up of military power and the waging of war were recognized by Bacon as indispensable. The internal affairs of a state must, therefore, be ordered accordingly. The profession of arms must be given first place as it was in Sparta and Rome, for "no nation which doth not directly profess arms, may look to have greatness fall into their mouths. . ." Therefore, "for empire and greatness it importeth most, that a nation do profess arms as their principal honour, study, and occupation. . ." [24] Moreover, care must be taken that the people of

[20] "We are much beholden," he says in one place, "to Machiavel and others, that wrote what men do, and not what they ought to do." E. A. Abbott, *Francis Bacon, an Account of His Life and Works* (London, 1885), p. 83.

[21] Essay XLVII, "Of Negotiating," *The Works of Francis Bacon,* by Basil Montague; 3 vols. (Philadelphia, 1852), I, 53.

[22] Essay VI, "Of Simulation and Dissimulation," *Ibid.,* p. 15.

[23] Oscar Kraus, *Der Machtgedanke und die Friedensidee in der Philosophie der Engländer Bacon und Bentham* (Leipzig, 1926), pp. 4-5. It was a fundamental assumption of Bacon's foreign policy that "the increase of any estate must be upon the foreigner, for whatsoever is somewhere gotten, is somewhere lost" (Essay XV, "Of Seditions and Troubles," *op. cit.,* I, 23).

[24] Essay XXIX, "Of the True Greatness of Kingdoms and Estates," *op. cit.,* p. 38.

such a nation should not be too much occupied with "sedentary and within-door arts, and delicate manufactures" lest their robustness and martial spirit suffer.[25]

Bacon contended that war was not only necessary as a means of achieving empire, but that it was essential for the preservation of the health of states. In this he anticipated the thought of certain militaristic writers of the nineteenth century.[26] "No body," he asserted, "can be healthful without exercise, neither natural body nor politic, and, certainly, to a kingdom, or estate, a just and honorable war is the true exercise." Civil wars, to be sure, he regarded as "like the heat of fever," to be forestalled, among other things, by distracting the minds of dissatisfied subjects from internal affairs to foreign warfare.[27] But "a foreign war is like the heat of exercise, and serveth to keep the body in health; for, in a slothful peace, both courages will effeminate, and manners corrupt. . ."[28]

Like Machiavelli, this adviser of English monarchs was careful to point out that the expansion of a state must correspond to its inner strength and its ability to keep the prize of empire once it is grasped. The possession of gold is not nearly as important for this purpose as having a "stout and warlike" breed of men.[29] Such were the Romans, and the Empire that they achieved stands as a model for all kingdoms aspiring to greatness. Quite consistently with these views, Bacon advocated a warlike, aggressive policy for England. In 1619, in a memorandum for the King entitled a *Short View of Great Britain and Spain,* he contended that there could never be a secure peace between England and Spain on account of the latter's iniquity, and that England, as the greatest naval power of the world, was in a favorable position and had the duty to seize the Indies and implant the true faith in these new lands.[30] It was not necessary to wait for injury from Spain, one gathers from his essay *Of Empire,* for "a just fear of an imminent

[25] Bacon pointed out that in the days of Sparta, Athens, and Rome such tasks could be given over to slaves, but that since Christianity had largely abolished slavery the next best thing was for a state to employ strangers for such occupations. (*Ibid.*) On the other hand, like Machiavelli, he was opposed to the hiring of mercenary soldiers. A veteran national army was the only real reliance of a state aspiring to greatness. (*Ibid.*, p. 37.)

[26] See especially Ch. XII.

[27] Abbott, *op. cit.*, pp. 144, 148, 151.

[28] Essay XXIX, *op. cit.*, I, 38.

[29] Essay XXIX, *Ibid.*, I, 36; Kraus, *op. cit.*, pp. 20-21.

[30] Abbott, *op. cit.*, pp. 278-279.

danger though there be no blow given, is a lawful cause of war." [31] On the other hand, Bacon tells us in the *Essays* that when a state resolves to make war on another it is important to be in a position to make out some sort of a case for its action, "for there is that justice imprinted in the nature of men, that they enter not upon wars (whereof so many calamities do ensue) but upon some, at the least specious, grounds and quarrels." [32] In the memorandum advocating a war with Spain, it will have been noted, the imponderables were duly taken into account.

In strong contrast with the nationalism and stark realism of Machiavelli and the imperalism of Bacon was the internationalism and idealism of the great Dutchman, Desiderius Erasmus (1466-1536). To practical statesmen the Florentine's realism was far more congenial than it was to the humanists of northern Europe. For the humanism which spread north of the Alps after 1500 was somewhat different in character from that of the Italian renaissance. In the first place the Northern humanists remained Christian rather than pagan in outlook, finding their inspiration and guide in the Bible, however, rather than in medieval church dogma. Some, in fact, had a close affinity with the mystic sects of heretics of the Middle Ages who professed adherence to early Christian doctrine and, contrary to the position of the Church, opposed all war.[33]

In general, it may be said that the outlook of the humanists, at any rate in northern Europe, was essentially pacifist. Believing as they did in the worth and dignity of human life, and having as an ideal the development and cultivation of the individual so that he might realize his potentialities and get the greatest enjoyment out of life, they tended to regard war as a disturbing intruder, brutal, destructive of life, and fatal to civilized intercourse. This international, sometimes cosmopolitan, outlook was strengthened in men like Erasmus who traveled widely from country to country and contracted friendships on the basis of intellectual affinities uninfluenced by considerations of language, race, or nationality. On the other hand, the humanists were usually but little interested in politics, and one finds more declamation against war in

[31] *Works,* I, 27.
[32] Essay XXIX, *Ibid.,* I, 38.
[33] For a discussion of the pacifist views of such medieval sects as the Moravians, Anabaptists, Lollards, and Hussites see Lange, *op. cit.,* pp. 47-66.

their writings than concrete, constructive suggestions for the improvement of international relations.[34]

Erasmus was a native of Rotterdam, but he traveled and resided in England, France, Germany, Italy, and Switzerland, and in outlook was a European rather than a Hollander. Not only did he correspond with every important writer of his time in the various countries, but he had friendly intercourse with Pope Leo X, Francis I of France, and Henry VIII of England. His views on war were partly the reflection of his temperament and intellectual affiliations. Refined and sensitive, its coarseness shocked him and its arbitrary character repelled him. Erasmus was a man who always taught moderation, the avoidance of extremes. War in any case can hardly be regarded in any other light than as a drastic and extreme method of international adjustment. But as it was waged in his day, it was certainly an enterprise lacking in all the restraints and amenities normally obtaining among individuals of culture and refinement. Moreover, Erasmus, who has sometimes been spoken of as the "Voltaire of the Renaissance," was inclined to examine manners and institutions from the point of view of their rationality as well as from their conformity with religious principles, and his denunciation of war was on the ground of its stupidity as well as its wickedness. He thought war was an unnatural institution. In one of the articles in the *Adages, Dulce Bellum Inexpertis,* he says that Nature arms all animals with the exception of man. The latter alone depends upon the help of others of his kind; he is made for mutual aid and friendship, and war is the negation of all that is human. It is, therefore, made by man rather than foisted upon him by Nature. Man suffers from innumerable natural afflictions not of his making, and beyond his control—earthquakes, floods, etc. Why should he introduce yet another calamity of his own volition? [35]

Erasmus felt that religion was used too often as a cloak for the concealment of the real motives actuating princes and their advisers to make wars—ambition, anger, and greed; and with biting irony he sought to expose the sham and pretense so frequently to be found in the justifications urged for resorting to war. For example, in an imaginary "colloquy" in hell between two devils, Charon and Alastor, on the success of the Furies in spreading ruinous wars and dissensions

[34] Lange, *op. cit.*, pp. 136-137. [35] *Ibid.*, pp. 159-161.

throughout the world, Erasmus has them say in the course of the dialogue: [36]

CHARON. Right, but men's minds are variable; and what if some Devil should start up now to negotiate a peace? There goes a rumour, I can assure ye, of a certain scribbling fellow (one Erasmus they say) that has entered upon that province.

ALASTOR. Ay, ay: but he talks to the deaf. There's nobody heeds him nowadays. He writ a kind of a Hue and Cry after Peace, that he fancied to be either fled or banished; and after that an epitaph upon Peace Defunct, and all to no purpose. But then we have those on the other hand that advance our cause as heartily as the very Furies themselves.

CHARON. And what are they, I prithee?

ALASTOR. You may observe up and down in the courts of Princes certain Animals; some of them tricked up in feathers, others in white, russet, ash-colored frocks, gowns, habits; or call 'em what you will. These are the instruments, you must Know, that are still irritating Kings to the thirst of War and Blood under the splendid notion of Empire and Glory: and with the same art and industry they inflame the spirits of the Nobility likewise and of the Common People. Their sermons are only harangues in honour of the outrages of Fire and Sword under the character of a just, a religious, or a holy war. And which is yet more wonderful, they make it to be God's Cause on both sides. God fights for us, is the cry of the French pulpits; and what have they to fear that have the Lord of Hosts for their Protector? Acquit yourselves like men, say the English, and the Spaniard, and the victory is certain; for this is God's cause, not Caesar's. As for those that fall in the battle, their souls mount as directly to Heaven as if they had wings to carry 'em thither, arms and all.

CHARON. But do their disciples believe all this?

ALASTOR. You cannot imagine the power of a well dissembled Religion, where there's youth, ignorance, ambition, and a natural animosity to work upon. 'Tis an easy matter to impose, where there is a previous propension to be deceived!

But all of the wars envisaged in the time of Erasmus were not between Christians. There was still much talk of carrying the cross against

[36] As given by J. A. K. Thompson, "Desiderius Erasmus," in *The Social and Political Ideas of Some Great Thinkers of the Renaissance and Reformation*, ed. by F. J. C. Hearnshaw (London, 1925), pp. 168-169. The translation is by Sir Roger L'Estrange (1699).

the crescent as a religious duty as well as in the name of defense. But, unlike Dubois, he was opposed to such enterprises. "If what we want is really to expand our Empire, if it is the wealth of Turkey we are after, why cover our mundane greed with the name of Christ?"[37] On the other hand should the Turks take the offensive and force a war on Europe, in spite of all honest efforts made to avoid it, there would be no alternative to taking up arms in self-defense. Erasmus did not carry his pacifism to the point of non-resistance.[38]

Nevertheless, at times he approached a peace-at-any-price position. In the *Complaint of Peace,* written about 1515, he expresses the opinion that occasions will arise when it will be necessary to purchase peace even though the price be extremely high, for war with its fearful toll of human life, and its great drain of treasure, would cost even more. Almost any sacrifice is justified that will avoid the disruption of education, and the arts and sciences, and that will prevent the prosperity of the land from being destroyed.

In the *Praise of Folly* (1511), written in the home of Sir Thomas More, and dedicated to this close friend, he attacked war as a stupid enterprise, from an economic point of view as well as in other respects. It does not pay either side engaging in it,[39] and he suggests in this connection that if one cannot have the mind of a statesman he might at least show the sense of a shopkeeper.[40] He is not even disposed to admit that war demands intelligence, except the special and limited kind of military intelligence of the commanders. As for the other participants, they are made up of parasites, brigands, bandits, clowns, blockheads, debtors, and in general the scum of humanity rather than men of intelligence.[41] And the physical courage shown by these people did not impress him, for he considered the moral courage of men of wisdom and character—the courage to govern desire, conquer rage, and suppress illegitimate ambitions—as the rare type of courage to be prized.

[37] Translation taken from Stawell, *op. cit.,* p. 89.

[38] Lange, *op. cit.,* pp. 172-173.

[39] This anticipates the position of Norman Angell (*infra,* pp. 307-308), although Erasmus does not think it necessary to give a bill of particulars. As a matter of fact it would have been difficult to show in his day that from an economic point of view, war did not pay the people of any state waging it.

[40] Benjamin Franklin was to make the remark about two hundred years later that "it is never good business to knock your customers on the head."

[41] At this period the employment of foreign mercenaries and adventurers was

Erasmus refused to acknowledge that the wars of his time were waged for the sake of justice or for the welfare of the people. They originated rather in the ambitions of princes. The latter, instead of developing their skill in winning wars, should use their intellectual powers to prevent them.[42] And neither they nor their ministers should have the right to start a war without obtaining the full and unanimous consent of the people; for it is upon these, he holds, that its burden chiefly falls. This sounds like the suggestion of a popular referendum, although popular rule, even in domestic affairs, was not to come about until long after his time, and Erasmus probably did not consider the far-reaching implications of his suggestion or the manner in which it might be carried out. Nevertheless, he was clearly not satisfied with the Roman practice, which, as he says, glorified a "just" war, and accepted all wars as just if the prince declared them to be. For the prince, says Erasmus, may be either a child or a fool.

Referring to another theory, advanced during the Middle Ages, that war is permissible just as the use of force is admittedly justifiable against a wrongdoer within the state, Erasmus was quick to detect the flaw in the reasoning. He insisted that the cases were not analogous, that "in the courts a man is condemned and suffers according to law, in battle each party treats the other as guilty." Moreover in war innocent persons on both sides are made to suffer. "To the man who complains that it is unjust for the wrongdoer to escape punishment, I reply it is far more unjust for millions of innocent men and women to undergo intolerable suffering." [43]

But if war is to be ruled out, except as it may be clearly forced upon a state in spite of all its endeavors, what is to take its place? How are disputes to be settled? Erasmus was confronted with the same question which Dubois attempted to answer, and he answered it in the same way. He did not believe empire was the solution, for emperors are fallible. "There is no doubt that a unified Empire would be best if we could have a sovereign made in the image of God, but, men being what they are, there is more safety among Kingdoms of moderate

common, national standing armies in the modern sense not having been developed. Machiavelli, in his *Art of War* and other treatises on politics, was a strong advocate of the replacement of mercenaries by national soldiers.

[42] L. K. Born, "Some Notes on the Political Theories of Erasmus," *Journal of Modern History*, Vol. II (June, 1930), No. 2, p. 233.

[43] Translations taken from Stawell, *op. cit.*, p. 88.

power united in a Christian league." [44] And, as Erasmus doubtless realized, there was more likelihood of the princes of such kingdoms accepting arbitration. For arbitration, as he saw it, was the solution. Apparently he regarded the arbitral function as properly belonging to the Pope and other officers of the Church, although it is not clear that he would not have favored a mixed tribunal of laymen and ecclesiastics, as did Dubois. Anticipating the objection that a prince submitting a dispute to arbitration ran the risk of an unjust decision, Erasmus answers characteristically that an occasional biased decision will not cause the evil and suffering occasioned by resort to the "irrational and doubtful decision of war." [45]

Finally, Erasmus seems to have deplored the making of so many treaties. In the first place he was inclined to the belief that if nations intended to keep faith with one another, written agreements were superfluous; and in any case he regarded many of the treaties of his time, such as treaties of alliance, as "nothing but war measures" designed to serve the selfish ends of the parties. On the other hand, contrary to the position of his contemporary, Machiavelli, he insisted that once a treaty has been made every effort should be made to live up to the spirit as well as the letter of the agreement, and that failure on the part of one of the parties to fulfil some small clause should not be used by the other as a pretext for the violation of the entire treaty.[46]

It is evident that Machiavelli and Erasmus, both products of the Renaissance, were the antithesis of each other in method and in outlook.[47] In a sense, the former spoke for the man of action who is looking for results here and now, and is willing to pay the price of immediate success; the latter, for the thinker and observer who is pained at much in the human scene, is disinclined to accept things as they are, and wants to "mould them more to the heart's desire." Erasmus, like many such, was able to grasp and suggest sound principles of action without quite knowing how to work out the details of their application.

Sir Thomas More (1478-1535), English humanist, was a close friend of Erasmus, and his views on international relations, in so far as they

[44] Stawell, *op. cit.*, pp. 90-91, Lange, *op. cit.*, p. 175.

[45] Born, *op. cit.*, p. 236.

[46] L. K. Born, "Erasmus on Political Ethics," *Political Science Quarterly*, Vol. XLIII (Dec., 1928), No. 4, pp. 534-535.

[47] The same contrast holds in the case of Bacon and Erasmus.

are revealed in his writings, were in general much the same. But More, who was at one time Speaker of the House of Commons, and rose to the position of Chancellor under Henry VIII, was necessarily more affected by nationalist prepossessions than his friend. His views on the relations of states are principally to be found here and there in the *Utopia*[48] (1516), especially in the chapter "On Warfare."

The Utopians regarded warfare between nations as "a thing very beastly," but unhappily not always avoidable. In certain cases they considered it justifiable. Thus the Utopians thought that not only wars of defense were justified but also wars for the purpose of driving enemies from their friends' lands, and for the purpose of freeing a subject people from oppression. On the other hand, war for commercial reasons was not to be undertaken. But it is interesting to observe that they did not look upon a war for expansion of territory in an unfavorable light, but regarded it under certain circumstances as the most justifiable of all wars. Thus, if in spite of their attempts to check their population the Utopians found that they were outrunning their means of subsistence, it was proper for them to seek land which had not been fully occupied. If the inhabitants should resist, then the Utopians should drive them out. "For they count this the most juste cause of warre, when anye people holdethe a piece of grounde voyde and vacaunt to no good nor profitable use, kepying other from the use and possession of it, which notwithstanding by the law of nature ought thereof to be nouryshed and relieved." This is very nearly the whole economic case for imperialism, stated in its simplest terms. It lies at the bottom of nearly all the discussions that have dealt with the economic aspects of imperialism from that day to the present time.

Nevertheless the Utopians disliked war and regarded it as tending to corrupt those waging it. For that reason they used mercenaries as far as possible, and selected for the purpose the worst scoundrels they could find. They paid them good wages in order that they could be sure to retain their services. Moreover, the Utopians considered that they were rendering the world a real service by putting as many as possible of these undesirables in the way of being slaughtered.

The Utopians were chary of entering leagues, principally because

[48] A brilliant satire on the society of his day in England, and a description of the ideal communistic society on the island of Nowhere, which an imaginary traveller from the famous island gives to More.

they observed that the members too frequently broke their word, but also because leagues cause men "to think themselves born adversaries and enemies of one another; and that it is lawful for the one to seek the death and destruction of the other, if leagues were not." Like Erasmus, the Utopians of More's creation thought "that men be better and more surely knit together by love and benevolence than by covenants of leagues, by hearty affection of mind than by words." Both Erasmus and More wanted what is known today as "moral disarmament."

In the period of the Renaissance and Reformation, it need hardly be remarked that the ideas of Machiavelli and Bacon were far more congenial than those of Erasmus and More to rulers intent not only on throwing off the restraints and controls of Church and Empire, but impatient of the restrictions of any law not made by themselves. The former represented rampant individualism in the field of international relations, the latter the tolerant spirit of the humanists who could not reconcile the warlike and imperialistic enterprises of states with their convictions of the unity of the human species.

REFERENCES

Bede, J., *Social Theories of the Middle Ages* (London, 1926), pp. 206-212.

Born, Lester K., "Erasmus on Political Ethics," *Political Science Quarterly*, Vol. XLIII (Dec., 1928), No. 4, pp. 520-543.

Butler, G., *Studies in Statecraft* (Cambridge, Eng., 1920).

Constantinescu-Bagdat, E. C., *Études d'Histoire Pacifiste,* 3 vols. (Paris, 1924-1928), Vol. I, *La "Querela Pacis" d'Erasme.*

Detmold, C. E., ed. and trans., *Historical, Political and Diplomatic Writings of Machiavelli;* 4 vols. (Boston, 1882), Vol. II.

Donnadieu, L., *Essai sur la Théorie de l'Équilibre* (Paris, 1900).

Dunning, W. A., *A History of Political Theories, Ancient and Medieval* (New York, 1902), Ch. XI.

Dupuis, C., *Le Principe d'Équilibre et le Concert Européen* (Paris, 1909).

Erasmus, *Erasmus Against War,* ed. by J. W. Mackail (Boston, 1907).

Erasmus, *Institutio Principis Christiani,* English translation, with introduction by P. E. Corbett (London, 1921). Grotius Society Publications No. 1.

Ferrari, J., *Histoire de la Raison d'État* (Paris, 1860).

Hearnshaw, F. J. C., ed., *The Social and Political Ideas of Some Great Thinkers of the Renaissance and Reformation* (London, 1925).

Hill, D. J., *A History of Diplomacy in the International Development of Europe,* 3 vols. (New York, 1921-1925), Vol. I, pp. 359-418, Vol. II, pp. 152-158, 308-311.

Hoijer, O., *La Théorie de l'Équilibre et le Droit des Gens* (Paris, 1917).

Kaeber, E., *Die Idee des Europäischen Gleichgewichts in der Publizistischen Literatur vom 16 bis zur Mitte des 18 Jahrhunderts* (Berlin, 1906).

Lange, C., *Histoire de l'Internationalisme* (Christiania, 1919), Chs. VI, VII.

Machiavel, N., *Oeuvres Politiques de Machiavel,* ed. by Charles Louandre (Paris, 1851).

Morley, Lord J., *Machiavelli* (London, 1897).

Murray, R. H., *History of Political Science from Plato to the Present* (Cambridge, Eng., 1926), Ch. IV.

Myers, P. V. N., *History as Past Ethics* (Boston, 1913), Chs. XVI, XVII.

Potter, P. B., *Introduction to the Study of International Organizations* (New York, 1922), Ch. VII.

Redslob, R., *Histoire des Grands Principes du Droit des Gens* (Paris, 1923), Ch. II.

Smith, Preserved, *Erasmus: A Study of His Life, Ideals, and Place in History* (New York, 1923).

Stawell, F. M., *Growth of International Thought* (London, 1930), Ch. IV.

Watson, J., *The State in Peace and War* (Glasgow, 1919), pp. 86-87, 247-248.

Wright, R. F., *Medieval Internationalism* (London, 1930), pp. 93-106.

CHAPTER VIII

THE SEVENTEENTH CENTURY: INTERNATIONAL LAW

THE new political environment and enlarged horizons of the sixteenth century, suggested in part in the preceding chapter, led necessarily to the development of juridical theory to harmonize with and cover the new conditions. By 1500 England, France, Spain, and Portugal had already definitely taken form as national kingdoms with distinctly national languages and literatures, and rulers ready to assert their respective nations' independence of all outside authority.[1] And, highly significant of the trend of the times, theologians as well as lawyers now begin to come to the defense of national monarchs against the pretensions of Emperor and Pope. In Spain, for example, Franciscus de Victoria (1480-1549), famous Franciscan, denied that the Pope might exercise a temporal jurisdiction above that of princes; and Fernando Vasquez (1509-1566) made the sweeping assertion that no man whether Pope or Emperor, and not even Christ himself, had ever been even *de jure* lord of the whole earth in temporal matters.[2] When such statements can be made by doctors of theology, it is evident that the unitary base of the Christian society of the Middle Ages no longer exists. There is now a plurality of "sovereign" states. How are their relations to be regulated? Are there any ties by which they may be regarded as bound together in a single society? These were new questions to be discussed and answered.

Other circumstances, related to this political development, led to subordinate inquiries involving particular interstate relations. The discoveries of new lands across the Atlantic and of new trade routes with

[1] As early as the thirteenth century there were statutes in England which forbade obedience to all authorities other than the Crown, and in the fourteenth century proceedings in the law courts, customarily conducted in Latin, were required to be conducted in English. From this time on, the vernacular supplanted Latin in parliament as well. See A. N. Holcombe, *Foundations of the Modern Commonwealth* (New York, 1923), p. 137.

[2] T. A. Walker, *A History of the Law of Nations* (Cambridge, Eng., 1899), p. 149.

the East had led to a commercial revolution in which the Italian and German city-states lost their commercial supremacy to the new national states, and the latter engaged in a colonial and commercial rivalry world-wide in extent. For as national consciousness and royal power grew in the various states the national spirit was carried into commerce, and state policies designed to foster and develop national commercial monopolies were adopted. Thus trade tended to lose its private character and came to be regarded in each country as a competitive national enterprise to be regulated, subsidized, and supported by the state against the national policies and the arms of other states. Among other questions raised by these developments was that of the freedom of the high seas for purposes of commerce and intercourse. As early as 1255 certain rules embodied in the *Consolato Del Mare* had been adopted by Venice and were recognized by the city-states as authoritative for the commerce of the Mediterranean. But new questions involving the use of vast ocean areas were now to arise; and beyond these oceans lay strange lands and strange peoples. Were there any principles upon which particular nations could lay claim to these lands, and rule the inhabitants? These were questions which could not be answered simply by appeal to ready-made medieval formulas or exclusively to the old Church authorities; for the old authorities were no longer accepted, and the old formulas could not always easily be stretched to cover problems much more vast and varied than any confronting the medieval world. Nevertheless a science of international law embodying principles by which these, and other, questions relating to rules of warfare may receive an authoritative answer is not to be evolved without reference to past thought and without drawing on old principles. This will be evident in reviewing some of the theories of the forerunners of the "father of international law," Grotius.

One of the outstanding theologians of the early sixteenth century was the Spaniard, Franciscus de Victoria. In 1526 he became professor of theology at the University of Salamanca, where he remained until his death twenty years later. Although he did not write down his views for publication, some of his pupils gathered together and preserved certain of his learned discourses upon which his reputation rests.[3] So

[3] In 1557, several years after his death, a collection of thirteen *Relectiones,* dealing with various questions from the point of view of a theologian, but one with a remarkable breadth of view, were published at Lyons.

highly was he esteemed that Pope Paul III invited him to attend the Council of Trent, and Charles V often submitted questions to him on the affairs of the Indies, and other matters which bothered the Emperor's conscience. In fact, Victoria's views come down to us principally in the form of discussions of and answers to concrete questions. His *De Indis,* written in 1532, raises the question of the title of the Spaniards to dominions in the New World; and the *De Jure Belli Hispanorum in Barbaros,* designed to complete the *De Indis,* goes into the question of the circumstances under which war may be justified, and the manner in which it may be waged. Together they constitute a brief treatise, the first to appear, on the law of peace and war, and entitle the author to a very high, perhaps the highest, rank among the early forerunners of Grotius.

The discussion in the first *Relectio* on the Indians [4] is designed to answer three questions: (1) By what right did the Indians come under Spanish sway? (2) What rights did the Spanish sovereigns obtain over them in temporal and civil matters? (3) What rights did these sovereigns obtain over the Indians in spiritual and religious matters? In his discussion of these questions Victoria draws upon a wide variety of authorities—Aristotle, the Holy Scriptures, the Church fathers, the Schoolmen, church councils, the canon law, and the writings of civilians. In order to answer the first question, Victoria proceeded systematically by an examination of connected questions to a final conclusion. Admitting, on the authority of Aristotle, that people of the character of the Indians might properly be regarded as slaves by nature, he nevertheless pointed out that when the Spaniards came they were actually in peaceable possession of property both publicly and privately. Rejecting the propositions that the Indians could lose true ownership on account of sin or infidelity, or that for these reasons Christians were entitled to seize their lands and goods, Victoria concluded that the Indians "had true dominion in both public and private matters, just like Christians, and that neither their princes nor private persons could be despoiled of their property on the ground of their not being true owners." [5] The

[4] For English translation of the two *Relectiones* from which quotations will be taken, see Franciscus de Victoria, *De Indis et De Iure Belli Relectiones,* tr. by John Pawley Bate (Washington, 1917), Carnegie Classics of International Law, ed. by J. B. Scott, copyrighted by Carnegie Endowment for International Peace.

[5] Victoria, *op. cit.,* Sec. I, pp. 127-128, paragraphs 23-24.

position of Victoria at this point represents an advance over medieval conceptions.[6]

Victoria next addresses himself to the reputation of certain alleged titles of the Spaniards to extend their dominion over the Indians. He refused to admit world lordship on the part either of the Emperor or Pope that would entitle the Spaniards to occupy the lands of the Indians. As regards the alleged right to these lands by virtue of discovery, the claim was inadmissible because, as previously stated, the Indians were already in occupation and were true owners of the land. Thus the Spaniards have no more title to the lands of the Indians, merely because they discovered them, than the Indians would have to Spain if they discovered it. To the contention that the Indians had refused to accept the Christian faith, although they had been advised to do so, and that therefore the occupation of their lands was lawful, Victoria likewise entered a denial. If the Indians are admonished to hear and reflect upon religious matters over a period of time, and those seeking to convert them demonstrate in their own lives the value of the Christian faith, the Indians are bound to receive the faith or be guilty of mortal sin. But, concludes Victoria, who evidently regarded example more important than precept, this apparently has not been done. "Now I hear of no miracles or signs of religious patterns of life, nay, on the other hand, I hear of many scandals and cruel crimes and acts of impiety. Hence it does not appear that the Christian religion has been preached to them with such sufficient propriety and piety that they are bound to acquiesce in it. . ."[7] And even if this were true and the Indians had refused to accept the faith, it would still not entitle the Spaniards to make war upon them and despoil them of their property. Although this is humane doctrine, it is to be observed that there is hardly anything in it not readily derived from medieval authorities.

On the other hand, in his discussion of titles under which he considers that the Spaniards may legitimately extend their dominion over the Indians, Victoria definitely takes advanced ground. He asserts that on the grounds of "natural society and fellowship," the Spaniards had the right to travel and reside in the lands of the Indians, as long as they did not harm the latter. This principle of the right of intercourse between nations Victoria derives from the law of nations (*ius gentium*)

[6] Lange, *op. cit.*, pp. 273-274.
[7] *Op. cit.*, Sec. II, p. 144, paragraph 14.

"which either is natural law or is derived from natural law." According to this law all nations regard it as inhumane to mistreat visitors and foreigners unless the latter have misbehaved: Human friendship is rooted in nature for, quoting from Ecclesiastes, "every animal loveth its kind." It is therefore against nature to shun the society of other peaceful human beings. Victoria also advances additional "proofs" of the same general nature. He then advances the specific proposition that the Spaniards have the right to trade with the Indians, bringing the latter what they need, and receiving in exchange those things of which they have a surplus. This is legitimate if no harm is done the Indians, and its denial would be contrary to natural and divine law. A third proposition was that the Spaniards were entitled to such harmless rights and privileges as the Indians granted to their own citizens and to foreigners as well. "For if the Spaniards may travel and trade among them, they may consequently make use of the laws and advantages enjoyed by all foreigners."[8] Finally, says Victoria, children born of Spaniards domiciled in the country of the Indians may not be deprived of citizenship or of the advantages enjoyed by other citizens, for by the law of nations he is a citizen who is born within the state.[9] Victoria then eliminates the possibility of a second nationality by asserting that "whoever is born in any one state is not a citizen of another state." Victoria also asserts in effect that citizenship may be acquired by naturalization when he says that any persons who wish to acquire a domicile in some state of the Indians, by marriage or in some other manner by which foreigners acquire citizenship, may not be prevented from doing so, and from enjoying all the privileges of other citizens provided they also share the burdens of citizenship. Thus Victoria briefly, it is true, outlines a theory of the acquisition of citizenship by birth, and by naturalization.

Now if the Indians try to prevent the Spaniards from exercising any of the foregoing rights under the law of nations, reason and persuasion must first be employed. If this is of no avail, even though all possible efforts are made, and the Indians use force, the Spaniards may defend themselves in all necessary ways. It is always permissible to repel force by force. And if to obtain security it is necessary for the Spaniards to occupy the states of the aborigines and subject them to their rule,

[8] Victoria, *op. cit.*, Sec. III, p. 153, paragraph 4.
[9] This is based on the Justinian Code.

this also is lawful. And if the Indians persist in resisting, the Spaniards may avail themselves of all the rights of war, in order to bring them to complete subjection, and may punish them according to the degree of their offense. "This, then, is the first title which the Spaniards might have for seizing the provinces and sovereignty of the natives, provided the seizing be without guile or fraud and they do not look for imaginary causes of war." [10]

Another possible title, suggested by Victoria, is that obtained in connection with the propagation of the Christian religion. Just as persons have the right of travel, trade, residence, and citizenship in other states, so Victoria declares that Christians have the right to preach and proselyte in the states of the Indians. It is not lawful to carry on war against them when they merely refuse to accept the faith, but if the Indians obstruct Evangelistic efforts, all means necessary may be used to convert them, including the occupation of their lands, the deposition of their rulers, and the prosecution of war against them.

In the *Second Relectis On the Indians,* or *On the Law of War Made by the Spaniards on the Barbarians,* Victoria treats of the laws of war. Following St. Augustine and other authorities, he declares that it is lawful for Christians to wage both defensive and offensive wars. As regards defensive war, any private person may wage it if necessary for the protection of his person, property, or goods. Victoria's second proposition is that every state has authority to declare war and wage it not only in self-defense but for the purpose of avenging itself and exacting reparation for wrongs suffered. The authority representing the state for this purpose, as Aquinas shows, is, in the natural order of things, the prince.

Victoria follows Aquinas also in holding that a war must have a just cause. Difference of religion, he repeats, is not a just cause, nor extension of Empire. Neither is the personal glory of the prince. "For a prince ought to subordinate both peace and war to the common weal of his State and not spend public revenues in quest of his own glory or gain, much less expose his subjects to danger on that account." [11] There is but one just cause of war, says Victoria succinctly, and that is the violation of a right. But not every wrong justifies war against the wrong-doer any more than every offense of persons within the state

[10] Victoria, *op. cit.,* Sec. III, p. 156, paragraph 8.
[11] *Ibid.,* p. 170, paragraph 12.

merits the most extreme punishment. The punishment in each case should correspond to the measure of the offense.

Victoria recognizes and faces another difficulty. If the prince is vested with the sole power of deciding whether a war is just, is it enough that he believes he has a just cause?—"for although it is not a common occurrence for princes to wage war in bad faith, they nearly always think theirs is a just cause."[12] Victoria's recognition of this widely observed trait of human beings did not, however, lead him to the logical position taken, for example, by Dubois and Erasmus. He faced a *de facto* situation, the actual internal power, and independence of outside authority of the national monarchs and the disposition of the latter to maintain that independence. Doubless for this reason he stopped short of suggesting that alleged "just causes" he placed before unprejudiced parties for examination and decision. Nevertheless he sought to prevent hasty or frivolous wars by laying down the proposition that the prince should consult unbiased persons,—apparently, though, from among his own countrymen!—before beginning a war. "It is essential for a just war that an exceedingly careful examination be made of the justice and causes of the war and that the reasons of those who on grounds of equity oppose it be listened to. For (as the comic poet says) 'A wise man must make trial of everything by words before resorting to force,' and he ought to consult the good and wise and those who speak with freedom and without anger or bitterness or greed, seeing that (as Sallust says) 'where these vices hold sway, truth is not easily distinguished.' This is self-evident."[13] Victoria said further that the influential persons of the state ought to examine into the causes of a war about to be undertaken, for "they can avert the war, supposing it to be unjust, if they lend their wisdom and weight to an examination into its causes." Victoria does not regard the common people as capable of understanding or exerting influence in the matter, but he says emphatically that "war ought not to be made on the sole judgment of the king, nor, indeed, on the judgment of a few, but on that of many, and they wise and upright men."[14]

It had generally been assumed and taught by theologians of the Middle Ages that in any war justice was wholly on one side, and

[12] Victoria, *op. cit.*, p. 173, paragraph 20.
[13] *Ibid.*, p. 173, paragraph 21.
[14] *Ibid.*, p. 174, paragraph 24.

guilt on the other. But Victoria anticipates cases in which there are "apparent and probable reasons on both sides," by setting forth what should be done in certain hypothetical cases. Thus, if one monarch claims and has possession of a disputed territory, the true ownership of which is doubtful, he holds that it would not be lawful for another claimant to try to take it by force of arms. In such a case the party in possession has the better position. Now since "princes are judges in their own cases, inasmuch as they have no superior," it is incumbent upon them to proceed in the matter as an ordinary judge would do, and the latter in case of doubt would never dispossess the party in possession. Incidentally, by taking this position Victoria accepts the theory that it is proper for a prince to exercise both the functions of accuser and judge. He only admonishes the prince not to forget that he is performing a judicial function.[15]

As regards rules of warfare, Victoria hardly advances beyond the theoretical position of the ancients. Although he denies that it is lawful in itself to kill innocent persons such as women and children, "even in war with the Turks," he admits that it may be done deliberately in case of military necessity. Likewise, non-combatants may be despoiled of their goods to the extent that it may be necessary to the effective waging of war, though this should not be done wantonly. Moreover, if an enemy refuses to restore things wrongfully seized and no other way is open, the injured party may recoup his losses from innocent as well as from guilty. As regards the question of the lawfulness of carrying off and enslaving innocent persons, Victoria takes a position somewhat similar to that taken by the Greeks toward the barbarians: "And so when a war is at that pass that the indiscriminate spoliation of all enemy-subjects alike and the seizure of all their goods are justifiable,

[15] The position of the theologians in the Middle Ages had been that, in the case of a dispute between princes over a matter in which the blame was partly on one side and partly on the other, war was inadmissible. (Hans Wehberg, *The Outlawry of War* [Washington, 1931], p. 2). In such cases the logical alternative was arbitration. By the time of Victoria and Suarez, however, the older view was becoming undermined. Suarez, for example, admitted that a sovereign who, after careful study, came to the conclusion that right was more probably on his side than on that of his opponent, might declare war.

By the end of the sixteenth century, the tendency to justify wars in which there might be culpability on both sides was marked, and the right of subjects to exercise any judgment as to the justice of a war decided upon by their sovereign was practically no longer recognized. Luigi Sturzo, *The International Community and the Right of War* (London, 1929), p. 181.

then it is also justifiable to carry all enemy subjects off into captivity, whether they be guilty or guiltless. And inasmuch as war with pagans is of this type, seeing that it is perpetual and that they can never make amends for the wrongs and damages they have wrought, it is indubitably lawful to carry off both the children and the women of the Saracens into captivity and slavery. But inasmuch as, by the law of nations, it is a received rule of Christendom that Christians do not become slaves in right of war, this enslaving is not lawful in a war between Christians. . ." [16] It is noticeable that the liberal spirit which pervades much of Victoria's work is absent at this point. Perhaps it is too much to expect even a theologian always to rise above the prejudices of his time. In general, he takes the position that war should be waged only to obtain one's rights, defend one's country, and realize peace and security. Thus when victory has been achieved it "should be utilized with moderation and Christian humility, and the victor ought to deem that he will deliver the judgment whereby the injured state can obtain satisfaction. . ." [17] One fears that this is a counsel of perfection.

Francisco Suarez (1548-1617), another eminent Spanish theologian and philosopher, ranks with Victoria as one of the earlier precursors of Grotius who, while still approaching human problems in the spirit and with the method of the medieval Scholastics, nevertheless are becoming conscious of new times and the necessity of solving new problems. He was a member of the Society of Jesus, and taught philosophy at Segovia and theology at Rome as well as at the universities in Spain and Portugal. He was a voluminous writer but treated only incidentally of international relations. His views on this subject are principally to be found in his Treatise on Law and God the Legislator.[18]

In this work he distinguishes between the law of nature (*ius naturale*) and the law of nations (*ius gentium*), as was common among the theological jurists of the time. *Ius naturale* is God-made law implanted in the human soul and enabling it to distinguish between right

[16] *Op. cit.*, p. 181, paragraph 42.

[17] *Ibid.*, p. 187, paragraph 60. It is interesting to note that it never seems to occur to Victoria that the party in the wrong may sometime win. Does he, as Lange suggests (p. 279), regard war as a sort of judgment of God, giving victory to the right?

[18] *Tractatus de Legibus et Deo Legislatore* (Coimbra, 1612). Suarez also discusses certain phases of the relations between states in his *Tractatus de Charitate*, Disputatio XIII, De bello; the *Tractatus de Fide*, Disputatio XVIII, Sec. II, No. 8; and the *Opus de Triplici Virtute Theologica*, Disputatio on War in section on Charity.

and wrong. It is above all human law, is universal, immutable, and eternal. Its precepts are inevitably deduced from nature. On the other hand, the *ius gentium* is man-made law and arises from the concurrent judgments of nearly all the peoples of the earth. It is therefore founded upon custom and not upon nature. Suarez includes in the *ius gentium* such matters as the rights of diplomatic agents, the law of war, alliances, and treaties of peace. And then in a single famous passage he reveals so much insight and states his views so cogently on behalf of the necessity of such law between states that it has been quoted many times by modern writers. He says: "The human race, however divided into various peoples and kingdoms, has always not only its unity as a species but also a certain moral and quasi-political unity, pointed out by the natural precepts of mutual love and pity which extends to all, even to foreigners of any nation. Wherefore, although every perfect State, whether a republic or a kingdom, is in itself a perfect community composed of its own members, still each such State, viewed in relation to the human race, is in some measure a member of that universal unity. For those communities are never singly so self-sufficing but that they stand in need of some mutual aid, society, and communion, sometimes for the improvement of their condition and their greater convenience, but sometimes also for their moral necessity and need, as appears by experience. For that reason, they are in need of some law by which they may be directed and rightly ordered in that kind of communion and society. And although this is to a great extent supplied by natural reason, yet it is not so supplied sufficiently and immediately for all purposes; and, therefore, it has been possible for particular laws to be introduced by the practice of those nations. For just as custom introduced law in a State or province, so it was possible for laws to be introduced in the whole human race by the habitual conduct of nations; and that all the more, because the points which belong to this law are few, and approach very nearly to natural law; and, being easily deduced from it, are useful and agreeable to nature; so that, although this law cannot be plainly deduced as being altogether necessary in itself to laudable conduct, still it is very suitable to nature, and such as all may accept for its own sake." [19]

[19] *Tractatus de Legibus et Deo Legislatore,* Vol. II, Ch. XIX, p. 5. The translation is taken from David Jayne Hill, *World Organization and the Modern State* (New York, 1911), pp. 81-82. Copyrighted by Columbia University Press.

It will be recognized that much of this sounds like a restatement of what was generally accepted medieval doctrine, such as the completeness of states in the sense that they form wholes for certain purposes, yet are parts of a larger whole. But the theological emphasis is less in evidence, and the recognition of an actual interdependence of states and the need of law, from a practical utilitarian point of view, is clearly indicated. The passage is likewise significant for what it fails to include. There is no suggestion of any common superior as the divine agency for the application of this law to the various states. Apparently its immediate validity is to be sought in the voluntary consent of the society of states.

Suarez follows Victoria (who in turn goes back to St. Augustine) in holding that inasmuch as the rulers of states have no temporal superior, it is lawful for them to wage war against outside offenders just as it is their prerogative to punish crime within their states. But he attempts, as Victoria did not, to meet the objection that this makes the prince a party in a conflict and at the same time a judge as to its merits. Admitting that this is so, Suarez contends that wrong must be punished, and that whatever faults this method may have, there is no better way that is feasible. In the case of individuals there is an authority above them entrusted with the maintenance of justice, but in the case of states there is no such authority.[20]

Nevertheless, Suarez holds that all possible and honest means should be canvassed to the end of avoiding war. If, for example, arbitration can be resorted to without fear of its employment resulting in injustice, it will be a better means than war and should be used. For, says Suarez, in effect, surely the Creator has not left human affairs in such a critical state that every sort of conflict between states must be settled by war. This would ultimately be contrary to justice. Besides it would result in the strong always getting more than the weak, and would make the size of one's forces the measure of his rights, "which would be as absurd as it is barbarous." So far one feels that Suarez is facing the issue squarely, and that as a result he admits that justice stands a better chance of being served by the employment of arbitration than by a contest of arms. However, sufficiently serious objections

[20] A. Vanderpol, *La Doctrine Scolastique du Droit de Guerre* (Paris, 1919), pp. 368-369. French translation of *De Bello*, pp. 362-412. See also Lange, *op. cit.*, pp. 287-288.

occur to him that he is led to conclude that there is not even a moral obligation to have recourse to it. In the first place, there is the difficulty attendant upon the selection of arbitrators. A prince is likely to be suspicious of foreign judges. Moreover, a sovereign acting in good faith can have his rights in any particular controversy with other princes examined by men of wisdom and prudence. If they regard his case as good, there is no need to appeal to others. In a just judgment there are two different objects to be sought. In the first place, there is the examination into the question at issue and the determination of right as between the two parties. Science and prudence are required at this stage, and war is not employed in the matter, but it is rather upon the findings of the inquiry that war is based. There is thus no apparent reason for having recourse to arbiters. In the second place, there is the question of the vindication of a right once it is clearly established. At this point the sovereign himself must have jurisdiction, and there is no reason for him to have recourse to arbitration, although he ought to accept fair proposals if they are offered to him.[21] The weakness of this reasoning is apparent when one reflects that in such a case as Suarez has supposed two sovereigns on opposite sides of a dispute select men of "wisdom and prudence," normally, we may assume, from within their respective kingdoms, to advise them. It is rather too much to expect impartiality of men selected in such fashion.

Albericus Gentilis (1552-1608), an Italian jurist, is to be noted as another representative figure among the forerunners of Grotius, and one upon whom the latter relied heavily at certain points. Gentilis approached interstate relations from the point of view of the lay jurist. Indeed he is especially noteworthy for his efforts to liberate the law of nations from theology, and make it an autonomous science. Gentilis was a Protestant and, fearing the inquisition, left Italy and resided in Germany, and later in England, where he became professor of law at Oxford in 1587.[22] He also took up practice in the Admiralty Court, and was so highly regarded that the government in 1584 sought his advice in a serious matter involving the Spanish ambassador. As a result, he wrote the *De Legationibus* (London, 1585), a treatise on the character and status of ambassadors which was of great value in help-

[21] Lange, *op. cit.*, pp. 289-291.
[22] In view of the circumstances related, it is not surprising that his books were placed on the Index.

ing to "formulate and establish the principles and practice of modern diplomacy." [23]

From the point of view of general international theory, however, the single work of Gentilis of most importance is the *De Jure Belli,* which appeared in 1588 and 1589 in three volumes.[24] In this work he incidentally reveals his ideas on the character of the international community, treats certain aspects of the law of nations, and discusses at length the problem of war and peace. Employing the historical rather than the narrower theological approach he showed greater appreciation than Victoria and Suarez of the part played by custom in providing a foundation for the law of nations, and of the necessity of paying more attention to later historical developments instead of relying largely upon biblical history or that of Greek and Roman times. The law of nations (*ius gentium*) which, as Lange points out,[25] Gentilis does not seem clearly to distinguish as law between, instead of law common to, all nations, he nevertheless traces to the sociability of the human species, and the reciprocal needs and interdependence of men. And in his treatment of the theory of war and its legitimacy it is clear that Gentilis is thinking of *ius gentium* as law applying to the relationship between states.

Gentilis' discussion of the law of war reveals at various points how different his temper was from that of his predecessors among the theologians. In his definition of war he follows these, Victoria excepted, in holding that it is a relationship between states, but his position is perhaps more clearly defined. On both sides there must be public authorities waging it. Thus operations against pirates may not be regarded as war. The contending parties in all wars are independent sovereigns or peoples subject to no higher jurisdiction. When disputes arise between sovereigns, there are two alternative methods by which they may be settled—by discussion or by force of arms. It is highly desirable that the first alternative be followed, and in fact sovereigns have submitted many disputes to arbitration. When they have done so, however, they

[23] W. S. M. Knight, in *Encyclopaedia of the Social Sciences,* VI, 616.

[24] *De Jure Belli* (1612 ed.), tr. by John C. Rolfe; 2 vols. (Oxford, 1933), Classics of International Law. See also T. E. Holland, *Studies in International Law* (Oxford, 1898), pp. 1-39.

[25] *Op. cit.,* p. 297. It is to be noted also that Gentilis departed from the position of the earlier theologians in holding that "war may be justly waged by both sides." See Gentilis, *op. cit.,* pp. 31-33.

have acted by their own free will. Since there is no higher authority to compel independent sovereigns to have recourse to arbitration, it follows that when they will not do so the judgment of war is a necessity. Gentilis admits many just causes of war, but it is significant that he denies that a war may justly be made on behalf of religion. Religion is properly considered "a right existing between God and man; it is not a human right, that is, a right between man and man." Christians wage war justly against the Turks, not because of the difference in religion, but because the Turks, like the Spaniards, are constantly seeking universal domination.[26]

Although, as already observed, Gentilis holds that in the absence of a supreme jurisdiction above all princes, war is a necessity, he denies that it is the natural condition of men. War between the Greeks and barbarians, he says, was not natural, nor are the Saracens and Christians natural enemies. All men by nature are kin, and there is no natural discord between them whatever race they may be or whatever religious faith they may profess.[27] On the other hand, there are natural causes of war, such as self-defense. A war of self-defense may be begun before one is actually attacked if it is to anticipate aggression already planned or reasonably believed to have been planned. Another natural cause of war is the denial of something granted by nature such as "innocent passage, navigation, and commerce." [28]

Gentilis' conception of the solidarity of human kind, and of the moral obligations of states to prevent injustices in international relations is indicated in his assertion that a just war may be fought by a state in the defense of another state. Men individually owe one another mutual aid, says Gentilis, and the same rule holds for states. If any state seeks to injure another, and if a state is unjustly attacked, all the others should rally to its defense. On the other hand, he concludes that a state is not legally obligated to undertake such a war, and of course he does not visualize a *system* whereby collective action might be taken by states against one of their number in case of threatened or actual injury.[29] The net result, therefore, would seem to be that each state individually, unless it is allied with others, will be free to calculate whether its own interests will be served by aiding a state that has been

[26] *De Jure Belli,* Bk. I, Chs. I-IX.
[27] *Ibid.,* Ch. XII.
[28] *Ibid.,* Chs. XIII, XIV.
[29] *Ibid.,* Ch. XV.

attacked, which is something that one imagines it would have felt free to do in any case. Nevertheless it is clear that the intent of Gentilis was that the law of nations should give moral support to a law-abiding state, and pause to a state contemplating injury to others.

Gentilis is well aware that when a war breaks out each of the contending parties is disposed to insist that it has embraced the just cause. He is not the first writer to make such an observation, but he follows it with an admission, which runs contrary to the usual assumptions of the theologians, that it is not always the just cause that prevails in war. Nevertheless he apparently feels that when injustice triumphs there is nothing to be done about it. The successful evil doer must be left to a deserved infamy, to his own bad conscience, and eternal expiation [30] —a position more theological than logical.

As for the rules for conducting war, to which Gentilis devotes much thought and labor, it may be said that they are enlightened and humane and embody the best thought and practice of the past, but not much that is new. The value of his contribution to the subject is enhanced, however, by his elimination of matters connected with military tactics and similar topics which were dealt with in older treatises, but do not properly have a place in a treatise on the law of war.

Hugo Grotius (1583-1645) is justly entitled to the tribute usually paid to him of being the founder of the science of international law. Although he was unquestionably indebted heavily to many predecessors including Victoria, Suarez, Ayala,[31] and Gentilis, who contributed inspiration and ideas in various parts of the field, it remained for the great Dutchman to elaborate suggested principles and work out a complete system which was to attain such authority and become such a landmark that today writers on international law are designated as forerunners or successors of Grotius. At fifteen years of age he was already being spoken of as the "miracle of Holland," holding his own with the best minds of his day in philosophy and jurisprudence, and amazing people with the range of his knowledge. So highly was he

[30] Lange, *op. cit.*, p. 303. These moral sanctions could not have had much potency in the period in which Gentilis lived. It needed something stronger than a bad conscience, or the fear of future punishment to deter the self-seeking monarchs of that day.

[31] Baltasar Ayala (1548-84) was a Spanish jurist and political theorist. His *De Jure et Officiis Bellicis et Disciplina Militari,* published in 1582, was often cited by Grotius in the latter's great treatise.

regarded, indeed, that at this early age he was sent as an attaché with an embassy from the Netherlands to France.

His first work, *De Jure Praedae Commentarius* (Commentary on the Law of Prize) was written at the age of twenty-one and was occasioned by his being hired by the Dutch East India Company to act as counsel in a case involving the right of the Dutch to trade in the East and West Indies. In 1609, when the Company was engaged in negotiations with Spain concerning navigation and commerce in Eastern waters and needed the aid of Grotius again, he was asked to detach Chapter XII of the Commentary and publish it under the title of *Mare Liberum*.[32] The thesis of *Mare Liberum* represented a departure from the generally accepted thought of the Middle Ages on maritime dominion, which was in general that states may acquire dominion over seas and oceans as in the case of land areas. For example the Danes claimed the dominion of the Baltic, Venice of the Adriatic, and the English of the seas about the British isles, and such claims were admitted by the medieval lawyers. Exclusive control was regarded as flowing from dominion over such bodies of water and therefore the right to prohibit the citizens of other nations from trading, navigating, or fishing in such waters, or to levy tolls and exact customs dues for such privileges. The foundation for such claims lay partly in the fact that the seas were infested with pirates and it was highly desirable to have some authority responsible for keeping them in check.[33] After the overseas discoveries, Spain and Portugal sought and secured a religious sanction [34] for claiming between them the vast expanse of the Atlantic as well as dominion in East Indian waters. It was in opposition to such claims that Grotius wrote his *Mare Liberum.* Here again others had preceded him in challenging the position of those contending for *mare clausum*—the closed sea.[35]

Grotius took the position, which we have already seen upheld by

[32] For some reason the remainder of the work was not given out for publication. It first came to public attention when published in 1868.

[33] Walker, *op. cit.*, pp. 162-166.

[34] In 1493 Pope Alexander VI drew a line from pole to pole 100 leagues west of the Azores, and as Lord of the Isles of the Ocean, gave all land and sea west of it to Spain, and all east of it to Portugal. Accordingly, Spain and Portugal forbade foreign ships to sail in their respective seas.

[35] For example, Ferdinand Vasquez (1509-1566), Jean Bodin (1530-1596), and Gentilis (1552-1608) all challenged claims to dominion over the high seas, although Bodin's position was more qualified.

Victoria,[36] that nations have a natural right to communication and trade with one another. He contended that God had ordained that nature should not provide every country with all of life's necessities, but that they should be so distributed that an exchange of products would be required for the benefit of all. Otherwise nations would have a feeling of self-sufficiency and would lack sociability. Commerce thus being essential in the natural order of things, and the freedom of the seas being necessary for the carrying on of commerce, it follows that no power has the right to close them. Moreover in the very nature of things, all attempts to monopolize the sea are bound to fail, for it cannot be physically appropriated. Its immensity, its lack of stability, and its want of fixed limits all prevent the possibility of its being seized and enclosed and so possessed by any state. Grotius does not define "the sea" of which he is writing. Apparently he is contesting the dominion of any and all states anywhere on the sea rather than merely contending for the freedom of outer seas.[37]

The fame of Grotius rests upon his really great work, *De Jure Belli et Pacis*[38] (1625), which was the product of maturer years and ripened judgment. The *De Jure Praedae* was the work of a youthful, though brilliant, advocate of special interests; the latter work, although an expansion of the earlier one, was written entirely from the point of view of the general interests of mankind. The reason for its being undertaken and its content as well were influenced by the character of the times. Grotius, it may be remarked, was born amidst "war's alarums." Spain and the Netherlands had been at war for twenty years. Shortly after his birth, William of Orange was assassinated, and savagery and retaliation were the order of the day. In the background were the edict of the Spanish inquisition, condemning all of the inhabitants of his native country to death as heretics, and the terrible massacre of St. Bartholomew's Day, in France. Finally, it was during the most devastating

[36] *Supra*, pp. 139-140.

[37] In the great work, *On the Law of War and Peace* (Oxford, 1925), Bk. II, Ch. III, Grotius is more definite, and clearly holds that bays and inner seas may come under dominion. An answer to Grotius was made by John Selden in his *Mare Clausum* (London, 1635). See P. B. Potter, *The Freedom of the Seas in History, Law, and Politics* (New York, 1924), Ch. IV, on the Grotius-Selden controversy.

[38] (*On the Law of War and Peace.*) English translation by Francis W. Kelsey in the Classics of International Law, ed. by J. B. Scott, copyrighted by Carnegie Endowment for International Peace; 2 vols. (Oxford, 1925), Vol. II. This translation will be used henceforth in quotations from this work.

struggle that Europe had ever endured, the Thirty Years' War, that *On the Law of War and Peace* was written. It was hardly a matter for surprise, therefore, that the main concern of Grotius was with the law of war, the current savagery of which he desired to mitigate, and that his treatment of the law of peace seems to be rather the interpolation of an afterthought. On the other hand, it was the work of one who would have liked to see peace prevail between nations, and was conceived in a broad humanitarian spirit. In this connection Scott [39] remarks that the great treatise was "international from its origin. . . The work of a Dutchman, the treatise was worked out in France, written in Latin, the international language of the day, printed in Paris, which was already a cosmopolitan centre, and exposed for sale at the fair of Frankfort, a free city of that Confederation of Germanic nations which was the Holy Roman Empire."

Grotius goes back to the law of nature for the foundation of his system, and at the outset distinguishes between the nature of the lower animals and that of man. Man has "an impelling desire" for the society of his own kind, and, alone among the animals, has the faculty of speech as a special instrument with which to gratify it. He also has as his peculiarly human endowment the faculty of reason, and the power to discriminate between what is good and what is harmful for him. It is from these traits that law, for the maintenance of social order, has its source. Although Grotius traces these natural traits ultimately to God, the law of nature to him was not a narrow theological conception but, based on the universal attribute of human reason, was as wide as humanity itself, and therefore capable of serving as a common ground upon which all men, regardless of race or creed, might unite to erect a universal system of law between as well as within nations. The time had passed when Church or Empire could perform such a service, for religious unity had disappeared, and authority had been discarded. It was to fill the breach that Grotius offered the law of nature defined as "the dictate of right reason." [40] It may be remarked that the Grotian

[39] *Ibid.*, Introduction.

[40] As contrasted with the theological conception of the Middle Ages that the law of nature was the unrevealed (as contrasted with the Scriptural and canon law) law of God planted by him in the consciences of men. For elaboration of the contrasting conceptions, see F. J. C. Hearnshaw, in *Encyclopaedia of the Social Sciences,* I, 100; W. A. Dunning, *Political Theories from Luther to Montesquieu* (New York, 1905), pp. 164-166.

conception was not original—it was essentially that of the Stoics and Cicero.[41]

As contrasted with the law of nature—that unalterable system of rights rooted in the reality of things, and deduced unerringly by the best minds of all times and places by a process of right reason—Grotius recognized the existence of a *ius gentium* or law of nations. This law does not originate from a sure process of reasoning, but "yet is clearly observed everywhere."[42] It is human and volitional law determined by the consent of all or of many nations, and its content is to be determined by reference to constant practice and usage and by the testimony of the learned.[43] It is occasioned by consideration for the welfare of the great aggregate of nations just as the civil law is for the welfare of the aggregate of the individuals within a state. The law of nations, in so far as it could be distinguished from natural law,[44] was utilized by Grotius to supplement natural law in the system he developed. But *ius gentium,* or the practices of states in their relations with one another, was not always as advanced as Grotius thought desirable, and inasmuch as he wanted to improve international relations he made *ius naturale* the ultimate foundation of his system to which he could look for support.[45]

Grotius takes the position at the outset that "no association of men can be maintained without law," and, contrary to Machiavelli, that the rule of expediency is no more fitting between states than it is within states. "For since . . . the national who in his own country obeys its laws is not foolish, even though, out of regard for that law, he may be obliged to forego certain things advantageous for himself, so that nation is not foolish which does not press its own advantage to the point of disregarding the laws common to nations.[46] The reason in either case is the same. For just as the national, who violates the law of his country in order to obtain an immediate advantage, breaks down that by which the advantages of himself and his posterity are for all future time

[41] *Supra,* p. 83.

[42] *De Jure Belli,* p. 40.

[43] *Ibid.,* Bk. I, Ch. I, Sec. XIV, pp. 1, 2.

[44] W. A. Dunning, *op. cit.,* pp. 175, 176, points out that Grotius failed in his effort to distinguish between the law of nature and the law of nations. In the final analysis, both rested upon "the opinions of the publicists."

[45] Walker, *op. cit.,* p. 332.

[46] Other passages make it clear that Grotius, though using the phrase "common to nations," at this point is really thinking of the law *between* nations.

assured, so the state which transgresses the law of nature and of nations cuts away also the bulwarks which safeguard its own future peace."[47] To those who denied that the standard of justice which is upheld as between individuals within the state is applicable to nations and their rulers, contending that individual citizens need law for their protection on account of their weakness, but that great states have the means within themselves for their protection and can dispense with justice, Grotius replied: "There is no state so powerful that it may not some time need the help of others outside itself, either for purposes of trade, or even to ward off the forces of many foreign nations united against it. In consequence we see that even the most powerful peoples and sovereigns seek alliances, which are quite devoid of significance according to the point of view of those who confine law within the boundaries of the states."[48]

Law is necessary in the relations between nations not only in time of peace but it is also essential in time of war. "Some people," says Grotius, "imagine that in war all laws are in abeyance. On the contrary war ought not to be undertaken except for the enforcement of rights; whence once undertaken, it should be carried on only within the bounds of law and good faith . . . in order that wars may be justified, they must be carried on with not less scrupulousness than judicial processes are wont to be."[49] This has a very familiar ring. Victoria, Suarez, Gentilis, and many others had looked upon war in much the same way, some at least regarding it as a means of invoking the judgment of God, and most of them professing to believe that "victory crowns the right." In the *De Jure Praedae* Grotius asserted in effect that a study of the outcome of wars would show that God frequently awarded victory to the party having right on his side.[50] In the *De Jure Belli,* he contends that history reveals the great moral value in war of "the consciousness that one has justice on his side," and that historians "often attribute victory chiefly to this cause." It is rather curious, but it does not seem to occur to him that frequently, if not, indeed, usually, both sides have the benefit that is derived from such "consciousness." Grotius does admit that "unjust enterprises" occasionally succeed, but he does not feel that one should be disturbed about it, for the unworthy

[47] *De Jure Belli,* p. 18.
[48] *Ibid.,* pp. 21, 22.
[49] *Ibid.,* p. 25.
[50] See Lange, *op. cit.,* p. 316.

winner is likely to lose and the just loser is likely to gain in other ways. "Even for winning friendships, of which for many reasons nations as well as individuals have need, a reputation for having undertaken war not rashly nor unjustly, and of having waged it in manner above reproach, is exceedingly efficacious. No one readily allies himself with those in whom he believes that there is only a slight regard for law, for the right, and for good faith." [51] One infers from this and other like statements of Grotius that in the long run, if not immediately, Right triumphs and immoral Might suffers penalties for the disregard of law and justice.

It will be seen from the foregoing that Grotius accepts war as an element in the system of international relations and looks upon it as in the nature of a judicial process. In this connection it may be observed that Gentilis was more advanced in his notion of war, in one respect at least, than Grotius, for the former's clear cut definition made it an armed contest exclusively between public authorities.[52] Grotius, on the other hand, includes armed contests between private individuals, defining war as "the condition of those contending by force. . ." He makes his definition wide enough to include private war, "since in fact it is more ancient than public war and has, incontestably, the same nature as public war; wherefore both should be designated by one and the same term." [53] Grotius admits that private war is harder to justify since the establishment of courts to settle disputes between individuals. "For although public tribunals are the creation not of nature but of man, it is, nevertheless, much more consistent with moral standards, and more conducive to the peace of individuals, that a matter be judicially investigated by one who has no personal interest in it, than that individuals, too often having their own interests in view, should seek by their own hands to obtain what they consider right; wherefore equity and reason given to us by nature declare that so praiseworthy an institution should have the fullest support." [54] On the other hand, Grotius concludes that private war is not a violation of the law of nature in cases where judicial processes may not be available, and in certain cases it is even permitted by the law of the Gospel.[55]

[51] *De Jure Belli,* p. 27.
[52] *Supra,* p. 148.
[53] *De Jure Belli,* Bk. I, Ch. I, Sec. II, p. 1.
[54] *Ibid.,* Bk. I, Ch. III, Sec. I, p. 2.
[55] *Ibid.,* Bk. I, Ch. III, Sec. II, pp. 1, 2; Sec. III, pp. 1-9.

It is unnecessary for our purposes to follow the extended discussion of Grotius on the subject of causes of war and rules for its conduct.[56] Suffice it to say, as regards the former, he treated the subject from the point of view of just causes, unjust causes, and doubtful causes of war, and took the position that in the case of public wars the appropriate public authorities in each state were to pass upon their own case. It is only in his discussion of cases where there is a doubt that Grotius suggests methods whereby disputes may be settled by means other than war, and even so his suggestions are quite brief and incidental. However, he mentions three methods. The first method is that of conference, which he recommends by quoting with approval the words of Cicero: "Since there are two methods of settling a difference, the one by argument, the other by force, and since the former is characteristic of men, the latter of beasts, we should have recourse to the second only when it is not permitted to use the first." [57] Grotius, however, drops the matter without any suggestions as to the nature of such a conference. The second method, arbitration, is given more, though still scanty, attention. Grotius suggests that "it would be advantageous, indeed in a degree necessary, to hold certain conferences of Christian powers, where those who have no interest at stake may settle the disputes of others, and where, in fact, steps may be taken to compel parties to accept peace on fair terms." [58] Brief as this is, it envisages three things that remind one of the plans of Dubois and Poděbrad [59] for the international organization of Christendom: the organization of conferences of the Christian states, the setting up of arbitration tribunals for the settlement of international disputes, and finally the imposition of sanctions for the enforcement of fair decisions. The third method, that of peaceful settlement by lot, is not discussed by Grotius, but he does suggest that when kings have disputes of a private character they might settle the matter and save

[56] It should be noted, however, that although Grotius assumes that in most instances justice will be found on one side, the laws of war take no account of this. The rights and obligations flowing from them apply equally to both sides. As regards those nations not participating in a war the merits of which are doubtful, Grotius advises strict impartiality. In a case in which one side is clearly in the wrong, he has this to say: ". . . it is the duty of those who keep out of a war to do nothing whereby he who supports a wicked cause may be rendered more powerful, or whereby the movements of him who wages a just war may be hampered. . . ." (*De Jure Belli*, Bk. III, Ch. XVII, Sec. III, p. 1.)

[57] *Ibid.*, Bk. II, Ch. XXIII, Sec. VII, p. 1.

[58] *Ibid.*, Sec. VIII.

[59] *Supra*, pp. 105-113.

their peoples from much suffering by engaging, after the manner of the Franks and other earlier peoples, in single combat.[60]

In the course of his work Grotius, like his predecessors with the exception of Gentilis, summoned a host of witnesses—poets, historians, philosophers and theologians—and cited many precedents from Biblical as well as Greek and Roman history to bolster his position or "embellish" his thought. Indeed, in his desire to gain acceptance for what should be, he takes great pains to show what has been. In fact his work is essentially the gathering together and synthesizing of the thought of the past, and working it into a system of rules for the interstate conduct of nations in war and in peace. He was definitely conservative in the sense that he felt more progress could be made by making haste slowly and taking a middle position which would be less vulnerable to attack and less likely to be disregarded. For this reason he found it necessary to criticize men like Erasmus who were less inclined to compromise with war and other undesirable practices. He says: ". . . but their purpose, as I take it, is, when things have gone in one direction, to force them in the opposite direction, as we are accustomed to do, that they may come back to a true middle ground. But the very effort of pressing too hard in the opposite direction is often so far from being helpful that it does harm, because in such arguments the detection of what is extreme is easy, and results in weakening the influence of other statements which are well within the bounds of truth. For both extremes therefore a remedy must be found, that men may not believe either that nothing is allowable, or that everything is." [61] When he says this, he is, of course, thinking of practices in war, but it characterizes his attitude in general. It is doubtless the reason for his failure to go farther than to suggest that Christian states *ought* to avoid war whenever possible and resort to arbitration or some form of peaceful settlement, which was the position of the Theologians. And one must admit that to have worked out a system of arbitration and included the requirement that monarchs *must* resort to it would certainly have been regarded as "extreme" by them and would not have been acceptable.

But if Grotius could not bring himself to accept fully the radical ideas of Erasmus, although fundamentally in sympathy with the posi-

[60] *De Jure Belli,* Bk. II, Chap. XXIII, Secs. X, XI.
[61] *Ibid.,* p. 29.

tion of the great humanist, he was totally unprepared, on the other hand, to follow the Machiavellian School. In fact the Grotians and Machiavellians represented two opposing and irreconcilable conceptions of the state and of the relations of states with one another. Machiavelli, and later Hobbes [62] and Spinoza, exalted expediency as the source of all law; Grotius traced its source to the natural impulse of men to associate. Machiavelli, and his followers, regarding the state at bottom as a predatory enterprise, held that it might feel free to break faith with others to achieve its ends; Grotius throughout his treatise and at the very end emphasizes the necessity of basing international relations on good faith: "And good faith should be preserved, not only for other reasons but also in order that the hope of peace may not be done away with. For not only is every state sustained by good faith, as Cicero declares, but also that greater society of states. Aristotle truly

[62] Thomas Hobbes (1588-1679) famous English philosopher, contrary to Grotius, asserted that "Men have no pleasure but on the contrary a great deal of grief in keeping company. . ." His analysis of human nature as nasty and brutish and unsocial laid the foundation for his contract theory and the defense of absolutism. It also led to his fatalistic view concerning international relations. Nations like individuals before the latter are coerced by a superior authority, are with respect to each other in a state of nature, which is a state of war. The rulers of states "because of their independency, are in continual jealousies and in the state and posture of gladiators; having their weapons pointing, and their eyes fixed on one another. . ." (*Leviathan* [New York, 1907], Ch. XIII.) There is no law over them and considerations of international justice and good faith are not applicable. "To this war of every man, against every man, this also is consequent, that nothing can be unjust. The notions of right and wrong, justice and injustice have there no place. Where there is no common power, there is no law: where no law, no injustice. Force, and fraud, are in war the two cardinal virtues." (*Ibid.*) Logically, as one writer (George E. G. Catlin, *Encyclopaedia of the Social Sciences*, VII, 396) has pointed out, the Hobbesian analysis "dictates an international state" that shall make the reign of law universal rather than merely statewide.

Baruch Spinoza (1632-1677), Dutch-Jewish philosopher, held views similar to those of Hobbes on international relations, and apparently was considerably influenced by the latter. States live in a state of nature (war) but they are not under the same necessity of establishing law between each other that drove men in the state of nature to accept a superior authority. For states are able to guard themselves against oppression by their neighbors as individuals are not. (*The Chief Works of Benedict de Spinoza,* tr. from the Latin, with an introduction by R. H. M. Elwes, 2 vols. [London, 1883], I, 306.) Spinoza, although taking the position of the medieval theologians, that war should be made only for the sake of peace, followed Machiavelli in holding that, if necessary, cities of the enemy may be utterly destroyed and their inhabitants removed. (*Op. cit.*, I, 325.) Moreover, treaties between states remain in force only so long as "fear of hurt or hope of gain, subsists." Every state has a right to break its contract when it can do so with impunity, or when it no longer gains anything from it. (*Op. cit.*, I, 307.) See also H. Lauterpacht, "Spinoza and International Law," *The British Year Book of International Law* (1927), pp. 89-107.

says that, if good faith has been taken away, all intercourse among men ceases to exist.[63]

REFERENCES

Brière, Yves de la, *La Conception du Droit International chez les Théologiens Catholiques* (Paris, 1930).

Dickinson, E. D., *The Equality of States in International Law* (Cambridge, Mass., 1920), Ch. II.

Dunning, W. A., *Political Theories from Luther to Montesquieu* (New York, 1905), Ch. V, pp. 137-142.

Grotius, Hugo, *De Jure Belli Ac Pacis*, tr. by F. W. Kelsey; 2 vols. (Oxford, 1913-1925), Vol. II. Classics of International Law, ed. by J. B. Scott.

——————, *Mare Liberum* (1609), ed. by J. B. Scott (Washington, 1916).

Hershey, A., *Essentials of International Public Law and Organization* (rev. ed., New York, 1927), pp. 59-72.

Holland, T. E., *Studies in International Law* (Oxford, 1898).

Janet, P., *Histoire de la Science Politique;* 2 vols. (Paris, 1887), Vol. II, pp. 227-234.

Knight, W. S. M., *The Life and Works of Hugo Grotius* (London, 1925). (Grotius Society Publications).

Korff, Baron S. A., "An Introduction to the History of International Law," *American Journal of International Law,* Vol. XVIII (1924), pp. 246-259.

Lange, C., *Histoire de l'Internationalisme* (Christiania, 1919), Ch. VIII.

Laurent, F., *Histoire du Droit des Gens* (Bruxelles, 1861-1870), Vol. X, pp. 477-495.

Meulen, J. ter, *Der Gedanke der Internationalen Organization in Seiner Entwicklung* (1300-1889); 2 vols. (The Hague, 1917-1929), I (1300-1800), 153-159.

Murray, R. H. *The History of Political Science from Plato to the Present* (Cambridge, Eng., 1926), pp. 186-198.

Nys, E., *Les Origines du Droit International* (Paris, 1894).

Pillet, A. (ed.), *Les Fondateurs du Droit International* (Contents: F. de Victoria, A. Gentilis, F. Suarez, Grotius, Zouch, Pufendorf, Bynkershoek, Wolf, Wattel, de Martens.) (Paris, 1904).

[63] *De Jure Belli,* Bk. III, Ch. XXV, Sec. I. For the further development of international juridical thought, see Amos S. Hershey, *Essentials of International Public Law and Organization* (rev. ed., New York, 1927) pp. 71-101, with footnote references, and bibliography, pp. 123-124. See also article and bibliography on "International Law" by Edwin M. Borchard, in *Encyclopaedia of the Social Sciences,* VIII, 157-175. Except for certain absolutely indispensable fundamentals, the domain of juridical theory lies beyond the scope of the present work.

Potter, P. B., *The Freedom of the Seas in History, Law, and Politics* (New York, 1924), Chs. II, III, IV.

Redslob, R., *Histoire des Grands Principes du Droit des Gens* (Paris, 1923), pp. 195-209.

Scott, J. B., *The Spanish Origins of International Law* (Washington, 1928).

Selden, J., *Mare Clausum* (London, 1635).

Stawell, F. M., *Growth of International Thought* (London, 1930), pp. 121-131.

Vanderpol, A., *La Doctrine Scolastique du Droit de Guerre* (Paris, 1919), pp. 362-412.

Victoria, Franciscus de, *De Indis et De Iure Belli Relectiones,* ed. by Ernest Nys (Washington, 1917). Classics of International Law, ed. by J. B. Scott.

Walker, T. A., *A History of the Law of Nations* (Cambridge, Eng., 1899), Pt. I, Ch. III.

White, A. D., *Seven Great Statesmen* (New York, 1910), pp. 55-110.

Wright, Herbert, *Catholic Founders of Modern International Law* (Washington, 1934).

CHAPTER IX

THE SEVENTEENTH CENTURY: INTERNATIONAL ORGANIZATION

The work of Grotius aroused great interest and won widespread approval outside the circles of the narrower theologians, but it can hardly be said that it appreciably influenced international practices. Here, for example, is a picture of the war that was to continue to rage for nearly a quarter of a century after the publication of the *De Jure Belli:* "The Thirty Years' War . . . marked the lowest state of degradation to which Europe had descended since the time of primitive barbarism. In that desperate conflict, the basest passions mingled with the noblest purposes and the most heroic sacrifices in the effort to settle by brute force questions of the deepest moral and religious significance. A hireling soldiery, ready to fight for pay under any standard, making war its profession, sacked populous cities, murdered the inhabitants, devastated a great part of Central Europe, and left behind it a scene of ruin, suffering, and desolation which centuries were required to repair. Multitudes were homeless, two-thirds of the houses in Germany having been destroyed; yet so great was the loss of life that only half the remainder were occupied. An entire generation had known little but tales of slaughter; and war, in its most brutal and disgusting forms, had come to appear to those who in their entire lives had witnessed nothing else as the natural and permanent condition of mankind." [1]

In the second half of the seventeenth century the Thirty Years' War gave place to other conflicts. The dynastic ambitions and predatory enterprises of divine-right monarchs were not to be denied by definitions of "unjust wars." Louis XIV paid this much homage to Grotius—or was it to the teachings of Machiavelli?—that when he initiated his wars of conquest he was careful to *seem virtuous.* When German territories were annexed, they were annexed "legally" by

[1] D. J. Hill, *World Organization and the Modern State,* p. 91. Copyrighted by Columbia University Press.

Chambers of Reunion.[2] In reality, *raison d'état,* in practice the "reason" of the absolute monarchs of the day, was the dominating factor in the determination of foreign policies. The Grotian system, after all, in the final analysis, left the matter of justice in every question arising in international relations to the conscience and private judgment of each ruler. It was inevitable that the responsibility and strain would prove too great. Exhortation and appeals to princely consciences were not enough. Apparently a more drastic remedy was needed. Therefore certain thinkers worked out plans of international organization designed to provide a common authority to which nations would agree to look for the settlement of serious differences which they would otherwise be unable to solve peaceably, and which would inquire into conflicting territorial claims.

Chronologically, the first of these seventeenth century plans was contributed by a more or less obscure but acute Frenchman, Émeric Crucé (1590-1648), and published in 1623 under the title of *Le Nouveau Cynée.*[3] In it his advice to princes [4] was in striking contrast with that given by Machiavelli, and was based upon a fundamentally different conception of state relationships. For example, the thought that one state will gain through the losses suffered by others, which was as-

[2] The Chambers of Reunion were special courts set up by Louis and subservient to his wishes. Their task was to judge what territory might be annexed as a result of the revival of ancient feudal rights. When they adjudged that a particular district should belong to Louis, the King duly executed the judgment with his army. From the point of view of the French King, this unilateral justice left nothing to be desired.

[3] The title was apparently suggested by an incident in the life of Cyneas, an orator and diplomat of Thessaly in the service of King Pyrrhus. In a conversation between the two, as related by Plutarch, Cyneas takes occasion to ask the King what he intends to make out of the victory for which he is hoping when he attacks the Romans. The King answers that such a victory will enable him to become master of all Italy. Cyneas asks, what then? The King answers that he can then take Sicily. The conversation goes on after this fashion until the King has conquered (in his imagination) about everything there is to conquer, whereupon Cyneas asks: "But when we have conquered all, what are we to do then?" To which the King jovially replies that "we will take our ease, and be merry." Cyneas then asked a question that one would not expect a diplomat to ask of his King: "And what hinders us from drinking and taking our ease now, when we have already those things in our hands, at which we propose to arrive through seas of blood, through infinite toils and dangers, through innumerable calamities, which we must both cause and suffer?" The answer of the King is not recorded. (T. W. Balch, *Émeric Crucé* [Philadelphia, 1900], notes 39, 40.)

[4] The work was addressed: "To the Monarchs and Sovereign Princes of the present time." Like Machiavelli's *Prince,* it was intended as a guide for rulers; but unlike the *Prince* it attempts to point out to them "the means to assure your state by the establishment of a universal peace."

sumed in the *Prince,* ran counter to the conviction of the interdependence of states held by Crucé, who says: "There are those who . . . think so little of strangers that they consider it a prudent policy to sow among them dissensions, in order to enjoy a more secure quiet. But I am of a different opinion and it seems to me that when one sees the house of his neighbor burning or tumbling down that one has as much cause for fear as compassion, because human society is a body of all whose members have a common sympathy, so that it is impossible that the sickness of one shall not be communicated to the others. Now this little book contains a universal polity, useful to all nations alike and agreeable to those that have some light of reason and sentiment of humanity." [5] If one compares the thought of this quotation from the introductory part of Crucé's project with the Prolegomena of Grotius' *De Jure Belli,* he will observe at once that they start out on their respective enterprises from essentially the same premises.

Crucé seems to have been of a decidedly practical bent, and inclined to examine callings and institutions from the point of view of their utility. Accordingly he disparages the calling of the soldier and glorifies that of the merchant. ". . . there is no occupation to compare in utility with that of the merchant who legitimately increases his resources by the expenditure of his labor and often at the peril of his life, without injuring or offending anyone: in which he is more worthy of praise than the soldier whose advancement depends upon the spoil and destruction of others." [6] He was interested in all the practical arts from farming which "nourishes a state" and trade which "enriches it" to manufactures and the mechanical arts. If princes saw to it that their subjects were employed in these ways, Crucé thought the latter would not seek amusement in war. On the other hand, he was inclined to steer clear of theology, which was responsible for so much of the strife of his time, as something which "surpasses our capacity." And he thought that grammar, poetry, and history were "more specious than profitable." Even jurisprudence he regarded as unnecessary,[7] although the essence of his plan lies in its provisions for the substitution of peaceful judicial processes for the arbitrary decisions of war.

[5] See English translation of *Le Nouveau Cynée,* from the Preface of which this quotation is taken, by T. W. Balch under title of *The New Cyneas of Éméric Crucé* (Philadelphia, 1900). See also by same author, *Éméric Crucé* (Philadelphia, 1900) for extracts from the latter's treatise.

[6] Crucé, *op. cit.,* p. 30.

[7] *Ibid.,* pp. 29, 46, 47.

Crucé anticipated Adam Smith in his liberal views concerning international trade. Although he did not advocate complete freedom of trade, he was certainly opposed to the prevalent mercantilist restrictions of his day. "It is reasonable," he says, "that the Prince levies a few honest pennies on the merchandise which is brought in and taken out of his territory: but he must in so doing use moderation as much as he possibly can, and especially about the merchandise necessary to life. . . ." [8] Crucé also advocated the improvement of waterways and the cutting of canals not only for the purpose of improving transportation within states but for the encouragement of commerce between them. For he always kept in mind the benefits of an unimpeded worldwide intercourse. "What a pleasure it would be, to see men go here and there freely, and mix together without any hindrance of country, ceremonies, or other such differences, as if the earth were as it really is, a city common to all." [9] Now some of the obstacles in the way of travel and trade during Crucé's time were the varying systems of weights and measures, and the diversity in the monetary systems of the different countries. Moreover, the tendency of impecunious monarchs to debase their currencies aggravated the situation. Crucé condemned the latter practice and in addition made the revolutionary proposal that all countries should "agree to a general regulation, by which not only gold and silver, but also merchandise should be sold by an equal weight in all countries." [10]

Crucé believed that these things could be achieved, but not without the establishment of universal peace among the nations, and he presented many arguments for the complete eradication of war. In this respect he occupied a position identical with that of Erasmus, and different from that of his contemporary, Grotius, who clung to the belief that some wars were necessary to execute justice. Crucé rejected the assertion that wars could never be eliminated between peoples widely separated by geography and culture, for there was among all of them "the similarity of natures, true base of amity and human society. Why should a Frenchman wish harm to an Englishman, a Spaniard, or a Hindoo? I cannot wish it when I consider that they are men like me, that I am subject like them to error and sin and that

[8] *Ibid.*, p. 31.
[9] *Ibid.*, p. 36.
[10] *Ibid.*, p. 210.

all nations are bound together by a natural and consequently indestructible tie, which ensures that a man cannot consider another a stranger, unless he follows the common and inveterate opinion that he has received from his predecessors." [11]

It was inevitable that Crucé should take account of the religious wars raging over Europe as he was working upon his plan, and recognize theological prejudices as one of the serious obstacles to the attainment of the peace he desired to see established. His outlook on the question of religion was almost wholly modern. "Is it necessary to wage war for the diversity of ceremonies, I will not say of religion, since the chief object of these lies in the adoration of God, who demands rather the heart of men, than the exterior worship and sacrifices, of which so much parade is made? Not that I wish to conclude to the disdain of ceremonies; but I say that we should not persecute those who do not wish to embrace ours." [12] In any event, Crucé did not believe that it was ever possible by force of arms to compel men to become believers in a religion distasteful to them, although they might be forced to become hypocrites. And finally Crucé urged that men were not competent to punish and correct the mistakes of faith. In such matters, only God, "who sees hearts and the most secret thoughts," is in a position to judge.[13]

For the maintenance of peace Crucé recognized that the rulers of his day held the key position, and he felt that if they were to take an enlightened and courageous stand they would secure the necessary support from their respective peoples. In this connection his analysis of the character of the different groups to be found within any nation is not without acuteness. There were admittedly, he said, a certain number of "miscreants," men who were disposed toward war and would have to be counted on as opposing a policy of peace. On the other hand, the prince may count on the support of a number of good men who are to be found in every community. In between there are the weak and timid people who "do neither good nor harm, and line themselves up always on the side of the strongest." They may, therefore, be depended upon to support their prince and the good people.

[11] Crucé, *op. cit.*, p. 48.

[12] *Ibid.*, pp. 50, 51. Moreover, he pointed out that experience had shown Henry IV of France "that it was easier to maintain two religions in peace than to preserve one by war."

[13] *Ibid.*, pp. 57, 58.

All of these united will comprise two thirds of the people of the country and will be able to "down the other and you will see all these firebrands supple as a glove to the commands of their monarchs."[14]

It goes without saying that Crucé was opposed to imperialism, for the ambition of a prince to extend his domains was normally realized only by means of war. But Crucé addressed some additional arguments to rulers, designed to convince them of the undesirability of seeking to rule over vast territories. In the first place, he pointed out "that it is more difficult to keep a province than to subjugate it: because conquest rests only upon force. But the conservation depends in addition upon the prudence of the victors, upon a continuous happiness, and upon the good will of the subjects, which are three very rare things. . ."[15] It is a very difficult matter, says Crucé, to retain the good will of subjects who have to be governed from a great distance, and who therefore do not come in contact with the prince. "For it is difficult to love or respect a thing that one does not see." Moreover, the lieutenants of the prince, upon whom he is compelled to rely for the government of his distant territories, feeling that they are out from under his watchful eye, will often be guilty of avarice and cruelty toward the people entrusted to their charge, and seek to usurp power on their own account.

Crucé realized that merely to admonish princes to abstain from coveting and seizing their neighbors' territories, and from fighting out their quarrels, was not enough. The peace must be organized. He therefore proposed that some neutral city, conveniently located, and at which all nations would be able to keep ambassadors permanently, should be selected as the seat of an international organization. He regarded Venice as the ideal place for such a purpose. Whenever differences should arise between sovereigns, the ambassadors of all the nations would assemble and pass judgment after hearing the arguments of the ambassadors of the contending nations. Apparently the advice of the great republics represented would be sought, but they would not have a vote except in a case in which the Assembly was evenly divided. In such an event, they would be called upon to break the tie.[16] Crucé made no reservations as to questions suitable for decision by the Assembly. Every type of question was to be submitted, and all were to be

[14] *Ibid.*, pp. 80, 81.
[15] *Ibid.*, pp. 96, 97.
[16] *Ibid.*, pp. 60, 70.

settled by vote of the majority. Moreover, the princes were to be sworn to regard decisions taken as inviolable law. Crucé anticipated refusal of a sovereign to accept a decision and suggested the use of force, if necessary, to secure compliance: ". . . if anyone rebelled against the decree of so notable a company, he would receive the disgrace of all other Princes, who would find means to bring him to reason."[17]

This ambitious plan was impossible of realization at the time, and in some respects was more logical than realistic. For example, all of the nations of the earth were to be represented in Crucé's organization for peace, no matter how distant they might be, which was quite logical if the end in view is *universal* peace: "As for Persia, China, Ethiopia, and the East and the West Indies, they are lands far distant, but navigation remedies that inconvenience, and for such good object, one must not refuse a long voyage."[18] The state of transportation in the seventeenth century hardly justified this easy optimism, even had the state of mind of all of these countries been receptive to such suggestions. On the other hand, there was justification for maintaining the theoretical universality of membership. Crucé had no axe to grind. His league was not intended to serve the interest of any one nation, and was not intended to be directed against any. The plans of Dubois and Poděbrad were not disinterested, as we have seen, and so far from envisaging universal peace they contemplated war against the Turks. Now Crucé not only proposed to bring the Turks into the universal organization which he outlined but, in his discussion of the order of precedence to be accorded the various princes, he actually suggested that the Emperor of the Turks should have a place of honor second only to that of the Pope, while the "Christian Emperor" was to have third place. It is hard to see how religious toleration could go farther than this, but it is equally difficult to understand why Crucé thought, if, indeed, he did, that such an arrangement would have a chance of acceptance in his age.

[17] Crucé, *op. cit.*, p. 61. In another place he says specifically that the princes would be obligated "to pursue with arms" anyone opposing a decision of the Assembly. *Ibid.*, p. 73. It must be noted, however, that Crucé's idea was that the Assembly would "meet discontents half way, and would appease them by gentle means, if it could be done. . ." *Ibid.*, p. 73. This was not only good logic but good sense, considering that he was seeking ". . . a peace which is not patched up, nor for three days, but which is voluntary, equitable, and permanent. . ." *Ibid.*, p. 194.

[18] *Ibid.*, p. 61.

Another feature of Crucé's plan is worthy of attention. He proposed virtually the freezing of the territorial *status quo* of the various nations which, if accepted, would have ruled out all wars of conquest. As a necessary condition of a general peace he held that there should be a "limitation of the monarchies, so that each Prince remains within the limits of the lands which he possesses at present, and that he does not pass beyond them for any pretences." [19] Anticipating, however, that some prince may be "offended by such a regulation" Crucé urges rather curiously, and somewhat strangely for him, that the boundaries of the various kingdoms have been drawn by the hand of God, and that he "takes them away and transfers them when and where it seems good to him. . ." The prince is therefore advised to accept his present status, and not attempt to recover any lands he may at one time have possessed. However, Crucé knew his monarchs well enough to understand that such an admonition might not be sufficient. And so he deserted logic, which would have suggested that the matter of the limits of kingdoms be left to God as in the past, and offered the practical suggestion that if a prince still felt aggrieved he might present his case to the others. Says Crucé: ". . . if he has some things to complain of, let him address himself to this great assembly, as to the most competent judge that can be imagined. This is the principal way of establishing universal peace, and upon which all the others depend. It is in this way that a beginning must be made." [20]

Would the princes of Crucé's time take his suggestions seriously? Crucé himself had his doubts, but like other choice spirits of all ages he preferred to "play for the verdict of history" rather than for an immediate triumph. For he said, in concluding his appeal for a peaceful world: "As for me I can in this only bring wishes and humble remonstrances, which perhaps will be useless. I have wished, nevertheless, to leave this testimony to posterity. If it serves nothing, patience. It is a small matter, to lose paper, and words. I shall protest in that case like Solon of having said and done what was possible for me for the public good, and some few who read this little book, will be grateful to me for it, and will honor me as I hope with their remembrance." [21]

Fifteen years after the appearance of *Le Nouveau Cynée,* the Duke

[19] *Ibid.,* p. 78.
[20] *Ibid.,* pp. 78, 79.
[21] *Ibid.,* p. 226.

of Sully, minister of finances and close adviser to Henry IV of France, published the first instalment of his memoirs, in two volumes. These, with the third and fourth volumes published in 1662, twenty-one years after his death, contain, among a wide variety of other matter, the *Great Design* formerly attributed to Henry IV, but regarded by most competent scholars within recent years as Sully's own.[22] This plan for the peace of Europe is much better known than that of Crucé, and has gained a prestige which doubtless would not have been accorded it had it not been supposed to have been the dream of the great French King. Apparently it was written, for the most part, at any rate, during the latter years of Sully's life, after Henry IV was assassinated and the minister, having lost his high office, was living in retirement. In Sully's various references to the *Great Design,* there are many discrepancies and inconsistencies, and one is left in some confusion as to precisely what was intended, and doubt as to how much pure fiction was interwoven among authentic documents by the astute minister. That a certain amount of fictitious material was incorporated in the memoirs is no longer open to question.

The gist of the *Design,* according to Sully, was "the establishment of an universal most Christian republic . . . composed of all those Kings and potentates who profess the name of Christ."[23] The professed object was to attain peace throughout Christendom. According to Sully, the cooperation of Queen Elizabeth of England was sought and an agreement on such a policy was actually reached shortly before the Queen's death. Whether this was true or not, further negotiations, which Sully says he carried on with her successor, James I, came to naught. Certain matters, however, seem to be uncontradicted in connection with the policy of Henry, and as these are definitely related to the *Great Design* and are of intrinsic interest, they deserve mention. Among the "désirs" of Henry was religious toleration in Europe. He set the example by a liberal religious policy in France, but something more than a good example was needed for Europe. Sully declares that the King favored the recognition and mutual toleration throughout Europe of the

[22] The full title of the memoirs is *Mémoires des Sages et Royales Oeconomies d'Éstat Domestiques, Politiques et Militaires de Henri le Grand,* 4 vols. (Amsterdam and Paris, 1638-1662). For a good discussion of the question of authorship, with citations of scholars who have given the matter close study, see Lange, *Histoire de l'Internationalisme* (Christiania, 1919), op. cit., pp. 434-445.

[23] B. Butler, *Studies in Statecraft* (Cambridge, Eng., 1920), p. 75.

three principal confessions that had already established themselves—Roman Catholic, Lutheran, and Calvinist. However, in certain states—such as Italy, where the Catholic faith was clearly preponderant—a single confession would be allowed. In others, Sully contemplated the toleration of a plurality of faiths. The object thus seems to have been not to assure the right of private judgment in matters of religion, but to establish a sort of political equilibrium, as Lange [24] says, between the confessions and thus get rid of one potent source of controversy within and between states. Sully also proposed to utilize the old hatred of the Turks for the closer cementing of the "good and perfect union" of the Christian states. War is to be carried on against them continually. This will not only tend to draw all Christians together as such but will furnish an outlet for the fighting energy of the Christian nations.[25]

It is agreed by historians that the foreign policy of Henry IV was motivated largely by a desire to reduce the excessive holdings and power of the House of Austria.[26] It is not surprising, therefore, to discover that this object is prominent in the plan or plans of pacification found in the *Mémoires*. A European federation, according to Sully, was a necessity for the realization of peace, but such a federation was not possible as long as the ambitious and oppressive House of Austria dominated the continent and held vast territories beyond. There must be a rectification of this situation if such a plan was to be successful. The dominant powers must agree to some diminution of their territories. At one time Sully proposed that the King should use force in the freeing of the Dutch provinces from Spain and the taking of other territories such as Alsace and Lorraine. But in later parts of the *Mémoires* the emphasis shifts from force and craft to persuasion. The other states are to make representations in a friendly fashion that Spain give up some of her European territories, and Sully even suggests at one point that France should submit to arbitration her own claims to certain

[24] *Op. cit.*, p. 471. Sully was, for example, not an advocate of the toleration of the smaller dissident sects.

[25] Lange, *op. cit.*, pp. 473-474. Stawell, *op. cit.*, pp. 118-119.

[26] The Spanish branch of the House had by 1600 acquired the following territories: Spain, the Two Sicilies, Milan, Franche Comté, the Belgian Netherlands, Portugal, and a huge colonial empire; the Austrian branch included Austria and its dependencies, Hungary, Bohemia, and the title of Holy Roman Emperor. (C. J. H. Hayes, *A Political and Social History of Modern Europe*, 2 vols. [New York, 1919], I, 219.)

regions. Above all, he stresses the point that France should not seek for herself any of the territory which might be given up by the Hapsburgs. The aim was not to be the aggrandizement of France or any other power, but the establishment of an equilibrium in which none would be so powerful as to cause fear and concern among the others.[27]

Perhaps the most significant idea to be found in Sully's discussion of the *Great Design* is that any redistribution of territories resulting in changes of government should take account of the sentiment of nationality of the people concerned instead of being determined arbitrarily: ". . . in every attempt at new combinations . . . care must be taken to respect the natural dispositions and peculiar characteristics of peoples and races and thus guard against the folly of trying to unite in any one State . . . men whose differences of temperament or diversity of language, law and tradition are so great as to be incompatible." [28] Here is a clear recognition of a new principle destined to play an increasingly important part in the formation of states in the 19th century and in our own day. It is at this point that Sully seems to grasp what Crucé apparently did not see—that the arbitrary will of even a majority of princes will be too frail a foundation for the attainment of peace, and that a broader foundation must be sought. Crucé, on the other hand, proposed to start with the territorial *status quo* undisturbed, although, as we have seen, he conceded that princes feeling themselves badly used might have their claims to additional territories examined. In an age of absolutism in government, Crucé's plan was, it would seem, more in accord with the spirit of the times. More than a century and a half was to elapse before the wishes of nationalities rather than the desires of princes was actually to play any part anywhere in the redistribution of territories.

The details of the specific plan of organization proposed varied as it was discussed in different places in the *Mémoires*, but as it finally took form apparently in the mind of Sully, it was as follows. Europe was to be divided into fifteen states. First, there were to be six hereditary monarchies: France, Spain (reduced to the Peninsula, the Balearic islands, Azores, and her New World possessions), Great Britain, Denmark, Sweden, and a new Italian Kingdom embracing Savoy, Piedmont,

[27] Lange, *op. cit.*, p. 457. Stawell, *op. cit.*, pp. 108, 115-116.

[28] As translated in Stawell, *op. cit.*, p. 110. See also Lange, *op. cit.*, p. 468, for passage in French.

and Lombardy. In the next group of states, there were to be five (or six) elective monarchies: the Papacy, the Empire, Poland, Bohemia, and Hungary. Finally there were to be four republics: the Swiss (to be enlarged by the addition of Alsace, Lorraine, and the Tyrol), the Netherlands, the Republic of Venice, and a new republic comprising certain states in the north of Italy.[29] Russia was not included, but might be admitted should she take the initiative and ask to join the Confederation. Until such time, however, Sully thought her remoteness and backward condition would make her admission inadvisable. Thus the Confederation envisaged by Sully was to be restricted to the Christian states of Western Europe, at least in the beginning.

The fifteen powers were to form a General Council consisting of sixty-six persons chosen from the members of the Confederation roughly in proportion to their individual importance. The selection of the sixty-six representatives would be made every three years. They would have the functions of deliberating on any matters affecting the member states, and of composing their differences of whatever nature. The Grand Council might be divided into committees, to function in different localities in the consideration of territorial changes and other questions.[30]

Sully's exposé of the *Great Design* reveals at once a desire to distribute territories and power in Europe so as to secure an equilibrium of forces, and a disposition to avoid doing violence to the sentiment of nationality in the process of redistribution. It is not clear, however, that a strict regard for the wishes of nationalities would have also insured the establishment of an equilibrium. For the basis of the latter is mathematical, a matter of mechanics, whereas the recognition of nationality involves at least the subordination of considerations of physical forces, and the introduction of imponderables into the settlement. It may be remarked, however, that a recognition of the right of certain

[29] Taken from Stawell, *op. cit.*, p. 111. See also Butler, *op. cit.* p. 74, *ter Meulen, op. cit.*, p. 165, G. Butler and S. Maccoby, *The Development of International Law* (London and New York, 1928), p. 12, Lange, *op. cit.*, pp. 463-468, for varying arrangements proposed. It should be noted that Sully did not assume that a new territorial *status quo* should be fixed for all time. Like Crucé, however, he took the position that future changes should be a matter for the deliberation of the representatives of the Confederation rather than that they should be determined by individual states. (Lange, *op. cit.*, pp. 468-469.)

[30] See ter Meulen, *op. cit.*, p. 165, for a variation of this plan of organization which appears elsewhere in the *Mémoires.* It is to be observed that Sully even proposed that the councils should have power to accommodate disputes between sovereigns and their own subjects. See ter Meulen, *op. cit.*, p. 167.

nationalities, such as the Dutch, the Bohemians, and the Hungarians, to a separate political existence did fit in with Sully's aim of reducing the power of the Hapsburgs, and thus with the attainment, theoretically, of something like an equilibrium of forces. The *Mémoires* do not reveal that Sully envisaged in any detail a judicial procedure for the pacific settlement of questions that would arise between the members of the Confederation, although the regional councils were apparently to be invested with the authority to compose differences in their respective localities. Nor does he suggest any system of sanctions for the enforcement of decisions taken by the deliberative body of "the most Christian Republic." In both of these matters, but especially in the first, Crucé was the more definite, although it seems clear that both he and Sully were agreed in principle.

The *Great Design,* whatever its origins, and whatever its shortcomings, was to create quite an impression among peace advocates of later generations. It may be observed also that the principle of religious accommodation along the lines suggested in the *Mémoires* was written into the treaties of Westphalia. Likewise the House of Austria was constrained to accept a diminution of territory and power in that general settlement of 1648. But the more drastic medicine of Confederation, Europe was not ready to take.

The idea of European Confederation found support, however, in still another quarter. In the seventeenth century a new religious sect, the Society of Friends (Quakers) arose. Its essential doctrine was that there is an inner light in each individual to guide his footsteps. By it he not only is enabled to choose the right way of living, but is equipped to interpret the Scriptures themselves without the aid of any external authority. This doctrine led to an extreme individualism among the Quakers and logically to passive resistance to authority in so far as it might attempt to constrain men to do what their consciences tell them is wrong. By the same logic, it was opposed to the arbitrary and coercive institution of war. The Quakers were agreed that it was contrary to the spirit and precepts of the Gospel.

One of the most prominent members of this sect was William Penn (1644-1718), son of an English Admiral who, incidentally, was much distressed and scandalized at his son's apostasy. Penn is perhaps best known for the founding of the Pennsylvania colony and his unique and successful method of dealing with the Indians. But his *Essay towards the*

Present and Future Peace of Europe [31] likewise entitles him to a high place among the pioneer thinkers in the field of international federation. Penn wrote toward the end of the seventeenth century, when new wars launched by the ambitions of Louis XIV were raging in Europe. It is unnecessary to recount his indictment of war except to remark that it turned principally upon its economic wastage rather than upon its inconsistency with Christianity. His approach was quite that of the man who appreciates a comfortable orderly existence and deplores war because, as Penn says, "like the Frost of '83, [it] seizes all these Comforts at once, and stops the civil Channel of Society." [32]

In analyzing the causes of wars, Penn declared that ambition and appetite and the "Pride of Conquest" were usually the real ones. Mentioning the formula which one runs across frequently among the theologians of the Middle Ages that "Peace is the end of War," Penn remarks that in reality the war-makers are interested in gratifying certain ambitions rather than in achieving peace. Nevertheless, says Penn, as war cannot in any sense be justified except on the ground that a wrong has been committed for which redress has been refused, men advance justice as a reason.

Penn then takes up the question of the "Ways and Methods by which Peace is Preserved" within countries and points out that in order to avoid confusion, disorder, and injustice men give up their freedom to act as they individually please and submit to rules of their own making: "No Man is Judge in his own Cause, which ends the Confusion and Blood of so many Judges and Executioners." Government, then, is established as a means of justice, and justice in turn is a means of peace. For "so depraved is Human Nature, that without Compulsion some Way or other, too many would not readily be brought to do what they know is right and fit, or avoid what they are satisfied they should not do." Now it is necessary for states to resort to similar ways and means if peace is to be realized in the relations between them.

Penn's specific suggestion was that the sovereign princes of Europe agree among themselves to give up the state of nature as between states for the same reason that individuals within states surrendered their

[31] The full title was *An Essay towards the Present and Future Peace of Europe, by the Establishment of an European Dyet, Parliament, or Estates.* The *Essay* was published in 1693-94.

[32] The text from which this and the following quotations are taken is that published by the American Peace Society (Washington, 1912).

right to be a law unto themselves, i.e., the desire to secure peace and order. In order to give effect to their resolution, they should establish a "General Dyet, Estates, or Parliament" composed of their representatives, and draw up rules of justice "for Sovereign Princes to observe one to another." The "Imperial Dyet" was to meet yearly or at least once in two years, or whenever occasion should demand, and should hear all disputes not taken care of by ordinary diplomatic methods. Penn, though a Quaker, was ready to face the possibility that compulsion might be required and to recommend "that if any of the Sovereignties . . . shall refuse to submit their Claim or Pretensions to them, or to abide and perform the Judgment thereof, and seek their Remedy by Arms, or delay their compliance beyond the Time prefixt in their Resolutions, all the other Sovereignties, United as One Strength, shall compel the Submission and Performance of the Sentence, with Damages to the Suffering Party, and Charges to the Sovereignties that obliged their Submission." Penn thought, however, that no sovereignty would dare to flout the judgment of the "Sovereign Assembly."

Fresh conquests, under Penn's plan, would not be tolerated by the Confederation he suggested, but he did not propose to freeze the *status quo*. A prince who has in the past been despoiled of certain territory will be entitled to lay claim to it before the "Sovereign Court" and have his case determined, but he may not take up arms to vindicate his claim. And Penn recognizes that a good title to territory may be acquired by "a long and undoubted Succession," by election, by marriage, and by purchase. He also concedes that conquest in the past has been recognized as conferring a legal title, but he considers that such a title is, "morally speaking," questionable. If, however, a conquest has been confirmed by a treaty of peace, Penn confesses that it is "an Adopted Title; and if not so Genuine and Natural, yet being engrafted, it is fed by that which is the Security of Better Titles, Consent." Penn senses the fact that such a title, secured under duress, may leave the fire of war still smouldering though the flame may be for the moment extinguished. But he does not draw the conclusion that a title acquired by means of a treaty forced upon a losing party is tainted. Nevertheless its validity may be brought up for collective consideration by the injured party.

Penn realized that the question of representation and voting strength in the Diet presented a problem in view of the inequality of size and wealth of the different states, and he proposed that the number of representatives of each sovereignty be proportioned as nearly as possible according to the personal revenues of the Prince and the value of the entire territory over which he ruled.[33] A three-fourths majority must be obtained for the passage of any measure or the taking of any decision by the Diet. Penn's reason for the latter suggestion was, oddly enough, that it would take a good deal of money to buy so many votes and that it would therefore be an aid against treachery.[34]

Answering possible objections, Penn was not inclined to think that opposition to his plan on the ground that men would become effeminate without war was well founded. This danger could be obviated, he declared, by introducing a sufficiently severe discipline in the education of youth, by requiring simplicity of living and the building up of habits of industry. They should be taught these things that will give them an understanding of "how to be useful and serviceable, both to themselves and others: and how to save and help, not injure or destroy." As for the objection that a régime of peace would be dangerous to a country, as it would lack soldiers to defend itself against attack, Penn did not think that after his plan had been put into operation any nation would keep an army large enough to threaten the safety of the others. But if necessary the Confederation could order the reduction of the forces of any nation so that every sovereignty should have a small force.

Another objection which Penn anticipated and which he answered in interesting fashion was that if princes and states agreed to give up war, and to undertake the obligations outlined they would surrender their sovereignty. He points out that "they [would] remain as Sovereign at home as ever they were," but that they would not exercise sovereignty over one another: "And if this be called a lessening of their Power, it must be only because the great Fish can no longer eat up the little ones, and that each Sovereignty is equally defended from Injuries,

[33] He made a tentative proposal that the Empire of Germany should have twelve representatives; France, ten; Spain, ten; Italy, eight; England, six; Portugal, three; Sweden, four; Denmark, three; Poland, four; Venice, three; the Seven Provinces, four; the Thirteen Cantons and "Little Neighboring Sovereignties," two; Dukedoms of Holstein and Courland, one; and if Turkey and Russia were included, as Penn felt they should be, each should have ten representatives. Altogether there would be ninety representatives.

[34] Penn specifies also that the language used should be either Latin or French.

and disabled from committing. . ." But Penn's whole plan was devised to get away from the Logic of the Fish,[35] and the state of nature between states which made that logic inevitable.[36]

REFERENCES

Beales, A. C. F., *The History of Peace* (New York, 1931), pp. 28-33.

Butler, G., *Studies in Statecraft* (Cambridge, Eng., 1920), Chs. IV, V.

————, and Maccoby, S., *The Development of International Law* (London, 1928), pp. 11-14.

Carré, H., *Sully, Sa Vie et Son Oeuvre, 1559-1641* (Paris, 1932).

Crucé, É., *The New Cyneas of Émeric Crucé,* tr. by T. W. Balch (Philadelphia, Pa., 1909).

Hirst, M. E., *The Quakers in Peace and War* (London, 1923).

Knowles, G. W., ed., *Quakers and Peace* (London, 1927). Grotius Society Publications No. 4.

Lange, C., *Histoire de l'Internationalisme* (Christiania, 1919), pp. 395-476.

Louis-Lucas, P., *Un Plan de Paix Générale et de la Liberté de Commerce au 17e Siècle: le Nouveau Cynée d'Émeric Crucé* (Paris, 1919).

Meulen, J. ter, *Der Gedanke der Internationalen Organisation in Seiner Entwicklung* (1300-1889), 2 vols. (The Hague, 1917-1929), I (1300-1800), 143-152, 160-179.

Murray, R. H., *The History of Political Science from Plato to the Present* (Cambridge, Eng., 1926).

Penn, W., *An Essay toward the Present and Future Peace of Europe* (Washington, D. C., 1912).

Stawell, F. M., *Growth of International Thought* (New York, 1930), Ch. V, and pp. 131-139.

Sully, M. de Bethune, duc de, *The Great Design of Henry IV from the Memoirs of the Duke of Sully, and the United States of Europe,* by E. E. Hale with introduction by E. D. Mead (Boston, 1909).

————, *Sully's Grand Design of Henry IV* (London, 1921). Grotius Society Publications No. 2.

[35] *Supra,* p. 45.

[36] For plan of union of Christendom into a "Christian Commonwealth" published in 1710 by John Bellers, also a Quaker, see ter Meulen, *op. cit.,* pp. 177-179.

CHAPTER X

THE EIGHTEENTH CENTURY: THE ENLIGHTENMENT

FROM the point of view of the conduct of international relationships, one sees little difference whether he is considering the seventeenth century or the eighteenth century. Possibly Machiavellian aims and methods were even more shamelessly in evidence in the latter. In the former period religious wars and dynastic struggles largely characterized the relations of the different states of Europe; in the latter century the conflicts were more frankly and definitely political, but were even more extensive in character and more far-reaching in their effects. A new state, Russia, begins to play a part on the European stage, with ambitions of her own. Seeking a "window on the west," she came into collision with Sweden in the north; and, entertaining ambitions for an outlet on the Black Sea, she had a contest of arms with Turkey. Finally, to prove how well she was westernized, she participated along with Prussia and Austria in the vulture-like dismemberment of Poland. It was an age when such "Grand Designs" had far more prospect of success and approval than those of a Crucé or a Sully. Beyond Europe, contenders for empire fought for mastery and enlarged domains in America and India, without taking the trouble to read their Grotius.

The struggle for power and wealth was not with arms alone. National commercial policies were likewise calculated to promote the welfare of the nation as such and increase national strength. Various expedients were adopted to overreach or ruin trade rivals and achieve a favorable balance of trade: outright prohibition of certain kinds of foreign goods, heavy duties on others, bounties and subsidies for home producers, the monopolizing of colonial markets for the benefit of the mother country. These policies were regarded as essential to national well-being, and they yielded rulers tangible results. The more prosperous the merchants and traders of a country became, the more taxes they would be able to pay. Wars cost money and the keeping and administering of conquered territories could not be accomplished without strong national treasuries. Thus trade warfare and armed conflict went hand in hand throughout most of the eighteenth century.

Quite another picture was presented in the realm of philosophy and of political and economic ideas, and toward the end of the century new conflicts were to be staged in their defense. The movement of thought referred to was known as the *Enlightenment*. Its beginnings may be traced back to the Renaissance, but in the eighteenth century the movement attained a volume and momentum and definiteness that justifies our calling it the Age of the Enlightenment. For this century was a century of challenge not only of the remnants of medieval doctrine which had survived the onslaughts of earlier thinkers, but also of newer dogmas of Divine Right. Authoritarianism from whatever quarter and of whatever kind was subjected to the pure white light of reason. Reason was exalted to the point that the philosophers of the period felt it could illuminate all things, and furnish an answer to all questions struggling humanity might ask. The aid of a supernatural agency was unnecessary. Man, by the use of reason alone, could come to comprehend the world in which he lives, and work out his own destiny. All that was necessary was to discover and act in accordance with the laws of nature, and human progress and perfectibility would follow. Sir Isaac Newton's discoveries, tending to show the orderliness of the physical universe and its obedience to natural laws, confirmed and stimulated philosophers in the pursuit of the laws of social life, and in their efforts to bring mankind into conformity and harmony with the world of nature. There was much, indeed, in their outlook that suggests the ancient Chinese view of nature and man's place in it,[1] and likewise these "children of the Enlightenment" had much in common with the philosophy of the Stoics. It may be remarked also that the Enlightenment was not confined to any one country, although its great center was France.[2] "The philosophical empire was an international domain of which France was but the mother country and Paris the capital." [3]

The whole trend of thought which has just been outlined led men

[1] *Supra*, p. 18. It may be noted also that Chinese philosophy and life held a great attraction for the French philosophers of the Enlightenment.

[2] In France, among a host of writers may be mentioned Montesquieu, Voltaire, Rousseau, Diderot, Turgot, Quesnay, Condorcet; in England, Locke, Hume, Bolingbroke, Ferguson, Adam Smith, Priestley; in Germany, Leibnitz, Lessing, Herder; in America, Franklin and Jefferson.

[3] Carl Becker, *The Heavenly City of the Eighteenth-Century Philosophers* (New Haven, Conn., 1932), p. 34.

to think, as did the Chinese and Stoic philosophers and, with important qualifications, the Christian theologians, in terms of humanity rather than in terms of particular peoples. The "climate of opinion" was entirely favorable to the acceptance and propagation of ideas of cosmopolitanism, internationalism, and pacifism, and by the same token unfavorable to the acceptance of war and the advocacy of restrictive, "unnatural" national trade policies.

Interference with the "natural" flow of goods from one country to another by various governmental restrictions was condemned by a group of writers in France known as the Physiocrats,[4] and the theories of the latter were taken up by a number of English economists of whom the most famous was Adam Smith. Their general position was that government should keep hands off industry and trade, and refrain from all activity in the economic field. For such interference with the natural order of things was unwise from every point of view. It is unnecessary to go into the ramifications and implications of the new doctrines, but it must be noticed that they tended to make the individual and not the nation the trading unit,[5] and thereby to remove one of the most bitter sources of rivalry and enmity between nations. And in so far as they emphasized the mutual benefit to be derived by nations from unrestricted international trade, they promoted economic internationalism. Thus, says Hume, in criticizing the policy of England in placing restrictions on external trade in order to secure a balance of specie, money should be left to circulate according to natural laws, and only harm can come from adopting artificial means to interfere with it. Moreover, such policies "deprive neighboring nations of that free communication and exchange which the Author of the world has intended, by giving them soils, climates, and geniuses, so different from each other."[6] And to the argument that the international trade of a nation is benefited by keeping down rivals, Hume declared that "the increase of riches and commerce in any one nation, instead of hurting, commonly promotes the riches and commerce of all its neighbors; and . . . a state

[4] Among the most prominent Physiocrats were Quesnay, Gournay, Turgot, and Dupont de Nemours.

[5] In France, even internal economic unity was not achieved until the Revolution, and in other states of Western Europe there were also shackling restrictions. In fact, in France the theory of free trade was developed principally as a reaction against minute governmental regulation of internal trade. Nevertheless it was in complete harmony with the philosophic thought of the time.

[6] David Hume, *Essays and Treatises*, 2 vols. (London, 1772), I, Essay V, 337.

can scarcely carry its trade and industry very far, where all the surrounding states are buried in ignorance, sloth, and barbarism." [7]

Pacifism was quite pronounced among the men of the Enlightenment. In this connection mention must be made of Fénelon (1651-1715) who, though too early, and perhaps fundamentally too conservative to be included among the philosophers of the eighteenth century, had great influence on French thought. He was scathing in his denunciation of war and regarded the warlike policies of Louis XIV with great aversion. He urged France to restore the conquests which had been made. The building up of empires was unwise not only because of the fear and hatred engendered and the fact that they are unstable and of short duration, but because of the moral effect on the conquerors. A great power superior to all others is always tempted to abuse its power and soon succumbs to the temptation. A wise and just prince should therefore not desire to pass on to his successors extensive territories and power, but should rather seek to hold a position of equality among the nations. True strength and real superiority lie not in vast territories and strong fortifications, which arouse the jealousy and hate of one's neighbors, but in a well-ordered populous state in which the people are devoted to agriculture and the necessary arts. Superiority of this nature is not difficult to acquire, and it does not arouse envy. It is better calculated than wars of conquest to render a people invincible.[8]

Montesquieu (1689-1755), although classed as one of the men of the Enlightenment, was an empirical thinker whose philosophy was based upon a study of the past and an examination of the present rather than upon abstract political speculation. He was therefore inclined to view political institutions in the light of their time and, while

[7] Hume, *op. cit.*, I, Essay VI, 341. Hume, however, was not a free trader in the absolute sense. Nor was Adam Smith, his famous contemporary. The latter, in his *Wealth of Nations*, 2 vols. (London, 1776), held that there was a fundamental economic interdependence between nations, but he was not prepared to carry the doctrine of *laissez-faire* as far as the Physiocrats.

[8] See his *Examen de Conscience sur les Devoirs de la Royauté* (1734); also C. Lange, "Histoire de la Doctrine Pacifique et de son Influence sur le Développement du Droit International," *Recueil des Cours*, Vol. XIII (1926), Pt. III, pp. 295-296, Académie de Droit International (Paris, 1927). Cited henceforth, Lange, "Histoire." For further views of Fénelon on pacifism, see E. Constantinescu-Bagdat, *Études d'Histoire Pacifiste;* 3 vols. (Paris, 1924-1928), II, *De Vauban à Voltaire* (Paris, 1925), pp. 87-104. Other pacifist writers of the late seventeenth and early eighteenth centuries were Vauban (1633-1707), Bois-Guillebert (1646-1714), and Boulainvilliers (1658-1722). Discussions of the views of these writers may be found in Constantinescu-Bagdat, *op. cit.*

interested in reform, was not a true revolutionary as was Rousseau. The relatively conservative character of Montesquieu's thought is reflected likewise in his views on international relations. While others might, for example, deliver slashing attacks on war and call for its complete eradication, Montesquieu accepted it, reluctantly it is true, as an unfortunate necessity, and thought rather of means of preventing as far as possible unjust wars by a balance of power. Thus, believing as he did in small republics rather than in large monarchies, yet realizing their weakness as against large and powerful nations, he proposed the solution of republican federations. Montesquieu assumed that republics, as contrasted with monarchies, were inclined toward peace: "The spirit of the monarchy is that of war and aggrandizement; the spirit of the republic is that of peace and moderation." Montesquieu, however, did not believe that war could be eliminated; human nature was too incorrigible, and even republics could not be depended upon to maintain their spirit. Some wars, perhaps many, could be avoided, but he hoped, like Grotius, to see all wars conducted with restraint. Deploring, for example, the invention of gunpowder and other cruel modes of destruction, he nevertheless believed that nations could be brought to place a limit on war's destructiveness, and that if a still more cruel means should be devised, it would be "prohibited by the law of nations and the nations would, by unanimous consent, bury this discovery." [9] With our hindsight we can see that he might better have been a pessimist at this point. Montesquieu's conservative temper led him once into a paradoxical position which drew forth the lightning of Voltaire. Montesquieu had pointed out that nations are in a different situation from that of the citizens within a nation. The latter can take their cases to a tribunal instead of attacking their antagonist, unless, indeed, they have to defend themselves against an actual physical attack. But between nations, the right of natural defense sometimes entails the necessity of one's attacking another when it sees that the continuance of peace would lead to its own destruction. Voltaire (1694-1778) subjected this to the following merciless analysis: To justify an attack upon your neighbor in the midst of peace, you must be sure that he will destroy you if he becomes powerful. But you cannot be sure of this unless he has already made preparations for your destruction. In such an event, it is he who commences the war. Continuing, Voltaire de-

[9] Constantinescu-Bagdat, *op. cit.*, II, 204-205.

clared in effect: You could not find a more obviously unjust reason for war. It would be impossible for you to attack your neighbor on the excuse that he intended to attack you unless you were yourself prepared to attack him—which meant, on your own argument, that you had given him the right to attack you. Thus you kill your neighbor, who is not attacking you, for fear he may be in a position to do so; you risk the ruin of your own country in the hope that you may ruin, without reason, that of another.[10]

Voltaire was a pessimistic pacifist who hated war because of its irrationality, stupidity, and the oppression and cruelty involved in it, but thought it as inevitable among men "as among other carnivorous animals." Nevertheless this did not prevent him from attacking it savagely and uncompromisingly, if superficially, although it rendered him completely skeptical of the value of "projects of peace" and kept him most of the time in the ranks of the destructive critics. The flavor of his criticism may be gathered from the less gruesome portion of a passage in *Candide* in which he describes an imaginary battle of the Bulgarians: "There was never anything so gallant, so spruce, so brilliant, and so well disposed as the two armies. Trumpets, fifes, hautboys, drums, and cannon made music such as Hell itself had never heard. The cannons first of all laid flat about six thousand men on each side; the muskets swept away from this best of worlds nine or ten thousand ruffians who infested its surface. The bayonet was also a sufficient reason for the death of several thousands. The whole might amount to thirty thousand souls. Candide, who trembled like a philosopher, hid himself as well as he could during this heroic butchery. At length, while the two kings were causing Te Deum to be sung each in his own camp, Candide resolved to go and reason elsewhere on effects and causes."[11] Candide had many more adventures, saw not only war but many other terrible evils which afflicted the world of affairs, and finally reached the conclusion, as he advised his companions, that "we must cultivate our garden."[12] Many philosophers have come to this conclusion sooner

[10] Constantinescu-Bagdat, *op. cit.*, II, 203-204.

[11] *Candide,* Ch. III. Translation taken from edition of Universal Library (New York, 1931).

[12] At the time Voltaire was writing *Candide,* Bernis, the Foreign Minister of France, disillusioned and crushed by the state of affairs in France and the sufferings of the soldiers in the badly managed war with Frederick the Great, decided to retire to the country "to cultivate cabbages." (K. Martin, *French Liberal Thought in the Eighteenth Century* [Boston, 1929], p. 265.)

or later, but not Voltaire. He had more things to say about war. He classed it with famine and pestilence and remarked that it combined the evils of both. It was different from them, however, in that they were the gift of Providence whereas war arose out of "the imagination of three or four hundred persons scattered over the surface of the globe under the name of princes or ministers. . ." [13] The wars of Voltaire's day were in fact dynastic struggles, and no one was his equal in stripping them of all sham and pretense and baring the ugly side:

A genealogist proves to a Prince that he is the direct descendant of a Count whose relatives had made a family compact three or four hundred years before with a House whose very memory is now forgotten. This House claimed distant rights over a province whose last possessor had died of apoplexy. The prince and his council conclude without difficulty that this province belongs to him by divine right. It is in vain that the province, which is at a distance of some hundreds of leagues from him, protests that it does not know him; that it has no desire to be governed by him; that, to promulgate laws for people, it is at least necessary to have their consent: all this talk does not even reach the ears of the prince, whose right is clear beyond dispute. Forthwith he finds a great number of men who have nothing to lose; he clothes them in coarse blue cloth at a hundred and ten sous the ell, puts a border of broad white ribbon on their hats, makes them turn to the right and to the left, and marches to glory.

Other princes who hear of this preparation take part in it, each according to his power and . . . multitudes fight desperately against each other, not only without having any interest in the affair, but without even knowing what it is all about. . .

The amazing thing about this infernal enterprise, is that each chief of the murderers has his flags blessed, and solemnly invokes the aid of God before going out to exterminate his neighbor.[14]

Rousseau (1712-1778) likewise passionately indicted war as an outrage to humanity, and was scathing in his denunciation of those who defended it by such sophistries as we have just seen exposed by Voltaire. Rousseau's position, however, has not always been understood, for he was not always clear and consistent in his treatment of the subject in his different works.[15] That he regarded tyranny and war as "the

[13] *Dictionnaire Philosophique,* 3 vols. (Éditions de Cluny, Paris, 1930), II, 168-169, article *Guerre.*

[14] *Ibid.*, pp. 170-172.

[15] Rousseau's views on war and peace are scattered through his various works and, except for his *Projet de Paix Perpétuelle,* are offered in connection with his

greatest plagues of humanity," there is no room for doubt. However, liberty was to him the most precious of all things, and in its defense even war became a sacred duty. Indeed, so highly does he regard a war for liberty that he would not entrust it to the hands of mercenaries. On the other hand, he refuses to exalt military heroes. Those who distinguish themselves in battle are brave men, to be sure, but the true heroes are those who do their duty day by day in civil life without ostentation, having the public welfare rather than personal glory at heart. And it is in peace and not in war, he remarks, that public well-being is found.[16] In Rousseau's view, war was directly due to the passion of princes to make conquests and rule over others, and to the desire of despots to find means of maintaining themselves. As the state grows larger, it is easier for them to dispense with liberty. But Rousseau was not content with such a superficial analysis, which was more truly the method of Voltaire. He turned to an analysis of social institutions and found war inherent in their imperfections. "The first thing I notice in looking at the state of mankind is a palpable contradiction which makes all stability impossible. As individuals, we live in the civil state, under the control of the Law; as nations each is in the state of nature. And it is this which makes our position worse than if such distinctions were unknown. For, living as we do at once in the civil order and in the state of nature, we find ourselves exposed to the evils of both conditions, without winning the security we need in either. The perfection of the social order lies, doubtless, in the union of force and Law. But such a union is only possible when force is controlled by Law; whereas, so long as the prince is regarded as absolutely uncontrolled, it is force alone which speaks to the subject under the name of Law and to the foreigner under the name of reason of State . . . in both cases, brute force reigns under the empty name of justice."[17]

treatment of other subjects. See his *Émile* (1762), *Contrat Social* (1762), *Les Confessions* (1782), *Discours sur la Vertu la Plus Nécessaire aux Héros* (1751), *Discours sur l'Origine de l'Inégalité* (1755).

[16] Constantinescu-Bagdat, *op. cit.*, II, 283, 291-293.

[17] Fragments of an "Essay on the State of War," *A Lasting Peace and the State of War* (Constable and Co., London, 1917), by Jean Jacques Rousseau, tr. by C. E. Vaughan. The constructive analysis of Rousseau is also of the highest importance, but may better be deferred until projects of international organization are discussed. It is not to be supposed that pacifist thought was confined to French philosophers in the eighteenth century. In England, Addison (1672-1719), in his *Essays of the Spectator* (1711-12), and Swift in *Gulliver's Travels* (1726), as well as Bentham in his various works, attacked war. In America, Benjamin Franklin (1706-1790) was an outstanding pacifist; and in Germany, Kant and many others held pacifist and cosmopolitan convictions.

We may now turn to the cosmopolitan views of certain representative thinkers of the century. The eighteenth century has been called the "Age of Cosmopolitanism." [18] In the realm of the philosophers this was largely true, especially if we contrast their thought with that of the nineteenth century. "The Enlightenment, continuing the tradition of the Renaissance, reabsorbed stoic philosophy into Western culture and in this way cosmopolitanism entered into a new epoch of significance. Princes, diplomats, poets, scholars and other intellectuals became its spokesmen. . . While cabinets continued to wage war, intellectuals posted up constructive theories of peace. . ." [19]

Although cosmopolitan views were widespread, they found their most congenial soil in Germany, which was cut up into a number of small states whose rulers were despots who could not usually be characterized as "enlightened" or liberal. Advanced thinkers were excluded from positions of power and responsibility and subjected to a galling censorship. In 1794, for example, Kant was reprimanded by the king of Prussia for "misusing" his philosophy. Thus the tendency was for liberal-minded thinkers to seek outlets for their intellectual energy and sympathy for their views among other reformers and intellectuals beyond the frontiers,[20] and to have their cosmopolitan tendencies strengthened. For example, Lessing (1729-1781) held that religious, class, and state divisions separating mankind could be overcome only by the ideal of humanity. Love of country, to him, was "at best but an heroic vice." Patriotism which obscured one's duties to humanity was not something to cultivate. "To be praised as a zealous patriot is the last thing I desire—a patriot, that is, who would teach me to forget that I must be a citizen of the world." [21] Goethe (1749-1832) philosophized in much the same vein, and in phrases that remind one of the Greek cynics: "If we find a place where we can rest with our belongings, a field to support us, a house to shelter us, have we not a Fatherland?" And Schiller (1759-1805), too: "I write as a citizen of the world who serves no prince. I lost my Fatherland, to exchange it for the great world. What is the greatest of nations but a fragment?" [22]

[18] G. P. Gooch, *Nationalism* (New York, 1920), p. 11.

[19] M. H. Boehm, "Cosmopolitanism," *Encyclopaedia of the Social Sciences,* IV, 460.

[20] Gooch, *op. cit.,* p. 12.

[21] *Ibid.*

[22] Schiller fled from Württemburg, where he had been compelled to go to a military school and learn to become a military surgeon, after the Duke of Württemburg had forbidden him to write "comedies." He had already written several

But these "flashes of cosmopolitan lightning" did not represent the most characteristic reactions of the men of the Enlightenment to the political world. They were by no means indifferent to the state [23] and to international relationships and, preoccupied with human welfare as they were, and recognizing the imperfections of human institutions, they were bound to want to do something about it, or at least try to point the way to better things. It was an age of projects, from the *Encyclopédie* to that grandest of all projects, the Revolution, which the elderly Kant hailed with joy, exclaiming, "Lord, let now Thy servant depart in peace; for mine eyes have seen Thy salvation." [24] It is, therefore, not surprising that the more constructive-minded thinkers should have attempted a reëxamination of a field in which human imperfections were most in evidence, that of international relations, and to reason men into improving it.

The first great project of constructive internationalism of the eighteenth century was the plan of the Abbé de Saint-Pierre (1658-1743). Interested in the natural sciences and politics, rather than theology, the Abbé sought to apply the method of science, and even of mathematics, to affairs of state. At one time he is said to have had the ambition to become a minister in the French government, but later he resigned himself to the task of influencing statesmen through his writings. If he did not succeed in this, it was certainly through no lack of industry. He was an indefatigable worker and put out a great many projects on a variety of subjects. He even ventured to write one with the title, *Project for Making Dukes and Peers Useful*, something which was attempted in drastic fashion in 1789. Desiring also to make them—the princes—harmless, he wrote another book which was to cause scoffing in some quarters but was to bring him renown in others: *A Project for Making Peace Perpetual in Europe*. The occasion for

tragedies and lyric poems and was greatly discontented with the life of an army surgeon. Repression was not as successful with him as it had been with the young Frederick the Great.

[23] For example, Rousseau in his first draft of the *Contrat Social* said: "We conceive the Society of the whole after the model of our own societies. The building-up of little commonwealths sets us dreaming of the great, and we do not really become Men until we have learned to be Citizens. Which shows what we ought to think of those self-styled cosmopolitans who, while they profess to base their love of country on their love of mankind, make their love of all the world an excuse for loving nobody at all." (Quoted in Stawell, *op. cit.*, p. 149.)

[24] Quotation from W. Durant, *The Story of Philosophy* (Garden City, N. Y., 1926), p. 307.

this particular contribution was the War of the Spanish Succession, which lasted from 1702 to 1713, and was conducted on a larger scale than Europe had ever known. The good Abbé was distressed by the suffering it entailed and, perhaps above all, by its irrationality. He set himself the task of enlightening the princes on the subject and finally produced a peace plan, elaborated in three volumes comprising about twelve hundred pages. The style was unattractive and there were many repetitions.[25] It was, however, not the work of a cloistered recluse, as one might perhaps surmise from the time that must have been consumed in writing it and other projects. Saint-Pierre gave up the life of a scholar, spent some time at the royal court, made many acquaintances, and mingled a great deal with persons of influence. This gave him an opportunity, as he said in a letter to a friend, to observe disinterestedly the center of the world stage and the principal actors, and to form his judgments for the shaping of a plan to improve matters.[26]

The Project was, according to the Abbé's statement, inspired by the plan of the Great King Henry IV, and was modeled after it. Perhaps this was a little judicious advertising on the part of the Abbé, who naturally wanted his plan read by people of consequence. At any rate, it is more nearly like that of the obscure Crucé on certain vital matters. Saint-Pierre contemplated an organization of the Christian states of Europe into a federal union, and in the volumes published in 1713 spoke of the desirability of a defensive alliance with a similar Asiatic union, which Europe would try to have formed, for the preservation of mutual possessions, and the protection of commerce.[27] On the other hand, he definitely followed Crucé rather than Sully in providing that the union of the various states should be based on the territorial *status quo* existing at the time of its formation rather than that it

[25] Two volumes were published at Utrecht in 1713, and a third in 1717. In 1729 the author published an abridgment at Rotterdam. The Abbé made some changes in the third volume and in the abridgment. For English translation of the abridgment, see H. H. Bellot, in Grotius Society Publications (London, 1927), No. 5. See also W. E. Darby, *International Tribunals* (4th ed., London, 1904), for extensive English translation from the *Project*.

[26] J. ter Meulen, *Der Gedanke der Internationalen Organisation in Seiner Entwicklung (1300-1899)*, 2 vols. (The Hague, 1917-1929), I (1300-1800), 181. H. H. Post, *La Société des Nations de L'Abbé de Saint-Pierre* (Amsterdam, 1932), p. 137.

[27] ter Meulen, *op. cit.*, pp. 189, 200. In the third volume, which was dedicated to the Prince Regent, Saint-Pierre apparently thought his plan would arouse more interest and support by suggesting once more that the Christian union should expel the Turks from Europe. In this respect he followed Sully.

should seek to establish and maintain a balance of power.[28] It is to be observed also that under Saint-Pierre's original plan, the political *status quo within* states was to be preserved, although he seems to have given up the idea later.[29] One can understand, however, that such an arrangement might be a good talking-point with princes, for it would protect them against revolution. The heart of the plan, on the other hand, was not likely to make an appeal to ambitious rulers. They were to agree to renounce for themselves and their successors the right to resort to war for any purpose other than to carry out a judgment of the allied states, and to consent to have all their differences settled by the general assembly.

Saint-Pierre follows Crucé again in the attention he gives to the matter of sanctions. He was convinced that to be effective the union must have force behind it to be used, if necessary, for the execution of its decisions: "The sword is not less necessary to Justice than the scales." [30] Thus if any of the members of the Alliance should refuse to execute the collective judgments and rules, should negotiate treaties contrary to its obligations as a member, or should make preparations for war, the Grand Alliance was to force it by arms to comply as well as to make reparation for any wrongs inflicted by its arms, and reimburse the Grand Alliance for the cost of bringing it to terms. It must also be pointed out that the Abbé proposed that when fourteen of the twenty-four states had entered, the union should be regarded as formed. Henceforth any state refusing to enter was to be regarded as an enemy of the Alliance and the members of the latter should force it to become a member.[31]

One of the conspicuous features of the Abbé's plan was its attention to the possibilities of constructive action on the part of the Alliance in promoting the common interests of its members. As he envisaged it, the union was to be far more than an organization to prevent war and to punish transgressors. It was to be equipped with various bureaus to handle different matters of common interest. One, dealing with public

[28] Erasmus, in the *Querela Pacis,* also suggested that the princes once for all fix their frontiers. They should then agree not to sell or cede their territories under any circumstances (Constantinescu-Bagdat, *op. cit.,* II, 111). Under Saint Pierre's plan, arrangements already made in the Treaty of Utrecht, 1713, as well as other past treaties still applicable, were to be adhered to henceforth.

[29] Lange, "Histoire" *loc. cit.,* p. 306. ter Meulen, *op. cit.,* p. 190.

[30] ter Meulen, *op. cit.,* p. 201.

[31] Lange, "Histoire," *loc. cit.,* 307. ter Meulen, *op. cit.,* p. 192.

law, was to work out an international commercial law for the better ordering of commerce between the subjects of the different states. Such matters as the standardization of weights and measures and the coinage systems and reform of the calendar were also dealt with.[32] This interest in economic matters and the promotion of trade, to which Crucé also had given considerable attention, is one of the signs of the times. A new class, the bourgeoisie, is coming into prominence. And it is demanding consideration not for the interests of nobles, whose energies have been devoted largely to war, but for the welfare of bankers, merchants, manufacturers, and traders whose predilection is for the pursuits of peace. In England this class had already aided in overthrowing monarchs and had established some claim for consideration; in France it was to rise up, before the century was spent, with cries of revolution.

The work of the Abbé created rather widespread interest among the intellectuals of the time, in spite of its formidable character, and drew forth many comments. Frederick the Great, who, before coming to the throne, had written against the views of Machiavelli and upon whose enlightenment the Abbé placed great reliance, read and commented on the Project in the following language: "The thing is most practicable; for its success all that is lacking is the consent of Europe and a few similar trifles." [33] The Prince, who, a few years after his *Anti-Machiavel,* carried on war against Maria Theresa in the best Machiavellian fashion, could certainly be counted upon to withhold his consent and, in lieu of argument, use the weapon of ridicule against it. Many others, among them Leibniz, Voltaire, Cardinal Fleury, and Kant, discussed and criticized the Abbé's scheme. And Rousseau found it such "a solid sensible" plan that he remarked that if it should not be adopted by princes, it would not be the fault of the Project but of the princes. Moreover he undertook, at the request of Madame Dupin, friend of the Abbé, the task of editing and abridging it, changing it here and there, and in fact treating the original with such great freedom that it became infused with his own thought.[34] In an independent essay he subjected the Abbé's plan to the most acute and searching criticism.

Rousseau's criticism, however, did not find fault with the substance

[32] ter Meulen, *op. cit.*, pp. 197, 200.
[33] *Ibid.*, p. 218.
[34] See English translation by C. E. Vaughan of *A Lasting Peace through the Federation of Europe,* by Jean Jacques Rousseau (London, 1917), Introduction, p. 7.

of the plan. He regarded it as altogether reasonable and sound and clearly in the interest of the princes and peoples of Europe. But Rousseau was not among those optimists of the Enlightenment who felt that institutions based on reason would necessarily prevail. The Abbé, he thought, "would have been a very wise man had he not been so absurdly reasonable." Rousseau did not object to the use of reason, but he considered it a very frail support for one's plans for society. In a letter to Mirabeau, he made this clear. "Men are led very seldom by their reason, and very often by their passions. It is easy to prove that the true interest of the despot is to obey the Law; that has been admitted for a generation. But who is there that is guided by his true interest? Only the sage, if he exists. It follows that you assume your despots to be so many sages. My friends! you must allow me to tell you that you give too much weight to your calculations, and too little to the heart of man and the play of passion. Your system is excellent for Utopia; for the children of Adam it is worth nothing."[35] And so the good-hearted Abbé, who labored to prove to princes absolutely, because mathematically and statistically, all that he had written, had, in the judgment of Rousseau, labored in vain.

For a full appreciation of Rousseau's insight, the entire essay should be read.[36] But certain of his observations may be given as illustrating the tenor of his thought about the Abbé's plan and the prospect, in general, of a federation of Europe. He points out that one must distinguish between real and apparent interest in politics as in morals. The real interests of princes would be served by European federation. But their apparent interest is "found in the state of absolute independence which frees sovereigns from the reign of Law only to put them under that of chance."[37] Kings are animated by two desires: to extend their dominions, and to achieve a more absolute rule over their subjects. They may hide their real purposes under beautiful phrases about "the happiness of their subjects," the "good of the community," or "the glory of the nation"; but these are merely pretexts. Now the Abbé's proposal would not only stereotype the frontiers of Europe, but also it would fix the constitution of each state so that if it would guarantee princes against the rebellion of their subjects, it would likewise

[35] Rousseau, *op. cit.*, Introduction, p. 16.

[36] *Ibid.* His statement of Saint-Pierre's Project is to be found on pp. 36-90; his criticism of Saint-Pierre's Project, on pp. 92-112.

[37] *Ibid.*, p. 95.

protect the latter against the tyranny of their princes.[38] No sovereign would consent to a system which would compel him to be just not only toward foreigners but also toward his own subjects.

Rousseau also declared that there was a reciprocity between war and despotism, that "war and conquest without, the encroachments of despotism within give each other mutual support. . ." Enslaved people give money and men to the support of war establishments and conquest, and large armies are used to keep the people in subjection. The people of a conquering nation are no better off than the conquered. " 'I have beaten the Romans,' so Hannibal used to write to Carthage, 'send me more troops. I have exacted an indemnity from Italy, send me more money.' That is the real meaning of the Te Deums, the bonfires and rejoicings with which the people hail the triumphs of their masters." [39]

Among the advantages which the Abbé had declared would follow from the adoption of his plan was uninterrupted commerce between nations. Rousseau agrees but points out that the advantage is common to all and will therefore be appreciated by none. "For such advantages make themselves felt only by contrast, and he who wishes to increase his relative power is bound to seek only such gains as are exclusive." [40]

If princes would spurn peace on the basis of the Abbé's plan, said Rousseau, the same would be true of their ministers. The interests of the latter are always opposed to those of the people. Moreover, they can make their positions more secure in war by becoming indispensable to the king, and they can also utilize the occasion of a war to advance their own interests in a variety of ways. On the other hand, a lasting peace would rob them of many important resources. Thus, like their royal masters, they may be depended upon to "turn into ridicule" any plan for permanent peace, no matter how practicable it may be.

And finally, says Rousseau, "given the good will that we shall never find in princes or their ministers," there is another obstacle, for ". . . it would be essential that all the private interests concerned, taken together, should not be stronger than the general interest, and that everyone should believe himself to see in the good of all the highest good to which he can aspire for himself." [41] Rousseau thought this very unlikely,

[38] In the unabridged proposals of Saint-Pierre, the internal constitutions of the members of the Grand Alliance were to be guaranteed by the Alliance. See ter Meulen, *op. cit.*, p. 190.

[39] Rousseau, *op. cit.*, p. 97.

[40] *Ibid.*, pp. 99-110.

[41] *Ibid.*, p. 101.

and that in the absence of spontaneous popular agreement force would have to be used. "Things of public utility," he observed, "are seldom brought in but by force, for the simple reason that private interests are almost always ranged against them."[42]

Rousseau's conclusion from this analysis was inevitably dismal: "No Federation could ever be established except by a revolution. That being so, which of us would dare to say whether the League of Europe is a thing more to be desired or feared? It would perhaps do more harm in a moment than it would guard against for ages."[43] Thus Rousseau by the process of reason demonstrated that the inherent reasonableness of the Abbé's plan would not carry the day against passion.

In Jeremy Bentham (1748-1832) one is reminded strongly of Saint-Pierre in many respects. Here again we find a man strongly imbued with a desire to pull men and nations out of the mire and set them on the road to happiness, and ever sanguine that his demonstrably reasonable proposals will meet with approval. Appealing always to reason and practical advantage, he writes to rulers, the Tsar of Russia at one time, the President of the United States at another, suggesting various reforms.[44] His *Plan for an Universal and Perpetual Peace*[45] was but one of many projects on a great variety of matters. He was ambitious to "maximize" human happiness by applying to social relationships "the experimental method of reasoning" employed by chemists and physicians. All social institutions were tested by their utility, their capacity to minister to "the greatest happiness of the greatest number" of people. And in his writings on the reform of international relations his proposals always had in view "the common and equal utility of all nations."

In his peace plan, the approach of Bentham differs from that of his Continental precursors in that he did not propose a complete and logical

[42] Rousseau, *op. cit.*, p. 111.

[43] *Ibid.*, p. 112. In later years Rousseau expressed the opinion that some day the people might get tired of being the victims of the pastimes of their monarchs and compel the latter to agree to lasting peace. He thought peoples would be much less inclined toward war and would "fight only for their real interests, and for large ones, while Kings do so from mere pride; because they are surrounded by men who love war, and because they always abuse the power entrusted to them." (*Ibid.*, pp. 9-10.)

[44] E. Briout, *L'Idée de Paix Perpétuelle de Jérémie Bentham* (Paris, 1905), pp. 5-6.

[45] Text in the Grotius Society Publications No. 6 (London, 1927), with an introduction by C. John Colombos.

scheme for European federation, but advanced two fundamental propositions as the basis for a more restricted project recommended to all nations, but particularly to England and France. The first proposition was that the armaments of the nations composing the European system should be reduced and fixed at a certain point, and second that the distant dependencies of each state should be emancipated. For many years Europe had been an armed camp, and there was no doubt that when Bentham wrote the situation was quite like that pictured by Montesquieu: "The disease increases in virulence and of necessity becomes contagious. For as soon as one Prince increases his troops the rest of course do the same; so that nothing is effected thereby but the public ruin. Each Monarch keeps as many armies on foot as if his people were in danger of being exterminated. . ." [46]

Bentham's belief was that if Great Britain and France could agree on his fundamental propositions "the principal difficulties would be removed to the establishment of a plan of general and permanent pacification for all Europe." [47] Such a plan "might be considerably facilitated" by setting up a Common Court of Judicature to which nations could take their differences. This he later refers to as a "Congress or Diet" to which each nation would send deputies. It would have the power of giving its opinion on matters submitted to it, of circulating such opinion in all of the states, and, after a certain time, putting a "refractory state under the ban of Europe." [48]

It is apparent that Bentham thought that the master key to the situation lay in his second proposition. He argued that it was "not to the interest" of either Great Britain or France that they should retain their dependencies,[49] and that if they were to give them up they would no longer have anything to fear from each other. Certainly neither England nor France would entertain any thought of permanent conquest of each other's homeland. Thus they would have no further need for large armed establishments and could safely dispense with them. And yet he recognizes that the matter is not quite so simple, for there are other nations to be considered: "On the subject of troops, France says to England: Yes, I would voluntarily make with you a treaty of dis-

[46] As quoted in K. Martin, *French Liberal Thought in the Eighteenth Century* (London, 1929), p. 263.

[47] Bentham's *Plan for an Universal and Perpetual Peace, loc. cit.*, p. 13.

[48] *Ibid.*, pp. 13, 30-31.

[49] This was an argument commonly used by English anti-imperialist writers in the nineteenth century. *Infra*, Ch. XIII.

arming, if there were only you; but it is necessary for me to have troops to defend me from the Austrians. Austria might say the same to France; but it is necessary to guard against Prussia, Russia, and the Porte. And the like allegation might be made by Prussia with regard to Russia." [50] Nearly a century and a half after Bentham wrote this, statesmen gathered to discuss a plan for general disarmament, had to face this as one of their major problems.[51] Bentham suggested the difficulty, but offered no clear way out. He believed, apparently, that a general agreement for the reduction of the armaments of the various nations could be reached and that when it was embodied in a treaty and presented to the people any prejudices they might have against it would be dissipated. For they would see how much it would cut down their contributions and would immediately "feel the relief it brought them. They would see it was for their advantage it was calculated, and that it could not be calculated for any other purpose." [52] An attentive reading of Rousseau might have tempered Bentham's optimism on this question. But it is evident that intellectually he had a closer affinity with Saint-Pierre.

On the subject of sanctions, Bentham suggested the use of force only as a last resort, while really feeling that it would not be necessary. He placed great reliance on the power of public opinion to bring a nation to accept the decrees of the Court, and suggested a way in which it might be made to function in order to avoid having recourse to force. "But the necessity for the employment of this recourse would, in all human probability, be superseded forever by having recourse to the much more simple and less burthensome expedient of introducing into the instrument by which such Court was instituted a clause guaranteeing the liberty of the Press in each State, in such sort that the Diet might find no obstacle to its giving, in every State, to its decrees and to every paper whatever, which it might think proper to sanction with its signature, the most extensive and unlimited circulation." [53] Here again it is evident that Bentham had great faith in the disposition and capacity of people to assimilate facts and respond to reason.

Bentham also struck a vigorous blow at secret diplomacy, anticipating many of the arguments made by the proponents of open diplomacy

[50] Bentham's *Plan, loc. cit.*, p. 22.
[51] *Infra*, Ch. XIX.
[52] Bentham's *Plan*, p. 27.
[53] *Ibid.*, p. 31.

within recent years. Although his criticisms were directed particularly against British practice, he made it clear that his arguments applied likewise to the practice of secrecy of Departments of Foreign Affairs in general: "My persuasion is that there is no State whatever in which any inconveniences capable of arising from publicity in this Department would not be greatly overbalanced by the advantages, be the State ever so great or ever so small, ever so strong or ever so weak, be its form of government pure or mixed, single or confederated, monarchical, aristocratical, or democratical."[54] Bentham went so far as to maintain, for England at any rate, that all stages of negotiations with other powers ought to be revealed not only to Parliament but to the public at large, and above all that "secrecy ought never to be maintained with regard to treaties actually concluded."[55] For, argued Bentham, if the people have no knowledge of what is going on they have no opportunity to stop the pursuit of policies or measures which may lead to war. The people, therefore, should have such a check on their Ministers.

Among the eighteenth-century rationalists who made contributions to the theory of international relations, Immanuel Kant (1724-1804) deserves a foremost place. A professor of logic and metaphysics at the University of Koenigsberg, Kant led the life of a teacher and philosopher and never took an active part in public affairs. He was familiar, however, with the writings of Saint-Pierre and Rousseau, as well as their forerunners, and was an interested and keen observer of the international relationships of his time. Moreover, he brought a trained and powerful mind to bear on the subject. Nor was he willing to admit that philosophers had nothing to offer practical statesmen. In connection with his own plan for perpetual peace, he stated that the views of philosophers should receive consideration in the councils of states inasmuch as the statesman necessarily tends to be conservative. It is the business of his office "to apply existing laws, not to investigate the necessity of improving them. . ." On the other hand, Kant remarked: "It is not to be expected or even desired that Kings should philosophise, or that philosophers should become Kings; for the possession of power inevitably destroys the free judgment of reason. But it is necessary for their own enlightenment that Kings, or a sovereign people (i.e., a nation of self-governing equals), should not allow the class of philosophers

[54] *Ibid.*, p. 36.
[55] *Ibid.*, pp. 31-32.

to vanish, or to sink into silence, but rather should allow them the right of free speech, for since this class is by its nature incapable of intrigues and conspiracies, such a course is above the suspicion of propaganda." [56]

In his *Idea of a Universal History from a Cosmopolitan Point of View* (1784), Kant regards man's history as one of gradual evolution. Originally, on account of his egoistic, unsociable, and acquisitive nature his condition was one of anarchy. But nature used these very traits of mutual antagonism to bring about the development of man's capacities. The resistance of his fellow-creatures to his desires and inclinations had the effect of awakening all his latent powers, aroused him out of a disposition toward sluggishness and desire for mere comfort, and spurred him on to seek glory and possession and power. But nature also endowed him with reason. Through it he learned that he must live in human society in order to have freedom so as to give scope to his desires and develop his capacities. And so "selfishness is forced to discipline itself" and accept laws and government. Between these organized societies, says Kant, nature decrees a similar process of evolution. For her purpose she uses war, destroying here, building there, achieving partial federations, but ever working toward the ultimate establishment of law and government in international relations. For as men become more enlightened, and the costs of war to all nations become increasingly heavy at the same time that their freedom to live and develop is diminished, nations will be led, however unwillingly, to abandon their anarchical state and seek an international régime of law, just as individuals were reluctantly brought to the acceptance of government.[57]

In the same work [58] Kant emphasizes the importance, indeed the necessity, of this development in the sphere of international relations if mankind is to realize its destiny. As Rousseau had pointed out that to abandon the state of nature for particular societies and retain it as between them was worse than for it to have survived in both, so Kant declared that a satisfactory constitution for civil societies could

[56] Kant's *Perpetual Peace*. Translation by Helen O'Brien. Grotius Society Publications No. 7 (London, 1927), Addendum II, pp. 42-43. This translation will be followed in further excerpts.

[57] ter Meulen, *op. cit.*, pp. 314-317. Stawell, *op. cit.*, pp. 196-198.

[58] *Idea of a Universal History,* in De Quincey's Works; 15 vols. (Edinburgh, 1863), Vol. XII.

not be attained until the external relations of states were brought under a reign of law. On the other hand, in his *Perpetual Peace* (1795) Kant envisages an organized international society made up of states with republican constitutions.[59] For such states, he asserts, will give the power to declare war into the hands of their citizens. Like Rousseau, Kant was inclined to believe that if the people of the different countries were given such a decision, "nothing is more natural than that they should think long before beginning such a terrible game, since they would have to call down on themselves all the horrors of war, such as, to fight themselves; to pay the cost of war out of their own pocket; miserably to repair the devastation it leaves behind; and to add to the over-abundance of misery they would themselves have to bear the burden of debts which, owing to ever new wars, could never be paid off and would thus embitter peace itself. . ." But in states with despotic constitutions, says Kant, the Sovereign enters on a war lightheartedly. "He abates nothing of his feasts, sports, pleasure palaces or court festivities etc., through the war, and can therefore declare war as a sort of pleasure-party on the slightest provocation, negligently leaving its justification, for decency's sake, to the diplomatic corps ever ready to hand for this service." [60]

Before nations can set about the organization of a definitive peace, however, Kant specified that they must agree to certain preliminary articles; for certain evils must be removed.[61] In the first place, they must agree to abandon the all too frequent practice, when they are for the moment too exhausted to continue a war, of making treaties with the mental reservation that they will resume war at the first opportunity. In the second place, they must agree that no state may acquire another by inheritance, exchange, purchase, or gift. For a state is not a piece of property; it is "a society of people over which no one but itself has the right of command or disposal." This was, of course, revolutionary doctrine, for the rulers of Europe had always done precisely these things as of right. Standing armies must also eventually be given up because

[59] Kant drew a distinction between the republican and autocratic principles as follows: "The republican principle is that of separation of the executive from the legislative power; the despotic that of an arbitrary execution by the State of laws made by itself, i.e., the ruler substitutes his own for the general will." (*Perpetual Peace,* Pt. II.)

[60] *Ibid.*

[61] His *Perpetual Peace* was put into the form of a treaty with six preliminary articles, three definitive articles, certain addenda, and an appendix.

of their evil effects. "They incite (other states) to outbid each other in unlimited numbers of armed forces, and, as peace finally becomes more costly than a short war on account of the expenditure on armies, these themselves become the causes of wars of aggression undertaken in order to reduce this burden." On the other hand, Kant held that the "voluntary exercise of citizens skilled in arms, undertaken periodically to insure the safety of themselves and of the state against attacks from without," is quite a different matter. By the time of Kant, nations were more and more resorting to the expedient of floating foreign as well as domestic loans for the purpose of carrying on war. In another preliminary article he proposed to make it impossible for a state to contract a debt "for external state enterprises," although it might still borrow within or from outside the state for internal enterprises of public utility. Another practice which Kant held should be forbidden altogether to a state was that of forcibly interfering with the constitution and government of another. Even in case of an internal conflict, the intervention of another state was not to be allowed. And finally, states at war must abstain from such conduct as will destroy mutual trust and thus render a future peace impossible. There is, of course, nothing new in this. The admonition was one often given by the theologians of the Middle Ages. Kant recognized that some of the foregoing prohibitions could not be immediately and completely put into effect, but no unnecessary delay should be admitted.

In Kant's view, perpetual peace would not be realized merely by the banning of certain practices. Like Hobbes, he held that peace is not a natural state. In a state of nature men are disposed toward war. If, then, peace is to be realized, it must be "instituted." In addition to the establishment of republican constitutions in all states, there must be a federation of free states established by a special international treaty. International law without this must remain as impotent as law within societies would be if no governmental organization were established. "The conception of the law of nations as containing the right to war is really meaningless, for this right is supposed to be based on the one-sided principle of deciding what is right by force, not on universally valid, external laws, which limit the freedom of each in the same degree. . . For states having relations with one another there can reasonably be no other method of escaping from the lawless condition which connotes only wars than by renouncing their uncivilized, lawless freedom, like private individuals, and subjecting themselves to compulsory public laws, thus forming an international State (*civitas gentium*) which would gradually extend and finally include all the peoples of the world." [62]

In his assessment of human nature, Kant, as has been seen, agreed in part with Hobbes. But Hobbe's analysis led him to the support of despotic government within states and to accepting as inevitable a continuing "state of nature" or state of war between them. Kant, on the other hand, influenced by Rousseau at many points, defended republicanism, which he already saw emerging in America and in France, and envisaged the ultimate development of an effective régime of law between nations. He also repudiated the contention of Machiavelli and his supporters that states should not be disturbed by ethical considerations in their dealings with one another. Like Grotius, he contended that good faith is an essential in all public dealings and that morals can never be discarded. "Right must be held sacred by man, however great the cost and sacrifice to the ruling power. Here is no half-and-half course. We cannot devise a happy medium between right and expediency, a right pragmatically conditioned. But all politics must bend the knee to the principle of right, and may, in that way, hope to reach, though slowly perhaps, a level whence it may shine upon men for all time." [63] Thus Kant rules out *raison d'état* along with despotism, in whose atmosphere, after all, it would seem to be more congenial than in the climate of republics.

REFERENCES

Beales, A. C. F., *The History of Peace* (New York, 1931) pp. 33-37.

Becker, C. L., *The Heavenly City of the Eighteenth Century Philosophers* (New Haven, Conn., 1932).

Bentham, J., *Plan for An Universal and Perpetual Peace* (London, 1927). Grotius Society Publications, No. 6.

Borner, W., *Das Weltstaatsprojekt des Abbé de Saint-Pierre* (Berlin and Leipzig, 1913).

Briout, E., *L'Idée de Paix Perpétuelle de Jérémie Bentham* (Paris, 1905).

Bury, John, *The Idea of Progress* (London, 1920).

[62] *Ibid.,* second definitive article. The third definitive article limited the rights of men as citizens of the world "to the conditions of universal hospitality."

[63] *Ibid.,* Appendix I, for elaboration of this idea.

Constantinescu-Bagdat, E. C., *Études d'Histoire Pacifiste,* 3 vols. (Paris, 1924-1928), Vol. II, *De Vauban à Voltaire* (Paris, 1925).

Darby, C. E., *International Tribunals* (4th ed., London, 1904).

Drouet, Joseph, *L'Abbé de Saint-Pierre* (Paris, 1912).

Dunning, W. A., *A History of Political Theories from Luther to Montesquieu* (New York, 1905), Chs. XI-XII.

Fénelon (F. de Salignac de la Mothe), *Oeuvres Choisies* (Paris, 1871).

Gargaz, Pierre-André, *Project of Universal and Perpetual Peace* (New York, 1922).

Hibben, J. G., *The Philosophy of the Enlightenment* (New York, 1910).

Hume, David, *Essays and Treatises,* 2 vols. (London, 1772), Vol. I, Part II, Chs. I, V, VI.

Kant, Immanuel, *Perpetual Peace.* English translation by Helen O'Brien in Grotius Society Publications No. 7 (London, 1927); also English translation by M. Campbell Smith (London, 1903), including introduction and notes.

Kayser, E. L., *The Grand Social Enterprise; A Study of Jeremy Bentham in His Relation to Liberal Nationalism* (New York, 1932), Ch. IV, and bibliography, pp. 94-103.

Kraus, O., *Der Machtgedanke und die Friedensidee in der Philosophie der Engländer* (Leipzig, 1926), pp. 33-64.

Lange, C., "Histoire de la Doctrine Pacifique et de son Influence sur le Développement du Droit International," *Recueil des Cours,* Vol. XIII (1926), pp. 294-335, 347-352, Académie de Droit International (Paris, 1927).

Martin, K., *French Liberal Thought in the Eighteenth Century* (Boston, 1929), Ch. X.

Olphe-Galliard, G., *La Morale des Nations* (Paris, 1920), Ch. VII.

Meulen, J. ter, *Gedanke der Internationalen Organisation in Seiner Entwicklung* (1300-1889); 2 vols. (The Hague, 1917-1929), I (1300-1800), 180-339.

Post, H. H., *La Société des Nations de l'Abbé de Saint-Pierre* (Amsterdam, 1932).

Rousseau, J. J., *A Lasting Peace Through the Federation of Europe; and The State of War,* English translations by C. E. Vaughan (London, 1917), and by E. M. Nuttall (London, 1927).

Rozemond, S., *Kant en de Volkenbond* (Amsterdam, 1930).

Saint-Pierre, L'Abbé de, *Projet Pour Rendre la Paix Perpétuelle en Europe;* 3 vols. (Utrecht, 1713-1717). *Abrégé du Projet de Paix Perpétuelle* (Rotterdam, 1729).

Seroux-d'Agincourt, *Exposé des Projets de Paix Perpétuelle de l'Abbé de Saint-Pierre* (Paris, 1905).

Smith, Preserved, *A History of Modern Culture,* 2 vols. (New York, 1930-1934), Vol. II, *The Enlightenment, 1687-1776.*

Stawell, F. M., *Growth of International Thought* (London, 1929), Chs. VII-IX.

Voltaire, F. M. A., *Candide.* (New York, 1931). Universal Library series.

————, *Dictionnaire Philosophique,* 3 vols. (Éditions de Cluny, Paris, 1930), II, 168-175, article "Guerre."

CHAPTER XI

THE NINETEENTH CENTURY: NATIONALITY AND NATIONAL SELF-DETERMINATION

THE rise of the modern nations as national states [1] has already been noted, and the consequences of the new development in international relationships and theory have been related. At the close of the Thirty Years' War, legal recognition of the new international society was recorded in the treaties of Westphalia. The feeble Holy Roman Empire was to linger on until Napoleon should deliver the *coup de grâce* in 1806, but after the peace of Westphalia the several German princes were recognized as sovereign, and competent to declare war, make peace, and otherwise rule over their states without the intervention of the imperial Diet, which continued to meet as a diplomatic body concerned only with trivial matters.

The new states, however, were by no means homogeneous. They were not intimately bound together, as had been true of the primitive tribal communities or "nations" of earlier times, by ties of blood, language, religion, customs, and traditions. The nations of the early modern period were larger and not so closely knit. Racially they were mixed; and different languages and dialects were still spoken within their borders. There was no clear stamp of nationality on them. Even in the case of England,[2] where conditions were peculiarly favorable to the early growth of a single nationality, there were the Irish, Welsh, and Scotch [3] nationalities, all more or less self-conscious. And in France there were Flemings, Normans, Basques, Bretons, varying dialects, and divergent customs. To a greater or less extent, the same may be said about the other national states. On the other hand, in each one of these

[1] The terms "nation," "national state," and "state" are generally used interchangeably to designate the modern state.

[2] Used in the sense of the English state.

[3] In 1603 the crowns of England and Scotland were joined by a personal union. A corporate union was not achieved until 1707 when the Kingdom of Great Britain was established.

various states was a particular nationality which formed the nucleus and furnished the governing authority, as well as the official language, of the state. And at the head of each one was a more or less autocratic monarch to whom all of the nationalities within the kingdom rendered obedience and gave support in his struggles with other states.

During the centuries between the time of the emergence of the first national states at the beginning of the sixteenth century and the French Revolution, the welding process was continued, and a deepening consciousness of nationhood developed. Monarchs might lead their peoples into wars to satisfy their own personal ambitions and achieve glory for their dynasties rather than from any solicitude for the welfare of their subjects, but these wars nevertheless were a powerful factor in developing a separate consciousness of kind among English, French, Spanish, Dutch, and other nationalities. The Hundred Years' War between England and France undoubtedly stimulated the growth of nationality in both states. English aggression, in the first place, developed a spirit of solidarity in France against the invader and in time made for a feeling of unity among Frenchmen engaged in a common enterprise of hardship and suffering and danger for *la douce France* against an alien intruder. But at the end of the struggle the English, too, had their memories of defeats and victories for Merry England. And later the exploits of Drake, the defeat of the Spanish Armada, and similar enterprises, played their part in deepening the sentiment of an English breed.

> So long as flashes English steel
> And English trumpets shrill,
> He is dead already who doth not feel
> Life is worth living still.

The same process was chiefly responsible for welding the Netherlands into a nation. Prior to the attempt of the Spanish to dominate and oppress them, the Dutch failed to unite. In the face of the Spanish tyranny and in the course of its overthrow, they developed a spirit of nationality and became a united nation.

Up to the time of the French Revolution, however, the sentiment of nationality was exploited by the rulers of the several states in the carrying out of their own designs rather than in the realization of the aspirations of their subjects. The peoples of these states had no voice in determining the character of the enterprises undertaken or the objects for which they fought. Moreover, the monarchs freely disregarded the sentiments of other nationalities whenever it suited their convenience. The three partitions of Poland in the latter part of the eighteenth century were but the most flagrant of countless instances of the disregard of national feelings when they stood in the path of ruthless ambition; in fact in the sixteenth, seventeenth, and eighteenth centuries, it was customary rather than exceptional for princes to seize territories and barter peoples about as if they were cattle. In an age of absolutism, the will of the prince was the only thing that mattered.[4]

The coming of the French Revolution, with its doctrine of the Rights of Man, destroyed the old system of absolutism in France and set forces in motion that were to challenge it in all parts of the world. "Men are born and remain free and equal in rights. . . The object of every political association is the maintenance of the natural and imprescriptible rights of man. . . The principle of all sovereignty resides in the nation. . . Law is the expression of the general will."[5] These doctrines had definite implications for the external relations of peoples. The doctrine of popular sovereignty, which denied the validity of any internal rule not based on popular consent, was regarded as containing also the corollary that no change of sovereignty affecting an important human group was legal without the consent of the people concerned. Thus the doctrine of the rights of man, of general application to human beings, led to the more specific assertion that settled groups of men having common ideals and mutual sympathies should have the right to determine their political destiny. Thus was the answer given to de Mably's protesting question raised under the *ancien régime:* "Can free nations, without degrading themselves, dispose of a people without their consent, and give them to a master as you would a flock in a farm?"[6]

[4] Lord Acton points out that there were special reasons for Poland's being obnoxious to the dynastic rulers of the time. It was an elective monarchy and its political institutions were distasteful to absolute rulers. "A monarch without royal blood, a crown bestowed by the nation, were an anomaly and an outrage in that age of dynastic absolutism. The country was excluded from the European system by the nature of its institutions. It excited a cupidity which could not be satisfied. It gave the reigning families of Europe no hope of permanently strengthening themselves by intermarriage with its rulers, or of obtaining it by bequest or by inheritance." *The History of Freedom and Other Essays* (London, 1909), p. 275.

[5] *The Declaration of the Rights of Man and the Citizen* is quoted in full in F. S. Marvin, *The Evolution of World Peace* (London, 1921), pp. 98-99.

[6] Gabriel Bonnot de Mably (1709-1785). Quotation taken from biography by E. A. Whitefield, *Gabriel Bonnot de Mably* (London, 1930), p. 285. Historically,

But Louis XIV and the other sovereigns of France had not acted in accord with any such principles, and French boundaries reflected rather what despotism had been able to achieve and retain in the competitions of power of the European states from the sixteenth century onwards.[7] The revolutionists did not propose to raise the question as to how far the then existing frontiers might coincide with the wishes of the people within them, but they embodied in the constitution of 1791 and called to the attention of the European Powers the renunciation of all future wars of conquest. And when a year later war broke out with these Powers and French armies crossed the frontiers, they did so at first in the conviction that it was necessary in their own defense and then to free other peoples from the yoke. On November 19, 1792, the National Convention pledged itself by decree to "accord fraternity and succour to all peoples who may desire to recover their liberty. . ." It was not long, however, before the revolutionists determined that oppressed peoples should be freed and become democratic whether they desired it or not, for a decree of December, 1792, read: "The French nation declares that it will treat as enemies every people who, refusing liberty and equality or renouncing them, may wish to maintain, recall, or treat with a prince and the privileged classes; on the other hand it engages not to lay down its arms until the sovereignty and independence of the people whose territory the troops of the republic shall have entered shall be established, and until the people shall have

de Mably's question had been asked and answered in the negative by those jurists in the Middle Ages who held the social contract theory of the origin of the state. If a ruler desired to transfer territory to another, the express consent of the people was held to be necessary, for such a transfer involved a change in the original contract upon which the state was founded. E. Wittman, *Past and Future of the Right of National Self-Determination* (Amsterdam, 1919), pp. 75-76. For the connection between the social contract theory and the self-determination of nationalities, see also Robert Redslob, *Le Principe des Nationalités* (Paris, 1930), pp. 5-7.

[7] It should be noted, however, that as early as 1562 the principle of the self-determination of nationalities was asserted and officially endorsed in a particular case. Francis I of France, after his defeat and capture at the battle of Pavia in 1525, promised to cede Burgundy to the Emperor Charles V. The Burgundians objected and, apparently under the coaching of the King's lawyers, claimed that Francis could not cede Burgundy without first consulting the Burgundians. The consultation was held June 4, 1526, resulting in the latter refusing to be separated from France. Charles V demurred at this method of solution, but Francis I declared: "Il est fondé en droit qu'on ne peut nulle villes ou provinces contre la volonté des habitants et sujets transférer en autre, sinon par leur consentement exprès." (René Johannet, *Le Principe des Nationalités* [Paris, 1923], pp. 63-64.) It is doubtful whether Francis saw in this principle anything more than a useful expedient in his desire to keep Burgundy.

adopted the principles of equality and founded a free and democratic government." [8]

During the first stages of the Revolution, plebiscites were held in good faith to determine whether certain districts said to desire French sovereignty should be annexed. Before the war broke out with the other Powers, petitions had come from Avignon and the Comtat Venaissin asking for annexation to France. The revolutionary government would not agree to annexation, however, until two years later, and then only after a plebiscite had apparently confirmed the asserted desire of the inhabitants. During the war, when French forces entered Savoy and Nice, the plebiscite was also used to determine whether the people of these districts desired to come under French sovereignty.[9] But the revolutionists soon lost their early idealism. Political expediency and military necessity got the upper hand, and it was assumed that conquered peoples desired not only to be freed from the yoke of their former masters but wanted French rule.[10]

With the advent of Napoleon, the Revolution entered a phase in which the ambition of one man was to determine the destinies of peoples throughout Europe. To be sure, he so far recognized Polish nationality as to create the Grand Duchy of Warsaw, and he also set up an Italian Kingdom, brushing away petty rulers with a ruthless hand. But this was not national self-determination, and it was not liberty, although it had the effect of mightily stimulating such sentiments among the peoples affected. The sovereigns opposed to the new conqueror took advantage of the feeling and announced that they were fighting for the liberty of peoples. But there were no plebiscites ordained at Vienna when the diplomats of the victorious powers met to decide what to do about France, Europe, and the rights of man.

The principle of national self-determination announced by the revolutionaries of France was clear in the sense that it denied the right to barter about from sovereignty to sovereignty territories inhabited by civilized peoples, as rulers had customarily done in the past. It was

[8] As quoted in C. J. H. Hayes, *A Political and Social History of Modern Europe*, 2 vols. (New York, 1916), I, 504. Ardent revolutionaries argued that no free people can wish for a tyrant and that if a majority chooses one it is a sign that there has been coercion by the masters of the people. Therefore, first of all when French armies march into a province they must see that the privileged classes are dispossessed and the old authorities displaced by persons taking the oath of liberty and equality. This will clear the way for a genuine manifestation of the popular will. (E. Wittman, *op. cit.*, pp. 42-44.)

[9] Sarah Wambaugh, *A Monograph on Plebiscites* (New York, 1920), pp. 6-7.

[10] Wittmann, *op. cit.*, pp. 44-54.

rooted in the theory of the social contract and was a logical derivation from the doctrine of popular sovereignty. But what was meant by "peoples"? Must a people be a "nationality"? What are the criteria of a nationality? The answers to these questions would decide the nature and the number of states that would make up the international community and thereby have far-reaching consequences for international relations. We may therefore turn to the views of some of the writers who expressed themselves on the subject during the revolutionary period and through the period of the movements for national unification in the nineteenth century.[11]

It is perhaps not an accident that the chief contribution to the subject of nationality in the eighteenth and early nineteenth centuries should have been by Germans. The conditions which produced a cosmopolitan outlook among certain thinkers influenced others to work for the development of a national spirit. At the beginning of the eighteenth century, Germany comprised about eighteen hundred separate and practically sovereign territories varying in size and form of government. The Holy Roman Empire, the only tie uniting them, was moribund, and for the most part there was no sentiment favorable to its resuscitation. In general, mercantilist policies were followed by the rulers of the different states; innumerable tariff barriers were set up, and the growth of economic unity was prevented. Religious particularism was also a disuniting factor. And with the decline of Latin the upper classes turned to French rather than to German as a medium of conversation, correspondence, and literary expression, just as they tended to assimilate French culture in general. To add to the lack of unity, there were sharp divisions and stratifications between the classes in Germany, the nobility maintaining an arrogant attitude of superiority and aloofness from the other classes. It was in this environment that Herder and other German writers pondered the subject of nationality.[12]

[11] The inherent difficulties in the application of the principle of the self-determination of peoples were recognized by some of the French revolutionary leaders. Carnot, for example, pointed out that if the principle were to be applied without limitation it would mean that every village would have the right to decide whether it desired to separate from the state to which it belonged. This would lead to the disruption of states. Carnot held that it was not possible to recognize that the different territorial parts of a state have such a right. Nor was the right, in his opinion, to be advanced to prevent a state from annexing territories absolutely indispensable to its defense. Wittmann, *op. cit.*, pp. 54-55.

[12] Robert R. Ergang, *Herder and the Foundations of German Nationalism* (Columbia Studies in History, Economics, and Public Law, Columbia University Press. New York, 1931), Ch. I.

Johann Herder (1744-1803) was born in East Prussia, and attended the University at Koenigsberg, where he became a great admirer of Kant. The latter interested him in history and philosophy, and the study of natural science. Kant's lectures on physical geography seem to have made a deep impression on him and may account for Herder's emphasis on physical factors in his own treatment of the development of nationalities. He also came under the influence of Rousseau, as a student of Kant was likely to do, and developed a strong feeling of the necessity of a back-to-nature movement for his generation.[13]

Herder was not interested in politics or particular states, although Prussian militarism and despotism, and imperialistic policies everywhere, repelled him; but in elaborating a philosophy of nationality and national differences he was led to the consideration of political as well as cultural aspects of the subject. Like the other men of the Age of Enlightenment, he regarded the purpose of history as the development of humanity. "In all states, in all societies, man had nothing in view, and could aim at nothing else, but humanity, whatever may have been the ideas he formed of it." But the advancement of humanity necessitates the grouping of human beings who singly could not develop their highest virtues and talents, by which humanity is served. The group for this purpose, declared Herder, is the nationality, and the perfection of the national group is the means of attaining perfection of the individual and of humanity at large. On the other hand, he held that each nationality was an individual organic unit, and that the development of its individuality was an end in itself. Moreover, as in the case of all organisms, national groups grow, mature, and decay after making their contribution to civilization. Each national organism possesses inherently a soul which is its creative and regulative power, "the mother of all culture upon the Earth." And the individuality of each national group expresses itself in its language, literature, religion, custom, art, science, law, which together make up the sum of its peculiar culture.

In his explanation of the origin of the different national cultures, Herder rejects the theory of the multiple origin of races, contending that man constitutes a single species throughout the earth, and that

[13] Ergang, *op. cit.*, pp. 57-58, 60. The most systematic presentation of Herder's views is to be found in *Ideen zur Philosophie der Geschichte der Menscheit* (1784). English translation under the title *Outlines of a Philosophy of the History of Man*, 2 vols. (London, 1803). The work was never completed, but it contains the complete expression of his philosophy of history.

nationalities are all "branches from one stem" and "plants from one primitive nursery." Their differentiation and development of peculiar qualities are due chiefly to the physical environment. "As every region of the earth has its peculiar species of animals which cannot live elsewhere, and consequently must have been born in it, why should it not have its own kind of men?" As for the members of a national group, "the constitution of their body, their way of life, and the pleasure and occupations to which they have been accustomed from their infancy, and the whole circle of their ideas are climatic. Deprive them of their country and you deprive them of everything. Had the power which constructed our earth given its mountains and seas a different form; had that great destiny which established the boundaries of nationalities caused them to originate elsewhere than from the Asiatic mountains; had the eastern part of Asia possessed an earlier commerce and a Mediterranean Sea which its present situation has denied; the whole current of culture would have been altered. For on the whole earth nature has effected more permanent differences by mountains than by any other means. Here nature sitting upon her eternal throne sends out rivers and storms, and distributes the inclinations and often the destiny of nationalities in the same manner as the climate." [14]

Other factors contributing to the moulding of nationalities, in Herder's opinion, were education, intercourse or non-intercourse with other national groups, tradition, and heredity. As regards non-intercourse, Herder wrote: "A secluded national group which lives far from the sea-coast and is separated from intercourse with other national groups by mountains, a nationality which derived its knowledge from a single place . . . may acquire great peculiarity of character and retain it long; but this continued peculiarity will be far from giving it that useful versatility which can be gained only by active competition with other nationalities." Herder does not attribute everything in connection with the development of nationality to environmental influences. In time as a result of the play of numerous forces upon the national soul the individuals of a nationality acquire a particular stamp which is passed on to future generations. So deep is this stamp, indeed, that it will remain even after the members of a nationality have lived for several generations in another environment. "The climate," says Herder,

[14] Translations from the *Ideen* as given in Ergang, *op. cit.*, pp. 90, 92. By permission of Columbia University Press.

"stamps on each its mark or spreads over it a slight veil, but not sufficient to destroy the original national character."

Herder had no patience with the views of cosmopolitanism held by many men of the Enlightenment, and one can appreciate that his conception of nationality made such an ideal empty and meaningless if not actually iniquitous. In ironic vein, he remarked: "All national characters, thank God, have become extinct! We all love one another or, rather, no one feels the need of loving anyone else. We associate with one another, are all completely equal-cultured, polite, very happy! We have, it is true, no fatherland, no one for whom we live; but we are philanthropists and citizens of the world." [15] To attempt to merge the peoples of the world into a single unit was, from Herder's point of view, an unwise interference with Nature.

Nationality, according to Herder, was a product of Nature, but the members of a national group should not accept passively what Nature has given. Moreover, he declared that most nationalities were "still in their childhood" and had great potential energies which, however, might lie dormant if not released. The duty of the individuals within a national group, therefore, was to cultivate the peculiar genius of the group and to avoid cramping its development with artificial rules and regulations. Nor should they seek to imitate other nationalities, either ancient or modern, for this would likewise be contrary to Nature and would prevent true progress. This was general counsel to all nationalities, but Herder felt that the Germans of his time were especially in need of the admonition, for they had been conspicuously guilty of sins both of omission and commission with respect to their nationality, and he wanted them to become conscious of the dignity of their own heritage. To that end, he urged educational reform, including the substitution of the teaching of German for Latin and French and the placing of a much greater emphasis on the study of German history. The German people must also steep themselves in native poetry, literature, folksongs, and folk-ways, and cultivate everything found to be typically German.[16] But Herder did not seek to stimulate a narrow arrogant spirit of superiority among Germans. Nationalities, the German included, were different, individual. Each could make its contribution to

[15] Ergang, *op. cit.*, p. 96. By permission of Columbia University Press.

[16] C. J. H. Hayes, *Historical Evolution of Modern Nationalism* (New York, 1931), pp. 31-32. Ergang, *op. cit.*, Ch. IV.

humanity by cultivating its particular genius. But there was nothing in Herder's thought that suggested the singling out of a particular nationality as superior to all the rest.

If nationalities are natural organisms, and if their development is to be encouraged, may this not be best achieved and their potentialities best realized by their attainment of statehood? As one might surmise, Herder gives an affirmative answer: "The most natural state is *one* nationality with one national character. This it retains for ages, and this is most naturally formed when it is the object of its native princes; for a nationality is as much a plant of nature as a family, only with more branches. Nothing therefore appears so indirectly opposite to the end of government as the unnatural enlargement of states, the wild mixings of all kinds of people and nationalities under one scepter. The human scepter is far too weak and slender for such incongruous parts to be engrafted upon it. Glued together indeed they may be into a fragile machine, termed a machine of state, but it will be destitute of inner life and mutual sympathy of the parts . . . the very politics which produced them are those that play with men and nationalities as with inanimate substances. But history sufficiently shows that these instruments of human pride are formed of clay, and, like all other clay, will crumble to pieces or dissolve." [17] Herder, therefore, vigorously denounced imperialism and wars of conquest. It was unnatural to form an empire by forcing together a number of nationalities and provinces, and the product was not a body politic but a monstrosity. Thus, although Herder did not go so far as to declare that all nationalities should be granted the right to determine their own political destiny, his thought clearly pointed in that direction.

Johann Fichte (1762-1814), another German philosopher of the revolutionary period and sympathetic with much of the thought of the Enlightenment was, like Herder, more interested in the cultural than the political aspects of nationalism. Prior to the disastrous battles of Jena and Auerstadt and the French occupation of Prussia, he held cosmopolitan views, regarding Europe as the fatherland of the truly cultured European and advising his countrymen that one "need not fret about the fortunes of particular states." [18] The following year, however,

[17] Ergang, *op. cit.*, pp. 243-244. By permission of Columbia University Press.
[18] G. P. Gooch, *Nationalism* (London, 1920), p. 14.

he delivered a series of *Addresses to the German Nation*[19] in the Academy building in Berlin, designed to arouse Germans to the spiritual perils threatening their nationality and to galvanize them into action to combat foreign influences. Although Fichte suggested only the use of spiritual weapons[20] to stem a spiritual invasion rather than arms to repel the physical invasion, his addresses had the effect of arousing a will to resistance which expressed itself in the War of Liberation of 1813-1815.

Fichte's views on nationality and the national state can, however, not be fully understood without attention to an earlier work written during the pre-Napoleonic phase of the French Revolution when its idealism was less alloyed and its aggressiveness less pronounced. In *The Closed Commercial State,*[21] Fichte worked out a system in which the national state was the unit of economic life, and regulated minutely the work and wages of producers and distributors. His inspiration was perhaps, in part at least, derived from France under the Jacobin régime, when an attempt was made to realize economic self-sufficiency by a system of state control of industry and trade.[22] The state visualized by Fichte was a natural unit in that it was sufficiently extensive to be economically self-sufficing. In its commercial policy, it was to steer clear of mercantilism on the one hand and free trade on the other. For mercantilism led to international rivalry and wars, and free trade led to the exploitation of the individual. Moreover, the idea of international free trade, in Fichte's opinion, was out of date. The national state, with its separate government and national system of law, should likewise be economically independent of other countries and should close its frontiers to their commerce, or at least to everything that could be produced within its own borders.

In his *Reden,*[23] delivered several years later and with the German nationality (there was no unified German national state) in mind, he adheres to the same view. The German, he says, does not need to trade outside Germany. "The abundant supplies of his own land, together with his own diligence, afford him all that is needed in the life of a civilized

[19] *Reden an die Deutsche Nation* (Berlin, 1808). Translation by R. F. Jones and G. H. Trumbull under the title *Addresses to the German Nation* (Chicago and London, 1922.) Copyrighted by the Open Court Publishing Company.

[20] *Addresses to the German Nation,* p. 227.

[21] A translation of *Der Geschlossene Handelstaat* (Tübingen, 1800).

[22] Hayes, *op. cit.,* pp. 263-264.

[23] P. 203.

man; nor does he lack skill in the art of making his resources serve that purpose. As for acquiring the only true advantage that world-trade brings in its train, viz., the increase of scientific knowledge of the earth and its inhabitants, his own scientific spirit will not let him lack a means of exchange." Fichte, however, did not propose in either of these works to eliminate foreign intellectual contacts. In the work of 1800, he was favorable to foreign travel, but proposed that it should have government authorization and should be restricted to members of the intellectual class; in the *Reden*,[24] he admits that "an interaction of culture and education" may be of benefit to the individual as long as his own national individuality is not submerged by it. And finally Fichte's closed commercial state would not need a large military establishment for commercial rivalry with other states, the main cause of war, would disappear with the abandonment of world commerce. And freed from the demands and distractions of war, the people would be able to develop their individual capacities and their culture.

Although the *Reden* were animated by a single practical purpose, and were exclusively for German consumption at the time they were delivered, they nevertheless reveal more fully than anything else Fichte's conception of nationality. In contrast with his position in *The Closed Commercial State,* in which he indicated that nature determined the boundaries of national states by reference to their needs for economic self-sufficiency, he held that a people's habitat was a result rather than the cause of its essential character. The factor of outstanding importance to Fichte was language. "Men," he declared, "are formed by language far more than language is formed by men." [25] And, referring to these matters in one of his last addresses, he elaborated his thought as follows: "To begin with and before all things: the first, original, and truly natural boundaries of States are beyond doubt their internal boundaries. Those who speak the same language are joined to each other by a multitude of invisible bonds by nature herself, long before any human art begins; they understand each other and have the power of continuing to make themselves understood more and more clearly; they belong together and are by nature one and an inseparable whole. Such a whole, if it wishes to absorb and mingle with itself any other people of different descent and language, cannot do so without becoming

[24] P. 206.
[25] *Op. cit.,* p. 46.

confused, in the beginning, at any rate, and violently disturbing the even progress of its culture. From this internal boundary, which is drawn by the spiritual nature of man himself, the marking of the external boundary by dwelling-place results as a consequence; and in the natural view of things it is not because men dwell between certain mountains and rivers that they are a people, but, on the contrary, men dwell together—and, if their luck has so arranged it, are protected by rivers and mountains—because they were a people already by a law of nature which is much higher." [26]

There was no exaltation of the state in Fichte's writings. The nationality is the supremely important entity, the state merely furnishing the necessary conditions of peace and security to the end that the nationality may realize its fullest possibilities. ". . . the State, merely as the government of human life in its progress along the ordinary peaceful path, is not something which is primary and which exists for its own sake, but is merely the means to the higher purpose of the eternal, regular, and continuous development of what is purely human in this nation." [27] Like Herder, Fichte thought of each nationality as developing and making its peculiar contribution in accordance with, and as a part of, a divine plan unfolding through the ages.

Although Fichte was interested in the state only as a means, he was not indifferent to the danger that its power might be used to thwart rather than encourage the development of nationality, and this was apparently what he feared and expected from an alien rule. Referring to those persons who had expressed the opinion, before and after the French occupation, that even if the Germans should lose their political independence they would still retain their language and literature and therefore always remain a "nation," he declared them "vain comforters." Upon what did they base their hopes? "Those men now living and mature, who have accustomed themselves to speaking, writing, and reading in the German language, will no doubt go on doing so; but what will the next generation do, and, more important still, the third generation? What counterpoise do we propose to place in the hearts of these generations that will hold the scale against their desire to please, by speech and writing, the race with which all glory rests and which has

[26] Reden, p. 198.

[27] *Ibid.*, p. 123. Fichte does not make a distinction between state and government.

all favors to distribute?" But even if German language and literature should survive the loss of political independence, what sort of literature could it be? A writer with any depth or worth desires to influence public life and the life of the people. "He can, therefore, only write in a language in which the governors think, in a language in which the work of government is carried on, in the language of a people that forms an independent State." [28]

Fichte asserted that "wherever a separate language is found, there a separate nation exists," and that such a nation has the right to set up a government of its own and lead an independent existence. He was thus in agreement with Herder on the question of the right of national self-determination, although they differed on the relative emphasis placed on physical environment and language in the formation of nationalities. Fichte also expressed the opinion that when a people had lost its independence it was then its duty to give up its language and allow itself to be assimilated by its conquerors in order that unity and peace might be attained.[29]

In the meantime, while philosophers speculated on the nature and political implications of nations and nationalities, a decision was reached on the battlefields of Europe, and in 1814-1815 the Congress of Vienna met to undo the work of Napoleon and to restore, as far as expedient, the situation in Europe as it was in 1789. It did not entirely ignore nationality [30] in the settlement, but the principle of legitimacy rather than that of nationality was in general followed in the redistribution of territory, in so far as the restoration of thrones and territories was compatible with certain other aims. These were to punish revolutionary France and those states that had been friendly to her, and to reward those that had joined the coalition against her. Moreover, the settle-

[28] *Ibid.*, p. 190.

[29] *Ibid.*, p. 191. This was certainly what Fichte hoped the Germans would not do. The logical alternative, then, was armed resistance. It must be remembered, however, that he was delivering his addresses in a city garrisoned by the French invaders and that to counsel resort to armed force might not have been accepted by the French with the same indifference that they showed toward his exhortation to Germans to resist them with spiritual weapons. In any case, a number of internal reforms, which would take time, were necessary before armed resistance would have a prospect of success.

[30] For example, the greater part of the Grand Duchy of Warsaw, although being transferred to Russia, was recognized as a constitutional kingdom united with Russia through the common sovereignty of the Tsar who was to rule as a "limited" monarch. The hope that it might continue to exist as a national entity and serve as a buffer state was blasted by the extension of Russian autocratic rule over it.

ment was designed to reestablish a European equilibrium, and this entailed allocations of territory quite regardless of the wishes of the people inhabiting it.

Perhaps the most flagrant disregard of nationality occurred in the Italian settlement. Italy became once more a "geographic expression." The despotic rulers of the various states and duchies existing in 1789 were restored to their thrones. The Pope was restored to rule over the States of the Church; the grand duchy of Tuscany, and the duchies of Parmia and Modena were reestablished; in the south, the Kingdom of the two Sicilies was restored; in the north, an enlarged Sardinian Kingdom was established; and finally Lombardy-Venetia was given to Austria. The latter was also given a general oversight in Italian affairs, and set herself to prevent the growth of liberal ideas.[31] But French revolutionary doctrines of liberty and equality had gained a foothold during the Napoleonic régime; and most of the peninsula had experienced a unified administration, so that in spite of all efforts to stamp it out, a movement for a united Italy grew up.

The most eloquent advocate of the unification of Italy was Giuseppe Mazzini (1805-1872), and it was he who supplied the movement with a supporting theory.[32] Steeped in the philosophy and literature of the French Revolution and of medieval Italy, he began to wear mourning for his "enslaved" country at the age of twenty-two and dedicated his life to her freedom. In 1830 he founded Young Italy, an organization of Italian intellectuals under forty years of age pledged to work for the liberation of Italy from foreign and domestic tyrants and to establish a unified Italian Republic.[33] He was opposed to the establishment of an Italian monarchy, believing that it would be conservative and back-

[31] Thus the Emperor of Austria instructed the professors of the University of Pavia (in Lombardy) as follows: "Your duty is less to make learned men than faithful subjects." H. Rose, *Nationality in Modern History* (New York, 1916), p. 76.

[32] Pasquale Stanislao Mancini (1817-1888), Italian jurist and statesman, must also be mentioned. In his inaugural lecture as professor of international law at the University of Turin on Jan. 22, 1851, "Della Nazionalita come fondamento del diritto delle genti," he developed his concept of nations as a natural society of men bound together by a common history, customs, and language and possessing territorial unity. Such a community, having consciousness of moral unity, has the right to form a state. Like Mazzini, he advocated Italian independence on the basis of the existence of an Italian nation or nationality.

[33] Mazzini later founded Young Europe for those who believed in the establishment of the principles of liberty, equality, and fraternity everywhere, and special associations for various nationalities such as the Poles, Hungarians, and Irish who desired freedom.

ward, and therefore would stand in the way of the accomplishment of Italy's mission. Moreover, Italy had in the past realized her greatest achievements under republican régimes, which seemed best fitted to the Italian genius.[34]

Mazzini has been called the exponent of "cosmopolitan nationalism." The ultimate goal of all his teaching was the service of humanity. Nations were but the necessary means for the attainment of the higher ends of humanity. "You are men before you are citizens or fathers," he declared to his countrymen, and he insisted that their first duties were to humanity. "Ask yourselves whenever you do an action in the sphere of your Country or your family, *if what I am doing were done by all and for all, would it advantage or injure Humanity?* and if your conscience answers, *It would injure Humanity,* desist; desist, even if it seem to you that an immediate advantage for your Country or your family would ensue from your action. Be apostles of this faith, apostles of the brotherhood of nations, and of the unity of the human race—a principle admitted today in theory, but denied in practice."[35] But nations are necessary, for each isolated person could do very little for humanity; he is too weak and humanity is too vast. Association, therefore, is necessary.

What is to determine the character and limits of this association? At this point, Mazzini gives his conception of nationality. God originally divided Humanity into distinct groups in different parts of the world, and so planted the seeds of nations. The lines in his design were clearly marked out, for Europe at least, by rivers, mountains, and other geographical features. But conquest and greed mutilated it in time so that it has remained undisturbed in only a few places. Nevertheless, Mazzini believed it would be restored. "Natural divisions, the innate spontaneous tendencies of the peoples will replace the arbitrary divisions sanctioned by bad governments, the map of Europe will be remade."[36] As for Italy, Nature had given her more clearly-defined boundaries than was true of any other country in Europe. On one side were the Alps, on the other the sea. But to Mazzini the final test of nationality was apparently not geography, after all, but language. In

[34] Rose, *op. cit.*, p. 79.

[35] *The Duties of Man and Other Essays,* tr. by Ella Noyes (London, 1907), pp. 49-50, Everyman's Library series. The first four chapters under the title of "The Duties of Man" appeared in 1844, the remaining eight in 1858.

[36] *Ibid.*, p. 52.

describing the God-given boundaries of Italy, he says: "As far as this frontier your language is spoken and understood, beyond this you have no rights"; and ". . . you should have no joy or repose as long as a portion of the territory upon which your language is spoken is separated from the Nation." [37]

That nationalities, wherever existent, must attain statehood and form a brotherhood of free peoples in order to contribute to human progress, was a cardinal tenet of Mazzini. Every nationality had a mission. He was, of course, primarily interested in that of Italy, which was to lead the nations with the banner of Liberty and Association to a new realization of unity.[38] Italy was not to be content merely to seek internal reforms: "Do you answer that it is enough for you to organize better the government and the social conditions of your own country? It is not enough. No people lives today exclusively on its own produce; you live by exchange, by importation and exportation. An impoverished foreign nation, in which the number of consumers diminishes, is one market the less for you. A foreign commerce upon which a bad administration brings crises or ruin, produces crises or ruin in yours. The failures of England and America bring about Italian failures." [39] The failure to recognize this economic interdependence, and the "stupid presumption" of nations that they were capable of solving independently their political, social, and economic problems was, in Mazzini's view, fatal to the welfare of all.[40]

Mazzini's central thought was that the way of progress for mankind lay in educating men to a sense of duty to humanity, to their country, to their family, and to themselves. The French Revolution, with its Declaration of the Rights of Man, was stressing a false principle. The single right possessed by man is the right to be unobstructed in the fulfillment of his duties. Upon such a theory, man is enabled to rise up and free himself from obstacles, fight for the freedom of his nationality to determine its own way of life. But political systems must be based not upon rights but upon duties. Men must be taught and encouraged to sacrifice rather than acquire. A system of rights leads

[37] *Duties of Man,* pp. 53, 55.

[38] This supreme mission must be Italy's, in Mazzini's belief, for England had become "a land of timid compromise," and France had embraced the erroneous principle of the Rights of Man. Rose, *op. cit.,* pp. 84-5.

[39] *Duties of Man,* p. 49.

[40] Sydney M. Brown, "Mazzini and Dante," *Political Science Quarterly,* XLII (1927), 84. The quotation is from *Foi et Avenir.*

to the conception of politics as a struggle of individuals and classes, each seizing what it can for itself, and disregarding the rights of others. But societies must be based upon duty, in order to have a foundation for orderly and peaceful progress.[41] Thus nationalities have the right to form national states in order to fulfill their duties to humanity. These duties come first, and it is only from them that rights emanate.

John Stuart Mill (1806-1873) discussed nationality in connection with his treatment of representative government, and endorsed, with certain qualifications, the principle of national self-determination.[42] He defined a nationality as "a portion of mankind united . . . by common sympathies which do not exist between them and any others, which make them cooperate with each other more willingly than with other people, desire to be under the same government, and desire that it should be government by themselves, or a portion of themselves exclusively." [43] A number of causes may contribute to the formation of a nationality, such as race, language, religion, and geography, but the strongest of all, Mill declared, is "identity of political antecedents"—the possession of a national history with its accumulation of recollections of a common life and common ideals.

Mill believed that whenever the members of a nationality became strongly conscious of the bonds uniting them and desired to form a government and a state of their own, there was a *prima facie* case for granting them their independence. From the point of view of the functioning of representative government, such a course was desirable, he said, for a state made up of different nationalities, speaking different languages, and with different social and political conceptions, could not provide the foundation for a united public opinion. But without this, representative government, in Mill's opinion, could not exist. His conclusion, therefore, was that in general free institutions require that, as far as possible, the boundaries of states should coincide with those of nationalities. On the other hand, Mill was aware that on account of geographic hindrances, and the intermingling of nationalities in certain parts of Europe, the application of the principle was not always feasible or desirable. For example, he thought it better that the Basques and Bretons should be brought within the current of French nationality, and

[41] *Duties of Man,* pp. 8, 11, 15.
[42] The question is discussed in *Considerations on Representative Government* (London, 1861), Ch. XVI.
[43] *Ibid.,* p. 308.

that the Welsh and Scots should be members of the British "nation," rather than that they should seek a separate political existence. Moreover, he held as a general proposition that "whatever really tends to the admixture of nationalities, and the blending of their attributes and peculiarities in a common union, is a benefit to the human race."

Ernest Renan (1823-1892), in a brilliant analysis of what constitutes a nation,[44] went more deeply into the subject than Mill and rejected all of the external criteria advanced by previous writers as determinants of nationality. The tendency of some to confound nationality with race was shown to be an error, Renan pointing out that none of the nations of Europe is inhabited by a pure race but that their inhabitants are made up of a mixture of races. Nor did he find the objective test of language satisfactory. He observed that different nations, such as England and the United States, speak the same language and, on the other hand, that in a single nation such as Switzerland three languages are spoken. Likewise nations exist in spite of religious diversity within their boundaries. Admitting that community of economic interests constitutes a powerful bond between men, he declared that common interests are not enough, that "a Zollverein is not a country." That geography has been an influence in forming nations and that natural frontiers have played a part, he likewise admitted. But the doctrine of natural frontiers, he observed, had been arbitrarily used as an excuse for the extension of political boundaries by force, whereas in reality natural features have no necessary relation to the existence of nationalities.

What, then, is a nation? To Renan, it is a soul, a spiritual principle. It is not something which can be improvised. It exists when a people possesses in common a rich legacy of memories, when they desire to live together, and to keep the heritage which they have received. The social capital upon which a national idea is based is a heroic past, great men, glory. The conditions essential to the existence of a nationality, then, are the sharing of common glories and sufferings in the past when great deeds were accomplished together, and the wish to go forward to new achievements. Thus, with Renan, nationality becomes a state of mind developed by a people under favoring conditions rather than something to be determined objectively by the application of tests of race, language, religion, or geography, Logically, then, a nationality

[44] In a discourse at the Sorbonne, March 11, 1882, under the title "Qu'est-ce qu'une nation?," in *Discours et Conférences* (6th ed., Paris, 1919), pp. 277-310.

can only be discovered by consultation of the people to which the issue is presented, rather than by the application of external criteria to them [45]; and such is the position of Renan. Moreover, he held the view that it is never in the true interests of a national state to annex or retain a people against its will, that the single legitimate criterion for the determination of its political destiny should be the wish of the people concerned.[46]

The advocates of the principle of nationality as the basis of statehood were not allowed to win their case by default. They were subjected to searching criticism in the course of the nineteenth century, not only from conservative upholders of imperialism, who saw in the principle of national self-determination a disintegrating force, but from certain liberal and radical quarters as well. John Stuart Mill perhaps expressed the prevailing liberal thought of the century on the subject and, except for the followers of Karl Marx who looked forward to the day when the workers of all nationalities would make common cause against their capitalistic masters, socialist thought in general aligned itself with the liberals who sympathized in principle with all nationalities struggling for freedom and independence. On the other hand, one finds in the French anarchist Pierre-Joseph Proudhon (1809-1865) a scathing critic of the principle of nationality and of the pleas of particular nationalities who were demanding their independence in the 30's and 40's. Proudhon justified the partitions of Poland, denied the validity of the pleas of Italian patriots for a united Italian state, and in general upheld the work of the Congress of Vienna. A lover of liberty, equality, and peace, he supported the treaties of 1815 because they sought to establish a political equilibrium between and within the states of Europe and thus, in his judgment, contributed to the attainment of these far distant goals.[47]

[45] Per contra, German writers, in making a case for the annexation of Alsace in 1870, contended that even though the sentiment of the inhabitants favored France, they were German in origin, character, and language, and thus being of German nationality, they belonged within the German state. W. E. H. Lecky, *Democracy and Liberty* (New York, 1896), I, 477. It may be added that French and Italian writers have also used objective tests of nationality exclusively as justifications for extending the national frontiers.

[46] It may be observed, however, that Renan's definition of a nation (nationality) does not define it, and would leave the door open to any group of people which had "accomplished great things in common" and "felt themselves a nation" to seek statehood. Renan apparently recognizes this, but contents himself with the remark that no principle should be pushed to excess.

[47] *Du Principe Fédératif* (Paris, 1868), pp. 284, 318.

Proudhon's justification of the partitions of Poland and his opposition to the Polish aspiration for independence were based on his belief that peace and social equality and progress were and would continue to be furthered by the incorporation of the Poles in other states. The Polish nobility had been corrupt, devoid of public spirit, arrogant, and oppressive in the days of Poland's independence, and it was still the same. The independence of the Polish nationality, therefore, would result merely in two or three million Polish nobles, who had no sympathy with the democratic and equalitarian aspirations of peoples, once more entrenching themselves in power, exploiting the people, and blocking the paths of social progress. The Polish masses would lose rather than gain by Polish independence, and in any case an attempt to resurrect the Polish state would unleash a war which would retard European progress.[48]

Proudhon's love of liberty and equality, resulting in his dislike for coercive governmental institutions, led him naturally to favor federal as opposed to unitary political systems. He hoped that the growth of great centralized states was merely transitory and that the twentieth century would open the era of federations in which the conditions of social equilibrium would be realized. In so far, therefore, as the proponents of the principle of nationality had in mind a world of unitary states ruled in each case by, and exclusively in the interest of, a particular nationality, Proudhon rebelled against the conception, for the freedom of smaller groups would be sacrificed.[49] Thus he argued against the establishment of a united Italian kingdom principally on the ground that it meant the inclusion in a single centralized state of a number of small states such as the Kingdom of Naples, Sicily, the states of the Church, and Tuscany, as well as the inclusion of members of the Italian race living within the frontiers of Austria, France, and Switzerland.[50] His idea of a federal system was the union of a number of small states, democratically organized under the protection of a federal government which would guarantee order, justice, stability, and peace, but would not absorb the liberties of any of the groups within it. Nation-

[48] *Du Principe Fédératif*, pp. 286-314; C. Bougle, *La Sociologie de Proudhon* (Paris, 1911), pp. 249-251.

[49] "Je m'incline devant le principe de nationalité comme devant celui de la famille: c'est justement pour cela que je proteste contre les grandes unités politiques qui ne me paraissent être autre chose que des confiscations de nationalités." (As quoted in Bougle, 253.)

[50] *Op. cit.*, pp. 282-285.

alities, as well as other groups would find freedom and security in such political systems.[51]

Another French critic of the principle of nationality was the philosopher Charles Bernard Renouvier (1815-1903). Like Proudhon, he was a strong believer in individual liberty, which he placed above the ideal of national unity. And for reasons similar to those that caused Proudhon to advocate federal political systems Renouvier opposed the centralized state and supported the idea of the existence of various forms of autonomous groups within it. He regarded the conception of nationality as not only mischievous but historically false. War and the events of history, he asserted, had long since destroyed the small natural groups of antiquity based on intimate ties of kinship, religion, language, and customs. In the modern national states, characterized by intellectual and physical diversity and by various moral aptitudes on the part of the groups composing them, a higher civilization is possible than formerly. Men of all races, languages, and beliefs with common ideas of justice may be embraced within them under the social contract.[52] All that is essential for the foundation of the rational state is morality and right. The things that all the citizens have in common should be the common concern, differences of belief and custom, on the other hand, should be respected by all.

Renouvier denied the claims of nationalities, therefore, to a separate political existence except in the most flagrant cases of prolonged oppression and where historical, geographical and other conditions clearly justify separation. Thus a nationality as defined by Mill, and which, according to him, would *ipso facto* have a *prima facie* case for independence, would, according to Renouvier, have no such claim. A heavy burden of proof, on the other hand, would have to be borne by it before it should receive consideration. In all doubtful cases, he held, the superiority of the principle of the state over that of nation-

[51] *Ibid.*, pp. 237-242. See also René Johannet, *op. cit.*, pp. 263-276, for interpretation and discussion of Proudhon's views on the subject of nationality.

[52] Renouvier recognized the Social Contract theory as a fiction, but a fiction that "has its real counterpart in the nature of things. The theoretical assumption of a contract anterior to any particular convention is a form given to the two-fold principle, both of the free and reasoned consent given by the individual to the society in which circumstances have placed him, and of his duty to respect its laws, under condition of his liberty being guaranteed within limits." *Philosophie Analytique, III*, p. 635, as quoted in Roger Soltau, *French Political Thought in the Nineteenth Century* (New Haven, Conn., 1931), p. 309.

ality should be recognized. In cases of injustice and oppression, normally every effort should be made to reform the state to the end of securing justice within it, rather than unchain a war with all its evils. Moreover, whether a state may have had its origin in injustice or not, if it has been long established and ties have been formed, associations established, and implicit consent given, it has a higher claim than that of the nationality that would break away from it.[53]

Another vigorous attack upon the doctrine of nationality by a liberal was made by the English historian, Lord Acton (1834-1902).[54] A witness of the revolutionary uprisings of 1848 and of the nationalist movement in Italy and Central Europe, his reactions to the doctrine of nationality were quite different from those of his contemporary, John Stuart Mill. Both men were liberals, but the liberalism of Mill led him to support the theory of nationality on the grounds of human liberty. Acton, on the other hand, saw a new absolutism inherent in the doctrine. For the theory of nationality demands for the nation, says Acton, the subordination of all other interests and traditional rights and requires the establishment of a uniformity of institutions for all groups within it. "It overrules the rights and wishes of the inhabitants, absorbing their divergent interests in a fictitious unity; sacrifices their several inclinations and duties to the higher claim of nationality, and crushes all natural rights and all established liberties for the purpose of vindicating itself. Whenever a single definite object is made the supreme end of the State, be it the advantage of a class, the safety or the power of the country, the greatest happiness of the greatest number, or the support of any speculative idea, the State becomes for the time inevitably absolute. Liberty alone demands for its realization the limitation of the public authority, for liberty is the only object which benefits all alike, and provokes no sincere opposition." [55]

Acton contended, on the other hand, that States such as the British and Austro-Hungarian Empires furnished the best conditions for political diversity and freedom. In his opinion, the presence of several nations with their varying customs within a state constituted "a firm

[53] C. B. Renouvier, *Science de la Morale,* 2 vols. (Paris, 1908), II, 238-292; *La Critique Philosophique,* 2 vols. (Paris, 1872-1873), II, 81-89.

[54] John Emerich Edward Dalberg-Acton, *The History of Freedom and Other Essays* (London, 1909), Essay IX on "Nationality," pp. 270-300; originally appeared in *Home and Foreign Review,* July, 1862.

[55] *Ibid.*, p. 288. Excerpt quoted by permission of The Macmillan Company, publishers.

barrier against the invasion of the government beyond the political sphere which is common to all into the social department which escapes legislation and is ruled by spontaneous laws." Moreover, he declared that inferior races were benefited by their inclusion within a state having intellectually superior peoples, and that nations in the stage of decay were revitalized by contact with a more vigorous race. But the process of fertilization and regeneration could take place only within the bounds of a single state.

To make the boundaries of states and nationalities coequal was to insure stagnation and deterioration such as happens to men who cut themselves off from contact with their fellows. Acton assumed, however, that in such states there might still be minor nationalities whose lot would inevitably be an unhappy one. For, he declared, "The greatest adversary of the rights of nationality is the modern theory of nationality. By making the state and the nation commensurate with each other in theory, it reduces practically to a subject condition all other nationalities that may be within the boundary. It cannot admit them to an equality with the ruling nation which constitutes the State, because the State would then cease to be national, which would be a contradiction of the principle of its existence. According, therefore, to the degree of humanity and civilization in that dominant body which claims all the rights of the community, the inferior races are exterminated, or reduced to servitude, or outlawed, or put in a condition of dependence." [56]

Another critic of the doctrine of nationality, W. E. H. Lecky (1838-1903), the Irish historian, regarded it as in general a disintegrating force.[57] He admitted that in so far as it called for government to be

[56] *Ibid.*, pp. 297-8. Excerpt quoted by permission of The Macmillan Company, publishers. The theory of nationality as developed by J. W. Burgess (1844-1931), the American historian and political scientist, may be cited as containing the very implications so obnoxious to Acton. Burgess, however, arrives at his conclusions on the basis of his theory of the superior political capacity of some nations and the lack of political genius of others. Those lacking political capacity may properly be attached to and subjugated by the superior nations, who may, if they find it expedient, stamp out the language, literature, religion, and customs of the nationalities subject to them. And sound policy, Burgess thought, would dictate that the state containing several nationalities should seek to "develop ethnical homogeneity," language uniformity, and homogeneous institutions and laws. *Political Science and Constitutional Law,* 2 vols. (Boston, 1890), Vol. I, Chs. I-IV.

[57] See *Democracy and Liberty,* 2 vols. (Longmans, Green & Co., publishers. New York, 1896), Vol. I, Ch. V, for his discussion of nationality.

based upon the free consent of the great masses of the world's population, it made for peace and justice, and that in so far as it repudiated the wanton extinction of a nation or its oppression by another it was a sign of moral progress; but it had been used for less worthy and even dangerous designs. On the one hand, it had been utilized by rulers bent on conquest to furnish the justification for their annexations, and on the other it had been used by revolutionists to justify rebellion within states. Lecky disliked and distrusted democracy in general, and he regarded the advocates of the doctrine of nationality as disturbers of peace "by deliberately kindling democratic, socialist, or nationalist risings." Moreover, he declared that it was difficult to discover the true opinion of an alleged nationality, the consultation of the members of the community not being satisfactory. "A plebiscite is very rarely the unforced, spontaneous expression of a genuine national desire. It is usually taken to ratify or indemnify an accomplished fact. It is taken only when there is no doubt about the result, and a strong centralized Government has, on such occasions, an enormous power of organizing and directing. In all countries a great portion, in most countries a large majority, of the people take no real interest in political affairs, and if a great constitutional or dynastic question is submitted to their vote by a strongly organized Government, this Government will have no difficulty in dictating the response." [58]

To recognize the validity of the principle of nationality, according to Lecky, was to endanger the entire public order of Europe; for practically all countries, including Switzerland, Belgium, and the Austro-Hungarian Empire, contained districts with distinct racial and religious elements and thus had the materials with which a separatist agitation might be kindled and the dissolution of the state threatened. A state should not be exposed to the dangers of disintegration involved in the doctrine that nationalities should be free at any time to sever their connection with the state of which they are a part. "As in marriage the conviction that the tie is a life tie, being supported by all the weight of law and opinion, is sufficient in the vast majority of cases to counteract the force of caprice or temporary disagreement, and produce acquiescence and content, so, in the political world, the belief in the sovereign authority of the State, and in the indissoluble character of national bonds, gives stability and unity to a nation. Divorce in fam-

[58] *Democracy and Liberty*, p. 480.

ilies, and revolution in States, may sometimes be necessary, and even desirable, but only under very grave and exceptional circumstances."[59] Empires must, therefore, for the sake of their own preservation refuse to tolerate secessionist movements within their territories, meeting the wishes of localities, as far as possible, by varying political institutions and laws. On a final analysis, Acton and Lecky are found to be substantially in accord in their attack on the principle of nationality and on the doctrine of national self-determination. Lecky, however, writing more than three decades after Acton,[60] had more abundant historical material in the national developments of the later period upon which to base his observations and opinions.

Johann Kaspar Bluntschli (1808-1881), Swiss-German jurist and political theorist, gave a qualified endorsement of the principle of nationality. He asserted that nationalities have a natural right to the use of their language and literature and that States have a duty even to promote the use of the languages of their nationalities "so far as the general interests of civilization are not injured thereby."[61] Likewise, a nationality has the right to its own customs provided they are not injurious to the State or to society. On the other hand, the unity and harmony of the State demand that its legal institutions take precedence over those of its nationalities. In principle, therefore, Bluntschli held that "differences of nationality must give way before the unity and equality of law and justice."[62] The assumption so far is that nationalities develop their cultural life within multi-national states. Bluntschli in fact held that "a national State may embrace various nationalities, and even a State which is distinctively based on nationality may gain in breadth and variety by the inclusion of foreign elements, which serve to establish and keep open communication with the civilization of other peoples."[63] It is natural, however, for well-developed self-conscious nationalities, said Bluntschli, to seek the full expression of their personality in a State of their own. Can the principle of "a State for each People" be justified? Bluntschli's conclusions were that "not every people is capable of creating and maintaining a

[59] *Ibid.*, p. 482.

[60] Acton wrote his *Essay on Nationality* in 1862; Lecky published *Democracy and Liberty* in 1896.

[61] *The Theory of the State* (3rd ed., Oxford, 1895), p. 94. But the State may find it advisable to select one language exclusively for State purposes. (*Ibid.*)

[62] *Ibid.*, p. 95.

[63] *Ibid.*, p. 105.

State, and only a people of political capacity can claim to become an independent nation. The incapable need the guidance of other and more gifted nations; the weak must combine with others or submit to the protection of stronger powers. . . Strictly speaking only those peoples in which the manly qualities, understanding and courage, predominate are fully capable of creating and maintaining a national State. Peoples of more feminine characteristics are, in the end, always governed by other and superior forces." [64] Who, then, shall decide whether a particular nationality has the necessary capacity to form a state? In the existing state of international law, said Bluntschli, the decision cannot be made by human judgment. In the last analysis, the strength of the aspiring nationality will be the criterion: "As a rule it is only by great struggles, by its own sufferings and its own acts, that a nation can justify its claim." [65] Finally, it should be observed that Bluntschli sounded a note against the view that nationality should be regarded as the highest limit of political development. Humanity should be placed first in the scale of values. Therefore, the establishment and competition of nationalities, itself necessary for the development of humanity, must be followed by the combination of the various organized peoples in a higher unity under law.[66]

REFERENCES

Acton, J. E. E. Dalberg-, *The History of Freedom and Other Essays* (London, 1909), Essay on "Nationality," pp. 270-300.

Aulard, A., *Le Patriotisme Français de la Renaissance à la Révolution* (Paris, 1921).

Barlow, Joel, "A Letter to the People of Piedmont on the Advantages of the French Revolution," *Political Writings* (2nd ed., New York, 1795).

Bluntschli, J. K., *Theory of the State,* tr. by Ritchie, Matheson, and Lodge (2nd ed., Oxford, 1892), Bk. II, Chs. I-IV.

Brown, S. M., "Mazzini and Dante," *Political Science Quarterly,* XLII (1927), 77-98.

Burgess, J. W., *Political Science and Comparative Constitutional Law,* 2 vols. (Boston and London, 1890-1891), Vol. I, Chs. I-IV.

Dewey, John, *German Philosophy and Politics* (New York, 1915).

[64] *Ibid.*, p. 103.
[65] *Ibid.*, p. 106.
[66] *Ibid.*, p. 105.

Dunning, W. A., *A History of Political Theories from Rousseau to Spencer* (New York, 1920), Ch. VIII.

Ergang, R. R., *Herder and the Foundations of German Nationalism* (New York, 1931).

Fichte, J. G., *Addresses to the German Nation,* translation of *Reden an die Deutsche Nation* (Berlin, 1808) by R. I. Jones and G. H. Turnbull (Chicago and London, 1922).

Gooch, G. P., *Nationalism* (London, 1920), Chs. I-IV.

Hauser, H., *Le Principe des Nationalités, Ses Origines Historiques* (Paris, 1916).

Hayes, C. J. H., *Essays on Nationalism* (New York, 1926), Chs. I, II.

————, *Historical Evolution of Modern Nationalism* (New York, 1931).

Hegel, G. W., *Philosophy of History,* tr. by J. Sibree (London, 1857).

Holcombe, A. N., *The Foundations of the Modern Commonwealth* (New York and London, 1923), Ch. IV.

Holtzendorff, Franz von, "Le Principe des Nationalités et la Littérature Italienne du Droit des Gens," *Revue de Droit International et de Législation Comparée,* II (1870).

Johannet, René, *Le Principe des Nationalités* (2nd ed., Paris, 1923).

Lecky, W. E. H., *Democracy and Liberty,* 2 vols. (New York, 1896), Vol. I, Ch. V.

Lieber, F., *Fragments of Political Science on Nationalism and Internationalism* (New York, 1868).

MacIver, R. M., *The Modern State* (Oxford, 1926), pp. 121-133.

Mancini, P. S., *Della Nazionalità come Fondamento del Diritto del Genti* (Turin, 1851).

Marvin, F. S., ed., *The Evolution of World Peace* (London, 1921), Essays VI, VII, VIII.

Mazzini, Giuseppe, *The Duties of Man and Other Essays* (London, 1912). Everyman's Library series.

Mill, John Stuart, *Considerations on Representative Government* (London, 1861).

Nys, E., *Le Droit International,* 2 vols. (Paris, 1912), Vol. I, Sec. II, Ch. II.

Pi y Margall, F., *Las Nacionalidades* (Madrid, 1882).

Redslob, R., *Histoire des Grand Principes du Droit des Gens* (Paris, 1923), pp. 415-423.

————, *Le Principe des Nationalités* (Paris, 1930).

Reisner, E. H., *Nationalism and Education Since 1789* (New York, 1922).

Renan, Ernest, *Discours et Conférences* (6th ed., Paris, 1919), pp. 277-310.

Rose, J. H., *Nationality in Modern History* (New York, 1916).

Savigny, F. C. von, *System of the Modern Roman Law,* tr. from German by William Holloway (Madras, 1867), Secs. VII-X.

Stawell, F. M., *Growth of International Thought* (London, 1929), pp. 225-232.

Stocks, J. L., *Patriotism and the Super State* (London and New York, 1920), Sec. II on "Nationalism."

Wambaugh, Sarah, *A Monograph on Plebiscites* (New York, 1920).

Wittmann, E., *Past and Future of the Right of Self-Determination* (Amsterdam, 1919), Ch. II.

CHAPTER XII

THE NINETEENTH CENTURY: WAR AND PROGRESS

THE typical philosophers of the Enlightenment, it will be recalled, were thoroughly imbued with the belief that man by taking thought could add many cubits to his moral stature, and by discovering and following natural laws through the process of reason could capture the secrets of social progress, and ultimately reach perfectibility. In their view, man had his social destiny largely in his own hands, neither being the victim of blind chance nor an automaton having his course irrevocably determined for him in accordance with a divine Plan beyond his understanding and not subject to his will.[1] In the nineteenth century, partly due to the reaction against the philosophy of the Enlightenment, but chiefly to the rise of the science of biology, progress came to be regarded in many quarters as a phenomenon largely if not entirely beyond the control of man's will. It was determined by Nature, not nurture, and came about automatically and inevitably as a result of the human struggle for existence and the elimination of the unfit. Thus it had its foundation in conflict rather than in cooperation.

The idea of strife and conflict as a vital part of the eternal scheme of things was nothing new. The early Greek thinkers recognized struggle as a universal phenomenon in animate nature, and Empedocles anticipated, however crudely, the theory of evolution through the "survival of the fittest" as early as the fifth century B.C. In ancient India, as we have seen, the idea of the state as an organism, which grows, struggles with like organisms, and in due course declines, was conceived long before the Christian era. Struggle also figured prominently in many of the ancient religions. The conception of a dualism of good and evil forces in perpetual conflict with each other was basic in Christian theology, and became embedded in the thought of medieval Christendom. But until the late eighteenth century, and more particularly the

[1] The Physiocrats and classical economists as a class must be excepted. For them, progress was determined largely by natural forces, although it might be impeded by the unwise action of men.

first half of the nineteenth century, ideas of universal and eternal conflict connected with evolution were arrived at largely by deductive processes of reasoning or by way of divine revelation. They might not be without benefit of clergy, but they were without benefit of science, at least in the modern experimental sense.

Such was, for example, the view of human history set forth by the German philosopher Georg Wilhelm Friedrich Hegel (1770-1831). Hegel wrote during the period of the reaction from the doctrines of the French Revolution, for which, incidentally, he entertained great enthusiasm in his youth, but prior to the rise of biological science, and its influence on philosophical and historical writings. He succeeded Fichte as professor of philosophy at the University of Berlin, and came to enjoy the doubtful reputation of being the "official philosopher" to the Prussian government whose patronage he enjoyed. To Hegel the state was an individual, a kind of collective person, and an "absolute, fixed end-in-itself" with a single will, and guiding mind. He divided history into different stages in each of which a particular "world people" represents or reflects the "world-spirit" before sinking into decadence and yielding its place to its successor. The relations of states to one another are completely anarchical. The individual will of each state determines its action without the restraints of law or ethical obligation, for the state has no higher duty than to maintain itself. Emphasizing constant change in human affairs and perpetual strife between opposites, he regarded war as inevitable and indeed not unbeneficent. For out of the struggle of nations comes the divine judgment, the selection of the nation which shall give the "universal idea" to mankind. The nation which is defeated shows itself no longer worthy of reflecting the world spirit. Victory and survival in the struggle, therefore, was in the Hegelian philosophy the test of national righteousness. Moreover, Hegel claimed that "through war the ethical health of peoples is preserved as the movement of the winds preserves the seas from the corruption into which they would be brought by a settled calm, and the peoples by a lasting, not to say perpetual peace." [2]

[2] His views on these matters are to be found principally in his *Vorlesungen über die Philosophie der Geschichte* (Berlin, 1837). English translation under the title *Philosophy of History,* by J. Sibree (New York, 1899). See also John Dewey, *German Philosophy and Politics* (New York, 1915), pp. 117-118, and A. C. Armstrong, "Hegel's Attitude on War and Peace," *Journal of Philosophy,* Vol. XXX (Dec. 7, 1933), pp. 684-689.

The views of Hegel and of the power theorists who preceded him were those of historians and philosophers. Was it possible to find a solid scientific foundation for their interpretation of human history? Many nineteenth century political "realists" thought that such a scientific sanction was furnished by Charles Darwin (1809-1882) in his *Origin of Species by Means of Natural Selection* (1859), in which he set forth a complete theory of the evolution of plant and animal life.[3] His concept of evolution in its main features may perhaps be put as follows. Nature constantly brings many more individuals of every species of plant and animal into existence than can find standing room or opportunity to live. This disparity between the demand for room and sustenance and the available supply results in a struggle for existence. This struggle takes place between members of the same species, between members of different species, and is carried on by all against environmental conditions such as heat, cold, and disease. In this threefold struggle those individuals of a species that have the qualities whether of cunning, or speed, or strength, or thickness of fur, or resistance to disease, or whatever best fits them to cope with the enemies and forces encountered in the particular environment in which they find themselves, are selected by nature for survival and the reproduction of their kind. The much greater number in every species succumb in the struggle that they must wage, and leave no progeny. Among the survivors, who inherit the qualities of their progenitors, though with variations, the struggle goes on, countless millions in each species being eliminated. Those that survive are selected because of the variations in their inheritance that make them better adapted to their environment. In this way, in time new species are developed. Man himself, according to the

[3] Darwin was not the first writer of the nineteenth century to broach a scientific theory of evolution. He was anticipated by the Frenchman Lamarck, among others. In 1830 Sir Charles Lyell, one of Darwin's countrymen, published his *Principles of Geology,* in which he worked out an evolutionary theory of the development of the earth, contending that it was the product of gradual and constant change over long ages and that the process was still going on. In 1852 Herbert Spencer, in his *Essay on the Development Hypothesis,* and in 1855, in his *Principles of Psychology,* advanced a theory of evolution. Darwin was indebted to Thomas Malthus' *Essay on Population* (1798) for his idea of natural selection. Malthus had pointed out the constant tendency of human population to outrun the means of subsistence, and the consequent struggle for existence. Darwin applied the concept to the entire organic world. Finally, his hypothesis of the evolution of species through natural selection was worked out independently by Alfred Russel Wallace. The two men first made a public statement of their theory of evolution independently in 1858.

evolutionists, has developed as a result of this process of variation, selection, and heredity, although Darwin recognized that in social evolution man's social instincts and habits, his moral sense, and his intellectual powers have been of chief importance in his evolution.[4]

The Darwinian theory at first met with furious resistance from most theologians and with skepticism from some scientists. On the other hand, it was almost immediately taken over by writers in politics and sociology, applied to phenomena in the field of the social sciences, and invoked to support and condemn all kinds of "isms." [5] Moreover and above all it was generally assumed, although with relatively little support from the ranks of the biologists themselves, that evolution and progress were one and the same thing.[6] The phrase "survival of the fittest" was given an ethical connotation and utilized by exponents of extreme nationalism, socialism, and imperialism, as well as by other special pleaders in support of their particular notions. To those nationalists who regarded national states as struggling organisms, or those who looked upon them as persons or as being endowed with individual souls and particular aspirations or "missions," the theory of evolution through struggle and natural selection was highly suggestive. To the racialists, who were impressed with the disparity in civilization and achievement between different races, and who identified race with nationality, it provided an explanation and justification of group conflict and the domination of superior races. To expansionists, it was utilized to reconcile nationalism with imperialism. To militarists, it furnished conclusive proof of the inevitability of war. To pacifists in general, it presented a challenge which was met partly by a complete or qualified acceptance of the validity of the hypothesis as applied to plants and

[4] See his *Descent of Man* (London, 1871), Chs. III-V, XXI. On page 618 he says: "Important as the struggle for existence has been and even still is, yet as far as the highest part of man's nature is concerned there are other agencies more important. For the moral qualities are advanced, either directly or indirectly, much more through the effects of habit, the reasoning powers, instruction, religion, etc., than through natural selection; though to this latter agency may be safely attributed the social instincts which afforded the basis for the development of the moral sense."

[5] It has been pressed into service on behalf of socialism, individualism, progressivism, conservatism, militarism, pacifism, nationalism, racialism, and imperialism.

[6] As Todd points out, "Progress is evolution measured by an assumed standard of human values. Evolution may or may not spell progress; progress is only one among many possible turns to evolution. . ." (A. J. Todd, *Theories of Social Progress,* (New York, 1918), pp. 94–95.)

lower animals and a more or less complete denial of its applicability to human societies.

Among the writers who, during the nineteenth and early twentieth century, discussed the question of the relation of war to human progress, at least four main positions may be distinguished. There were those who regarded war as a natural phenomenon associated with the evolutionary process, but who were disposed to doubt or deny that the evolutionary process means progress.[7] Others looked upon war as an eternal element in the cosmic process and were inclined to regard it as the chief, if not the sole, cause of human progress.[8] A third group took the position that in the course of the development of human civilization war played an essential and on the whole a beneficial part, but that it has accomplished its work and is not only no longer necessary but actually a retarding influence.[9] Finally, there were those who insisted that the progress of mankind has taken place in spite of war and that it has always been a retarding influence.[10] The writers whose views have been selected for presentation are merely representative of a great number who have written on the subject.[11]

Herbert Spencer (1820-1903), the English sociologist and contemporary of Darwin, applied the theory of evolution to political and social institutions, and held that in the progress of civilization two stages could be distinguished, the military and the industrial. The industrial type of state represented an advance over the militant type, although in the earlier stages of civilization war was held to be as indispensable an element among social groups as struggle was among lower organic forms. "We must recognize the truth that the struggles for existence between societies has been instrumental to their evolution. Neither the consolidation and reconsolidation of small groups into larger ones, nor the organization of such compound and doubly compound groups, nor the concomitant developments of those aids to a higher life which civilization has brought would have been possible without inter-tribal

[7] Among others, Ludwig Gumplowicz in *Der Rassenkampf* (Innsbruck, 1909) and *Outlines of Sociology* (Philadelphia, 1899); and Gustav Le Bon in *The Psychology of Peoples* (London, 1899).

[8] S. R. Steinmetz, *Die Philosophie des Krieges* (Leipzig, 1907); Karl Pearson, *National Life from the Standpoint of Science* (London, 1905).

[9] Franklin Giddings, *Principles of Sociology* (New York, 1896); Ludwig Stein, *Einführung in die Soziologie* (Munich, 1921).

[10] Jacques Novicow, *La Critique du Darwinisme Social* (Paris, 1910); George Nasmyth, *Social Progress and the Darwinian Theory* (New York, 1916).

[11] See list of references at end of chapter.

and inter-national conflicts. Social cooperation is initiated by joint defense and offense; and from the cooperation thus initiated all kinds of cooperations have arisen. Inconceivable as have been the horrors caused by the universal antagonism which, beginning with the chronic hostilities of small hordes tens of thousands of years ago, has ended in the occasional vast battles of immense nations, we must nevertheless admit that without it the world would still have been inhabited by men of feeble types sheltering in caves and living on wild food."[12] War, he declared, was responsible not only for the development of political organizations, but for initiating the organization of labor and laying the foundation of industrialism, for developing in men the power of continuous application through its coercive discipline, and for stimulating the arts and inventions.[13]

On the other hand, Spencer was just as certain that "the conclusion of profoundest moment to which all lines of argument converge, is that the possibility of a high social state, political as well as general, fundamentally depends on the cessation of war." For all of the benefits to be expected, he declared, have already been secured, and its work is done. Henceforth only evil can come from its employment, and only good from its abandonment. But Spencer did not expect this truth to have much effect on the course of events. He felt it was too far in advance of the time, and that the forces slowly working in the general direction of permanent peace could be only slightly facilitated by demonstrating its necessity.

Thomas Huxley (1825-1895), the English biologist and philosopher, was an eloquent exponent of the theory of evolution. He also accepted in general the principle of natural selection as an explanation of the structural evolution of plants and animals. But he rejected the notion that "men in society, men as ethical beings, must look to the same process to help them toward perfection." Admitting that in the earlier stages of civilization the struggle for existence among men tended to eliminate those less fitted to adapt themselves to their environment, quite regardless of ethical fitness, he was not prepared to admit, as were Spencer and the other individualists of his day, that ethical prog-

[12] *Principles of Sociology*, 3 vols. (New York, 1891-97), II, 241.

[13] *Ibid.*, II, 264. The American sociologist, Lester F. Ward (1841-1913), took substantially the same position. See his *Pure Sociology* (New York, 1903), p. 238, and article in *American Journal of Sociology*, March, 1905, p. 594. See also Steinmetz, *op. cit.*, Ch. II.

ress could be made by keeping hands off Nature. "Social progress means a checking of the cosmic process at every step and the substitution for it of another, which may be called the ethical process; the end of which is not the survival of those who may happen to be the fittest in respect of the whole of the conditions which obtain, but of those who are ethically the best."[14] Huxley admitted that the development of an ethical society among men could not be rapid. Man's nature and training over millions of years were heavy and enduring obstacles. However, he saw "no limit to the extent to which intelligence and will, guided by sound principles of investigation, and organized in common effort, may modify the conditions of existence, for a period longer than that now covered by history. And much may be done to change the nature of man himself. The intelligence which has converted the brother of the wolf into the faithful guardian of the flock ought to be able to do something towards curbing the instincts of savagery in civilized men."[15] But Huxley was by no means certain that the struggle for existence among individuals and between nations would ever completely give way to a reign of universal peace. Certainly no great progress toward such an ideal could be expected, he declared, as long as man continued to allow the natural tendency of "unlimited multiplication" of human beings to go unrestrained. For in such a contingency mounting populations must insure "a struggle for existence as sharp as any that ever went on under the regime of war."[16] Thus while Spencer saw an inevitable, if slow, natural process working toward peace, which man could do little to retard or accelerate, Huxley believed that the only hope of attaining such a state was for man constantly to interfere with and put a curb upon Nature.

Among writers of the nineteenth century in the field of history and politics who regarded war as an essential and beneficent part of the divine plan, none, perhaps, had a wider influence than the German patriotic historian, Heinrich von Treitschke (1834-1896). There was soldier-stock on both sides of his family, and after entering politics and coming into close contact with the Prussian military caste, whose system he later saw triumph in the wars with Denmark, Austria, and France, he was converted from liberal views to the position of an apologist

[14] *Evolution and Ethics* (New York and London, 1893). The Romanes Lecture.
[15] *Ibid.*
[16] *Collected Essays* (New York, 1896-1902), essay on "The Struggle for Existence in Human Society."

for war and an advocate of the settlement of national destinies by might.[17] The most complete statement of his position is to be found in *Die Politik*.[18] Treitschke was wary about attempting to apply principles of natural science to the social science field, and while the idea of struggle is extremely prominent in his philosophy, he does not rely upon Darwin and the natural scientists for his inspiration, but upon Machiavelli and practical "blood and iron" statesmen such as Bismarck, "the real heroes of history."

Like Machiavelli he viewed the State as Power,[19] and declared that "the essence of the State consists in its incompatibility with any power over it."[20] He parted company, however, with those who regarded the State as an organism. The State differed, he said, from innumerable organisms in having a conscious will. To regard it as an automatically developing organism was to invite indolence. States must be understood as "the great collective personalities of history, thoroughly capable of bearing responsibility and blame."[21] They arose in the first place through war, and although as time goes on wars will become shorter and less frequent they will never cease.[22] Nor should they. For Treitschke regards the independent sovereign state as the supreme political attainment of man. The idea of a universal empire is "odious" to him, and any higher restraining authority unthinkable. States may and should unilaterally annul treaties when in their individual judgment the circumstances under which such treaties were signed have changed.[23] Treitschke recognizes that states may very well disagree on such matters. In such a case, their only recourse is to war, which is "the form of litigation by which States make their claims valid."[24] Moreover, war may be the only remedy for vindicating the national honor, which must

[17] See H. W. C. Davis, *Political Thought of Heinrich von Treitschke* (London, 1914), p. 1 *et passim.*

[18] English translation, *Politics,* 2 vols. (New York, 1916). They were made up from the notes of his lectures to classes at the University of Berlin, where he was appointed professor in 1874.

[19] *Op. cit.,* p. 84. It is to be noted, however, that Treitschke, unlike Machiavelli, had an ethical end in mind. The State "is Power *in order to protect and to further the highest welfare of the human race.*" (I, 85; II, 588.)

[20] *Ibid.,* I, 28.

[21] *Ibid.,* I, 17-19.

[22] *Ibid.,* I, 69.

[23] *Ibid.,* I, 19; II, p. 596. Nevertheless, Treitschke insisted that a State must be restrained by "conscience and reason" and that it would defeat its own ends by following the principle of "despising faith and loyalty." (II, 587.)

[24] *Ibid.,* I, 66; II, 597.

be preserved at all costs. "We mistake the moral laws of politics if we reproach any State with having an oversensitive sense of honour, for this instinct must be highly developed in each of them if it is to be true to its own essence. The State is no violet, to bloom unseen; its power should stand proudly, for all the world to see, and it cannot allow even the symbols of it to be contested. If the flag is insulted, the State must claim reparation; should this not be forthcoming, war must follow, however small the occasion may seem; for the State has never any choice but to maintain the respect in which it is held among its fellows." [25]

But Treitschke was far from feeling that war was an unhappy form of international adjustment. Indeed, he declared that pacifists, who would do away with it, were "simply unintelligent." [26] Fortunately, mankind need not fear any such prospect, for "the God above us will see to it that war shall return again, a terrible medicine for mankind diseased." [27] This medicine Treitschke looked upon as "the one remedy for an ailing nation." [28] By its therapeutic powers individuals are raised out of the slough of selfishness, political parties are purged of their hatreds, and nations are reinvigorated. Its sublimity inspires in Treitschke the following passage: "We have learned to perceive the moral majesty of war through the very processes which to the superficial observer seems brutal and inhuman. The greatness of war is just what at first sight seems to be its horror—that for the sake of their country men will overcome the natural feelings of humanity, that they will slaughter their fellow-men who have done them no injury, nay, whom they perhaps respect as chivalrous foes. Man will not only sacrifice his life, but the natural and justified instincts of his soul; his very self he must offer up for the sake of patriotism; here we have the sublimity of war. . . He who knows history knows also that to banish war from the world would be to mutilate human nature." [29] Moreover, Treitschke saw in war the divine agency for testing nations, and winnowing the wheat from the chaff. "Brave peoples alone have an existence, an evo-

[25] *Ibid.*, II, 595. Excerpt quoted by permission of The Macmillan Company, publishers.
[26] *Ibid.*, I, 30.
[27] *Ibid.*, I, 69.
[28] *Ibid.*, I, 66.
[29] *Ibid.*, II, 395-6. Excerpt quoted by permission of The Macmillan Company, publishers.

lution, or a future; the weak and cowardly perish, and perish justly." [30] Thus a State must not make the mistake of neglecting its strength "in order to promote the idealistic aspirations of man. . ." If it does this, "it repudiates its own nature and perishes." [31] In Treitschke the old idea of war as the means of discovering the judgment of God appears once more. He was enough of a historian, however, to recognize that war's verdicts have frequently been reversed. A State emerges victor over an antagonist today; tomorrow, in another contest with the same foe, it may be vanquished. What has Treitschke to say to this? "It is important not to look upon war always as a judgment from God. Its consequences are evanescent; but the life of a nation is reckoned by centuries, and the final verdict can only be pronounced after the survey of whole epochs." [32] Over a short period of time, a State may seem not to get its just deserts, said Treitschke; but "in the course of the world's history a Divine ordinance is perceptible." [33]

The American admiral and naval historian, Alfred T. Mahan (1840-1914) who commanded great respect for his erudition in naval matters, and who was one of the delegates to the first Hague Conference, was one of the most eloquent defenders of the use of force in international relations.[34] Although perhaps not as extreme as Treitschke in his views as to the rôle of war in the life of states, he was as convinced that it represented a permanent and necessary element in human affairs. He regarded power (force) as "a faculty of national life; one of the talents committed to nations by God." [35] Like Treitschke, he looked upon States as persons, with God-given talents for which they must give an account, with vital interests which they must safeguard, and honor which they must, if necessary, fight to preserve.

States, like persons, must keep their consciences alive. Rather than do or endure wrong, an individual may, if necessary, appeal to the "higher law," and take matters into his own hands. In precisely the same way, but with even more reason, nations must resort to arms when, in their judgment, right cannot otherwise be enforced. This, ac-

[30] Treitschke, *op. cit.*, I, 21.
[31] *Ibid.*, I, 24.
[32] *Ibid.*, I, 66.
[33] *Ibid.*, I, 11.
[34] See his *Armaments and Arbitration, or the Place of Force in the International Relations of States* (New York, 1912). Mahan's writings exerted quite an influence on the mind of his admirer, Theodore Roosevelt.
[35] *Some Neglected Aspects of War* (London, 1907), p. 47.

cording to Mahan, is not for the purpose of getting a judgment of God on the matter at issue, for the state itself renders the judgment. ". . . a state, when it goes to war, should do so not to test the rightfulness of its claims, but because, being convinced in its conscience of that rightfulness, no other means of overcoming evil remains." [36] Mahan admits that a nation's conscience may be "often clouded or misguided, by passion or by interest," but this does not disturb him, for he does not regard it as an important consideration. "It is not the accuracy of the decision," he says, "but the faithfulness to conviction, that constitutes the moral worth of an action, national or individual." [37] Mahan was opposed to agreements binding nations to arbitrate disputes that might arise in the future. The conscience of a nation must be kept free to judge each case as it arises. It must determine whether a particular question involves the "vital interests" of a nation, and if it does it must not be submitted to arbitration, for the nation has an obligation to posterity not to submit a matter involving a vital interest to an outside tribunal.[38]

Mahan not only believed that war may be regarded as one of the fixed institutions of mankind, but he looked upon it, along with other types of organized force, as providing the necessary condition for progress.[39] "Upon organized force," he declared, "depends the extended shield, under which the movements of peace advance in quietness, and of organized force war is simply the last expression." Mahan, however, unlike many other war apologists who shared his general point of view, looked upon war as an artificial man-made institution rather than a natural phenomenon. Indeed, its great virtue lay in the fact that men could employ it to "measurably control, guide, delay, or otherwise beneficially modify" natural forces which they are powerless to prevent. Mahan looked upon war as performing the same type of service as that rendered by the dikes of Holland in obstructing the North Sea in its natural tendency to swallow up the land, or the levees that restrain and

[36] *Ibid.*, p. 30.

[37] *Ibid.*, p. 32.

[38] *Ibid.*, Preface, xvii. Like Treitschke (II, 598-599) Mahan did not think international arbitration tribunals could give impartial decisions (*Ibid.*, p. 100).

[39] He opposed compulsory arbitration and disarmament, fearing that under a peaceful regime nations and men would gradually lose their powers of individual initiative, and that with its fighting energy lost European civilization might not survive. *Armaments and Arbitration,* p. 10.

guide the course of the Mississippi River. In much the same way, according to Mahan, war acted as a regulator and adjuster of the movements of peoples. It was a preventive agency necessary to check and guide the strong material impulses of nations.[40]

The English mathematician and eugenist, Karl Pearson (1857-), was, in the decade preceding the Great War, one of the staunch defenders of war as the great agent of human progress. He declared that communities of men are as subject to biological laws of struggle as communities of ants or herds of buffaloes. And, he added, it is fortunate for man that this is true. It was out of struggle for existence between human groups that man evolved the social instinct. Those tribes with the greater social feeling survived and passed this trait down to their posterity. Moreover, race struggles resulted in the survival of those races that were mentally and physically fitter. By this means only could a high state of civilization have been developed. And, according to Pearson, it is only by war that this civilization can be retained. Were man to give up war, he would stagnate. But as regards the struggle between individuals and classes within the state, he admits that it may be lessened or suspended within limits without danger to the national stock. In fact, he recommends an artificial limitation of the internal struggle so that the nation may be in better position to wage the external struggle. This is and must be continuous, taking the form not only of recurrent war, but of economic and commercial rivalry. And in this struggle a nation must look to its brains as well as its brawn. "The nation, however prosperous, however hardy, however big, will fail when it comes to a crisis, when it is suddenly placed in a new environment, unless it has organized brain-power controlling its nervous system right away to the smallest outlying points. Hardihood, big battalions, command of the purse, may enable us to struggle through in either peace or war so long as we have only to meet small or semi-organized opponents, but they will not avail when great nation meets great nation; then it is the codified experience and the organized brain-power which tell in the struggle." [41] This is true, he says, because the struggle is no longer a blind and unconscious brawl, as it was in the

[40] Mahan, *op. cit.*, pp. 87-90, 92-93. Mahan also compared war to the police, who prevent an outburst of crime in the community. The analogy is obviously faulty, but is frequently advanced by military men.

[41] Pearson, *op. cit.*, pp. 14-15.

days of barbaric tribes, but "has become more and more the conscious, carefully directed attempt of the nation to fit itself to a continuously changing environment." [42]

Among the more extreme defenders of war on biological grounds, in the years immediately preceding the Great War, was General Friedrich von Bernhardi. In his *Germany and the Next War* (London, 1912) he undoubtedly expressed the convictions not only of the blatant militarists of Germany but in general those of extreme militarists everywhere. He accepted without reservation the theory of natural selection, as he understood it, as an explanation of progress throughout the world of nature, and applied it practically without qualification to the affairs of men and nations. It is clear that he was not very familiar with the true position of Darwin, Huxley, and the other biologists. On the other hand, he relied heavily throughout on the German historian, von Treitschke.

Bernhardi held that of all the laws of nature, that of struggle was basic, that it resulted in progress, and that two kinds of struggle were to be distinguished in human affairs. There was the intra-social struggle, which was one between ideas, institutions, customs, and social systems, within each state; and there was the extra-social struggle between "societies, nations, and races" known as war. "In the extra-social struggle, in war, that nation will conquer which can throw into the scale the greatest physical, mental, moral, material, and political power, and is therefore the best able to defend itself. War will furnish such a nation with favourable vital conditions, enlarged possibilities of expansion and widened influence, and thus promote the progress of mankind; for it is clear that those intellectual and moral factors which insure superiority in war are also those which render possible a general progressive development. They confer victory because the elements of progress are latent in them. Without war, inferior or decaying races would easily choke the growth of healthy budding elements, and a universal decadence would follow." [43]

Bernhardi admitted that in war a number of weak nations may combine and overcome temporarily a strong nation. But in the long run, he declared, the strong nation will prevail against greater numbers

[42] *Ibid.*, pp. 36-37. For an extended examination and criticism of Pearson's thesis see J. A. Hobson, *Imperialism* (London, 1902) Pt. II, Ch. II.

[43] Bernhardi, *op. cit.*, p. 12. Excerpt quoted by permission of Edward Arnold and Co., publishers, London.

because of its greater vitality and because the allied nations "have the seeds of corruption in them." It may be remarked that this over-simplification is helpful to the author in reaching the conclusion that war in the long run assures the survival of the fittest, but in the real world of nations the "seeds of corruption" are apparently not distributed by nature with such foresight that vitality and virtue can be assured an eventual victory against the "big battalions" of numerous foes.

Not only is war, according to Bernhardi, the supreme agent for the determination of the fitness of nations to survive, but frequent resort to it is necessary to prevent national decay.[44] On this matter he embellishes his argument with a stanza from Schiller:

> Man is stunted by peaceful days,
> In idle repose his courage decays.
> Law makes the world the same.
> But in war man's strength is seen.
> War ennobles all that is mean;
> Even the coward belies his name.

On account of war's ennobling effects on human character through its calling forth the virtues of constancy, pity, magnanimity, unselfishness, and heroism among the members of each national group, Bernhardi regarded its employment as a duty and attempts to maintain peace as "detrimental to the national health."[45]

The writers whose views have been examined thus far have in all instances stressed the fact of struggle in the organic world, and most of them have emphasized the importance historically of war in the life of man, and have regarded it as definitely connected with human progress. One of the first writers to question the importance and value of struggle within species as a factor in evolution, and more particularly to criticize war as a main cause of progress was the Russian scientist and sociologist, Peter Kropotkin (1842-1921). As a result of observations of animal and plant life made in the course of his Eurasian travels, and suggestions contained in a lecture *On the Law of Mutual Aid* delivered by the Russian scientist Kessler in 1880, Kropotkin con-

[44] *Cf.* Theodore Roosevelt, *The Strenuous Life* (New York, 1905), p. 6. "In this world the nation that has trained itself to a career of unwarlike and isolated ease is bound, in the end, to go down before other nations which have not lost the manly and adventurous qualities."

[45] Bernhardi believed also that healthy national organisms must expand or decay, that Germany had a mission to extend her Empire and her culture, and seek world supremacy.

ceived and developed the idea of mutual aid as a law of nature and one of the chief factors of evolution.[46] Kropotkin did not deny the fact of struggle, nor the survival of the fittest. What he was at pains to try to demonstrate by an impressive number of examples and illustrations was his thesis that among men as well as among animals the struggle that makes for survival is the struggle of the members of a species *together* against the difficulties of their environment, rather than competition within the species. Throughout nature, he declared, the most sociable animals are those that prove to be the fittest and "sociability appears as the chief factor of evolution, both directly, by securing the well-being of the species while diminishing the waste of energy, and indirectly, by favoring the growth of intelligence."[47] The progress of man, Kropotkin contended, has occurred as a result of the practice of mutual aid rather than by competition and war. Historians and chroniclers, with a predilection for the dramatic side of history, have overlooked and failed to record the peaceful life of the great masses of people, and have given such an undue prominence to struggle and war as to present a distorted picture of the life of man.[48]

By far the most searching and vigorous criticism, however, of the doctrine that human progress is dependent upon war was undertaken by Kropotkin's countryman and contemporary, the sociologist Jacques Novicow (1849-1912).[49] Denying that war ever had been useful in any way to the human race, Novicow asserted that those who looked upon it as a necessary and beneficent form of the struggle for existence were guilty of the error of ignoring the physical universe and the struggle of man with his environment for food, shelter, clothing, etc. This struggle, unlike war, must be waged ceaselessly and continuously and there is, even among the most war-like peoples, an enormous difference between the amount of time and energy thus spent in productive eco-

[49] The most complete statement of his position is to be found in a relatively tween 1891 and 1896. (He lived in England after 1886. The political climate was less severe on professed anarchists.) They were put in book form and published under the title of *Mutual Aid—A Factor of Evolution* (London, 1902).

[47] *Mutual Aid,* pp. 50, 52.

[48] *Ibid.,* p. 92.

[49] The most complete statement of his position is to be found in a relatively late work, *La Critique du Darwinisme Social* (Paris, 1910). Also important is his *La Guerre et ses Prétendus Bienfaits* (Paris, 1894). He hated Russian despotism, and took up his residence in France and wrote in the French language. German militarism was often used as a horrible example in his attacks on militarism and war.

nomic activity requiring the cooperation of human beings and that spent in war between them. It is this struggle, and not "collective homicide," that is responsible for the development of civilization, according to Novicow.[50] Just as geological change has come about in the main through the slow processes of erosion by wind and water rather than by earthquakes and convulsions, so has human evolution been due to slow and invisible and complicated processes rather than to war and other cataclysms. The great inventions of fire, the wheel, the sail, the steam engine, the locomotive, the telephone and telegraph, and so on, have all contributed greatly to the progress of the human race, but these and a thousand other inventions, including even gunpowder, were not made for the purpose of war. They were originally made solely for the struggle with the physical universe.[51]

Novicow denied just as vigorously that war has served the cause of progress by weeding out the weak and unintelligent races and perpetuating those physically and mentally strong. Admitting that the white race is superior to all others, he denies that this is due to natural selection and the elimination of inferior races, for it is a minority among the peoples of the world. The so-called inferior races greatly outnumber it.[52] The more intelligent nations have not been selected by war as against the backward ones. On more than one occasion, savage and barbarous hordes have extirpated the finest and most brilliant civilizations, and as long as war lasts the highest nations intellectually will succumb to the lower, more brutal types.[53] As a matter of fact, he declared, war results in a reverse selection. The best youthful specimens of a nation are selected for combat, so that the better the man the better the chance he has to be killed and the less chance he has to perpetuate his kind. The weaker are left behind to marry and propagate the race.[54] Natural selection, as contrasted with this artificial

[50] *La Critique du Darwinisme Social,* pp. 38-39. Norman Angell (pseudonym for R. N. A. Lane), in his *Great Illusion* (New York, 1910), seems to have been indebted for this and many other ideas to the earlier works of Novicow: *La Politique Internationale* (Paris, 1896); *Les Luttes entre Sociétés Humaines et leurs Phases Successives* (Paris, 1893); and *La Guerre et ses Prétendus Bienfaits* (Paris, 1894).

[51] *La Critique,* p. 182. This unqualified assertion, like many others in Novicow's work, would probably be difficult to prove.

[52] *Ibid.,* p. 185.

[53] *Ibid.,* p. 373.

[54] *Ibid.,* p. 164. This is also in substance, the position taken by Darwin, *op. cit.,* p. 151. For a similar point of view by more recent writers, see David Starr Jordan, *War and the Breed* (Boston, 1915); Vernon Lyman Kellogg, *Military Selection and*

selection, takes place in the economic competition between individuals. In so far as there is equality of opportunity, the most gifted are able to assure their economic welfare, and the mortality is much lower among them than among the poorer classes.[55]

Novicow regarded the indirect losses of war as more injurious than the losses in killed and wounded. For the indirect losses arise out of war as a process of dissociation. War divides instead of uniting peoples in a common effort. By association men do not merely add, they multiply, the vital power of the individual and of society; by the dissociation of war, there is not merely a subtraction, but a division, of vital powers; for war interferes with the vital circulation of the social organism, and causes a rupture of the biological equilibrium. Thus, in the view of Novicow, war is, today at least, pathological. It is a social disease; for, since the growth of communication and interdependence of the peoples of the earth, the entire human race constitutes a single social organism.[56]

Had it not been for war, according to Novicow, mankind would have advanced much further, not only intellectually, socially, and economically, but politically.[57] He took issue with Spencer and other writers who contended that war must be credited with the welding of small political groups into the nations of today, and asserted that its influence had been in exactly the opposite direction. It has always retarded the union of peoples because it has created hates and implacable resentments between groups. Thus the wars between England and Scotland delayed the union of those two countries. The war of 1870, likewise, has been the principal impediment to the realization of a federation of Europe. And had it not been for war, world federation would long since have been realized.[58] War and conquest have resulted in the formation of unnatural, polyglot states that oppose themselves to the rational political organization of humanity. For government to

Race Deterioration in Carnegie Endowment for International Peace Studies in the Causes and Results of War (Oxford, Eng., 1916), pp. 159-202.

55 Novicow, *La Critique,* p. 186.

56 *Ibid.,* Ch. X, for an elaboration of this organismic conception in relation to war.

57 In his earlier work, *Les Luttes,* Novicow attributed the origin of the territorial state to the need of kinship groups for an organization for collective attack and defense, but in his *La Critique* he maintains that war not only was not responsible for the origin of the state but often actually delayed its formation.

58 *La Critique,* pp. 126-127. An extended discussion of these matters is also to be found in *La Justice* (Paris, 1905), pp. 251-367.

function satisfactorily, each nationality should constitute a separate state. War has in the past operated in most instances to prevent or retard the realization of this, and will continue to be a retarding factor, for imperial states will resort to it to put down the aspirations of their peoples for separate statehood.[59]

In another work in which he takes issue with the fatalism of the war apologists, Novicow says:

"No grim fatality obliges us to massacre one another eternally like wild beasts. . . . The Darwinian law in no wise prevents the whole of humanity from joining in a federation in which peace will reign. Within the federation of humanity the same will take place as takes place within each state. Here struggle has by no means disappeared but goes on under the form of economic competition, lawyers' briefs, judges' sentences, votes, party organizations, parliamentary discussions, meetings, lectures, sermons, schools, scientific associations, congresses, pamphlets, books, newspapers, magazines—in short, by spoken and written propaganda. And we must not suppose that these methods have been preferred to bloodshed because men have become better. Idylls play no part in the question. These methods have been preferred because they were found to be the most effective, therefore the quickest and easiest. . . . All the methods of struggle just enumerated are constantly employed in normal times among 381,000,000 of English subjects inhabiting 25,000,000 of square kilometers. They could be equally well employed by 1,480,000,000 men inhabiting 135,000,000 square kilometers. Then the federation of the entire globe would be achieved."[60]

A somewhat different and more dispassionate approach is to be found in the writings of William Graham Sumner (1840-1910), the American political and social scientist. Viewing the past of mankind, he held that the most primitive peoples had in general been peaceful. They united in groups in order to carry on the struggle for existence against Nature to greater advantage. As civilization developed, however, these groups came into collision, and entered into a more or less intense competition of life. War arose out of this intergroup competition as a fundamental condition of human existence.[61] Hunger, love, vanity, and the fear of superior powers were underlying motives. But, says Sumner, "while men were fighting for glory and greed, for revenge

[59] *La Critique,* p. 314.

[60] *War and Its Alleged Benefits,* pp. 102-103. This is the English translation of his *La Guerre et ses Prétendus Bienfaits* (Paris, 1894), by Thomas Seltzer, published in 1911 by Henry Holt and Company, New York.

[61] *War and Other Essays* (New Haven, Conn., 1911), pp. 3-10.

and superstition, they were building human society. They were acquiring discipline and cohesion; they were learning cooperation, perseverance, fortitude, and patience." [62] And wars of conquest, he declared, must be credited with having destroyed the effete and made way for the viable. On the other hand, war has been carried on at such a heavy cost in life and capital that the evolution of civilization has been greatly retarded.[63] But Sumner apparently believed that it would not have taken place at all had not warlikeness as well as peacefulness characterized human beings. He regarded military discipline as educative, and competition in war as fruitful in sharpening men's ingenuity and inventiveness. On this matter, his position is in sharp contrast with that of Novicow. "In history the military inventions have led the way and have been afterwards applied to industry. Chemical inventions were made in the attempt to produce combinations which would be destructive in war; we owe some of our most useful substances to discoveries which were made in this effort. The skill of artisans has been developed in making weapons, and then that skill has been available for industry." [64]

Sumner also credits war with having produced political institutions and classes and with having developed the highly organized society of the present. Moreover, he regarded it as a rejuvenating agent. "In long periods of peace the whole societal structure becomes fixed in its adjustments and the functions all run into routine. Vested interests get an established control; some classes secure privileges and establish precedents, while other classes form habits of acquiescence. Traditions acquire a sacred character and philosophical doctrines are taught in churches and schools which make existing customs seem to be the eternal order of nature. It becomes impossible to find a standing-ground from which to attack abuses and organize reform. . . By war new social powers break their way and create a new order." [65] But the new order is never what was wanted, Sumner remarks. It has within it new evils mixed with the old ones. War and revolution work in a haphazard fashion and are always attended by great evils. Yet Sumner sees no other way in which the good could have been attained, for the neces-

[62] *Ibid.*, p. 15.
[63] *Ibid.*, p. 16.
[64] *Ibid.*, p. 30. It is doubtful whether this position can be sustained. Both Sumner and Novicow would have done better to qualify their statements.
[65] *Ibid.*, p. 31.

sary statesmanship and the required popular sense and virtue for national solutions of human affairs have in the past been absent.

What of the future? Sumner admits that the "iron spur of the nature-process," one form of which has been war, is frightful and cruel, but if men are to escape force and bloodshed they will have to embrace the only alternatives, "more knowledge and more reason." And Sumner was not at all optimistic when he was writing on the subject in 1903. He felt that there was danger in the fact that people were becoming saturated with the literature of humanitarianism and complacently allowing themselves to be convinced that the world was inevitably advancing along the path of "progress" toward peace and brotherly love while at the same time their statesmen were constantly preparing for war. Sumner entertained a firm belief that "what you prepare for you will get," and he prophesied quite accurately the outcome. "What will come of the mixture of sentimental social philosophy and warlike policy? There is only one thing rationally to be expected, and that is a frightful effusion of blood in revolution and war in the century now opening." [66]

The War came, and certain thoughtful men were led to further appraisal of the validity of the philosophy of force and fatalism which they felt had played a large part in bringing it on. Among these was the eminent English political historian and statesman, James Bryce (1838-1922). In an article on "War and Human Progress," [67] written during the war, Bryce examined the question both from the biological and historical points of view. On the biological side he contributed nothing new, but this historical discussion was on the whole fresh and suggestive. He looked at progress from the point of view of the economic advancement, intellectual development, and moral betterment of mankind, and attempted to define these three kinds of progress.[68] He admitted in the first place as an historical fact that war has often been accompanied by an advance of civilization, and therefore that war and

[66] *War and Other Essays,* p. 30. Like Spencer, whose sociological writings influenced his thinking, Sumner did not think men could accomplish very much in attempting to reform the world at any point. The most that they could do would be to modify slowly the tendencies of some of the forces at work. See *op. cit.,* Ch. VIII, on "The Absurd Effort to Make the World Over."

[67] *Atlantic Monthly,* September, 1916. Citations are taken from reprint in *International Conciliation,* November, 1916, No. 108. Published by Carnegie Endowment for International Peace.

[68] *Ibid.,* pp. 13-14.

progress may be regarded as compatible. But, like Novicow, he was unwilling to assume that the concurrence of the two proves that war has caused the advance. For example, were the undeniable contributions of Rome to the intellectual progress of mankind to be credited to her great conquests? Bryce conceded that the wars and military triumphs of Rome caused an exaltation of spirit in the Roman people as well as disciplining them, and developing their political capacity. Their intellectual development, however, he was inclined to attribute largely to Hellenic influences. Moreover, he noted that the creative epoch passed after a short time and a decline set in all along the line, although the fighting continued and increased. Like Jordan,[69] he was inclined to the belief that the waning strength and economic decay of the Empire were largely due to the exhaustion of the old Roman stock by warfare.

In the history of Prussia, Bryce found the single clear instance in which a state throve on the trade of war. Referring to the Prussian successes of 1864, 1866, and 1870 in the wars with Denmark, Austria, and France, Bryce said: "Ever since those victories her industrial production, her commerce, and her wealth, have rapidly increased, while at the same time scientific research has been prosecuted with the greatest vigor and on a scale unprecedentedly large. These things were no doubt achieved during a peace of forty-three years. But it was what one may call a belligerent peace, full of thoughts of war and preparations for war. There is no denying that the national spirit has been carried to a high point of pride, energy, and self-confidence, which has stimulated effort in all directions and secured extraordinary efficiency in civil as well as in military administration. Here, then, is an instance in which a state has grown by war and a people has been energized by war." [70]

Nevertheless, Bryce felt that a final verdict on the basis of this "single instance" could not then be given. Would Prussia be successful in the war then being waged? Even if not defeated, might not its material prosperity be arrested and its domestic tranquillity impaired? And might not the national character suffer deterioration? The Romans were very proud of the world dominion in the time of Augustus, but already decline was setting in. Moreover, said Bryce, "the advance of any single state by violent methods may involve greater harm to the world than the benefits which that state expects to gain, or than those which it

[69] *War and the Breed,* pp. 128-140.
[70] Bryce, *loc. cit.,* p. 18.

proposes to confer upon its neighbors by imposing its civilization upon them." [71]

Bryce was not prepared to concede that in the absence of war a nation will inevitably stagnate. Some states have been both peaceful and unprogressive, he said, but it is not clear that their peacefulness caused their unprogressiveness. The Chinese, so often used as a horrible example of what a pacific temper will do to a people, had early produced a great civilization, but had made little further progress, not because they fought relatively little, but because they were isolated from the rest of the civilized world and enjoyed no stimulating contacts. For the same reason, according to Bryce, the Japanese, a military people, for many centuries made no more progress than the Chinese.

Bryce next cited instances in which long continued war had not been accompanied by progress, and periods of comparative peace in which outstanding achievements could be recorded. The Thirty Years War, for example, had not only brought no progress, but had put Germany back two centuries in her development. On the other hand, "the age that produced More and Bacon and Harvey, Sidney and Spenser and Shakespeare," in England was relatively free from war. Other instances likewise tended to show, in Bryce's opinion, that the proofs of progress through war were far from adequate. Progress, he pointed out, is affected by so many things besides war and peace that in almost any given case it is impossible to say that human advancement has been due chiefly to the one or the other.

Bryce regarded the argument that the best races and states have established their position by war as unsound, and commented as follows: "All the races and states have fought, some better, some worse. The best fighters have not always succeeded, for they may have been fewer in number. There is no necessary connection between fighting quality and intellectual quality. True it is, that some of the intellectually gifted peoples have also been warlike peoples. The Greeks were; so are the French and the Germans. But the Turks, who are good fighters, are good for nothing else. . . Where the gift for fighting goes with the gift of thought, the success achieved by the intellectual race in war is not a result but a symptom, an indication or evidence of an exceptional natural force. Those races and states that are now in the front rank of civilization have shown their capacity in many other fields

[71] Bryce, *loc. cit.*

besides that of war. All that can safely be said to be proved by history is that a race which cannot fight or will not fight when a proper occasion arises, as, for instance, when it has to vindicate its independence, is likely to go down, and be subjected or absorbed. Yet the fact that a state is subjected or absorbed does not prove its inferiority. There is no poetical justice in history. The highly gifted race may be small, like Israel, or too much divided to maintain itself, like the Hellenes of antiquity. From 1490 to 1560 Italy was the prey of foreign invaders; but she was doing more for human progress in art and letters than all the other European states put together." [72]

Denying, in conclusion, that war can be regarded, speaking generally, as a cause either of material, intellectual, or moral progress, Bryce stated his view as to the main causes of progress. It is due in part, if not to strife, to competition. But above all it is to be attributed to thought, which war usually hinders. "It is the race that knows how to think, rather than the far more numerous races that excel in fighting rather than in thinking, that have led the world. Thought, in the form of invention and inquiry, has given us those improvements in the arts of life and in the knowledge of nature by which material progress and comfort have been obtained. Thought has produced literature, philosophy, art, and (when intensified by emotion) religion—all the things that make life worth living. Now, the thought of any people is most active when it is brought into contact with the thought of another, because each is apt to lose its variety and freedom of play when it has worked too long upon familiar lines and flowed too long in the channels it has deepened. Hence, isolation retards progress, while intercourse quickens it." [73]

Bryce admitted that war has at times been the agent through which contact between peoples has been established, but contended, nevertheless, that fruitful contacts have more frequently been established in periods of peace. The tonic theory of Treitschke and the others, he absolutely rejected, holding that the future progress of mankind was to be sought in the stimulus of peaceful cooperation among nations.[74]

[72] *Ibid.*, p. 22.
[73] *Ibid.*, p. 27.
[74] In this chapter all of the views given are characteristic of nineteenth-century thought, although, as will have been observed, in a few instances works cited or analyzed were published in the early years of the twentieth century before the shock of the World War. Bryce's reflections on the subject were published during the War.

REFERENCES

Bagehot, W., *Physics and Politics* (New York, 1876).

Barnes, H. E., "A Sociological Criticism of War and Militarism," *Journal of International Relations,* Vol. XII (Oct., 1921), No. 2, pp. 238-265.

Bernhardi, F. von, *Germany and the Next War,* tr. by A. H. Powles (London, 1912).

Boas, Franz, "An Anthropologist's View of War," *International Conciliation,* March, 1912, No. 52, pp. 5-14.

Brinton, D. G., *Races and Peoples* (New York, 1890).

Bryce, James, "War and Human Progress," *Atlantic Monthly,* CXVIII (Sept., 1916), 301-315. Reprinted in *International Conciliation,* November, 1916, No. 108, pp. 3-27.

Constantin, N. A., *Le Rôle Sociologique de la Guerre* (Paris, 1907).

Darwin, Charles, *The Descent of Man* (London, 1871).

Ellis, Havelock, *Essays in War Time* (Boston and New York, 1917).

Giddings, F., *Studies in the Theory of Human Society* (New York, 1922).

Gumplowicz, L., *Der Rassenkampf* (2nd ed., Innsbruck, 1909).

Hobhouse, L. T., *Democracy and Reaction* (New York, 1905), Chs. III, IV.

Hobson, J. A., *Imperialism* (London, 1902), Pt. II, Ch. II.

Huxley, Thomas, *Collected Essays* (New York, 1896-1902).

Jahns, M., *Ueber Krieg, Frieden und Kultur* (Berlin, 1893).

Jordan, David Starr, *War and the Breed* (Boston, 1915).

Kellogg, V. L., *Beyond War* (New York, 1912).

Kidd, Benjamin, *Social Evolution* (rev. ed., New York and London, 1915), Ch. II.

Kropotkin, Peter, *Mutual Aid* (London, 1902).

Lagorgette, J., *Le Rôle de la Guerre* (Paris, 1906).

Lamprecht, K., *Krieg und Kultur* (Leipzig, 1914).

Lea, Homer, *The Valor of Ignorance* (New York, 1909).

Letourneau, C., *La Guerre dans les Diverses Races Humaines* (Paris, 1895).

Mahan, Alfred T., *Armaments and Arbitration* (New York and London, 1912).

————, "The Place of Power in International Relations," *North American Review,* CXCV (Jan., 1912), 28-39.

————, *Some Neglected Aspects of War* (London, 1907).

Mason, O. T., *Origins of Invention: A Study of Industry Among Primitive People* (London, 1895).

Mitchell, P. C., *Evolution and the War* (London, 1915).

Molinari, G. de, *Grandeur et Décadence de la Guerre* (Paris, 1898).

Nasmyth, George, *Social Progress and the Darwinian Theory* (New York, 1916).
Nicolai, G. F., *The Biology of War* (New York, 1918).
Novicow, Jacques, *La Critique du Darwinisme Social* (Paris, 1910).
——————, *Les Gaspillages des Sociétés Modernes* (Paris, 1899).
——————, *La Justice* (Paris, 1905).
——————, *Les Luttes entre Sociétés Humaines et leur Phases Successives* (3rd ed., Paris, 1904).
——————, *War and Its Alleged Benefits,* tr. by Thomas Seltzer (New York, 1911).
Osborn, Henry Fairfield, *From the Greeks to Darwin* (New York, 1905).
Pearson, Karl, *National Life from the Standpoint of Science* (2nd ed., London, 1905).
Proudhon, P. J., *La Guerre et la Paix* (Paris, 1869).
Ratzenhofer, G., *Wesen und Zweck der Politik,* 3 vols. (Leipzig, 1893).
Simmel, G., *Soziologie* (2nd ed., Munich, 1923).
Sorokin, P., *Contemporary Sociological Theories* (New York and London, 1928), Ch. VI.
Steinmetz, S. R., *Die Philosophie des Krieges* (Leipzig, 1907).
Sumner, W. G., *Folkways* (Boston, 1907).
——————, *War and Other Essays* (New Haven, Conn., 1911).
Tarde, G., *Social Laws* (New York, 1899).
Thomson, J. A., *Biology and the War* (London and New York, 1915).
Todd, A. J., *Theories of Social Progress* (New York, 1918), Chs. XVIII-XIX.
Treitschke, Heinrich von, *Politics,* tr. by Blanche Dugdale and Torben de Bille, 2 vols. (New York, 1916).
Vacher de Lapouge, Georges, *Les Sélections Sociales* (Paris, 1896).

CHAPTER XIII

THE NINETEENTH CENTURY: NATIONAL EXPANSION AND IMPERIALISM

THE rise of the modern national states and the overseas discoveries set the stage for the development of a type of imperialism different from that of the ancient and medieval periods. The growth of Roman power and the success of Roman arms and diplomacy made possible the establishment of a universal rule over the Western world. The break-up of the Empire did not mean the abandonment of the ideal of universalism which persisted throughout the Middle Ages. But the rise of self-conscious national states, substantially equal in power, made the dream of a restoration of the old empire, or the realization of a new one embracing all of Europe, quite impossible. Apparently the most that any state could expect to achieve permanently on the Continent was a relatively small expansion of its frontiers. But overseas there was a new world, inhabited by relatively weak peoples, into which imperially-minded states might expand and compete for empire.

Economic motives, as well as national power and glory, unquestionably played a great part in the pursuit of overseas domains by the European powers in the seventeenth and eighteenth centuries. During this period, trade expansion resulted in such an increase in manufacturing that home markets became glutted and a fierce rivalry for foreign markets developed. Mercantilist restrictions, however, so limited these markets that they offered no solution. Colonies then came to be regarded as highly important as markets for manufactured goods and as sources of supply of the necessary raw materials. They could be monopolized for both purposes and colonizing states saw in them a valuable means of enhancing national wealth and power.

But during the latter part of the eighteenth century a change in the "climate of opinion"[1] in Europe took place which affected the attitude, especially in England and France, toward colonial ventures. Anti-im-

[1] *Supra*, Ch. X.

perialism, which figured more or less prominently in the thought of liberals in Europe, and particularly in England, throughout the first half of the nineteenth century, may be partly explained in connection with the following facts. In the latter years of the preceding century, imperial states suffered heavy losses of colonial territory as a result of wars and revolutions. In 1763 France lost a large part of her empire to England. A couple of decades later, England's American colonies revolted and won their independence. Finally Portugal was to lose Brazil, and Spain, most of her colonies in the New World. These events raised doubts in some intellectual circles as to the desirability and value of imperial possessions, and in others offered confirmation of the unwisdom of seeking or holding a colonial domain. In the case of the British, there was a powerful reason in addition for a renunciation of imperial ambitions. The series of mechanical inventions in the latter years of the eighteenth century in England enabled her to manufacture so cheaply that she immediately gained an enormous advantage over her rivals, could dispense with colonial restrictions, and undersell all competitors in the European market, which became better than that of the colonies.[2]

The philosophy of the period of the Enlightenment, with its emphasis upon natural laws and its doctrine of a natural order of things bearing upon social institutions,[3] might also be regarded as anti-imperialistic in its implications. Eighteenth-century writers, such as Rousseau, favored the small state as the natural political unit. Just as nature had set limits to the stature of a normal man, so had she set bounds to the size of a well-governed state.[4] From the international point of view, as well as from the standpoint of the internal welfare of a state, it must be democratically governed. For democracy, in his judgment, could only function in states of small size. On the other hand, an international federation of states could only be realized in a society of democratic states.[5] The theory of nationality was likewise considered anti-imperialistic in its essence and in its implications. If nationalities were in all cases allowed to determine their political affiliations, and set up separate states at will, according to the earlier doctrine any particular state, it is true, might be large or small; but, contrary to the case of a

[2] P. T. Moon, *Imperialism and World Politics* (New York, 1926), pp. 15-16.
[3] *Supra,* Ch. X.
[4] J. W. Garner, *Introduction to Political Science* (New York, 1910), pp. 94-95.
[5] *Supra,* pp. 191-194, for Rousseau's views on international government.

truly imperialist state, it would be based on consent. The chief attack on imperialism, however, came from the Physiocrats in France and economists like Adam Smith in England. According to the Physiocrats, the welfare and prosperity of each state depended upon the adjustment of economic processes and institutions to natural laws, and the removal of mercantilist restrictions on industry and trade within and, to a large extent, between nations as well. They regarded the forcible acquisition or retention of colonies and the policy of artificially restricting their economic life and monopolizing their trade as economically unsound. And, following Turgot, they were inclined to think, and to be quite undisturbed by the reflection, that "colonies are like fruits which cling to the tree only till they ripen."

Adam Smith (1723-1790) was in general agreement with the Physiocrats on this question. Although realizing that national pride would stand in the way of a state's voluntarily emancipating its colonies, he declared that England would be better off without colonial responsibilities. If the colonies were freed, she could still trade freely with them, but would not have the expense of holding and protecting them.[6] Jeremy Bentham argued in much the same way, but looked at the question from the point of view of international relations as well. The holding of distant dependencies, he contended, increased the chances of war by increasing the number of possible subjects of dispute. Moreover, he held that men are not as much interested in avoiding war when it is carried on in distant parts as when it is nearer home.[7]

The most vigorous and hard-hitting of the English anti-imperialists of the Manchester School, writing past the middle of the century, was Goldwin Smith (1823-1910).[8] The argument that England had a "mission" or a "responsibility" in India or elsewhere moved him to remark that "a 'mission,' historically speaking, is little more than another name for a tendency to rapine," and that "responsibility" is often used "to defend

[6] *An Inquiry into the Nature and Causes of the Wealth of Nations*, 2 vols. (London, 1776), Bk. IV, Ch. VII. Josiah Tucker, Jeremy Bentham, Joseph Hume, Richard Cobden, and others expressed a similar point of view.

[7] *Plan for an Universal and Perpetual Peace.* In England after the Napoleonic Wars some writers, known as the Colonial Reformers, advocated retention of the English colonies in order to relieve unemployment and overpopulation at home. See C. A. Bodelsen, *Studies in Mid-Victorian Imperialism* (New York, 1925), pp. 16-17.

[8] Regius professor of modern history at Oxford, 1858-1866; professor of English and constitutional history at Cornell, 1868-1881.

the retention of what you have got in those special cases where the retention is very unprofitable to the nation at large, but profitable or agreeable to a class."[9] Smith was contemptuous of sentimental arguments on behalf of imperialism, and devoted himself principally to the task of demonstrating that the dependencies of England were unprofitable and dangerous. By retaining them, England risked entanglements with other Powers. Admitting that at one time, when there was a universal prevalence of commercial monopoly, England had been economically justified in holding dependencies and monopolizing their trade, he contended that now that nations were more and more following free trade policies the original reason for having dependencies could no longer be advanced.[10] If the colonies were buying more English goods than foreign goods they were doing so not for reasons of sentiment induced by their political connection, but because they found it to their economic advantage to do so. The American colonies, he pointed out, bought more from England after they had attained independence than before. He also declared that the imperialist contention that colonial markets are safer than foreign markets was unsound. A colonial market was especially precarious, he said, because of the tendency of the colonists to set up the same manufactures as the mother country. Nor could Smith agree that colonies were valuable as homes for surplus population, for most of the emigrants from the United Kingdom went to the United States rather than to the English colonies. Moreover, Smith doubted the efficacy of emigration as a solution of the problem of over-population, for he regarded it as draining off the strong and the fit and leaving the weak. And, from a military point of view, he contended that territories scattered all over the globe and incapable of defending themselves or meeting the cost of their defense, were a source of weakness rather than strength.

All of the foregoing arguments were addressed to Englishmen, and were concerned with the question as to whether the British Empire was a paying proposition. But Smith was in reality quite as much concerned with principles as with profits. His opposition to imperialism was perhaps ultimately based on his regard for the principle of nationality. England, by keeping the colonies in subjection, no matter how benevolent her intentions, was preventing them from developing their own

[9] *The Empire* (London, 1863), pp. 257-258.
[10] *Ibid.*, pp. xx, 6.

national character.[11] In discussing the case of the Ionian islands, which the Congress of Vienna had placed under the protection of Great Britain, Smith declared that Great Britain should give effect to their desire to be joined to Greece, without quibbling over the question of the racial make-up of their inhabitants and without considering whether they would benefit by the change. The only relevant matter, he said, was their own desire. "We have constructed good roads in Ionia and kept up a good police; but England has testified in a hundred constitutional struggles that good roads and a good police are not the highest objects of national existence. The Ionians are forcibly held down by a foreign soldiery. When this is said, all is said, at least to hearts which owe allegiance to the cause of freedom. To play the gaoler of a people struggling for national existence is a part which can no longer be pressed on a great and generous nation. . . If the principle of nationality is a true principle, why should not England embrace it frankly, and take the strength and the greatness which a frank adhesion to a true principle never fails to bring?" [12]

In England, Germany, and France, the views of the anti-imperialists exerted considerable influence well past the turn of the nineteenth century. They were not always reflected in English and French foreign policy, both countries adding somewhat to their imperial domains, and neither one officially evidencing a strong desire to give up imperial responsibilities already incurred.[13] Nevertheless, prior to the Seventies, the English government on several occasions failed or refused to annex territories that might easily have been had; and the efforts of France to enlarge her colonial domain were spasmodic, and met at times with effective internal opposition. Nor did Germany immediately launch herself on an imperial career after the attainment of unification. Bismarck was for a number of years opposed to a policy of expansion and rejected several opportunities to make colonial acquisitions.[14]

[11] *The Empire,* p. 3.

[12] *Ibid.,* pp. 232, 241. Smith discussed the question of the Ionian islands in a series of letters to the *Daily News* in 1862 and 1863. In 1864 England ceded the islands to Greece. There were, however, limits to Smith's advocacy of national self-determination. He regarded the struggles of Ireland for independence as "treason" and approved the suppression of rebellion there apparently on the ground of preserving "national unity." (*Ibid.,* p. ix.)

[13] Although in 1865 a committee of the House of Commons went so far as to recommend that Britain give up all holdings on the West African coast, with the exception of Sierra Leone, and annex no more territory in that region.

[14] Moon, *op. cit.,* pp. 19-24.

In the meantime, however, forces were at work which eventually led to a mad race for colonies, or at least political control over "backward peoples," on the part of the European powers and, in a lesser degree, affected the policy of the United States as well. During the last quarter of the nineteenth century, England rapidly lost the lion's share of the world's trade which she had enjoyed prior to the industrial rise of Germany, the United States, France, and other powers.[15] Moreover, all of the principal industrial nations began to find themselves producing surpluses of manufactured goods which must find wider foreign markets. But none of them desired to admit goods from other countries similar to those for which their own manufacturers were seeking markets, and, with the exception of Great Britain, they began to build high tariff walls. Under these circumstances, the only alternative, in the opinion of a growing number of business men and politicians as well as other groups within these countries, was to seek colonies and monopolize their markets.

On the other hand, the unprecedented and growing output of manufacturers in the chief industrial countries created a demand for cotton, rubber, and other raw materials and minerals in such quantities that new sources of supply often had to be sought outside the manufacturing country. To insure a steady supply of these essential products as well as other tropical or semi-tropical products, such as sugar, tea, coffee, and cocoa, the untapped areas of "backward peoples" now became necessary. But the unembarrassed exploitation of such areas normally required the extension of political control by the interested country. It must be able to establish an orderly administration over the area in question, and secure exclusive economic rights.

About the beginning of the twentieth century another economic factor became important. In the chief industrial countries large fortunes were made and surpluses of capital accumulated too great to be reinvested at a satisfactory rate of return in the home country. The holders of such capital then looked abroad. Other advanced and politically stable countries offered in some instances opportunities for profitable

[15] For example, between 1870 and 1903 British iron-masters expanded their business 50%, but during the same period their American competitors increased their business by 966% and the Germans theirs by 609%. In the export trade, English exporters increased their sales by 45% from 1870 to 1900, but American exports were nearly quadrupled and German exports were doubled. (Moon, *op. cit.*, p. 26.)

investment, but the chances for the largest profits were to be found in the more speculative enterprises in the undeveloped areas of backward peoples. In the latter case, however, conditions often developed under native administration which jeopardized these enterprises and caused investors to bring pressure on their governments to intervene. Intervention often led to outright annexation or the establishment of some form of political control designed to safeguard investments and perhaps promote the establishment of new enterprises.[16]

There was still another surplus that presented a problem to certain industrial nations whose populations grew rapidly along with their industrial development, and made the competition of life within their borders more difficult. A nation with a "surplus population" was disinclined to have its progressive elements, seeking greater economic opportunities by emigration abroad, "lost to the national flag." This inevitably occurred if they migrated to underpopulated but advanced and nationally self-conscious countries. On the other hand, if additional standing-room could be found for them by the annexation of rich territories occupied by primitive peoples, this would be preferable, argued the imperialists, from an economic and from a political point of view as well.

In the second half of the nineteenth century the "scientific" justification for imperialism was, as we have observed in the preceding chapter, at hand. It was "natural" and, to some, it was essential to human progress, for strong nations to struggle for aggrandizement, and for the superior "races" to prevail. Given this biologic urge on the part of healthy "races," and the presence of accessible "backward races," and the logic of imperialism is inescapable. It needs, indeed, no further defense or explanation. It is independent of time and place and, finally, whether one regards imperialism as brutal or beneficent, it is no more a question of man's choice than is an earthquake. From this point of view, however, imperialism can be regarded as entirely consistent with the theory of subjugation and annexation of weaker nationalities and

[16] It must be remembered, also, that the imperialism of the last half century, involving the exploitation on a large scale of distant and formerly almost inaccessible areas, was made possible for the first time by the revolution in transportation and communication which came about with the development of the fast steamship, the telegraph, telephone and other space-annihilating inventions of more recent years.

backward peoples by states claiming statehood on the basis of nationality.

Ludwig Gumplowicz (1838-1909), Polish sociologist and professor of law at the University of Graz, looked upon imperialism as a natural phenomenon. Influenced by the Darwinian concept of the struggle for existence and the Spencerian idea of evolution, he regarded civilization as the product of perpetual struggle, first between primitive racial groups and later between the larger national states arising out of struggles in which the weak groups are conquered by the strong and brought into subjection. In all group struggles, as contrasted with the competition of individuals, ethical considerations and moral principles are altogether lacking. This is as true, according to Gumplowicz, in the case of civilized states as it was in the conflicts between primitive social groups, and there is nothing to be done about it. "Blind natural law controls the action of savage hordes, of states and of societies." [17] The "most natural tendency" of states, he declared, "is incessant increase of power and territory." [18] Their success in securing additional spoils will depend upon their ability in assimilating conquered peoples and attaining internal unity. But in any case, according to Gumplowicz, the law of their being will drive them toward expansion. "So necessary and so strong is the tendency to foreign conquest that no state can escape it what ever may be the feeling of the ruler at the time. The method will vary with the circumstances; and unfavorable circumstances will be circumvented or overcome." [19] Thus the greatest states have attempted to rule the world and have only ceased their striving when they have met with catastrophe and ruin.[20]

A similar point of view, extended and elaborated, however, into a philosophic system, was presented several years later in the works of the

[17] *The Outlines of Sociology,* pp. 146-148. Translation by Frederick W. Moore (Philadelphia, Pa., 1899) of *Grundriss der Soziologie* (Vienna, 1885).

[18] *Ibid.,* pp. 150.

[19] *Ibid.,* p. 151. In an earlier work, *Der Rassenkampf* (Innsbruck, 1883), p. 166, Gumplowicz attempts to trace from primitive times the various forms in which the natural tendency of the state to augment its power and extend its authority is manifested.

[20] Gumplowicz regards this as a "social law" observable not only in the growth of states but also in the struggle among groups within states for wealth, power, and property. The tendency of all is to seek expansion without limit until the "crash" comes. (*Ibid.,* p. 152.)

Frenchman, Ernest Seillière (1866-).[21] The latter traced the principal source of human actions to a fundamental tendency in both individuals and groups, whether nations, races, or classes, toward aggrandizement. This tendency, which Seillière called imperialism,[22] he regarded as a corollary of the instinct of self-preservation found in all organisms. To Seillière, therefore, social reformers like Bentham and Cobden were just as imperialistic as Cecil Rhodes, the only difference being that the former were pursuing different objects. Imperialism may be irrational and mystical or it may be rational. At first, according to Seillière, man's will to power, whether one is considering the individual or a group, was almost altogether mystic; that is, the support of a divine ally was sought for it. This, Seillière asserted, was the basis of the imperialism of Gobineau,[23] Chamberlain,[24] and Rhodes.[25] The essential of this type of imperialism, as exhibited by nations, is the pretension of a race or nation that it particularly has superior merit and divine support in its struggle to rule less favored groups; and the tendency to disregard realities in the attempt to realize its objectives. This type of imperialism has its dangers for the group practicing it. On the other hand, rational imperialism seeks its objects by checking its mystic enthusiasm in the light of reason or accumulated human experience. Seillière regards this type of imperialism with approval.[26]

Among English writers who began to arise in the Eighties to a vigorous defense of British imperialism, the historian J. R. Seeley (1834-1895), professor of modern history in Cambridge, commanded a great

[21] See *La Philosophie de l'Impérialisme,* 4 vols. (Paris, 1903-1908); and *Introduction à la Philosophie de l'Impérialisme* (Paris, 1911).

[22] Hobbes called it the desire for power; Nietzsche, the will to power.

[23] Arthur de Gobineau (1816-1882), French diplomat and race mystic. His chief work was his *Essai sur l'Inégalité des Races Humaines,* 4 vols. (Paris, 1853-1855). Translation of Book I by Adrian Collins (London, 1915).

[24] Houston Stuart Chamberlain (1855-1927), though born in England, became a naturalized German citizen and ardent race mystic who created an ideal "Teutonic" race largely out of his imagination. His *Die Grundlagen des Neunzahuten Jahrhunderts,* 2 vols. (Munich, 1899), however, was taken seriously by many Germans, and greatly stimulated German nationalism and race pride. This work was translated into English by John Lees under the title *The Foundations of the Nineteenth Century* (London, 1910).

[25] Cecil John Rhodes (1853-1902), British empire builder, early dedicated himself to the task of spreading the rule of the British race over Africa, where he had made a fortune in the Kimberley diamond fields, and as much of the remainder of the earth as possible.

[26] *Introduction à la Philosophie de l'Imperialisme,* Preface and Section I.

deal of attention.[27] Englishmen are still fond of repeating his remark about the casual way in which the British Empire was supposed to have been acquired. "We seem, as it were, to have conquered and peopled half the world in a fit of absence of mind." [28] But Seeley felt that Englishmen should slough off this absent-mindedness and deplorable indifference, and become conscious of England's "destiny." The expansion of the English race into Canada and Australia, he asserted, was due to "natural causes," but he denied the ripe-fruit doctrine of Turgot and the little Englanders that eventual separation from the mother country was "natural" and therefore inevitable. Seeley was, however, not impressed by what he called the "bombastic" school of imperialist opinion. Mere bigness, for example, he did not regard as necessarily important. He declared that during most of the historical period very large states had usually been of a low type. To point out, therefore, that the British Empire was one "upon which the sun never sets" was not sufficient to win his approval. Nor did Seeley take seriously the argument that the Empire should be preserved regardless of other considerations, as a point of honor and out of respect for the heroes who had won it. He even declared that the fact that such an immense empire had been built up did not necessarily prove that Englishmen were possessed of "invincible heroism, or supernatural genius for government." [29]

Seeley distinguished between the "possessions" of England, such as India, and the "colonies," such as Canada and Australia. He admitted that it was not clear that India should have been acquired in the first place, and its value to England might be regarded as doubtful. Nevertheless, he was sure that "the experiment must go forward. . ." [30] On the other hand, "Greater Britain," consisting of the English-speaking "colonies," represented a process of "natural expansion." For the most part, these colonies were acquired without conquest, and were in reality a normal extension of the English race rather than an empire. Such a

[27] His *Expansion of England* (London, 1883), comprised two courses of lectures delivered to his students. The book was very popular, 80,000 copies being sold in two years. Lord Rosebery is said to have been converted to imperialism after reading it. It also seems to have earned Seeley knighthood. (Moon, *op. cit.*, p. 39.)

[28] *Op. cit.*, p. 8.

[29] *Ibid.*, pp. 293-294.

[30] *Ibid.*, p. 305.

type of expansion can only be regarded with pleasure. It affords a much-needed outlet for superfluous population and new markets for the mother country.[31] Does it mean an undue enlargement of the English state? Seeley is sure that it does not, for times have changed. Since the development of representative government and federalism, and the shortening of distances by steam and electricity, much larger states are politically feasible than was true in the past. The United States, for example, has shown the possibility of combining free institutions with indefinite expansion. And Englishmen must realize, said Seeley, that the question is not whether England shall choose to be a small state among small states, but whether she shall be a small state among larger ones now springing up in the world, such as Russia and the United States. "Is not this a serious consideration, and is it not especially so for a state like England, which has at the present moment the choice in its hands between two courses of action, the one of which may set it in that future age on a level with the greatest of these great states of the future, while the other will reduce it to the level of a purely European Power looking back, as Spain does now, to the great days when she pretended to be a world state."[32] To Seeley, there was no question as to the choice England should make, for he was convinced a great destiny was reserved for her.

Another representative of British imperialist thought whose approach, however, was quite different from that of Seeley, was the historian J. A. Cramb (1862-1913), professor of modern history at Queen's College, London, and occasional lecturer on military history. His theory of imperialism is best stated in his *Reflections on the Origins and Destiny of Imperial Britain,* originally a course of lectures delivered in 1900, and inspired by the war between England and the Boers in South Africa.[33] Cramb's imperialism was based upon a race mysticism centering about the conviction that certain races are "dowered with the genius for empire," and that a race so endowed "is compelled to dare all, to suffer all, to sacrifice all for the fulfillment of its fate-appointed

[31] Seeley, *op. cit.,* pp. 296-298.

[32] *Ibid.,* p. 301. J. A. Froude (1818-1894), contemporary of Seeley, Regius Professor of Modern History at Oxford, was likewise a supporter of English imperialism for reasons similar to those emphasized by Seeley.

[33] His *Germany and England* (London, 1914), is also revealing. Cramb was an admirer of Prussian militarism, and it was characteristic of him to see and approve the ancient Teutonic spirit of Germany expressing itself in German imperialism in the years before the War.

task."[34] Seeley would doubtless have classified Cramb as a "bombastic" imperialist. Both men were fond of using the word "destiny" in connection with British imperialism, but Seeley presumably thought its use justified from a careful historical study of the "unparalleled," "profound" and "persistent" expansion[35] of England, whereas Cramb was inclined to rely more largely upon inspiration than upon investigation, and to read a nation's destiny in its "race." An "imperial race" such as the Teutonic (of which the Anglo-Saxon race is a branch) is destined for a career of imperialism. Not so other races, such as the Slav. In this race Cramb declares that "the innate energy, the determining genius for constructive politics which marks races destined for empire, everywhere is wanting."[36]

Cramb regarded the war in the Transvaal as a conflict between two principles, "the dying principle of Nationality, and the principle which, for weal or woe, is that of the future, the principle of Imperialism."[37] The former, though useful in the building up of the state system of Europe, Cramb seems to think is now outdated, at least for "imperial races."[38] Such races *must* go forward even though in the process other races have to be conquered. "In political life, in the life-history of states, as in religions, as in intellectual and social history, change and growth, or what we now name Evolution, are perpetual, continuous, unresting. The empire which has ceased to advance has begun to recede. Motion is the law of its being, if not towards a fuller life, motion toward death. Thus in a race dowered with the genius for empire, as Rome was, as Britain is, Imperialism is the supreme, the crowning form, which in this process of evolution it attains. The civic, the feudal, or the oligarchic State passes into the national, the national into the imperial, by slow or swift gradations, but irresistibly, as by a fixed law of nature."[39]

[34] *The Origins and Destiny of Imperial Britain* (London, 1915), p. 13. This is a reprint of the course of lectures delivered in 1900. It was published in 1915, apparently as anti-German war propaganda, although Cramb himself had certainly been a spiritual ally of the chauvinists and imperialists of Germany as he had been of the English imperialists.

[35] Seeley, *op. cit.*, pp. 16, 308.

[36] Cramb, *The Origins and Destiny of Imperial Britain*, p. 131.

[37] *Ibid.*, p. 90.

[38] He seems to lean toward a doctrine of relativity. "It is one thing," he says, "to exalt the grandeur of this ideal for Italy or for France, but it is another to assume that it has final and equal grandeur in every land and to every State." (*Ibid.*, p. 94.)

[39] *Ibid.*, p. 91. Excerpt quoted by permission of E. P. Dutton and Co., Inc., pub-

Another racialist whose views led to imperialism was the American historian and political scientist, J. W. Burgess. Although believing that the modern national state, based on nationality, is the highest form of political organization the world has achieved, Burgess was not prepared to admit that "every nation must become a state." For nations are not equally endowed with political capacity. The "Celt," for example, "has almost none," the Asiatic nations are also conspicuously deficient, the Greek and the Slav have little.[40] Rome, it is true, showed great political genius in establishing a universal Empire and in this achievement solved the problem of the defense of the state against external foes. But such a political régime, in Burgess' opinion, had nevertheless a serious defect. It did away with the benefits of "contact, competition and antagonism" between states and sank the world in a "universal reign of peace, which means, in the long run, stagnation and despotism."[41]

It is the Teuton, according to Burgess, who has shown the supreme political genius. The modern national state, far superior to anything the world had known before, is the creation of Teutonic elements.[42] Their outstanding superiority in the field of government, therefore, authorizes them "to assume leadership in the establishment and administration of states."[43] Moreover, as Divine Providence has entrusted them with "the mission of conducting the political civilization of the world," they must see to it that the balance of power always remains in their hands and, if necessary to the accomplishment of this end, they may deprive other elements of their political rights. And they must have a colonial policy as one of their primary duties. Backward

lishers and holders of copyright. Cramb was also convinced of "the might, the majesty, and the mystery of war (*ibid.*, p. 125), and of its permanence in the life of states. The effect of imperialism was to "greaten and exalt the character of war." (*Ibid.*, p. 147.)

[40] *Political Science and Constitutional Law,* 2 vols. (Boston and London, 1890-1891), I, 4. The Celtic (Irish) element seems to have shown considerable political genius in New York City, where Burgess taught, as well as in other American cities. A few years after Burgess passed judgment on the Asiatic as possessing a low order of political genius, Japan was rapidly forging to the front as a Great Power. And within recent years the light of political genius has been burning rather low in Teutonic states.

[41] *Ibid.*, pp. 35, 36, 38.

[42] Burgess stated that Teutonic elements were dominant in the creation of Spain, Portugal, Italy, France, Belgium, England, Denmark, Norway, Sweden, Germany, Holland, Switzerland, Austria, and the United States. Some of these peoples are certainly entitled to be surprised by this inclusive statement.

[43] *Op. cit.*, p. 39.

peoples have no rights to the lands they inhabit and the Teutons, according to Burgess, may properly oust them and take possession. Only civilized states can acquire titles to lands. Finally Teutons may interfere in the affairs of any states that do not reach their standards and "righteously assume sovereignty over them."[44] In brief, the position of Burgess seems to be that Teutonically-ruled states or those regarding themselves as Teutonic are entitled, on account of their superior political genius, to bring all other peoples into subjection, and establish empires for themselves throughout the earth.

The American sociologist, Franklin H. Giddings (1855-1931), who, like Burgess, taught at Columbia University for a number of years, came forth as an ardent imperialist at the time of the Spanish-American War. Although not disposed to catalogue "races" according to their political genius with the completeness and assurance exhibited by Burgess, he looked upon the English-speaking democratic nations, Great Britain and the United States, with favor as against the state he regarded as their only dangerous rival, autocratic Russia; and hoped they would unite their forces and expand their influence and power so that they would win out "in the international struggle for existence." [45] Giddings, like the social Darwinists, was given to the use of phrases such as "cosmic law" and prone to regard certain social phenomena as inevitable. Thus he was convinced "that the combination of small states into large political aggregates must continue until all the semi-civilized, barbarian and savage communities of the world are brought under the protection of the larger civilized nations." [46] Likewise he asserted that "the war with Spain was as inevitable as any event of nature" and that "at this particular stage in the development of the United States, territorial expansion is as certain as the advent of spring after winter." [47] Why? Because the American people have reached a stage where they have surplus energy to expend and surplus manu-

[44] *Ibid.*, pp. 46-47.

[45] Before Giddings, the American historian John Fiske had already settled the matter when he wrote that "the work which the English race began when it colonized North America is destined to go on until every land on the earth's surface that is not already the seat of an old civilization shall become English in its language, in its political habits and traditions, and to a predominant extent in the blood of its people." (*American Political Ideas* [New York, 1902], p. 143.)

[46] *Democracy and Empire* (New York and London, 1901), Preface.

[47] *Ibid.*, p. 270.

factures to sell. If an anti-imperialistic policy should be adopted and the surplus energy thus denied an outlet, Giddings feared it would discharge itself in anarchistic and socialistic movements within and work all sorts of mischief.[48]

The general views of Giddings on the advantages of imperialism may be seen in connection with his advocacy of the retention of the Philippines by the United States after the victory over Spain in 1898. In order to push surplus American manufactures in the Far East, it is necessary, he pointed out, to have greater trade facilities there. And the best way to make our demand for such facilities effective is by "maintaining our sovereignty over some territory, however small, in that quarter of the world." [49] On the other hand, such trade with the Far East as Americans already possessed would be lost to Russia and the other Powers, he declared, if the Philippines should be given up. The Philippines and other tropical territories of politically backward peoples should be taken and held as territorial possessions by white races who should govern them in the interests of the world at large and of the native inhabitants.[50] This is the only way in which the civilized world can continue in its economic conquest of the natural resources of the earth. The increased responsibility involved in an imperialist career operated as a "powerful moralizing influence" on states accepting such responsibility, and tended to develop their capacity for government and administration.

Giddings rejected as unjustifiable the assumption that democracy and empire are incompatible. He contended that both England and the United States were becoming more democratic each year although pursuing a colonial career, and that democratic institutions had grown up in the English dominions and were also developing in India and the lesser

[48] *Democracy and Empire*, p. 274.

[49] *Ibid.*, p. 283.

[50] This is essentially the position taken by Benjamin Kidd in his *Control of the Tropics* (New York, 1898). It also found a vigorous supporter in Theodore Roosevelt. Kipling gave poetic expression to it in the well-known lines:

> "Take up the White Man's Burden—
> Send forth the best ye breed.
> Go bind your sons to exile
> To serve your captive's need;
> To wait in heavy harness,
> On fluttered fold and wild—
> Your new-caught, sullen peoples
> Half-devil and half-child."

dependencies. His idea of a modern democratic empire was one in which the imperial government should in general confine itself to providing for imperial defense, suppressing conflict between different parts of the empire, and requiring the local administration to attain "a certain standard of life and property." [51]

Treitschke, whose views on war and progress have already been noted, was also an imperialist. His theory of the State as Power led him inevitably to regard the size of a state as vital and to look upon expansion as necessary. He seemed to think that the very existence of Germany as a state of first rank depended upon her ability to become an overseas power, and that if she did not expand outside Europe there was grave danger that England and Russia would divide the world between them.[52] In any event, he agreed with the poet that "wide horizons liberate the mind." Great states he apparently regarded as the nurseries of great thoughts and great deeds, whereas small states were capable only of developing a sort of parish-pump political outlook; and he thought the time might come "when no State will be counted great unless it can boast of territories beyond the seas." [53]

Perhaps the most penetrating of the critics of the new imperialism to enter the lists about the beginning of the twentieth century was the liberal-radical British Economist, J. A. Hobson (1858-). In his *Imperialism* (London, 1902), Hobson examined the question in both its economic and political aspects and brought an indictment against imperialism on both counts. A follower of John Stuart Mill in his views on nationality,[54] and an internationalist and pacifist [55] in his outlook on international relations, Hobson regarded imperialism as a perversion of the nature and purpose of nationalism: "It is a debasement of this genuine nationalism, by attempts to overflow its natural banks and absorb the near or distant territory of reluctant and unassimilable peo-

[51] Giddings, *op. cit.*, p. 11. See David Starr Jordan, *Imperial Democracy* (New York, 1901), pp. 3-179 especially, for an extended criticism of the position of Giddings, and a plea for the United States to decide against imperialist adventures.

[52] *Politics*, I, 33.

[53] *Ibid.*, I, 36. For a defense of the small state see H. A. L. Fisher, *Studies in History and Politics* (London, 1920), for essay on "The Value of Small States." It was written in 1915 in the midst of the World War apparently as a polemic against the German position. The British government, it will be remembered, had announced that England was fighting for the rights of small nationalities.

[54] *Supra*, pp. 221-222.

[55] See, among other works, his *Towards International Government* (London, 1915).

ples, that marks the passage from nationalism to a spurious colonialism on the one hand, Imperialism on the other."[56] Colonialism, as exemplified in the British self-governing dominions, populated by British stock was, however, legitimate, according to Hobson, for it represented "a genuine expansion of nationality." On the other hand, he condemned the typical cut-throat imperialism of the Great Powers. "Not only does aggressive Imperialism defeat the movement toward internationalism by fostering animosities among competing empires; its attack upon the liberties and the existence of weaker or lower races stimulates in them a corresponding excess of national self-consciousness. A nationalism that bristles with resentment and is all astrain with the passion of self-defence is only less perverted from its natural genius than the nationalism which glows with the animus of greed and self-aggrandisement at the expense of others."[57]

From an economic point of view Hobson, having the British Empire in mind, contended that imperialism does not pay, if the general interest, as contrasted with special interests,[58] of the country supporting such a policy, is the criterion. For example his analysis of the trade of Great Britain led him to conclude that her internal industry and trade were far more important than her external trade, and that of the external trade that with foreign countries was more important and valuable than that with her possessions.[59] The argument that colonies provided a needed outlet for surplus population Hobson met by the contention that Great Britain was not over-populated, and that it was not likely to be in the future, on account of a diminution in the rate of increase. Admitting that imperialism furnished some employment to the military and official classes, and to missionaries, engineers, prospectors, etc., Hobson pointed out that altogether this represented an insignificant contribution toward the unemployment problem.[60] On the other hand, the imperialistic rivalries of the Powers were responsible for the growth

[56] *Imperialism,* p. 4.
[57] *Ibid.,* p. 9.
[58] J. M. Robertson, in his *Patriotism and Empire* (London, 1900), p. 187, was among those who anticipated Hobson's thesis. He declared: "The only interests really furthered by fresh expansion are those of the speculative trading class, the speculative capitalist class, the military and naval services, the industrial class which supplies war materials, and generally those who look to an imperial civil service as the means of employment for themselves and their kin." Robertson's "counter-ideal" is also essentially the same as that of Hobson. (Pp. 202-204).
[59] *Imperialism,* p. 44.
[60] *Ibid.,* pp. 46-50.

of large armaments, militarism, and wars which placed a heavy financial burden on the governments and peoples of the countries concerned.

Hobson contended, nevertheless, that imperialism had an "economic tap-root" that sustained it in spite of the fact that its benefits to the country as a whole were illusory, and that it was a dangerous and "depraved choice of national life." Certain classes and interests were served by imperialism. For example, there are manufacturers who produce more goods than can be profitably sold at home, and there are capitalists who cannot find opportunities for remunerative investments within the country. But, Hobson contends, this need not be so. The demand for new markets and new fields for investment is due not to industrial progress, but to the "mal-distribution of consuming power which prevents the absorption of commodities and capital within the country. The over-saving which is the economic root of Imperialism is found by analysis to consist of rents, monopoly profits, and other unearned or excessive elements of income, which, not being earned by labor of head or hand, have no legitimate *raison d'être*. . . . Let any turn in the tide of politico-economic forces divert from the owners their excess of income and make it flow, either to the workers in higher wages, or to the community in taxes, so that it will be spent instead of being saved, serving in either of these ways to swell the tide of consumption—there will be no need to fight for foreign markets or foreign areas of investment." [61] Thus Hobson's analysis was essentially that of socialist theorists, but his remedy was that of social reform rather than socialism. He felt that a sound scheme of taxation, which would bear heavily on "unearned increments of land values" and on "profits in trades which, by virtue of some legal or economic protection screening them from close competition, are able to earn high rates of interest or profit," would provide the remedy.[62]

Hobson also condemned imperialism from the political standpoint. Speaking of the British Empire, he asserted that so far from enlarging

[61] *Ibid.*, p. 91. In any case, Hobson was opposed to the policy of extending government aid and protection to investors who, investing capital abroad with expectation of large profits, and with full knowledge of the risks involved, yet called upon government when difficulties were encountered. (*Ibid.*, pp. 379-381.) A similar attitude was taken by H. N. Brailsford, *The War of Steel and Gold* (10th ed. rev., London, 1918), pp. 240-241.

[62] *Op. cit.*, p. 103. For a criticism of Hobson's position on the economic side, see E. M. Winslow, "Marxian, Liberal, and Sociological Theories of Imperialism," *Journal of Political Economy*, Vol. XXXIX (Dec., 1931), No. 6, pp. 732-737.

the area of British liberty in the world, as Englishmen often contended, it had—the Dominions excepted—"increased the area of British despotism." For the most part, the Empire was autocratically governed from Downing Street, and this despotic and expensive imperial rule had unfortunate reactions upon home politics as well, for democratic institutions cannot flourish at home while autocratic methods are employed abroad.[63] Furthermore, social reforms such as improvement of public education, housing, and labor conditions, which require large expenditures of public money, are postponed or abandoned because growing military expenditure for imperial purposes drains the public purse. Hobson added that, "every social reform involves some attack on vested interests, and these can best defend themselves when active Imperialism absorbs public attention. When legislation is involved economy of time and of governmental interest is of paramount importance. Imperialism, with its 'high politics,' involving the honour and safety of the empire, claims the first place, and, as the empire grows, the number and complexity of its issues, involving close, immediate, continuous attention, grow—absorbing the time of the government and of Parliament."[64] Yet representative institutions are not adapted to the handling of the vast issues and complicated problems of empire, and in practice the executive arm of the government is given a free hand, party government is weakened, and popular control tends to become nominal in foreign affairs[65] and of less influence in the conduct of public affairs generally.

Hobson recognized the great support given imperialism by the unqualified application of the Darwinian theory to human affairs by such men as Karl Pearson,[66] and devoted a chapter to a refutation of their doctrines. His position in general was that mankind is not doomed to

[63] Another liberal English writer, L. T. Hobhouse, takes the same position. In his *Social Evolution and Political Theory* (New York, 1911), p. 144, he says: "We cannot deny principles of liberty to Orientals, or for that matter to Zulus, and yet maintain them with the same fervor and conviction for the benefit of anyone who may be oppressed among ourselves. We cannot foster a great bureaucratic class without being impregnated at home by its views of government. We cannot protect a great dependency from without except by remaining a great military and naval power, and to all these necessities our own body social must accommodate itself." A similar point of view was expressed by W. G. Sumner, in *War and Other Essays* (New Haven, Conn., 1911), pp. 292, 346; and J. G. Godard, *Racial Supremacy* (London, 1905), pp. 33-35.

[64] *Op. cit.*, p. 149.

[65] For a similar point of view, see L. T. Hobhouse, *Democracy and Reaction* (New York, 1905), p. 147.

[66] *Supra*, pp. 244-245.

maintain a crude struggle for existence by means of recurrent wars in order to achieve advances in civilization through natural selection. The beneficence of struggle and competition he did not deny, but he argued that in the case of man the struggle can and must, in the interest of greater progress, proceed on a higher plane. In much the same fashion as Novicow, he asserted: "Individuality does not suffer but greatly gains by the suppression of the lower struggle; there is more energy, greater scope for its expression, a wider field of close competitors; and higher and more varied forms of fitness are tested and evoked. It is not even true that the struggle ceases to be physical; the strain and the support of the higher forms of struggle, even in the topmost intellectual and moral planes, are largely physical; the health and nervous energy which take part in the struggles of the law or literature or on any intellectual arena are chief requisites if not the supreme determinant of success. In all the higher forms of struggle an elimination of the physically unfit is still maintained, though the criteria of physical unfitness are not quite the same as in the primitive human struggles." [67]

Hobson also denied that imperial expansion was a natural necessity on account of the working of the law of diminishing returns. There was no inexorable law that a nation must, sooner or later, either expand its land area in order to have a sufficient food supply, or evade the law by producing a constantly growing surplus of manufactures for which markets must be found so as to get money to purchase food from abroad. Hobson insists that there are other alternatives whereby war and expansion may be avoided. Man may work out an adjustment "by a progressive mitigation of the law of diminishing returns in agriculture and the extractive arts, and by limiting the rate of growth of population." [68] Even in the past, he points out, these rational checks have to some extent operated to resist or postpone the operation of the law of diminishing returns. There is reason to believe, he adds, that such progress may be made in agriculture and the arts in the future that the operation of the law may even be reversed.[69] Likewise he advocates and expects a development of the tendency toward a rational restriction of the "natural" growth of population, as a necessary complementary means of economic adjustment. This is the alternative to imperialism

[67] Hobson, *op. cit.*, pp. 182-183.
[68] *Ibid.*, p. 186.
[69] *Ibid.*, pp. 187-189, for elaboration of this view.

and there is nothing to prevent man by deliberate conscious choice from embracing it.

Hobson does not advocate, however, that each nation must confine itself solely to the intensive cultivation of its own vineyard. There is still the problem of backward peoples inhabiting rich and extensive areas of the earth. May they take refuge behind the principle of nationality and ask to be allowed to do as they please with the given area they happen to occupy, regardless of consequences to the rest of the world? Assuredly not, answers Hobson. This would be not only impossible, for there will be no halt in the development of the world's resources, but in the final analysis it would not be ethically defensible. Absolute nationalism cannot be admitted. In principle, when the interests of the world require the development of the resources of a backward people, the latter should not be allowed to interpose a veto, and even "some element of compulsion" against them may be resorted to if necessary. But this cannot safely be left to some self-appointed nations because they call themselves "trustees of civilization." [70] For the object should be "the safety and progress of the civilization of the world, and not the special interest of the interfering nation." [71] And it is too much to expect, declares Hobson, that imperial nations will pursue a course of conduct in which the common interest and the interests of the subject people will receive first consideration. What, then, is the solution? Hobson asserts that the right to exercise control over backward peoples should only be granted to a nation on condition that it "is accredited by a body genuinely representative of civilization, to which it acknowledges a real responsibility, and that it is in fact capable of executing such a trust." [72] Such a body as Hobson had in mind must not be a "self-chosen oligarchy" of dominant nations likely to act in collusion for the exploitation of backward peoples. That, in his opinion, is a real danger to be guarded against.

It will thus be seen that Hobson's regard for nationality in principle and his rejection of imperialism both in principle and practice did

[70] Mr. Joseph Chamberlain, speaking at the Birmingham Chamber of Commerce, November 13, 1896, said that "as fast as we acquire new territory and develop it, (we) develop it as trustees of civilization for the commerce of the world." President McKinley, in his message of December 3, 1900, announced that the Philippines were "an unsought trust which should be unselfishly discharged. . . ."

[71] Hobson, *op. cit.*, p. 245.

[72] *Ibid.*, p. 251. This anticipates the mandate system. *Infra*, Ch. XVIII.

not blind him to the dangers involved in a doctrinaire acceptance of the extreme demands of nationality to exclusive consideration; nor did it prevent his seeing that some of the things being done by modern imperialism must go forward. With the welfare of the international community in mind, however, he looked in the direction of international control as a solution. This was his answer both to irresponsible nationalism and irresponsible imperialism. Hobson was, however, ahead of his time. The World War, in part certainly a resultant of competing and irresponsible imperialisms, intervened before a partial attempt was made, in the establishment of the mandate system, to apply on a fairly large scale the principle for which he contended.[73]

REFERENCES

Angell, Norman, *The Great Illusion* (4th ed., New York and London, 1913), Pt. I.

Barnes, H. E., *Sociology and Political Theory* (New York, 1924), pp. 83-86, 182-185.

Bentham, J., *Works,* ed. by Bowring, 11 vols. (Edinburgh, 1843), Vols. II-IV.

Bérard, V., *British Imperialism and Commercial Supremacy,* tr. by H. W. Foskett (London and New York, 1906).

Bodelsen, C. A., *Studies in Mid Victorian Imperalism* (New York, 1924).

Bonnecase, J., *Philosophie de l'Impérialisme et Science du Droit* (Bordeaux, 1932).

Brailsford, H. N., *The War of Steel and Gold* (10th ed. rev., London, 1918).

Brie, F., *Imperialistische Stromungen in der Englischen Literatur* (Halle, 1928), pp. 83-270.

Bryce, J., *The Relations of the Advanced and the Backward Races of Mankind* (Oxford, 1903). The Romanes Lecture, 1902.

Burgess, J. W., *Political Science and Comparative Constitutional Law,* 2 vols. (Boston and London, 1890-1891), Vol. I, Chs. III, IV.

Cramb, J. A., *Germany and England* (London, 1914).

————, *The Origins and Destiny of Imperial Britain* (London, 1915).

Dawson, W. H., *Richard Cobden and Foreign Policy* (London, 1926), Ch. IX.

[73] The principle of international control in Morocco was recognized by the Algeciras Conference (1906), although no machinery for its realization was provided in the agreement reached. Walter Lippmann, in his *Stakes of Diplomacy* (New York, 1915), pointed out the need for the establishment of permanent international agencies in such sore spots to supervise the enforcement of international agreements concerning them. See *infra,* pp. 411-412.

Fisher, H. A. L., *Studies in History and Politics* (London, 1920), pp. 161-179.

Fiske, J., *American Political Ideas* (New York and London, 1902), pp. 101-152.

Gazeau, J., *L'Impérialisme Anglais, son Évolution: Carlyle-Seeley-Chamberlain* (Paris, 1903).

Giddings, F. H., *Democracy and Empire* (New York and London, 1901).

Godard, J. G., *Racial Supremacy* (Edinburgh and London, 1905).

Gumplowicz, L., *The Outlines of Sociology,* tr. by F. W. Moore (Philadelphia, Pa., 1899), pp. 150-153.

Hobhouse, L. T., *Democracy and Reaction* (New York, 1905).

Hobson, J. A., *Imperialism* (London, 1902).

——————, "Socialistic Imperialism," *International Journal of Ethics,* XII (Oct., 1901), 44-58.

Hovde, B. J., "Socialistic Theories of Imperialism Prior to the Great War," *Journal of Political Economy,* XXXVI (1928), 569-591.

Jordan, D. S., *Imperial Democracy* (New York, 1901), pp. 3-179.

Keller, A. G., *Colonization* (Boston, 1908).

Kidd, Benjamin, *The Control of the Tropics* (New York, 1898).

Leroy-Beaulieu, P., *De la Colonisation chez les Peuples Modernes* (3rd ed., Paris, 1891-1902).

Le Play, P. G. F., *La Réforme Sociale en France,* 3 vols. (7th ed., Paris, 1887), Vol. III, Ch. LI, Sec. VIII; Ch. LIII, Sec. V.

Lippmann, Walter, *The Stakes of Diplomacy* (New York, 1915).

Lugard, Sir Frederick, *The Rise of Our East African Empire* (Edinburgh and London, 1893).

Merriam, C. E., and Barnes, H. E., *A History of Political Theories of Recent Times* (New York, 1924), pp. 508-539.

Moon, Parker T., *Imperialism and World Politics* (New York, 1926).

Noske, G., *Kolonial-Politik und Sozialdemokratie* (Stuttgart, 1914).

Pavlovich, M., *The Foundations of Imperialist Policy* (London, 1922).

Ratzel, F., *Politische Geographie* (Munich, 1893).

——————, *Der Staat und Sein Boden* (Leipzig, 1897).

Reinsch, P. S., *World Politics* (New York and London, 1900).

Robertson, J. M., *Patriotism and Empire* (3rd ed., London, 1900).

Robinson, E. van Dyke, "War and Economics," *Political Science Quarterly,* Vol. XV (Dec., 1900), No. 4, p. 581.

Schuyler, R. L., "The Rise of Anti-Imperialism in England," *Political Science Quarterly,* Vol. XXXVII (Sept., 1922), No. 3.

Seeley, J. R., *The Expansion of England* (London, 1883), pp. 440-471.

Seillière, E., *Introduction à la Philosophie de l'Impérialisme* (Paris, 1911).
————, *La Philosophie de l'Impérialisme,* 4 vols. (Paris, 1903-1908).
Smith, Adam, *An Inquiry into the Nature and Causes of the Wealth of Nations,* 2 vols. (London, 1776).
Smith, Goldwin, *Canada and the Canadian Question* (London, 1891).
————, *The Empire* (London, 1863).
Sprietsma, C., *We Imperialists: Notes on Ernest Seillière's Philosophy of Imperialism* (New York, 1931).
Sumner, W. G., *Earth Hunger and Other Essays* (New Haven, Conn., 1913), pp. 31-64.
————, *War and Other Essays* (New Haven, Conn., 1911), Chs. XIV, XV.
Vaccaro, M. A., *Les Bases Sociologiques du Droit et de l'État* (Paris, 1898), pp. 473 ff.
Woolf, L., *Economic Imperialism* (New York and London, 1920).
————, *Empire and Commerce in Africa* (London, 1919).

CHAPTER XIV

PACIFISM AND INTERNATIONALISM TO THE WORLD WAR

It has been shown that pacifist thought and doctrine, like the opposing conception of a world essentially characterized by perpetual strife, reaches far back into antiquity. It was not until the development of modern science in the nineteenth century, however, that a doctrine of the inevitability and even beneficence of war as a nature process was formulated and seriously discussed.[1] Likewise, although pacifism and internationalism had always claimed to be in accord with natural and divine law, it was not until the nineteenth century that pacifists and internationalists pushed the boundaries of their influence beyond a small circle of theologians and philosophers by organizing an international peace movement and making a varied appeal to statesmen and men of affairs. Denying the thesis of the "Social Darwinists" that Nature has decreed group struggle in the form of war between human societies until the end of time, they reasserted the fundamental unity of the human race both morally and biologically, refused to allow the theory of evolution to be appropriated by the supporters of war, and contended that, rightly understood, the evolutionary theory did not constitute a barrier to the ultimate realization of universal peace.[2]

The immediate cause of the formation of peace societies in the United States and England in 1815 and in the following years [3] was the

[1] See Ch. XII.

[2] *Ibid.*, for view of Novicow and others.

[3] Peace societies were founded in New York, Massachusetts, and Ohio in 1815. In 1828 the state peace societies were fused into the American Peace Society. In England, an independent movement resulted in 1816 in the establishment of the British "Society for the Promotion of Permanent and Universal Peace." The first peace society on the European continent was established by the Comte de Sellon in 1830. For the entire peace movement, including bibliography, see A. C. F. Beales, *The History of Peace* (London and New York, 1931). Especially valuable on the side of theory is Christian Lange's "Histoire de la Doctrine Pacifique, et de son Influence sur le Développement du Droit International," *Recueil des Cours*, Vol. XIII (1926), Pt. III, Ch. XVII, pp. 171-426, Académie de Droit International. For American Pacifism up to the time of the Civil War, see M. E. Curti, *The American Peace Crusade 1815-1860* (Durham, N. C., 1929).

protracted warfare in Europe during the Napoleonic era. The spectacle of nations calling themselves Christian still resorting to the brutal and sinful method of war for the settlement of their differences was repellent to all sincere Christians, and altogether unjustifiable under any circumstances, according to the belief of the Christian sects such as the Society of Friends. Unlike the Roman Catholic Church and most Protestant Churches as well, which, though deploring war in general, still admitted that certain wars might be regarded as "just,"[4] the Quakers and individual clergymen among other Protestant sects regarded *all* war, whether "defensive" or otherwise, as "criminal" on the ground that it involved the taking of human life which the Scriptures and the founder of Christianity held as sacred and inviolable.

The peace movement, though preserving its own identity, may also be regarded as an aspect of the humanitarian movement of the nineteenth century. The latter, designed to reduce human suffering and improve the conditions of life for mankind in general, expressed itself within states in efforts to improve the conditions of the laboring masses, provide special protection for women and children in industry, effect penal reform, reduce poverty and in other humane measures to ameliorate the conditions of the less fortunate members of society. The slave traffic, which was international in scope, was denounced in principle at the Congress of Vienna and the Powers agreed that it should be suppressed. In view of these manifestations of a more humane spirit, or, if one prefers, of a more enlightened selfishness, that were to become more marked in the course of the nineteenth century, it was natural that war should come under renewed scrutiny and that the pacifist ideal should receive more widespread endorsement. All humanitarians, whether single-minded pacifists or factory reformers or anti-slavery crusaders, could agree that war, whatever justification might be advanced in its behalf, was inhumane, and frequently entailed misery and suffering for great numbers of innocent human beings. They were therefore disposed to go along with the pacifists and seek its eradication. Those less sanguine of the possibility of achieving a warless world were in any case sympathetic with all efforts to humanize the conduct of war as far as possible and alleviate the suffering caused by it.

[4] For a recent statement of the Roman Catholic position, see *International Relations from a Catholic Standpoint*, translated from the French and edited for the Catholic Union of International Studies (Irish Section) by Stephen J. Brown (London, 1932), Pt. I, Ch. V.

Supplementing the more strictly pacifist thesis which was characterized largely by a negative criticism of war and which relied chiefly on building up a public opinion that would demand universal peace, the internationalist thought of the nineteenth century was more constructive in character and perhaps more realistic. Although differing widely on many matters, internationalists, with the exception of certain socialist and syndicalist groups, were in agreement in accepting the separate national states as the basis for the international society they hoped to see perfected. They rejected the idea, entertained by many pacifists, of working for a world state and a cosmopolitan order. Such a development, in the opinion of many, was neither likely nor desirable. It would make the world dull and drab, and lead to stagnation. The preservation of the national state was regarded as essential to the maintenance of cultural richness and variety. On the other hand, internationalists argued for the development of a world federal system in which states would maintain their separate identity, but would regulate their relations and seek the vindication of their rights and the guarantee of their security by accepting a measure of international government sufficient to enable them to promote their common interests and to dispense with war. Internationalists contended that in the absence of such an organization of international society the moral pleas of pacifists to statesmen to give up war would continue to fall upon deaf ears. Moreover, they were prepared to invest an international organization with the authority to use force—including war—if necessary, on behalf of the international community to ensure respect for international obligations and regard for the world's peace.

The founders and leaders of the early peace societies were divided on one fundamental question. Should pacifists, like many of the early Christians, refuse to support in any way war for any purpose, or should they recognize the legitimacy of some wars, for example those of self-defense? It was the old question with which the medieval theologians had wrestled. David L. Dodge, the New York Merchant who founded the first peace society in the United States, took an absolutist position as, eventually, did William Ladd, the founder of the American Peace Society.[5] In 1838, the latter wrote: "I do *not* believe that a Christian has the right to take life in self-defense. I ought not to fight in defense

[5] Lange, *loc. cit.*, p. 364; Curti, *op. cit.*, p. 68.

of life, liberty, or religion, much less for property; but to leave vengeance to God, to whom it belongs." [6]

The most thorough-going exposition of the non-resistant attitude of the early English pacifists was to be found in a work by the Quaker, Jonathan Dymond.[7] He inquired into the causes of war and challenged their validity. He was convinced that its continued acceptance was due to the fact that, like the slave trade which endured so long, people took it as a matter of course and failed to inquire into its justification or necessity. "We acquiesce in it, as we acquiesce in the rising of the sun, without any other idea than that it is a part of the ordinary processes of the world." [8] Dymond also recognized that there is something in war "which glitters and allures," and makes men willing to expose themselves oftentimes willingly to hardships and dangers. The military profession is exalted, and soldiers who die heroes' deaths have always been favorite topics for historians, biographers, and poets. Fully examined, however, and tested by Christian standards and precepts, all this is hollow and false. Bravery is not a quality to be exalted. The mastiff and the game-cock possess it. Moreover, bravery requires many dispositions incompatible with Christianity—animosity, resentment, the desire to retaliate, injure, and destroy. Christianity requires something finer: courage, "a calm, steady determination of purpose, that will not be diverted by solicitation, or awed by fear." [9] Patriotism, which Dymond asserted was "the great foundation of the soldier's glory," was also subjected to merciless analysis. "We contend that to say generally of those who perish in war that 'they have died for their country,' is simply untrue; and for this simple reason, that they did not fight for it . . . men have commonly no such purity of motive, . . . no such patriotism. What is the officer's motive to entering the army? We appeal

[6] Quoted in Beales *The History of Peace*, p. 60.
[7] The full title was *An Inquiry into the Accordancy of War with the Principles of Christianity and an Examination of the Philosophical Reasoning by Which it is Defended: With Observations on Some of the Causes of War, and on Some of its Effects*. It was first published in 1823. The third edition (Philadelphia, Pa., 1834) is the one hereinafter cited. For the views of other integral pacifists, see G. E. Beckwith, ed., *The Book of Peace, A Collection of Essays on War and Peace* (Boston, 1845); A. Ballou, *Christian Non-Resistance in All its Important Bearings, Illustrated and Defended* (Philadelphia, Pa., 1846); and F. J. and W. P. Garrison, *William Lloyd Garrison* (New York, 1885).
[8] *Op. cit.*, p. 11.
[9] *Ibid.*, pp. 28-32.

to himself. Is it not *that he may obtain an income?* And what is the motive of the private? Is it not *that he prefers a life of idleness to industry,* or that he had no wish but *the wish for change?*" Having entered the army, a soldier fights "because fighting is a matter of course to a soldier, or because his personal reputation is at stake, or because he is compelled to fight, or because he thinks nothing at all of the matter; but seldom, indeed, because he wishes to benefit his country."[10]

The argument that war was justified when waged for the maintenance of a balance of power was also considered inherently unsound by Dymond. In a changing world in which thousands of circumstances are constantly operating to destroy the equilibrium between nations, it is impossible to maintain an equipoise. In any case, he regarded the *desire* to resort to a system in which "an equality of the means of destruction" was recognized as the only means of preventing nations from tearing each other to pieces was a confession of wickedness.

That economic motives, as well as human inertia and human passion, contribute to the outbreak of wars, was also recognized by Dymond. Many individuals make money out of every war, and various industries are benefited by it. Support can therefore be expected from such quarters. The most systematic and powerful support, however, comes from those in the middle and higher ranks of society who regard trade as vulgar, and who traditionally take up the profession of arms as one which "unites gentility with profit." Fighting and destruction thus become their business. In this way those of higher rank and wealth and influence in the country accept and promote wars.[11]

The single test avowedly applied by Dymond in determining whether war is ever justified was its compatibility with the "will of God" as revealed in the Scriptures and as expressed in the precepts and declarations of Christ.[12] By voluminous quotations and painstaking analysis, he undertook to show that by that test no Christian could take up arms under any circumstances. He denied the validity of the familiar defense of war on the ground that there is no common superior to protect a state from the violence of another, as there is in the case of individuals within the state, and that each state must protect itself by war. This, he contended, was fallacious in that it assumed that

[10] Dymond, *op. cit.*, p. 34. Quoted by permission of the American Peace Society, (Founded 1828), 734 Jackson Place, Washington, D. C.

[11] *Ibid.*, pp. 19-22.

[12] *Ibid.*, pp. 49, 150.

individuals gave up the right to war against one another in view of the fact that there were laws to which they could look for protection, whereas the duty to refrain from violence was antecedent to man-made rules and had no connection with them.[13] Admitting that God had planted in man the instinct of self-preservation, he denied that this gave either to an individual or to a nation a right of self-defense. This, as well as other instincts, is subject to abuse, and God in his wisdom instituted a superior law regulating and restraining the instincts. Thus, to restrain the instinct of self-preservation from expressing itself in the form of violent self-defense, there are the biblical precepts: "Resist not evil"; "Overcome evil with good"; "Do good to them that hate you"; "Love your enemies"; "Who smiteth thee on one cheek. . ."

Dymond did not deal with religious arguments to the complete exclusion of practical considerations. For example, he denied the practicability of attempting to classify wars as aggressive and defensive, and insisted that "if Christianity allows defensive war, she allows all war—except indeed that of simple aggression . . . the aggressor is difficult of discovery; for he whom we choose to 'fear,' may say that he had previous 'fear' of us, and that his 'fear' prompted the hostile symptoms which made us 'fear' again. The truth is, that to attempt to make any distinctions upon the subject, is vain. War must be wholly forbidden, or allowed without restriction to defense; for no definitions of lawful or unlawful war, will be, or can be, attended to. . . There is no hope of an eradication of war but by an absolute and total abandonment of it."[14]

The majority of the early nineteenth century Christian pacifists, however, if we except the Friends, were not convinced that such an absolutist position of non-resistance was sound. Noah Worcester, whose *Solemn Review of the Custom of War*[15] was to take its place as one of the classics in the early American peace movement, disavowed any attempt to prove that the people of a nation might not "defend their lives, their liberties, and their property" against an armed invader; he was interested rather in inquiring whether it might not be possible to effect a change "in the present views of mankind" so that the occasion for a "defensive" war would never arise. William Ellery Channing (1780-1842), another pioneer of the American peace movement, was

[13] *Ibid.*, pp. 99-100.
[14] *Ibid.*, pp. 135-136.
[15] Published in 1817.

also opposed to the doctrine of non-resistance. He pointed out that to follow to the letter the precept, "Resist not evil," would result in annihilating all government and leaving one's family, friends, and country to the violence of a wrong-doer. Rather than allow this, for example, a nation might properly require its citizens to engage in war. On the other hand Channing insisted that war must not be undertaken until every effort has been made to secure justice and the redress of legitimate grievances. Moreover, he took the position that the presumption must always be against its necessity and justice. As a general rule, he contended, "war does not and cannot repair injuries. Instead of securing compensation for past evils, it almost always multiplies them. As a general rule, a nation loses incomparably more by war than it has previously lost by the wrong-doer."[16] Channing advanced another objection to war that one associates with the internationalist thesis of the present day but hardly expects to find among pacifist utterances of the early decades of the nineteenth century. "War can hardly spring up between two great countries without extending beyond them. This fire naturally expands."[17] Fully appreciating and deploring the human suffering and destruction caused by war, Channing did not regard this as its chief evil. He observed that famine, pestilence, natural catastrophes, and man's inhumanity to man in periods of peace were constantly taking a heavy toll of human life. In common with the religious pacifists of his day, however, he abhorred it chiefly because it involved planned and deliberate fratricide. As such, it outraged his sense of the dignity and divinity of human beings. "The evil," he declared, "is moral evil. War is the concentration of all human crimes. Here is its distinguishing, accursed brand. Under its standard gather violence, malignity, rage, fraud, perfidy, rapacity, and lust. If it only slew men, it would do little. It turns man into a beast of prey. Here is the evil of war, that man, made to be the brother, becomes the deadly foe of his kind; that man,

[16] W. E. Channing, *Discourses on War* (Boston, 1903), p. 66. Channing also recognized that, as in the case of individuals, nations are not competent to judge dispassionately when they are involved in disputes, and that a nation should therefore always "desire" to refer its disputes to "an impartial umpire." *Ibid.*, p. 68.

[17] *Ibid.*, p. 74. This was uttered in a lecture delivered in 1838 and had special reference to war between England and the United States, which seemed to threaten at the time. Such a war, Channing declared, would not only affect these two countries, but on account of the growing interdependence of countries as a result of the development of world commerce, would result in "deranging more or less the intercourse of all other communities. . ." (*Ibid.*)

whose duty it is to mitigate suffering, makes the infliction of suffering his study and end; that man whose office it is to avert and heal the wounds which come from nature's powers, makes researches into nature's laws and arms himself with her most awful forces, that he may become the destroyer of his race." [18]

Channing, in common with the other Christian pacifists of the early nineteenth century in England and the United States, believed that a warless world could eventually be realized by educational propaganda appealing to men's minds and hearts throughout the world. Likewise Channing and other pacifists who justified fighting under some circumstances, as well as absolutists like Dymond, were agreed that public opinion based on an enlightened Christian attitude, rather than physical force, should be relied upon to hold nations to their pledges. They therefore rejoiced at the pronouncement of the European rulers in the treaty of the Holy Alliance in 1815 in which the sovereigns pledged themselves to adopt for the only rule of their conduct in their political relations with their subjects and with other governments "the precepts of justice, of charity, and of peace." To the pacifists this pronouncement was by no means to be characterized as "a piece of sublime mysticism and nonsense," as Castlereagh put it, but an auspicious sign that even autocratic rulers were beginning to be touched by the light of truth and inclined toward the gentle ways of peace. Inspired by this declaration and by the strong peace sentiment expressed in President Madison's last message to Congress, Channing prepared on behalf of the Peace Society of Massachusetts a memorial to Congress asking whether the American government might not respond to "the solemn profession of pacific principles lately made by several distinguished sovereigns of Europe" with "corresponding professions." Stating that they were aware of the fact that the public declarations and the actual conduct of rulers had often shown discrepancies, the memorialists nevertheless asserted their belief "that the solemn assertion of great and important principles by men of distinguished rank and influence has a beneficial operation on society by giving to these principles an increased authority over the consciences of those by whom they are professed; by reviving and diffusing a reverence for them in the community; and by thus exalting the standard of *public opinion,* that invisible sovereign to

[18] *Ibid.,* p. 81.

whose power the most absolute prince is often compelled to bow, and to which the measures of a free government are entirely subjected." The memorialists concluded by stating that "we are desirous that our government should unite with the governments of Europe in a distinct and religious acknowledgement of those principles of peace and charity on which the prosperity of states and the happiness of families and individuals are alike suspended." In addition, they asked Congress to undertake an inquiry to discover the methods the government might employ to promote peace among nations.[19] Altogether, the thought embodied in this memorial reminds one strongly of the American position as expressed over a hundred years later at the time of the campaign for the "Kellogg Pact."[20]

The first American pacifist of the period to make an outstanding contribution on political methods and agencies for the realization of the ideal was William Ladd (1778-1841). In his *Essay on a Congress of Nations,* published in 1840,[21] he proposed a concrete plan for international organization which henceforth represented perhaps more nearly than any other prior to the World War the American conception of the proper means of organizing peace. Taking the Swiss Diet and Court of Judges as his "nearest working model," he advocated the establishment of a Congress of Nations and a Court of Nations. On the other hand, inspired by the American political system, he stressed the point that the former body, composed of ambassadors from nations willing to enter the association, should exercise legislative powers, and should be separated from the Court, which should have exclusive judicial functions. Moreover, he took the Supreme Court of the United States as his model for a Court of Nations. Unlike the Congress of Ambassadors, which would be a transient body of shifting personnel, meeting periodically, the Court of Nations was to be a permanent body of judges appointed for good behavior. The first and most important task of the Congress was to reach an agreement on the principles of international law and frame a code upon which the Court's decisions could be based.[22]

[19] Channing, *op. cit.,* Introduction by Edwin D. Mead, pp. xx-xxi.

[20] See Ch. XVI.

[21] Ladd's plan is contained in *Prize Essays on a Congress of Nations,* published by the American Peace Society (Boston, 1840).

[22] Ladd asserted, however, that the Court might be set up before all the points of international law had been settled. Until this should be achieved, it could decide cases, when necessary, on the basis of generally accepted principles.

Another feature of Ladd's plan which, however, was typical of the pacifist thought of his time, was the omission of an executive organ. As he stated it, public opinion was to be the executive. Like other Americans of his day, he regarded standing armies as "always dangerous to liberty," and international schemes involving such means of enforcement were quite unacceptable.[23] Ladd, therefore, refused to rely upon physical power—"fleets and armies"—to compel obedience to the laws of the Congress of Nations, or to the decrees of the Court. He contended that the publicists who formulated principles of international law had no power to compel the acceptance of these principles, yet the opinions of these men had always been treated with respect. Likewise, he pointed out, arbitrators have never had the military power to enforce their awards.[24] In Ladd's opinion, the fear of punishment was not the reason for most men obeying the laws of the state; and therefore those advocating the use of arms for the enforcement of an international court's decrees were in error. He contended that "it will be found, that where one man obeys the laws for fear of the sword of the magistrate, an hundred obey them through the fear of public opinion." [25] Ladd expressed confidence that "even now, *public opinion* is amply sufficient to enforce all the decisions of a Court of Nations" . . . and that "already there is no civilized nation that can withstand the frown of public opinion." Accordingly he concluded, confidently: "It is therefore necessary, only to enlighten public opinion still farther, to insure the success of our plan." [26]

Although Ladd recognized the value of arbitration of national differences, and rejoiced in its application, the ideal to be pursued, he argued, was a Court of Nations. Arbitration was not entirely satisfactory, because an umpire had no fixed and universally acknowledged law of nations to guide him in his decisions. In cases in which the circumstances were similar, therefore, different umpires often differed in their decisions, with the result that their awards had less moral authority, and that no "body of international common law" could be built up. Moreover, said Ladd, it was not to be expected that an umpire

[23] *Op. cit.*, *p.* 563.

[24] Ladd proposed that the Court of Nations should judge only cases submitted to it by the mutual consent of the parties concerned; consequently, in his opinion, its decisions would be as well obeyed as those of umpires.

[25] *Op. cit.*, pp. 519, 599-600.

[26] *Ibid.* Over a century later, American advocates of the outlawry of war were to take substantially the same position.

could approach his task as objectively "as a bench of eminent jurists, selected from the most renowned in their own country for their talents, integrity, and experience, and translated from the highest judicial stations in their own nation to fill the highest judicial station in the world. . ." [27]

Ladd and the other peace advocates realized, however, that the ideal could be attained only as a result of a long process of education. In the meantime, frontier disputes and other irritating controversies troubled the relations between Great Britain and the United States and demanded immediate attention. The two governments had as early as 1794 given support to the principle of international arbitration by providing in the Jay Treaty of that year for the arbitration of certain outstanding differences.[28] Why should they not develop a policy of submitting all their otherwise insoluble disputes to this peaceful process? Many pacifists in the two countries decided to concentrate their attention on the spread of the idea of arbitration.

The most distinct contribution to the arbitration movement during the first half of the nineteenth century was made by William Jay, who thus carried on the work of his father, John Jay. In 1842, William Jay's *War and Peace: the Evils of the First, and a Plan for Preserving the Last,* was published. After the manner of many of his pacifist contemporaries, he argued that the final extinction of hoary evils such as the slave trade showed that war likewise could in time be eliminated by the building up of a public opinion against it, and by the creation of international agencies of peaceful settlement. Ultimately a world tribunal could be achieved; but Jay was convinced that, "under existing circumstances, the idea of a congress of nations for the extinction of war, is utterly chimerical." [29] On the other hand, he thought an important step toward the ideal could be taken if some one nation would set the others an example by seeking an all-inclusive arbitration treaty with a friendly state. For various reasons,[30] he believed that the United States could best undertake the experiment. He therefore proposed that in our next treaty with France, our former ally and a nation

[27] Ladd, *op. cit.*, pp. 603-604. Here Ladd anticipates some of the arguments advanced on behalf of the establishment of a world court by the American delegates to the Second Hague Conference.

[28] The Jay Treaty marked the revival of international arbitration and the beginning of its use in the modern period.

[29] *Op. cit.*, p. 79.

[30] *Ibid.*, p. 80.

with which we had "no rivalry . . . in commerce or manufacture," we should suggest an article pledging the two powers to submit to arbitration *all* disputes not yielding to negotiation that might arise in the future, and to abide by the award.[31] Unlike more radical proposals to disband the army and navy, he thought this suggestion would "shock no prejudice, and excite no reasonable alarm." It was important, however, that nations should agree in advance of the breaking out of controversies that they would submit them to arbitration, for when high tension has developed and public passions have become inflamed, nations are not disposed to listen to arbitration proposals. Jay thought that if the stipulation he proposed could be written into a treaty with France, other nations would gradually be won over to the idea and finally when the practice became universal and led to the establishment of a Court of Nations the nations could beat their swords into ploughshares and their spears into pruning hooks. Could nations be depended upon to observe such sweeping obilgations? Jay was confident that a sufficient guarantee could be found in "national interest" and in "public opinion." "Every government that felt disposed to violate such a treaty would be conscious that by doing so it would be sacrificing substantial interests for precarious advantages; exchanging the blessings of continued peace for the hazards and calamities of war." If a government, in violation of its pledge to abide by an arbitration award, attempted war it would "shock the moral sense of mankind" and conflict would probably "be prevented or speedily terminated by the interference of other powers interested in enforcing treaties for the preservation of peace."[32] Jay's confidence in the ultimate success of an appeal to reason and to the enlightened self interest and aroused consciences of men was quite typical of the pacifist thought of his day.

Concurrently with the rise of the peace societies and the elaboration of pacifist arguments against war, the free trade movement was

[31] *Ibid.*, p. 82. Several generations later (1911), President Taft attempted unsuccessfully to get the United States Senate to consent to such a treaty with France and Great Britain.

[32] *Ibid.*, pp. 62-63. Jay's idea was taken up by peace societies in England and the United States and from 1842 to 1854 superseded Ladd's plan in the support it received from pacifists. Vigorous efforts were made to have the American Congress and the British House of Commons approve resolutions for stipulated arbitration, as suggested by Jay. However, though the pacifists developed considerable strength in the British House, and succeeded in getting a favorable report from the Foreign Relations Committee of the American Senate in 1851, they were unable to get either government to endorse the plan. See M. E. Curti, *op. cit.*, Ch. IX.

developing in England. They were both reformist movements, aiming at the improvement of the conditions of mankind. Both of them rested upon a fundamental assumption—the essential unity of the human race. And in fact prior to the nineteenth century the relationship between peace and free trade was pointed out or inhered in the views of Grotius in the seventeenth century and Montesquieu, Josiah Tucker, and others in the century following. Grotius ultimately based his thesis on the freedom of the seas on the contention that God, in order that man *should not lack sociability,* had deliberately avoided making countries completely self-sufficient and thus made trade between them natural and necessary.[33] Montesquieu, in 1748, laid down the dictum that "peace is the natural effect of trade. Two nations who traffic with each other become reciprocally dependent." [34] Tucker, writing in 1763 on *The Case of Going to War,* advanced the essentials of the Grotian argument on behalf of the cause of peace.[35] It was perhaps natural, therefore, that during the first half of the nineteenth century, when pacifists and free traders began to develop campaigns on behalf of their respective causes they should contract a defensive and offensive alliance against the forces of the opposition. For a period the two movements coalesced, although the pacifists of the early peace societies for the most part continued to rely chiefly on religious and humanitarian arguments in their propaganda.[36]

Outstanding among the pacifists who did stress the importance of free trade in connection with their peace activities was the "learned blacksmith," Elihu Burritt (1810-1879). Burritt was a tremendous factor in the peace movement, writing, traveling, and speaking on behalf of the cause in Europe as well as in the United States, and perfecting a technique of organization and publicity of quite a remarkable character. He was not content to rest the pacifist case solely on the teachings of Christianity. From his studies in philology he discovered additional evidence in common roots and related word forms of the soli-

[33] *Supra*, p. 152.

[34] *The Spirit of the Laws*, tr. by Thomas Nugent, 2 vols. (Cincinnati, Ohio, 1873), Vol. I, Bk. XX, Ch. II, p. 365.

[35] "In the *natural* world, our bountiful Creator hath formed different Soils, and appointed different Climates; whereby the inhabitants of different Countries may supply each other with their respective Fruits and Products; so that by exciting a reciprocal Industry, they may carry on an Intercourse mutually beneficial, and universally benevolent." (*Op. cit.*, p. 32.)

[36] Helen Bosanquet, *Free Trade and Peace in the Nineteenth Century* (Christiania and New York, 1924), p. 71.

darity of mankind.[37] His interest in free trade and his visualizing its connection with peace grew out of studies preparatory to delivering a lecture on *The Anatomy of the Earth.* He became so impressed with the unity of the globe and with the interdependence of its parts that the lecture became metamorphosed into an address on peace. Friendly commerce, he contended, "is a condition provided and established in the very anatomy of the globe." Obstructions to commerce, and the blight of war were out of harmony with the constitution of nature.[38]

The free trade thesis in relation to peace was developed during the first half of the nineteenth century by writers in France as well as in England and the United States.[39] It challenged the position of the protectionists that the way to achieve national security was to protect one's country against foreign goods and achieve and maintain economic independence. On the contrary, the free traders argued, the mutual dependence of nations makes for national security and international peace. In England, they asserted that the safety of Great Britain from famine and from war depended upon her adoption of the policy of drawing her supplies from as wide an area of the outside world as possible. Crops would not fail everywhere in the same year, and England would not be at war with all the countries supplying her at the same time. Sir Robert Peel, in introducing the Free Trade Bill into Parliament in 1846, expressed the belief that it would constitute a new bond of peace, for other nations would follow suit and national animosities connected with trade rivalries would be dissipated. And John Stuart Mill, writing in the following year, confidently asserted that "it may be said without exaggeration, that the great extent and rapid increase of international trade, in being the principal guarantee of the peace of the world, is the great permanent security for the uninterrupted progress of the ideas, the institutions, and the character of the human race." [40]

[37] See Merle E. Curti's article in the *Encyclopedia of the Social Sciences,* III, 78; also Beales, *op. cit.,* pp. 71-74 *ff.*

[38] Bosanquet, *op. cit.,* pp. 73-74. Another enterprise to which Burritt devoted himself which was connected with the promotion of international intercourse and, as he felt, peace was the reduction of ocean postage. Senator Charles Sumner, eloquent and zealous American pacifist, brought Burritt's proposal for Universal Ocean Penny Postage before the Senate in 1852, and John Bright, the English Quaker pacifist and free trader, introduced it in the House of Commons. Burritt lived to see the substance of his proposal adopted.

[39] Frédéric Bastiat, Horace Say, Joseph Garnier, and Émile de Girardin in France, like Richard Cobden and John Bright in England, and Burritt in the United States, regarded protective tariffs as breeders of war.

[40] As quoted in Bosanquet, *op. cit.,* p. 78.

The towering figure among the free traders and internationalists of the first half of the nineteenth century was, however, Richard Cobden (1804-1865). It was he more than anyone else who was responsible for the reversal of English policy after his entry into Parliament, and for the repeal of the Corn Laws. Although his first and most intensive activity was in the furtherance of free trade, he looked upon the accomplishment of this as of the most vital import to peace, and by 1842 had decided to work with and lend his strong support to the leaders of the peace crusade. An understanding of his views as to the relationship of the two movements may be gained from the following extract from a letter to a friend: "They are one and the same cause. It has often been to me a matter of the greatest surprise that the Friends have not taken up the question of Free Trade as the means—and I believe the only human means—of effecting universal and permanent peace. The efforts of the Peace Societies, however laudable, can never be successful so long as the nations maintain their present system of isolation."[41] Free trade, he was convinced, would result in the destruction of colonialism and would thus strike at the chief source of modern wars. By making countries dependent upon one another and drawing peoples closer together in beneficial intercourse, governments would be robbed of their power "to plunge their people into wars."

Cobden's views on international relations were in harmony with his general political philosophy. He belonged to a school which looked upon government as an evil, though unfortunately some government was necessary on account of the frailties of human nature. But governments were to be entrusted only with such powers as were indispensable for protection against predatory and hostile elements within and outside the state. Unhappily, therefore, police and *some* armament were necessary. But governments should keep hands off the peaceful activities of their citizens, leaving the "sphere of anarchy" as wide as possible. This principle of *laissez-faire* in internal concerns had as its complement the principle of non-intervention in foreign affairs. In fact, Cobden urged that there should be "as little intercourse as possible between Governments." If governments could not be trusted to manage affairs decently and intelligently within the state, still less could foreign offices, weighed down with conservative traditions and saturated with false notions of

[41] Bosanquet, *op. cit.*, p. 48 for quotation; also J. A. Hobson, *Richard Cobden, the International Man* (New York, 1919), pp. 36-37.

the necessary antagonisms of peoples and the desirability of planting the flag throughout the world, be expected to act with intelligence and restraint.[42] His convictions on this matter were strengthened and confirmed as the result of extensive travels on the European continent during which he took pains to meet men of affairs, elicit their views, and study peoples and conditions.[43] The "spirited foreign policy" of the imperialistically-minded Lord Palmerston was the opposite of all that Cobden believed in, and was, in his judgment, thoroughly mischievous.[44] Cobden believed not only that there was no conflict between the interests of the individual and those of the nation, but that the interests of both were identical as well with the interests of all other nations. Cooperation and mutual aid were therefore called for. The Palmerstonian foreign policy was, on the other hand, aggressive and competitive in spirit and purpose. It led to intervention in the affairs and relationships of other states in accordance with the doctrine of the balance of power, which Cobden believed to be false and dangerous, because for one thing, it was ambiguous. International jurists and statesmen had never agreed upon a definition. Nor could they, in his opinion, for it was impossible to discover a measure of the "power" by which to estimate the claims of the various states. Moreover, were it possible to establish a "balance," it could not be maintained because it would not be possible to provide against "the peaceful aggrandizements which spring from improvement and labor."[45] As a matter of fact, each state, Cobden pointed out, insisted on arbitrarily defining and attempting to achieve a balance of power in terms of its own fancied interests at any particular time.

Threatened disturbance of the equilibrium by any Power was a sufficient cause for either diplomatic or military intervention by any of the others. Cobden, on the other hand, contended that every state had the right and duty normally to manage its own affairs and work out its own destiny without hindrance from others. Cobden's position, it may be observed, was logical in view of his own philosophy. He was merely extending the individualistic doctrine of *laissez-faire* to the

[42] Hobson, *op. cit.*, p. 36. It should be observed that Cobden was all for furthering the contacts and intellectual as well as commercial intercourse of *peoples*.

[43] Hobson says: "Hardly any other English statesman has taken so much trouble to equip himself for the wider art of statecraft. Cobden knew ten times as much as did his great antagonist, Lord Palmerston. . . ." (*Op. cit.*, p. 52.)

[44] *Ibid.*, Ch. V.

[45] *Ibid.*, pp. 33-34.

foreign relations of states. States, like individuals, are better off when they are put on their own, allowed to develop self-reliance, and given the freedom to develop their capacities. Occasionally, he admitted, in extreme cases in which the welfare of other peoples was clearly jeopardized by the action of a Power, intervention might be justified on the grounds of national duty and urgent national interest. But it is evident, as the following statement of his position in regard to intervention on behalf of the freedom of struggling nationalities will show, that he felt few worthy cases would arise: "I yield to no one in sympathy for those who are struggling for freedom in any part of the world; but I will never sanction an interference which shall go to establish this or that nationality by force of arms, because that invades a principle which I wish to carry out in the other direction—the prevention of all foreign interference with the nationalities for the sake of putting them down."[46] Thus normally he would have English policy follow the maxim of George Washington's Farewell Address.[47] Otherwise, England would be drawn into alliances with the military powers of the continent, and would be compelled not only to maintain a large navy, but also to build up a large land armament.[48] This in turn would mean the diversion of large sums of money, as well as attention and energy that might better be devoted to improvement of internal conditions, and the fostering of agriculture, industry, and trade.

Cobden recognized that peace was a "far-off divine event," capable of attainment only after long and arduous efforts in the enlightenment of mankind. Temperamentally, he was not satisfied with abstract thinking on the subject of war and peace and the adoption of an absolutist position. He was disposed to go forward to the goal by stages through the achievement of concrete results rather than attempt to immediate realization of the ideal. Thus the "stipulated arbitration" of John Jay made more of an appeal to him than the proposals of William Ladd

[46] W. H. Dawson, *Richard Cobden and Foreign Policy* (London, 1926), pp. 97-98, 104; Hobson, *op. cit.*, p. 387.

[47] "The great rule of conduct for us in regard to foreign nations is, in extending our commercial relations, to have with them as little political connexion as possible."

[48] Cobden's sense of honor and fair play was also shocked at the fact that intervention in practice usually took the form of diplomatic or military pressure against small and weak states. (Dawson, *op. cit.*, p. 99.) The less advanced peoples should be treated with patience and given every opportunity to develop their own potentialities. This should not only be a principle of English policy, but also one Cobden hoped to see universally adopted as a principle of international law.

for a World Congress and Court, and he threw his support toward securing an arbitration treaty between England and France. If these two countries could be induced to sign an agreement to submit all their future differences to arbitration, Cobden was optimistic enough to believe that their example would be followed by the other nations.[49]

Cobden's opposition to growing armament expenditures further illustrates his international outlook. Regarding some wars as hateful necessities in an imperfect world, he accepted the necessity of some armament for a nation. But the armament rivalry, already in his day taking shape, was a foolish "beggar-my-neighbor game" with no justification whatever. Here, too, he urged that England and France, colonial and naval rivals, should agree to a reciprocal limitation of arms. To the argument that the safety of the country would be endangered, Cobden frankly asserted that England should "trust something to Providence as well as to her good intentions and good conduct toward other countries. Were she to do so, other nations could be induced to follow suit.[50] In Cobden's day the evils of private manufacture and sale of armaments were not as evident as they were to become later, although doubtless one is surprised for the moment when he learns that Cobden was consistently opposed to government manufacture, and insisted that everything in connection with armament be left to private enterprise. This position, however, was logical for an adherent of the Manchester School, opposed to all state interference in industry and trade.[51]

Looking backward, it is plain that Cobden's faith in international trade as a means of bringing peoples together in the bonds of peace was unjustified. International commerce was to grow enormously, but trade and colonial rivalry were to grow with it. Free trade was substantially realized, as far as England was concerned, but it had no appreciable effect in developing a pacific attitude and a more enlightened British foreign and colonial policy. Nor was the British example followed, as Cobden expected it would be, by other nations. In place of free trade, protectionism and imperialism became the order of the day. Cobden's strenuous endeavors in behalf of a policy of non-intervention for Great Britain did contribute toward England's avoidance of certain

[49] Hobson, *op. cit.*, pp. 55-57; Dawson, *op. cit.*, Ch. VI.
[50] Dawson, *op. cit.*, Ch. VII. Hobson, *op. cit.*, p. 387.
[51] Dawson, *op. cit.*, pp. 162-163

wars;[52] and if one regards constructive internationalism, involving a system of collective guarantees by the nations, for the maintenance of peace and justice as quite impossible of attainment in his day, non-intervention was defensible as the only practicable alternative.

The first distinctively peace society was founded on the European continent in 1830 by the Comte de Sellon (1782-1839), at Geneva, although nine years earlier the *Société des Amis de la Morale Chrétienne,* organized to work for the improvement of the spiritual and physical condition of man, became interested in the peace movement as a part of its liberal and humanitarian program.[53] On the other hand, peace doctrines were advanced by the early French socialists who, although they might subscribe to the free trade ideas of the spokesmen of the middle class, were interested in more far-reaching and radical changes in the social order on behalf of the masses of the Fourth Estate everywhere. By their day, war had become of vital interest to these masses, because it was no longer confined to a fighting class but, since the Revolution,[54] reached into the homes of workingmen whenever necessity required. The pacifism of the socialists, who wanted a new economic and social order in which the workers of all countries would be emancipated, tended even more than that of the Free Traders to start and end with the economic factor. The "class struggle," with the advent of the Marxians at any rate, cut across national lines and linked up the workers of all countries against the possessing classes. Logically, therefore, the socialist dogma, as it came to be developed, was more consistent with a cosmopolitan world society than with internationalism. Moreover, in the belief of revolutionary Marxians, although this

[52] Lord Morley, in his *The Life of Cobden,* 2 vols. (London, 1881), II, 158-159, asserts, in speaking of the contribution of John Bright and Cobden to the peace cause: "They were routed on the question of the Crimean war, but it was the rapid spread of their principles which within the next twenty years made intervention impossible in the Franco-Austrian war, in the American war, in the Danish war, in the Franco-German war, and above all, in the war between Russia and Turkey."

[53] Lange, *loc. cit.,* p. 370.

[54] Conscription of certain non-exempt groups of the King's subjects for temporary service in the army to supplement his mercenaries was resorted to in France as early as 1688. See article by Elbridge Colby, on "Conscription" in *Encyclopaedia of the Social Sciences,* IV, 220. It was not until 1798, however, that the principle of conscription was incorporated in the Constitution, enabling the French Army to require military service from every able-bodied citizen between the ages of twenty and twenty-five.

was not true of all socialistic thinkers, ultimate peace could not be realized until revolutionary wars of the Fourth Estate against their masters had succeeded in establishing a socialistic economy.[55] Their immediate appeal, therefore, was not against all war—the "class war" was a necessary preliminary to universal peace—but against international war. It was useless to appeal to class-controlled governments, however, to abstain from this form of "capitalistic rivalry." The plea must be addressed to the workers to refuse to fight in such wars. This was an approach and a specific appeal quite different from that of most of the middle class pacifists.[56]

The leader of the early French Socialist School, Saint-Simon (1760-1825), accepted as a basic assumption of his social theory the idea that the whole of mankind is a unit and that it is the duty of society to work for the amelioration of the moral and physical existence of the poorest class. He envisaged an industrialist state, organized and controlled by the intellectually élite, in which war would be suppressed. In 1814, he published *De la Réorganisation de la Société Europèene,* in which he suggested that a beginning might be made to organize the countries of Europe into a wide union if England and France would take the initiative. In time, he prophesied, the peoples of this Continent would be united and would place the general interest above national interests. The Golden Age in which the social order would be perfected and interests harmonized was, however, in his opinion, far distant. Before its achievement could be realized, new and frightful wars and revolutions would afflict Europe.[57] The followers of Saint-Simon, likewise animated by religious sentiments and imbued with a passion for social justice, emphasized the importance of universal peace as a foundation for the type of society to which they aspired—a so-

[55] See Ch. XXII for complete treatment of the socialistic theory of international relations.

[56] It should be pointed out, however, that the appeal to the class consciousness of workingmen was apparently conceived by a non-Marxian American society, the National Association for Promoting the Political and Social Improvement of the People, two years before the famous *Communist Manifesto* of Marx and Engels. The laboring men of America were exhorted not to be "seduced" to go to war for the enrichment of aristocracy, the common enemy. And Elihu Burritt, in the fifties, began urging "a parliament of the workingmen of Christendom" and "an organized strike of the workingmen of Christendom against war." (Curti, *op. cit.,* pp. 114-115, 150).

[57] J. ter Meulen, *Der Gedanke der Internationalen Organisation in seiner Entwicklung* (*1300-1889*), 2 vols. (The Hague, 1917-1929), II (1789-1889), 205-212.

ciety in which all mankind would be united through fruitful work, the love of which would displace the fever for war.[58]

The most thoughtful and elaborate treatment of the peace question from a member of the Saint-Simon-Fourier group in France was published in 1842 by Constantin Pecqueur (1801-1887), French social philosopher and reformer, under the title, *De la Paix, de son Principe et de sa Réalisation.* He suggested various indirect ways which would contribute towards the attainment of peace such as the spread of Christian ethics, and the education of the poor to an understanding that only through peace can their lot be improved. The educators of youth, in the different countries, should think and teach in terms of all humanity as a single great family rather than with partiality for a particular people. The promotion of the association and cooperation of scholars and men distinguished in art and letters in different countries would also have a beneficial influence. Congresses should be held to seek freedom of trade, uniformity of weights and measures, a common language, and a code of international law. Standing armies should be abolished and a system of military defense like that of the Swiss should replace them. Railroad systems should be extended beyond national frontiers in order to increase trade and communications between peoples. Moreover, states should engage in cooperative undertakings, including colonization,[59] in which workers of different lands should work together. Capitalists likewise should share in the great common enterprise. In this way, also, understanding between nations would be furthered and world unity promoted. Finally, Pecqueur advocated the extension of popular education in the different countries, and regarded the fact that bankers and financiers were already in a position to cause princes to listen to advice as an influence tending to restrain the latter from rushing heedlessly into war. As the principal direct means of attaining peace, Pecqueur advocated the formation of a federation of nations modeled along somewhat the same lines as the American federal union. The world federation would include a parliament, a court of justice, and a plural executive composed of the heads of the various united states. The latter would retain their own parliaments which, however, would henceforth have the functions of provincial legislatures.

[58] ter Meulen, *op. cit.,* II, 194-205, 212-218, for the views of Charles Fourier, Victor Considérant, and other religious and Utopian socialists of the period.

[59] Pecqueur states that the colonies must not belong to one state. Apparently he envisages a collective ownership by the nations and common exploitation.

In this way the more or less absolute power of the different states would be merged into a collective unit, and peace would be maintained by the common institutions and united strength of all.[60]

The idea of a United States of Europe as a necessary preliminary or as an alternative to world organization has always been more or less prominent in pacifist thought, especially in France. As long as there were no important powers outside Europe, and wars of consequence were always between European states, as well as for other obvious cultural reasons, this was to be expected. By the nineteenth century, however, other continents had begun to attain importance, and new states were rising to positions of prominence. Nevertheless, the idea persisted.[61] Napoleon I actually tried by means of the sword to "create a great federative system in Europe. . ."[62] Saint-Simon, Considérant, and others of their school adhered to the same idea. And in his presidential address at the International Peace Congress at Paris in 1849, Victor Hugo lent it the support of his eloquence. After pointing out that at one time people would have thought it absurd to suggest that independent Burgundy, Normandy, Brittany, and Provence would one day be merged in France, he said: "Well, then, you at this moment say—and I say it with you—we who are assembled here, say to France, to England, to Prussia, to Austria, to Spain, to Italy, to Russia—we say to them, 'A day will come when from your hands also the arms you have grasped will fall. A day will come when war will appear as absurd and be as impossible, between Paris and London, between St. Petersburg and Berlin, between Vienna and Turin, as it would be now between Rouen and Amiens, between Boston and Philadelphia. A day will come when you, France—you, Russia—you, Italy—you, England—you, Germany—all of you, nations of the Continent, will, without losing your distinctive qualities, and your glorious individuality, be blended into a superior unity, and constitute a European fraternity, just as Normandy, Brittany, Burgundy, Lorraine, Alsace, have been blended into France. A day will come when the only battlefield will be the market open to commerce and the mind opening to new ideas. A day will come when bullets and bombshells will be replaced by votes, by

[60] See ter Meulen, *op. cit.*, pp. 257-267, for a more thorough exposition of Pecqueur's international views.

[61] Its basis in the twentieth century is treated in Ch. XX.

[62] F. M. Stawell, *Growth of International Thought* (London, 1929), pp. 213-214.

the universal suffrage of nations, by the venerable arbitration of a great Sovereign Senate, which will be to Europe what the Parliament is to England, what the Diet is to Germany, what the Legislative Assembly is to France. A day will come when a cannon will be exhibited in public museums, just as an instrument of torture is now, and people will be astonished how such a thing could have been.' "[63] Hugo was also hopeful that this desirable consummation was not far away, basing his hope on the speed with which space was being annihilated by rapid transportation and communication. These and other manifestations of progress he assumed would at no distant day cause "the cessation of international animosities, the effacing of frontiers on the maps, and of prejudices from the heart. . ."

In the program of the *Ligue International de la Paix et de la Liberté,* founded in 1867 by the Frenchman, Charles Lemonnier (1806-1891), the United States of Europe was also an objective.[64] Along with it, as one of the "bases of permanent peace," the pacifists of this school reaffirmed the idea of Rousseau and of Kant that monarchical systems must give way to democratic governments. This might entail war, as Rousseau had surmised, but it was regarded as providing the necessary foundations for peace. The Lemonnier School looked upon standing armies as "an absolute obstacle to the peace and liberty of peoples," advocated their abandonment, and the substitution of an "army of peace" controlled by the United States of Europe and employed to prevent or punish acts of aggression by any of the members.[65]

During the second half of the century, as war weapons improved and the cost and deadliness of armament increased, pacifist agitation for "the simultaneous disarmament of all nations," to use the formula adopted in 1859 by the American Peace Society, became more insistent and eventually was to receive serious consideration in official quarters. In 1863, and again in 1870, Napoleon III of France made gestures to the other European powers toward calling an International Dis-

[63] For text of the address see *World Peace Foundation Pamphlet Series,* Vol. IV (Oct., 1914), No. 6, Pt. 2.

[64] Beales, *op. cit.,* pp. 120-121.

[65] The inclusion of this sanction was criticized by the Peace Society in England. The latter took the position that nations should first be induced to disarm; that then they would not have the *power* to commit acts of aggression, and that sanctions would be superfluous. Moreover, they asserted that "the army of peace must be a moral and not a military organization." (Beales, *op. cit.,* pp. 120-122.) Pacifists and internationalists are still split on this issue. See Chs. XV and XVI.

armament Conference; but, although the idea was generally applauded, the conference did not take place.[66] In the English Parliament in the Seventies the increased expenditures for armament were severely criticizd, not only because of the heavy drain on the treasury, but because competitive arming on the part of the European nations was arousing national fears and resentments and thereby endangering peace rather than providing security. At about the same time, disarmament proposals were brought forward in the Austrian and German Reichstags. The leader of the movement in the Austrian Chamber proposed that the Dual Monarchy should "take the initiative in a general disarmament." [67]

It was in connection with the desire to work effectively for disarmament and arbitration that the idea of forming an Inter-Parliamentary Union took shape. The first suggestion came from the German pacifist, Edward Lowenthal, in 1874. He advocated a universal Parliamentary Peace Union with a membership recruited from every legislature in the world. In the following year the Austrian pacifist, Adolf Fischoff, worked out a definite scheme for an annual conference at which members of the proposed Union would meet and discuss ways and means of furthering the cause of disarmament and arbitration in the several parliaments. In 1889, the Inter-Parliamentary Union became a reality and a factor henceforth in the pacifist movement.[68]

In the Eighties, the peace movement entered the Scandinavian countries, where from the first it aroused interest and support on the part of the press and many public officials in a campaign for arbitration and disarmament. The position taken was that Norway, Sweden, and Denmark were self-contained nations, and were sufficiently remote geographically from the troubled regions of Europe, as well as politically disinterested and harmless, that they could afford to test out a policy of disarmament and arbitration. That this agitation was taken seriously is evidenced by the fact that in 1883 a motion in the Swedish Rigsdag, for the permanent neutralization and disarmament of Sweden as an example to the world, received 70 out of 182 votes.[69]

The first definite interest and support for the cause of disarmament by a great European power, however, came from an unexpected quar-

[66] Beales, *op. cit.*, p. 111.
[67] *Ibid.*, p. 153.
[68] *Ibid.*, pp. 153-154.
[69] *Ibid.*, p. 182.

ter, i.e., autocratic Russia. What was its origin? It appears that in 1898 the Russian Minister of War was informed that the Austrian government had placed an order for a new type of artillery, and he desired to have Russia supplied with the same kind. This, however, would mean a heavy additional outlay and the Finance Minister, M. Witte, far more interested in the industrial and commercial expansion of Russia than in the expansion of her military expenditures, made an energetic protest. He suggested that Russia should open negotiations with the Austrian government for an agreement pledging the two countries not to increase their artillery, but the Russian cabinet is said to have vetoed the suggestion on the ground that it would be interpreted abroad as a sign of weakness. At this point, an attaché of the Ministry of Foreign Affairs drew the attention of his superiors to the work of the Inter-Parliamentary Union. He had attended its seventh conference in 1896 and had written a report of its activities for his government. He now proposed that Russia reinforce its work with an appeal to the several governments to consider a limitation of armaments. At first repudiating the idea, the Tsar later agreed and the International Peace Conference of 1899 resulted.[70] Political questions were excluded from the program, but the Russian government submitted a plan for a limited military and naval holiday. National rivalries, fears, and jealousies, however, prevented agreement on this, the chief aim of the conference.

It has also been suggested that the Tsar and his ministers may have been strongly influenced in the decisions for an international conference by a remarkable book on war by a Polish Jew, Jean de Bloch (1836-1902). Bloch rose from poverty to become a wealthy banker and financier in Poland and the president of important railroad systems. As a young man, he had studied war and had written pamphlets on military subjects. Reaching the conviction that war was the great menace to the economy of states, he finally devoted years to an intensive study of the subject, finally producing his monumental *La Guerre* (Paris, 1898-1900) in six volumes, translated from the Russian.[71] In

[70] Lange, *loc. cit.*, pp. 403-404.

[71] An English translation, by R. C. Long, of the last volume under the title *The Future of War*, in which Bloch summarizes his conclusions, was published at New York in 1899. It also contains an introduction by Edwin D. Mead, and a conversation with the author by W. T. Stead.

this work Bloch examined in great detail the fundamental causes and the social and economic effects of war, as well as its technical conduct. His main thesis was that war between the Great Powers had become a physical impossibility from a military, economic, and political point of view. Summarizing his conclusions in a conversation with W. T. Stead, he declared: "The very development that has taken place in the mechanism of war has rendered war an impracticable operation. The dimensions of modern armaments and the organization of society has rendered its prosecution an economic impossibility, and finally, if any attempt were made to demonstrate the inaccuracy of my assertion by putting the matter to a test on a great scale, we should find the inevitable result in a catastrophe which would destroy all existing political organization."[72] Explaining his meaning further, he said: "When we say that war is impossible we mean that it is impossible for the modern state to carry on war under the modern conditions with any prospect of being able to carry that war to a conclusion by defeating its adversary by force of arms on the battlefield. No decisive war is possible. Neither is any war possible, as I proceed to show, that will not entail, even upon the victorious Power, the destruction of its resources and the break-up of society. War therefore has become impossible, except at the price of suicide."[73] The World War came and disproved part of Bloch's thesis. After a long and bitter struggle, carried on in large part along the lines prophesied by Bloch, and resulting in the tremendous losses and dislocations that he predicted, one side did emerge victorious on the field. Nor have the victors gone down in a common ruin—yet. But eighteen years later they are still striving to liquidate that War, and to avoid another which, in the opinion of many statesmen, might, as Bloch predicted, irretrievably ruin them.

In the years immediately preceding the World War, perhaps the most widely read and influential of all the peace advocates was Norman Angell,[74] the English publicist. In 1909, he published a pamphlet under the title of *Europe's Optical Illusion,* which he expanded in the following year into his famous book, *The Great Illusion, a Study of the Relation of Military Power to National Advantage* (New York, 1910). In the

[72] *Ibid.,* Preface, p. xi.
[73] *Ibid.,* p. xxxi.
[74] Ralph Norman Angell Lane.

years before the War it was translated into a number of different languages, went through several editions, and made a profound impression. It attracted interest, however, not because it advanced new ideas—Bentham, Novicow,[75] Bloch, and others had anticipated Angell's thesis for the most part—but in the trenchant, forceful, and attractive manner in which they were presented. He challenged the notion, widely accepted when he wrote, that territorial expansion is essential to national well being, and that political and military power are necessary in a world of competitive national units. He attempted to prove on the other hand that this doctrine "belongs to a stage of development out of which we have passed; that the commerce and industry of a people no longer depend upon the expansion of its political frontiers; that a nation's political and economic frontiers do not now necessarily coincide; that military power is socially and economically futile, and can have no relation to the prosperity of the people exercising it; that it is impossible for one nation to seize by force the wealth or trade of another, to enrich itself by subjugating, or imposing its will by force on another; that, in short, war, even when victorious, can no longer achieve those aims for which people strive."[76] He then entered into an analysis of the economic and financial interdependence of peoples and nations throughout the civilized world in support of his contentions.[77] He was convinced that disarmament and peace could only be brought about by changing the old and erroneous notions. Until this should be done, the attempt to set up peace machinery would be largely futile. The Hague Conferences, for example, "represented an attempt not to work through the reform of ideas, but to modify by mechanical means the political

[75] However, Novicow's writings were not known to the English-speaking world and appeared to be new to most readers. Angell acknowledged his debt to Novicow, especially for his biological treatment. See fourth American edition (New York, 1913), p. 184, note.

[76] *Ibid.*, p. x. Quotation by permission of G. P. Putnam's Sons. The American philosopher, William James, also an avowed pacifist, thought the program of Angell and the others was deficient in not recognizing the service of war and militarism in preserving among men "ideals of hardihood," service, and discipline. They must therefore present a "moral equivalent." Such an equivalent, James suggested, might be furnished by universal conscription of the young men of the country for a certain period during which they would be required to work at road-building, tunnel-making, mining, and many other kinds of tasks. Here they would be subjected to military hardihood and discipline, would "get the childishness knocked out of them, and . . . come back into society with healthier sympathies and soberer ideas." ("The Moral Equivalent of War," *International Conciliation,* February, 1910, No. 27.)

[77] For a painstaking attempt to demolish the position of Angell, see G. C. Coulton, *The Main Illusions of Pacificism* (London, 1916).

machinery of Europe, without reference to the ideas which had brought it into existence." [78]

In the United States, at the time of the publication of Angell's book, a great step was taken in the campaign to "change people's ideas" in the direction he and other pacifists and internationalists sought. Andrew Carnegie, multi-millionaire steel magnate, following the lead of Alfred Nobel [79] in 1897 and Edwin Ginn [80] in 1910, contributed a large sum of money for the establishment of the Carnegie Endowment of International Peace. The conception of the Trustees of the Endowment, as stated by the Director, Nicholas Murray Butler, President of Columbia University, was not only to carry on propaganda but also to conduct painstaking research into the legal and economic incidence of war, and the advantages to be derived from an "organization of the world into a single group of cooperating nations. . . ." President Butler was aware, as was Angell, of the importance of teaching people to think in new terms. An international mind must be developed, and in his opening address as chairman of the Lake Mohonk Conference on International Arbitration in May, 1912, he defined it as follows: "The international mind is nothing else than the habit of thinking of foreign relations and business, and that habit of dealing with them, which regards the several nations of the civilized world as friendly and cooperating equals in aiding the progress of civilization, in developing commerce and industry, and in spreading enlightenment and culture throughout the world. It is as inconsistent with the international mind to attempt to steal some other nation's territory as it would be inconsistent with the principles of ordinary morality to attempt to steal some other individual's purse. Magnitude does not justify us in dispensing with morals." [81]

Another American university president and scientist, David Starr

[78] *Ibid.*, p. 369. For the ideas to which he refers, review Chs. XII and XIII, and see Ch. XV.

[79] Alfred Nobel, the Swedish inventor of dynamite, founded the Nobel Peace Prize, consisting of a diploma, a gold medal, and one hundred and fifty thousand Norwegian kroner, to be awarded each year to the man or woman who, during the year, had made the greatest contribution to the cause of peace.

[80] Edwin Ginn, wealthy American publisher, who became interested in pacifism, left a legacy for the establishment of the World Peace Foundation at Boston. It has, like the Carnegie Endowment, done much to publicize and forward the peace movement.

[81] N. M. Butler, *The International Mind* (New York, 1912), pp. 102-103. Quotation by permission of Charles Scribner's Sons.

Jordan (1851-1931) of Stanford University, added his voice and pen to the movement at about the beginning of the twentieth century. Although he attacked war from many angles, his chief contribution, growing out of his interests and training in biological science, was his demonstration by means of research and investigation of war's disastrous effects on the human species through its selection of the fittest for disability and death. This reverse selection, he contended, leaves a larger proportion of the weaker and less promising to perpetuate the species. The race is thereby weakened.[82]

We have seen that in the early nineteenth century war was attacked as inconsistent with Christianity, as repugnant to human dignity, and spiritually destructive. The efforts of the religious pacifists were in time strongly supported by free traders and humanitarians and social reformers who were, so to speak, natural allies. Interest in plans of international organization, reminiscent of schemes such as those of St. Pierre and Kant, was revived, disarmament was advocated, and arbitration as a substitute for war in the settlement of international disputes was supported. If one examines carefully the peace literature of the period, he realizes that most, if not all, of the main problems of international society, as they have been revealed clearly in the period since the World War, were anticipated by one writer or another, although few profound studies were made of any of them. In the decade before the World War, leaders in the movement were beginning to advance the theory that war was not only an unnecessary evil from many points of view, but that armed conquest did not pay; indeed, that in view of its constantly mounting costs and the close economic and financial dependence of countries on one another, war could only be waged on any considerable scale at an unbearable sacrifice to victors and vanquished alike.

With the coming of the World War, the international atmosphere became so poisoned that pacifists had practically to cease their organized activities, and most of them in all countries concluded shortly that efforts to stop the conflict would be futile—that the only way out was through. The direction of their thought, as the years dragged on, was toward the immediate realization at the end of the War of an

[82] See especially *The Blood of the Nation* (Boston, 1902), *The Human Harvest* (Boston, 1907), and *War's Aftermath* (Boston, 1914). On other aspects see Jordan's *The Unseen Empire* (Boston, 1912), *Ways to Lasting Peace* (Indianapolis, Ind., 1916), *Democracy and World Relations* (Yonkers, N. Y., 1918).

effective international organization to make a similar conflict in the future impossible.

REFERENCES

Amos, S., *Political and Legal Remedies for War* (London, 1880).

Ballou, A., *Christian Non-resistance in All Its Important Bearings, Illustrated and Defended* (Philadelphia, Pa., 1846).

Beales, A. C. F., *The History of Peace* (London and New York, 1931).

Beckwith, G. C., *The Peace Movement, or War and Its Remedies* (Boston, 1868).

——————, ed., *The Book of Peace, a Collection of Essays on War and Peace* (Boston, 1845).

Bloch, J. S., *The Future of War* (New York, 1899).

Bolles, J. A., *Essay on A Congress of Nations* (Boston, 1839).

Bosanquet, H., *Free Trade and Peace in the Nineteenth Century* (Christiania and New York, 1924).

Bouvet, F., *La Guerre et la Civilisation* (Paris, 1855).

Brailsford, H. N., *The War of Steel and Gold* (10th ed. rev., London, 1918).

Burritt, E., *Lectures and Speeches* (London, 1869).

Butler N. M., *The International Mind: An Argument for the Judicial Settlement of International Disputes* (New York, 1912).

Channing, W. E., *Discourses on War,* ed. by E. D. Mead (Boston, 1903).

Clarkson, T., *Essay on the Doctrines and Practice of the Early Christians as They Relate to War* (3rd ed., London, 1818).

Cobden Club Essays, ed. by J. W. Probyn (2nd ed., London, 1872).

Cones, S. E., *War and Christianity* (Boston, 1842).

Curti, M. E., *The American Peace Crusade 1815-1860* (Durham, N. C., 1929).

Dawson, W. H., *Richard Cobden and Foreign Policy* (London, 1926).

Dodge, D. L., *War Inconsistent with the Religion of Jesus Christ* (Boston, 1905).

Duncan, P. B., *The Motives of War* (London, 1844).

Dymond, J., *An Inquiry into the Accordancy of War with the Principles of Christianity* (Philadelphia, Pa., 1834; reissued New York, 1876).

Fried, A. H., *Handbuch der Friedensbewegung,* 2 vols. (rev. ed., Leipzig and Berlin, 1911-1913).

Hemmenway, J., *The Daily Remembrancer on Peace and War* (New Vienna, Ohio., 1875).

Hervé, G., *L'Internationalisme* (Paris, 1910).

Hill, D. J., *World Organization as Affected by the Nature of the Modern State* (New York, 1911).

Hobson, J. A., *Richard Cobden, the International Man* (New York, 1919).

Huber, M., *Die Soziologischen Grundlagen der Internationalen Gesellschaft* (Berlin, 1928).

Hugo, V., "The United States of Europe; Presidential Address at the International Peace Congress, Paris 1849," *World Peace Foundation Pamphlet Series,* Vol. IV (Oct., 1914) No. 6, Pt. 2.

James, W., *The Moral Equivalent of War* (New York, 1910).

Jay, W., *War and Peace* (New York, 1919).

——————, *The Blood of the Nation* (Boston, 1902).

——————, *The Human Harvest* (Boston, 1907).

Jordan, D. S., *The Unseen Empire* (Boston, 1912).

——————, *War and the Breed* (Boston, 1915).

——————, *War's Aftermath* (Boston, 1914).

Kobatsch, R., *Internationale Wirtschaftspolitik* (Vienna, 1907).

Krehbiel, E., *Nationalism, War and Society* (New York, 1916).

Ladd, W., *Essay on a Congress of Nations,* ed. by J. B. Scott (New York, 1916).

Lagorgette, J., *La Rôle de la Guerre* (Paris, 1906).

Lange, C., "Histoire de la Doctrine Pacifique," *Recueil des Cours,* Vol. XIII (1926), Pt. III, Ch. XVII, Académie de Droit International (Paris, 1927).

Levi, L., *The Law of Nature and Nations as Affected by Divine Law* (London, 1855).

——————, *War and Its Consequences, with Proposals for Establishing a Court* (London, 1881).

Macnamara, H. T. J., *Peace, Permanent and Universal* (London, 1841).

Marchand, P. R., *Nouveau Projet de Traité de Paix Perpétuelle* (Paris, 1842).

Mead, E. D., *Literature of the Peace Movement* (Boston, 1911).

Merz, J. T., *History of European Thought in the Nineteenth Century,* 4 vols. (Edinburgh, 1896-1914).

Meulen J. ter, *Der Gedanke der Internationalen Organisation in Seiner Entwicklung (1300-1889),* 2 vols. (The Hague, 1917-1929).

Novicow, J., *La Fédération de l'Europe* (Paris, 1901).

——————, *War and Its Alleged Benefits* (New York, 1911).

Pecqueur, C., *Des Armées dans leurs Rapports avec l'Industrie, la Morale et la Liberté; ou les Devoirs Civiques des Militaires* (Paris, 1842).

Renault, L., *Les Deux Conférences de la Paix, 1899 et 1907* (Paris, 1908).

Richard, H., *Standing Armies and Their Influence upon Nations* (London, 1868).

Roberts, S., *Thoughts on War* (London, 1834).

Stokes, W., *A Permanent European Congress in Lieu of War* (3rd ed., London, 1861).

Sumner, C., *The True Grandeur of Nations* (Boston, 1845), Waterman Pamphlets, Vol. XXXIX, No. 8.

———, *Speeches* (Boston, 1854), No. 5, *The War System of the Commonwealth of Nations.*

Suttner, B. von, *Memoirs, 2 vols.* (Boston, 1910).

Veblen, T., *An Inquiry into the Nature of Peace* (New York, 1919).

Worcester, N., *A Solemn Review of the Custom of War* (Hartford, Conn., 1817).

Wright, H. C., *Defensive War Proved to Be a Denial of Christianity and the Government of God* (London, 1846).

CHAPTER XV

THE BALANCE OF POWER AND THE LEAGUE OF NATIONS SYSTEM

THE World War was the logical outcome of the commonly accepted notions and practices of international relations of the nineteenth century. These notions and practices, an inheritance in part of preceding centuries, and based on intellectual inertia and the conservative temper of mankind, always fearful of new ideas, retained their mastery over the minds of statesmen in general. And this was true despite the fact that the century witnessed revolutionary changes in transportation and communication, a tremendous increase in industrial output, as a result of the invention and constant improvement of labor-saving machinery and the development of large-scale production, and finally the growth of international trade on a scale never before even remotely approached.[1] These developments of course, were not altogether without consequences in the field of governmental policy. As capital and trade flowed over national boundaries, there was a demand on the part of business interests in particular that governments protect and facilitate international intercourse by agreements with other countries involving the establishment of international unions and administrative organs. Pressure from commercial interests, for example, forced governments to accept and act upon the principle that waterways flowing between or through several states must be subject to international regulation and control. Thus such international organs as the European Commission of the Danube were set up by international agreement to improve such waterways, establish rules of navigation, fix tolls, and otherwise facilitate their use by the community of nations. Likewise the demands of growing business and social intercourse caused the formation of the Universal Postal Union in the last quarter of the century. States agreed to abandon their freedom in the sphere of postal communication, fix rates, and otherwise lay down rules for service outside national bound-

[1] See Ch. XIII.

aries by agreement in periodical Postal Congresses; and to establish a Postal Bureau to administer the affairs of the Union between Congresses. By 1914, more than 45 Public International Unions, dealing with telegraphic communications, matters of health and sanitation, railroad transportation, and a great variety of other matters, were in existence.[2] These rapid developments upon which pacifists and internationalists, especially toward the close of the nineteenth century, placed great reliance as visible and concrete evidence of the soundness of their contentions and as indications of the swift triumph of their cause, were accompanied, however, by others which, as has been seen, were not so reassuring.[3]

Another unifying agency utilized at one time or another from the time of the Congress of Vienna to 1914 was the Concert of Powers. In the years following the Congress, a number of conferences were held at fixed periods by the representatives of England, Russia, Prussia, and Austria. These were "to facilitate the execution of the present treaty" and to be "devoted to the great common interests and to the examination of the measures which at each of these periods shall be judged the most salutary for the repose and prosperity of the Nations and for the upholding of the peace of Europe." After France was admitted to the Concert in 1818, it became truly representative of all of the principal European powers. These powers were less interested, however, in the maintenance of peace than in the suppression of revolutionary movements and the maintenance of the *status quo*. Moreover, if they did not ignore the views and wishes of the smaller states, they were, nevertheless, inclined to regard themselves as competent to make decisions affecting the interests of these states whenever necessary. Opposed to the aspirations of nationalities, hostile to the democratic concept, and in general opposed to liberal ideas, the Concert lost the support of England and, after 1822, was abandoned. In the second half of the nineteenth century, however, the principle of concerted action, especially for the disposition of troublesome questions involving the interests of the powers and the peace of Europe, was revived. The Near East was the chief trouble zone and demanded much attention. Russia, the "big Slav brother" of the Balkan peoples under Turkish rule, was am-

[2] See for extended discussion of these developments and their significance, L. S. Woolf, *International Government* (Westminster, Eng., 1916), Part II.

[3] See, for example, Chs. XII and XIII for notions and policies in support of militarism and imperialism.

bitious for a "window on the Mediterranean." Convinced that the "sick man of Europe" was too feeble to protect his territories, the Tsar attempted to get English approval for a plan of dismemberment, and, failing to do so, picked a quarrel with Turkey on his own account. The other powers failed to avert the Crimean War which resulted in 1854, but a coalition of nearly all the Great Powers under the leadership of England was formed against Russia and dictated the peace at the Congress of Paris in 1856. At this Congress the Concert of Powers issued the Declaration of Paris, aimed to regulate and protect neutral trade in time of war.[4] In 1864, the Concert sought to humanize warfare and ameliorate suffering by adopting rules neutralizing the hospital corps of armies in the field. In order to carry out the convention, Red Cross societies were eventually to be organized in every civilized country in the world.

The Concert of Europe succeeded in averting, or at least localizing, several wars during the latter part of the nineteenth century and the first decade of the twentieth century. When in 1867 Holland proposed to sell Luxembourg to France and it became apparent that this might lead to war between France and Germany, the powers intervened and at a conference held in London brought the matter to a satisfactory issue by collectively guaranteeing Luxembourg's neutrality in future wars. The Concert, however, failed to prevent a Russo-Turkish War in 1877 principally because, although the subject peoples of Turkey clamored for independence on the basis of nationality, and Turkish rule had been notoriously cruel and oppressive, England and the other powers hesitated to proceed to collective intervention. Gladstone, the liberal, could declaim against the "unspeakable Turk," but England had imperial responsibilities in India and imperial statesmen hesitated to do anything that might further weaken the convenient "sick man" who stood in the way of the aspirations of powerful Russia. The freeing of the subject peoples in the Balkans did not insure peace in that region, although the Concert was able in 1885 to localize the Serbo-Bulgarian War, the Cretan War of 1897, and the Balkan Wars of 1912-1913. On occasion the Concert was enlarged by the inclusion of non-European states. This occurred at the time of the Boxer uprising in China against the "foreign devils" in 1899-1900, when the

[4] See article "Declaration of Paris" by George Grafton Wilson in *Encyclopedia of the Social Sciences,* V, 48-49.

United States and Japan cooperated with the European powers in a collective intervention.[5] Again in 1906 the United States participated along with the European Powers in the Algeciras Conference to settle the status of Morocco. In this instance the Concert was apparent rather than real. Actually two hostile groups of states, led by France and Germany, respectively, confronted each other, with the United States not openly favoring either, but actually leaning toward the side of France and the Entente. A settlement was finally reached, although accepted by Germany only under pressure, and the World War was postponed.[6]

The Concert system assumed that there were certain common interests of the community of states that demanded collective consideration and decision by agreement. It operated on occasion, as has been seen, to prevent war. On the other hand, it was oligarchical in composition and spirit, relied on no body of popular opinion, and was animated in its decisions by no avowed principles upon which a permanent structure of peace could be reared. It left the Great Powers ultimately free to do pretty much as they pleased as long as they did not tread on the toes of powerful neighbors in the process. The rights and interests of small states were given little consideration, and decisions taken were too often based on expediency rather than founded on justice.

A far more sinister development, however, was dividing Europe into two armed camps in the decade prior to the World War. This was the system, if it can be called such, of alliances and ententes involving all of the Great Powers and many of the lesser states of Europe, contracted avowedly to insure the security of the contracting parties and preserve peace and the *status quo* through the maintenance of a balance of power. This old conception has already been discussed to some extent, but its challenge in the course of the nineteenth century caused it to be scrutinized more carefully than before by a number of opponents and defenders. It may be remarked at the outset that by the phrase *balance of power* is generally understood a principle of action, not a principle or rule of law, although from the Peace of

[5] Herbert Adams Gibbons, *An Introduction to World Politics* (New York, 1922), pp. 146-151.

[6] Pressure from President Roosevelt seems to have been decisive in procuring Germany's assent. The settlement put France in a favorable position to extend her control in Morocco.

Utrecht in 1713 until the World War numerous important treaties were designed to establish or preserve the balance of power against any state or combination of states seeking to attain hegemony over the others. Whatever adverse criticism may today be advanced against the concept, it had many defenders up to 1914. In the seventeenth century, the French prelate Fénelon gave an explanation of the use and justification of the doctrine which its advocates in the nineteenth century could still quote with approval: "To hinder one's neighbor from becoming too strong is not to do harm; it is to guarantee one's self and one's neighbors from subjection; in a word it is to work for liberty, tranquillity, and public safety; because the aggrandizement of one nation beyond a certain limit changes the general system of all nations, connected with it. . . The excessive aggrandizement of one may mean the ruin and subjection of all the other neighbors. . . This attention to the maintenance of a kind of equality and equilibrium between neighboring states is what assures peace for all." [7] According to Fénelon, therefore, when one power sought undue aggrandizement the others were justified in uniting against it. However, he qualified the doctrine in the following language: "But that such confederacies for restraining the growing power of a state may be lawful the danger must be real and pressing; the League defensive or no further offensive than a just and necessary defence requires; and such bounds must be set to it as it may not entirely destroy that Power which it was formed only to limit and moderate." [8]

In the nineteenth and early twentieth centuries, the principle of the balance of power was defended by various writers on historical and theoretical grounds. It was pointed out that in the absence of a supreme international authority capable of enforcing justice, it was the only means by which small states could preserve their existence and the community of states could compel respect for international law. Historically, it was asserted, it had proved to be a detriment to grandiose ambitions and an agent of justice. Some writers even justified, or at least condoned, the partition of Poland by Russia, Austria and Prussia on the ground that the Poles were politically so weak and disorganized

[7] Quotation taken from article by Sidney B. Fay on "Balance of Power" in *Encyclopedia of the Social Sciences,* II, 396.

[8] Quotations taken from Sir Geoffrey Butler and Simon Maccoby, *The Development of International Law* (London and New York, 1928), p. 66.

that in the absence of the balance-of-power principle Russia would have taken the whole of Poland and thereby would have added to her already great power and become a greater menace to other states. As it was, Poland was divided, the other two participating states getting such a proportion as would relatively increase their strength in relation to that of Russia. Most apologists for the system of equilibrium, however, would probably deny, as some definitely did, that this was a proper application of the principle, and assert that it was used as a cloak for plain robbery, just as other nefarious acts have been committed in the name of morality, of religion, of liberty, of justice and equity. In fact, there were supporters who denied that the system of "compensations," calling for territorial additions all around (for the Great Powers) when one power expands at the expense of a weaker state or "backward people," has any legitimate connection with the system of political equilibrium.[9]

The general position of Stieglitz is perhaps fairly representative of the proponents of the balance of power who regard it as an indispensable means of maintaining a community of states. The foundation of his theory lay in the conception that the group of civilized states forms a single organism properly proportioned throughout. If one state becomes preponderant, the organism becomes deformed, and suffers complete disorganization in the same way that the equilibrium of an individual is destroyed if, for example, there is an abnormal growth of the head or any of the limbs. The member of the Union, therefore, that aspires to a position of predominance is to be regarded as the common enemy of the entire group, for it presents the same danger to all. The most natural, and at the same time the most efficacious, way to deal with such an aspirant is to form coalitions and alliances against him. Isolated action would be dangerous and ineffective, whereas concerted action is energetic and decisive and results in the reestablishment of the equilibrium. Thus in accepting the principle of political equilibrium as one of the rules of conduct of states, and in recognizing it as a guarantee and a defense of the international community, the members of the community will be free to pursue their legitimate individual ends in security. Stieglitz denied that the principle was inconsistent with the internal development of states and that it took no account of growth

[9] Alexander De Stieglitz, *De l'Équilibre Politique, du Légitimisme et du Principe des Nationalités*, 3 vols. (Paris, 1893-1897), I, 243.

and change. It was rather a principle of political wisdom and prudence designed to check conquest, prevent the realization of inordinate ambitions for political supremacy, and disregard for the fundamental interests of other states.[10]

On the other hand, the principle was attacked on various grounds by a number of writers, especially in the years before the outbreak of the World War. David Jayne Hill, writing after the development of the Triple Alliance and Triple Entente pointed out the transitory character of alliances, the attempts of rivals to undermine them, the desperate efforts to prevent their destruction, and the resultant feeling of uneasiness and insecurity. His fundamental objection, however, was that the system was founded on the assumption that states are naturally and inevitably hostile political entities, "that the society of nations as a whole cannot by general agreement exist upon terms of peace and justice, and that security can be obtained only by balancing one group of states against another in such a manner as to check the power of one group by the power of another. In the perfection of the physical balance of forces, upon this theory, lies the sole effective guarantee that peace will prevail, and that international justice will not be constantly violated." [11] It is clear from this passage that Hill followed Grotius, not Machiavelli, in his international outlook. Such a "mechanical conception," said he, relying entirely on physical forces, and divorced from all considerations of ethics, means ever increasing armaments, and leads to the vicious corollary of "compensations." Thus justice has been disregarded, "nationalities dismembered, whole nations effaced from the map, and distant continents partitioned by ruthless expropriation or compliant transaction." [12]

Other writers pointed out that, for another reason as well, the balance of power never meant security. The meaning always in the minds of statesmen is not an equilibrium of forces as when a scale is evenly balanced, but a balance on their own side or the sort of balance one has

[10] *Op. cit.*, pp. 232-238, 247-248. Note also the statement of Lingelbach, *The Annals of the American Academy of Political and Social Science,* XVI (July, 1900), 10: The principle underlying the doctrine and practice has been that the existing distribution of territory and power among the principal states at any one time is so essential to law and order in the society of nations that a disturbance of the *status quo* constitutes a valid ground for intervention.

[11] D. J. Hill, *World Organization as Affected by the Nature of the Modern State* (New York, 1911), pp. 131-132.

[12] *Ibid.*, p. 134.

when he has money to his account at the bank. As each one of two opposing groups of powers ostensibly formed to maintain an equilibrium is thinking in terms of the bank balance and is constantly struggling to augment its forces, the outcome is eventually war.[13] It was also declared by a writer a few months before the World War when the Concert of Europe was practically shattered: "Equipoise between two rival groups, if ever it could be attained, would mean a condition intolerable to the human mind. It would mean stagnation and stalemate, the throttling and hand cuffing, not of one nation, but of all. It is for liberty of movement, for opportunity to carry out their national purposes, that all Powers strive. In a Concert (of Power) that liberty is sought through the amicable adjustment of interests around a Council-Board, and just in so far as Powers form permanent groups which support each other in issue after issue on the principle of 'my ally right or wrong' does any Concert governed by the disinterested opinion of neutrals become impossible. Without a Concert the group system means that all negotiation, even when it is outwardly courteous, is carried on with the knowledge that arguments are weighed by the number of army corps and guns and ships which each combination can muster. The evil reaches its climax when all the Great Powers are regimented, as they are today, in one group or the other, and none of them is free, without some measure of disloyalty to partners, to approach any question with an open mind or consider any aspect of it save its reaction upon the interests of these partners."[14]

Criticism of the doctrine as a "mechanical conception" was based on the contention that to attempt to appropriate a law of statics and erect it into a principle to be applied in a dynamic, sentient world was at bottom unrealistic. In the effort to determine what constitutes a balance of power as between nations, many factors must be taken into account, among them population, territory, resources, armaments, allies. None of these is a constant. The populations of some nations at any particular time are growing, those of others are declining; perhaps those of still others are standing still. But in any case one of the

[13] G. Lowes Dickinson, *The International Anarchy, 1904-1914* (New York, 1926), pp. 5-6.

[14] H. N. Brailsford, *The War of Steel and Gold* (10th ed. rev., London, 1918), pp. 28-29. The tendency was clearly seen after 1904 for the members of the Triple Entente to present a united front on all issues regarded as of vital importance to any one of them, and a similar tendency could be seen in the Triple Alliance.

bases of power is shifting to some extent, at least, among any group of nations that might be taken. The acquisition of new territories also tends to alter the balance, perhaps strengthening, but possibly weakening the possessor. New resources are discovered and utilized or new techniques developed to increase the power of a certain nation in relation to others. And strength in armament is constantly changing and being affected by changes in other directions. Under these conditions, therefore, it was contended that no satisfactory equilibrium is possible for any length of time and that a balance of power system cannot be relied upon either to maintain peace and the *status quo* or to prevent the strong from oppressing the weak.[15]

A brief survey of international political conditions in Europe, especially in the decade preceding the World War, may serve further to account for the various positions taken on the question of the utility of a political system based on the balance of power, and to account for the sentiment that developed during the War for an alternative system. With the defeat of France and the completion of the unification of Germany in 1870, a new and formidable power appeared on the European stage. Although Bismarck attempted to divert the thoughts of France from a war of revenge for the recovery of Alsace-Lorraine by diplomatically isolating her [16] and, at the same time, adopting a benevolent attitude toward French colonial aspirations, the dismissal of the Iron Chancellor and the development of a more aggressive foreign policy by Emperor Wilhelm II after 1890 aroused French fears and revived French antagonism. In the meantime, the German drive for colonies and markets and the adoption of a big navy policy began to alarm England.[17] As late as 1898, the latter was on the verge of war with France as a result of imperial rivalry in the Sudan, and was sounding out Germany for an alliance; but by 1904 the two countries, in the face of the militancy of a powerful common rival, were constrained to compose their differences and form the Entente Cordiale. Three years later,

[15] See article by Sidney B. Fay, *loc. cit.*, pp. 397-398.

[16] In 1872, he formed the Dreikaiserbund, in which Russia and Austria agreed to work with Germany for the maintenance of the *status quo*. In 1879, Russia withdrew on account of Bismarck's support of Austria as against Russia on a Balkan issue; but in 1882 Italy, incensed at France's seizure of Tunis, joined Germany and Austria in the Triple Alliance.

[17] The building of a large navy had been no part of Bismarck's policy, and until Germany embarked on such a policy England was not disturbed because, as Bismarck expressed it, "a land cat cannot carry on war against a water rat."

England came to terms with another rival, Russia, by the adjustment of conflicting colonial policies and the formation of the Anglo-Russian Entente. As France had already (1895) formed an alliance with her erstwhile bitter Russian enemy in order to break her isolation and have a powerful friend on Germany's flank, the path was now clear for the formation of the Triple Entente by the three powers. Moreover, the Anglo-Japanese alliance, directed against Russia when it was originally contracted in 1902, was renewed in view of growing German ambitions for a larger place in the sun in the Far East. Thus the English policy of "splendid isolation," which had been preserved from the time of the Crimean War, was abandoned. Prior to the agreements with Russia and France that have been mentioned, England remained outside the balance of power and, as one writer expressed it, held the scales. Afterwards she definitely aligned herself with one of the two rival groups and played the game accordingly.

The Moroccan affair reveals a great deal about the spirit and methods of European diplomacy during this period and the way in which it was paving the road to Armageddon. Principally for commercial and strategic reasons Great Britain was interested in the fate of Morocco, which was in 1904 under the technical sovereignty of its Sultan but was actually coming under foreign control; but after her decision to form an Entente with France she was willing for a price to give the latter country, which had annexationist aspirations, her blessing. In a secret understanding, therefore, she agreed to allow France a free hand in Morocco in return for the recognition of her own freedom of action in Egypt. The French government reached another secret understanding with Spain, and purchased Italy's consent by generously conceding her the Turkish province of Tripoli in Africa. In the meantime, Germany became suspicious that all was not well, and on the advice of the Chancellor, the Kaiser landed at Tangier in March, 1905, and made a speech in which he pointedly spoke of the Sultan of Morocco as an "independent sovereign." This challenge was promptly answered by an announcement from the other camp that a British squadron would visit Brest in July, and that a French squadron would visit Portsmouth in return. These gestures were not in the nature of diplomatic pleasantries; the parties concerned were in deadly earnest, and a serious situation developed. Germany insisted, on the basis of the Treaty of Madrid which recognized the Open Door in Morocco, that the situation demanded collective handling. France, whose Russian ally was locked in a struggle with Japan, finally reluctantly consented on the advice of President Roosevelt, one of the few American statesmen subscribing to the system of the balance of power,[18] to an international conference to determine the status of Morocco. At this conference held at Algeciras in 1906, a compromise arrangement was finally agreed upon after President Roosevelt had thrown his weight in favor of the plan and had applied diplomatic pressure on Germany. Within a few years France went ahead and absorbed Morocco, "compensating" Germany with some territory in Equatorial Africa.[19]

In the following years the tension in the international atmosphere increased, even though this and other issues between France and Germany, and between the latter and England, were "settled" by negotiation. Each side moved in secrecy, although all parties gave the appearance of frankness by publishing some of their agreements and denying or evading answers as to others. Thus Germany was greatly disturbed in the years before the War at the rumor that England and France had entered into a naval convention which contemplated war against her. That Sir Edward Grey denied the existence of a secret agreement with France on the subject, did not convince the Germans that no kind of understanding had been reached. On the other hand, France was nervous when negotiations were proceeding between England and Germany in 1912 over the Bagdad railway. The French ambassador at London notified the British that rumors of a rapprochement between England and Germany were weakening the Entente, and that Poincaré was going to be interpellated on the matter in the Chamber of Deputies. Sir Edward Grey's reply that only minor questions were being discussed with the Germans did not altogether relieve French uneasiness. The nervousness of France was even more eloquently disclosed in a report of the Russian minister at Berlin in February, 1914, that Ambassador Cambon was opposed to a naval holiday which England had been seeking with Germany, "as all savings [of Germany] on the navy would go to the army and be used against France in a

[18] It is perhaps not generally known that Roosevelt was a firm believer in the balance of power system and, as far as he could, followed a foreign policy consistent therewith. See especially Tyler Dennett's *Roosevelt and the Russo-Japanese War* (New York, 1925).

[19] For a good discussion of the Moroccan Question, see G. P. Gooch, *History of Modern Europe, 1878-1919* (Henry Holt & Co., New York, 1923), Ch. X.

future collision." [20] By 1914 Poincaré, expressing the fatalism that had spread among the statesmen of the Great Powers, is reported to have said: "In two years the war will take place. All my efforts will be devoted to preparing for it." [21] Soon after, however, the "shot that was heard round the world" was fired in the Balkans, and another crisis—this time destined to be fatal—developed. At the last moment, Sir Edward Grey sought to bring the Great Powers together into a conference which would undertake to mediate the issue between Russia and Austria-Hungary, but no Concert was possible now and his efforts met with failure. It is the consensus of opinion that few if any statesmen really wanted war, but Lloyd George said several years later that it "was something into which they glided, or rather staggered and stumbled. . ." The situation was described even more aptly by an English historian [22]: "The root of the evil lay in the division of Europe into two armed camps, which dated from 1871, and the conflict was the offspring of fear no less than of ambition. The Old World had degenerated into a powder magazine, in which the dropping of a lighted match, whether by accident or design, was almost certain to produce a conflagration. No war, strictly speaking, is inevitable; but it requires rulers of exceptional foresight and self-control in every country to avoid catastrophe. . . Blind to danger and deaf to advice as were the civilian leaders of the three despotic empires (Austria-Hungary, Russia, and Germany), not one of them, when it came to the point, desired to set the world alight. But though they may be acquitted of the supreme offence of deliberately starting the avalanche, they must bear the reproach of having chosen paths which led straight to the abyss. The outbreak of the Great War is the condemnation not only of the clumsy performers who strutted for a brief hour across the stage, but of the international anarchy which they inherited and which they did nothing to abate."

In the early days of the War, scarcely anyone was prepared to believe that it would be a long struggle of attrition. German military strategists were said to have thought it would be a "short and merry one" like those waged by victorious Prussia in the Sixties and in 1870. And many Englishmen, certainly, thought of it in terms of a glorified

[20] Gooch, *op. cit.*, p. 528, for quotation.
[21] Dickinson, *op. cit.*, p. 346.
[22] Gooch, *op. cit.*, p. 559.

Boer war of short duration, in which England would play a gallant and successful rôle as the defender of Belgium and of the rights of small nations against a brutal and aggressive enemy. As the romance faded, however, and the nations settled down to a long, grim, and ghastly struggle of trench warfare, as Bloch had predicted, war propaganda was resorted to in all the belligerent countries designed to enlist and maintain the utmost public support. The peoples on both sides were inoculated with the belief that the enemy was guilty of the most diabolical and fiendish acts and that he must be pursued and destroyed as one would destroy a mad dog. Germans wrote ferocious "songs of hate" about "perfidious Albion," and articles about decadent and degenerate France. In the Allied countries, the Kaiser was pictured as another Attila and the German people, as savage "Huns." As the struggle dragged on and millions of lives were sacrificed, the atmosphere became so poisoned that men normally of a liberal and sane temper came, in many instances, to accept the thesis that the War was solely the work of the cruel and heartless enemy.

From this conception of the War there grew logically in the minds of many a corresponding conception of the type of peace that must be made at the end. On the side of the Allied and Associated Powers, for example, the current view was that it must be a "war to end Prussianism," and the "Prussian" and Pan German ambition to dominate Europe and the world.[23] After victory was assured, therefore, the victors must first of all divest Germany of her strength and then adopt the necessary political and economic measures to keep her in a state of impotence for the future. During the War, an Inter-Allied Conference was held in Paris for the expressed purpose of preserving the economic as well as the political solidarity of the Allies after the War by a system of tariffs and other restrictive measures against the Central Powers. The Peace Settlement, to be imposed on the defeated Powers after a "knock-out," was to restore the balance once more—the "bank balance"—by reduction of territory and population, laying down economic restrictions, by the imposition of a large indemnity, and by other measures. The balance was then to be maintained by a close and enduring alliance among the victors with, perhaps, the assistance of neu-

[23] The German view was that a circle of enemies, jealous of Germany's great energy and progress, had surrounded the Fatherland with a ring of steel. These fetters must be broken and Germany accorded her place in the sun before peace could reign.

trals willing to join. In this way, it was declared, Europe could henceforth be freed from the menace of new wars. This rather naïve assumption that only the Central Powers could ever harbor designs that would lead to war, was, perhaps, equalled by the assumption that the ties which held the Allies together in a life-and-death struggle would prove strong enough to resist the centrifugal forces that always operate in time of peace.[24]

Fundamentally opposed to this conception was that of most of the internationalists throughout the world. Those in the countries fighting the Central Powers were likely to subscribe in part to the indictment of Germany in view of the sword-rattling policy of the German government in the years before the War, its disposition to oppose the extension of the principle of arbitration, and its insistence on the necessity of increasing German armaments on land and sea. Nevertheless they were not to be diverted from the view that the root cause of the War was the failure to work out a method of social control in the international sphere. The governments of all the Great Powers and those of most of the lesser ones, imbued with a strong sense of nationalism, and disinclined to listen to any proposals that might infringe upon their sovereignty, had contributed in varying degrees to the maintenance of the "international anarchy" which led to the World War. The remedy, therefore, was to abandon rather than to reconstitute a balance of power. The opposite principle, that of a Concert of Power, must now be accepted and embodied in a permanent organization representative, however, of great and small, and capable of seeing that justice was done and peace assured. In view of the tremendous loss of life, the enormous wastage of economic resources, and the social and economic dislocations the War visited on all of the belligerents, as well as its disturbing effects in every country, it was held that the world could not stand the strain of another such conflict. The "race

[24] The point of view outlined was assiduously cultivated by the Northcliffe press in England, and probably came to represent the conviction of millions of Englishmen. It is also safe to say that it was quite as widely held in France. Official spokesmen of France, such as Poincaré, Clemenceau, and Tardieu, fully subscribed to the "guilty nation" theory, although they were too realistic to expect that they could count on the perpetuation of the alliance against Germany. Among expressions of this general point of view, see article by L. P. Jacks on "Punishment and Reconstruction," *Hibbert Journal,* XV (April, 1917), 373-381, and J. M. Robertson, *The Future of Militarism* (London, 1916), who however was not disposed to feel that it would be wise to keep Germany in durance vile by economic and other penalties and thus "divide the world into two hostile trading groups. . . ."

between education and catastrophe" must, therefore, be to the swift. An international organization must immediately be set up and put in operation at the conclusion of the war, and internationalists started during the conflict to educate public opinion in their several countries to the necessity.[25]

It was inevitable, however, that the concrete plans designed to give effect to the principle should show considerable variation. A number of questions involving other principles had to be considered and answered before any permanent international organization could be set up. Was it to be an organization merely to settle disputes likely to lead to war between nations, or was it to have positive functions as well? Was it to be a super-state, or were nations to retain their sovereignty, limiting its functions to the holding of discussions, giving of advice, and the rendering of decisions when asked to do so? Was it to be a new Concert of Powers controlled by the Great Powers, or were small states to be represented and have a voice in its deliberations? Should it be an organization of diplomatic representatives following the precedent of the Hague Conferences, or should another principle of national representation be followed, looking toward a League of Peoples rather than a League of Governments? Should it be endowed with physical sanctions, or should reliance for the effective carrying out of its decisions be placed upon public opinion and the good faith of its members? Other questions more closely connected with the War also had to be answered. Should the enemy states be admitted immediately; should it be linked organically with the entire peace settlement or divorced therefrom; and should it be supplemented by, or acknowledge the legitimacy of, regional or other types of defensive alliance, or be recognized as a complete substitute for them? These were perhaps the main issues, and on nearly all of them there was a variation of viewpoints. The different schools of opinion and some of the more significant individual contributions to the subject, therefore, deserve some attention.

[25] Among the principal organizations formed for the realization of this objective was the League to Enforce Peace, in the United States; the Union of Democratic Control and the League of Nations Society, in England; the Association for a Society of Nations, and the League of the Rights of Man, in France; and the Central Organization for a Durable Peace, in Holland. For an account of the German conception of a League, see Ernst Jäckh, "L'Idée de Société des Nations en Allemagne Pendant la Guerre," *L'Esprit International,* Vol. III (July, 1929), No. 11, pp. 393-415.

The Union of Democratic Control, formed in London in October, 1914, and numbering among its members Ramsay MacDonald and Norman Angell, adopted a program which probably reflected in general the views of left wing liberal and right wing labor internationalists not only in England but in other countries as well. It regarded the balance of power system as a failure, and approved the institution of a European concert and of an international council to settle disputes. The conspicuous feature of the program, however, was the emphasis placed upon popular as contrasted with autocratic control. It laid down the principle that no province should be transferred by one government to another without the consent of the inhabitants expressed in a plebiscite.[26] Other articles were addressed to British foreign policy. Executive control and secret commitments must be abandoned and parliamentary control established. Every treaty concluded must have the sanction of Parliament. Great Britain should work for the inclusion in the peace settlement of provisions for a radical reduction of armaments by all of the belligerents, and should also seek nationalization of the manufacture of the arms and munitions of war and the prohibition of their export from one country to another. Great Britain should also set herself against an economic war after the War, and should work for the maintenance and extension of the principle of the Open Door.[27] It will be noticed that this program reflected the belief so frequently found in the utterances of pacifists and internationalists, not only in the nineteenth century but much earlier, that rulers and ruling groups are predisposed toward war and that the masses are pacifically inclined; and that the secret and irresponsible conduct of foreign policy further endangers peace by the opportunity that it gives for intrigue and by the nervousness and suspicion that it excites. In its advocacy of a drastic reduction of armament, it was also endorsing what became one of the main planks of the pacifists in the course of the preceding century.

Adherents to the principle of organizing the world for peace, with few exceptions, were not prepared to advocate a super-state. It was perhaps realized that whatever the theoretical merits of a world state, it could be realized only, if at all, by intervening stages of international

26 *Infra*, pp. 206-208, for origin of this practice during the French Revolution.
27 Lange, "Histoire," pp. 412-413.

organization.[28] In France and Belgium, however, there were some who adhered to the super-state idea, although not in the sense of a unitary world state. An interesting and original plan for a federal Union of States was submitted to the French League for a Society of Nations by H. Lepert. There was to be a central legislature and a system of central courts. Acts of the central legislative body were to be binding on the several states, as were the decisions of the central courts. There was to be a central ministry or executive organ appointed by, and to serve at the pleasure of, the legislature. An international police force was to be established. The central courts were to pass only provisionally upon matters not covered by international law, afterwards referring the question raised to the legislative assembly.[29]

Another proposal for a super-state was submitted by the Belgian, M. Paul Otlet, to the French Society. A novel feature of the plan was that only half of the representatives in the central parliament were to be appointed by the governments of the member states; the others were to be selected by transverse sections of society, representing international associations and unions. Thus labor, capital, education, science, and other groups would each have representation as such. Separate representation in the central parliament was provided also for distinct nationalities within each state. The parliament was to be competent to pass legislation binding on the states and, except when it made legislation optional, acts of the central legislature were to supersede local laws. Moreover, except as it might delegate its authority, the central government was to administer its affairs in the several states through its own officials.[30]

In the United States, the greatest interest centered about the establishment, at the conclusion of the War, of a League to Enforce Peace. Ex-President Taft, President Lowell of Harvard, and other prominent

[28] Kant, over a century earlier, regarded a state of nations or super-state as the ideal form of international association, but he thought it unattainable, for states jealous of their sovereignty, "reject *in hypothesi* what is correct *in thesi.* Hence, instead of the positive idea of a world republic, if all is not to be lost . . . a federation averting war, maintaining its ground and ever extending over the world, may stop the current of this tendency to war and shrinking from the control of law. But even then there will be a constant danger that the propensity may break out." See Campbell-Smith's translation of the *Essay on Perpetual Peace,* pp. 128-129.

[29] Theodore Marburg, *Development of the League of Nations Idea,* 2 vols. (New York, 1932), II, 767-768. This work, edited by J. H. Latané, contains a wealth of documents and the correspondence of Theodore Marburg, chairman.

[30] *Ibid.,* p. 768.

men became convinced that permanent international machinery must be devised and set up at the end of the War for the settlement of international differences. The proposals adopted by the organization set up by the group were regarded as embodying a "practical program" that would stand a chance of acceptance by the various governments. It was, therefore, fairly conservative. Recognizing two classes of disputes, it proposed appropriate international organs for the handling of each.[31] The signatory powers forming the League were to agree to submit all "justiciable questions," or those of a legal nature involving such matters as the interpretation of a treaty, to an international court of justice for decision. The idea in the minds of the framers of the League program was to develop the so-called Hague Court of Arbitration into a true judicial tribunal with a fixed panel of judges who would base their decisions on the rules and principles of international law. As far back as 1907, at the Second Hague Conference, the United States used its influence on behalf of such a court, and had it not been for a deadlock over the question of selecting the judges, it would probably have been established. The second article of the League program provided that "all other questions arising between the signatories and not settled by negotiation, shall be submitted to a council of conciliation for hearings, considerations and recommendation." In the latter case, involving the ascertainment of questions of fact rather than questions of law, and an attempt to get the parties to accept a solution in accord with the facts after passion had died down, the League was merely proposing to extend the usefulness of a piece of international machinery which had already been tried and found useful.[32] The third part of the League

[31] Compare with Articles XIII, XIV, and XV of the Covenant which also recognize this distinction. See Appendix for text of the Covenant.

[32] The Hague Convention for the Pacific Settlement of International Disputes, adopted by the First Hague Conference in 1899, gave international standing to the principle of the Commission of Inquiry, and promoted its use in the following provisions. "In differences of an international nature involving neither honor nor vital interests, and arising from a difference of opinion on points of fact, the Signatory Powers recommend that the parties, who have not been able to come to an agreement by means of diplomacy, should, as far as circumstances allow, institute an International Commission of Inquiry, to facilitate a solution of these differences by elucidating the facts by means of an impartial and conscientious investigation." In the Wilson administration the United States concluded some thirty-five treaties providing for the appointment of commissions of inquiry in advance of the occurrence of disputes between the signatories. No class of dispute was reserved from the procedure of automatic inquiry, if the parties could not settle it by the ordinary methods of diplomacy. A period of one year was given for the Commission to make its investigation and report, and in the meantime the parties

program pledged the signatories of the proposed League to the joint use of economic and military sanctions against any member going to war or committing hostile acts against any of the others without first having submitted its case to the courts or to the conciliation procedure. In the program adopted in 1915, it was not proposed to use forceful measures against a signatory resorting to war after having complied with this procedure. It was felt that this "would be imposing obligations far greater than the nations can reasonably be expected to assume at the present day; for the conceptions of international morality and fair play are still so vague and divergent that a nation can hardly bind itself to wage war on another, with which it has no quarrel, to enforce a decision or a recommendation of whose justice or wisdom it may not be itself heartily convinced." [33] It is to be observed, however, that in its "victory program," adopted after the Armistice (November 23, 1918), when ideas of the necessity of a "strong peace" were in the air, and when there seemed a good prospect of inducing statesmen to go further, it was provided that sanctions should be used for enforcing the decisions of the Court as well as for refusal to take a case before the Court in the first place.[34] The fourth part of the League program provided that the signatories should agree to hold conferences from time to time "to formulate and codify rules of international law, which, unless some signatory shall signify its dissent within a stated period, shall thereafter govern in the decisions of the judicial tribunal. . ." It was regarded as highly essential that the statute law of the world be developed in order to contribute to the growth of international law upon which it was intended that the court should rely in making its decisions.

It is to be remarked also that although the program of 1915 was exclusively concerned with the settlement of disputes, and no permanent diplomatic or political organization with positive functions was provided for, the intervening years in which contacts were made and discussions held with other League groups in Europe as well as in the

pledged themselves not to go to war. The theory was that this would not only give an opportunity for the discovery of all relevant facts, but also that the "cooling-off period" would enable nations to view the facts dispassionately and thereby be in a frame of mind to compose their differences. For discussion of this method, see P. B. Potter, *Introduction to the Study of International Organization* (3rd ed., New York, 1927), pp. 153-156.

[33] A. Lawrence Lowell, "A League to Enforce Peace," *World Peace Foundation Pamphlets*, Vol. V (Oct., 1915), No. 5, Pt. I, p. 7.

[34] Marburg, *op. cit.*, II, 799.

United States brought a somewhat changed perspective. The "victory program" of 1918, for example, included permanent legislative, executive, and administrative organs with corresponding functions. The administrative organization was "for the conduct of affairs of common interest, the protection and care of backward regions and internationalized places, and such matters as have been jointly administered before and during the war."[35] It was held that the objects sought must be attained "by methods and through machinery that will insure both stability and progress, preventing on the one hand any crystallization of the *status quo* that will defeat the forces of healthy growth and change, and providing, on the other hand, a way by which progress can be secured and necessary change effected without recourse to war."[36] A "representative congress," in addition to its task of codifying international law, was to "inspect the work of the administrative bodies and to consider in public any matter affecting the tranquillity of the world or the progress or betterment of human relations."[37] The "executive body" was "to act in case the peace of the world is endangered."[38] In view of the ideas reflected in this later program, it is not surprising that the League to Enforce Peace found itself sufficiently in agreement with the fundamentals of the Covenant of the League of Nations when the latter was framed to be able to give the instrument unqualified endorsement.[39]

An examination of the numerous proposals of individuals and societies made during the War period on behalf of a League of Nations reveals that the great majority subscribed to the principle of physical sanctions of one kind or another to compel, if necessary, the members of the League organization to abide by their pledged word.[40] It has already been observed that the League to Enforce Peace was in line with the majority opinion on this point, but there were in the United States some prominent opponents of the idea. The position taken against sanctions by many of the leaders of the early peace movement

[35] Compare with Article XXIV of the Covenant of the League of Nations, also with Article XXII.

[36] Marburg, *op. cit.,* II, 798. Compare with Article XIX of the Covenant. See Appendix.

[37] Compare with Article III, paragraph 3 of the Covenant.

[38] Compare with Article IV, paragraph 4 of the Covenant.

[39] Marburg, *op. cit.*, II, 799.

[40] See C. van Vollenhoven, *War Obviated by an International Police* (The Hague, 1915), for collection of opinions of a number of prominent men in different countries on the need for armed sanctions.

in this country was still endorsed by the American Peace Society, as was perhaps to be expected, and by a number of individuals. James Brown Scott, whose name is best known in connection with his advocacy of the development of international law and international organization on the judicial side, decried any proposal to introduce collective force under any circumstances as a sanction in international affairs. He agreed that there should be a world court and that nations should pledge themselves to take "justifiable" cases to it and to abide by awards, but he would then rely on their "good faith" and on the pressure of public opinion to insure their compliance with the decisions of the court. It was upon "that greatest of sanctions, a decent respect to the opinions of mankind," that Scott pinned his faith.

David Jayne Hill was also a member of the non-force school, in spite of the fact that he was prepared to favor the establishment of an international legislature to make laws binding at least on a limited group of powers who were to form the nucleus for an ultimately wider union including "all responsible and socially inclined nations." Dr. Hill believed that such nations would respect their obligations without being forced to do so; but he was opposed, in any case, to provisions in advance for the use of force in given contingencies, arguing that it would tend to perpetuate the *status quo*. In lieu of this, he believed that a declaration by the League states as to "what should constitute just and unjust causes of war" would suffice to warn prospective aggressors that they could not count on the sympathy of neutrals if they violated the rules.[41]

One of the most thoughtful, realistic, and penetrating discussions of the principles upon which a League of Nations should be based was contributed in 1917 by H. N. Brailsford, British publicist and member of the Independent Labour Party.[42] He anticipated the question, upon which a difference of opinion developed at the time of the Peace Conference two years later, as to whether a League of Nations should be linked with the peace settlement or should be considered separately by contending that the making of the peace and the establishment of a

[41] Marburg, *op. cit.*, II, 773-774. See also statement of the position of Nicholas Murray Butler, likewise classed by Marburg as belonging to the non-force school. See, however, Butler's *The International Mind* (New York, 1912) for his opinion that an international police will be needed for the rare cases in which a nation may flout its obligations.

[42] Under the title, *A League of Nations* (2nd ed. rev., New York, 1917).

permanent international organization constitute a single problem and that the questions they presented must be settled as a whole. Suggesting the principle that President Wilson and General Smuts were later to support, Brailsford declared that the various national, colonial, and economic questions raised by the War must be given a solution that would "help the creation, and ensure the harmonious working," of the League.[43] Among other measures, in this connection, he suggested that the League have as one of its organs "an International Commission to insure free access for the trade of all the signatory Powers to raw materials, and other natural resources."

Much of the discussion current in Allied circles during the War, even among some advocates of a League, assumed that a drastic treaty must be imposed on Germany, involving the seizure of her colonies, the confiscation of her fleet, and the strangulation of her economic life, and that thereupon a League of Nations should be established to insure peace and justice. To Brailsford, such an attempt to "mix a settlement by force with a League based on conference" was bound to be fruitless. Granted that the German mind was permeated with the idea that the world is such that a nation must be either hammer or anvil, such an idea could not be eradicated by an endeavor to make Germany the anvil. The conviction would merely be confirmed. On the same line of reasoning, Brailsford argued against the principle of an exclusive league of victors. If the League started as an anti-German organization, it would be difficult for it later to evolve into a broader association. We would then be back to the balance of power, for Germany would still be strong, and, resenting the discrimination, would build up a competitive hostile group.[44]

The revelation of secret treaties, contracted between 1915 and 1917 by the various Entente powers, and looking toward the division of territorial spoils at the end of the war, confirmed Brailsford and others in their distrust of the traditional methods of diplomacy. He pointed out that even those nations claiming the title of advanced democracies allowed a small number of officials to conduct their foreign affairs without the checks which democracies employ in connection with questions of internal policy and administration. The democratic principle should rule in both spheres, and to this end Brailsford suggested that gov-

[43] *Ibid.*, Preface.
[44] *Ibid.*, pp. 18, 95.

ernments might well be pledged to consult their peoples on major issues of foreign policy, and particularly to secure the consent of their parliaments before going to war. Should a treaty providing for a League of Nations be agreed upon, it should be ratified by the parliaments of the signatories and finally submitted for approval to the peoples of the several states.[45]

In Brailsford's opinion, any League, to be a success, must meet two tests. It must not only be so constituted as to assure its members of an impartial handling of disputes submitted to it, but it must also be prepared to afford them an opportunity of effecting reasonable changes in the established order of things when changes are needed. Failure to take account of the world's growth and need for change, and a rigid insistence upon an established *status quo,* would be fatal. On the other hand, the League must have at its command a preponderance of military and naval force sufficient to prevent any of its members from resorting to aggression instead of invoking peaceful procedure.

It is apparent from the foregoing remarks in opposition to a static peace that Brailsford did not conceive the functions of the League to consist solely in settling disputes. This "negative conception of peace" which meant the "bare avoidance of war" would have no general appeal, he contended, and in fact would not insure peace. The attempt, for example, to settle economic disputes between nations as they arose would be "hazardous and unsatisfactory." The League, therefore, must anticipate and forestall economic conflicts as far as possible by the appointment of international commissions to maintain the Open Door for capital and trade, and to ensure free access to raw materials in an open market. Although Brailsford recognized that universal free trade could not be realized immediately, it was nevertheless a goal toward which the League should strive.[46]

The question of alliances in relation to a League was also given attention. Theoretically, Brailsford pointed out, the continued resort to alliances would seem to be incompatible with the League method. Offensive alliances would imply that war would be waged under some circumstances without regard for the League, and defensive alliances

[45] This procedure was later adopted by Switzerland. The "great and solemn referendum" proposed by President Wilson on the Covenant was mixed up in the presidential election of 1920 in the United States with a number of other contentious questions.

[46] *Op. cit.,* pp. 271-294.

would imply a doubt either as to the good will of the members of the League or of its ability to provide protection against aggression. The War, however, had tended to cement the alliances of the contending combinations of powers, and if the Entente countries should impose heavy terms on Germany at the end of the War, they would have to maintain their partnership in order to enforce them. In such a case, however, the idea of a League of peace would have to be abandoned. On the other hand, assuming a fair peace, the problem, in Brailsford's opinion, was to insure the defensive character of alliances rather than attempt to rule them out completely. This might be accomplished by having the signatories of the League treaty make a declaration that they would in no case furnish armed support to any Power, ally or otherwise, if that Power either resorted to war without first having submitted its case to the League and followed the prescribed procedure of peaceful settlement, or became involved in war by reason of failure to submit to this procedure or to carry out an award or recommendation of the appropriate League organs. Under these stipulations, an innocent and loyal member of the League would be able to depend on the support of allies, and a disloyal and aggressive Power would the more surely suffer isolation.[47]

The proposed League system carried with it necessarily, in Brailsford's opinion, the abandonment of the conception of neutrality in any case in which the League might have to resort to arms against an aggressor.[48] All members would be expected to give active or at least passive aid against such a state. Anticipating the danger to which a small state adjacent to a strong Power would be exposed if it were expected to use its forces against the latter on behalf of the League, Brailsford suggested that different situations must be taken into account in determining the obligations of League members in this matter. States entering the League might accordingly be entitled to make reservations as to the type of sanction, if any, that they would be obligated to employ against a lawless member.[49]

[47] *Ibid.*, pp. 178-194.

[48] Brailsford suggests a simple test of aggression: refusal to refer any dispute that has not yielded to diplomacy, to the Court or Council of the League.

[49] *Op. cit.*, p. 304. After the League of Nations became a reality, this question was raised by a prospective member, Switzerland. The League Council, although pointing out that "the conception of neutrality of the members of the League is incompatible with the principle that all members will be obliged to cooperate in enforcing respect for their engagements," recognized the special position of Switzer-

The resistance of the Central Powers collapsed in October, 1918, and first Austria-Hungary and then Germany asked for an armistice and peace negotiations on the basis of President Wilson's speech of January 8, 1918, containing the Fourteen Points. These points or principles represented the American government's conception of the foundation upon which peace must be based. The Fourteenth Point read: "A general association of nations must be formed under specific covenants for the purpose of affording mutual guarantees of political independence and territorial integrity to great and small states alike." [50] Eventually the victorious Allied and Associated Powers agreed to the enemy's request that peace be founded on the Wilson program,[51] and thus both victors and vanquished pledged themselves to establish an "association of nations" as a part of the peace settlement. As a matter of fact, not only had the problem of the formation of such an association or League been engaging the attention of private individuals and associations for several years prior to the Armistice, but the French and British governments, as well as those of neutral countries, as early as 1917, had appointed committees to study the question.[52]

The French conception of a League of Nations is interesting and important, not because it was to be incorporated in the Covenant (for the chief architects of the League were the British and Americans), but because it explains so much in the French attitude and policy in the post-war years on the questions of armaments, sanctions, and security. The chairman of the official French committee appointed to study the question and report a draft convention for a League was Léon Bourgeois (1851-1925), an outstanding French philosopher, statesman, and pacifist who had represented France at both Hague

land geographically and as a state with a long tradition of neutrality which had been and still was guaranteed by international agreements. Switzerland was therefore admitted with the understanding that she would be expected to cooperate "in such economic and financial measures as may be demanded by the League of Nations against a Covenant-breaking state," but was relieved of the obligation to participate in the use of military force or allow foreign troops to pass over or utilize her territory. C. Howard-Ellis, *The Origin, Structure, and Working of the League of Nations* (Boston and New York, 1928), quotes the Council resolution in full, p. 102.

[50] For text of speech, see W. H. Cooke and Edith P. Stickney, *Readings in European International Relations Since 1879* (New York and London, 1931), pp. 546-551.

[51] With a reservation in regard to the Point concerning the freedom of the seas, and an interpretation of the ones dealing with the evacuation and restoration of invaded territories.

[52] See Marburg, *op. cit.*, II, 831-838.

Conferences. In his *Pour La Société des Nations,* published in 1910, Bourgeois had expressed confidence in the progress that had been made at The Hague, and took occasion to answer critics who regarded the agreements reached at the Conferences as of doubtful value on account of the failure to provide an international military sanction to support them. Had not great military states carried out the awards of arbitration tribunals, although the latter had no force with which to back their awards? In view of this fact, Bourgeois was confident that a similar good faith could be relied upon in the case of the multilateral Hague Conventions, in the support of which so many nations were interested. The pressure of universal public opinion, he declared, would hold nations to their contracts.[53] Four years later, the multilateral treaty providing for the neutrality of Belgium had become a "scrap of paper," and France was fighting for her life. It is not surprising that the Bourgeois of this period should have an altered conception. Whether the report of the French Ministerial Commission for the League of Nations, which was under his chairmanship, fully expressed the personal views of Bourgeois, it is, of course, difficult to say; but on the question of the principle of a league as against a return to the balance of power he was, in contrast to the cynical Clemenceau,[54] a strong supporter of the League. But first of all he wanted Germany punished. The League was to be established by the Allies alone, after which trustworthy neutral states might be admitted; but Germany was to be excluded for an indefinite period. On this point he declared: "The Society of Nations has a universal character but, because of its very aims, it can be established only between nations which are free, which are faithful to their pledged word, which have discharged all the obligations resulting from past offenses and which can give to one another the necessary guarantees in fact and in law."[55] However, Germany was eventually to be admitted to the League, for "no one dreams of classing forever the states of the world into two camps."

[53] *Op. cit.,* pp. 278-284.

[54] The "Tiger" was openly contemptuous of the idea of a league, and frankly a believer in the balance of power system. On the eve of the Peace Conference, he announced in the Chamber of Deputies that if entrusted with the making of peace he would work for a treaty based on the old principle.

[55] Marburg, *op. cit.,* II, 772. Thomas G. Masaryk, the great Czech statesman, took a similar position. He was in favor of a League, but he apparently wanted the "free peoples who fought together" to hold the balance of power within it "rather than allow Germany to tip the scales in her favor." (*Outlook* [New York], April 16, 1919, p. 647.)

Ultimately peace can only be founded in law which affords justice for all nations great and small. Bourgeois, in accord with what was undoubtedly the official French viewpoint, was not in favor of a League which should require nations absolutely to abandon their sovereignty, but he would have them accept obligations to submit all their disputes to peaceful settlement and endow the League with the authority to enforce its decisions by diplomatic and economic measures and by international military sanctions if necessary. And "so long as certain great Powers remain outside the Society of Nations, the international force must be maintained at a strength which will insure its triumph and the maintenance intact of the common patrimony which the rule of law will secure to the peoples thus freely associated." [56] Thus Bourgeois completely abandoned the position he had earlier taken on the question of sanctions.

It is generally agreed that the most determined and eloquent advocate of a League of Nations during the later months of the War and after the Armistice was President Wilson. It may even be doubted whether a League would have come into existence in 1920 had it not been for his grim insistence that it be among the first questions considered at the Peace Conference and that it be made "an integral part of the general treaty of peace." [57] He was chairman of the Commission on the League of Nations which was charged by the Peace Conference with the task of working out a plan, and was therefore one of the fathers of the Covenant.[58] His own original contributions to the Covenant were slight, but he had, prior to the end of the War, studied many plans for a League and had incorporated into a draft of his own a

[56] Marburg, *op. cit.*, II, 772-773. See also William Rappard, "The League of Nations as an Historical Fact," *International Conciliation* (June, 1927), No. 231, pp. 287-288, published by Carnegie Endowment for International Peace.

[57] In this he was strongly supported by Lord Robert Cecil and General Smuts. Not only, however, was there considerable opposition in those European circles that were hostile or indifferent to making the League the central task or even a major interest of the Peace Conference, but Wilson's own Secretary of State, Lansing, was opposed to it, as was Senator Lodge, chairman of the Foreign Relations Committee of the United States Senate.

[58] On this Commission, the five Great Powers—the United States, Great Britain, France, Italy, and Japan—were represented, with two delegates each; and nine smaller Powers were also given representation. The most outstanding and influential members were, in addition to its chairman, the British delegates General Jan Smuts and Lord Robert Cecil. Among other distinguished members were Léon Bourgeois of France, M. Hymans of Belgium, Wellington Koo of China, and M. Venizelos of Greece.

number of ideas that were later to form an essential part of the Covenant.[59]

As regards membership in the League of Nations, Wilson's view was apparently similar to that of Bourgeois and the other framers of the Covenant. The League must not be composed merely of a group of Allied and Associated Powers, but should in principle, at any rate, be a universal association of nations. However, after the entry of the United States into the War the President drew a sharp line between autocratic and democratic systems of government and many times expressed the conviction that autocratic governments could not be trusted to keep their engagements. In fact, the War was "to make the world safe for democracy." To Mr. Wilson, this was not merely an effective war slogan, but a statement of a fundamental issue which divided the Allied and Associated Powers and their enemies. The position he took in an address of May 3, 1917, was, therefore, logical. The League, he said, was to be limited to a "partnership of democratic nations," for "no autocratic government could be trusted to keep faith within it." An insistence on the rigid application of this test, however, would certainly have excluded one of the Allies, Japan, from the League and would at least have put others in the doubtful column. And on the other hand Germany, metamorphosed into a republic as the victors were discussing her fate, had at least met all formal requirements for admission to a league of democratic nations. The same was true of Austria. But neither one of these nations was at first admitted to the League. Fear and resentment played an important rôle, especially in the exclusion of Germany.

Wilson's conception of a League differed from that of the League to Enforce Peace and other plans emphasizing the judicial aspect of international organization. He felt that they placed too much faith in "mere machinery," especially judicial machinery. This arose in part, doubtless, from his impatience with lawyers and the strictly legal way of approaching human problems. In working over Colonel House's draft for a League, which Wilson took as a starting point for his own plan, he eliminated the provision for a world court.[60] Wilson's dislike

[59] Actually, Wilson drew up three different drafts as a result of critical study and suggestions from various sources, among them Colonel House, General Smuts, and David Hunter Miller, his legal adviser at the Peace Conference.

[60] Howard-Ellis, *op. cit.*, pp. 70-71; 78-79. See also David Hunter Miller, *The Drafting of the Covenant*, 2 vols. (G. P. Putnam's Sons, New York and London, 1928), I, 42.

of elaborate machinery of any kind is to be attributed to his feeling that machinery cramps and stifles growth. It is impossible, he contended, for those framing a fundamental law, especially one that shall apply to the entire world, to foresee and plan for all contingencies. He, therefore, exerted his influence to keep the Covenant as free as possible from detail; and, in explaining the Draft Covenant, which the Commission submitted to the Peace Conference, he pointed out that one of its chief virtues was that "it is not a straitjacket but a vehicle of life." [61]

Wilson's conception of the primary function of a League was that it should guarantee the territorial integrity and political independence of its members. Several years earlier he had supported a treaty with the countries of Latin America providing that "the High Contracting Parties in this solemn covenant and agreement, hereby join one another in a common and mutual guarantee of territorial integrity and of political independence under republican forms of government." [62] This represented an attempt to make the Monroe Doctrine a partnership arrangement rather than a unilateral declaration. Wilson's idea was now to extend the principle to the entire world. What the United States through the Monroe Doctrine had done for the Western world, the League of Nations was now to do for the world as a whole.[63] It was by reason of this conception of the League's main *raison d'être* that Wilson later spoke of Article X [64] as "the heart of the Covenant" and absolutely refused to have it eliminated or tampered with.[65]

In the matter of sanctions, Wilson's position seems to have changed from what it had been prior to the War. In 1913, at any rate, he had supported his pacifist Secretary of State, William Jennings Bryan, in the negotiation of a number of treaties obligating the contracting parties to submit their disputes of whatever nature to international com-

[61] See *International Conciliation* (March, 1919), Special Bulletin, p. 360. For the entire address, see pp. 355-364.

[62] See his address of January 6, 1916, before the Second Pan-American Scientific Congress.

[63] Marburg, *op. cit.*, II, 764; Rappard, *op. cit.*, p. 281; Miller, *op. cit.*, I, 42; II, 370.

[64] The article reads: "The members of the League undertake to respect and preserve as against external aggression the territorial integrity and existing political independence of all members of the League. In case of any such aggression or in case of any threat or danger of such aggression the Council shall advise upon the means by which this obligation shall be fulfilled." See Appendix for complete text of Covenant.

[65] Ray Stannard Baker, *Woodrow Wilson and World Settlement*, 3 vols. (Garden City, N. Y., 1922), I, 320, 332.

missions of inquiry. These treaties contained no provisions for sanctions of any kind.[66] Wilson, on the other hand, emphasized the importance of sanctions for the League of Nations. In his address to the United States Senate on January 22, 1917, he said: "It will be absolutely necessary that a force be created as a guarantor of the permanency of the settlement so much greater than the force of any nation now engaged or any alliance hitherto formed or projected, that no nation, no probable combination of nations could face or withstand it. If the peace presently to be made is to endure, it must be a peace made secure by the organized major forces of mankind." [67] Later, in expounding the Covenant to the Peace Conference, he pointed out that sanctions had not been stressed, but that the League had been provided with the means of enforcing international obligations: "Armed force is in the background in this program, but it is in the background, and if the moral force of the world will not suffice, the physical force of the world shall. But that is the last resort, because this is intended as a constitution of peace, not as a league of war." [68]

Wilson did not propose, however, that the nations should be asked to guarantee an unjust peace. The peace must be just to the small nations as well as to the great, and to the vanquished as well as to the victors. Justice also demanded that territorial changes should be based as far as possible on the principle of self-determination. An unjust peace, he contended, would not last and would not be worth guaranteeing. It would be the duty, however, of the League of Nations to correct the defects or injustices of the peace treaties as they should be revealed or seek their alteration by negotiation as changing conditions might require adjustment.[69] This attitude was consistent with his conception that the Covenant should be a "vehicle of life." [70]

Lord Robert Cecil, also one of the fathers of the League, conceived of an association more nearly along the lines of the pre-war Concert of Powers, or a perpetuation of the Allied Supreme War Council.

[66] But see Felix Morley, *The Society of Nations, Its Organization and Constitutional Development* (Washington, 1932), p. 6, for view that by the autumn of 1914 Wilson was thinking in terms of physical guarantees.

[67] Rappard, *op. cit.*, p. 282, for quotation.

[68] *International Conciliation* (March, 1919), p. 360. The text of the entire address is also contained in this same issue.

[69] Miller, *op. cit.*, I, 42. Article XIX of the Covenant was intended to cover this.

[70] For texts of the various Draft Covenants drawn up by Wilson, see Miller, *op. cit.*, II, 12-15, 65-93, 98-105, 145-154.

He was, of course, in favor of a permanent organization, and he contemplated the creation of various organs such as a Permanent Court, a General Conference, and a Secretariat, as well as linking various international bodies already in existence to the League organization. But he was quite frank in declaring that the Great Powers should have exclusive control. To that end, the Council, which was to be the directing and controlling organ, was to be composed exclusively of representatives of the Great Powers. The General Conference, representative additionally of the other members of the League, was to meet normally but once in four years. Except for the exclusion of Bolshevist Russia as a "definitely untrustworthy and hostile state," Cecil was not particularly concerned about excluding other states, remarking that "it is desirable not to be too rigid in scrutinizing qualifications, since the small powers will in any case not exercise any considerable influence." [71]

As regards the primary function of the League, Cecil seems to have regarded it as that of preventing war between states by providing machinery for the discussion and conciliation or the legal decision of disputes.[72] He was conservative in his desire to avoid "a large invasion of sovereignty," and in his feeling that it was not feasible to require that disputes involving the vital interests of states should be submitted to an international court whose awards were to be enforced by arms. On the other hand, he believed that a League, by providing alternative methods of peaceful settlement, and forbidding nations from going to war in any particular case until they had given them a fair trial, could interpose a powerful barrier against war. His conception is well expressed in the following excerpt from one of his addresses: "The most important step we can now take is to devise machinery which, in case of international disputes, will, at the least, delay the outbreak of war, and secure full and open discussion of the causes of the quarrel. For that purpose . . . all that would be necessary would be a treaty bind-

[71] Miller, *op. cit.*, II, 61-64, for Cecil's Draft Sketch of a League of Nations; also Vol. I, Ch. V, for a discussion of Cecil's proposals, including his "Notes on a Permanent Court."

[72] Cecil, perhaps somewhat influenced by the Smuts conception, envisaged a number of positive functions for the League, but they were rather in the nature of addenda. In his concluding remarks on the draft Convenant before the Peace Conference, he said: "And finally, we have thought that if the world is to be at peace it is not enough to forbid war. We must do something more than that. We must try and substitute for the principle of international competition that of international cooperation. . ." *International Conciliation* (March, 1919), Special Bulletin, p. 373.

ing the signatories never to wage war themselves or permit others to wage war till a formal conference of nations had been held to enquire into and, if possible, decide upon the dispute. It is probably true, at least in theory, that decisions would be difficult to obtain for the decisions of such a conference, like all other international proceedings, would have to be unanimous to be binding. But since the important thing is to secure delay and open discussion, that is to say, time to enable public opinion to act and information to instruct it, this is not a serious objection to the proposal. Indeed, from one point of view, it is an advantage, since it avoids any interference with national sovereignty except the interposition of a delay in seeking redress by force of arms. That is the essential thing, and to secure it, the treaty would require each of the signatories to use their whole force, economical as well as military, against any nation that forced on war before a conference had been held. To that extent, and to that extent only, international coercion would be necessary." [73]

The position of another one of the prominent fathers of the Covenant, General Jan Smuts, is conveyed in its general outline in the following paragraph of his remarkable pamphlet, "The League of Nations: a Practical Suggestion," written on the eve of the Peace Conference: " . . . my reflections have convinced me that the ordinary conception of the league of nations is not a fruitful one nor is it the right one, and that a radical transformation of it is necessary. If the league is ever to be a success it will have to occupy a much greater position and perform many other functions besides those ordinarily assigned to it. Peace and war are resultants of many complex forces, and those forces will have to be gripped at an earlier stage of their growth if peace is to be effectively maintained. To enable it to do so, the league will have to occupy the great position which has been rendered vacant by the destruction of so many of the old European empires and the passing away of the old European order. And the league should be put into the very forefront of the programme of the peace conference, and be made the point of departure for the solution of many of the grave problems with which it will be confronted." [74]

This discloses the basic idea of Smuts, elaborated further on, that the League should not be designed mainly as an instrument to ward off

[73] Rappard, *loc. cit.*, 284-285, for quotation.
[74] The Smuts Plan is printed as Document 5 in Miller, *op. cit.*, Vol. II.

or prevent the outbreak of future wars, but as an institution to be knit into the fabric of the common international life of states. It should become so necessary and function so vitally in ordinary peaceful intercourse that it would be irresistible when it had occasion to deal with a war situation. The Peace Conference should, therefore, regard the establishment of a League of Nations as "a primary and basic task," for only through a League could a stable solution of the many economic, territorial, and other problems confronting the Conference be found. Specifically, there was the problem of the disposition of the peoples and territories split off from the Russian, Austrian, and Turkish Empires. These peoples should not be annexed, and yet for the most part they had not had sufficient political training to justify the expectation that they would immediately be able to dispense with aid and guidance. Here was a task which only the League could undertake. It should become the reversionary or successor of the Empires, and be given the authority where necessary, to administer and ultimately to dispose of these territories and peoples in accordance with the principle of self-determination. During the period of tutelage the League might appoint some other state as its agent or mandatory to carry on the necessary administration, but in all cases the League should retain its control.

The Covenant of the League of Nations was chiefly the work of these men—Wilson, Cecil, and Smuts, and it reflects to some extent the varying conceptions of all of them as conditioned and modified by the interchanges that took place in the League of Nations Commission, and by the thought of many publicists and statesmen of the War period. The conflict, of course, did not work a sudden revolution in their thought on international relations, and produce ideas unknown to the nineteenth century. The War provided a driving force, however, and instilled a sense of immediacy that made for more searching and penetrating discussions of the major problems of international affairs and their relation to the creation of a League of Nations. From another point of view, the framers of the Covenant of the League built upon institutional foundations laid in the course of the nineteenth century and the cooperative agencies they were compelled to set up during the War. The Council [75] of the League of Nations was the Concert of Powers made permanent, enlarged to insure representation of the smaller states, and given a more or less clearly defined though not altogether

[75] Covenant, Article IV.

exclusive field of juridisction, including not only the settling of disputes, but also the general direction of other activities of the League. The Assembly [76] was patterned after the Hague Conferences, representing all of the members of the League on a basis of equality, and expected to develop into a "law-making" body. The Hague Court of Arbitration and the attempt at the Second Hague Conference to establish a World Court of Justice pointed the way to the Permanent Court of International Justice which was not created at the time the Covenant was drafted, but was foreseen and provided for as a necessary part of the peace machinery.[77] It was also true that the International Labor Organization, affiliated with the League had its inspiration in developments of the nineteenth century.[78]

The Covenant reflected the views of all of the framers in its provisions for a loose association or confederation of states rather than a super-state.[79] Its language throughout testifies that this was their intent. In the preamble, "*The High Contracting Parties* . . . agree to this Covenant of the League of Nations." Although the organization itself is intended to be permanent the right of individual members to withdraw is specifically recognized. (Article I.) Moreover, no organ of the League is endowed with authority to command a member to do anything. For example, the Council is entrusted with the task of formulating plans for the reduction of armaments, but no scheme is to be effective until "adopted" by the several governments. (Article VIII.)

[76] Covenant, Article III.

[77] The Covenant, in Article XIV, provided that "The Council shall formulate and submit to the members of the League for adoption plans for the establishment of a Permanent Court of International Justice. . ." This was the constitutional basis for the Court which was later created. See A. Hammarskjöld, "The Place of the Permanent Court of International Justice Within the System of the League of Nations," *International Journal of Ethics,* Vol. XXXIV (Jan., 1924), No. 2, pp. 146-156.

[78] See Covenant, Article XXIII (a); also Howard-Ellis, *op. cit.,* Ch. VIII and Francis Wilson, *Labor in the League System* (Stanford, Cal., 1935), Ch. XI.

[79] For an opposite point of view shared by few writers, see David Jayne Hill, *Present Problems in Foreign Policy* (New York, 1919), especially pp. 109-110. He claimed that the Covenant is not in the nature of a treaty, but that the League which it creates is "a distinct corporate entity, exercising a will not identical with that of all the separate members, is organized with power to coerce other states not belonging to it, to act under its own rules and by its own judgment, and even to dictate the form of government and degree of authority to be exercised over wide areas and great populations subjected to its control." For a good discussion of the nature of the League from the point of view of an American authority on international law, see C. G. Fenwick, *International Law* (New York, 1934), index under "League of Nations."

Under Article X, the Council is to "advise" as to the means to be adopted to carry out its stipulations. Under Article XIII, it is to "propose" the steps to be taken should a state fail to carry out an arbitral award or judicial decision. And in other cases the word "recommendation" is used.

On the other hand, the members of the League, under the terms of the Covenant, surrender their freedom of action in a number of matters that were regarded before the War as in the nature of sovereign rights. They agree to submit all disputes, whether affecting "national honor or vital interests" or any other matters reserved before the War for national decision, to some form of peaceful settlement, and not to go to war against a state accepting an award. They likewise agree in any case not to go to war for a specified period after an award is made. Moreover, they agree to use jointly economic and, if necessary, military measures against a state resorting to war in defiance of the procedure provided.[80] Furthermore, although the principle is recognized that disputes within the "domestic jurisdiction" of states are not reviewable by the League, the Council is given authority to decide in case of doubt whether any particular dispute falls within the League's jurisdiction.[81] It is to be noted also that members of the League give up (Article X) the time-honored right of conquest and agree to use concerted action against any member violating the territorial integrity and political independence of another.[82] This was a large order, and it need occasion no surprise, although it cannot but cause distress, that the practice has not always reached the level of the theory.

In the formation of the Covenant the political, as contrasted with the legal, concept of a League largely prevailed. That is, its main organs, the Council and Assembly were political organs, whereas the sponsors of the League to Enforce Peace, for example, wanted a world court as the central institution, and legal decisions increasingly to take the place of diplomatic and political processes of peaceful settlement. The Covenant provides in considerable detail for the peaceful settlement of

[80] The Covenant anticipates the case of a dispute in which one or more non-League states are involved by seeking (Article XVII) to bring them into the League system on terms of equality for the purpose of settling the particular difference. If any state refuses and resorts to war against a member of the League, collective sanctions may be employed against it.

[81] See Article XV, paragraph 8.

[82] Article XIX provides a basis, however, for peaceful change of frontier, and for modification of treaties.

disputes by the Council and by the Assembly, but gives less attention to arbitration and judicial settlement. It did provide, however, for the creation of a Permanent Court of International Justice as a necessary supplement to the League's activities in the cause of peace, and therefore paved the way for increasing recognition and use of strictly juridical processes in the League system.

The ideal of a universal association was suggested and its desirability assumed, although it was not immediately provided for under the terms of the Covenant. The ex-enemy states were for the time being not admitted to membership, although there was considerable sentiment among the neutrals in favor of their immediate entry. In fact, not all neutral states were invited to become original members of the League. However, an invitation was extended to thirteen of them,[83] and others were admitted later. In principle, it is to be noted, the Covenant looks in the direction of universality, and in practice all of the ex-enemy states were members within a few years.

Finally, it is to be observed, the Covenant embodies the newer conception of "diplomacy by conference" as a regular, rather than as a sporadic, means of adjusting international disputes and promoting the common interests of the family of nations. Pre-war diplomacy, so largely characterized by formal diplomatic notes, by secret conversations and agreements, by conspicuous visits of the heads of states to show solidarity against a potential common enemy, or by ultimatums and a show of force to extort concessions, was in general popular disfavor; and men like Wilson and Cecil were determined that it should be replaced, as far as possible, by open diplomacy, and by multilateral agreements. This view is particularly in evidence in Article XVIII of the Covenant, which requires henceforth the registration of all treaties or international engagements as a condition precedent to their juridical validity, and Article XX in which the League members agree to abrogate "all obligations or understandings *inter se* which are inconsistent with the terms" of the Covenant. This was directed at alliances involving the pursuit of selfish objects at the expense or in disregard of the interests of the international community.[84]

[83] See annex to the Covenant.

[84] For an attempt to supplement and strengthen the Covenant see text of "Protocol for the Pacific Settlement of International Disputes," also the "General Act of 1928," in Appendix.

REFERENCES

Angell, N., *America and the New World State* (New York and London, 1915).

Baker, R. S., *Woodrow Wilson and World Settlement,* 3 vols. (Garden City, N. Y., 1922).

Bourgeois. L., *Pour la Société des Nations* (Paris, 1910).

Brailsford, H. N., *A League of Nations* (and ed. rev., New York, 1917).

Butler, G., and Maccoby, S., *The Development of International Law* (London and New York, 1928), Chs. XV-XVII.

Buxton, C. R., ed., *Towards a Lasting Settlement* (London, 1916).

Cooke, W. H., and Stickney, E. P., *Readings in European International Relations Since 1879* (New York and London, 1931).

Corbett, P. E., "What is the League of Nations?" *British Year Book of International Law, 1924,* IV, 119-148.

Dickinson, G. L., *The Choice before Us* (New York, 1917).

Duggan, S. P., ed., *The League of Nations, the Principle and the Practice* (Boston, 1919).

Fanshawe, M., *Reconstruction; Five Years of Work by the League of Nations* (London, 1925).

Gonsiorowski, M., *Société des Nations et Problème de la Paix,* 2 vols. (Paris, 1927).

Guerreau, M., *L'Organisation Permanente du Travail* (Paris, 1922).

Hammarskjöld, A., "The Place of the Permanent Court of International Justice Within the System of the League of Nations," *International Journal of Ethics,* Vol. XXXIV (Jan., 1924), No. 2, pp. 146-156.

Hervé, G., *L'Internationalisme* (Paris, 1910).

Hicks, F. C., *The New World Order, International Organization, International Law, International Coöperation* (Garden City, N. Y., 1920).

Hobhouse, L. T., *Questions of War and Peace* (London, 1916).

——————, *The World in Conflict* (London, 1915).

Hobson, J. A., *Towards International Government* (London, 1915).

Hoijer, O., *Le Pacte de la Société des Nations* (Paris, 1926).

Howard-Ellis, C., *The Origin, Structure, and Working of the League of Nations* (Boston and New York, 1928).

Jäckh, E., "L'Idée de Société des Nations en Allemagne Pendant la Guerre," *L'Esprit International,* Vol. III (July, 1929), No. 11, pp. 393-415.

Jones, R., and Sherman, S. S., *The League of Nations from Idea to Reality* (2nd ed., London, 1929).

Kobatsch, R., *Internationale Wirtschaftspolitik, ein Versuch ihrer Wissenschaftlichen Erklärung auf Entwicklungsgeschichtlicher Grundlage* (Vienna, 1907).

Lange, C. L., "Histoire de la Doctrine Pacifique et de son Influence sur la

Développement du Droit International," *Recueil des Cours,* Vol. XIII (1926), Pt. III, pp. 171-426, Académie de Droit International (Paris, 1927).

Lansing, R., *The Peace Negotiations* (Boston and New York, 1921).

Lawrence, T. J., *The Society of Nations, Its Past, Present, and Possible Future* (New York, 1919).

Lorwin, L. L., *Labor and Internationalism* (New York, 1929).

Mahaim, E., "L'Organisation Permanente du Travail," *Recueil des Cours,* Vol. IV (1924), Pt. III, pp. 65-223, Académie de Droit International (Paris, 1925).

Marburg, T., *A League of Nations,* 2 vols. (New York, 1917-1919).

Marvin, F. S., ed., *The Unity of Western Civilization* (London and New York, 1915), Ch. XII.

Miller, D. H., *The Drafting of the Covenant,* 2 vols. (New York and London, 1928).

Minor, R. C., *A Republic of Nations* (New York, 1918).

Morley, F., *The Society of Nations, Its Organization and Constitutional Development* (Washington, 1932), Ch. XVI.

Mowat, R. B., *The Concert of Europe* (London, 1930).

Munch, P., *L'Origine et l'Oeuvre de la Société des Nations* (Copenhagen, 1923-1924).

Novicow, J., *La Fédération de l'Europe* (Paris, 1901).

Perigord, P., *The International Labor Organization* (New York, 1926).

Phillimore, W. G. F., *Schemes for Maintaining General Peace* (London, 1920).

Politis, N., *La Justice Internationale* (Paris, 1924).

Pollard, A. F., *The League of Nations in History* (London and New York, 1918).

Pollock, F., *The League of Nations* (London, 1920).

Rappard, W. E., *International Relations as Viewed from Geneva* (New Haven, Conn., 1925).

Ray, J., *Commentaire du Pacte de la Société des Nations* (Paris, 1930).

Redslob, R., *Théorie de la Société des Nations* (Paris, 1927).

Riches, C. A., *The Unanimity Rule and the League of Nations* (Baltimore, Md., 1933).

Scott, J. B., *The Hague Peace Conferences of 1899 and 1907,* 2 vols. (Baltimore, Md., 1909).

Schmitt, B. E., *Triple Alliance and Triple Entente* (New York, 1934).

Schücking, W., *Der Bund der Völker* (Leipzig, 1918).

————, and Wehberg, H., *Die Satzung des Völkerbundes* (Berlin, 1931).

Smuts, J. C., *The League of Nations, A Practical Suggestion* (London, 1918).

Solano, E. J., ed., *Labour as an International Problem* (London, 1920).

Temperley, H., *A History of the Peace Conference of Paris*, 6 vols. (London, 1920-1924).

Voorhees, D., "The League of Nations: A Corporation, Not a Superstate," *American Political Science Review*, Vol. XX (Nov., 1926), No. 4, pp. 847-852.

Webster, C. K., *The League of Nations in Theory and Practice* (Boston and New York, 1933).

Williams, B. S., *State Security and The League of Nations* (Baltimore, Md., 1927).

Williams, J. F., *Chapters on Current International Law and the League of Nations* (London and New York, 1929).

——————, *Some Aspects of the Covenant of the League of Nations* (London, 1934).

Wilson, F., *The Origins of the League Covenant* (London, 1928).

Wilson, F. G., *Labor in The League System* (Stanford University, 1934).

Woolf, L. S., *The Framework of A Lasting Peace* (London, 1917).

——————, *International Government* (Westminster, Eng., 1916).

CHAPTER XVI

THE OUTLAWRY OF WAR

THE League of Nations system, as has been shown, is the political and legal expression of the aspirations of internationalist thinkers whose point of view and activities during the century prior to the outbreak of the World War have been recorded.[1] It did not, however, fulfill the hopes of the absolute pacifists, who were unqualifiedly opposed to all war for whatever purpose it might be undertaken. From their point of view, the Covenant fell short in some respects and went too far in others, some even regarding the League set up under it as a "war-breeder." The reasons for this attitude, in so far as it may be dissociated from the partisan considerations that were prominent in the controversy in the United States in 1919 and 1920 over the question of American membership, were largely as follows: The Covenant does not proscribe all war. It is true that it clearly points in the direction of eliminating all private wars, as shown in the preamble[2] of the Covenant, but the articles that follow do not in all cases forbid a member from resorting to war on its own account. In fact, war is clearly permitted under certain circumstances, and forbidden in others. Members of the League are obligated not to go to war until after they have submitted a dispute "either to arbitration or judicial settlement or to inquiry by the Council, and they agree in no case to resort to war until three months after the award by the arbitrators or the judicial decision, or the report by the Council" (Article XII, paragraph 1). Should the case be taken to arbitration or submitted to judicial settlement, the award is binding and war may not be resorted to against a party complying with the judgment rendered (Article XIII, paragraph 4). On the other hand if the dispute is submitted to the Council, the

[1] *Supra,* Ch. XIV.

[2] The intent of the framers and of the nations accepting League Membership, as expressed in the preamble, is "to promote international cooperation and to achieve international peace and security by the acceptance of obligations not to resort to war," as well as by other means.

process is in principle that of mediation and the parties are not obligated to accept the Council's report. If, however, the report is unanimous (the parties in dispute excepted), war may not be waged against the party accepting its recommendation (Article XV, paragraph 6). If a dispute is claimed by one of the parties and is found by the Council to lie "solely within the domestic jurisdiction of that party," the Council is henceforth without jurisdiction and apparently, therefore, war may be undertaken without violating the covenant. (Article XV, paragraph 8.) [3]

All of the foregoing cases are concerned with the threat of war, and the extent to which its actual occurrence may be prevented between members of the League. But Article XI, paragraph 1, of the Covenant declares that "any war or threat of war, whether immediately affecting any of the members of the League or not, is hereby declared a matter of concern to the whole League, and the League shall take any action that may be deemed wise and effectual to safeguard the peace of nations." And under Article XVII, if a serious dispute arises between a League member and another state, or between two non-League states, the latter shall be invited to "accept the obligations of membership in the League for the purpose of such dispute, upon such conditions as the Council may deem just." A non-member state, however, is not obliged to accept the League's invitation, but if it not only refuses to do so but makes war on a League member, the League may resort to the sanctions provided for in Article XVI against it. If non-member states have a serious controversy and both refuse to accept a League invitation, "the Council may take such measures and make such recommendations as will prevent hostilities and will result in the settlement of the dispute" (Article XVII, paragraph 4). It is evident, then, from what has been said, that the provisions of the League Covenant indicate acceptance of the principle that war by any states anywhere is of such danger to the members of the international community that the League may require states that have not been able independently to compose serious differences to try, at least, the machinery devised for the purpose by the framers of the Covenant. The resort to war is made more difficult by interposing delay before the outbreak of hostilities and by inviting disputants to select one or more of the various

[3] But see Hans Wehberg, *The Outlawry of War,* tr. by E. H. Zeydel (Washington, 1931), p. 10, for a different opinion.

procedures for peaceful settlement contained in the Covenant. On the other hand, it is obvious that the framers of the Covenant did not interdict all wars, and if collective military action against an offender by members of the League is regarded as war, they have definitely sanctioned and provided for what some writers call public war, or war by representatives of the international community on its behalf.[4]

A movement for the complete "outlawry of war" originated in the United States in 1919 in opposition to the conceptions embodied in the Covenant of the League. The Peace Settlement, and more particularly the drastic Treaty of Versailles, came as a shock to American liberals. Regarding the acceptance by the Allies of President Wilson's principles of peace as a commitment to make a just and durable peace, they were unprepared for a treaty that in many respects seemed harsh and indefensible. The Wilson program, they had felt, offered the best prospect of ushering in an era of peace. The Versailles Treaty, they were sure, contained the seeds of future wars. They turned away from it, therefore, in many instances with a sense of disillusionment and chagrin that the great crusade had not been, after all, a "war to end war." Many regarded the League Covenant, even apart from its provisions, as tainted in view of the fact that it was intertwined with the Treaty, that the ex-enemy states were excluded from the League, and that the latter was endowed with economic and military sanctions to enable it to maintain the new *status quo*. It was, therefore, in their view, nothing more than the alliance of the victors perpetuated for the purpose of enforcing an unjust settlement upon the defeated powers. The United States should have nothing to do with it, for it was not a league of peace but a league of war. For example, John Dewey, the American phi-

[4] Clyde Eagleton, who does not regard the use of armed force by the League under Article XVI of the Covenant as war, accepts J. B. Whitton's list of seven cases in which "war remains licit: (1) When one disputant refuses to abide by the award or unanimous recommendation of the Council, war against it is permitted to all other members; (2) When both refuse, there seems to be no limitation at all upon the right to make war; (3) When the Council is unable to reach a unanimous decision, freedom of action is reserved; (4) If the Council admits that the matter is one which by international law is solely within domestic jurisdiction, it has no control; (5) Civil wars, in which belligerency is recognized, are wars under international law, but are not covered in the Covenant; (6) If the arbitral award or recommendation of the Council is not given within a reasonable time, the state involved would appear to recover its liberty of action, although this situation is improbable; (7) States not members of the League, not bound by the Covenant could claim the right to wage war in accordance with the international law existent before the creation of the League." (*International Government* [New York, 1932], p. 528.)

losopher, who had been a strong supporter of the Wilsonian program, and an advocate of a democratic League of Nations designed "to further common interests,"[5] said in 1920 after the Senate had rejected the Covenant: "Quite probably it is fortunate for us that nationalistic ambitions and imperialistic aggressions were so undisguisedly powerful in the peace negotiations. We owe monuments to Clemenceau, Sonnino, and Balfour. Probably in our excited idealism nothing less flagrant than the exhibition they gave could have averted our becoming innocent and ignorant accomplices in the old world game of diplomacy. As it was, the contrast between prior professions and actual deeds was so obvious as to evoke revulsion."[6]

The idea of the outlawry of war was first broached during the last year of the World War by Salmon O. Levinson, a Chicago lawyer.[7] In 1919, Mr. Levinson and Senator Philander C. Knox, one of the most energetic of the group of Senate irreconcilables, formulated the plan for the outlawry of war, around the central ideas of which a number of more or less prominent Americans later rallied.[8] The plan called for "a Conference of all civilized nations" to create and codify international law. The basic provisions of the code would include the following:

1. The further use of war as an institution for the settlement of international disputes shall be abolished.

2. War between nations shall be declared to be a public crime, punishable by the law of nations.

3. War shall be defined in the code and the right of defense against actual or imminent attack shall be preserved.

4. All annexations, exactions, or seizures, by force, duress or fraud, shall be null and void.

[5] *Characters and Events,* 2 vols. (New York, 1929), II, 602-614.

[6] *Ibid.,* p. 615.

[7] "The Legal Status of War," *New Republic,* XIV (March 9, 1918), 171-173.

[8] Among the supporters of the idea were John Dewey, Senator Wm. E. Borah, Raymond Robins, Rev. John Haynes Holmes, Rev. C. C. Morrison, J. Reuben Clark, Jr., and Judge Florence E. Allen. Senator Borah introduced resolutions in the Senate on behalf of the outlawry of war on February 14, 1923, December 9, 1926, and December 12, 1927. On September 4, 1920, Senator Harding, while campaigning for the presidency, is reported as having said: "If I catch the conscience of America, we'll lead the world to outlaw war." As President he voiced the same idea. President Coolidge, in his annual message to Congress of December 3, 1924, gave the movement encouragement in the following words: "Much interest has of late been manifested in this country in the discussion of various proposals to outlaw aggressive war. I look with great sympathy upon the examination of this subject. It is in harmony with the traditional policy of our country, which is against aggressive war and for the maintenance of permanent and honorable peace." (Quoted in Wehberg, *op. cit.,* p. 19.)

5. An international court with affirmative jurisdiction over purely international disputes shall be created and modelled as nearly as may be on the jurisdiction of the United States Supreme Court over controversies between states. All purely international disputes as defined by the code shall be decided and settled by the international court sitting as a judicial body, which shall be given jurisdiction over all parties to a dispute upon the petition of any party to the dispute or of any signatory nation.

6. All nations shall agree to abide and be bound by and in good faith to carry out the orders, decrees, and decisions of such Court.

7. One nation cannot summon another before the International Court except in respect to a matter of international and common concern to the contending nations, and the jurisdiction of the court shall not extend to matters of governmental, domestic or protective policy unless one of the disputing parties has by treaty or otherwise given another country a claim that involves these subjects. The classes of disputes excluded from the jurisdiction of the international court should be specifically enumerated in the code and not be left open to the flexible and dangerous distinction between justifiable and non-justifiable controversies.

8. The court should sit in the hemisphere of the contending nations; and if the disputants live in opposite hemispheres, then in the hemisphere of the defendant nation.

9. National armaments to be reduced to the lowest point consistent with domestic safety and with the necessities of international requirements.

10. All nations shall make public report once each year setting forth fully their military and naval armaments, structural and chemical. These reports to be verified by authorized committees.

11. The doctrines of military necessity, retaliation and reprisal which are open to such flagrant and abhorrent abuse, shall be eliminated.[9]

It will thus be seen that the advocates of the outlawry of war proposed to reach the goal of a warless world, not by a progressive evolution, which is the idea implicit in the League Covenant, but by a revolutionary act. Until war is made a "public crime," they contended, it is useless to establish leagues and courts for its suppression. It must be recognized that until it is "outlawed" it remains as in the past, an established, respectable, legal institution in the same sense that marriage, the church, and the school are institutions. At present, "Society is not organized for peace; it is actively organized for war."[10] The same procedure, therefore, must be followed as was adopted when

[9] Salmon O. Levinson, *The Outlawry of War* (Chicago, 1921), pp. 11-12.
[10] C. C. Morrison, *The Outlawry of War* (Chicago, 1927), pp. 91-92.

the world decided to get rid of such evils as duelling and slavery. Duelling, the outlawrists assert, is analogous to war, which is "duelling on an international scale."[11] The institution of duelling, like war, was also at one time "thoroughly legal, and had so woven itself into the presuppositions of society's thinking that a man was virtually compelled to uphold his 'honor' by resorting to the duel on the slightest occasion of injury or affront. The arbitrament of the sword was accepted as establishing the 'honor' of the victor. But when the conscience of society penetrated the absurdity, the irrelevance, and the moral repugnance of the institution, it was disestablished by law and disappeared."[12] It is contended that war, like duelling, has its own code; for example, it is pointed out that a large part of international law is taken up with the regulation of war. This being true, it is contended that "war . . . is within the law, sanctioned and sustained by the law, just as duelling carried on under the *code duello* was within the law, sanctioned and sustained by the law."[13]

The Levinson plan for the outlawry of war embodied a throughly legalistic conception. In this it expressed the strong American predilection for legal formulae and judicial supremacy. Levinson, Knox, and Borah—all lawyers—were thoroughly representative of the widespread American opinion that when one wants to get rid of an evil it can be done most easily and effectively by passing a law against it. Levinson expressed this viewpoint in defending his program of outlawry: "In dealing with any other form of evil one's first impulse is to have the legislature or congress pass a law making the practice illegal and criminal. If that is the way to deal with ordinary grievances, why not try the beaten path with the greatest of all wrongs? We want not 'laws of

[11] Morrison, *op. cit.*, p. 98.

[12] *Ibid.*, p. 99. It is at least doubtful whether duelling has largely disappeared as a result of the laws against it. Social change, better judicial methods, an altered perspective have probably been the chief factors in its decline, and the laws have rather reflected the changed conditions and newer outlook.

[13] *Ibid.*, p. 100. Levinson, *op. cit.*, p. 313. Quincy Wright, however, points out that modern publicists have abandoned the old Roman conception of war. A "state of war" is not regarded as legal or illegal, but rather "as an event, the origin of which is outside of international law although the law prescribes rules for its conduct differing from those which prevail in time of peace." On the other hand, although customary international law does not make war illegal, bilateral and multilateral treaties involving practically all civilized nations do "outlaw" it in stipulated areas or for certain objects or in given circumstances. See his articles, "Changes in the conception of War," *American Journal of International Law*, Vol. XVIII (Oct., 1924), No. 4, p. 755, and "The Outlawry of War," *American Journal of International Law,* Vol. XIX (Jan., 1925), No. 1, pp. 75, 86, 89.

war' but 'laws against war' as we have laws against murder and burglary."[14] Levinson's plan, therefore, was simple and to many internationalists a bit naïve in placing a legal ban on war and providing exclusively judicial machinery for the settlement of all classes of disputes not specifically enumerated as belonging within the domestic jurisdiction of states. It called for no political machinery or international diplomatic processes, and no organization for continuous international cooperation in matters of common concern to nations. It was regarded, indeed, as embodying a different principle from that upon which the League of Nations was founded, a principle distinctively American. Interestingly enough, it commanded the support of Dewey on these very grounds, that it simply "outlawed" war, and provided a code and a court in its place, although during the war he seems to have visualized quite a different type of organization. In November, 1918, for example, he declared that "the real problem is one of organization for more effective human association and intercourse," and that a League "whose main purpose is to enforce peace by an extension of legal mechanisms of controvery and litigation is idealistic and academic."[15]

At that time he visualized an organization of nations growing out of common everyday necessities, and operating "to meet the commonplace needs of everyday life with respect to food, labor, securing raw materials for the reparation of a devasted world. . ." If such an organization were realized, the legal and political mechanisms for dealing with disputes and conflicts of interests would follow in due time. "But," he declared, "there is all the difference in the world between a system of courts, laws, decisions, and coercive enforcements which rests upon an organized system of wants and satisfactions, and which gives that system added security and a system which, taking no constructive care for common interests, spasmodically attempts to keep peace by bringing into play legal devices."[16] Dewey was apparently visualizing an economic League, and it is clear that the League of Nations of the Covenant, even though it had as one of its aims the promotion of international cooperation, did not come up to his specifications. One would have thought, however, that the Levinson plan would altogether fail

[14] *Op. cit.*, p. 14, Cf. also Frances Kellor and Antonia Hatvany, *Security against War*, 2 vols. (New York, 1924), II, 780-781.

[15] *Op. cit.*, Ch. II, pp. 603-604.

[16] *Op. cit.*, pp. 604-605.

to meet them. This did not prove to be the case. Not only had Dewey become convinced that "the political approach to the abolition of war is hopeless,"[17] but he had been converted to the idea that "an international court based on carefully codified law that makes war a crime, having as full jurisdiction in cases of honor as in other cases, is the sole practicable road to the goal" of peace.[18]

The establishment of a supreme international court beyond which there would be no appeal is of the essence of the ideas of Levinson, Morrison, and indeed all of the leaders of this school of thought. In the original plan of 1919, Levinson made no mention of any other international agencies, except the conferences for codification; but others of the group have since admitted the usefulness of diplomatic and political agencies in a supplementary and subordinate capacity.[19] The outlawrists seem to object to the Permanent Court of International Justice mainly on the ground that it is subordinate to the "political" League of Nations,[20] and that it operates under a system of international law in which war is "legal." The proponents of outlawry, therefore, have demanded a "real court" in place of the "League court," based on a code of law which will abolish war in its first article. It is recognized that a complete code will take time and will need periodic revision, but Levinson thought an adequate one could be framed in two years.[21] And Morrison argues that the decision to outlaw war will in itself enormously simplify the problem of codification, for the codifiers then need only concern themselves with the laws of peace.[22] It was proposed in the Levinson plan not only to define in the code disputes "purely international" in character, and therefore subject to the "affirmative" (compulsory) jurisdiction of the Court, but also to enumerate the classes of disputes that should be specifically excluded

[17] *Op. cit.*, p. 667.

[18] *Ibid.*, pp. 669-670.

[19] *Op. cit.*, p. 64; Dewey, *op. cit.*, pp. 682-690.

[20] The Permanent Court is a part of the League system of peaceful settlement as the Supreme Court of the United States is part of the American system of government. It was also in a loose sense created by the League. The Supreme Court was also created by a political organ, the Congress of the United States. In neither case can it be said that the court is subordinate to the political authority, but the Supreme Court of the United States is generally conceded to be at the pinnacle of the American system, whereas the Permanent Court of International Justice cannot be said to occupy a similar place in the League system.

[21] *Op. cit.*, p. 17.

[22] *Op. cit.*, p. 162. Senator Borah, however, has favored the codification of the law of maritime war. See Wehberg, *op. cit.*, p. 23.

from the Court's jurisdiction.[23] In the case of the United States, Morrison assumes that such questions as the Monroe Doctrine, immigration, the tariff, and allied debts would never be suitable for decision "by a tribunal of any sort." Disputes over such questions must, therefore, be settled by the parties out of court by some process of conciliation, or left to time, "or not settled at all." To attempt to provide for the compulsory settlement of such questions, in Morrison's opinion, would tend to cause war rather than enable nations to escape it. On the other hand, the absolute prohibition in the first article of the outlawry plan would remain, although it would not prohibit a nation from using arms to defend itself. In whatever way nations might decide to settle such disputes as were not suitable for decision by the international court, they might not go to war over them.

Critics of the outlawry school have not failed to point out, however, that the very questions which are loaded with the most dynamite are the ones that the outlawrists would apparently withhold from the court's jurisdiction, and that inasmuch as they all recognize the continued legitimacy of military action for defense, a wide gap is opened for war to enter. Walter Lippmann, for example, has stated in effect that the outlawry plan is vitiated by the introduction of "a set of reservations which withdraws from the scope of the code and the competency of the court many, if not most, of the major policies which cause disputes. Finally, it disembowels the outlawry of war by legalizing wars in defense of those major policies which are excluded from the competence of the court and the code." [24] The outlawrists, however, contend that if war were "cut out of the legal tissue of civilization," many disputes that now assume great importance either would not arise or would be settled with relative ease. Morrison even declares: "Were the war system not inherent in the presuppositions and purposes of the nations the disputes which now lead to fighting would be enormously reduced. Abolish the institution of war and you will abolish most of the 'causes' of war." [25] For example, the Monroe Doctrine would disappear if war were abolished. At present it is "part of the war system of the United States." But if the war system were cut out root and branch, there would be no need for it, inasmuch as its "ultimate *raison d'être* . . . is

[23] *Op. cit.*, pp. 11, 12.
[24] "The Outlawry of War," *Atlantic Monthly*, August, 1923.
[25] *Op. cit.*, p. 195.

to keep Europe from transplanting her warring national interests to this continent and so drawing the United States into the conflicts of the old world. We have to protect the Monroe Doctrine by war, but it is war that produces the Monroe Doctrine." [26] Morrison also believes that the economic causes of wars would lose their importance if the "war system" were discarded. "The wars which are said to spring from economic competition," he contends, "are really not the effect of natural economic conflict, but are induced artificially by the presence of military systems in association with competing economic interests. Left to itself, divorced from and no longer supported by the war system, the world's international commerce would wear a changed countenance." [27]

Finally, the outlawry of war school is apparently almost unanimous in its conviction that physical compulsion should not be used either to compel nations to take their cases to the court under the code, or to abide by an award, or to refrain from committing the "crime" of going to war. Levinson, however, in his earlier advocacy of outlawry, indicated some uncertainty in the matter. He declared that the Court should have the power to enforce its decrees "against all war criminals," [28] but was inclined to feel that force might be dispensed with as far as the Court's civil judgments were concerned. Nevertheless he admitted that "much may be said in favor of an international force, or a force contributed to by various nations to aid in the execution of the international court's civil decrees as well as its criminal judgments." [29] The other leading American exponents of outlawry, however, place their reliance on the good faith of nations and upon the power of public opinion to make the outlawry of war effective. One of the principal objections they advance to the League Covenant is the inclusion of provisions for collective economic and military sanctions against states resorting to war in violation of their undertakings under the Covenant. From the point of view of the outlawrists, the use of joint military force, even on behalf of the international community, would still be "war," and therefore is not to be tolerated. Dewey says, for example, of internationalist critics of the outlawry idea that reliance must be

[26] Morrison, *op. cit.*, p. 196.

[27] *Ibid.*, pp. 196-197.

[28] Borah, however, would have each nation agree "to indict and punish its own international war breeders or instigators. . ." See his Senate resolution of December 20, 1922, quoted in Kellor and Hatvany, *op. cit.*, p. 790. Dewey also accepts this procedure, *op. cit.*, p. 676, as does Morrison, *op. cit.*, p. 204.

[29] Levinson, *op. cit.*, pp. 18-19.

placed on the good faith of nations: "They plead for the abolition of war . . . and for its retention as a means of coercion. For what else does an international army, even though called a police force, mean in substance? Abolish war, and at the same time keep war up our sleeves! The contradiction is more than merely logical. it means the perpetuation of that attitude of mind that perpetuates war." [30] Morrison points out that the great majority of treaties contain no provisions for the use of military sanctions, to guarantee their execution, that they rest solely on the honor and good faith of the parties, and that this has been sufficient. Treaties have seldom been broken, but when they have been it has been "under the operation of the war system!" [31] This system demands a superior allegiance, and being accepted as legal and righteous, obscures and confuses the sense of honor of nations and causes them to break their plighted word when military necessity commands. If the nations solemnly renounced the system, this compulsion would be removed and complete reliance could be placed on their good faith. In any case, Morrison argues, all treaties rest ultimately upon the plighted word of nations. For example, the Locarno Pact calls for the use of military sanctions under certain circumstances.[32] Suppose the circumstances occur, and France calls upon England for help against Germany under the Locarno Pact, and England fails to respond. There are no sanctions for that contingency. Reliance is placed upon the honor and good faith of the parties. Then, inquires Morrison, if nations, as in this case, are trusted to keep their word to go to war even when it does not directly concern them, can they not be depended upon to keep a pledge not to resort to war? In his opinion, the chances are much better that they can be depended upon in the latter case.[33]

However convincing the case against sanctions and armed establishments might appear to Americans whose freedom from powerful and dangerous neighbors put them in an exceptionally favorable position against external aggression, it was perhaps inevitable that it should fail

[30] Dewey, *op. cit.*, p. 676.

[31] Morrison, *op. cit.*, pp. 181-183.

[32] The treaty referred to included Great Britain, France, Germany, Italy, and Belgium as signatories. The parties undertook severally and collectively to guarantee the frontiers between Belgium and Germany, and between France and Germany, as established by the Treaty of Versailles. Germany and France also agreed not to resort to war against each other except in self-defense, or in compliance with international obligations under the Covenant. If the treaty is violated and one of the states is attacked, the other signatories pledge themselves to come to its aid.

[33] *Op. cit.*, pp. 185-190.

to convince European continental states with frontiers exposed to traditional enemies or to powerful neighbors dissatisfied for one reason or another with the territorial *status quo*. They could not share the optimism of the American outlawrists as to the magic change that would take place once the nations had "outlawed" war. Nor were they willing to scrap the League and the Permanent Court of International Justice and abandon the League peace system in favor of a new Court and a code. They preferred to retain, improve, and work through the institutions already established. On the other hand, the outlawry plan made a strong appeal to many American religious pacifists who inherited the tradition of uncompromising opposition to all war,[34] and to others who felt that it offered a truly American alternative to the League of Nations, which was widely regarded as embodying distinctively European ideas. Under the outlawry plan, as many seemed to view it, the Monroe Doctrine would be safe, the United States could "get out of Europe," and yet could save the world from war if it really cared to be saved, by an infallible American method. The problem, therefore, from the point of view of American and European internationalists and pacifists who were not too completely wedded to particular formulae or too rigidly opposed to the examination of ideas that were not home-grown, was to build a bridge between the two schools of thought. Men like Professor James T. Shotwell and President Nicholas Murray Butler of Columbia, and David Hunter Miller and others, recognized the League of Nations not only as a going concern but, in spite of deficiences, as a useful institution deserving of support by the United States. On the other hand, they realized that along with a very real American idealism there was a strong isolationist tendency that expessed itself in a distrust of Europe and a fear of "involvement," and that it must be taken into account in any plan of rapprochement.

In 1927, Professor Shotwell, who had been particularly active in attempting to work out a plan whereby organized official cooperation between the League and the United States might be realized, inspired M. Briand, French Foreign Minister, to make a declaration to the American people that was to have far-reaching consequences.[35] M.

[34] Morrison denies that the outlawry movement is a pacifist movement or that he is a pacifist "in the current restricted use of the term as one who for conscience' sake refuses, under any circumstances, to have any share in the existing war system." (*Op. cit.*, p. 208.)

[35] David Hunter Miller, *The Peace Pact of Paris* (New York, 1928), p. 7.

Briand's message, sent on the occasion of the tenth anniversary of the entrance of the United States into the World War, suggested that in order to further the cause of peace in general, "France would be willing to enter into an engagement with America mutually outlawing war. . ." He continued: "The renunciation of war as an instrument of national policy is a conception already familiar to the signatories of the League Covenant and the Locarno treaties. Any engagement subscribed to in the same spirit by the United States toward another nation, such as France, should greatly contribute in the eyes of the world to enlarge and fortify the foundations on which the international policy of peace is being erected. . ."[36] The proposal, after some discussion in the press, struck a spark in the United States, and the American government was eventually influenced to state its readiness to enter into diplomatic conversations with the French government to determine whether an agreement of the nature proposed by the French Foreign Minister might not be reached between the two countries.[37] This was followed by a draft treaty from M. Briand which served as a basis for discussion and negotiation. In this "Pact of Perpetual Friendship," as M. Briand called it, the French government and the government of the United States agreed in the name of their respective peoples to renounce war "as an instrument of their national policy towards each other," and never to seek the solution of any dispute that might arise between them by any other than pacific means. The proposed treaty quite equaled in its simplicity the solution advanced by the outlawrists; and the renunciation of war, though qualified and limited to two countries, seemed to offer a point of departure for the goal of outlawry.

After carefully considering the French proposal, the American government responded favorably, and suggested that France and the United States should seek the adherence of the principal powers (excluding Russia, whose government had not been recognized by the United States) to such a treaty, and that subsequently "all the other nations of the world" should be invited to become signatories. This momentous

[36] *Ibid.*, p. 7, for quotation.

[37] For a full account of the part played by Nicholas Murray Butler and other leaders in arousing American public opinion and in causing the American government to become interested in the Briand proposal, see James T. Shotwell, *War as an Instrument of National Policy and its Renunciation in the Pact of Paris* (New York, 1929), Chs. VII-IX.

proposal immediately raised certain questions that led to further correspondence, and the clarification of important issues. It also brought the United States government, for the first time since 1919, back to the quest for world peace in concert with the other nations. The American proposal to convert the treaty into a multilateral pact drew a reply from France to the effect that she would in such a case have to confine the renunciation to "all wars of aggression," since she had obligations under the Covenant, the Locarno agreements, and other conventions that might require her to go to war in the defense of these international agreements.[38] Later she agreed to retain the original unqualified statement, but with the understanding that such renunciation did not impair her right to fulfill obligations under the treaties mentioned nor the right of self-defense.

The negotiations of the multilateral treaty brought out certain important viewpoints that deserve attention.[39] The American Secretary of State, Mr. Kellogg, objected to the introduction of a reservation of self-defense in the treaty as being superfluous and perhaps harmful. Article I of the treaty should therefore contain the declaration, unqualified as regards this matter, that the signatories renounce war "as an instrument of national policy in their relations with one another."

In support of his position, Mr. Kellogg declared in sweeping language that the right of self-defense "is inherent in every sovereign state and is implicit in every treaty. Every nation is free at all times and regardless of treaty provisions to defend its territory from attack or invasion and it alone is competent to decide whether circumstances require recourse to war in self-defense." [40] This statement could not but satisfy the most timorous and conservative. If it is understood that each nation is to be the sole judge in such a case there could hardly be any reason for making a specific reservation. Moreover, said Mr.

[38] For draft of an alternative multilateral treaty proposed by France, see Shotwell, *op. cit.*, pp. 288-290.

[39] Only certain leading ideas that were brought out will be treated. A good account of the negotiations, however, and texts of the documents and correspondence may be found in Miller, *op. cit.*

[40] Extract from his note of June 23, 1928, to the other governments. Text in Miller, *op. cit.*, pp. 213-219. Excerpt on pp. 213-214. Referring to Mr. Kellogg's statement, Manley O. Hudson remarks: "That statement would paralyze much that has been done in recent years; it is opposed to the whole current of our thinking about war; it is a denial of the very basis of the Covenant which requires any state's use of force to be justified before a collective judgment." (*Progress in International Organization* [Stanford University, Calif., 1932], p. 97.)

Kellogg, expressed recognition of the right of self-defense is undesirable. "Inasmuch as no treaty provision can add to the natural right of self-defense, it is not in the interest of peace that a treaty should stipulate a juristic conception of self-defense since it is far too easy for the unscrupulous to mold events to accord with an agreed definition." [41] Mr. Kellogg's position as to the right of self-defense of a nation seems to have been essentially the same as that of the proponents of the outlawry of war, and he and they seem to be in agreement that each nation remains the judge whenever a question arises as to whether it is using arms in self-defense, although it must answer to world "public opinion." On the other hand, Senator Borah and Mr. Levinson seemed to feel, when they were advocating complete outlawry of war "as an institution," that it was desirable to stipulate formally that the right of self-defense remained unimpaired.[42]

That the "right of self-defense," individually interpreted, was capable of great elasticity was suggested, prior to the signing of the "Briand-Kellogg Pact," by the reservation made by the British Government, often referred to as the British Monroe Doctrine. Sir Austen Chamberlain, British Foreign Secretary, advised the American government that: "There are certain regions in the world, the welfare and integrity of which constitute a special and vital interest for our peace and safety. His Majesty's Government have been at pains to make it clear in the past that interference with these regions cannot be suffered. Their protection against attack is to the British Empire a *measure of self-defense.*[43] It must be clearly understood that His Majesty's Government in Great Britain accept the new treaty upon the distinct understanding that it does not prejudice their freedom of action in this respect." [44] Sir Austen delicately added, without mentioning the Monroe Doctrine by name, that the American government "have comparable interests any disregard of which by a foreign power they have declared they would regard as an unfriendly act." [45] It may be remarked that

[41] *Ibid.*, p. 214.

[42] See Morrison, *op. cit.*, pp. 50-51 and 62. For position of Morrison, see pp. 207-211; for that of Dewey, *op. cit.*, p. 680.

[43] My italics.

[44] See British note of July 18, 1928. Text in Miller, *op. cit.*, pp. 196-200.

[45] It is interesting to note that Secretary Kellogg discreetly made no rejoinder or allusion to Sir Austen's declarations on these points. His silence indicated acquiescence. A determined unsuccessful effort was made by certain of the Irreconcilables to have the Senate attach a reservation of the Monroe Doctrine when the Treaty came before that body for its "advice and consent." See D. F. Fleming,

the "comparable interests" referred to were at least confined to a specified region, the Western Hemisphere. The British reservation, however, referred only to "certain regions," and considering the extent and dispersion of the British Empire, might conceivably take in vast areas.[46]

On the question of sanctions, the Briand-Kellogg Pact [47] was in full accord with the tenets of outlawry as far as the text is concerned, and as far as the intent of the American formulators is revealed. It would, of course, have had no chance of being accepted by the United States Senate, and probably would not have had the powerful support of Senator Borah, had it obligated the United States in advance to use armed force along with the other signatories against a violator. All that is provided, therefore, is that "any signatory power which shall hereafter seek to promote its national interests by resort to war should be denied the benefits furnished by this treaty." These benefits were the presumed security from invasion or aggression by the other signatories that the treaty was intended to furnish. Should one of the parties violate its obligations, however, the others would recover their freedom of action and might resort to war against it.[48] Senator Borah stated the position

The Treaty Veto of the American Senate (New York, 1930), pp. 255-268, for a discussion of the Senate debate in which this and other "understandings or interpretations" were advocated.

[46] In this connection, the Soviet Government took the position that the signatories of the Pact "have a right exactly to know where the freedom of action of the British Government begins and where it ends." It said further that to recognize the right claimed by the British Government "would come to justifying war and might be taken as a contagious example by other signatories of the Covenant who by reason of equal rights would also take upon themselves the same liberty with regard to other regions and the result would be that there would probably be no place left on the earthly globe where the Covenant could be put in operation." Quotation from Soviet note of Aug. 31, 1928. Text in Miller, *op. cit.*, pp. 263-268. Egypt, Persia, and Turkey also objected to the British reservation for fairly obvious reasons.

[47] Officially, it has been called the "Pact of Paris" and the "Treaty for the Renunciation of War." Although on account of "practical considerations" only fifteen states were invited to become original signatories, and the ratification of this number was sufficient to bring the Pact into force, invitations were immediately extended to forty-eight other nations to adhere. It was, therefore, like the League Covenant, intended to include all civilized states. For text of the Pact, see Appendix.

[48] In his note of June 23, 1928, in which he took pains to state his understanding of the obligations of the proposed treaty, Mr. Kellogg said that "there can be no question as a matter of law that violation of a multilateral anti-war treaty through resort to war by one party thereto would automatically release the other parties from their obligations to the treaty-breaking state." Miller, *op. cit.*, pp. 213-219, for text of note.

of one who was both prominent in the outlawry movement and conspicuous as an advocate of the Briand-Kellogg Pact, when he said, according to the *New York Times* of March 25, 1928: "Another important result of such a treaty would be to enlist the support of the United States in cooperative action against any nation which is guilty of flagrant violation of this outlawry agreement. Of course, the Government of the United States must reserve the right to decide in the first place whether or not the treaty has been violated, and second, what coercive measures it feels obliged to take. But it is quite inconceivable that this country would stand idly by in case of a grave breach of a multilateral treaty to which it is a party."

A comparison of the fundamental features of the Briand-Kellogg Pact with the Covenant of the League of Nations reveals certain obvious differences. In the first place, the Pact has a single aim—to have the drunkard take the pledge that he will not use war as an instrument of national policy. The Covenant, on the other hand, commits its members in less specific terms, but in a great variety of ways against war as a normal method of settlement, and in addition indirectly attempts to promote peace by making the League an agency of international cooperation. It must be observed also that each of the signatories of the Pact of Paris remains legally competent to determine whether its use of armed force in any particular case is permissible under the Pact, whereas the members of the League surrender such a right in connection with their obligations under the Covenant. The Covenant stipulates specific methods and provides definite permanent machinery for the settlement of international disputes, whereas the Pact does not do so. Its signatories, however, in Article II agree that "the settlement or solution of all disputes or conflicts of whatever nature or of whatever origin they may be, which may arise among them, shall never be sought except by pacific means." And a great variety of pacific means are today available including arbitration tribunals, the Permanent Court of International Justice, the various organs of the League of Nations, commissions of inquiry and conciliation. Finally, it may be recalled, the Covenant definitely anticipates the question of enforcement of League obligations by providing in some detail for the employment of economic and military sanctions, whereas the Pact leaves the question to the conscience of each signatory and to public opinion.[49]

The Pact may likewise be contrasted with the outlawry plan already discussed. It makes no mention of a code or a court, although it would seem to imply a court as well as other "pacific means." An even more fundamental difference, however, would seem to lie in the fact that the signatories of the Pact do not outlaw war in the sense that they declare it "illegal" or a "crime" under international law. They merely state in solemn manner that they renounce it "as an instrument of national policy." They are therefore free to use it apparently for other purposes, particularly in self-defense.[50]

The Pact has had fulsome praise in high quarters. President Coolidge asserted in his annual message to Congress in 1928 that "the observance of this covenant, so simple and so straight-forward, promises more for the peace of the world than any other agreement ever negotiated among the nations."[51] Others have pointed out that, as a great multilateral treaty which nearly every civilized nation of the world has ratified, it has great moral value and that henceforth governments will not be able to lead their peoples into wars that are not clearly for defense.

On the other hand, the Pact has been criticized adversely on various grounds. For example, one writer declares:

> The Kellogg Pact, despite its appearance, is not a renunciation of the use of military force by the signatory States for any purpose for which States have resorted to force in the recent past. It is a moral symbol and

[49] Miller, *op. cit.,* Ch. XX, also stresses the fact that the Pact, differing from the League Covenant and most modern treaties, is perpetual. Members may withdraw from the League, but there is no provision for signatories of the Pact withdrawing. Whether they may legally do so, nevertheless, is a matter upon which legal authorities are not in complete agreement.

[50] Dr. Morrison, however, contends that the renunciation of war is "the first half, the harder half of the outlawry of war," for until war is renounced, it remains unchallenged within the legal system of international society, and all the leagues or courts or arbitration treaties "are little less than futile." He considered that when the Treaty came into effect the military obligations under the League Covenant and the Locarno pacts were morally, if not legally, indefensible. The "other half" of outlawry—the establishment of an adequate mechanism of peace—he thought logically followed renunciation. (*Time and Tide* [London], August, 1928, Supplement, *Foreign Affairs,* pp. 25-26.)

[51] Quoted in Fleming, *op. cit.,* p. 255. In a peace pamphlet issued in October, 1928, Nicholas Murray Butler also wrote: "The Pact of Paris, signed August 27, 1928, renouncing War as an instrument of national policy, marks the longest step forward since the noble movement to lift civilized nations above the barbarity and cruelty of international war began." *A Program of Peace* (New York, Oct. 1, 1928).

a diplomatic gesture. It is perhaps an "outlawry of war" in a narrow legal sense. But it is not a pledge on the part of any State to refrain from military violence in the pursuit of diplomatic objectives, nor does it offer any assurance that such violence will not encounter resistance, with armed conflict resulting. It does not require any particular State to submit any particular controversy to any particular mode of pacific settlement. . . To a much greater degree than is true of most treaties, it is a scrap of paper binding no one to anything. It is capable of becoming something more than an idle gesture only when governments and peoples modify fundamentally the traditional attitudes and values which have bred war in the past and will breed war (by another name) in the future.[52]

Another American writer in the field of international law,[53] who represents the most extreme reaction against the Pact, takes the position that the character of the Treaty was completely changed as a result of the British and French reservations. Mr. Kellogg's proposal to France had called for the outright and unconditional renunciation of war, he says, which would have been a progressive step. But with the various reservations the Treaty *"constitutes no renunciation or outlawry of war, but in fact and in law a solemn sanction for all wars mentioned in the exceptions and qualifications."* "Moreover," he declared, "it would be difficult to conceive of any wars that nations have fought within the past century or are likely to fight in the future, that cannot be accommodated under these exceptions." From the point of view particularly of American interests and policy the writer also regarded the treaty as injurious. According to his analysis the United States is "bound by League decisions as to aggressors and League policy generally but without any opportunity to take part in the deliberations leading to League conclusions." Under the circumstances, he concludes, it would have been better and safer for the United States to have become a member and then have been entitled to a part in League deliberations on matters of important consequence.

Manley O. Hudson, another American, eminent in the field of international law, but of a different school, has perhaps expressed the view of League of Nations internationalists in general on the Pact when he says: "It furnishes a useful peg on which insistence may be hung,

[52] Frederick L. Schuman, *International Politics* (McGraw-Hill Book Co., Inc., New York, 1933), p. 682.

[53] Edwin M. Borchard, "The Kellogg Treaties Sanction War," *The Nation* (New York), CXXVII (Sept. 25, 1928), 234-236.

it serves as a *point de départ* in discussion, it stands as a landmark by which mariners may steer who choose to use it for that purpose . . ." but "War will not disappear from men's minds because of a pronunciamento. It will not lose its appeal because of a moral ukase. It will not be ended by a fiat. Institutions, methods, habits are needed to assure that intelligence will be brought to bear when situations become acute, and these mean international organization." [54]

REFERENCES

Allen, D., *The Fight for Peace* (New York, 1930), Ch. X.

Bénès, E., "La Renonciation à la Guerre et le Pacte de la Société des Nations," *L'Esprit International* (July, 1930), No. 15, pp. 323-329.

Borchard, E. M., "The Kellogg Treaties Sanction War," *The Nation,* CXXVII (Sept. 5, 1928), 234-236.

Clark, J. R., Jr., "The Pacific Settlement of International Disputes," *Unity* (Oct. 4, 1923).

Council on Foreign Relations, *Survey of American Foreign Relations, 1928* (New Haven, Conn., 1929), Sec. II, Ch. II, "Pact of Paris," pp. 387-413.

Dewey, J., "Outlawry of War," *Encyclopaedia of Social Sciences,* XI (1933), 508-510.

———, *Characters and Events,* 2 vols. (New York, 1929), Vol. II, Bk. IV.

Dumont-Wilden, L., "La Guerre hors la Loi," *Revue Politique et Littéraire, Revue Bleue,* LXVI (April 21, 1928), 239-242.

Fenwick, C. G., "War as an Instrument of National Policy," *American Journal of International Law,* Vol. XXII (Oct., 1928), No. 4, pp. 826-829.

Fischer, L., *The Soviets in World Affairs,* 2 vols. (London, 1930), II, 774-780.

Fleming, D. F., *The Treaty Veto of the American Senate* (New York, 1930), Ch. XI.

Harley, J. H., "The Outlawry of War," *Fortnightly Review,* CXXIV (Sept., 1928), 289-300.

Hoijer, O., *La Sécurité Internationale et Ses Modes de Réalisation,* 4 vols. (Paris, 1930), Vol. II, Ch. VII.

Howard-Ellis, C., *The Origin, Structure and Working of the League of Nations* (Boston, 1928), pp. 327-342.

Kellogg, F. B., "The War Prevention Policy of the United States," *Foreign Affairs,* Special Supplement to Vol. VI (April, 1928), No. 3, pp. i-ii.

[54] *Op. cit.,* pp. 95, 96. For a similar view see Olof Hoijer, *La Sécurité Internationale et Ses Modes de Réalisation,* 3 vols. (Paris, 1930), II, 255-257.

Levinson, S. O., "The Legal Status of War," *New Republic,* XIV (March 9, 1918), 171-173.

———, "A Law to End War," *The Forum,* Vol. LXXI (Jan., 1924), No. 1, pp. 1-8, Pt. 1 of "Can War Be Outlawed?"

Lippmann, W., "The Outlawry of War," *Atlantic Monthly,* CXXXII (Aug., 1923), 245-253.

Miller, D. H., *The Peace Pact of Paris; or a Study of the Briand-Kellogg Treaty* (New York, 1928).

Mirkine-Guetzevitch, B., "La Renonciation à la Guerre et le Droit Interne," *L'Esprit International,* Vol. IV (Oct. 1, 1930), No. 16, pp. 546-562.

"The Pact of Paris with Historical Commentary by J. T. Shotwell; Text of Treaty and Related Documents," *International Conciliation* (Oct., 1928), No. 243, pp. 445-532.

"The Preservation of Peace," *Proceedings of the Academy of Political Science,* Vol. XIII (Jan., 1929), No. 2, Pt. 1, "The Renunciation of War as an Instrument of National Policy."

Salter, J. A., *The United States of Europe, and Other Papers* (London, 1933), Ch. XIV.

Schuman, F. L., *International Politics* (New York, 1933), pp. 672-685.

Shotwell, J. T., *War as an Instrument of National Policy and Its Renunciation in the Pact of Paris* (New York, 1929).

———, "Plans and Protocols to End War; Historical Outline and Guide," *International Conciliation* (March, 1925), No. 208, pp. 79-109.

Stimson, H. L., "The Pact of Paris: Three Years of Development," *Foreign Affairs,* Special Supplement, Vol. XI (Oct., 1932), No. 1, pp. i-ix.

United States. Treaties, etc., "Treaty for the Renunciation of War; Text of the Treaty, Notes Exchanged, Instruments of Ratification and of Adherence, and Other Papers." This contains documentary history of the "Kellogg Pact" or "Treaty of Paris." *United States Department of State, Miscellaneous Publications,* No. 468 (Washington, 1933).

Wehberg, H., "Der Pakt von Locarno," *Wörterbuch des Völkerrechts und der Diplomatie,* 3 vols. (Berlin, 1929), III, 977-995.

———, *The Outlawry of War,* tr. by E. H. Zeydel (Washington, 1931).

———, "Die Amerikanische Kriegsächtungsbewegung," *Die Gesellschaft,* II (July, 1928), 13-23.

Wheeler-Bennett, J., ed., *Documents on International Affairs, 1928* (London, 1929). See Kellogg Pact.

Wright, Q., "Changes in the Conception of War," *American Journal of International Law,* Vol. XVIII (Oct., 1924), No. 4, pp. 755-767.

———, "Future of Neutrality," *International Conciliation* (Sept., 1928), No. 242, pp. 353-442. Contains also Borah resolution for Outlawry of War introduced into the Senate of the United States on December 12, 1927; and draft treaty for renunciation of war, prepared by the United States, June 23, 1928.

———, "The Outlawry of War," *American Journal of International Law,* Vol. XIX (Jan., 1925), No. 1, pp. 75-103.

Wright, Q. and Eagleton, C., "Neutrality and Neutral Rights following the Pact of Paris for Renunciation of War," *Proceedings of The American Society of International Law,* Twenty-fourth annual meeting, April 23-26, 1930, pp. 79-114.

CHAPTER XVII

NATIONALITY AND NATIONAL MINORITIES

1. NATIONALITY

AT Vienna, in 1814, the statesmen of the victorious coalition against Napoleon met to square accounts with France, and redraw the map of Europe. At Versailles, in 1919, the representatives of the victorious Allied and Associated Powers came together on a similar errand, although some of the actors had changed rôles. France was one of the leading powers that had united against the latest bid of a Great Power for European hegemony, and Germany was the Power that was now in Coventry. In 1814, outside French revolutionary circles, the principle of nationality was in most quarters regarded as dangerously subversive of existing political systems, and as far as expediency would allow it was rejected as a basis for territorial changes. But a hundred years later, it had completely displaced the rival principle of legitimacy, and was ostensibly the foundation upon which the territorial settlements at the end of the World War were based.

That this principle should completely triumph, however, was perhaps no more to be expected than that the principle of legitimacy should exclusively prevail at the Congress of Vienna. The World War left a heritage of bitterness and resentment that inspired the victors with an overwhelming desire to take revenge, especially on the acknowledged leader of the Central Powers. In 1919, allied statesmen were united in regarding Germany as the sole instigator of the War, and of one mind as to the necessity of completely breaking her power. The items of the settlement, however, are not to be attributed chiefly to a blind yearning for revenge, but, to a great extent, to the fear that without drastic measures Germany would later on strike again. Fear, revenge, and, in addition, ambition all played a part in the decisions of the victors as expressed in the several treaties with the defeated countries, and each one of the powers had special objectives which influenced the demands that it made. Britain and certain of her Dominions were interested in seeing that Germany should be shorn of her strength on the sea and relieved of her colonies; France was desirous of weakening her by cutting down her territory, resources, and population, reducing her armament to a police-force basis, presenting her with a staggering bill of reparations, and surrounding her with buffer states and allies whose interests would likewise be to prevent her from again becoming a Great Power with corresponding ambitions; Italy was not only desirous of "redeeming" Italian-speaking districts held by Austria-Hungary, but ambitious to expand in the Levant and in Africa; Japan was determined to oust at least one European Power from Asia, and to inherit its holdings.

The Peace Settlement was to a certain extent a compromise between those among the victors who were chiefly animated by a desire for revenge and the spoils of victory, and those who took the long view and sought to utilize the opportunity to lay the foundations of a new world order in which the democratic principle of the consent of the governed should have a secure place. In the case of the latter, the principle of nationality was taken seriously, although its application inevitably presented difficulties. The course of events, as well as the conviction of certain allied statesmen, reenforced by President Wilson, made these countries the champions of the principle of nationality and the right of self-determination. The first act of Germany which could give her opponents a clear-cut issue with a popular appeal was the violation of the neutrality of Belgium. It was in vain that the German Chancellor expressed his regret to the English ambassador that military necessity allowed the German government no other course, and that at the conclusion of the War Germany would make amends to Belgium. Here was a small nation, under the collective guarantee of the Powers that her neutrality would be respected by them, the unwilling victim of one of the signatories of the Treaty. Could the others be indifferent to or condone such an act? The issue seemed simple to the members of the House of Commons, who loudly cheered Sir Edward Grey when he quoted Gladstone's expressed conviction on the subject of the independence of Belgium: "We have an interest in the independence of Belgium which is wider than that which we may have in the literal operation of the guarantee. It is found in the answer to the question whether, under the circumstances of the case, this country, endowed as it is with influence and power, would quietly stand by and witness the perpetration of the direst crime that ever stained the pages of history, and thus become participators in the sin."[1]

The invasion of Belgium was the occasion for Britain's entry into the War and the declaration of Prime Minister Asquith that she was fighting for the freedom of small nations. It also tended to focus attention anew on the question, first raised in ancient Greece,[2] and discussed much later by Rousseau,[3] Comte and others, as to the value of the small state. In 1915, Herbert Fisher, a member of the British Ministry, contributed a paper on the subject to a series of war pamphlets, in which he sprang to the philosophical defense of small states. He did not contend that the world should be made up entirely of small political units, but rather that they had distinct and useful contributions to make as members of international society. They were of value to "humanity at large," and to the Great Powers as well, by reason of the fact that they could not indulge in the luxury of large armaments and aggressive foreign policies. Their size forbade the hot pursuit of power, and disposed them toward a peaceful, law-abiding existence. And standing outside the armed and vigilant rivalries of the large states, they were performing a service by lessening the general tension and narrowing the field of inflammable controversy. As buffer states between Great Powers, taking no part in the quarrels of the latter, and interposing a physical barrier to discourage them from resorting to war, the small states had definitely contributed, said Fisher, to the maintenance of peaceful relations. On the other hand, the forceful extinction of a small state worked an injury to it and to the despoiler. "No historical state can be driven out of its identity without suffering a moral impoverishment in the process. The evil is not only apparent in the embitterment and lowering of the citizens of the conquered community, whether they are compelled to the agonies of a Polish dispersion, or linger on nursing their rights and wounded pride in the scene of their former independence, but it creates a problem for the conqueror which may very well harden and brutalize his whole outlook on policy. It is never good for a nation to be driven to the employment of harsh measures against any portion of its subjects."[4] Fisher contended that the small states

[1] See Cooke and Stickney, *Readings in European International Relations Since 1879* (New York and London, 1931), pp. 412-418 for text of Grey's speech.
[2] *Supra,* Chap. IV.
[3] *Supra,* Chap. X.
[4] *Studies in History and Politics* (The Clarendon Press, Oxford, 1920), pp. 173-174.

deserved to be preserved also because they added an element of richness and variety not to be found in "the set type which is imprinted by steady and powerful governments upon the life and behaviour of the larger powers." Moreover, small states such as Switzerland and Denmark had proved valuable as laboratories for social experiment. Fisher admitted, however, that these latter advantages may be realized within imperial systems in which small states are allowed practically complete freedom to order their internal life, as in the case of the British Dominions, and in a federal system such as that of the United States.[5]

The general point of view expressed by Fisher could not but lend encouragement to dissatisfied peoples within the enemy empires who might harbor aspirations to achieve complete political independence and set up political establishments of their own on the basis of a principle that had demanded recognition ever since the days of the French Revolution. The polyglot empire of Austria-Hungary, and the Turkish Empire contained many such peoples; and within the German empire as well there were groups which disliked the iron Prussian rule and policy of assimilation, and were ready to listen to the voice of a deliverer. In fact, the outbreak of the War was the signal for immediate activity among leaders of several of the subject peoples, especially the Czechs. In December, 1914, Thomas G. Masaryk, professor of philosophy at the University of Prague and the leader of the Czech Nationalist movement, began to organize a campaign in the various Allied States on behalf of a completely independent Czechoslovak state. At about the same time, Nationalist leaders of the Jugoslavs started a movement for the establishment of a Jugoslav State to be composed of Serbs, Croats, and Slovenes, who were declared to be "all members of one and the same nation, with all the necessary conditions for the formation of an independent state" [6] The Poles also became active early in the War, demanding the resurrection of a free and united Poland.

[5] For a similar point of view, see T. J. Masaryk, *The Problem of Small Nations in the European Crisis* (London, 1916), Inaugural Address delivered at the University of London; also E. Baie, *Le Droit des Nationalités* (Paris, 1915), pp. 87-90. P. B. Potter, *Introduction to the Study of International Organization* (New York, 1922), pp. 7-11, points out the desirability of a large number of small states from the point of view of the growth and enrichment of international law. For an opposite viewpoint, see H. L. McBain and Lindsay Rogers, *The New Constitutions of Europe* (New York, 1922), pp. 55-56. For a criticism of the creation of new states at the end of the War, see also Paul Scott Mowrer, *Balkanized Europe* (New York, 1921), and for the view that the small state is an anachronism in the world today, see A. E. Zimmern, *Nationality and Government* (New York, 1918), p. 72.

[6] Statement of "Jugoslav Committee," as quoted in F. Lee Benns, *Europe since 1914* (rev. ed., New York, 1934), p. 128.

The theoretical basis for the claims of the nationalities in general was formulated in a set of principles put forth by a conference of delegates of different nationalities held in Paris in 1916.[7] It was declared that the right of nationalities, whether large or small, to live, to develop their characteristics, and to dispose of themselves was a primordial right, for only free nationalities can furnish the *milieu* necessary for the development of man's faculties. The right of each nationality, as in the case of individual rights, must be limited by the equal right of other nationalities and secured by mutual respect for, and adhesion to, certain principles regulating their relationships. Good international understanding, the only basis of a durable peace, depends upon a number of factors, but among the first conditions is the satisfaction of the legitimate aspirations of nationalities. Such nationalities, whether composed of people having a common origin and having the same language and traditions, or resulting from the voluntary association of different ethnical groups, have the right to determine their own destiny. There should be no annexations or transfers of territory contrary to the wishes and interests of such peoples. These statements of principle covered the case not only of the single nationality that desired separate statehood but seemingly brought within the principle any heterogeneous group or groups that might desire to unite and form a state.

Liberal elements in the Allied countries for the most part not only sympathized with the desire of oppressed peoples everywhere, but also were inclined to assume the soundness of the principle of nationality and, in general, to look with favor upon the pretensions of nationally self-conscious peoples to statehood. Moreover, the leaders of the states allied against the Central Powers, whether liberal or not, were not unmindful of the potency of the appeal to the principle of self-determination. If dissatisfied peoples under the sovereignty of the Central Powers could be brought to look forward to freedom in the event of the victory of the Allies, the unity of the Central Powers would be weakened and their strength impaired. On the other hand, to the extent that the Allied countries themselves possessed unreconciled subject peoples, "self-determination" might be a two-edged sword. The British Empire, for example, was not altogether a Commonwealth of Free Nations, but included the peoples of India, already stirring with nationalistic aspirations, and the chronically intransigent Irish nationality. In fact, in the

[7] Alphonse de Heyking, *La Conception de l'État et l'Idée de la Cohesion Ethnique* (Paris, 1927), pp. 86-87.

midst of waging war on behalf of "submerged" nationalities, England had to put down an Irish rebellion. On the whole, however, to invoke the principle as against the enemy had a two-fold advantage. It gave the peoples of the Allied countries a worthy cause, in addition to that of the sanctity of treaties, for which to continue fighting, and thus tended to bolster their morale, and *per contra* could be used in devastating fashion to break down the morale of the millions of subject peoples fighting in the enemies' ranks. It therefore came to constitute the chief avowed war aim of the Allied Nations. In 1916, after the Central Powers, then in an advantageous military position, had made a peace proposal to the Allies, the latter replied in general terms that they were continuing the war "for the defense of the freedom of nations," for the "recognition of the principle of nationalities, and of the free existence of small states." When President Wilson shortly afterwards asked both the Allies and the Central Powers to state in specific terms the objects for which they were fighting, the Allied Powers in their answer called for "the restitution of provinces formerly torn from the Allies by force or against the wishes of the inhabitants; the liberation of the Italians, as also of the Slavs, Rumanes, and Czecho-Slovaks from foreign domination; the setting free of the populations subject to the bloody tyranny of the Turks. . . ." [8]

With the entry of the United States into the War, the principle of nationality received additional powerful support. President Wilson identified it with the democratic principle and put the war of the Allied and Associated Powers on the high plane of a great crusade to "make the world safe for democracy." In his speech to the Senate on January 22, 1917, he declared: "No peace can last, or ought to last, which does not recognize and accept the principle that governments derive all their just powers from the consent of the governed, and that no right anywhere exists to hand peoples about from sovereignty to sovereignty as if they were property." His Fourteen Point program contained a number of democratic principles upon which the peace must be based, but the master-principle for territorial settlements was that of nationality. One of the reasons for Italy's having entered the war on the side of the Allies was her desire to recover *Italia Irredenta*. In Wilson's ninth

[8] For the complete statement of War aims, as given in the notes to the German government, and the reply to President Wilson, see Cooke and Stickney, *op. cit.*, pp. 476-479, 482-484.

point, he declared for a rectification of Italy's frontiers "along clearly recognizable lines of nationality." [9] As regards the peoples of Austria-Hungary, the farthest he would go at the time was to say that they "should be accorded the freest opportunity of autonomous development," although later the victorious powers decided the subject nationalities should have complete freedom. A similar "opportunity of autonomous development" was demanded for the various nationalities under Turkish rule. On the other hand, Wilson declared that "an independent Polish state should be erected which should include the territories inhabited by indisputably Polish population. . ." [10] It is thus evident that President Wilson stood for the safeguarding of the separate existence of nationalities in the various enemy states, but that he did not support the application of the principle of self-determination in all cases.[11] As a matter of fact, to grant the right of self-determination to every nationality within the enemy empires ambitious to become an independent state would have produced the greatest confusion and have led to very unhappy results. As it was, there were those who criticized the soundness of the principle itself.

Among the critics of the commonly accepted view during the War that nationality was a political principle of the first importance, perhaps none put the case more cogently than Alfred Zimmern. In a paper read before the Sociological Society in London in 1915, on the subject of "Nationality and Government," and in later addresses during the War, he took definite issue with the position of John Stuart Mill,[12] and put himself squarely behind that of Lord Acton,[13] asserting that the "theory that the nation-state is the normal and proper area of gov-

[9] *Ibid.*, p. 549. The secret Treaty of London, signed in 1915, between Italy and the Allies, as the price of Italy's entrance into the War, was clearly based on the principle of horse-trading rather than on that of nationality. Italy was out for additional territory largely regardless of nationality. For text of the Treaty, as well as the secret negotiations of Italy with both sides prior to her entry into the War, see *ibid.*, pp. 444-459.

[10] *Ibid.*, pp. 549-550.

[11] The Fourteen Point speech, as a matter of fact, does not contain any specific reference to "self-determination." In his Four Point speech to Congress of February 11, 1918, however, he declares that "self-determination is not a phrase. It is an imperative principle of action, which statesmen will henceforth ignore at their peril." Nevertheless, when he was flooded with petitions from subject nationalities at the time of the Peace Conference, he took the position that autonomy within the state rather than secession should be the aim of nationalities, and that there should be no change of sovereignty by conquest.

[12] *Supra*, pp. 221-222.

[13] *Supra*, pp. 226-227.

ernment . . . is one of the most formidable and sinister forces on the side of our enemies and one of the chief obstacles to human progress at the present time." [14] Those who assume that the division of Europe into a number of states on the basis of nationality would assure peace are in error even if such a division were possible. The record of the typical national states—Germany, Italy, France under Napoleon III, and the Balkan states—does not compare favorably with "the two great international states, the British and American Commonwealths." [15] And this was to be expected, for to base a state on nationality is to base it on something "partial, arbitrary, and accidental" rather than on some "universal principle such as justice, democracy, or collective consent. . ." Men desiring better international relations, therefore, and a better political organization of the world "must set their hope, not in the Nation-State, which is only a stage, and in the West an outworn stage, in the political evolution of mankind, but in States which, like the great governing religious systems of the past, like Medieval Christendom and Islam, find room for all sorts and conditions of communities and nations." [16] In other words, a liberal empire, allowing its various nationalities the fullest cultural expression, and even encouraging them in the maintenance of their traditions, was the true ideal in Zimmern's view. But Zimmern was well aware that actually nationalities in many parts of Europe had been cruelly oppressed by ignorant and brutal governments seeking to stamp out their separate culture. This oppression had been responsible for these nationalities becoming politically conscious and desiring to form separate national states. He reluctantly admitted that their aspirations in this direction would probably have to be satisfied at the conclusion of the War, but he was not at all sanguine as to the beneficial effects of such a consummation. A nationality long oppressed, bitter over old wrongs, unaccustomed to a normal, salutary social existence, is not to be expected to exhibit a healthy outlook of tolerance, and an understanding of its responsibilities.

Another prominent Jewish figure, Israel Zangwill, expressed similar views in a brilliant address on "The Principle of Nationalities," delivered in London in 1917. He contended that the real needs of national-

[14] See *Nationality and Government* (New York, 1918), p. 46. The volume contains articles and essays on other subjects as well.

[15] Lecture on "The Passing of Nationality," delivered at King's Hall, London, November 23, 1917.

[16] *Op. cit.*, pp. 64-65.

ities were not political independence, but freedom from oppression, and that political independence did not lead to happy results. "Indeed, a triumphant nationality tends from its initial momentum to expand further, and even to feel that it is a privilege for other nationalities to be incorporated with the chosen people. Thus arises in every successful people the sense of a Mission."[17] Thus, the Kaiser's notion of the country's divine mission was not to be regarded as any departure from "the normal law of Nationalities." Zangwill, however, did not object to "missions" if national states found them "not in making other peoples miserable but in making their own people happy."[18] This type of mission he called Intensive Imperialism, and remarked that unfortunately it still awaited its Alexander. For these reasons, and the additional consideration that the setting up of new national states would, in particular instances, result in the destruction of the economic unity of regions from which they were carved, Zangwill warned that statesmen should not lightly break up the existing historic unities.[19]

Writing from the point of view of a lawyer and defender of constitutional authority, Robert Lansing, American Secretary of State under President Wilson, but highly critical of some of the guiding principles espoused by the President at the Peace Conference, condemned the principle of self-determination without qualification. He contended that, like the phrase, "the consent of the governed," it "could not be practically applied without imperiling national safety, always the paramount consideration in international and national affairs."[20] Apart from the difficult problem of determining the unit to which the principle of self-determination shall be applied, a point also made by Zimmern, Lansing regarded it as fundamentally dangerous. It furnishes an excuse for rebellions on the part of turbulent political elements against their governments, it provides a basis for the urging of territorial claims by avaricious nations, and in general introduces into domestic and international relations "a new spirit of disorder."[21]

[17] *The Principle of Nationalities* (London, 1917), pp. 51, 87. For a similar opinion, see Louis Le Fur, *Races, Nationalités, États* (Paris, 1922), p. 77.

[18] *Op. cit.*, p. 74.

[19] See Paul Scott Mowrer, *op. cit.*, for a post-war criticism especially of the break-up of Austria-Hungary and the establishment of the new states.

[20] *The Peace Negotiations* (Houghton Mifflin Co., Boston and New York, 1921), p. 96.

[21] *Ibid.*, p. 104. Criticism of the same tenor is made by Le Fur, *op. cit.*, pp. 82-89.

Other writers, without completely rejecting the principle of nationality, accepted it with caution, and were at pains to demonstrate that the popularly accepted doctrine of self-determination could by no means be regarded as embodying an absolute principle. The mere wish of a group of people regarding itself as a nationality (perhaps because interested propagandists within it so insisted), and desiring separate statehood, could not be regarded in itself as entitling such a group to a separate political existence. One writer, for example, laid down five conditions which an aspiring nationality must fulfill.[22] The most elementary condition was that a numerical majority of the people should desire "to safeguard their national cohesion if they were already in enjoyment of it or to acquire it if still deprived of it." In the second place, the claimant for statehood should have been at some time in the past a sovereign state, or should at least possess an indisputably distinct historical background. The author desired to rule out hastily improvised "nationalities" by an appeal to history.[23] The Ukrainians, for example, though said to desire political independence, had not had such a separate group existence historically as would entitle them to consideration. On the other hand, Norway could very properly form a state distinct from Sweden, as she did in 1900, for Norwegian history had been quite separate from that of Sweden up to 1814. But peoples with proper enough claims of historical affinities in many instances do not today desire separate statehood; and the writer is inclined to the belief that historical progress has consisted in the diminution rather than in the artificial increase in the number of sovereign states. The third condition for independent statehood is that the members of the nationality should possess governmental capacity. They should be able to establish a government capable of maintaining public order, and of discharging all the functions a modern government may be called upon to discharge. In the fourth place, the nationality must possess a sufficiently numerous population, a large enough territory, and adequate natural resources so that its economic and political independence will be sufficiently assured. A state weak in one or more of these re-

[22] Bernard Lavergne, *Le Principe des Nationalités et les Guerres, son Application au Problème Colonial* (Paris, 1921), pp. 18-32. The author uses "autonomy" in various parts of his discussion apparently in the sense of complete political independence or separate statehood. In presenting the gist of his ideas, I have used the less ambiguous phrase.

[23] However, he was careful to point out that he did not subscribe to a theory of *historical rights*.

spects would have a precarious existence. If weak in material resources, its economic viability would be jeopardized; if possessing rich resources but only a sparse population, it would not have the military or political strength to protect itself against aggression. As conditions are, the small states in any case will find themselves drawn by the force of economic and social attraction into the orbit of the larger states, for the progress of the technical arts, the perfection of means of transport, and the growing division of labor between peoples has within recent times rendered impossible the maintenance of national autonomy of very small human groups. The writer laid down as a final condition that the nationality in question must possess at least the elements of "modern scientific culture." A knowledge of modern developments in both the social and physical sciences was regarded as indispensable for the comprehension and employment of modern governmental and economic processes in the exploitation of its resources. The author next discusses the theory of nationalities in what he calls its "passive form." A nationality may not desire separate statehood but to be reunited with its mother country when the latter is contiguous or lies in close proximity to it. In principle, the sole condition of the reunion should be its own wish. But the matter is not as simple as it would appear. Some cases, such as those of the Alsace-Lorrainers and the Rumanians, are clear, and in his opinion, although the victorious Allies would not allow it, Austria should likewise have been granted the right to join Germany. But other cases present difficulty. Very frequently, for example, the nationality in question is not contiguous to the state it would join, nor very near. It may command a majority of votes in a limited area but be rather an enclave in the territory of the state which governs it, the latter having a majority of the population as a whole. Under these circumstances the writer does not believe the principle of self-determination can be allowed. In lieu of this, the government of the dominant race should be required to grant the nationality in question as large a degree of autonomy as possible.[24]

The prominent French authority on international law, Robert Redslob, likewise recognizes in the principle of nationalities a relative rather than an absolute value.[25] He points out that it finds an obstacle

[24] Lavergne, *op. cit.*, pp. 40-46, for discussion of problems presented in connection with particular European peoples.

[25] *Le Principe des Nationalités* (Paris, 1930), p. 85.

in the natural tendency of every state to maintain its integrity, so that there is an inevitable struggle between the dynamic phenomenon, the nation, "which has a natural tendency to constitute itself into a state," and the static phenomenon, the state, which just as naturally resists such a pretension. A nationality seeking freedom has a strong moral appeal; on the other hand a state, by the excellence of its institutions, the liberality of its policies, and by services rendered, may likewise occupy a strong moral position, and sometimes its preservation may offer a better guarantee of general peace than for a nationality to secede from it.[26] If the secession of a nationality would gravely affect the organic structure of the state, as the success of the Sonderbund of 1847 would have dismembered Switzerland, or the secession of the Southern states from the American Union would have mutilated the United States, only exceptional circumstances would justify the separation. If, for example, the governing nationality should have been guilty of grave abuses of elementary rules of right, secession might be justified. "The state can only invoke justice in favor of its preservation according as it respects justice itself."

Redslob condemns the artificial propagation of national consciousness. Deliberate appeals to a people based on doubtful theories of race, fictitious claims of other kinds, and attempts to revive memories of a community life in a distant past serve only egoistic ends. On the other hand, he regards a past history and the possession of memories of a past life in common as an essential foundation for the development of a national consciousness. A group desiring separate statehood need not have known state existence in the past, but it should have had an autonomous cultural life. If, in addition to a common history, it adds language, or religion, its claims will be further enforced. The plebiscite may be used as a test of its desires if proper safeguards are used. Care should be taken to avoid a decision on the basis of momentary impulsions; therefore, not merely one vote but a second plebiscite, after a period of delay, should be taken and every other means used to insure a genuine expression of the considered opinion of the population.[27]

[26] Cf. President Wilson's speech of January 24, 1918, in which he said that "all well-defined national aspirations shall be accorded the utmost satisfaction that can be accorded them *without* introducing new or perpetuating old elements of discord and antagonism that would be likely in time to break the peace of Europe and consequently of the world."

[27] *Op. cit.*, pp. 90-91, 119-123. On the question of the plebiscite as a means of

Another post-war critic of the principle of nationality, Olof Hoijer, delivers a rather severe indictment, some of the counts of which are especially worthy of note. He points out that the principle is defective in that it does not embody a clear-cut, precise, juridical conception, but rather a vague moral idea of indeterminate character. There is no single and universal criterion of nationality to be used when it is proposed to apply the principle in connection with the so-called right of national self-determination. Hoijer rejects the subjective test, among other reasons, because it makes the question of the political allegiance of a group, and perhaps the fate of the state of which it is a part, depend upon the capricious and fragile will of such a group exercised, it may be, in the heat of anger or enthusiasm. Such a process leads to anarchy rather than to tranquillity. If, on the other hand, this "capricious subjectivism" is abandoned in favor of objective tests, it is found that there are none that are infallible. And because of the vagueness and imprecision of the principle, it can be made to serve very precise and unworthy ambitions of conquest. Moreover, so far from the principle being an influence for peace, states based on nationality, with their emphasis on cultural differences and their tendency toward a "virulent collective egotism," furnish the conditions for the most sanguinary and passionate wars.

Like most of the other critics of the principle of nationality as the single foundation of the state, Hoijer stresses the importance of order and stability in the world, and the subordination of particular interests. He therefore places the interests of states ahead of those of nationalities. He argues, for example, that a state can permit one of its nationals to abandon it and go to another state, for the individual is not bound to the territory, but that a collectivity is inseparable from the territory where it lives, and a state's territory is one of its essential elements. The secession of any of the parts of a state, therefore, is a blow at its unity, and the state can hardly tolerate such secession without consenting voluntarily to its own ruin. A state ought, in equity, to possess more rights than a nation (nationality) by virtue of its greater responsibility and the fact that its duties are more precise and

testing the sentiments of a nationality, see the authoritative work of Sarah Wambaugh, *Plebiscites since the World War*, 2 vols. (Washington, 1933), Vol. I, Ch. XII. For adverse opinions as to the value of plebiscites, see Hoijer, *La Sécurité Internationale et ses Modes de Réalisation*, 3 vols. (Paris, 1930), I, 112; and Guido De Ruggiero, *The History of European Liberalism* (London, 1927), pp. 409-410.

extensive. It represents a more general end, public interest, whereas a nationality represents particular interests. On the other hand, Hoijer points out that nationalities also have rights which it is to the interest of a state to respect. A state which retains a nationality only by force, and fails to respect, as far as possible, its language, religion, traditions, or other particularistic expressions, will only irritate it, and arouse it to seek liberty and emancipation.[28]

If the principle of nationality leads to an acceptance of the doctrine of self-determination, it follows that the boundaries of states and nationalities should ideally coincide. In spite of the fact that the doctrine has gained wide acceptance, and that the victorious powers officially endorsed it, their actual decisions were not and could not be wholly in accord with it. Some of the difficulties involved have been cogently discussed by various writers in connection with the subject of boundaries. Not all of them, it may be observed, regard nationality as the first consideration in the drawing of a frontier, and few if any believe that it should or can be the sole consideration. In general, it may be said that those who place little faith in the possibilities of developing an international jurisprudence for accommodating the more serious differences that arise in the relationships of national states, and who therefore feel that a nation must rely in the future, as it has in the past, mainly on its own armed force to resist encroachments upon its territory and its rights, look askance at nationality frontiers unless they are at the same time of definite military value. Without, in most instances, denying that a frontier is stronger if it is morally defensible, they believe that in the long run a boundary that offers a natural obstacle or that is best adapted to military defense will be more stable than one based merely on "juridical conceptions." Sir Thomas Holdich, for example, declares that through the ages the boundaries that have been the most effective have been those marked by "strong natural geographic features."[29] In his view, the primary object in defining a

[28] *Op. cit.*, Vol. I, Ch. III.

[29] President Wilson's Secretary of State, Robert Lansing, expresses a similar opinion: "International boundaries may be drawn along ethnic, economic, geographic, historic, or strategic lines. One or all of these elements may influence the decision, but whatever argument may be urged in favor of any one of these factors, the chief object in the determination of the sovereignty to be exercised within a certain territory is national safety. . . With national safety as the primary object to be attained in territorial settlements, the factors of the problem assume generally, though not always, the following order of importance: the strategic, to which is

frontier is not to make it, as far as possible, an expression of the legitimate aspirations of a nationality; it is, rather, "to set up a defensive partition between contiguous states which shall prevent mutual trespass or illegal expansion into either territory. . ." [30] Natural frontiers in the form of high mountain barriers are therefore always to be preferred to any artificial frontiers.

An opposite point of view is to be found in L. W. Lyde's *Some Frontiers of Tomorrow,* published, as was Holdich's volume, during the War and with the coming peace settlement in mind. Lyde rejects the assumption that a *defensive* frontier is essential to the ending of recurring conflicts between neighboring states. Frontiers, instead of being selected for the purpose of keeping peoples apart, should be, as far as possible, "identified with geographical features which are associated naturally with the meeting of peoples and persons in the ordinary routine of peaceful intercourse." [31] They should therefore be drawn with the idea of inviting rather than making more difficult such intercourse, for "civilization is essentially progress in the art of living together, and the rubbing off of racial and other 'corners' by constant friction with others is the greatest step to that end." [32] A navigable river, therefore, is an ideal boundary and, from the point of view of Lyde, a high mountain chain would be one of the worst. However, there are other considerations that he would not have overlooked. In order that causes for friction may be minimized, he asserts that "natural political units should coincide with actual political units" as far as may be. Evidently with the Peace Conference in mind, he averred that disturbing boundary changes should be reduced to the minimum, but that they must be "sufficient to meet what may be called the legitimate demands of insistent national consciousness." [33] Nationality, therefore, is to be taken into account in boundary drawing, but apparently as subordinate to the first consideration. Finally, if the guiding principle in the transfer of territory cannot in any particular instance be the wishes of its inhabitants, "full weight must be given to the ca-

closely allied the geographic and historic; the economic, affecting the commercial and industrial life of a nation; and lastly, the ethnic, including in the terms such conditions as consanguinity, common language, and similar social and religious institutions." (*Op. cit.*, pp. 102-103.) See also Erno Wittman, *Past and Future of the Right of Self-Determination* (Amsterdam, 1919), pp. 171-179.

[30] *Political Frontiers and Boundary Making* (London, 1916), pp. 128, 147.

[31] *Op. cit.*, p. 2.

[32] *Ibid.*, p. 14.

[33] *Ibid.*, p. 17.

pacity—or incapacity—of the proposed new owner to assimilate others."[34]

Lavergne, in his discussion of the principle of nationalities in relation to boundaries, agrees with most other writers in taking the position that this and other principles must be conciliated. Denying emphatically that a nation has the right to annex contiguous territory inhabited by a foreign population whenever it regards such action as necessary for military defense or to enhance its economic position,[35] he recognizes, nevertheless, certain circumstances in which the principle of nationality may not be applied absolutely without doing an injustice. For example, certain states should be accorded free access over their own territory to the sea. It is possible for states like Switzerland, far removed from the sea, to exist and even prosper without such access. But for states such as Poland, he contends that it is a different matter. The possession of the Vistula up to the sea, and Danzig or a favorable spot for the establishment of a large port on the Baltic, are essential if Poland is to avoid economic suffocation, for she is bordered by hostile states on all sides.[36] Under the circumstances, says the writer in substance, the principle of nationality which, if applied absolutely, would stand in the way of this consummation, must give way sufficiently to enable Poland to possess the indispensable conditions of viability.[37] On the other hand, such boundaries are not to be regarded as necessarily permanent. If in several generations the industrial or other circumstances of the state have changed so that the extended frontier is not necessary, the territory should be restored unless in the meantime the population has become reconciled to the government of the foreign nationality.[38] As regards strategic frontiers, Lavergne also suggested that there

[34] Lyde, *loc. cit.* Lyde asserted, as regards the Germans, that "they are essentially lacking in the imperial faculty of assimilation, and . . . their machine-bound psychology makes them incapable of distinguishing between a paralysing uniformity, imposed with the ubiquitous uniform, and an imperial unity, based on an untrammeled diversity of detail such as draws the best freely from many sources." (*Ibid.*, p. 48.)

[35] *Op. cit.*, pp. 47-50, 55, 56.

[36] *Op. cit.*, p. 53.

[37] Writers during the War generally either overlooked or regarded as impracticable another possible alternative in such cases: a treaty guarantee of access to the sea over foreign territory. The Germans suggested this as an alternative to the "Polish Corridor," but for rather obvious reasons the suggestion made no appeal to the Poles.

[38] It would seem that this would be too much to expect from the occupying state unless it was convinced that its interests would clearly be served by relinquishment of the territory.

might be circumstances in which the principle of nationality might justifiably be disregarded. Italy, for example, was entitled to a defensive frontier in the High Alps, even though it meant the annexation of several hundred thousand German Austrians.[39]

2. NATIONAL MINORITIES

By virtue, in part, of the necessity of reconciling the principle of nationality with other principles and with economic and geographic realities, as well as with national policies, the map of Europe after the Peace Conference by no means reflected the complete triumph of the principle in the decisions that had been made. Nevertheless, as a result of the break-up of the Austro-Hungarian Empire into a number of national states, and of the excision of portions of the Russian, German, and Turkish Empires, the Peace Conference succeeded in reducing European minorities from perhaps 54,000,000 to about 17,000,000.[40] But there were the 17,000,000 to consider. If one uses the linguistic test, about one-fourth of the population of Jugoslavia, one-half the population of Poland, two-fifths of the population of Czechoslovakia, and over one-tenth of the population of Italy consisted of minorities after the Peace Settlement. Most of these people wanted, if not a different political allegiance, at least freedom of language, religion, and cultural institutions. But remaining within the boundaries of states that were dominated by a single nationality and were more or less dedicated to the proposition, "each people its state; the whole people one state," the prospect of their being tolerated as cultural units within such states was not bright. The ruling groups of the new states, and of those with large additions of territory containing minorities, anxious for their own future, and in many cases smarting from past injustices at the hands of those now constituting minorities within their borders, were not likely of their own accord to follow a policy of tolerance. It was

[39] *Op. cit.*, p. 52. Redslob, *op. cit.*, p. 100, is also in general accord. Both writers, however, recognize that the plea of "natural frontiers" has often been used to cloak imperial adventures.

[40] This is an approximation chiefly on the basis of language. There is no universal agreement as to what constitutes membership of a national minority. Linguistic affinities do not always connote other close affinities, as plebiscites have sometimes revealed. But language was taken as the chief criterion of nationality at the Peace Conference. By this test, as well as by others, German Austria should have been allowed to join Germany after the War. In this case, however, policy prevailed over principle, and the Austrians were refused the "right of national self-determination."

rather to be expected that they would seek to assimilate their minorities by forceful measures and attain unity by the old time-honored but usually unsuccessful method of compulsory uniformity. Under the circumstances, it was clearly a problem which the Peace Conference had to face. If nationalities could not be granted political independence, prudence dictated that at least they should be guaranteed against oppression in the states within which they were forced to remain. Otherwise, new nationality wars might be expected in the future.

There were precedents for the international protection of minorities upon which a system of international control might be built. As early as the seventeenth century, the principle of religious toleration was written into certain treaties ending "religious" wars. In 1814, when the Congress of Vienna decided to unite Belgium and Holland, two countries differing in language and religion, the Powers required guarantees from the new state that all sects should be equally treated in every respect. There was, however, no requirement that the languages should be put on a footing of equality. In 1830, the Powers exacted of Greece a pledge of religious freedom for different sects similar to that required of Holland in 1815. In 1856, at the Conference of Constantinople, which established Moldavia and Wallachia as independent provinces, guarantees of racial as well as religious liberty [41] were required and later embodied in the Convention of Paris of 1856. In 1878, at the Congress of Berlin, the Great Powers agreed to recognize Rumania, Serbia, Montenegro, and Bulgaria only on the condition that they would accept obligations to put all religious faiths within their territories on a basis of equality as regards civil and political rights. In the course of the nineteenth century, the Powers required Turkey, on several occasions, to make declarations that the welfare of the religious minorities in the Empire would be safeguarded, but they were of little avail, massacres of the Armenians especially being repeatedly resorted to by the Turks. Several years before the World War, the Powers took more drastic steps compelling Turkey to agree to the establishment of foreign inspectors-general in Anatolia and Macedonia where conditions had been intolerable. After the Young Turk revolution in 1908, however,

[41] It will be noted from the following that Moslems were not included in the international guarantee of equal political rights. "Moldavians and Wallachians of all Christian rites shall enjoy political rights. The enjoyment of these rights can be extended to other religions by legislative enactment." L. P. Mair, *The Protection of Minorities* (Christophers, London, 1928), p. 32.

foreign control was thrown off and a program of extermination of the Macedonians was undertaken. The Balkan Wars precipitated by this policy led to the division of this region between the small Balkan states.

The pre-war system of dealing with the minorities problem had fairly well established the principle that whenever the recognition of statehood was sought by any people, or whenever a state should acquire large additions of territory, pledges of fair treatment of minorities might be required by the other Powers.[42] On the other hand, the treaties embodying international guarantees were defective in certain respects. They were, in the first place, agreements inaugurated by, and under the guarantee of, the Great Powers alone, and they paved the way for the intervention of these Powers in the internal affairs of the small states whenever they were disposed to do so. However, should the Great Powers be divided by conflicting policies or rivalries of one sort or another, as was frequently the case, the small states might be able to evade their obligations with impunity. Moreover, there was no effective machinery for investigating complaints of infractions of the treaty rights of the minorities, and no international judicial machinery for the interpretation of the treaties that stipulated the rights that were to be protected. Finally, there was no system of enforcement for clear cases of violation.

With the establishment of the League of Nations, representative of both large and small nations, and equipped to deal with a variety of international problems, it was hoped that these defects might be eradicated. The Supreme Council, therefore, set up a Committee on New States and the Protection of Minorities, composed of the representatives of the United States, France, Great Britain, Italy, and Japan. The proposal, however, that the new states and those that had received large additions to their territories should accept guarantees "to protect the interests of inhabitants . . . who differ from the majority of the population in race, language, or religion," drew forth immediate protests. The Poles, for example, argued that such a requirement would be a serious invasion of Poland's sovereignty, that for certain states

[42] In practice this principle was not applied to large states. For example, Germany was not required to give any pledge as to the treatment of her minorities when she achieved unification in 1870. The same was true of Italy when she acquired additional territories with large minority populations at the end of the World War.

to be singled out and required to give such guarantees, whereas others such as Germany and Italy were not, was a humiliating discrimination against small states. The representatives of the other affected states reasoned in much the same fashion.[43] It was insulting to have to give international guarantees. Bratiano of Roumania argued that the protection of the minorities should be entrusted to the governments of the small states rather than placed under the supervision of the League of Nations.

President Wilson, in reply, undoubtedly voiced the sentiments of the Great Powers; ". . . Mr. Bratiano . . . suggested that we could not, so to say, invade the sovereignty of Rumania, an ancient sovereignty, and make certain prescriptions with regard to the rights of minorities. But I beg him to observe that he is overlooking the fact that he is asking the sanction of the Allied and Associated Powers for great additions of territory which came to Rumania by the common victory of arms, and that, therefore, we are entitled to say: 'If we agree to these additions of territory, we have the right to insist upon certain guarantees of peace.'" Mr. Bratiano, on the other hand, quite as certainly interpreted the feelings of the small states affected by the minorities treaties when he replied in substance that a sound political principle should be universally applied, and that the obligations the small states were being asked to accept should be extended to the other Powers as well.[44]

The arguments of Bratiano and the other representatives of the small states were in vain. In the covering letter to the President of Poland, when the Polish Minorities Treaty was submitted for M. Paderewski's signature, M. Clemenceau, President of the Peace Conference, summed up the position of the chief Powers on the subject as follows: "The Principal Allied and Associated Powers are of opinion that they would be false to the responsibility which rests upon them if on this occasion they departed from what has become an established tradition. In this connection I must also recall to your consideration the fact that it is to the endeavors and sacrifices of the Powers in whose name I am addressing you that the Polish nation owes the

[43] J. S. Roucek, *The Working of the Minorities System under the League of Nations* (Prague, 1929), Ch. II, gives a good account of the views of the representatives of the Great Powers as well as of the objections of the Poles, Rumanians, and others to the minorities treaties.

[44] Two great Powers, France and Italy, and two small states, Denmark and Belgium, received territory containing minorities after the World War, but they did not sign minority treaties.

recovery of its independence. It is by their decision that Polish sovereignty is being reestablished over the territories in question and that the inhabitants of these territories are being incorporated in the Polish nation. It is on the support which the resources of these Powers will afford to the League of Nations that for the future Poland will to a large extent depend for the secure possession of these territories. There rests, therefore, upon these Powers an obligation, which they cannot evade, to secure in the most permanent and solemn form guarantees for certain essential rights which will afford to the inhabitants the necessary protection whatever changes may take place in the internal constitution of the Polish State." [45]

The new dispensation resulted in arrangements for the international protection of minorities by the negotiation of ten treaties between the Principal Allied and Associated Powers on the one hand, and Poland, Czechoslovakia, Jugoslavia, Roumania, Greece, Armenia, Austria, Bulgaria, Hungary, and Turkey on the other.[46] All of the parties of the second part agreed that the principles laid down in the treaties should be part of the fundamental law of the state, and not subject to modification by any law, decree, or administrative act. The treaties stipulate that all of the inhabitants of these states, whether citizens or not, are entitled to what M. Clemenceau pointed out are "elementary rights which are, in fact, secured in every civilized state"—the protection of life and liberty, and religious freedom. In the second place, the citizens or nationals of the states are given additional specific guarantees. If they are members of a social, religious, or linguistic minority, they are put on a plane of equality as regards civil and political rights, with the dominant nationality. They are also guaranteed the free use of their own language and the right to establish religious, educational, or charitable institutions. The treaties even go so far as to provide that in towns and districts where a minority forms a "considerable proportion" of the population, the Government must provide instruction in the primary schools in the minority language, although it may make the language of the state compulsory in these schools. In these districts the governments must also allocate an equitable share of the public school funds allotted to educational, religious, or charitable purposes.[47]

[45] Quoted in L. P. Mair, *op. cit.*, pp. 35-36.
[46] R. L. Buell, *International Relations* (rev. ed., New York, 1929), p. 186.
[47] Mair, *op. cit.*, pp. 37-30.

All of these stipulations on behalf of the various minorities constitute international obligations, and are placed under the guarantee of the League of Nations. Any member of the Council of the League is entitled to bring to the attention of that body any question involving an alleged infraction or danger of infraction of the provisions of the minorities treaties, and the Council itself is vested with authority to hear complaints and take such measures as may be necessary to the end that the obligations assumed in the treaties may be faithfully performed. In case a difference of opinion arises as to the meaning or legal effect of the treaties, it is to be regarded as a dispute of an international character and submitted to the Permanent Court of International Justice for final decision.[48]

After the establishment of the League, the question of international protection for minorities in newly-established states about to seek admission was raised. Certain of these states, notably Esthonia and Latvia, strongly objected to outside interference, but they, as well as Albania, Finland, and Lithuania, were induced to sign declarations embodying the same principles and accepting substantially the same measure of League control as were contained in the minorities treaties.[49] It must also be noted that after the plebiscite in Upper Silesia, when the League fell heir to the disposition of the territory and divided it between Germany and Poland, both countries agreed by treaty to accept similar obligations as regards their respective minorities in the divided territory for a period of fifteen years, the first instance in which a Great Power has accepted League supervision.[50]

Since the establishment of the minorities system, two general conceptions concerning it have developed, as perhaps was to have been expected. On the one hand, it is regarded as in the nature of a temporary expedient adopted to prevent the forcible assimilation of minori-

[48] C. K. Webster, *The League of Nations in Theory and Practice* (Boston and New York, 1933), p. 209.

[49] Mair, *op. cit.*, pp. 49-57. The obligations of Finland, with respect to the Swedish minority in the Aaland Islands, went much further. These people had desired to be united to Sweden, but after full investigation the League decided that Finland should retain the islands but grant a large measure of autonomy to the inhabitants and specific guarantees of minority rights.

[50] It may be noted that some bi-national treaties between states having minorities have been voluntarily negotiated. Such treaties are not under international guarantee, but depend for their observance on the mutual interest of the two contracting parties. See Buell, *op. cit.*, p. 189. For the drafting of the various minorities treaties and discussion of their character, purpose, and results, see the excellent work of C. A. Macartney, *National States and National Minorities* (London, 1934).

ties. This view assumes, however, that in the course of time the various minorities will probably be peacefully assimilated to the dominant nationality,[51] and when this occurs the problem will have disappeared and international control with it. Some who entertain this conviction regard temporary international guarantees of fair treatment of minorities as necessary to the ultimate removal of the problem on the ground that attempts forcibly to stamp out minorities have always tended to stiffen their resistance to assimilation.[52] Others, however, notably from states that have been compelled to accept international control, regard it as an irksome and unnecessary invasion of sovereignty, and as tending artificially to encourage and prolong the existence of separatist movements. From this point of view, the imposition of international control tends to have the effect, even in the absence of intent, of creating unrest and making for the longer continuance of such control. Those who prefer to view the present system of international control as temporary are naturally opposed, in most instances, to any suggestions that look in the direction of establishing a positive system of League supervision, and demand that the treaties be given a strict interpretation insofar as they confer rights of inquiry and investigation by the League.[53]

On the other hand, a number of writers not only regard the principle of international protection of minorities as sound, but think that it will need to be embodied in a permanent institution of international control and supervision. The present system they regard as helpful but

[51] This was the position taken at the Council meeting of December 9, 1925, by the Brazilian delegate, Mello-Franco, and by Sir Austen Chamberlain. (Otto Junghann, *National Minorities in Europe* [New York, 1922], p. 93.)

[52] See, for example of this view, Louis Eisenmann, "Rights of Minorities in Central Europe." *International Conciliation* (Sept., 1926), No. 222, pp. 326-328. Published by the Carnegie Endowment for International Peace. The following quotation (p. 328) sums up his position: "Little by little the question will become more simple. Many groups, such as the German group of Jugoslavia, will disappear. This will take place more or less rapidly. Also many groups which still exist in Roumania, in Czechoslovakia, in Hungary, will probably be assimilated. It is only the compact and larger groups which will continue for a considerable time. Will they subsist pure? That is the question of the future. But no violence should be used. There should never be anything but natural assimilation. It is one of the services accomplished by the application of the principle for the protection of minorities to have established this fact."

[53] In January, 1923, Poland stated in a memorandum to the Council of the League that the minority treaties should be interpreted "and applied in a restricted and not an extended sense," and that the procedure adopted by the Council for the handling of minority cases should be modified accordingly. For specific suggestions, see Buell, *op. cit.*, p. 197, note 2.

inadequate, and various suggestions for its improvement and elaboration have been offered. As early as 1921, Professor Gilbert Murray pointed out to the Assembly of the League that the procedure for investigating minority complaints was defective,[54] and recommended the appointment of a "permanent commission to consider and report upon complaints addressed to the League, and where necessary to make inquiries on the spot." Murray, and those who were later to repeat the proposal, were animated by a desire to systematize and put on a more solid foundation the work of the League in relation to minorities by giving the Council the assistance afforded by a permanent impartial body of experts, similar in character to the Permanent Mandates Commission.[55] Such a body, although advisory, would have weight and authority by virtue of the fact that it could make an intensive study of minority problems, and make its recommendations on the basis of knowledge and free from the suspicion that they were animated by particular political preoccupations. The second part of the recommendation of Professor Murray was designed to afford the Commission an opportunity to secure first-hand information on troublesome questions rather than leave it to rely upon partial and *ex parte* evidence that might be submitted by aggrieved minorities and by the governments whose actions they were protesting. In the following year Professor Murray made a number of proposals for improving the procedure of the League, including the suggestion that "in some localities of mixed population" the League should station with the consent of the state concerned, resident agents who would "report impartially on the behaviour of both, or all, sections of the population." [56] The purpose here was to anticipate, and therefore perhaps avert, the development of serious disputes by a stoppage-at-the-source mechanism.

After the entry of Germany into the League, renewed attention was focused on the minorities system, especially as a result of complaints of the German minority in Poland that Germans were being mistreated. The suggestion of a Permanent Minorities Commission was renewed at the Ninth Assembly in 1918 by the Dutch representative and was supported by Stresemann of Germany as well as by others,[57] but this

[54] For a concise statement of this procedure, see Frederick L. Schuman, *International Politics* (New York and London, 1933), pp. 317-318.

[55] *Infra,* pp. 422-424.

[56] L. P. Mair, "The Machinery of Minority Protection," *Journal of the Royal Institute of International Affairs,* Vol. VII (July, 1928), No. 4, pp. 263-264.

[57] See Blanche E. C. Dugdale, "The Working of the Minority Treaties," *Jour-*

and other proposals mentioned met with strong opposition. It was declared in some quarters that under the treaties the League had no right to do more than hear complaints duly brought forward by a Council member, and that the elaboration of additional machinery was unwarranted. It was urged also that it would have the effect of stirring up agitation for independence and aggravating difficult situations. None of these proposals was adopted, but the Council of the League in 1929, by resolution, adopted certain less controversial procedural changes useful chiefly, perhaps, in that they provide fuller publicity in connection with the handling of minority questions, and help to insure more energetic treatment of them.[58]

More than one critic of the League system for the protection of minorities has pointed out that the Council of the League, which is charged with the chief responsibility for securing the observance of the obligations contained in the treaties, is a political body not ideally fitted to perform such a responsibility. In the Fifth Assembly, Count Apponyi, the Hungarian representative, expressed this view in the following language: "The Council is first and foremost a political body consisting of statesmen delegated by their respective Governments and having definite instructions. They are fully conscious of their international duties, but owing to the nature of things and to the position they hold they are mainly preoccupied with the political interests of the states they represent. A case must be a flagrant one . . . before a member of the Council will care to create a delicate situation between his own country and another, in order to do justice to a minority to which he is bound by no particular ties." [59] In the opinion of one writer,[60] the future remedy is already indicated in the treaties themselves. It is provided that if any dispute as to their meaning should arise between a signatory state and a state which is a member of

nal of the Royal Institute of International Affairs, Vol. V (March, 1926), No. 2, p. 91; C. A. Macartney, "The European Minorities," *Contemporary Review,* Vol. CXXXV (March, 1929), No. 759, pp. 350-355; H. B. Calderwood, "Should the Council of the League of Nations Establish a Permanent Minorities Commission?" *American Political Science Review,* Vol. XXVII (April, 1933), No. 22, pp. 250-259; Otto Junghann, *The Origin and Solution of the Problem of National Minorities* (Vienna and Leipzig, 1929), pp. 27-28.

[58] See Julius Stone, *International Guarantees of Minority Rights* (London, 1932), for a careful analysis of the procedure developed by the Council of the League.

[59] Quotation taken from C. K. Webster, *op. cit.,* pp. 218-219.

[60] D. Krstitch, *Les Minorités, l'État, et la Communauté Internationale* (Paris, 1924), pp. 300-301.

the Council, the difference is to be referred to the Permanent Court of International Justice. He says: "No one can deny that in international conflicts—and those between States and nationalities are the most acute—an equitable decision, taken after a profound examination of the situation by impartial judges, would be infinitely preferable to any examination by a political body." It is therefore suggested that minorities be recognized as having a juridical character and be allowed to appeal directly to an international judicial tribunal if unable to get justice within the state to which they belong.[61] Another writer expresses the same idea even more emphatically.[62] National minorities, he believes, can never receive adequate protection until they are organized as corporate bodies, and are able to appear in their own right before the Permanent Court of International Justice. In certain regions where minorities form a compact *bloc,* as do the Germans in Bohemia, there would be no difficulty, he declares, in basing their right to a separate personality on their ethnographic unity. Even in other instances where the minority was scattered among the ethnic majority, it would be possible to identify its members for such a purpose. It is true that, traditionally, only states are recognized as subjects of international law, but this doctrine, says the writer, has been shaken by a number of modern developments. For example, the League of Nations, which in principle is supposed to be an organization whose members are independent states, finds a place in its membership for the Dominions of the British Empire on a basis of legal equality with the members who are independent states. He then remarks that if the British Empire does not regard itself as menaced by the fact that its autonomous colonies enjoy independent representation in the League and the legal position of subjects of international law, one would not suppose that other states would endanger their prestige if their minorities were given the right to appear in legal proceedings before the Permanent Court.[63] Although several writers are in substantial agreement with this viewpoint,[64] the great majority are not prepared to go

[61] In 1925 Count Apponyi also contended that minorities should be treated as legal persons and privileged to plead their case before the Council. (L. P. Mair, *loc. cit.*, pp. 264-265.)

[62] Alphonse de Heyking, *op. cit.*, pp. 129-133.

[63] *Ibid.*, p. 132, for other examples cited by Heyking.

[64] See, for example, Rudolf von Herrnritt, *Nationalität und Recht* (Vienna, 1899); Karl Renner, *Das Selbstbestimmungsrecht der Nationen in Besonderer Anwendung auf Österreich* (Leipzig and Vienna, 1918); Otto Bauer, *Die Nationalitäten-*

so far. Not only would such a step be quite incompatible with the minority treaties, but in the opinion of many it would have a disintegrating effect on states.

The League system for the international protection of minorities was called for by the impossibility of granting statehood to many minorities who must therefore live under the government of a dominant nationality that might not be disposed to accord them cultural freedom. Until such governments should be able peacefully to assimilate their minorities, therefore, or demonstrate by a sustained policy of tolerance that international control is superfluous, the presumption is that international control will need to be maintained. Although the system was not intended to be applied universally, and perhaps was not regarded as being necessarily permanent, there is no inherent reason why it might not be extended to include all countries having minorities, and perhaps little reason to expect that the need for international control, in some areas, at any rate, will disappear at no distant date.[65]

Another solution of quite different character, however, was applied as a result of the World War to certain minority populations. This was to leave the frontiers of the states involved intact, but shift the minorities. Thus a wholesale exchange of minority populations was effected between Greece and Bulgaria and between Greece and Turkey. During the War, these minorities suffered many vicissitudes, and at its conclusion about two million of them were exchanged, the Greeks in Turkey and Bulgaria being sent to Greece, and the Turks and Bulgarians in Greece being sent to Turkey and Bulgaria. The transfers were effected by international agreement, the League of Nations assisting the countries concerned in the monumental task. There is probably almost unanimous agreement that this major operation on the minorities problem is not susceptible of being performed successfully except in limited areas. To the extent that the transfer is complete, it does remove altogether the minority problem in the countries concerned, and therefore the need for international protection, but even in the countries mentioned this was not altogether possible. It is an ex-

frage und die Sozialdemokratie, Marx-Studien, 2 vols. (2nd ed., Vienna, 1924), Vol. III; Otto Junghann, *op. cit.,* pp. 28-29, 34.

[65] For discussion of proposals to generalize the minorities regime, see H. B. Calderwood, "The Proposed Generalization of the Minorities Regime," *American Political Science Review,* Vol. XXVIII (Dec., 1934), No. 6, pp. 1088-1098; and Macartney, *op. cit.,* pp. 487-494.

ceedingly costly method, and, if the exchange is on a large scale, involves serious problems of economic readjustment likely to impose heavy burdens not only on the people concerned, but also on the treasuries of their states. Redslob [66] points out, also, a considerable moral loss involved in the particular case of the forced removal of the Greeks from Turkey, where they had served as a "spiritual bridge" between Asia and the West. He remarks also that the forced transplantation of a people [67] violates a primordial right to liberty, even though it results in the creation of national unity and reassembles in a common life the members of a nationality. Instead of being a solution, therefore, exchange of populations by force is a displacement which changes the problem. On the other hand, the voluntary or optional migration of a minority, although avoiding such a reproach, does not solve the problem, because it results in a fragmentary and partial, rather than a collective, movement of the populations, thus still leaving minorities in both countries.

REFERENCES

Ammende, E., ed., *Die Nationalitäten in den Staaten Europas* (Vienna, 1931).

Barker, E., *National Character* (London, 1927).

Boehm, M., *Das Eigenständige Volk* (Göttingen, 1932).

————, *Europa Irredenta* (Berlin, 1923).

Bordhin, Manz, *Das Positive Recht der Nationalen Minderheiten* (Berlin, 1922).

Brun, L. J., *Le Problème des Minorités Devant le Droit International* (Paris, 1923).

Buell, R. L., *International Relations* (rev. ed., New York, 1929), Ch. VIII.

Dominian, L., *The Frontiers of Language and Nationality in Europe* (New York, 1917).

Eisenmann, L., "Rights of Minorities in Central Europe," *International Conciliation* (Sept., 1926), No. 222, pp. 315-329.

Epstein, L., *Der Nationale Minderheitsschutz als Internationales Rechtsproblem* (Berlin, 1922).

[66] *Op. cit.*, pp. 164-165.

[67] In the case of the Greek and Turkish minorities, the exchange was compulsory and took place under conditions of great suffering and hardship. The reciprocal emigration of national minorities between Greece and Bulgaria was theoretically voluntary, but became largely compulsory. See the careful study of Stephen P. Ladas, *The Exchange of Minorities; Bulgaria, Greece and Turkey* (New York, 1932), especially pp. 720-736; also A. Wurfbain, *L'Échange Gréco-Bulgare des Minorités Ethniques* (Geneva, 1930); and Macartney, *op. cit.*, pp. 430-449.

Evans, I. L., "The Protection of Minorities," *British Year Book of International Law 1923-24*, IV, 95-123.

Fawcett, C. B., *Frontiers, A Study in Political Geography* (Oxford, 1918).

Fouques-Duparc, J. F., *La Protection des Minorités de Race, de Langue, et de Religion* (Paris, 1922).

Gibbons, H. A., *Nationalism and Internationalism* (New York, 1930).

Gennep, A. van, *Traité Comparitif des Nationalités* (Paris, 1922).

Hauser, H., *Le Principe des Nationalités* (Paris, 1916).

Herrnritt, R. von, *Nationalität und Recht* (Vienna, 1899).

Heyking, A. de, *La Conception de l'État et l'Idée de la Cohésion Ethnique* (Paris, 1927).

Hoijer, O., *Le Pacte de la Société des Nations* (Paris, 1926), pp. 489-506.

Holdich, T., *Political Frontiers and Boundary Making* (London, 1916).

Johannet, R., *Le Principe des Nationalités* (new ed., Paris, 1923).

Junghann, O., *National Minorities in Europe* (New York, 1932).

Krstitch, D., *Les Minorités, l'État, et la Communauté Internationale* (Paris, 1924).

Ladas, S., *The Exchange of Minorities; Bulgaria, Greece and Turkey* (New York, 1932).

Lansing, R., *The Peace Negotiations* (Boston and New York, 1921), Ch. VII.

Le Fur, L., *Races, Nationalités, États* (Paris, 1922).

Macartney, C. A., *National States and National Minorities* (London, 1934).

Masaryk, T. G., *The Making of a State* (New York, 1927).

Mowrer, P. S., *Balkanized Europe* (New York, 1921).

Muir, R., *Nationalism and Internationalism* (London, 1918).

Murray, G., "Self-Determination of Nationalities," *Journal of the Royal Institute of International Affairs*, I (1922), 6.

Rappard, W. E., *International Relations as Viewed from Geneva* (New Haven, Conn., 1925), pp. 40-59.

——————, *Uniting Europe* (New Haven, Conn., 1930), Ch. I.

Redslob, R., *Le Principe des Nationalités* (Paris, 1930).

Renner, K., *Das Selbstbestimmungsrecht der Nationen in Besonderer Anwendung auf Österreich* (Leipzig and Vienna, 1918).

Rose, J. H., *Nationality as a Factor in Modern History* (New York, 1916).

Rosting, H., "Protection of Minorities by the League of Nations," *American Journal of International Law*, XVII (October, 1923), 641-660.

Ruyssen, T., *Les Minorités Nationales d'Europe et la Guerre Mondiale* (Paris, 1924).

——————, *The Principle of Nationality*, tr. by John Mez (New York, 1916-1917).

Schuman, F. L., *International Politics* (New York and London, 1933), Ch. IX.

Stocks, J. L., *Patriotism and the Super-State* (London and New York, 1920).

Stone, J., *International Guarantees of Minority Rights* (London, 1932).

Temperley, H., *A History of the Peace Conference of Paris,* 6 vols. (London, 1920-1924), Vol. V, Ch. II.

Wambaugh, S., *Plebiscites Since the World War,* 2 vols. (Washington, 1933).

Wertheimer, F., *Deutschland, die Minderheiten und der Völkerbund* (Berlin, 1926).

Webster, C. K., *The League of Nations in Theory and Practice* (Boston and New York 1933).

Wittmann, E., *Past and Future of the Right of National Self-Determination* (Amsterdam, 1919).

Zangwill, I., *The Principle of Nationalities* (London, 1917).

Zimmern, A., *Nationality and Government* (New York, 1918), Chs. II-IV.

CHAPTER XVIII

IMPERIALISM AND THE PRINCIPLE OF INTERNATIONAL CONTROL OF BACKWARD AREAS

MODERN imperialism may be studied from two different points of view, both significant today. It may be viewed from the standpoint of the stabilization of the relation of imperial powers to subject peoples, or with reference to the relations of these powers to one another. In the early modern period, when Europeans first came into contact with backward peoples across the seas, the latter were conquered, their lands appropriated, and their lives exploited for the most part in brutal disregard of the rules of international intercourse laid down by such theologians as Victoria and Suarez and by lay jurists such as Gentilis and Grotius.[1] In an age when the tendency was strong to exalt the Machiavellian type of statecraft, it was difficult enough to get Christian states to observe toward one another the amenities and restraints advocated by the early writers on international law; toward infidels and heathen peoples it was quite impossible, in general, to expect the conquering forces of these same states to show any consideration. In these early centuries there are instances of the extermination of entire peoples, and the reduction of others to the most pitiless forms of slavery.

Real improvement in the treatment of backward peoples, or rather widespread abolition of some of the most inhumane practices, was not realized until after the growth, in the nineteenth century, of an organized humanitarian movement. The seeds of the movement were germinated, however, in the fertile soil of the eighteenth century. Even this late in modern history, advanced states like England, for example, were not above making profits from the wholesale delivery of slaves to the Spanish colonies.[2] Anti-slavery societies were organized in England as early as 1791, and it was largely due to their efforts that in 1807 the

[1] See *supra*, Ch. VIII.

[2] By the treaty of Utrecht in 1713 England was given a monopoly of the slave trade with the Spanish possessions, and agreed to supply 144,000 slaves within thirty years. Buell, *International Relations*, p. 275.

government of Great Britain prohibited Englishmen from participating in the African slave trade and in 1833 abolished African slavery in the British colonies. It was likewise due principally to the efforts of these societies that the mere negative opposition to chattel slavery broadened into an official interest in an amelioration of the unhappy conditions brought about in the lives of backward peoples by their involuntary association with their civilized masters.[3] In 1835, through the influence of the Aborigines Protection Society, a select committee of the House of Commons was appointed "to consider what measures ought to be adopted with regard to the native inhabitants of countries where British settlements are made, and to the neighboring tribes, in order to secure to them the due observance of justice and the protection of their rights, to promote the spread of civilization among them, and to lead them to the peaceful and voluntary reception of the Christian religion."[4] In 1837, the committee reported its findings that "the intercourse of Europeans in general . . . has been, unless when attended by missionary exertions, a source of many calamities to uncivilized nations." It then urged that Great Britain should assume the leadership in a movement throughout the world to eliminate the evils to both civilized and uncivilized peoples growing out of their unregulated contact.[5] The movement had its counterpart in America among the Quakers and, in France, under the revolutionary humanitarians Condorcet, L'Abbé Gregoire, and Mirabeau.[6] Partly as a result of the efforts of these leaders and their nineteenth century successors in the organized humanitarian and democratic movements, public opinion was aroused on occasion to demand colonial reforms.

Although the humanitarian movement in the early part of the nineteenth century was to a great extent motivated by religious considerations, the arguments used were often addressed to the purse as well as to the conscience, and were the more effective by their appeal to enlightened self-interest. In the course of time statesmen began to interest themselves in the problems of imperial administration. Enlightened colonial administrators began to stress the importance, in colonial areas, of conserving the health of the natives, improving their eco-

[3] Alpheus H. Snow, *The Question of Aborigines in the Law and Practice of Nations* (Washington, 1919), p. 7.
[4] *Ibid.*, pp. 8-9.
[5] *Ibid.*, pp. 10-13.
[6] Quincy Wright, *Mandates Under the League of Nations* (Chicago, 1930), p. 9.

nomic condition, and, in general, of adopting policies that would make for their greater contentedness and efficiency. Only in this way, it was realized, could a satisfactory labor supply be guaranteed, necessary raw materials and minerals produced, the expanding market for goods developed, and the maximum fruits of imperialism garnered. Accordingly, in the course of the nineteenth century, not only was slavery largely abandoned and restrictions placed upon the sale of liquor and firearms to natives, but also in some colonial areas humane labor policies were worked out, a certain amount of attention was given to protecting natives' rights to land, and some effort was made to give them the rudiments of education.

In the 1880's, as has been observed,[7] Great Britain, France, and other Powers began on a large scale to "stake out claims for posterity" in Africa, and to attempt to monopolize resources and markets. Nevertheless, a certain amount of give-and-take among these Powers was necessary for the fullest realization of their objectives. Accordingly, international agreements conferring reciprocal economic benefits were made, the neutralization or internationalization of certain areas was established by treaty, and occasionally joint administration of backward territories was attempted.[8] Certain matters, in fact, were recognized quite early in the century as requiring international cooperation for satisfactory results. At the Congress of Vienna in 1814 the Powers represented accepted the principle that all of them, whether possessing African colonies or not, had the right to participate in the consideration of cooperative measures that might be directed toward abolishing the above trade. This right was based in turn on the principle that the subject of the relationship between civilized states and backward peoples affected public morals and humanity, and as such was a matter for the collective decision of the Powers. In 1841 the five great European Powers signed a general treaty by which they agreed to cooperate in the suppression of the slave trade; and other later conventions, designed more effectively to stamp out the traffic, were also negotiated. The most significant step, however, was taken at the Berlin African Conference of 1884-85, when the Powers acknowledged an individual and collective responsibility for the welfare of the aborigines of Middle Africa. Following the lead of the United States, which became espe-

[7] *Supra,* Ch. XIII.
[8] Wright, *op. cit.,* p. 10.

cially interested in the region by reason of the discoveries of Sir Henry Morton Stanley, sent by the *New York Herald* to Africa to find the lost explorer Livingstone, the Conference recognized the private International Congo Association, which had already gained considerable foothold in the region, as a state. This action was intended to make the Congo basin a zone of international jurisdiction and control.[9] Plans for an international commission of surveillance fell through, however, and later a ruthless system of exploitation was carried on in the region until 1911, when protest on the part of the Powers finally caused its abandonment.

These developments in the spheres of national and international policy, to be explained in part by the growth of a more humane spirit and in part by the development of a better understanding of self-interest on the part of civilized states, led to the general acceptance of new concepts of imperial responsibility. When new dependencies were acquired by European states, less emphasis was placed upon the rights of the imperial owners and more upon their duties and the obligation to discharge their new responsibilities on behalf of civilization. To be sure, no imperial power was prepared to acknowledge the right of the international community to supervise the performance of the trust, but the principle, at any rate, was acknowledged, and furnished a foundation upon which in time guarantees might conceivably be based. Moreover, as Wright[10] has expressed it, "the conception of the dependency itself was shifting from that of a piece of property to a personality. The dependency came to be looked upon not merely as real estate but as a community with a corporate personality—adolescent, perhaps, unprepared for immediate independence, but capable of organic development. Thus the trust undertaken by the imperial power was not only for the administration of property but also for the development of a ward. It resembled guardianship or tutelage." This conception was based on the theory of nationality as it came to be developed and applied in the course of the nineteenth century.[11] It is true, however, that as regards backward peoples on the fringes of civilization, such as most of the native population of Africa and of the islands of the Pacific, the Kipling theory was undoubtedly the most widely held

[9] Snow, *op. cit.*, pp. 28-29.
[10] *Op. cit.*, p. 11.
[11] *Supra*, Ch. XI.

among imperial powers. It was assumed that these peoples were innately inferior and incapable ever of developing a type of civilization that would entitle them to recognition of separate statehood such as could be and was accorded, for example, to Turkey's subject nationalities. Thus the White Man's Burden could at the most be somewhat lightened by taming and training these peoples; it could never be laid down. In very few instances, certainly, was a different conception expressed in official quarters before the World War.[12]

It has already been seen that at least one prominent writer in the years before the World War was advocating the development of unappropriated areas inhabited by backward peoples by accredited nations under some form of international control.[13] During the War, the same writer developed this idea further in connection with his suggestions of a plan for a permanent league of peace.[14] The "chief modern cause of war," according to Hobson's analysis, is the competitive struggle of the governments of modern nations for economic privileges of one kind or another for powerful financial and trading groups of their nationals.[15] "The real origins," he declared, "of most quarrels between such nations have related to tariffs, railways, banking, commercial, and financial operations in lands belonging to one or other of the parties, or in lands where some sphere of special interest was claimed. Egypt, Morocco, Persia, Asia Minor, China, Congo, Mexico, are the most sensitive spots affecting international relations outside of Europe, testifying to the predominance of economic considerations in foreign policy. The stress laid upon such countries hinges, in the last resort, upon the need of 'open doors' or upon the desire to close doors to other countries. These keenly felt desires to safeguard existing foreign markets for goods and capital, to obtain new markets by diplomatic pressure

[12] President Roosevelt, in his annual message to Congress in 1904, expressed the hope that the Filipino would eventually be "able to stand, if not entirely alone, yet in some such relation to the United States as Cuba now stands," and pointed out that the policy of the United States, in contrast with that of other Powers having possessions in the Orient, was to "endeavor to develop the natives themselves so that they shall take an ever-increasing share in their own government." Quoted in Wright, *op. cit.*, pp. 13-14, note 24. Taft, Wilson, and other high American officials had much the same conception of the nature of the responsibility of the United States in the Philippines.

[13] J. A. Hobson, *Imperialism* (London, 1902), p. 251. Hobson's position on imperialism has been discussed previously.

[14] *Towards International Government* (George Allen & Unwin, Ltd., London, 1915).

[15] *Ibid.*, p. 142.

or by force, have everywhere been the chief directing influences in foreign policy, the chief causes of competing armaments, and the permanent underlying menaces to peace."[16]

The solution, in Hobson's opinion, can come only through the adoption of certain principles of international policy with respect to the development of the resources of backward countries, and the setting up of an international council or other representative body to frame the necessary legislation and settle the international disputes that cannot be prevented from arising. As in his earlier work, Hobson declares that backward peoples, unable or unwilling to develop rich resources, must not be allowed to stand in the way of the exploitation of such resources whenever it can be shown to be for the general good. At the same time, the backward people of a given area must be protected against injustice and exploitation. He insists, therefore, that "only so much interference, economic and political, as is required to achieve this end is *prima facie* justified."[17] This principle, although obviously salutary from one point of view, apparently stands in the way of the undertaking of educational and other positive measures for the purpose of developing as well as protecting the backward peoples. As a matter of fact, Hobson's chief concern was to devise means for the maintenance of peace and the development of cooperative in place of competitive action among the nations in the world's backward areas.

As regards the powers and activities of the international council for this purpose, Hobson suggested that it might be empowered to negotiate the "partition" of given areas in view of the "special political and economic interests of particular nations by virtue of accessibility or established connections." A special right of intervention by a particular state and the establishment of political control might be allowed under such circumstances, but the nation so privileged should be committed to the maintenance of an Open Door policy and "equality of opportunity for the capital and trade of other nations." This principle, he points out, was embodied in the Convention of Algeciras, but the stipulations of that treaty did not include adequate provisions for its execution. Although Hobson, in the plan which he suggests, does not enter into a discussion of the means of supplying such deficiencies, he devotes two chapters to the discussion and demonstration of the

[16] Hobson, *op. cit.*, pp. 128-129.
[17] *Ibid.*, p. 140.

necessity of international sanctions for any League of Nations machinery that may be set up.[18]

A plan embodying the same principles and designed to accomplish the same purposes, but not integrated with a world-wide permanent international organization such as Hobson envisaged, was also suggested during the War by the brilliant young American journalist, Walter Lippmann.[19] Inspired by the potentiality of international conferences such as that at Algeciras, meeting in a troubled area and seeking the solution of questions arising out of the contact of a backward people with civilized states, Lippmann proposed a series of permanent "miniature world legislatures" for the various areas of friction in different parts of the world. These "legislatures" would meet in the locality in which the tension existed, would legislate for the area, and then would meet from time to time to take stock of the situation, hear grievances, and make changes or apply additional remedies.[20] Lippmann put his finger on a grave weakness in the application of the idea embodied in the Algeciras and other international conferences of like purpose. He pointed out that "all these legislatures have had one great fault. They met, they passed laws, they adjourned and left the enforcement of their mandate to the conscience of the individual Powers. The legislature was international, but the executive was merely national. The legislature, moreover, had no way of checking up or controlling the executive. The representatives of all the nations would pass laws for the government of weak territories, but the translation of those laws into practice was left to the colonial bureaucrats of some one nation." [21] Thus, if the law were not carried out, the only appeal by those injured was to their own government, and redress could be brought about only through negotiation of the Powers, a highly uncertain and unsatisfactory process. Lippmann, therefore, stipulated that the "legislature" or "senate" which he proposed for the various backward areas should have its officials stationed in the locality to oversee the administration of its laws, keep informed as to the facts, and be in a position to state grievances. In time, as the system developed, the senate might well develop an international colonial civil service, and take more complete charge of the territory concerned. Eventually it "would become an upper house for

[18] *Ibid.*, Chs. VI, VII.
[19] *The Stakes of Diplomacy* (Henry Holt & Co., New York, 1915).
[20] *Ibid.*, pp. 133, 144.
[21] *Ibid.*, p. 131.

the government of the protected territory," associating with it natives organized into a lower house.[22] However, the ultimate success of such a plan was, in Lippmann's opinion, dependent upon the service it could render to the powerful economic and other groups interested in the affected areas. Their allegiance must be transferred from their own governments to the international governments of the localities. In order that this might be accomplished, the protection of the interests of such groups should be handed over to these international governments by the several national governments. Foreign traders and capitalists should therefore be told by their countrymen: "When you enter territory which is internationally organized you are expected to obey its laws and look to it for protection. We have backed you up hitherto because no adequate government existed in these backward states. Now it does exist, and we are no longer under any obligation to risk wars in order to protect you. If you are not satisfied with the treatment accorded you, appeal to The Hague, but appeal as a private citizen and not as one of our 'nationals.' We may, perhaps, if your case is good, help you by diplomatic argument to the international government. But you must under no circumstances feel that the military forces of this country are at your disposal."[23] This would contribute powerfully, in Lippmann's opinion, toward building up loyalty among such interested parties toward the international government that had their interests in its hands.

Lippmann's suggestions are interesting as embodying the particular, pragmatic approach to the problem. Like Hobson, he recognizes that the only possible solution lies in international control. On the other hand, his proposals call for the institution of separate local "world" parliaments as independent units to handle problems arising in the particular areas of disturbance. The difficulties in the way of the realization of a world parliament in the inclusive sense, with other appropriate organs of world government, he regards as insuperable for a very long time. In the meantime, however, problems requiring an international solution can be attacked in given regions of strain, and perhaps in time these "miniature world legislatures" will "become localized organs of a world state."[24] It may be noted also that his plan appar-

[22] *The Stakes of Diplomacy*, pp. 133, 134.
[23] *Ibid.*, p. 156.
[24] *Ibid.*, pp. 143-144.

ently contemplates the political education of the natives of these areas, and perhaps implies that an increasing measure of governmental responsibility shall be shared with them. But, like Hobson, he is concerned primarily with the elimination as far as possible, of what they both agree are the chief causes of modern wars, and he does not address himself to questions of the self-determination of peoples.

The same problem received the attention of the British Labour Party during the War and led to a series of proposals for international control and administration of backward areas which went much further than those of Hobson and Lippmann. A League of Nations should be established and all colonial areas in Africa should be internationalized and placed under its sovereignty. Its powers of administration would be delegated under a written constitution to international commissions similar in character to the European Commission of the Danube, and these Commissions would carry out their task with the single aim of serving the interests of the natives and preparing them by progressive stages for eventual independence. The economic interests of the non-natives and of European states would be taken into account only to the extent that absolute equality of commercial interests should be guaranteed to all. The members of the international commissions would be servants of the League of Nations, which would have the exclusive powers of appointment and dismissal. It is clear that the emphasis in this plan, in contrast with the plans of the two preceding writers whose views have been examined, is the safeguarding and tutelage of the backward peoples rather than the harmonizing of conflicting policies and the maintenance of peace between civilized states, although, of course, the latter object is also sought.[25]

The plans that have been discussed were necessarily framed with reference to the general requirements of a better world order at the end of the World War rather than with reference to specific political situations. During the conflict the political situation was fluid; and only toward the last, when victory appeared certain, was the policy of the Allied and Associated Powers definitely crystallized, and immediate problems connected with the setting up of new states and the transfer of territories inhabited by backward peoples definitely revealed. It then became clear that certain peoples on the western fringe

[25] J. Stoyanovsky, *La Théorie Générale des Mandats Internationaux* (Paris, 1925), pp. 7-8; also Quincy Wright, *op. cit.*, p. 26, and note 7.

of Russia were determined to set up independent political establishments, that the peoples of the Austro-Hungarian and Turkish Empires would have their aspirations for independence approved, and that Germany would have to surrender her sovereignty over her colonial possessions in Africa and the Pacific. In the preceding chapter, the principle of international protection of national minorities in the newly recognized succession states was discussed. But the peoples to be freed from Turkey, and those to be taken from under German colonial rule were not sufficiently advanced to be recognized as independent states; they presented essentially the problem of backward peoples. Those in the Near and Middle East, especially the Arab inhabitants of Palestine, Syria, and Mesopotamia, were politically self-conscious and had aspirations to form an Arabian federation but their political capacity was uncertain, the problem of minorities was likely to be exceedingly difficult, and altogether there was grave doubt as to the wisdom of granting them separate statehood. There were, however, more decisive reasons of a somewhat different order that stood in the way. England, France, Italy, and Greece had ambitions that conflicted with such a consummation. England desired to control Mesopotamia and territory at the eastern end of the Mediterranean Sea chiefly in order to protect her line of imperial communications with India and the Far East; France was interested in controlling Syria for political, sentimental, and economic reasons; Italy was eager for spoils and coveted the rich Anatolian region; and Greece not only was anxious to expand into Asia Minor, where there were large numbers of Greeks, but was willing to extend her political control farther. As regards the German colonies, arrangements for their distribution among the victors had likewise been made through secret treaties entered into during the War by the Allied Powers.

The openly avowed war aims of the victorious Powers, however, spoke of the freeing of subject peoples and the restitution of European territories seized by the enemy; they did not reveal the less lofty ambitions to annex extra-European territories of the defeated Powers. Nor was the United States, which was not a party to any of the secret agreements and was not in favor of a spoilsman's peace, disposed to agree to the transfer of a territory unless it could be reconciled with the principles upon which the Allies had agreed to make peace. Under these circumstances, and in view of the fact that liberal as well as radical opinion in the Allied countries was strongly opposed to the outright annexation of conquered territories, some other solution had to be found.

The general features of the system which was eventually to be adopted by the Peace Conference and applied to such territories were worked out by George Louis Beer, eminent American expert on colonial history. As a member of the staff of experts composing the American Commission of Inquiry, created by Colonel House at the request of President Wilson in 1917, to gather data and make reports on every kind of problem likely to come before the Peace Conference at the end of the War, Beer proposed a mandate system for Mesopotamia and most of the German colonies. The proposal seems first to have been made in a report on Mesopotamia completed for the Inquiry on January 1, 1918. He did not believe this territory should be returned to the "blasting tyranny" of Turkey, nor did he feel that the Arabs were sufficiently advanced politically to have their aspirations for an independent New Arabia, which would include Mesopotamia, satisfied. On the other hand, in the light of experience he was not prepared to advocate an international protectorate for the areas, which would involve direct international administration of the type that had already been attempted without much success in Egypt, Samoa, and the New Hebrides.[26] His recommendation was much like that advanced by Hobson.[27] The responsibility must be entrusted to a particular state acting on behalf of the international community. "Under modern political conditions," he concluded, "apparently the only way to determine the problem of politically backward peoples, who require not only outside political control but also foreign capital to reorganize their stagnant economic systems, is to entrust the task of government to that state whose interests are most directly involved." In the case of Mesopotamia, he asserted that the "international mandate" should be entrusted to the "British Commonwealth." In every such case, however, he stated that "There should be embodied in the deed of trust most rigid safeguards both to protect the native population from exploitation and also to ensure that the interests of other foreign states are not injured either positively or negatively." The open door should be guaranteed not only in the

[26] G. L. Beer, *African Questions at the Paris Peace Conference* (New York, 1923), pp. 419, 420-424.
[27] *Supra*, p. 278.

sense of equality of trade conditions, but "complete opportunity should be given to all nations to participate on an equal basis in the economic development of the country." [28]

In his discussion of colonial questions affecting the German possessions in Africa and the Pacific islands, Beer reasserted the principle that in the settlement of such questions "primary consideration must be the welfare of the native populations," and that the interests of the outside world must take second place. In order that these principles should be given effect, Beer proposed that for most of these territories different states should be appointed as mandatories on behalf of the League of Nations which, it was generally agreed, should be established. The terms of the mandates would vary according to the circumstances of the individual case, and in some instances annexation to adjoining territories was recommended. The special conditions and the appropriate action in each of the territories was then discussed and several specific suggestions were made as to the state best fitted to succeed to, or become the mandatory for, a given area.[29]

The general idea of a system of mandates for the former German colonies also won the approval of President Wilson. On his way to the Peace Conference in December 1918, he revealed his thoughts on the subject to the group of American experts on shipboard in expressing the opinion that "the German colonies should be declared the common property of the League of Nations and administered by small nations. The resources of each colony," he declared, "should be available to all members of the League. . ." [30] Although President Wilson apparently had not at that time envisaged the mandate system for the territories of the Near and Middle East and, as regards these territories, seems to have derived the idea from the South African statesman, General Jan Smuts, it is clear that the general conception was familiar to him before he came across the proposals of Smuts.

Although it is inaccurate to assert that the idea of the mandate system, as expressed in Article XXII of the Covenant of the League

[28] Beer, *op. cit.*, pp. 424-425.

[29] *Ibid.*, pp. 431-458. For tropical Africa, Beer recommended the establishment, as a part of the organization of the League of Nations, of a special international conference, which should meet at least every three years; of a special African court, which should hear cases involving the interpretation of international conventions for the area; and a permanent central bureau to collect, correlate, and study data necessary for the intelligent framing of international legislation. (*Op. cit.*, pp. 440-441.)

[30] David Hunter Miller, "The Origin of the Mandate System," *Foreign Affairs*, Vol. VI (Jan., 1928), No. 2, p. 281.

of Nations, originated with General Smuts, he commanded the greatest respect and exerted a powerful influence at the Peace Conference with his thoughtful discussion of the colonial problem and his specific proposals for a mandatory régime for certain areas. In his "Practical Suggestion" for a League of Nations, submitted December 16, 1918, he contended that the League rather than the individual victors should succeed to the territories split off from the Russian, Austrian, and Turkish Empires, for "if the peace really comes, not in the settlement of universal human principles and the dawning of a better order, but in a return of the old policy of grab and greed and partitions, then the bitterness of the disillusion would indeed be complete. Our victory would then be bitterer than Dead Sea fruit." The League, then, as successor to these territories, not only should provide for their administration, but also should determine their ultimate disposition. Smuts did not believe, however, that it would be wise for the League to attempt to administer the territories itself, pointing out that although international administration of matters limited in scope had worked satisfactorily, as testified by the success of the European Commission of the Danube and the Universal Postal Union, the political administration of large territories was a different matter. Whenever "joint international administration" [31] had been tried for the latter purpose, it had not been satisfactory. Smuts analyzed the reasons for failure as follows: "The administering personnel taken from different nations do not work smoothly or loyally together; the inhabitants of the territory administered are either confused or if they are sufficiently developed, make use of these differences by playing one set of nations off against the other. In any case the result is paralysis tempered by intrigue." Smuts therefore believed that the League would make a grave mistake which would shake its prestige should it attempt "too soon" to administer the people and territories entrusted to its care. It must first gain experience, and train an international civil staff to approach questions from a broad human point of view rather than from the national viewpoint, and to cooperate with one another unhampered by nationalistic prejudices.

[31] It is apparent that Smuts is thinking of cases of joint administration or condominium such as Great Britain and France established in the New Hebrides, rather than of international administration on behalf of an international organization of wide membership such as the League of Nations was intended to be. It may be, however, that he thought, in either case, weaknesses of the same order might appear.

In the meantime, in most cases in which the League was presented with the problems of administration in areas inhabited by backward peoples, it should appoint some state with a long experience in such matters to act on its behalf. In every such instance the "mandatory state" should furnish the necessary officials and undertake the administration of the territory, "subject to the supervision and ultimate control of the League. . ." As far as possible the principle of self-determination should be applied in such cases. Thus, the people of any such territory should be consulted before the appointment of a mandatory for it, and in general its wishes should determine the choice made. Moreover, if later it voices objections to the mandatory selected, on grounds found sufficient by the League, the latter may appoint another power as mandatory. In every case the League should issue a special charter defining the policy to be pursued by its agent, the mandatory state. "This policy," said Smuts, "must necessarily vary from case to case, according to the development, administrative or political capacity, and homogeneous character of the people concerned." Smuts also made the important suggestion that the League should keep in constant touch with conditions in the mandated areas, and perhaps might require periodic reports from the mandatory powers. The latter were not to be allowed to adopt policies redounding to their own special economic or military advantage, but, on the other hand, must be required to maintain the Open Door and equality of economic opportunity in the territories under mandate. Only sufficient military forces to provide for the internal protection of the territories should be allowed. This would prevent the mandatory state from drawing on such territories for additional man-power for its military forces.[32]

It will have been observed that Smuts, in his proposals for a system of international mandate, did not include the colonies of Germany in Africa and the Pacific. He claimed that a different principle should be applied in the case of the African colonies by reason of their being "inhabited by barbarians, who not only cannot possibly govern themselves, but to whom it would be impracticable to apply any idea of

[32] Smuts saw a great danger in the policy of arming the African natives and using them in wars between whites. In 1917, he had expressed himself on the subject at considerable length, concluding with the hope "that one of the results of this war will be some arrangement or convention among the nations interested in Central Africa by which the military training of natives in that area will be prevented, as we have prevented it in South Africa." Quoted in G. L. Beer, *op. cit.*, pp. 275-276.

political self-determination in the European sense." [33] He therefore held that the disposition of these territories should be made in accordance with the principles contained in the fifth point of President Wilson's Fourteen Point program. That point declared for a "free, open-minded, and absolutely impartial adjustment of all colonial claims, based upon a strict observance of the principle that in determining all such questions of sovereignty the interests of the populations concerned must have equal weight with the equitable claims of the government whose title is to be determined." [34] This was more conservative than the statement on the same matter in Lloyd George's War Aims speech which preceded the Fourteen Point address by only three days. Lloyd George said that in the disposition of the colonies the wishes and interests of the natives must have primary consideration, and that they were capable of choosing the sovereignty under which they desired to live. President Wilson, on the other hand, laid down the principle that the interests of the natives and the "equitable claims" of the government seeking a title to their territories should be given equal consideration. This in itself would preclude them from having a decisive voice in the matter of their disposal, and it is probable that President Wilson intended that the decision should ultimately be made for them. This was done when his suggestion that the mandate system should be extended to them was agreed to by Smuts and adopted by the Peace Conference.[35]

The mandate system written into Article XXII of the Covenant of the League of Nations definitely embodies, for the former Turkish territories in the Near and Middle East and for most of the German colonies, the principles of trusteeship, tutelage, and international supervision and control that had come to be accepted in the course of the nineteenth century. It may, perhaps, be said to represent a compromise between idealism and imperialism. The intention of certain of the Allied Powers to annex most of these territories was abandoned, but the interested Powers—the British Empire, France, Belgium, and Japan—and

[33] Lloyd George, in his statement of British War Aims, of January 8, 1918, was much more optimistic. He declared: "The natives live in their various tribal organizations under chiefs and councils who are competent to consult and speak for their tribes and members, and thus to represent their wishes and interests in regard to their disposal." (Text in Cooke and Stickney, *op. cit.*, pp. 538-545.)

[34] See Cooke and Stickney, *op. cit.*, p. 549. Full text of the address, pp. 546-551.

[35] For an excellent discussion of the immediate origins of the mandate system, with quite complete documentation, see Quincy Wright, *op. cit.*, Ch. II.

the British Dominions, the Union of South Africa, Australia, and New Zealand, were entrusted with the responsibility of administration and tutelage under the supervision of the League of Nations. In another aspect the system may be said to represent a compromise between outright annexation and international administration. The latter alternative, although theoretically preferable in that control and execution would both be in the hands of the League of Nations, representing the interests and purposes of the community of nations, had certain inherent weaknesses and was open to attack on the grounds suggested by Beer, Smuts, and other students of the problem.

The basic principle of the mandates system is stated in the first paragraph of Article XXII. To the territories and colonies formerly belonging to Germany and Turkey, "which are inhabited by peoples not yet able to stand by themselves under the strenuous conditions of the modern world, there should be applied the principle that the well-being and development of such peoples form a sacred trust of civilization and that securities for the performance of this trust should be embodied in this Covenant." Although the trusteeship principle for backward peoples had not only been recognized but also applied by the Powers in Morocco and elsewhere before the War, "securities for the performance of the trust" by the states exercising it had either been altogether lacking, or inadequate. In the absence of any permanent international organization of states such as the League of Nations, this was perhaps inevitable. Sporadic conferences of the representatives of a few interested Powers to inquire into the performance of the trust, or individual or even joint diplomatic protests at alleged infractions, could never quite meet the situation. Some permanently functioning central machinery, therefore, was clearly indicated as a *sine qua non*. With the establishment of the League of Nations, this was for the first time possible; and a problem, comparable in some respects to that presented by national minorities, was thereby made easier of solution.

President Wilson's original idea, conceived perhaps before he had had time to study the problem, that the responsibility of administering these territories should be entrusted to "small nations," was not adopted, but a more realistic formula was devised. The mandates were to be "entrusted to advanced nations who by reason of their resources, their experience or their geographical position can best undertake this responsibility, and who are willing to accept it. . ." It is difficult to quarrel with this formula as a broad statement of general principles applicable to the selection of a mandatory, even though it provided a foundation for the claims of the parties that had originally bargained among themselves to annex the territories in question.

The provision in Article XXII dividing the mandates into different classes likewise, perhaps, cannot be questioned in principle. Obviously the type of control and administration needed for the inhabitants of a small island in the Pacific would be quite different from that required in the case of territories such as Syria or Mesopotamia. The latter were relatively advanced and politically self-conscious. Nevertheless, it was questionable whether they were yet "able to stand by themselves," and thus be accorded an unqualified right of self-determination. It is assumed in Article XXII, however, that they "have reached a stage of development where their existence as independent states can be provisionally recognized subject to the rendering of administrative advice and assistance by a Mandatory until such time as they are able to stand alone." It was also provided that their wishes "must be a principal consideration in the selection of the Mandatory." In the case of other less developed peoples such as those of Central Africa, it was obvious that "advice and assistance" would not meet the requirements. There must be direct administration by the mandatory in the case of such peoples, but at the same time certain safeguards should be provided in their interests and certain guarantees on behalf of the interests of the members of the international community. Protection for both sets of interests is provided in the stipulation of Article XXII that "the Mandatory must be responsible for the administration of the territory under conditions which will guarantee freedom of conscience and religion, subject only to the maintenance of public order and morals, the prohibition of abuses such as the slave trade, the arms traffic, and the liquor traffic, and the prevention of the establishment of fortifications or military and naval bases and of military training of the natives for other than police purposes and the defense of territory, and will also secure equal opportunities for the trade and commerce of other Members of the League."[36] The formula for the government of the third

[36] This Open Door provision, it will be observed, applies only to "members of the League," and has been criticized for that reason. In principle, it would seem that it should apply to all states. On the other hand, it may be contended that states voluntarily remaining outside the League of Nations, and therefore sharing none of its responsibilities and contributing nothing to its maintenance, have no

class of mandate is such that, although the principles of trusteeship and international control are retained, the freedom of action of the mandatory may be circumscribed but little. To make this clear, it should be quoted in its entirety. "There are territories, such as Southwest Africa and certain of the South Pacific islands, which, owing to the sparseness of their population, or their small size, or their remoteness from the centers of civilization, or their geographical contiguity to the territory of the Mandatory, and other circumstances, can be best administered under the laws of the Mandatory as integral portions of its territory, subject to the safeguards above mentioned in the interests of the indigenous population." According to these stipulations the mandatory would not be required to maintain the Open Door in these areas even to members of the League.[37]

It is generally agreed that the feature which mainly distinguishes the mandate system from all previous attempts to apply the principle of international control to territories inhabited by backward peoples is that of continuous oversight by an international body. Each Mandatory is specifically obligated to render an annual report to the Council of the League of Nations. Moreover, in order that these reports shall not be merely nominal, it is provided in Article XXII that a Permanent Mandates Commission shall be constituted "to receive and examine the annual reports of the Mandatories and to advise the Council on all matters relating to the observance of the mandates."

The provision for such a Commission was of the greatest importance in that it supplied the necessary element of continuous international scrutiny of the stewardship of the mandatories of the League.[38] The following conception of the nature of its work and the qualities needed

ground for complaint. The government of the United States complained, however, on the special ground that, as one of the Allied and Associated Powers, whose victory made the disposal of the territories possible, it was entitled to any privilege enjoyed by the others. This claim was recognized in special treaties with the mandatory states.

[37] This has also occasioned criticism and can hardly be regarded as entirely consistent with the spirit of Article XXII and the avowed aims of the League as an agency of peace. See Wright, *op. cit.*, p. 47 and note 65, for criticism by Japan; also pp. 580-581 for Wright's own criticism.

[38] It is to be noted, however, that in addition to the Permanent Mandates Commission and the Council which, under the Covenant, is the organ of the League entrusted with the chief responsibility for the execution of the provisions of Article XXII, the League Assembly, the League Secretariat, and the Permanent Court of International Justice collaborate at certain points. See Quincy Wright, *op. cit.*, Ch. V, "The Agencies of League Supervision."

in its members was expressed prior to the formation of the Commission by the Honorable Ormsby-Gore, member of the British House of Commons, who was later to become a member of the Commission. It is notable as well for the view that is inherent in it of the entire system. "The commission must be so constituted that it can constantly bear in mind three points of view; international interests, since in modern civilization what affects one region of the world has repercussions in every other portion; national interests, since the right and dignity of the Mandatory Power or the Mandatory Dominion are intimately concerned; native interest, since the promotion of the welfare of the Mandated Territories is the primary object. Further, each of these must be considered from at least two aspects: the general and the special. Each area has its peculiar problems; for example, the native legal systems prevailing in tropical Africa are entirely unlike those which obtain in the ex-Ottoman territories. For all such questions experts are necessary, but it must be borne in mind that the expert is liable to grave errors as a result of his very specialization. He is apt to lose his sense of perspective and to force facts to agree with theories, rather than to shape theories according to facts; he inclines to become either unduly enthusiastic—even sentimental—or morbidly hostile and hypercritical. It is necessary, then, that the contributions of the experts—who are absolutely indispensable and whose investigations, conclusions, and advice should in all cases be sought and carefully considered—be controlled and correlated from a general point of view; and that experts and general advisors bear patiently the buffetings that each must give the other to attain the common weal."

"But the Mandates Commission," he declared, "must be more than a body of experts and general advisers studying problems at the seat of the League of Nations. This Commission is not, in a sense, dealing with problems at all; at least, it is not investigating them as abstract questions. It is concerned with human beings, and—whatever else it may forget—this it must always remember. Its members must possess all knowledge—native law, native religion, native psychology, native customs, methods of combating disease and vice, understanding of climatic, geographical and economic conditions, principles of colonial administration throughout the world from the beginning; all this, and more, must be familiar to them—but their knowledge is nothing unless it serves for the promotion of the welfare of those over whom for a time they exercise tutelage. . ." After stating the necessity of the members possessing tact and understanding in their delicate and complicated task, and warning against the danger of the Commission's degenerating into a bureaucracy, the writer made the following suggestive proposal. "It will do well to consider all problems concerning backward countries, whether they are under foreign tutelage as colonies or protectorates; or whether they are independent but in need of advice, assistance, or administration; and general international conventions for the promotion of the welfare of backward peoples, such as the convention for the control of traffic in arms and ammunition, or conventions which may prove necessary in future for the advancement of the less progressive nations, will best come within its domain. All peoples, whether in Mandated territories or not, may perhaps come to seek from it needed advice and counsel; and the reports which it publishes should not be merely perfunctory records, but must be fertile in suggestion for the future as well as data regarding past and present conditions." [39]

Various criticisms have been made against details of the mandates system,[40] and the way it has functioned in certain cases; scarcely any, however, have been directed against the ideas embodied in it, or against the principle of national administration under international control and supervision. However, President Wilson's Secretary of State, Robert Lansing, did oppose adoption of the system on the latter grounds as well as on others. He voiced the opinion that it "appeared to possess no peculiar advantages over the old method of transferring and exercising sovereign control either in providing added protection to the inhabitants of territory subject to a mandate or greater certainty of international equality in the matter of commerce and trade. . ." [41] He expressed the view that it would be better to transfer the territories to particular nations by treaties of cession "under such terms as seemed wise. . ." The adoption of the mandate system would also present a difficult question as to the location of sovereignty of the transferred territories, and this also troubled him.[42]

[39] Quotation taken from larger excerpt contained in Wright, *op. cit.*, pp. 137-138, by permission of University of Chicago Press. See also D. F. W. Van Rees, *Les Mandats Internationaux,* 2 vols. (Paris, 1927-1928), I, 136-141, for discussion of the rôle of the Permanent Mandates Commission.

[40] See, for example, the changes proposed in 1924 at the Twenty-second Interparliamentary Conference. Text published in *Advocate of Peace,* September-October, 1924, pp. 557-559.

[41] *The Peace Negotiations* (Boston and New York, 1921), p. 155.

[42] For other objections from the point of view of American policy, see *ibid.,* Ch. XIII.

A highly dispassionate view of the mandate system, given a decade after its inauguration, is presented in the exhaustive and authoritative work of Quincy Wright.[43] In his concluding chapter, he says: "It is believed that the system has advantages from the standpoint of the inhabitants of the area and of the world in general over the system of imperial control (whether under the form of colonies, protectorates, or spheres of interest) which has characterized the relation of advanced and backward peoples in the Eastern hemisphere, and also over the less precise system of self-determination qualified by the Monroe Doctrine, sporadic interventions, quasi-protectorates, receiverships, and occasional annexations by the United States which has characterized those relations in the Western hemisphere. . ."[44]

Wright and others[45] have also expressed the belief that the development of new principles and the realization of improvements in the mandated areas will eventually penetrate into other colonial areas as well. "Finally," he remarks, "as a by-product of the League's supervisory control of mandatory administration, rules, principles, and standards of broader application are being formulated. An international code of native rights and of the open door is developing. The territories under mandate include three important types of backward areas—the Moslem, the Negro, and the Oceanic (Polynesian, Melanesian, Micronesian) each of which includes other areas, now governed for the most part as colonies or protectorates. Thus principles found satisfactory to mandated territories will in most cases have a broader application."[46]

Several writers, convinced of the soundness of the mandate system in principle, and sufficiently impressed with its effectiveness or with its potentiality, have suggested that it should be extended to the colonial areas held by the various Powers. Buell, for example, says: "One of the greatest steps toward world peace would be a treaty signed by the ten leading colonial powers, guaranteeing the Open Door in their colonies and just treatment for the natives, as provided in the mandates, subject to the supervision of the Mandates Commission."[47] H. N.

[43] *Op. cit.*

[44] *Op. cit.*, pp. 584-585.

[45] See, for example, E. Van Maanen-Helmer, *The Mandates System in Relation to Africa and the Pacific Islands* (London, 1929), Ch. VIII; also R. L. Buell, *International Relations* (New York, 1929), p. 369, note 2, quoting M. Albert Sarraut.

[46] Wright, *op. cit.*, pp. 586-587. For suggested improvements, see pp. 587-588.

[47] R. L. Buell, *op. cit.*, p. 368. Wright, however, says: "The question of extending the system to other areas in the administrative sense is of less importance than the extension of its principles. . . The system now embraces typical areas

Brailsford also proposes that "The mandate system into which the Allies stumbled, because they were afraid to face public opinion with a naked claim to annex the German colonies, ought to be extended to all their non-self-governing possessions." [48] He goes further than most writers, however, when he suggests the possibility of working toward, and eventually realizing, international administration for the various colonial areas. He would like to see the Permanent Mandates Commission eventually form and develop a College of Colonial Administration, drawing its students impartially from all civilized nations, and providing an international staff of ripe experience to train them for the international colonial service. During a transitional period the colonies of the various countries would remain under their rule, subject to the general supervision of the League. The services should gradually be filled, however, by the graduates of the League's College of Colonial Administration who would be nominated, regardless of nationality, to places as vacancies should occur. In view of their common training, Brailsford asserts they would not find it difficult to work together. As a result of this gradual infiltration the colonies could finally be transferred to the League without destroying the continuity of their administration.[49]

—if more were added the Commission's administrative duties might swamp its scientific and investigatory functions." (*Op. cit.*, p. 588.)

[48] *Olives of Endless Age* (New York and London, 1928), p. 339. Another writer also proposes that the mandate system should be extended to "all territories predominately populated by the coloured child races, yet not organized as States. . ." In order to accomplish this the colonial possessions of the various states might be "vested in a great International Native Trust or Pool under the League of Nations, and redistributed on the mandatory principle amongst the states willing to share in the responsibility of administrating them . . . until their populations had been trained to manage their own affairs." States giving up colonies should be reimbursed for past expenditures on them. (W. H. Dawson, *The Failure of Empire and the World Price of Peace* [London, 1930], pp. 108-110).

[49] *Op. cit.*, pp. 343-346. Brailsford also makes an interesting suggestion in connection with the problem presented when bankers and concessionaires seek the intervention of their governments in support of claims or grievances against a weak or backward country. He would lay down the principle that the regulation of trade, investment, and other economic matters, when the nationals of one state carry on business within the territory of another, ultimately lies with the League of Nations. The protection of the interests of such persons or corporations, therefore, should be taken out of the hands of their states. Normally cases would come before the Courts in the country in which the investments are made, but appeal would lie to the courts of the League which might be established in two or three convenient centers, perhaps the Near East, the Far East, and The Hague. Plaintiffs should be invested with international legal personality in order that they might sue in their own right in international courts. The League might also train men to serve weak countries, on request, as impartial advisers. (*Ibid.*, Ch. IX.)

REFERENCES

Allier, R., *The Mind of the Savage* (New York, 1929). Appendix IV, "The New Doctrine of Colonization," by Albert Sarraut.

Antonelli, E., *L'Afrique et la Paix de Versailles* (Paris, 1921).

Baker, R. S., *Woodrow Wilson and World Settlement,* 3 vols. (New York, 1922).

Batsell, W. R., "The United States and the System of Mandates," *International Conciliation* (Oct., 1925), No. 213, pp. 269-315.

Baty, T., "Protectorates and Mandates," *British Yearbook of International Law, 1921-1922,* pp. 109-121.

Beer, G. L., *African Questions at the Paris Peace Conference* (New York, 1923).

Brailsford, H. N., *Olives of Endless Age* (New York and London, 1928), Ch. X.

Buell, R. L., *The Native Problem in Africa,* 2 vols. (New York, 1928).

————, " 'Backward' Peoples under the Mandate System," *Current History,* XX (June, 1924), 386-395.

————, *International Relations* (rev. ed., New York, 1929), Ch. XV.

Buxton, T. F., *The African Slave Trade and Its Remedy* (London, 1840).

Chirol, V., *The Occident and the Orient* (Chicago, 1924).

Cioriceanu, G., *Les Mandats Internationaux* (Paris, 1921).

Dawson, W. H., *The Future of Empire and the World Price of Peace* (London, 1930).

Earle, E. M., *Turkey, the Great Powers, and the Bagdad Railway* (New York, 1923).

Elliott, W. Y., *The New British Empire* (New York, 1932).

Evans, L. H., "Some Legal and Historical Antecedents of the Mandatory System," *Proceedings of the Southwestern Political Science Association Fifth Annual Convention,* March, 1924.

————, "The Emancipation of Iraq from the Mandates System," *American Political Science Review,* Vol. XXVI (Dec., 1932), No. 6, pp. 1024-1049.

————, "The General Principles Governing the Termination of a Mandate," *American Journal of International Law,* Vol. XXVI (Oct., 1932), No. 4, pp. 735-758.

Fayle, C. E., *The Great Settlement* (London, 1915).

Feinburg, N., *La Juridiction de la Cour Permanente de Justice Internationale dans le Système des Mandats* (Paris, 1930).

Gerig, B., *The Open Door and the Mandates System* (London, 1930).

Grant, A. J., and others, *Introduction to the Study of International Relations* (London, 1916), Ch. V.

Hobson, J. A., *Towards International Government* (London, 1915).

Hocking, W. E., *The Spirit of World Politics, with Special Studies of the Near East* (New York, 1932), Pts. IV-VII.

Hoijer, O., *La Sécurité Internationale et ses Modes de Réalisation,* 4 vols. (Paris, 1930), Vol. I, Ch. V.

Hudson, O., "The League of Nations and the Protection of the Inhabitants of Transferred Territories," *The Annals of The American Academy of Political and Social Science,* XCVI (July, 1921), 78-83.

Johnston, H., *A History of the Colonization of Africa by Alien Races* (new ed., Cambridge, Eng., 1913).

Kat Angelino, A. de, *Colonial Policy,* 2 vols. (The Hague, 1931).

Langer, W. L., "A Critique of Imperialism," *Foreign Affairs,* Vol. XIV, No. 1 (Oct., 1935), pp. 102-119.

Lansing, R., *The Peace Negotiations* (Boston and New York, 1921), Ch. XIII.

Lavergne, B., *Le Principe des Nationalités et les Guerres, son Application au Problème Colonial* (Paris, 1921), Ch. II.

Lindley, M. F., *The Acquisition and Government of Backward Territory in International Law* (London and New York, 1926).

Lippmann, W., *The Stakes of Diplomacy* (New York, 1915).

Lugard, Sir F., *The Dual Mandate in British Tropical Africa* (Edinburgh and London, 1923).

Maanen-Helmer, E. van, *The Mandates System in Relation to Africa and the Pacific Islands* (London, 1929).

Macdonald, A. J., *Trade, Politics, and Christianity in Africa and the East* (London, 1916).

Margolith, A. M., *The International Mandates* (Baltimore, Md., 1930).

Miller, D. H., *The Drafting of the Covenant,* 2 vols. (New York and London, 1928). Text of the Plan of General Smuts for a League of Nations in II, 23-60.

————, "The Origin of the Mandates System," *Foreign Affairs,* Vol. VI (Jan., 1928), No. 2, pp. 277-289.

————, *My Diary at the Conference of Paris,* 21 vols. (New York, 1924).

Millott, A., *Les Mandats Internationaux* (Paris, 1924).

Moon, P. T., *Imperialism and World Politics* (New York, 1926).

Morel, E. D., *Africa and the Peace of Europe* (London, 1917).

————, *The Black Man's Burden* (New York, 1920).

Olivier, Sir S., *The League of Nations and Primitive Peoples* (London and New York, 1918).

Peffer, N., *The White Man's Dilemma: Climax of the Age of Imperialism* (New York, 1927).

Permanent Mandates Commission, *Minutes* (Geneva, 1921-1935).

Potter, P. B., "Origin of the System of Mandates under the League of Nations," *American Political Science Review,* XVI (Nov., 1933), 563-583.

————, "Origin of the System of Mandates under the League of Nations, Further Notes," *American Political Science Review,* XX (Nov., 1926), 842-846.

Powell, E. A., *The Struggle for Power in Moslem Asia* (New York and London, 1923).

Rees, D. F. W., van, *Les Mandats Internationaux,* 2 vols. (Paris, 1927-1928).

Sarraut, P., *La Mise en Valeur des Colonies Françaises* (Paris, 1923).

Schnee, H., *German Colonization, Past and Future* (London, 1926).

Schuman, F., *International Politics* (New York and London, 1933), Ch. XV.

Smuts, J. C., *The League of Nations, a Practical Suggestion* (New York and London, 1918).

Snow, A. H., *The American Philosophy of Government* (New York and London, 1921), pp. 321-336.

————, *The Question of Aborigines in the Law and Practice of Nations* (Washington, 1919).

"Some Principles and Problems of the Settlement," *The Round Table,* IX (Dec., 1918), 88-113.

Stoyanovsky, J., *La Théorie Générale des Mandats Internationaux* (Paris, 1925).

White, F., *Mandates* (London, 1926).

Willoughby, W. C., *Race Problems in the New Africa* (Oxford, 1923).

"Windows of Freedom: America's Place in World Government," *The Round Table,* IX (Dec., 1918), 21-35.

Woolf, L., *Imperialism and Civilization* (London, 1928).

————, *Empire and Commerce in Africa* (London, 1919).

Wright, Q., *Mandates under the League of Nations* (Chicago, 1930).

CHAPTER XIX

DISARMAMENT AND SECURITY

PRIOR to the World War, it was generally taken for granted that the size of a nation's armament was its own affair, and that the use of its armed forces was a matter lying within its own discretion, due regard being paid to treaty obligations. Considerations of economy or of national advantage might, of course, suggest the desirability of limiting armament in given areas and under certain circumstances by international agreement, but disarmament as an international policy and objective was never seriously considered outside pacifist circles.[1] The single example of virtual disarmament deliberately followed as a policy on both sides of an extensive frontier for over a hundred years is provided by Canada and the United States. An Anglo-American agreement for the limitation of armaments on the Great Lakes to a police force basis was originally made in 1817. The agreement then adopted laid the foundation for the policy since adhered to whereby the three-thousand-mile boundary between Canada and the United States has remained unfortified and practically without artificial defense of any kind.[2]

The refusal of governments to take seriously proposals for disarmament, or even the reduction or limitation of armaments, on a large scale may be ascribed largely to nineteenth century conceptions of politics and the relation of armaments to the realization of national ambitions and purposes. The existence of national armaments was a fundamental necessity in the balance of power conception. Although theoretically limitation of armaments by international agreement was not incompatible with the maintenance of a balance of power, actually the system of equilibrium as it was developed in the years before the War created an atmosphere favorable to the constant augmentation

[1] See, however, Olof Hoijer, *La Sécurité Internationale et ses Modes de Réalisation*, 4 vols. (Paris, 1930), Vol. IV, Ch. I, for extended discussion of efforts made for the reduction of armaments prior to the World War.

[2] See R. L. Buell, *International Relations*, pp. 554-557, for discussion of this and other agreements for the limitation of armaments before the World War.

rather than to the reduction of armaments. In fact, the emphasis placed upon the enhancement of national power and the relatively slight interest shown in official circles in the development of international law as the ultimate guarantee of national security, made the discussion of international agreements for the limitation of armaments largely academic. The possession of large armaments was frankly acknowledged as the *sine qua non* for the admission of a state to the rank of a Great Power. It was widely accepted not only that the peace and security of a nation depended upon its ability to defend itself by force of arms and that *si vis pacem para bellum* was axiomatic, but also that armament merely sufficient for the defense of a nation's territory was not enough. A school of military writers following the Prussian Clausewitz [3] looked upon armament as the instrument of diplomacy.[4] In substance, their thesis was as follows: The policy of a state is directed toward defending and advancing its interests. In so far as it can achieve these objectives by the less expensive processes of diplomacy, it keeps its armament in reserve. It is regarded as essential in the conduct of negotiations, however, that the other state or states should be aware that the nation has arms and that it will use them if diplomacy fails to procure respect for its just claims. In this way, arms add force to the argument of the possessor, sometimes preventing unjust attack, in other cases compelling concessions that would not otherwise be granted. A diplomat without armed force behind him, according to this theory, will find his efforts for peace, or his attempts to have the interests of his state recognized by others, doomed to failure, for as Frederick the Great put it, "negotiations without arms are like notes without instruments." If, however, a diplomat can rely upon armed force equal or superior to that of the other state or states concerned, he is in a good position to extort concessions, or if necessary use "the last argument" of diplomacy, war, to achieve the desired results. It is obvious that, viewed in this way, armaments are necessary final arguments; that without them a nation

[3] Carl von Clausewitz (1780-1831), who served in the Napoleonic Wars and rose to the rank of general, wrote a treatise on war that has had great influence in military circles throughout the world, and especially in Germany. His *Vom Kriege,* 3 vols. (Berlin, 1832-1834) was translated by J. J. Graham under the title *On War* (London, 1873; new ed., 1908). Vol. I has been translated by T. D. Pilcher as *War According to Clausewitz* (London, 1918).

[4] A. T. Mahan, *Armaments and Arbitration* (New York, 1912), p. 81. See also, for an exposition of the Clausewitz point of view, Major Stewart L. Murray, *The Reality of War* (London, 1914).

loses its case—perhaps its very existence; and that therefore to consent to disarm is to insure impotence in world affairs, and possibly lead to extinction.

The experience of the World War seemed to liberal thinkers, as well as avowed pacifists and internationalists, to demand a new attitude on the part of governments toward armaments. All of the Great Powers that were swept into war in August, 1914, were well armed, but that fact had certainly not been sufficient to keep them at peace. Their armaments had not insured them against war and had not afforded them security. Germany, the most thoroughly prepared of all on land, was not thereby insured against inglorious defeat. Moreover, although no Great Power escaped being drawn into the struggle, several minor states, insignificant from the point of view of armed force, were able to preserve their neutrality and avoid attack. Armaments, then, had not provided security, although they had put a severe strain on national treasuries. Moreover, it was asserted that they had helped to poison the atmosphere of foreign offices and had thereby contributed to the holocaust. The nations, therefore, must agree to give up the toy which had been proved both expensive and dangerous.

Although such views were probably not widely held by the governing class of any nation,[5] President Wilson, General Smuts, and others among the framers of the League of Nations Covenant were influenced by them and included the reduction of armaments as an essential part of their peace program. In fact, the system they proposed was designed to afford international guarantees of national security and a procedure for the impartial consideration and judgment of the claims of great and small states. There would, therefore, no longer be any *raison d'être* for national armaments except to provide for domestic safety and to contribute to the enforcement of international obligations. The peace settle-

[5] By 1932, however, two British statesmen definitely placed themselves on record as accepting this view. Arthur Henderson, President of the Disarmament Conference that began its labors in that year, said: ". . . the existence of armaments has been itself a grimly fertile source of the mutual fears and suspicions which poisoned international life, paralyzed the will to peace, and flung the nations time and again into feverish competition in armaments. Modern history provides incontestable and overwhelming proof of the fallacy of the idea that the safety of a nation is in proportion to its strength in armaments." Sir John Simon, Secretary of State for Foreign Affairs, also stated categorically at the same time: "The proposition that the peace of the world is to be secured by preparing for war is no longer believed by anybody, for recent history manifestly disproves it." (League of Nations, *Conference for the Reduction and Limitations of Armaments;* Verbatim Record (rev.), February, 1932, Conf. D./P.-V. 1 to 18(1).)

ment provided for the immediate disarmament of Germany and the other defeated states to a police force basis, but the victorious powers were not inclined to follow suit, at any rate until fully satisfied that their late enemies had become penitent and pacific. Nor were they prepared in any case to disarm to "the lowest point consistent with domestic safety."[6] However, in the provisions of the Treaty that laid down the restrictions on German armament, they stated that these were necessary "in order to render possible the initiation of a general limitation of the armament of all nations."[7] More important, however, were the definite obligations undertaken by them and all other members of the League under Articles VIII and IX of the Covenant.[8]

In the discussion since the War on the subject of disarmament, several different schools of opinion have been revealed. In the first place some writers are still disposed to reject the thesis that large armaments necessarily contribute to the outbreak of military conflicts, regarding them as unimportant one way or another or as helpful to peace and security. The questions of war and peace, it is contended by an eminent American authority on international law, have in the past depended, and will continue to depend, "not so much upon the size of military establishments as upon the cultivation of the spirit and habit of justice, of self-control, of reciprocal recognition of rights and of forbearance."[9] When the Napoleonic wars broke out, remarks another writer, armaments were at a low ebb. The Civil War, likewise, could not be attributed to large armaments. If conflicting national policies come into collision, war in some form will occur whether nations are armed for it or not.[10] On the other hand, a nation that is adequately armed is a force for peace and justice, for "offers of conciliation are more easily heard, sug-

[6] See number four of Wilson's Fourteen Points. Although it will be recalled that the Wilsonian Fourteen Point program had been accepted as the basis of the peace, the revolutionary proposal to disarm to a police force basis did not find support among the framers of the Covenant, and President Wilson apparently did not defend it. The proposal to substitute "national safety" for "domestic safety" in Article VIII of the Covenant came from the Japanese delegation. See Florence Wilson, *The Origins of the League Covenant; Documentary History of Its Drafting* (London, 1928), p. 45.

[7] Introduction to the Military, Naval and Air clauses of Part V of the Treaty of Versailles.

[8] See Covenant in the Appendix.

[9] John Bassett Moore, "Disarmament: Glib Phrase or Stern Necessity?," *Literary Digest*, CXVII (May 12, 1934), 38-39.

[10] Admiral Sir Herbert Richmond, *Economy and Naval Security* (London, 1931), pp. 11-12.

gestions for arbitration receive a readier response, and international agreements are more closely adhered to, if the ultimate sanction behind them is force, rather than dependence upon the belief that law is its own sanction, or that the moral force of international public opinion will restrain to the pathway of peace governments that are not of good will." [11] Those who hold these convictions are often doubtful also of the value of disarmament conferences as promoters of peace. Such conferences, it is claimed, often do more harm than good because they focus public attention on the conflicting interests of the members of the conference, bring out and stress points of disagreement, and lead to bitterness and often either to an unwilling acceptance of limitation or such an exacerbation of national passions that the growth of armaments is stimulated rather than halted. Where they are not actually mischievous in this sense, disarmament conferences are foolish and futile as far as achieving any substantial results, for it is not armaments that cause wars but conflicts of policy. Moreover, every failure of a disarmament conference breeds public cynicism and distrust of the possibilities of any international understanding.[12]

The most radical proposals concerning disarmament to come from official quarters since the World War, with one exception, approach the problem from the point of view of domestic policy rather than from that of international policy. In the pacifist movement of the nineteenth cen-

[11] Rear Admiral W. C. Cole, "The Web of Trade in the Pacific and the Resultant Naval Strategy," *Proceedings of the Institute of International Relations, Sixth Session,* August 8-15, 1930, at Berkeley, California, p. 94. See also Richmond, *op. cit.,* Preface; and Rear Admiral W. L. Rodgers, "War in the Scheme of National and International Life," *American Journal of International Law,* Vol. XXVIII (July, 1934), No. 3, pp. 555-559. This point of view which emphasizes the importance of national armed preparedness is naturally almost universal among military and naval writers. Hector C. Bywater, the naval expert, asserts in *Navies and Nations; A Review of Naval Developments Since the Great War* (London, 1927), p. 271, with respect to the effort since 1921 for the reduction of naval armaments: "Resistance comes almost entirely from the professional interests concerned, who by training and tradition are antipathetic to the whole principle of disarmament. Glancing back over the past five years it will be found that the campaign against the restriction of war fleets has been organized by naval officers and their civilian associates."

[12] This point of view is in substance expressed and elaborated in Frank Simonds' *Can Europe Keep the Peace?* (New York, 1931), pp. 251-259. It should be pointed out, however, that Simonds and John Bassett Moore (*loc. cit.,* pp. 38-39) are at bottom pessimistic about international conferences in general because they do not find nations disposed to abate "claims of national right and national interest." Ultimately, therefore, according to their position, the unyielding temper of nations rather than the conference method is at fault.

tury, world disarmament came to be one of the major objectives,[13] and occasionally proposals were made that one or another of the Great Powers should take the initiative and set an example to the others by reducing its own armament. Needless to say, such proposals found little or no support in governmental circles at any time. Not only security, but also prestige, caused statesmen to turn a deaf ear to them. To disarm would be tantamount to the voluntary relinquishment of the rank of Great Power. It was otherwise, however, with small states with no possibilities of or pretensions to "greatness." In Denmark, where the peace movement struck deep roots, it was urged by pacifists that a good testing-ground for practical disarmament, as well as unreserved arbitration, was available. Denmark, being self-contained, so it was argued, and politically free from the entanglements of the power groups, could safely disarm without waiting for other nations to do so. Unsuccessful prior to the World War, the agitation was renewed after its conclusion and has resulted since 1925 in proposals sponsored by the Social Democratic Party in the Danish Parliament for the unilateral reduction of Danish armed forces to the status of a police force capable of maintaining internal order and fulfilling international obligations under the Covenant of the League of Nations. On behalf of this drastic proposal, it is asserted that in case of a war between major Powers, Denmark in any event would be unable to muster sufficient military force to preserve her neutrality, and that to attempt to do so would sweep her into the war on one side or the other. A small state with three and a half million people, and with a coast line longer than that of France, it is argued, must frankly recognize her military impotence. If she disarms, she will gain the world's sympathy and assistance more surely than by putting up a merely fictitious defense.[14]

Although small states have not as a rule been conspicuous in their advocacy of national armaments as the means of security, and on the other hand have naturally looked with favor on proposals for the reduction of the forces of the heavily armed states, they have not, in

[13] *Supra,* Ch. XIV.

[14] Julius Moritzen, "Disarmament in Denmark," *The Nation* (New York), December 9, 1925, pp. 655-656. Peter Munch, "Danish Disarmament and Neutrals," *The Nation* (New York), March 9, 1932, pp. 294-295. It is interesting to observe that not only have the proposals been opposed by the conservatives and others in Denmark, but also that in Sweden, for example, apprehension is expressed in certain circles that Danish disarmament will lessen security in the Baltic and throw a greater burden on Sweden and other Baltic states.

official quarters at any rate, shown any disposition to follow the Danish proposals for complete unilateral disarmament. Prominent men in private life, however, have even urged this step on Great Powers. The scientist, Albert Einstein, for example, asserts that "under present-day conditions, any one state would incur no appreciable risk by undertaking to disarm —wholly regardless of the attitude of other states. If such were not the case it would be quite evident that the situation of such states as are unarmed or partially equipped for defense would be extremely difficult, dangerous, and disadvantageous—a condition which is refuted by the facts." He then expresses the conviction that "the voluntary self-disarmament of one great nation would mean a decisive step forward."[15] Another advocate of disarmament by example is Arthur Ponsonby of the British Labour Party. Apparently believing the attempt to accomplish disarmament through international agreement will continue to be fruitless, and convinced that as long as any armaments exist the likelihood of war will remain, he has proposed that Great Britain independently should "proceed to disarm on a basis regulated by economic considerations and the methods necessary for the gradual disestablishment of the fighting services." The achievement of disarmament, in his opinion, cannot be realized step by step, and by common consent, but only by complete renunciation on the part of some important nation.[16]

Not only have the suggestions just recorded not struck a responsive chord in official circles among the Great Powers, but sweeping proposals for disarmament by agreement have not elicited serious consideration. During the decade in which the question has been considered and explored under the auspices of the League, the discussions have centered about limitation or the maintenance of the *status quo* of armaments, and, at the most, a substantial proportionate reduction of existing armed establishments. Far more radical proposals, however, have been made by Soviet Russia. In 1927 M. Litvinov, Soviet Commissar for

[15] Albert Einstein, *The Fight against War,* ed. by Alfred Lief (New York, 1933), pp. 23, 25. Einstein also supports conscientious objectors to war, and further urges that, in the event of another war, people should absolutely refuse to bear arms or do war service of any kind. *Ibid.,* p. 26.

[16] Arthur Ponsonby, "Disarmament by Example," *Journal of the Royal Institute of International Affairs,* Vol. VII (July, 1928), No. 4, pp. 228, 232. Léon Blum, the French socialist, also expresses the conviction that if some Great Power immediately following the World War had completely disarmed without depending upon any agreement with others, it would not only have run no risk of attack but also would have been followed by all others. (*Peace and Disarmament* [London, 1932], p. 153.)

Foreign Affairs, presented to the Preparatory Commission for the Conference on Disarmament of the League of Nations a "plan for general and complete disarmament" to be put into effect by international agreement. It called for the "complete abolition of all armed forces on land, on the sea, and in the air." This principle was to be realized by the destruction of all means of combat and all war stores, the dismantling of all fortresses and naval and air bases, the prohibition of military instruction, the elimination of military budgets, and the abolition of war ministries and military staffs, as well as by other measures.[17]

The avowed reason for the drastic and revolutionary proposals of the Soviet Government is that nothing less than general and complete disarmament will insure peace and security for the peoples. The mere limitation of armaments is rejected, as Litvinov said, "if only because, far from representing a step forward along the path of disarmament, it does not even diminish either the possibility or the horrors of war." He pointed out that in 1914 "the general level of armaments throughout the world was, both as to quantity and quality, lower than it is now, and yet it allowed of the development of a world war with all the horrors which are still fresh in the memory of mankind. But these horrors pale before the picture of a new war which the present condition of war materials presents to our imagination." [18] Reduction of armaments, he declared, may be helpful if sufficiently drastic, but will not be enough to prevent war. Given the capitalistic system existing in most countries, no treaties, agreements, or international organizations will be able to create real security for all countries. That security can be realized only through total disarmament.[19]

The general thesis that security is to be attained by disarming has

[17] For proposals on disarmament by Soviet Russia from 1921 to 1933, see Eugene A. Korovine, "The U.S.S.R. and Disarmament," *International Conciliation* (Sept., 1933), No. 292; for texts of proposals of 1927 and Draft Convention of 1928, see *ibid.*, appendix, pp. 313-315.

[18] *Soviet Union Review,* Vol. X (May, 1932), No. 5, p. 106.

[19] *Ibid.*, Vol. X (March, 1932), No. 3, p. 51; *ibid.*, Vol. XI (March, 1933), p. 56, in which the view is reiterated that ". . . the best, if not the only, guarantee of security for all nations would be total disarmament." On May 29, 1934, Litvinoff at the General Commission of the Disarmament Conference expressed the belief that irreconcilable differences had made the disarmament problem insoluble, and said once more: "We believed and still believe that a genuine renunciation of war cannot be effective without a complete renunciation of armaments; that so long as armaments exist there can be no guarantee of peace; that only one kind of peace is possible—an unarmed peace—and that an armed peace is only an armistice, an interval between wars. . ." *Ibid.*, Vol. XII (July, 1934), p. 154.

been advanced outside Soviet Russia as well. Some writers, indeed, claim that armaments lead to wars and insecurity, and that therefore the way to reduce the chances of war is to reduce armament and the way to eliminate war is to abolish armament.[20] Léon Blum's diagnosis is similar: "Armaments are no longer determined and justified by the risk of war; it is the armaments which create the danger of war. Every nation that seeks security in armaments must inevitably aim at being at least as strong as her neighbors. The spirit of competition on the one hand, and the spirit of professional imitation on the other, invariably prompt a nation to go one better than her neighbor. She no longer seeks equality, but superiority. Now, every nation who is stronger than her neighbors will some day inevitably be tempted to display her strength." [21] On the other hand, if the world would completely wipe out national armaments a very different spirit would prevail, leading to the employment of conciliation and arbitration in the settlement of differences between nations. This will not come about, however, until the present social order which has always contained the "physical seeds of war" has been supplanted by socialism.[22]

In the post-war years, the approach of the United States to the questions of peace and security have likewise been by way of disarmament. There has been, in general, little official interest in, and encouragement of, efforts to foster peace and attain security through international organization, and specifically an unwillingness to join the League of Nations or adhere to the Permanent Court of International Justice, the most outstanding achievements of the world up to the present time in the field of international political and judicial organization.[23] Never-

[20] G. N. Robbins, *Security by Disarmament* (London, 1932), pp. 19-22.

[21] *Op. cit.*, p. 115.

[22] *Ibid.*, p. 202. This was also the Soviet position. At the Seventh Plenary Meeting of the Conference for the Reduction and Limitation of Armaments (February 11, 1932), Litvinoff declared: "The Soviet delegation knows that the triumph of Socialist principles, removing the causes giving rise to armed conflicts, is the only absolute guarantee of peace. So long, however, as these principles prevail only in 1/6 of the world, there is only one means of organizing security against war, and that is total and general disarmament." (League of Nations, *Conference for the Reduction and Limitation of Armaments; Verbatim Record* (rev.), February, 1932, Conf. D./P. V. 7, p. 9.)

[23] In 1934, however, the United States reversed its former policy and became a member of the International Labor Organization. It should be remarked, however, that the International Labor Organization, though a part of the League of Nations system in a broad sense, is not involved in League commitments as regards peaceful settlement, and that its recent support by the United States does not represent a fundamental change of policy on the part of the government of the United States.

theless the United States has shown energy and initiative in the post-war disarmament efforts. It called the Washington Conference for the Limitation of Armaments in 1921, has been active in seeking further progress in the limitation and reduction of naval armaments, and has for a number of years cooperated in the movement under League auspices for a general reduction of all classes of armament. Along with most of the other Powers, however, it rejected the Soviet proposal for immediate and complete disarmament. On the occasion of the Russian proposal, Mr. Hugh Gibson, representing the United States, explained that armaments could be reduced only to the extent that the will to peace and confidence in peaceful methods of settling disputes was built up, and that the American government had never believed "that the suppression of armaments would alone and by itself have the effect of creating that confidence which is essential to the successful conclusion of our task." [24]

The foregoing viewpoints, however, including that of the United States even as qualified by Mr. Gibson, show a strong tendency to regard disarmament as an isolated and technical problem to be solved readily by men of good will and good sense.[25] Moreover, its solution will *ipso facto* solve the problem of security and provide the necessary guarantee of world peace. Although Blum's simple definition of security as "suppression of the material means of war" and "the suppression of all fears and apprehensions regarding the possibility of war" [26] would perhaps not be accepted without qualification by all who

[24] Quotation from Benjamin Williams, *The United States and Disarmament* (New York, 1931), p. 262. Succeeding conferences of the Inter-Parliamentary Union in 1925 and 1927 also went on record for a general reduction of armaments as one of the most important means of affording security to nations. (William Martin, *Disarmament and the Inter-Parliamentary Union* [Lausanne, 1931], p. 41.) See also proceedings of the Twenty-ninth Interparliamentary Conference held at Madrid, October 4-10, 1933, in which the preceding stand of the Interparliamentary Union was reaffirmed. Official spokesmen of Great Britain and Italy have taken a similar position.

[25] Frank Simonds remarks that Great Britain and the United States "view the question of disarmament as a single matter of economics and ethics." (*Op. cit.*, p. 286.) It is to be observed, however, that the United States has tended to regard disarmament as dependent upon and to be preceded by the organization of political security in the Far East where vital American interests are considered at stake. Since the almost universal acceptance by the nations of the Briand-Kellogg Pact for the renunciation of war, the United States has taken the position that the world has renounced war, except that waged in self-defense, and has agreed to seek the settlement of all disputes by pacific means; and that this obliges nations to scale down their armaments to a strictly defensive basis.

[26] *Op. cit.*, p. 151.

might be classed in this school, it accurately describes their general position. The simplicity of the approach has appealed to many who feel that the attempt to solve the problem of security by the indirect method of world organization inevitably leads to complexities and controversies that are practically insoluble. Many have pointed out that the attempts to attain security by means of guaranty treaties and other legal instruments such as the Locarno Pact, the Briand-Kellogg Pact, and the General Act of 1928 [27] for pacific settlement have so far failed, and that instead of armaments being reduced the competition in armaments has become more intense.[28] It is necessary, therefore, to get at the root of the evil. The political uneasiness existing in spite of all the pacts that have been signed "is generated chiefly by the mutual fear and distrust arising out of armaments" and the "first step to restore confidence should be taken in the direction of a general reduction of armament." [29]

A somewhat different position, but still one emphasizing the importance of dealing directly with the disarmament problem, was expressed by Baron Ramel of Sweden at the Seventh Plenary meeting of the Disarmament Conference,[30] and by M. Beelaeres van Blokland, delegate of the Netherlands at the Tenth Plenary Meeting. Asserting that the Covenant of the League of Nations and the various treaties such as those mentioned by M. Grandi as well as others, although not completely effective,[31] had strengthened the security of nations and that the general system of guarantees would grow, they voiced the opinion that the time had come to increase security by a reduction of armaments. The reduction of armaments is thus not regarded as the condition precedent to, or the single effective means of, attaining security, but it is looked upon as contributing to security, and, indeed, as an essential element in its fuller realization.

[27] See Appendix.

[28] This was the view advanced by M. Grandi of Italy at the Sixth Plenary Meeting of the Disarmament Conference in 1932. (League of Nations, *Conference for the Reduction and Limitation of Armaments; Verbatim Record* (rev.), 1932. Conf. D./P. V. 6, p. 2.) He also took the position that "there can be no security without disarmament."

[29] Address of Dino Grandi before the Foreign Policy Association in New York City, November 26, 1931.

[30] League of Nations, *loc. cit.*, Conf. D./P. V. 7(1), p. 9.

[31] The delegate of the Netherlands admitted that the guarantees of the League of Nations were not adequate in the Manchurian controversy of 1931, but pointed out that the League had succeeded in a number of cases. (League of Nations, *loc. cit.*, Conf. D./P. V. 10(1).)

Many who have been in close touch with the post-war movement for disarmament, however, have no faith in the efficacy of the direct approach and insist that disarmament and world peace alike are dependent upon the development and universal acceptance of international organization. Those adhering to this school regard themselves as realists and look upon those who contend that disarmament is the only road or the main road to security and peace, as misguided idealists who have failed to analyze the problem. There are points of similarity, indeed, between the position of these latter-day realists and that of Clausewitz and the other military and civilian writers of his school. They insist, for example, that wars arise out of conflicting national policies; that armaments do not cause wars, but that wars cause armaments. They do not, however, follow the older school in the assumption that war is in any event inevitable and that therefore competitive armaments are necessarily a luxury with which the world can never dispense. They think that armaments and war can and should be dispensed with, but they point out that they are not seeking a static peace, and that such an ideal is in any case unattainable. The Spaniard Salvador de Madariaga, in a penetrating discussion of the disarmament problem,[32] states the conditions that make a constant conflict of national policies inevitable in terms as frank as those of any blood-and-iron historian: "At any given time the world presents a certain net-work of facts recognized as law. Frontiers are defined, obligations and rights laid down, zones of influence recognized, debts acknowledged, limitations of sovereignty accepted, occupations of territory admitted, in fine, a system is established which constitutes, so to say, a zero of history, a starting-point, not for history which has none, but for our own thoughts. Then, life flows on and every day something happens, some change takes place which gradually makes the world of facts and forces move away from the world of law. This nation grows weaker; that nation stronger; this territory, once uninhabited, grows to be an important center of population; new national feelings appear where careless and self-ignorant masses were once herded together by a foreign power; the nation yesterday subjected grows stronger than its subjector; economic and financial currents are reversed. Between the static

[32] *Disarmament* (London, 1929). Señor de Madariaga, Professor of Spanish Studies at Oxford, has held a number of important diplomatic posts, and was for several years director of the Disarmament Section of the Secretariat of the League of Nations.

set of laws and the dynamic set of forces there appears thus a set of conflicts. At every point in the world disruptive forces begin to act. This may be said to be the normal state of the world as a whole."[33]

But Madariaga and those of his school do not draw the conclusions from this analysis that war is inevitable, whether one holds it baleful or beneficent, and that therefore disarmament conferences are ill-advised and futile. They are not satisfied with the way the *inevitable conflicts* are resolved. The militarily strong resolve them in the time-honored fashion of threats, intimidations, war; the weak bide their time, discontents spread, and wide-spread conflagrations sooner or later result. These, they say, are the fruits of *laissez-faire* in the field of international politics, and if a different kind of crop is desired, a new conception and a new method must be substituted for the traditional ones. In place of the isolated, partial, and haphazard solutions of conflicts of interests by individual nations on the basis of self-help, they insist that these conflicts must be considered *as a whole* and settled by the international community on the basis of a universally accepted procedure, and a universally accepted system of rights and obligations to be enforced by and on behalf of that community.

As things are now, according to Madariaga, there is a permanent world war. It is carried on normally by the ministers for foreign affairs whose successes in their contests with one another are dependent upon the strength of the fighting forces they have at their backs. When diplomacy fails, the war with arms begins. Thus armaments have been, and are today, instruments of policy, and "no disarmament is possible as long as no alternative instrument of policy is devised . . . and no reduction of armaments is possible as long as the utility of armaments as instruments of policy has not been reduced."[34] This can be accomplished only by the replacing of national rivalries by international co-operation. This, in turn, requires "a well-organized World Community."[35] Until the situation is faced and the alternative provided,

[33] *Disarmament*, pp. 37-38.

[34] *Ibid.*, p. 51. Soviet Russia, he asserts, was the first Great Power to propose complete disarmament because she was the first nation to evolve an alternative instrument of policy—proletarian revolutions throughout the world. The spreading of communist revolution, her only foreign policy, does not require Russian armaments and will succeed better if other nations disarm. (*Ibid.*, pp. 51, 52.)

[35] Madariaga's general position was anticipated prior to the Great War. See especially the position of C. van Vollenhoven, professor of law in the University of Leyden, in a paper on the Limitation of Armaments read before the Dutch

Madariaga contends that international conferences for disarmament are premature. In reality, they inevitably become armament conferences in which every delegation seeks a relative increase of armed strength, and disarmament proposals from any quarter are anxiously and suspiciously scrutinized in the fear that they will impair one's relative position, and therefore make it vulnerable in the war which all assume will come some day.[36]

The "organized World-Community" envisaged by Madariaga as the solution of the problem of disarmament already possesses its character in the Covenant of the League of Nations. This aims to prohibit war regardless of causes; to establish a system for the examination and peaceful solution of international controversies, on the one hand; and for "foreseeing conflicts by taking over as many of the national activities of the world on an international basis as is possible." The carrying out of the purposes of the framers of the Covenant by the simultaneous application of these three methods is the only road to disarmament.[37]

Most writers of this school, however, take the position that the Covenant needs to be not only faithfully applied, but also strengthened or supplemented by a multilateral agreement, including all important states, in which all international controversies will be subject to international jurisdiction and settlement, and a system of specific and automatic guarantees for the enforcement of international obligations accepted. In their view, the Covenant needs to be further implemented along the lines of the defunct "Protocol of Geneva,"[38] the object of which was "to facilitate the reduction and limitation of armaments . . . by guaranteeing the security of States through the development of methods for the pacific settlement of all international disputes and the effective condemnation of aggressive war."[39] The trilogy—arbitration,

Institute of Naval Officers in April, 1913. The text may be found in *War Obviated by an International Police* (The Hague, 1915), pp. 47-59.

[36] Madariaga, *op. cit.*, also Olof Hoijer, *op. cit.*, IV, 208, 216-217.

[37] Madariaga, "Disarmament: The Rôle of the Anglo-Saxon Nations," *Problems of Peace, Third Series* (London, 1928), p. 67. Lectures delivered at the Geneva Institute of International Relations, August, 1928.

[38] Although the Protocol for the Pacific Settlement of International Disputes, as it was officially named, was unanimously recommended to the members of the League of Nations by the 1924 Assembly, its ratification was finally defeated as a result of the withdrawal of British support after the defeat of Ramsay MacDonald, one of its sponsors, and the Labour Party by the Conservatives in 1924. See Appendix.

[39] See statement of the authors, Beneš of Czechoslovakia and Politis of Greece,

security, and disarmament—represents the formula of this school for the realization of the aspirations of the framers of the Covenant and of all those who seek a new and better world order. Under the Protocol, war except in self-defense was to be renounced; more precise obligations of pacific settlement, including compulsory arbitration, were assumed; and the "fissures" in the Covenant thereby closed. Finally, a system of physical sanctions was provided, binding all of the contracting states to cooperate against a state, found by the Council of the League of Nations to be an aggressor, "in the degree which its geographical position and its particular situation as regards armaments allow."

The failure of the Geneva Protocol meant the failure of the attempt to solve the problem of armaments, since many European continental states, as well as many disinterested individuals in all countries, have adhered to the position that a thoroughgoing system of peaceful settlement and a system of collective guarantees to provide the necessary security must precede or at least be a part of any general convention.[40] Moreover, alarmed by the rise of the Nazis in Germany and the militant attitude of the National Socialist government in Germany since 1933, France and certain other states have insisted that even though the necessary minimum of guarantees is agreed upon, disarmament must be arrived at by successive stages over a period of years. At each stage, "the reduction of armament must be proportionate to the degree of security. In the measure that mutual confidence and progress in international organization develop there will be an increase of security, and it will be possible to realize a greater reduction and thus to make a farther step toward total disarmament."[41]

in League of Nations, *Official Journal, Special Supplement,* No. 26 (1924), Records of the Fifth Assembly, Minutes of Third Committee, Annex. 13, p. 197.

[40] Hans Kelsen insists that League members, at least, must accept compulsory adjudication without any limitation; and obligations not to resort to war among themselves under any circumstances before the League can be armed for collective defense. When these conditions are fulfilled it should be given a monopoly of armaments, and this will be readily accepted, for national armaments will have lost their purpose. See English translation, issued by the Foreign Policy Association, of his article, "Disarmament and the Structure of International Law," which originally appeared in *Der Deutsche Volkswirt,* April 1, 1933.

[41] Nicholas S. Politis, "The Problem of Disarmament," *International Conciliation* (March, 1934), No. 298, p. 60. It is obvious that even general conceptions and principles of disarmament (a present-day political issue of vast importance) such as have been mentioned in this chapter are likely to be influenced, and perhaps conditioned, by the preoccupation of those holding them with the needs and in-

The post-war effort to solve the disarmament problem has inevitably revived the question of sanctions. Those who insist that international organization must be further perfected and that all civilized states must assume obligations in an international system of security before disarmament can be realized, maintain that a collective system of sanctions is necessary. They admit that some states will not be able, and should not be expected, to make a substantial military contribution to the enforcement of international agreements, but they insist that these states must agree to make such contribution as their special position and circumstances will allow to the common effort to restrain or coerce a state that breaks the law of the international community.[42] They claim that the pre-war notion of neutrality, which recognized the right of a nation to stand aside whenever it did not want to become involved in hostilities between belligerents, is inconsistent with an effective system for safeguarding the rights and interests of the international community and must be abandoned. Neutrality is an obsolete conception and must give way before the facts of the twentieth century and the imperative need of world solidarity against disturbers of the world's peace.[43]

terests of their several states. This is the more likely to be true when they are advanced by the official spokesmen of interested governments. For example, the tendency of official American spokesmen to stress the importance of the direct approach to disarmament, and their tendency to shy away from commitments to participate in international guarantees, is undoubtedly influenced by the traditional policy of isolation and the feeling that our best interests will be served by continuing to keep free from European entanglements. The British approach, which is similar but not as rigid, doubtless is conditioned by the location of the British Isles with respect to the Continent which in the past has enabled them to pursue a policy of "splendid isolation" varied by occasional intervention to preserve the balance of power on the continent; by a reluctance to adopt a policy which would not command the support of the Dominions, and which might lead to strained relations with the United States in connection with the imposition of sanctions. On the other hand, France and the other Continental victors in the World War feel more keenly the need for a pledged security on account of their geographical location in relation to the defeated and dissatisfied powers, as the only safe alternative to a dependence on their own armed strength. Finally, perhaps something must be attributed to the traditional preference of the Anglo-Saxons for the partial and pragmatic approach to political questions, and the French to seek logical solutions involving a symmetrical and complete plan of international organization. The position of the statesmen of other Powers can likewise be accounted for in part by similar geographic, historical, and political reasons.

[42] To the argument, advanced by the outlawry-of-war school (cf. Ch. XVI), that nations must rely ultimately on good faith as the sanction for international obligations, Madariaga replies that breaches of faith are not the only nor perhaps the main danger. Collective sanctions must be ready in order to cool national passions which often lead nations to an ill-considered course. (*Op. cit.*, p. 230.)

[43] C. Howard-Ellis, *The Origin, Structure, and Working of the League of Na-*

As regards the nature and method of organization of sanctions, there is a tendency among those who advocate strengthening and working through the League of Nations to agree that so-called "aggressive" weapons should either be abolished or, preferably, made a monopoly of the League of Nations so that it may have armament at its disposal at all times superior to that which may be left to the individual states as a result of the decisions of the World Disarmament Conference.[44] Convinced that as a practical matter force cannot be dispensed with, they regard the real problem as one of determining how force is to be used. Is it to be used, as in the past by, and at the discretion of, individual national states in the pursuit of selfish national interests, or is it to be used by an international authority to serve the interests and conserve the welfare of all? One writer contends that for the first time in the world's history it is possible for the international community to organize force on its own behalf if it will: "The application of science to the art of war," he reminds us, "has revolutionized the mechanism of war. No Great Power can in future wage a successful war unless it is equipped with the most up-to-date and modern weapons which the scientific discoveries and inventions of the nineteenth century have placed at its disposal. But, by applying the principle of differentiation of weapons to the national armouries and handing over the new weapons to the control of an international authority, the scientific achievements in the military sphere may be utilized to the advantage of mankind. They can be transformed into the custodian of peace."[45]

tions, pp. 326-327; C. G. Fenwick, "Neutrality and International Organization," *American Journal of International Law,* Vol. XXVIII (1934); Clyde Eagleton, *International Government* (New York, 1932), Ch. XIX; P. C. Jessup, "American Neutrality and International Police," *World Peace Foundation Pamphlets,* Vol. XI (1928), No. 3; Fenwick, *International Law* (2nd ed., New York, 1934), p. 173.

[44] The representatives of the United States contended at the Disarmament Conference, which was called by the League of Nations in 1932, that the more powerful weapons which modern science has evolved should be abolished in order to deprive aggressive nations of the physical means of successfully attacking their neighbors. With the power of defense thus restored, nations would feel and would be more secure. This, however, is quite different from the proposal to hand such weapons over to the League to be used in connection with the establishment of a system of collective sanctions. Officially, the United States seems not to be ready to support this more positive position.

[45] David Davies, "An International Police Force?" *Journal of the Royal Institute of International Affairs,* Vol. XI (Jan., 1932), No. 1, p. 83. See also by the same author, *The Problem of the Twentieth Century* (London, 1930), for an eight-hundred-page discussion of the question of sanctions. The proposal of Davies, as outlined above, is the heart of the proposal of the French government of Tardieu to the World Disarmament Conference in 1932. For similar viewpoints see, Madariaga, *op. cit.,* p. 294; and Oscar T. Crosby, "An International Justice of the Peace and his Constable," *Advocate of Peace,* Vol. XCIII (May, 1931), No. 2, p.

The proposals of the representatives of this school taken in their entirety would undoubtedly go far toward transforming the League of Nations into a super-state, as has been pointed out by certain critics [46] and freely admitted by some of their advocates.[47] The framers of the Covenant, as has been seen,[48] did not believe in the desirability or at any rate the possibility of setting up a superstate. They did not regard it as practicable to close the door absolutely to self-decision and self-help on the part of individual nations in all cases, although they attempted to provide various procedures suitable for the peaceful adjustment of all international controversies, and to encourage members of the League to employ them. They believed, doubtless, that time and experience would result in the further perfection of the processes they outlined, and that the habit of utilizing these processes would grow. The unsuccessful efforts toward disarmament have, to many of their successors such as Madariaga, Politis, Beneš, and others, emphasized the necessity of taking additional steps to improve international organization and insure international responsibility, even though this may mean the endowment of the League with powers the framers did not contemplate.

REFERENCES

The problems of disarmament have been discussed exhaustively by the Preparatory Commission for the Disarmament Conference, and in the Conference itself, which had its first sessions in Geneva in 1932. The *Minutes* of the meeting of the Preparatory Commission and the *Journal* of the Conference have been published by the League of Nations and furnish a complete record for the student interested in the theories voiced as well as the technical problems encountered.

Baker, P. J. N., *Disarmament* (London, 1926).

Barnes, G. N., "Security, Disarmament, and America," *Contemporary Review,* Vol. CXXXIII (March, 1928), No. 747, pp. 289-293.

Blum, L., *Peace and Disarmament* (London, 1932).

118; and Wm. McDougall, *Ethics and Some Modern World Problems* (New York, 1924), pp. 215-243. McDougall, however, though contending that the only way to bring about disarmament is to internationalize all air forces, commercial as well as military, did not propose that the "International Authority" which should be given a monopoly of air power should be the League of Nations. It would be set up by agreement of the Great Powers.

[46] See, for example, remarks of Sir Thomas Wilford of New Zealand concerning the French proposals at the Eleventh Plenary Meeting of the Disarmament Conference on February 16, 1932 (League of Nations, *loc. cit.,* Conf. D./P. V. 11(1), p. 11.)

[47] For example, Hans Kelsen, *loc. cit.* Madariaga is likewise not disturbed at the implications of his proposals.

[48] *Supra.,* Ch. XV.

Bywater, H., *Navies and Nations; a Review of Naval Developments since the Great War* (London, 1927).

Cecil, Lord Robert, "Facing the World Disarmament Conference," *Foreign Affairs,* Vol. X (Oct., 1931), No. 1, pp. 13-22.

Charques, R. D., *The Soviets and the Next War; The Present Case for Disarmament* (London, 1932).

Clausewitz, Carl von, *Vom Kriege,* 3 vols. (Berlin, 1832-1834). Translated by J. J. Graham as *On War* (London, 1873).

Cushendun, Lord, "Disarmament," *Journal of the Royal Institute of International Affairs,* Vol. VII (March, 1928), No. 2, pp. 77-93.

Degouy, A., "Le Désarmement du Danemark," *Revue des Deux Mondes,* XXXII (March 1, 1926), 91-105.

Dickinson, Lord J., "The Problem of Disarmament," *Nineteenth Century,* CXII (Sept., 1932), 272-278.

"Disarmament" articles by Viscount Cecil of Chetwood and Norman H. Davis and Texts of Official Documents, *International Conciliation* (Dec., 1932), No. 285, pp. 461-526.

Dulles, A. W., "The Disarmament Puzzle," *Foreign Affairs,* Vol. IX (July, 1931), No. 4, pp. 605-616.

———, "Some Misconceptions about Disarmament," *Foreign Affairs,* Vol. V (April, 1927), No. 3, pp. 413-426.

Engely, G., *The Politics of Naval Disarmament* (London, 1932).

Gerould, J. T., "Disarmament and Treaty Revision," *Current History,* XXXVII (May, 1933), 197-200.

Hoijer, O., *La Sécurité Internationale et ses Modes de Réalisation,* 4 vols. (Paris, 1930).

Jouhaux, L., *Le Désarmement* (Paris, 1927).

Kelsen, H., "Disarmament and the Structure of International Law," translated from the original in *Der Deutsche Volkswirt* (April 1, 1933), and issued by the Foreign Policy Association.

Kenworthy, J. M., and Young, G., *Freedom of the Seas* (London, 1928).

Korovine, E. A., "The U.S.S.R. and Disarmament," *International Conciliation* (Sept., 1933), No. 292, pp. 293-309.

Lavallaz, M. de, *Essai sur le Désarmement et le Pacte de la Société des Nations* (Paris, 1926).

Lefebure, V., *Scientific Disarmament* (New York, 1931).

Lyon, J., *Les Problèmes du Désarmement* (Paris, 1931).

McDougall, W., *Ethics and Some Modern World Problems* (New York, 1924), Appendix, pp. 215-243, for disarmament plan.

Madariaga, S. de, "Disarmament—American Plan," *Atlantic Monthly,* CXLIII (April, 1929), 525-538.

Mahan, A. T., *Armaments and Arbitration* (New York and London, 1912).

Martin, W., *Disarmament and the Inter-Parliamentary Union* (Lausanne, 1931).

Moore, J. B., "Disarmament: Glib Phrase or Stern Necessity?" *Literary Digest,* CXVII (May 12, 1934), 38-39.

Myers, D. P., *World Disarmament, Its Problems and Prospects* (Boston, 1932).

Politis, N. S., "The Problem of Disarmament," *International Conciliation* (March, 1934), No. 298, pp. 59-82.

Ponsonby, A., "Disarmament by Example," *Journal Royal Institute of International Affairs,* Vol. VII (July, 1928), No. 4, pp. 225-240.

Richmond, Sir Herbert, Admiral, *Economy and Naval Security* (London, 1931).

Robbins, G. N., *Security by Disarmament* (London, 1932).

Rodgers, W. L., "War in the Scheme of National and International Life," *American Journal of International Law,* Vol. XXVIII (July, 1934), No. 3, pp. 555-559.

Scialoja, V., "Obstacles to Disarmament," *Foreign Affairs,* Vol. X (January, 1932), No. 2, pp. 212-219.

Shotwell, J. T., "Disarmament Alone no Guarantee of World Peace," *Current History,* Vol. XXX (Sept., 1929), No. 6, pp. 1024-1029.

Spender, H. F., "Security and Disarmament: Cross Currents at Geneva," *Fortnightly Review,* CXXII n. s. (Nov., 1927), 600-609.

Steed, H. W., "Le Désarmement, Est-Il Possible?," *L'Esprit International,* Vol. V (July, 1931), No. 19, pp. 397-413.

Tabacovici, G. G., *Sécurité et Désarmement* (Paris, 1932).

Warner, E. P., "Aerial Armament and Disarmament," *Foreign Affairs,* Vol. IV (July, 1926), No. 4, pp. 624-636.

Wehberg, H., *Die Internationale Beschränkung der Rüstungen* (Stuttgart and Berlin, 1919).

Wheeler-Bennett, J. W., *Disarmament and Security Since Locarno, 1925-1931* (London, 1932).

——————, *Documents on International Affairs, 1933* (London, 1934), pp. 139-384 for documents on disarmament and security.

Williams, B. H., *The United States and Disarmament* (New York, 1931), Chs. I-IV, VII, XIV-XVII.

Wilson, F., *The Origins of the League Covenant; Documentary History of Its Drafting* (London, 1928), pp. 44-48 ff.

Zimmern, A., "Disarmament: the Decisive Phase," *Fortnightly Review,* CXXXVIII (Dec., 1932), 681-691.

CHAPTER XX

CONTINENTALISM AND REGIONALISM

IT WILL be recalled that the architects of the Covenant drew up the blue-prints of a world system. Implicit throughout this document is the fundamental assumption that the time has arrived for the political and judicial organization of the entire world on the basis of the continued existence of national states as sovereign entities, voluntarily taking membership and assuming obligations in a universal association. No lesser international organization by regions or continents was regarded as capable of meeting the needs of the Great Society of the twentieth century. The Council, the Assembly, the Secretariat, the International Labor Organization, and, when organized, the Permanent Court of International Justice, were intended to function on behalf of all of the states comprising the World Community rather than with reference to particular regions or continents. To be sure, the fact that the World War had been fought out in Europe and that it had left a legacy of new European problems meant that in the nature of things the League would have to be largely preoccupied for an indeterminate period with peculiarly European problems. Nevertheless, the war, though precipitated in Europe and working the greatest havoc on that continent, had swept in all of the principal states of the western hemisphere and the Far East, and had had far-reaching consequences for the states of every continent. As such, it was a world war, and if a similar catastrophe was to be avoided in the future and the fruits of interdependence were not to be bitter, the entire world must be organized and mobilized against it. This was the generally accepted theory upon which the League system was founded.

The quest for security, however, and the necessity of taking account of certain political realities required some concessions to the idea of regionalism. Even so, the priority of the principle of universalism over that of sectionalism was maintained.[1] National states and "fully

[1] Universalism, however, made little headway against the dogma of national

self-governing" dominions and colonies only were recognized for separate membership in the League and as entitled to represent their respective peoples. In theory, except as they might individually be entrusted with the administration of mandated territories, or collectively clothed in conformity with the Covenant with authority for the execution of international obligations, they had no legal standing outside their own territories. If the peace of the world, for example, should be threatened by anyone anywhere, the principle of League intervention on behalf of the interests of the international community was clearly laid down in the Covenant. On the other hand, a concession to an insistent demand by American spokesmen for the recognition of the Monroe Doctrine, and thereby the principle of regionalism, is to be found in Article XXI of the Covenant, which specifically accepts the validity of "international engagements" and "regional understandings like the Monroe Doctrine, for securing the maintenance of peace." [2] The French representative on the League of Nations Commission was opposed to the inclusion of a reservation of the Monroe Doctrine because France envisaged a universal system of guarantees, and it was feared that perhaps in some future crisis requiring the solidarity of all League members and involving collective intervention in Europe, the United States might interpret the Monroe Doctrine as forbidding her to participate.[3] After much discussion and President Wilson's assurance that the proposed article would not relieve the United States from playing its full part in the League system, the French reluctantly gave way.[4]

Regionalism, whether expressing itself in the movement of Pan-

sovereignty, and, as has been seen, the framers of the Covenant were careful to safeguard the latter as far as possible.

[2] This article apparently opens the door to the assertion of a policy of paramountcy by any member of the League in a region in which it feels it has special interests, as long as the "maintenance of peace" is the professed object. Although it refers to the Monroe Doctrine as a "regional understanding," the United States has always maintained that it is a policy which the American government reserves the right unilaterally to define, interpret, and enforce.

[3] It will be recalled that President Monroe's message included this statement: "In the wars of the European powers in matters relating to themselves we have never taken any part, nor does it comport with our policy so to do. It is only when our rights are invaded or seriously menaced that we resent injuries or make preparations for our defense." If "our rights" only were to be supported by the United States, the Covenant would lose much of its meaning. President Wilson, however, assured the French that if the territorial integrity of any European state were threatened, the United States would have a solemn obligation as a member of the League to render aid. Miller, *Drafting of the Covenant,* II, 372.

[4] *Supra,* p. 342, for discussion of President Wilson's position.

Americanism or for a Pan Europa or Pan Asia in which vast continental areas are included, or in national policies, agreements, or understandings involving less inclusive regions,[5] is perhaps usually motivated primarily by considerations of national security from external enemies. It is also, however, nearly always based on the desire to exploit more fully the political, economic, and social possibilities presented by the physical propinquity of organized peoples living within a particular area, and having as a consequence varied and frequent contacts. The Pan American movement, for example, was based on the assumption that the peoples of the western hemisphere, by virtue of their physical separation from Europe as well as their common revolutionary origin and the similarity of their formal political institutions, had a solid foundation upon which to build up mutually beneficial interests of an exclusive nature and a certain cultural and political[6] solidarity.

In the western hemisphere, the idea of the regional organization of the world has been put forth most completely and assiduously by the Chilean jurist and diplomat, Alejandro Alvarez. As early as 1910 he developed the thesis of a separate American international law,[7] and during the World War he began to expound his ideas with reference to the international organization of the world along regional lines, a task he has continued indefatigably to carry on.[8] In the earlier work he denied that all of the principles of international law developed in Western Europe were of universal validity. Multilateral conventions obtaining the adhesions of all states, he admitted to the first rank of rules having a juridical and universal character[9]; and rules derived from usages representing a general consensus among the nations over a considerable period of time were to be regarded as having a more or less juridical character. Usages in process of being established, pursuant to

[5] Existing or proposed groupings such as the Little Entente, the Balkans, the Baltic States, the Danubian Confederation, are examples in point.

[6] It has not comported with the policy of the United States, however, to allow the Pan American Union to develop into an American League of Nations, and the American government has discouraged such suggestions when they have been made in Latin American quarters, doubtless because such a development would restrict the freedom of action of the United States.

[7] *Le Droit International Américain* (Paris, 1910).

[8] See especially, "La Réforme du Pacte de la Société des Nations sur des Bases Continentales et Régionales; Rapport Presenté à la Ve Session de l'Union Juridique Internationale, Juin 1926," in *Séances et Travaux de l'Union Juridique Internationale, Fifth Session* (Paris, 1926); and *L'Organisation Internationale, Précédents de la Société des Nations et de l'Union Fédérale Européenne* (Paris, 1931).

[9] *Le Droit International Américain*, p. 11.

the needs of modern international life, upon which a consensus is commencing to be manifested, he also considered to have more or less the force of law to the extent that they are, for example, crystallized into conventions or are taken account of in decisions of arbitration tribunals. And finally, conventions of a very general, though not universal, character must be recognized as having considerable moral force for all the members of the international community.[10] But rules derived from a European consensus were not necessarily to be regarded as applicable, in the opinion of Alvarez, to the entire civilized world. More particularly the states of the New World, although of European origin and civilization, were born under new conditions and with an outlook different from that of Europe; and from the beginning they had rejected in their constitutions certain principles of European public law and had sought to apply new ones. Moreover, as members of this new community, they faced problems of international law of a distinctly American character, and had developed distinctively American doctrines and practices.[11]

Alvarez found the basis for an American international law and a distinctively American political system in the Monroe Doctrine.[12] In the first place, it proclaimed that between all of the states of the New World was a bond of continental solidarity in the common determination to maintain their political independence of Europe. This was essential to the realization of a new and better political system. The governments of Europe were monarchical and absolutist; the New World sought to establish and maintain republican and democratic political institutions. The Old World adhered to the system of the balance of power and political intervention. The New World desired to follow different paths and therefore could not tolerate the transplantation of that system to the American continent. Nor could it, according to the Monroe Doctrine, tolerate further colonization in the New World on the basis of occupation, although vast parts of the American hemisphere remained unoccupied and unexplored at the time the Doctrine was announced. This particular declaration, Alvarez pointed out, was contrary to the principles of international law according to which territory not under the effective sovereignty of any state must be regarded as *res*

[10] *Ibid.*, p. 12.
[11] *Ibid.*, pp. 18-19.
[12] *Ibid.*, p. 139.

nullius and consequently susceptible of acquisition by occupation. It constituted, then, an announcement of a principle distinctly American, subscribed to by all of the independent nations of the New World.[13]

The conception of an American international law, regional in origin although possibly of universal application, was given an official sanction as early as 1908 in a resolution adopted by the First Pan American Scientific Congress, which declared: "There are on this continent problems which are *sui generis* and of clearly American character; the States of this hemisphere have regulated, by means of more or less general agreements, matters which interest these States only, or which, if of universal interest, have not been found susceptible of world agreement, thus incorporating principles of American origin in international law. These topics taken together constitute what may be called 'American situations and problems in international law.'"[14] Out of these conceptions there grew, after the World War, a movement for the codification of an American international law. Certain proponents of this movement have taken care to state that their initiative is not designed to "derogate from the authority of the universal law, but to set forth in addition to the old law principles and rules which are found to relate to the special exigencies of the American Republics."[15] From their viewpoint, also, although a world-wide conference for the purpose is theoretically desirable and of the greatest use, regional conferences may also be of the highest service. As stated by Chief Justice Hughes of the United States: "Limited conferences may be not only of great value and necessary to the powers concerned, but through their success in dealing with special problems may confer general benefits upon the world."[16] As illustrative of his contention, Justice Hughes stated that such success as the Washington Conference for the Limitations of Armaments had was "due to the fact that it was limited as to participants and objects." Likewise he declared that Far Eastern questions

[13] *Le Droit International Américain,* pp. 133-142. Alvarez carried the argument much further than can be attempted even in summary form. Due appreciation of his position can be had only by careful reading of the entire book.

[14] Quotations taken from an address delivered at meeting of the American Society of International Law in Washington, April 23, 1925, by J. B. Scott, on "The Codification of International Law in America."

[15] See address of Charles Evans Hughes before the American Society of International Law in Washington, April 23, 1925. A similar point of view was expressed on the same occasion by James Brown Scott, President of the American Institute of International Law.

[16] *Loc. cit.*

could not have been dealt with as satisfactorily, had powers with no direct interest in such questions been invited to participate, and that "our Pan American conferences show the advantages of regional conferences where the powers concerned have questions to consider which are peculiar to themselves."[17]

The movement for American codification culminated in a report, in 1925, of a number of projects of conventions by a committee of the American Institute of International Law which had been appointed for the purpose at the request of the governing board of the Pan American Union. The committee's conception of an American international law and its relation to universal international law is succinctly stated in the following paragraphs of the second project:

2. The American Republics declare that matters pertaining especially to America should be regulated in our continent in conformity with the principles of universal international law, if that be possible, or by enlarging and developing those principles or creating new ones adapted to the special conditions existing on this continent.

3. By American international law is understood all of the institutions, principles, rules, doctrines, conventions, customs, and practices which, in the domain of international relations, are proper to the Republics of the New World.

The existence of this law is due to the geographical, economic, and political conditions of the American Continent, to the manner in which the new Republics were formed and have entered the international community, and to the solidarity existing between them.

American international law thus understood in no way tends to create an international system resulting in the separation of the Republics of this hemisphere from the world concert.[18]

The fundamental assumptions that lead the protagonists of a code of American international law to look upon efforts under the auspices of the League of Nations to work out a universal code as insufficient,

[17] *Ibid.*

[18] For the Thirty Projects, see *American Journal of International Law*, Vol. XX (1926), Special Supplement. Published by the American Society of International Law. The enterprise of codifying an "American" international law has met with opposition within Pan American circles chiefly on the ground of duplication of the efforts already under way by the League of Nations; and at the International Conference of American States held at Montevideo in December, 1933, it was agreed that the work of American codification should take account of, and as far as possible be coordinated with, that of the League. See Carlos Dávila, "The Montevideo Conference, Antecedents and Accomplishments," *International Conciliation* (May, 1934), No. 300, p. 133.

if not actually ill-advised, lead them also—with perhaps a few exceptions—to reject the League and the Permanent Court of International Justice as instrumentalities adequate for the needs of the entire world community, and to demand new or additional international organization along continental and regional lines. In fact, this is but the logical conclusion from the premise that the political systems and ideals of the European and American continents are basically different. Alvarez, therefore, was but following out this thought and his earlier contentions concerning an American international law when, in 1917, he criticized the plan of the League to Enforce Peace [19] chiefly on the ground of the universal character of its jurisdiction and the obligations of its members. He declared that the states of one continent have never had, and probably never will have, any direct interest in matters pertaining solely to those of another continent, and that in any case the American republics can not agree to have their juridical or political affairs subject to the intervention of European powers. On the other hand, the republics of the western hemisphere can not accept obligations requiring them to participate in the forceful settlement of questions arising on other continents.[20] Señor Alvarez then submitted a project [21] designed to avoid the faults of the plan of the League to Enforce Peace and result in the peaceful settlement of international controversies. He proposed the establishment of continental unions or councils of conciliation for each continent, composed of permanent delegates, one each being chosen by the several states of such continent from persons other than diplomats. Each council would have general surveillance of the interests of the continent which it represented, and the duty of

[19] *Supra,* pp. 330-333, for program of League to Enforce Peace.

[20] *L'Organisation Internationale,* pp. 49-52. William Jennings Bryan criticized the League to Enforce Peace on similar grounds in 1916, in a debate with William Howard Taft at the Lake Mohonk Conference on International Arbitration: "Now, three of the objections mentioned [the fourth was the proposal to use force rather than to rely on moral suasion, a fundamental error in Mr. Bryan's opinion] might be obviated if we divided the world into groups, the American group being entrusted with the maintenance of peace in the Western Hemisphere. I would be much more willing to join with the Republics of Central and South America in any plan that would compel the submission of all disputes in this hemisphere to investigation before war; I would be much more willing to do that than to favor a plan that would bind us to enforce decisions made by nations across the ocean, or even obligate us to join European nations in compelling investigation before war." (*International Conciliation* [Sept., 1916], No. 106, p. 24, published by the Carnegie Endowment for International Peace).

[21] This was presented at the second session of the American Institute of International Law at Havana in 1917.

facilitating economic intercourse and cooperation with other continents. It would also see that international laws were observed and properly applied; and in extreme cases of bad faith or refusal to carry out international obligations, it might resort to a system of graduated sanctions against an offending state.[22] Anticipating conflicts between states of different continents, Alvarez proposed that the councils of the continents involved should act as mediators. If, in spite of their efforts, the disputants engaged in war, each council would take such measures as it deemed suitable under the circumstances. A court of international justice "of a universal character, if possible, or at least continental," should also be established to hear cases that states might prefer to submit to it rather than to the council of conciliation. Neither organ, however, might act except at the request of the parties to a dispute.[23]

The creation of the League of Nations along universal lines drew forth criticism from Alvarez and a proposal for the reform of the Covenant in accordance with the regional principle. He was, of course, primarily concerned with the problem of international organization from the point of view of the interest of the New World. The American continent, he declared, ought not to have its destiny interwoven with that of Europe, but should be left free to develop itself in conformity with its own traditions and aspirations. Contrary to what Europe had been able to achieve, the western hemisphere had developed a continental solidarity under the name of Pan Americanism, which today leads to cooperation in matters of a political, juridical, economic, administrative, intellectual, scientific, and journalistic character. And thanks to historical conditions, geographic circumstances, and the political doctrines they have developed, they have made greater progress in international cooperation than has Europe.[24]

Alvarez found the Covenant of the League of Nations defective in the following respects: In the first place, it represented a hasty and premature attempt to organize at one time the international political

[22] *L'Organisation Internationale,* pp. 57-64. Alvarez shared the widespread American repugnance to use of armed force, and believed reliance should first be placed on public opinion to bring a recalcitrant nation to terms. If this failed, diplomatic relations with the offender would be broken off. Next in order would be the imposition of an indemnity, and the severing of economic relations. Armed force, employed collectively or by one or more states as the agents of the continental group, should be used only in the last resort, *Ibid.*, pp. 63-64.

[23] *Ibid.,* pp. 57-59.

[24] "La Réforme du Pacte de la Société des Nations sur des Bases Continentales et Régionales," *loc. cit.,* pp. 29, 33-36.

life of the entire world by a single pact very difficult to amend, at the same time largely ignoring the matter of international economic cooperation.[25] The Great Powers were consecrated by being given permanent seats in the Council and, by virtue of the excessive powers conferred on them, tend to dominate the Assembly.[26] Nor was the Covenant well conceived from the point of view of the peaceful settlement of international disputes. Under it the League has shown that it is not capable of resolving conflicts between the Great Powers. It assumes that the problem of peace and security is always universal in that it is always presented in the same way in both Europe and America; and that all states, without distinction as to continent, must intervene each time peace is menaced anywhere. It unites all of the states of the world, making no allowance for continental differences, and consequently extinguishes the individuality of the American continent. It thus prevents this continent from exercising a distinctive influence and from cooperating freely, notably in the economic sphere, with the other continents, especialy Europe. Finally, although it recognizes the Monroe Doctrine in the formula comprised in Article XXI, the full meaning of the article is left in doubt. Whatever the extent to which the article may go, however, the truth is that the political, economic, and juridical life of the European and American continents are different. In reality, there are two Leagues of Nations, that at Geneva and the Pan American Union, and, unfortunately, under the Covenant there is no bond of cooperation between them.[27] The League of Nations, he concluded, should be reformed in order that the situation may be remedied.

[25] Alvarez, *loc. cit.*, p. 44. See also his article, "Les Groupements Continentaux et la Réforme de la Société des Nations," *L'Esprit International,* January, 1927, p. 47.

[26] It may seem natural in any case that Alvarez, spokesman of a small state, Chile, should object to this recognition of the paramountcy of the Great Powers. He, as well as other representatives of this school of American thought, have regarded the Great Power system as one of the important matters upon which European and American thought differ, the American republics emphasizing at all times the legal equality of states regardless of size. However, Alvarez recognizes that the Great Powers in fact have a larger sphere of interest and responsibility than have small states, that they must bear a heavier burden in any international organization, and that it is only just that they should be given a special position. He seemingly contends only that all states should be recognized as possessing juridical equality, that the Council was given excessive powers under the Covenant, and that political bodies representative of continents should be in a position to control the exercise of such powers as legitimately should be accorded them. ("Les Groupements Continentaux et la Réforme du Conseil de la Société des Nations," *loc. cit.*, pp. 46-47.)

[27] "La Réforme du Pacte de la Société des Nations sur des Bases Continentales et Régionales," *loc. cit.*, pp. 45, 90. For elaboration of these points and the variation of the League conception from that of Pan Americanism, see pp. 46-81. Alvarez,

Alvarez offered two possible solutions of the problem. The first involved a thoroughgoing reform of the League in order that it might be acceptable to the greatest number of states possible; the second, its maintenance as a European League and the establishment of cooperative ties with the Pan American Union.[28] The essential bases for the reformation of the League he outlined as follows: It should first of all be clearly established that the universal organization is not only unopposed to continental or regional organizations, but that it presupposes them. Matters of world interest should be discussed and regulated by all active countries of the world by way of international conferences. Matters of continental or regional interest should be regulated by the countries of the continent or region concerned. If it is insisted, said Alvarez, that the universal League or the regional organizations should have the mission of settling disputes of a political character, those of a regional nature arising outside the American continent should be resolved by the organs which represent the states of the region concerned. In such a case the states of other continents can only employ friendly action unless they have a direct interest. In the latter case, they must make their observations to, or register their complaints with, the continental organs or institutions created to resolve the conflict.[29] In case of the aggression of a state against another of the same continent, the continental council, if it finds the attack unjustified, may appeal to the states directly interested, or to those that have signed a treaty of guarantee with the state attacked, to come to the aid of the latter. And if the council thinks it necessary, it may also address itself to other states that may be disposed to participate against the aggressor.

it may be noted, had in mind only two continental groups, Europe and America; for Asia and Africa did not have a group of independent states. The latter continents were attached by many ties to Europe and should be considered conjointly with it. (p. 99.) He seems to modify his position, however, in the article in *L'Esprit International,* January, 1927, "Les Groupements Continentaux et la Réforme du Conseil de la Société des Nations." Here he calls attention to a continental movement of rapprochement between certain states in Asia which may develop into a League of Asiatic Nations, and says: "Quoique moins puissant que les mouvements panaméricain et paneuropéen, il a cependant une importance considérable et surtout est une 'idée force' qui peut avoir un grand lendemain." (*Loc. cit.,* p. 52.) These three groups along with the British Commonwealth of Nations might, he suggests, be united by a common council and thus form a world association. (*Ibid.,* pp. 61-62.)

[28] This idea is elaborated briefly on pp. 112-114, and the project itself on pp. 145-153, of "La Réforme du Pacte de la Société des Nations sur des Bases Continentales et Régionales," *loc. cit.*

[29] *Ibid.,* p. 134.

In case a state of one continent is attacked by a state of another, the continental council of the former may take the case to the council of the continent from which the attack came or to the world council, to the end of finding the best means of stopping the aggressor.[30]

The world council as envisaged by Alvarez in the proposals he made in 1926 would differ materially in its organization from that of the present Council of the League of Nations. All of the Great Powers would have permanent seats as at present, and the Assembly would likewise freely choose a certain number of representatives, but in addition there would be a fixed representation chosen by continental and regional groups. Thus the states of the continent of Asia would be entitled to choose representatives, and regional groups such as the Little Entente, the Scandinavian countries, and the Baltic states would likewise have representation selected by themselves.[31]

Although Alvarez has been the most conspicuous, persevering, and ingenious New World exponent of continentalism and regionalism, the idea has appealed as well to others who, for one reason or another, have not been altogether satisfied with the League of Nations as constituted. Even as early as 1916, when the League to Enforce Peace plan was being agitated in the United States, William Jennings Bryan and his successor, President Wilson's Secretary of State, Robert Lansing, placed themselves in opposition to American membership in a world-wide

[30] In the repression of an aggressor, Alvarez advanced the formula of three concentric circles. In the first circle, the states immediately interested, as stated above, would act; in the second, the continental organization would take part; and if the conflict should take on a general intercontinental aspect, the third circle of states, or those of other continents, might intervene. M. Paul Boncour advanced a plan somewhat similar in principle at the Disarmament Conference in 1932. He, too, proposed to divide the world, for the purpose of applying sanctions, into three concentric circles. The innermost circle would include states bound together by pacts of mutual assistance. This group would apply the sanctions provided for in Article XVI of the Covenant. The other members of the League, with less precise obligations, would form the middle circle; and the outer circle would be composed of states bound by the Kellogg Pact and committed only not to aid an aggressor.

[31] "Les Groupements Continentaux et la Réforme du Conseil de la Société des Nations," *loc. cit.*, pp. 110-111. For the specific proposals as to the number of seats in each case, see p. 138; for the entire project, see pp. 133-142. It may be observed that the practice is apparently becoming established in the League of Nations of according representation to certain regional groups, although the Assembly formally elects all of the non-permanent members of the Council. Thus for several years Latin America has always had three representatives, the Little Entente has had one, and the British Dominions have had one. Some one of the countries in northern Europe that were neutral during the World War has also been given a place on the Council at each election.

League which would bind its members to submit all disputes to some form of peaceful settlement and use force against them in case of non-compliance. Mr. Bryan was opposed to the use of force altogether, but showed a disposition to consider some such agreement if confined to the states of the New World.[32] Mr. Lansing also rather tentatively suggested in a letter to President Wilson that the danger to our sovereignty and interests involved in the obligation to send armed forces to Europe or Asia and allow European nations to stop quarrels in the western hemisphere, "might be obviated by the establishment of geographical zones, and leaving to the groups of nations thus formed the enforcement of the peaceful settlement of disputes."[33] Short of this, he saw a danger both to the Monroe Doctrine and to Pan Americanism.

Still another American, the distinguished president of Columbia University, Nicholas Murray Butler, in 1922 found the League of Nations inadequate because "as now organized it does not correspond to the real conditions which exist in the world." He proposed, therefore, that "first, agreement should be had upon the principles of international law and international administration which are hereafter to prevail in the world," and then it might be practicable to divide the world into three administrative areas. Europe, Africa, and areas immediately adjoining them or long dependent upon Europe, would form one area; the American continents would form a second area; and the Orient, including Japan, China, and Siam, would form the third zone. There would thus be, in effect, a Monroe Doctrine for each area. Normally, each area would see to the maintenance of law and order among the states included within it. In serious and rare emergencies, however, Dr. Butler suggested that the forces of other areas might be called upon for assistance in restoring peace. He believed, however, that the occasions for such interventions would be "increasingly infrequent." That such a development would necessitate remodelling the Covenant and a change in the form of the League of Nations was admitted. In Dr. Butler's opinion, however, the League might "furnish the nucleus both for a world-wide conference to agree upon and formulate the rules of international law and conduct, and for a permanent consultative and administrative body representing the first of the three proposed admin-

[32] *Supra,* p. 456, note 20.
[33] *The Peace Negotiations* (Boston, 1921), p. 39.

istrative areas or regions. . .[34] More recently, however, Dr. Butler has not raised the question of a fundamental modification of the structure or curtailment of the functions of the League. On the other hand, on a number of occasions he has praised the contributions of the League and the Permanent Court of International Justice to the cause of peace, and has called upon the "responsible leaders of civilization" to strengthen the authority of the Court and "increase the prestige and uphold the authority of the League of Nations, which is now an established institution, a fully recognized and indispensable instrument of international intercourse and international association."[35]

As the War has receded into the past and the League has increased its membership and broadened its activities in all parts of the world and along many lines not connected with the peace treaties; and as disturbing events in Europe and the Far East have seemed to threaten the peace of the international community and even endanger western civilization, regionalist sentiment in the western hemisphere, in its most pronounced form at any rate, seems to be less in evidence. At the Pan American Conference at Montevideo in 1933, the commission of the League of Nations, which, in accordance with the universal mission of the League under the Covenant, had been attempting to bring peace between two nations of the New World—Paraguay and Bolivia—was invited to the closing session of the conference and greeted with enthusiasm. Moreover, a resolution was offered, stating among other things that "the American states reunited in this Conference are disposed to cooperate with the League of Nations in the application of the pact which created it."[36] Nevertheless, continentalism still has its adherents. Writing in 1934, Señor Dávila of Chile stated: "Two currents of thought are evident at present. One seeks to avail itself more thoroughly of the Geneva organization and to strengthen the relations of the American Union with the various international instruments developed by the League. The second appears desirous of building its own structure on this continent, fitted to the needs of the American republics, but in a

[34] *The Faith of a Liberal* (New York, 1924), pp. 36, 38-40. The views quoted were from an address delivered before the Institute of Arts and Sciences, Columbia University, October 17, 1922.

[35] *The Path to Peace* (New York, 1930), p. 167.

[36] Carlos Dávila, "The Montevideo Conference," *loc. cit.* The delegations from the United States and Brazil effected a modification of this part of the resolution, however; for, not being members of the League of Nations, they could not agree to cooperate in applying the League of Nations Covenant.

way paralleling the European organizations and cooperating with them." [37]

It is perhaps broadly true to say that a self-conscious continentalism is a natural outgrowth of historical developments in the New World, beginning with the independence movement of the North and South American colonies, the acceptance of republican principles, and the establishment of formal republican institutions. Moreover, the new states started their careers under environmental conditions favorable in many respects to the development of relatively peaceful collaboration. Pan Americanism, though not as robust as some of its adherents assert,[38] has nevertheless had enough nourishment from American soil to survive and develop, and enough promise to lead many to feel that a complete indigenous political and juridical system may grow out of it.

On the other hand, Europe, though nurtured in ideas of universalism by Church and Empire, took the path of particularism with the rise of the modern national states, became the battleground of ambitious monarchs, and developed hates and rivalries and traditions of violence that have destroyed to a great extent a sense of solidarity and thus hindered the attainment of political unity. The World War not only revived and aggravated old hatreds and bred new ones, but it dealt a staggering blow to Europe's economic life not only by the destruction of capital and the dislocation of markets, but by the carving up of empires and the addition of new states to the European community. Thus, as a prominent European points out, whereas in 1914 there were twenty-six customs barriers and thirteen monetary systems in Europe, today there are thirty-five customs barriers and twenty-seven monetary systems; and there are six thousand kilometers of new boundary lines.[39] The new states as well as the old have attempted to become economically self-sufficient as far as possible, so as to be in a less precarious position when the "next war" comes, and to that end have erected barriers of one kind or another against their neighbors' products and

[37] *Ibid.*, p. 132.

[38] No realistic view of Pan Americanism can overlook the fact that the states of the western hemisphere are confronted by linguistic, racial, political, economic, cultural, and even geographical barriers; and that, as the Pan Hispanic movement testifies, the Latin Americans are culturally closer to Europe than to the United States. See, for example, Fred Rippy, *Latin America in World Politics* (New York, 1928), Chs. XII, XIV-XVI; and C. H. Haring, *South America Looks at the United States* (New York, 1928).

[39] Count Carlo Sforza, "The Proposed Federation of European States," *Current History*, XXXII (July, 1930), 658.

adopted other economic policies ruinous to all concerned. These conditions, seemingly a bar to the realization of a united Europe, have at the same time convinced certain men that Europe must unite or perish.

The historic schemes for the organization of the states of Europe from Dubois to Kant were evolved when Europe was assumed to be the only continent of independent, civilized states, and when in fact the Far East and America were not as yet prepared to play an independent rôle in international relations. They might be directed against the Turk, as was true in the earlier period, but they were conceived in universal terms in the sense that Europe was regarded as comprising the civilized world. Such is not the case today; nor has it been since the development of civilizations in the western hemisphere and the rise of Japan in the Far East. Today, Europe is recognized as but one of three great cultural areas, and the problem facing European states, while still essentially one of security, has taken a different form, and is presented as one of regional organization by the recent proponents of Pan Europa.

The first, and perhaps most influential, exposition of the needs of present-day Europe, from the regionalist viewpoint, was written by Count Richard N. Coudenhove-Kalergi in 1923,[40] at a time when the French were occupying the Ruhr and Europe was in a dangerous state of tension politically, and in a condition of stagnation economically. Kalergi diagnosed Europe's sickness as "political, not biological." It was not that Europe was senile, but that "its inhabitants are killing and destroying one another with the instruments of modern science." They must cease doing so and form a democratic "ad hoc politico-economic federation," he declared, if they are to hope to continue to play a world rôle or even exist alongside four new World Powers that must now be reckoned with. These are three powerful federations, the British Commonwealth of Nations, Russia, and the United States; and the empire of Japan.[41] Kalergi's concept of European federation was political rather than strictly geographical. England, though physically almost attached to the continent, was not to be included, unless she chose to be; and Russia, though a continental European power, was definitely excluded. England was tentatively placed outside because

[40] Published under the title of *Pan Europe* (New York, 1926), with an introduction by Nicholas Murray Butler. Coudenhove-Kalergi was born in 1894. His father was a distinguished Austrian diplomat, and his mother a Japanese.

[41] *Op. cit.*, pp. 4-6, Chs. XII, XIV, XV.

with the overseas dominions she formed a League of her own with extra-continental interests. To include her, therefore, would, in Kalergi's opinion, cause Pan Europe to "gain in power, but lose in cohesion. . ."[42] On the other hand, there should be close and peaceful collaboration with the British Empire, for the interests of both were in the maintenance of peace, and a security pact guaranteeing England against a European attack should be made if the former were to be excluded from the European organization.[43] Kalergi would exclude Russia from the democratic European federation he envisaged because of the incompatibility between such a system and the absolutism of the Soviet regime. Confident that the supreme aim of the Bolshevik leaders was the break-up of the European democracies,[44] and that an invasion of Europe was certain if Russia should regain her strength before Europe succeeded in consolidating, he urged that federal union, with the superior military strength it would bring, was the only way to cause Russia to give up such a design. An entente and cooperative arrangements between the two systems should then be worked out, for each needed the other in the process of reconstruction.[45]

Kalergi turned to the western hemisphere for models upon which to construct a Pan European system. The United States in particular furnished the great object lesson for Europe. Its great wealth and power, according to Kalergi's analysis, had come from bringing forty-eight states into a federal union and establishing peace and freedom of commerce among them, just as Europe's ruinous condition had been brought about by her failure to learn the lesson of unity. Were she to follow the American example, Europe could expect to attain an equally favorable position. Kalergi proposed that Europe should take the United States as its economic model, and the Pan American Union as its political model. Although the latter was as yet not fully developed, it was, in Kalergi's opinion, on the way to becoming a Pan American League of Nations. In such developments he saw no basis for unhealthy intercontinental rivalry, but the beginning of world solidarity. "World-Britain, Pan-Europe, and Pan-America, all three of which are interested in the maintenance of world peace and of the territorial *status quo*,

[42] *Ibid.*, p. 38.
[43] *Ibid.*, pp. 43, 48.
[44] He was writing, it must be remembered, in 1923, before the spread of Fascism in Europe.
[45] *Op. cit.*, pp. 55, 58-59, 65, 67, 69.

and are united by the same political principles as well as by a common culture and descent, would for a long time to come serve as the invincible guarantors of a peaceful development of world civilization." [46]

Kalergi did not regard the League of Nations as a substitute for Pan Europe. Although since 1923 some of the specific criticisms which he made of the League have lost their point with new developments,[47] his fundamental criticism with reference to its structure raises a question that is still germane: "The Geneva League of Nations is inorganic; instead of organically grouping the peoples and states of the world according to their economic, cultural, and geographical affinities, it joins together mechanically, like bricks, large and small states, Asiatic and European, neighboring and distant, without regard to geography, history, culture, or economics." [48] In its present form, it constitutes a standing menace to Europe's independence. Non-European powers from all over the world are able, under the Covenant, to meddle in European affairs and make the Continent a center of political intrigues. This should be changed so that purely European problems would be settled exclusively by European states, leaving inter-continental questions to be decided by the Council of the League of Nations. This regionalism should be carried further, and the aim of the Pan European movement should be "to divide the League of Nations into groups and to replace the centralism of Geneva by an inter-state federalism." These groups would be the Pan American, the Pan European, the British, the Russian, and finally the two Mongolian groups, China and Japan. These "power-groups" would "roughly balance one another," and thus no one of them would be in a position to challenge the world community. The formation and recognition of such groups would, moreover, further serve the cause of peace by tending to localize possible wars.[49]

Kalergi not only continued to write and agitate on behalf of Pan Europe after 1923 but also founded the *Union Pan-Européene* through which committees were formed in each one of the states of Europe. Many prominent men were induced to serve on these committees, and M. Briand of France lent the prestige of his name to the organization by becoming its honorary president in 1927. Also, a monthly publication, *Pan-Europa*, published in French and German, was widely circu-

[46] Kalergi, *op. cit.*, pp. 70-75, 81, 84, 86.
[47] *Ibid.* See for example pp. 87-88, 90, 97.
[48] *Ibid.*, p. 89.
[49] *Ibid.*, pp. 91-102.

lated in Europe, and a number of Pan European conferences were held to popularize the idea. By 1925, Kalergi could predict that the "time is not distant when the League of Nations itself will have to deal with the question of creating a Pan-European Section." [50] Four years later, at the Tenth Assembly of the League of Nations, M. Briand loosed a *ballon d'essai* in the suggestion that peoples constituting geographical groups such as those of Europe should be linked together by some kind of federal bond. Stresemann of Germany, Beneš of Czechoslovakia, and others received the idea cordially; and in the following year M. Briand, acting for the French government, drew up a memorandum on the organization of a régime of European federal union and submitted it to the governments of Europe which were members of the League of Nations.[51]

The Briand memorandum embodied the main idea of Count Kalergi and the proponents of Pan Europe in proposing a special European political structure. At certain important points in M. Briand's exposition, however, there is clearly a change of emphasis, if not divergence from the viewpoint of the regionalists. Great stress is laid on the necessity that any Pan European organization must be "within the framework of the League," its purpose being to harmonize European interests "under the control and in the spirit of the League of Nations by incorporating in its universal system a limited system all the more effective." [52] More specifically, M. Briand declared in effect that the League of Nations would retain its jurisdiction in the settlement of disputes by saying that "the European Association, which could not be called on in such matters to exercise its good offices except in a purely advisory capacity would be without authority to treat thoroughly special problems, the adjustment of which has been entrusted by the Pact or by the Treaties to a special procedure of the League of Nations or to any other procedure expressly defined." In other words, the principle of universalism rather than that of regionalism seems to be upheld in the Memorandum, which reiterates that the League of Nations "is deeply attached to the idea of universality which remains its object

[50] "Three Years of Pan Europe," in *Pan Europe* (New York, 1926).

[51] "European Union and the League of Nations," *Geneva Special Studies,* Vol. II (June, 1931), No. 6, p. 5.

[52] See text of "Memorandum on the Organization of a Régime of European Federal Union," in Appendix. It may also be found in *International Conciliation,* June, 1930, Special Bulletin.

and its end even when it pursues or favors partial realizations." The League of Nations would not be "reformed," as both Alvarez and Kalergi contemplated, but would be served by a new instrumentality organized within the terms of Article XXI of the Covenant. Certain other principles in the Memorandum likewise demand attention. The "federal bond" M. Briand had in mind was not to bind or restrict that holy of holies, national sovereignty. "It is on the basis of absolute sovereignty and of entire political independence," he said, "that the understanding between European nations ought to be effected." [53] The federation was to be "built not upon the idea of unity but of union. . ." One of the most important tasks, M. Briand recognized, was to achieve economic union. He expressed the well-known official French viewpoint, however, in his insistence that the first point of attack must be the political problem. A political union must precede an attempt to achieve an economic union, because the problem of national security must be solved before progress on the economic plane can be achieved.[54]

The plan of M. Briand, although apparently requiring no modification of the Covenant and professedly designed to strengthen rather than weaken the League, has encountered the same fundamental objection that the more sweeping proposals of Alvarez and Kalergi have met. Many supporters of the League of Nations see in all of these schemes, whatever the intention of the authors, a blow at the principle of universalism and the weakening of the League of Nations. They see in them "a new particularism founded upon the continent." [55] On the other hand, the opponents of these "Pan" movements contend that nothing less than a universal association of states can answer the eco-

[53] M. Briand was careful to anticipate this and other fears that the union would be directed against other states or groups of states by denying that such was an object of the proposed union.

[54] By 1930, many prominent Europeans had come to support the principle of European union and more or less unqualifiedly endorsed M. Briand's plan. Among them were Louis Loucheur, Joseph Caillaux, Édouard Herriot, Joseph Barthélemy, Gustav Stresemann, Francis Delaisi, Paul Hymans, Carlo Sforza, Édouard Beneš, and Thomas Masaryk. As might perhaps be expected, in view of the acceptance of the idea of Pan Europe by the French government and its adoption as a policy, Frenchmen were conspicuously active in its support. See, for example, Édouard Herriot's *The United States of Europe* (New York, 1930). For the view of a prominent Italian, see Carlo Sforza, "The Proposed Federation of European States," *Current History*, XXXII (July, 1930), 658-662. For a German view, see Hjalmar Schacht, "The Pan-European Problem," *Yale Review*, XX (Dec., 1930), 217-233.

[55] See criticism by M. Cornejo of plan of reform of the League of Nations advanced by M. Alvarez, in *Séances et Travaux de l'Union Juridique Internationale, Fifth Session* (Paris, 1926), pp. 194-197.

nomic and political needs of the twentieth century. They deny the validity of the argument of Kalergi and others that the League is unnatural in that it represents an attempt to skip a necessary stage of social development by passing, at a bound, from the national phase to the universal phase and ignoring the intermediate, continental stage. What would be unnatural, they reply, would be to divide the world politically into continents. "The economic life of the world today is not European but world-wide," says the late William Martin, famous European journalist, apropos of the Pan European movement. "A continent is not an economic entity. That is why the League of Nations is an exact reflexion in the sphere of political and juridical organization of current economic realities. Contrary to what amateur theoretical advocates of sociological realism think, nature, in the case of the League, has made no leap and the framers of the Covenant were more clearly aware of the political and economic realities of today than their theoretical opponents." [56]

A similar point of view has been expressed by the English economist, J. A. Hobson.[57] The proposal to create a continental political structure alongside the League and duplicating its machinery at a critical time when the latter is struggling to establish, without reference to continents, "the beginnings of a pacific world-government . . . would inevitably constitute a challenge to Geneva, even if it kept the form and the pretense of a grouping of League members to further the purposes of the League." [58] On the economic side, Hobson contended that "the economic interdependence of European countries cannot be said to be so close, or so sufficient, as to warrant any common policy which would weaken their trade relations with the outside world. Mere contiguity counts less and less for purposes of personal and commercial

[56] "European Unity," in *Problems of Peace, Seventh Series* (London, 1933), pp. 167-168.

[57] "The United States of Europe," *The Nation* (New York), CXXIX (Oct. 30, 1929), pp. 484-485.

[58] The same thought has been elaborated by J. A. Salter: "The more the developing organization of the world becomes regional, the wider and richer the regions, the less chance will the universal organ have of making universal interests and principles ultimately prevail. A strong impetus would be given to the development of both the economic and political life of the world in large regional units. Movements and problems which might have been, and should have been, universal, will become regional. Unnecessary regional and local difficulties will be created. There will be a conflict between the regional and the central in which the latter would constantly tend to be weaker." *The United States of Europe, and Other Papers* (London, 1933), p. 116.

intercourse, sea barriers are less substantial than land, while air-traffic cancels all barriers. . . No separate effective economic organization of Europe is either practicable or desirable. Europe must always depend upon tropical and many other outside raw materials and food-stuffs for the maintenance of its life and industry." In the present-day world, therefore, according to the universalists, the regional or territorial principle of international organization is unsound. Organization according to function is a clear necessity. As economic and other activities are world-wide in character and consequences, so must the international organization of control be on a world scale. Loyalty must be to universal principles and not to some "sectional code." [59]

The proposal of the regionalists that the world's peace machinery should function in continental units has also encountered opposition from many League supporters on similar grounds. The prevention of war, it is said, is in its nature "universal" in that "the causes of war, its range if it breaks out, its effects, and the sanctions required to stop it, all tend to be world wide." [60] They challenge the position of Kalergi that representatives of non-European states in the League of Nations have interfered in European affairs and made the solution of European problems more difficult than would have been the case had Europe handled them alone. They assert that, on the contrary, non-Europeans acting in League bodies or on League commissions have on many occasions been distinctly helpful because they have had no selfish interests to defend or promote. It is quite essential, in fact, that the strong sense of difference that exists between European nations should be diluted with the cooperation of extra-European elements acting as arbiters or as conciliating agents.[61] The problem is in reality not that of divesting the League of its universal character but of making it actually universal by bringing all nations into it and giving it world-wide authority. The difficulties it finds today in its attempt to solve the problem of peace and security "are in direct proportion to the non-participation of extra-European countries. . . The obstacle which is wrecking all efforts to increase the legal security of European na-

[59] David Mitrany, "The Case against Pan Europa," *Current History*, Vol. XXXIII (Oct., 1930), No. 1, pp. 68-69. See also, by the same author, *The Progress of International Government* (New Haven, Conn., 1933), pp. 114-119.

[60] Salter, *op. cit.*, p. 114.

[61] Salvador de Madariaga, "The Disunited States of Europe," *Forum*, Vol. LXXXIV (Oct., 1930), No. 4, pp. 246-249; also William Martin, *Disarmament and the Inter-Parliamentary Union* (Lausanne, 1931), p. 169.

tions has been Great Britain's repugnance to accept any new obligation whatever without being certain beforehand that in case of international conflict the British fleet would not be on the other side to that of the United States." If the United States were in the League, it is further asserted, the sanctions provided in the Covenant could be made effective.[62]

Nearly all the opponents of the Pan Europa movement point out that it is quite chimerical to expect the European states, with their particularistic traditions and their present institutional differences and conflicting policies, to unite in any effective way. Moreover, many believe that if they were to succeed in doing so they would become a menace not only to the League but also to the rest of the world. In fact, many fear that the likely development, if not the main object, of such a union would be that of a militant aggressive imperialistic combination of states fighting for exclusive economic and other advantages.[63] Contrary to the League organization, in which the small states are in a position to voice their opinions and defend their interests, in the proposed European union, the Great Powers would be able once more to dominate over the others.[64] The Great Powers always tend to rely upon military force for the realization of their objectives, whereas the smaller states, lacking military power, are more inclined to support pacific settlement. For this reason, also, their standing and influence must be maintained.[65]

Still another fear, arising particularly from M. Briand's initiative on behalf of a European union, has been expressed most frequently in certain political quarters. Italian and German spokesmen especially, but others as well, have looked upon the plan as an attempt to consolidate the political and territorial *status quo* in Europe under French leadership. Regarding the settlements of 1919 as unjust and untenable,

[62] Martin, "European Unity," *loc. cit.*, pp. 169-170.

[63] See Romain Rolland, "Broaden, Europe, or Die!" *The Nation* (New York), CXXXVII (April 22, 1931), 443-445; David Mitrany, *loc. cit.*, p. 65. The latter regards such regional proposals as "only a revival of the old policy of the balance of power." The plan of European union has also been severely criticized on the ground that Russia and Turkey were to be left out. Some of the problems involved in attempting to define "Europe" were pointed out several years before M. Briand's Memorandum by A. B. Coolidge in "The Grouping of Nations," *Foreign Affairs*, Vol. V (Jan., 1927), No. 2, pp. 175-188.

[64] Martin, *loc. cit.*, p. 171.

[65] Madariaga, "The United States of Europe," *Nineteenth Century*, Vol. CVIII (Aug., 1930), No. 642, pp. 169-176.

they are inclined to insist that there must be a new deal before a European union can be seriously considered.[66]

Certain writers who are critical of any scheme of regionalism or continentalism that would tend to parallel the organization of the League of Nations and usurp its necessary functions, nevertheless recognize the possibility, and even desirability, of some regional devolution of function within the framework of the League and under its actual as well as theoretical control. Sir Arthur Salter admits, for example, that many international questions are in certain vital respects local or regional in character, and that in many instances regional arrangements are a necessary prelude to the extension and coordination of such arrangements on a larger scale. Minor matters between contiguous countries may be handled simply and directly by the countries themselves, provided their action is consistent with League principles. But more important matters involving large continental areas cannot safely be handled through regional machinery paralleling that of the League. In such cases, inasmuch as the League has an elastic organization, its own mechanism can be and should be used for the purpose desired.[67] Other writers, realizing the importance of having closer collaboration and, if possible, membership of the United States in the League, and aware of the American aversion to a uniform system of sanctions, have advanced various formulae to accomplish that purpose and make the League a more effective agency for peace. Professor Shotwell, for example, suggests that Article XVI of the Covenant should be amended because "it draws no distinction between nations which are endangered by threat of war at their very doors and those far distant peoples who would not normally expect to be drawn into war." He proposed a system of graduated responsibility as follows: "An 'optional clause' could be signed by those nations which agree to help each other to maintain peace. Its agreements would naturally be regional. The United States in its geographic isolation could limit itself to the responsibilities stated and implied in the Kellogg Pact: to renounce war

[66] See, for example, the official Italian reply to M. Briand's proposal in which the necessity of a change in the régime of the peace treaties is clearly implied as a necessary condition of European union. (*International Conciliation* (Dec., 1930), No. 265, pp. 667-671.) See also reply of the German government, especially p. 686, for a somewhat more guarded criticism of the same general tenor. Francis Deák, in "Can Europe Unite?," *Political Science Quarterly*, Vol. XLVI (Sept., 1931), No. 3, pp. 428-429, likewise criticizes the proposal from this point of view.

[67] Salter, *op. cit.*, pp. 114-115; Martin, *loc. cit.*, p. 172.

as the instrument of its policy, and to renounce aid to any nation violating it." [68] These and similar proposals are not designed to attack the fundamentals of League organization or the universality of its mandate, but are more in the nature of questions of procedure.[69]

REFERENCES

Alvarez, A., *Le Droit International Américain* (Paris, 1910).

——————, *L'Organisation Internationale, Précédents de la Société des Nations et de l'Union Fédérale Européene* (Paris, 1931).

——————, "La Réforme du Pacte de la Société des Nations sur des Bases Continentales et Régionales; Rapport Presenté à la Ve Session de l'Union Juridique Internationale, Juin, 1926," *Séances et Travaux de l'Union Juridique Internationale, Fifth Session* (Paris, 1926).

Apelt, W., *Vom Bundesstaat zum Regionalstaat* (Berlin, 1927).

Aragonés, E., *Los Temas Fundamentales de Hispanoamérica* (Madrid, 1927).

Aubert, L., *The Reconstruction of Europe* (New Haven, Conn., 1925).

Barthélemy, J., "Le Problème de la Souveraineté des États et la Coopération Européene," *Académie des Sciences Morales et Politiques* (Sept.-Oct., 1931), pp. 187-225.

Benda, J., *Discours à la Nation Européene* (Paris, 1933).

Beneš, E., *Les Problèmes de l'Europe Centrale* (Prague, 1932).

Bibliography on European Union, *Bulletin of the British Library of Political and Economic Science* (Sept., 1932), pp. 14-22.

Brian, A., "Memorandum on the Organization of a Régime of European Federal Union Addressed to Twenty-six Governments of Europe, May 17, 1930," *International Conciliation* (June, 1930), Special Bulletin, pp. 325-353.

Buday, K. de, "The Danubian Problem," *Nineteenth Century,* Vol. CXI (May, 1932), No. 663, pp. 544-556.

Coolidge, A. C., "The Grouping of Nations," *Foreign Affairs,* Vol. V (Jan., 1927), No. 2, pp. 175-188.

Cordier, A. W., "European Union and the League of Nations," *Geneva Special Studies,* Vol. II (June, 1931) No. 6, pp. 1-27.

Coudenhove-Kalergi, R. N., *Pan-Europe* (New York, 1926).

Crane, J. O., *The Little Entente* (New York, 1931).

[68] Quoted by George Kidd in "Changes in the League, Past and Proposed," *Geneva Special Studies,* Vol. V (1934), Nos. 7-8, p. 37.

[69] See, for example, David Mitrany, *The Progress of International Government,* pp. 104-114, who, however, suggests a scheme of regional devolution involving the setting up of regional courts and councils within the League constitution.

Dahriman, G., *Pour les États Confédérés d'Europe* (Paris, 1929).

Deák, F., "Can Europe Unite?" *Political Science Quarterly,* Vol. XLVI (Sept., 1931), No. 3, pp. 424-433.

De Chair, S. S., *Divided Europe* (London, 1931).

Delaisi, F., *Les Deux Europes* (Paris, 1929).

Demangeon, A., "Les Conditions Géographiques d'une Union Européene," *Annales d'Histoire Économique et Sociale,* Vol. IV (Sept., 1932), No. 17, pp. 433-451.

——————, *Le Déclin de l'Europe* (Paris, 1920). English translation: *America and the Race for World Dominion* (Garden City, N. Y., and Toronto, 1921).

European Federal Union: "Replies of Twenty-six Governments of Europe to M. Briand's Memorandum of May 17, 1930," *International Conciliation* (Dec., 1930), No. 265, pp. 655-748.

Ferrara, O., "L'Organisation des Continents; Panaméricanisme et Fédération Européene," *Académie Diplomatique Internationale* (Oct.-Dec., 1931), pp. 241-247.

Ferrero, G., "L'Europe, l'Extrême-Orient et la Société des Nations," *L'Esprit International,* Vol. VI (July, 1932), No. 23, pp. 339-347.

——————, *The Unity of the World* (New York, 1930).

Fleissig, A., *Paneuropa* (Munich and Leipzig, 1930).

Gratz, G., "Coopération Économique et Politique des États Danubiens," *L'Esprit International,* Vol. VI (July, 1932), No. 23, pp. 364-379.

Guggenheim, P., *Der Völkerbund* (Leipzig, 1932).

Haushofer, K., *Geopolitik der Pan-Ideen* (Berlin, 1931).

——————, "Pan-Europe?" *Foreign Affairs,* Vol. VIII (Jan., 1930), No. 2, pp. 237-247.

Herriot, E., *The United States of Europe,* tr. by R. J. Dingle (New York, 1930).

Huddleston, S., "European Federation," *The New Statesman,* Vol. XXXV (May 3, 1930), No. 888, pp. 109-110.

——————, "United States of Europe and the Entente," *The New Statesman,* Vol. XXXIII (Sept. 26, 1929), No. 856, pp. 701-702.

Hutchinson, P., *The United States of Europe* (Chicago and New York, 1929).

Jouvenel, B. de, *Vers les États-Unis d'Europe* (Paris, 1930).

Kohn, H., "Pan-Movements," *Encyclopaedia of the Social Sciences,* XI, 544-553, and bibliography.

Lange, R., *Vers un Gouvernement International? La Société des Nations et la Composition du Conseil* (Paris, 1928), Ch. IV.

Lauterpacht, H., "The So-called Anglo-American and Continental Schools of

Thought in International Law," *British Year Book of International Law, 1931*, XII, 31-62.

Lefcoparidis, X., "Le Mouvement vers l'Union Balkanique," *Affaires Étrangères*, II (March 25, 1932), 155-164.

Lothian, Marquess of, "The Place of Britain in the Collective System," *International Affairs*, Vol. XIII (Sept.-Oct., 1934), No. 5, pp. 622-650.

Loucheur, L., *Problème de la Coopération Économique Internationale* (Paris, 1926).

Madariaga, S. de, "The Disunited States of Europe," *Forum*, Vol. LXXXIV (Oct., 1930), No. 4, pp. 246-249.

————, "The United States of Europe," *Nineteenth Century*, Vol. CVIII (August, 1930), No. 642, pp. 169-176.

Marchal, J., *Union Douanière et Organisation Européene* (Paris, 1929).

Martin, W., "European Unity," *Problems of Peace; Seventh Series* (London, 1933), Ch. VII.

Mirkine-Guetzevitch, B. S., *La Doctrine Sovietique du Droit International* (Paris, 1926).

Mirkine-Guetzevitch, B. S., and Scelle, G., *L'Union Européene* (Paris, 1931).

Mitrany, D., "The Case Against Pan-Europa," *Current History*, Vol. XXXIII (Oct., 1930), No. 1, pp. 65-69.

Moreno Quintana, L. M., *El Sistema International Americana* (Buenos Aires, 1927).

Mower, E. C., *International Government* (Boston and New York, 1931), pp. 77-93.

Politis, N., "Le Projet d'Union Européene et la Société des Nations," *Revue de Droit International, des Science Diplomatiques et Politiques*, VIII (July-Sept., 1930), 201-211.

Raafat, W., *Le Problème de la Sécurité Internationale* (Paris, 1930), Pt. III.

Rolland, R., "Broaden, Europe, or Die!" *The Nation* (New York), CXXXII (April 22, 1931), 443-445.

Salter, J. A., *The United States of Europe, and Other Papers;* ed. by W. Arnold-Forster (London, 1933), Ch. IV.

Sá Vianna, M., *De la Non-Existence d'un Droit International Américain* (Rio de Janeiro, 1912).

Scelle, G., "Essai sur la Crise de la Société des Nations et ses Remèdes," *L'Esprit International*, Vol. VIII (April 1, 1934), No. 30, pp. 163-182.

Schacht, H., "The Pan-European Problem," *Yale Review*, Vol. XX (Dec., 1930), No. 2, pp. 217-233.

Sforza, Carlo, Count, "The Proposed Federation of European States," *Current History*, Vol. XXXII (July, 1930), No. 4, pp. 658-662.

Spaight, J. M., *Pseudo-security* (London, 1928).

Spender, J. A., "La Grande-Bretagne et l'Europe," *L'Esprit International,* Vol. VIII (Oct., 1934), No. 32, pp. 523-534.

Urrutia, F. J., *Le Continent Américain et le Droit International* (Paris, 1928).

Williams, R., *The League, the Protocol, and Empire* (London, 1925).

Wilson, F. G., "The International Labour Organization," *International Conciliation* (Nov., 1932), No. 284, pp. 401-441.

Wright, Q., and Kidd, G., "Reform of the League of Nations," *Geneva Special Studies,* Vol. V (1934), No. 7-8.

Yepes, J. W., "La Contribution de l'Amérique Latine au Développement du Droit International Publique et Privé," *Recueil des Cours,* Vol. XXXII (1930), Pt. II, pp. 691-799, Académie de Droit International (Paris, 1931).

Zimmern, A., "L'Idée d'une Fédération Européene à la Dernière Assemblée de la Société des Nations." *L'Esprit International,* Vol. V (Jan., 1931), No. 17, pp. 51-60.

CHAPTER XXI

INTEGRAL NATIONALISM

The Peace Settlement of 1919, in so far as it reflected Wilsonian conceptions, attempted to lay the foundations of a new world order in which a democratic international society of democratically organized states, recognizing that the well-being and safety of the members of that society required their relinquishment of the right to pursue their own several national interests in all circumstances, would accept that minimum of international government necessary to safeguard and advance the interests of the whole. Each nation would remain free to order its internal affairs as it pleased,[1] and would likewise retain its freedom in the conduct of its external relations except as the exercise of such freedom might imperil the peace of the international community. In the latter case, the society, acting through organs established for the purpose and in accordance with a prescribed procedure, might intervene to maintain or restore peace. It might also exercise such functions as its members might see fit to give to it for the promotion of the well-being of the interests of the whole. The League of Nations system, as we have seen, was organized to give effect to these principles. They were principles, one may add, that were not regarded as inimical to the national state, but rather as pointing the way to its preservation through the building of safeguards against destructive wars.

Integral nationalism, as defined by the author of the phrase, Charles Maurras, means the "exclusive pursuit of national policies, the absolute maintenance of national integrity, and the steady increase of national power—for a nation declines when it loses military might." [2] It may be distinguished, then, from the liberal-democratic, and humanitarian nationalism of the Mazzini and Wilson schools in its peculiar exaltation and tendency toward deification of the national state, and

[1] Except as it may have accepted obligations with respect to the treatment of its minorities.

[2] Quoted in C. J. H. Hayes, *The Historical Evolution of Modern Nationalism* (New York, 1931), p. 165.

in its reliance upon military might for the achievement of national ends. An examination of the creed and philosophy of its supporters reveals, in general, the following characteristics. Regarding national expansion as natural, and indeed necessary, for a healthy and virile state, and being inhibited by no democratic qualms about such a state imposing its will and extending its authority by force over unwilling peoples, it validates imperialism for states capable of mobilizing the necessary energy and power. War for the realization of national ends, which a career of imperialism is certain to involve, is, in any case, a tonic agent good in itself. The carrying out of great national designs by such a "God-bearing people" as integral nationalists—whether French, Italian, or German—have in mind, demands a high degree of centralization of power and the stamping out of individual freedom, class consciousness, local autonomy, and federal tendencies. Strong emphasis is laid on rigid discipline. The individual, after the fashion of the ancient Spartan, must give himself to the state in war and in peace, allow the thinking to be done by those in authority, and find his chief satisfaction in life in doing the part that may be assigned to him by the *duce* or *führer* for the advancement of state ends. This demands, in turn, the systematic and thorough inoculation of the children of the state with the nationalist ideology. They must be inspired with a national consciousness above all else. Their thinking in the field of government, at any rate, must be confined and concentrated on the restoration and enhancement of the position the state once occupied, if its position has been impaired, and toward the achievement of new glories for the future in civil or militant competition with less worthy "foreign" peoples. Constant propagandizing of the masses of the people to the end of inculcating the entire nation with the set of beliefs desired, and the forcible suppression of all counter beliefs or tendencies, is likewise regarded as justified and essential for the achievement of national ends. In the economic sphere, also, individual welfare must be subordinated and even sacrificed, if necessary, in order that the state may become as nearly self-contained as possible, and be thereby in a better position to deal with its external enemies.

The official acceptance and frank acknowledgment of the principles of integral nationalism for the guidance of state policy is a post-war phenomenon and is doubtless, in large part, a consequence of the economic dislocations caused by the World War, and the unhealthy political atmosphere generated by it. Many of the ideas that constitute its ingredients, however, have been the common property of the Machiavellis of ancient and medieval times and of the "Social Darwinists" and blood-and-iron writers of the nineteenth century.[3] To the extent that post-war integral nationalists have developed new ideas, they concern technique and mechanism rather than fundamental principles.

It is an interesting fact that integral nationalism has had some of its most eloquent spokesmen in certain circles in republican France. Among them one may select Maurice Barrès (1862-1923) and Charles Maurras (1868-) for special mention.[4] Barrès, influenced by the Nietzschean will-to-power and superman doctrines, was a strong proponent, in the early period of his productivity, of self-expression as the sole duty of man.[5] However, the nihilism to which this led seems to to have left him dissatisfied. Moreover, he came to the conviction that the individualism which he sought could be realized only under some form of organized society, and that régimes based on the egalitarian philosophy and doctrines of the French Revolution could not provide favorable conditions for its realization. This led him finally to espouse a national egotism looking in the direction of the authoritarianism of the *ancien régime*.[6] The nationalist philosophy which he developed was undoubtedly also greatly influenced by the hatred he conceived against the "barbarous" Germans who had invaded France when he was a boy and had unjustly seized Alsace-Lorraine. A war of revenge and the return of these fair provinces became one of his chief preoccupations.[7] In due course, a "man on horseback," General Boulanger, appeared upon whom he pinned great faith as *l'homme national* who would restore the military prestige of France and win back the lost provinces.

[3] See especially Chs. XII and XIII.

[4] Others who have more or less fully subscribed to the tenets of integral nationalism are Louis Dimier, Léon Daudet, Jacques Bainville, Paul Bourget, Jules Lemaître, and others of the Royalist *Action Française* group.

[5] See E. R. Curtius, *Maurice Barrès und die Geistigen Grundlagen des Französischen Nationalismus* (Bonn, 1921), pp. 37-52, for full discussion of his philosophy at this period; also Barrès, *Le Culte du Moi* (Paris, 1892).

[6] Roger Soltau, *French Political Thought in the Nineteenth Century* (New Haven, Conn., 1931), p. 380; also C. J. H. Hayes, *Historical Evolution of Modern Nationalism* (New York, 1931), pp. 188-189.

[7] Curtius, *op. cit.*, Ch. X, and Hayes, *op. cit.*, pp. 185, 200. Barrès, however, did not advocate the restoration of the Bourbons, because they had been responsible for the evils that led to the Revolution and the republican régime. He favored, rather, the establishment of a Caesarian republic.

But the "man of action" failed. Apparently a doctrine as well as a leader must be found, and Barrès set himself to the task.

The foundation upon which Barrès' doctrine of integral nationalism was erected consisted in a certain set of assumptions as to the power of race, ancestry, and native soil over the thoughts and lives of individuals.[8] One's race, he held, determined his thought processes so that liberty of thought was in reality non-existent. One's ancestors hold the living with chains to the past. A Frenchman thinks French thoughts, therefore, in whatever country he may live. And finally, one's native soil, where he was born and reared and where his parents and ancestors lived out their lives, evokes memories and awakens emotions connected with all that has gone before and inspires and gives value and meaning to life. Hence, those who uproot themselves from the soil of their native districts cut themselves off from communion with their ancestors and lose their individual and social usefulness.

Barrès felt the need of providing his country with a set of master-ideas that might serve to rally the entire nation behind a man-of-action who could then lead France forward to the great destiny for which she was intended. To this end, he advocated a return to the regionalism of the pre-revolutionary days in which individuals were intimately attached to groups. Give these groups a real share in the national government, unify them under a powerful military leader, and nationalism could recover from the weakening influences from which it was suffering under a centralized parliamentary system. Another thing that must be done is to prevent the further penetration of foreign words into the French language and eliminate those that have already secured a foothold. The language indigenous to French soil must be maintained in its purity if France is to remain France. For a somewhat similar reason, Barrès upheld Catholicism. The latter was a national tradition reaching far back into the past, and it thus provided an atmosphere within which Frenchmen could work and develop the highest aspirations.[9] And finally the traditional love of Frenchmen for heroes must be conserved, for one day a new Napoleon must be found to avenge the "frightful accident" of 1870.[10]

[8] See especially his *Scènes et Doctrines du Nationalisme* (Paris, 1902). My discussion is based largely on this work, on Curtius, *op. cit.*, and on Hayes, *op. cit.*, pp. 189-202, who has examined many additional works of Barrès and has drawn upon them for his analysis of Barrèsian nationalism.

[9] Curtius, *op. cit.*, Ch. XI.

[10] Hayes, *op. cit.*, p. 197; Curtius, *op. cit.*, Ch. VII.

The nationalism of Barrès was hostile to internationalism. Liberal nationalists who could work for disarmament, for the abandonment of war as a means of achieving national aims, and for international organization were foisting subversive doctrines upon the people. He regarded the Jews in France as chiefly responsible for the introduction of these dangerous ideas. They were indifferent to French traditions and interests, and cosmopolitan in their outlook because of their international financial affiliations. These and all other individuals and doctrines which would threaten those traditions upon which the life of France rests must be fought to the death.[11] The tasks which Barrès would have France undertake in the field of external policy were such as to demand soldiers, armament, and a militant leadership. In the first place, the lost provinces must be regained. Beyond that, France must consolidate and extend her colonial domain and thereby enhance her prestige. Here, too, was a tradition that must be revived. There was Syria, for example. French crusaders had established French influence there and French Catholic missions had carried on the French tradition. France should not abandon her interests but should secure Syria "as the bridgehead to Persia and India." [12] The efforts of France to extend her spheres of influence in Africa should likewise be continued. If it was not completely logical for Barrès to disregard the traditions of other peoples brought into subjection in the name of a French tradition of imperialism, it must be pointed out that he regarded the emotional and irrational as more important than the logical and intellectual in human affairs.

Charles Maurras (1868-) was born a few years after Barrès, and, as a young man, came under his influence and developed a doctrine of integral nationalism along Barrèsian lines.[13] The Dreyfus affair was the occasion for the beginning of a campaign of propaganda on behalf of a return to the traditional monarchy and the rehabilitation of France. In this movement Maurras took a most prominent part. He

[11] Freemasons, Protestants, Socialists, and resident foreigners or recently naturalized Frenchmen were among the alien influences that must be combated in order that they should not succeed in denationalizing France.

[12] *Une Conquête aux Pays du Levant*, II, 193, as quoted in Hayes, *op. cit.*, p. 201.

[13] The views of Maurras on the subject are most fully expressed in his *Enquête sur la Monarchie* (definitive edition, Paris, 1925). Other works are *Le Chemin de Paradis* (Paris, 1893), *Kiel et Tanger* (Paris, 1910), *La Politique Religieuse* (Paris, 1912), *Quand les Français Ne s'Aiment Pas* (Paris, 1916), *Les Conditions de la Victoire;* 4 vols. (Paris, 1916-1918), *Romantisme et Révolution* (Paris, 1922).

organized and led the *Action Française,* and won supporters among the French royalists, traditionalists, and in general the ultra-conservatives, including many Catholics.[14] The activities of the group have included the publication of a daily newspaper, the establishment of a publishing plant, the formation of propagandist societies throughout France, and the organization of the *Camelots du Roi,* a body of militant young men who lead street demonstrations and are active in various matters where muscle rather than mind is the chief requisite. In the doctrine of Maurras, strong emphasis is laid upon the necessity of relying upon force in the hands of a small governing class for the preservation of society. The freedom of republicanism, he insists, is a dangerous thing to be conferred upon the masses. Liberty can safely be entrusted, as in the past, only to an élite interested in maintaining social order. Individualism, indeed, is the great enemy that must be rooted out before a renaissance of French nationalism can come about. "Political life must rest for the greater part on the respect and worship of unconscious habits, all the stronger and more valuable as they are less felt. It is almost impious to bring them to consciousness. The great misfortune of our time is the necessity for every citizen to have a deliberately formed opinion on the State." [15] In the field of foreign affairs, Maurras and the *Action Française* are completely chauvinist. As expressed by Hayes,[16] "Throughout the writings of Charles Maurras and throughout the journalism which he has sponsored, his integral nationalism appears as a breeder of hatreds. He tirelessly preaches hatred of 'alien' influences within France: Jewish, Protestant, masonic, liberal republican, communist, and latterly, papal. He ceaselessly directs tirades against foreigners: Germans, Englishmen, Americans, Bolshevist Russians. Always he upholds a hundred-per-cent French nationalism, which is at once suspicious and forceful. He is ever expecting the worst, and ever preparing against it by counselling heavier armaments and more unyielding foreign and colonial policies." Although the group of integral nationalists in France have doubtless made their influence felt in the field of foreign policy by their incessant propaganda, the French people

[14] In 1926, perhaps because Maurras is an agnostic, the Roman Catholic Church, through the Pope, officially denounced the *Action Française* movement, although the latter has supported the Church as one of the great traditional institutions of France.

[15] Quotation taken from Soltau, *op. cit.*, p. 370.

[16] *Op. cit.*, p. 212.

do not as yet seem inclined to throw overboard the principles of the French Revolution and accept a régime of authoritarianism and a career of external expansion. They appear to believe that their safety lies in the maintenance, with perhaps slight concessions, of the political *status quo* in Europe, and that their interests require the consolidation of their present empire, rather than new adventures. They continue to place faith in parliamentary institutions and in a foreign policy emphasizing peace and stability and the necessity of developing international institutions to guarantee national security and promote the common interests of nations.

The successful propagation of integral nationalism demands certain favoring conditions. In Italy and Germany since the World War, a number of circumstances have combined to discredit parliamentary democracy and usher in political régimes based on conceptions of the totalitarian state. Italy emerged from the World War on the victorious side but, like her associates, at a frightful cost, and with an ambition for compensation and the spoils of a victor. England and France demanded and secured large territories under mandate, as well as making gains in other directions, at the expense of the defeated Powers. Italy, for her part, looked forward not only to the fruits of victory promised her by the Allied Powers in the Treaty of London in 1915, but developed ambitions for additional territory. As it turned out, her aspiration for *Italia Irredenta* was satisfied and, in addition, her frontier in the north was extended up to the Brenner Pass in order to give her a good strategic frontier. However, the "compensation" granted her in Africa by Great Britain and France was regarded by Italian statesmen as inadequate. The Turkish nationalists successfully repelled her attempts to get a foothold in Asiatic Turkey, and the rebellious Albanians helped to thwart her desire to make the Adriatic an Italian lake. Altogether, Italian nationalists and imperialists were inclined to feel, as they put it, that they had "won the war but lost the peace." [17] The failure of Italian statesmen to induce other nations to satisfy the maximum Italian demands caused a great deal of dissatisfaction in the ranks of strong

[17] A Fascist spokesman, Count Antonio Cippico, expressed this widely held view at the Institute of Politics in Williamstown, Massachusetts, in 1925, when he said that "all the great European Allies and even Japan, who swore they were waging the war of democracy against every form of imperialism, divided up among themselves the spoils of victory, excluding therefrom the most democratic country of them all, Italy." (*Italy, the Central Problem of the Mediterranean* [New Haven, Conn., 1926], p. 47.)

nationalists and a resentment not only against Italy's "faithless allies" but against her own "decrepit" statesmen who were accused of weakness and incompetence.

The disappointment, humiliation, and dissatisfaction engendered by these failures in the field of foreign policy were greatly aggravated by a chaotic economic and social situation within Italy with which succeeding post-war governments seemed unable to cope. In the aftermath of the War, all of the nations of Europe had to face severe economic problems. Old markets had been destroyed, industries had been demoralized or prostituted to war purposes, productive forces had been disorganized, huge national debts had been accumulated, and monetary systems deranged. But, with the exception of certain of the defeated countries, the Italian people after the War found themselves in more desperate straits perhaps than did any of the Continental peoples. Undoubtedly this was due in large measure to the discrepancy between population and resources, a situation that in the nature of things could not readily be remedied by any government. Italy could not produce enough food for her rapidly growing population. In order to purchase this food abroad, it was necessary to develop a manufacturing surplus for foreign markets. But Italy also lacked the basic raw materials, minerals, and fuels essential to this development. Many of these, therefore, likewise had to be imported in great measure from abroad. Other countries, such as Great Britain, had exported considerable capital prior to the War and had large interest-bearing investments with which to balance their international accounts. Italy had been able to accumulate no such investments, but, on the other hand, had to become a borrowing nation in order to make ends meet. The World War, far from affording a solution by reducing population, aggravated the problem. From 1914 to 1918, more than a million Italians returned to their native land. Moreover, the War imposed a tremendous drain on Italian resources, caused living costs to soar out of all proportion to incomes, and left in its wake serious economic disturbances and distress. At the same time, conditions in other countries were such that opportunities for Italian emigrants were greatly restricted, if the doors were not closed to them altogether.[18] Thus, thwarted in her ambitions to expand on the eastern shores of the Adriatic, in the Near East, and in Africa, in

[18] See C. E. McGuire, *Italy's International Economic Position* (New York, 1926), for study of Italy's economic problems.

order to have new homes for her emigrants under the Italian flag and new sources of raw materials for her manufactures, and faced with an increasingly serious economic situation at home, Italy was ready by 1922 to listen to revolutionary proposals and countenance extreme action.

More than a decade before the World War, a nationalistic spirit of an aggressive and imperialist character was observable in Italy. Up to about the beginning of the twentieth century, there was no manifest disposition in any important political group to prepare Italy to assume the rôle of a Great Power and seek a career of colonial expansion beyond *Italia Irredenta,* although English and French expansion in northern Africa had caused some concern and jealousy and had contributed toward sporadic Italian thrusts in northern and eastern Africa.[19] The successful Lybian war of 1911, however, although in part an evidence of a growing determination to have a share in the partition of Africa, was important as well for its effect in stimulating the national pride and imperialist aspirations. The Nationalist Association, formed by a small group of intellectuals in 1910, grew rapidly after 1911. Enrico Corradini, later to be recognized as one of the intellectual precursors of Fascism, founded the *Idea Nazionale,* a newspaper that helped powerfully in the forming of the public opinion of the younger generation. In 1913, the Nationalist Association developed into a political party, and later captured six seats in the Italian Parliament. Irredentist societies likewise were founded to carry on propaganda for the recovery of the Italian-speaking districts from foreign sovereignty and for the realization of Italy's "natural" frontiers.

The nationalists were impatient and contemptuous of a slow-moving parliamentary régime that tolerated, and even assumed, on the basis of liberal principles, rival political parties and classes. National unity and discipline must be attained, and a strong foreign policy pursued

[19] Francesco Crispi (1819-1901), however, exhibited authoritarian views and dreamed of the acquisition of a new Roman Empire. As President of the Council of Ministers from 1887 to 1891 and from 1893 to 1896, he was in a position to exert considerable influence in this direction. The disaster to Italian arms at Adowa in 1896, on the occasion of Crispi's endeavors to carve out an empire in Ethiopia, put an end to his career and for the moment to a forward foreign policy. But, twenty-eight years later, after the Fascists had come into power, a tablet to his memory was erected in the Chigi Palace and he was apotheosized as "the last hero of the *risorgimento* and the first of Italy's greatness." Moreover, Mussolini now (1936) seems to be intent on making Crispi's policy good by launching a large-scale offensive against Ethiopia.

in order to make good the demand of a new and rejuvenated Italy for a "place in the sun." Why should a vigorous and prolific Italy have to see hundreds of thousands of her sons and daughters each year forced to seek new homes under foreign flags? This "imperialism of the poor" must cease, but it will not cease until a united Italy, purged of the life-sapping liberal institutions and methods that make her impotent in the national struggle for existence, and seeking her inspiration in imperial Rome, shall demand new lands for her sons at the point of the sword.[20] It is to be observed, therefore, that this exuberant pre-war Italian nationalism, propagated by a small group of intellectuals and journalists who did not pretend that they spoke for the majority of the Italian people (they were contemptuous of majorities in any case), but who contended that they did represent "the true interests of the nation," was, like the French brand of Barrès and Maurras, reactionary. Just as the royalists of the *Action Française* in France harked back to the good old days of the *ancien régime,* so the Italian nationalists took ancient Rome as the model for the new Italian state they were seeking. However, they and the doctrinal spokesmen of the post-war Fascist state which has become the concrete expression of their aspirations, have drawn their ideology from a variety of sources, many of them foreign, so that in fact nationalist and Fascist doctrines may be said to have a more or less cosmopolitan origin.[21]

Integral nationalism requires a "man-on-horseback" as the incar-

[20] H. W. Schneider, *Making the Fascist State* (New York, 1928), pp. 1-5; J. S. Barnes, *The Universal Aspects of Fascism* (London, 1928), pp. 56-57; Hayes, *op. cit.,* pp. 213-216.

[21] Mussolini, for example, acknowledges his indebtedness not only to the Italians, Machiavelli and Vilfredo Pareto (1848-1923), but also to the German, Friedrich Nietzsche (1844-1900), the Frenchman, Georges Sorel (1847-1922), and the American philosopher, William James (1842-1910). See W. K. Stewart, "Mentors of Mussolini," *American Political Science Review,* Vol. XXII (Nov., 1928), No. 4, pp. 843-869. Nationalists such as Enrico Corradini, Francesco Coppola, Alfredo Rocco, Luigi Federzoni, Roberto Forges-Davanzati, and Maurizio Maraviglia also drew much of their inspiration from Maurras and Sorel. (Schneider, *op. cit.,* p. 102.) See *ibid.,* bibliography, pp. 365-385, for their works. Fascism naturally has found its strongest supporters among the nationalists and is largely indebted to some of them for the ideology it has developed since the March on Rome. See, for example, Alfredo Rocco, "The Political Doctrine of Fascism," *International Conciliation* (Oct., 1926), No. 223. Fascism derived its ideology in part from the Italian Idealists, Francesco De Sanctis, Silvio Spaventa, Benedetto Croce, and Giovanni Gentile. These in turn derived their inspiration from the great German philosopher, Hegel, although the Fascist apologist, J. S. Barnes, points out that they "contributed much to attenuate the German theses" and "to purge them of their gross materialism." (Barnes, *op. cit.,* p. 93.)

nation of national unity and authority. In France, the royalists still seek such a man, unless Colonel de la Rocque, leader of the Fascist *Croix de Feu* may be regarded as their choice; in Italy, the nationalists found him in Benito Mussolini. In the days before the War, Mussolini was a revolutionary socialist with syndicalist leanings. As a young man, he led a somewhat restless and turbulent life and served several terms of imprisonment in his own country and in Austria and Switzerland for organizing strikes of workingmen and for other subversive activities. As a Socialist who regarded the "class war" as the significant form of social struggle, Mussolini agitated against the Tripolitan War of 1911 and once more landed in prison. Four years later he again took his stand, along with other members of the Socialist party, against Italy's entrance into the World War. His fighting disposition, however, seems to have triumphed over his socialistic principles, for as early as October, 1914, he had definitely aligned himself with the interventionists who demanded that Italy should enter the War on the side of the nations allied against Austria and Germany. Expelled from the Socialist party as a renegade, he insisted that he still adhered to socialistic principles and suggested that the cause of the workers could best be furthered and the bourgeois state undermined by active participation in the War. "Do not believe that the bourgeoisie is enthusiastic about our interventionism," he declared at the meeting at which he was formally expelled from the Socialist party. "It is grumbling, accusing us of rashness, and evidently fears that the proletariat once armed with the bayonet will be able to use it for its own ends. Do not imagine that by tearing up my membership card in the Socialist party you can forbid my socialist faith or prevent me from continuing to work for the cause of socialism and of the revolution." [22]

From this moment, Mussolini not only spoke and wrote on behalf of Italy's entry into the World War, but also gave evidence as time went on of a new perspective in which the class war eventually was to be viewed as far less important than the struggle of nations.[23] In his campaign to convince the Socialists that they should support inter-

[22] Quoted in Schneider, *op. cit.*, pp. 9-10.

[23] In a discussion of Fascist doctrine in *Gerachia* (Dec., 1923), a Milan Fascist monthly, of which Mussolini was editor-in-chief, Enrico Corradini said: "The class struggle alone is a reality and a necessary condition of society, but it is subordinated (under Fascism) to a still higher reality—the struggle of nations." See *Living Age*, March 1, 1924, pp. 403-405.

vention, it is true that he held the picture before them of a proletarian revolution after the War in which the capitalist autocrats would be overthrown and a Socialist government installed in Italy. He insisted, however, that "war and socialism are incompatible only where taken in the universal meaning of the terms," that "every age and every people has its wars," and that, after all, "it is *blood* that gives motion to the clanging wheels of history." It was not until after the Fascist revolution, however, seven years later, that he advanced an ethical justification for war in general.

After his expulsion from the Socialist party, Mussolini founded a daily paper, *Il Popolo d'Italia,* and campaigned vigorously for intervention. When Italy entered the War, he saw active service for about a year and a half before a wound sent him to a hospital and eventually back to his journalistic tasks.[24] When the war ended, he gathered a group of young men about him, founded the *Fascio di Combattimento* (Union of Combat), and drew up a program of internal reforms of distinctly democratic and even revolutionary nature which was brought before the Italian people in the elections of 1919.[25] In the course of the ensuing two years, however, this program was thrown overboard. Italy was in a turmoil from strikes and labor disturbances engineered in part by communistic elements. Factories were seized and attempts were made to operate them by, and on behalf of, the workers. The Fascisti hesitated until the occupation of the factories had collapsed and then launched themselves against communism. This helped to attract to their standards a great many different elements which, for one reason or another, were dissatisfied with the government's post-war policies and wanted more vigorous action both at home and abroad. By their successes against the communists the Fascists gave some promise of being able to establish a strong government. Fighting their opponents with clubs and castor oil, they furnished the Italian populace with amusement at the same time that they aroused its respect.

[24] Benito Mussolini, *My Autobiography* (New York, 1928), pp. 43-49.

[25] Among his proposals were proportional representation, woman suffrage, abolition of the Senate, abolition of conscription, a national constituent assembly, an eight-hour day, minimum wage laws, participation of workers in the control of industry, national occupational councils, nationalization of all factories for the manufacture of arms and explosives, a heavy capital levy, revision of war contracts, and the sequestration of eighty-five per cent of all war profits. A foreign policy was also advocated, designed to increase the prestige of Italy and enable her to acquire Fiume and the entire Dalmatian coast.

Harassed business men, anxious to have labor disciplined and willing to accept lower wages, saw in the enemy of communism a possible saviour. Members of the middle class, as well as professional men, desirous of having law and order restored, were likewise attracted to a movement whose leaders had stepped into the breach and saved the country, as the Fascists contended, from Bolshevism.[26] Conservatives were further assured that they had nothing to fear from the Fascists when Mussolini, the erstwhile republican[27] and socialist, declared in September, 1922, in favor of the monarchy. In the following month, in which the historic "march on Rome" placed the Fascists in the seats of power, Mussolini indicated a further movement from the Left and foreshadowed the abandonment of parliamentary institutions. Democracy, he said, had performed a useful service in the nineteenth century, but "it is possible that the twentieth may see arise some other political force more powerful and better adapted to the needs of the country." [28]

The ideology of Fascism was developed after the event. According to Mussolini, "Fascism was not the nursling of a doctrine worked out beforehand with detailed elaboration; it was born of the need for action and it was itself from the beginning practical rather than theoretical. . ." [29] Put bluntly, the Fascists seized power, desired to retain it, met situations as they arose and developed ways and means of dealing with them. The institutions which they created, as well as the ideas of the state which they began to voice after the "march on Rome," were determined by their ambitions to retain power and create a strong and militant Italy that would demand a leading part in the world drama along with other Great Powers.[30] Perhaps it is not too much to say

[26] For a keen analysis by an anti-Fascist of the various elements and classes of the population which Fascism attracted, see Carlo Sforza, "Italy and Fascism," *Foreign Affairs,* Vol. III (April, 1925), No. 3, pp. 358-370.

[27] Mussolini has since explained that the Fascists had supported republicanism up to this time "for reasons of expediency." *International Conciliation* (Jan., 1935), No. 306, p. 9.

[28] F. Lee Benns, *Europe Since 1914* (New York, 1934), p. 356. For a good account of the various shifts assertedly made by Mussolini in his position on fundamental matters, see Sforza, *loc. cit.,* pp. 358-370.

[29] "The Political and Social Doctrine of Fascism," *International Conciliation* (Jan., 1935), No. 306. pp. 5-6. This is the translation of an article contributed by Mussolini to the *Enciclopedia Italiana* in 1932. In another place he expressed the characteristic contempt that integral nationalists frequently show toward the rational approach: "Intuition in the face of adventure rather than doctrine—the older faculty is the purer; my blood tells me what to do." *National Review* (London), November, 1925.

[30] Fascist ideas concerning international relations will, of course, receive chief

that their conception of the relation of the individual to the state, upon which the political, economic, and social structure of the Fascist state has assertedly been reared, was inspired principally by their objectives in the field of foreign policy. In the earlier years of the Fascist régime, Mussolini seems to have looked upon domestic matters as relatively unimportant and unworthy of his personal attention. One of the principal American analysts of Fascism says: "As a statesman he felt superior to them. Both by temperament and by his nationalist principles he was preoccupied with Italy's international relations and the urgent problems of diplomacy. His notion of the administration of the interior was that it was primarily a negative affair, a police job, which he might safely entrust to Bianchi, while he devoted himself to foreign politics." [31] In 1925 on one of the many occasions upon which the theme of empire occupied a large part of his discourse, Mussolini pointed out that to reach such a goal "we must resolutely abandon the entire phraseology and mentality of liberalism. The word of command can be only this: discipline. Internal discipline, in order that abroad we may present the granite block of a single national will." [32]

The discipline which Fascism regards as necessary is quite unattainable under a régime of liberalism in which governments are supposed to be for the purpose of furnishing the conditions necessary for the realization of life, liberty, and happiness by the governed. As expressed by one of the outstanding Fascist spokesmen whose statement of the political doctrine of Fascism has the endorsement of Mussolini: "For Fascism, society is the end, individuals the means, and its whole life consists in using individuals as instruments for its social ends." [33] That is to say, Mussolini and other Fascists who may collaborate with

attention in the discussion that follows in this chapter. No attempt will be made to deal comprehensively with Fascist doctrine. Certain aspects, however, that have a connection with, or implications for, the field of foreign affairs must receive attention. For an excellent treatment of Fascist political thought as a whole, see Frances W. Coker, *Recent Political Thought* (New York, 1934), Ch. XVII.

[31] Schneider, *op. cit.*, p. 116. Cf. Luigi Villari, *The Fascist Experiment* (London, 1926), p. 230, and especially speech of Mussolini before the Chamber, November 15, 1924.

[32] Benito Mussolini, *Discorsi del 1925* (Milan, 1926), p. 106. For a similar statement of the relation of discipline to empire see Mussolini's article on "The Political and Social Doctrine of Fascism," *loc. cit.*, p. 16.

[33] Alfredo Rocco, "The Political Doctrine of Fascism," *International Conciliation* (Oct., 1926), No. 223, p. 19. "Fascists make of the individual an economic instrument for the advancement of society, an instrument which they use so long as it functions and which they subordinate when no longer serviceable." (*Ibid.*, p. 20.)

him in the determination of policy, decide what social ends are worthy and in what way individuals may most effectively be used to achieve them. Individuals are not entirely deprived of their liberty, however, but only of that part which the government regards as "useless and possibly harmful." "The individual in the Fascist state," says Mussolini, "is not annulled but rather multiplied, just in the same way that a soldier in a regiment is not diminished but rather increased by the number of his comrades."[34] The comparison is an apt one, for Fascists, like other integral nationalists, constantly extol the virtues of discipline and unquestioning obedience for the masses—"theirs not to reason why"—and the leadership of a small élite. "Our concept of liberty," says Rocco, "is that the individual must be allowed to develop his personality in behalf of the state, for these ephemeral and infinitesimal elements of the complex and permanent life of society determine by their normal growth the development of the state." If, however, the growth is abnormal it may be as fatal to society as abnormal growths in living organisms. What is normal and what is abnormal is again seemingly for the Fascist physicians and metaphysicians to decide. "Freedom . . . is due to the citizen and to classes on conditions that they exercise it in the interest of society as a whole and within the limits set by social exigencies, liberty being, like any other individual right, a concession of the state."[35] According to *Il Duce,* however, the masses are not capable, except under skillful handling, of exhibiting either intelligence or unselfishness. They are quite as evil, deceitful, fickle, and cowardly as Machiavelli described them in *The Prince,* which Mussolini extols as "The Statesman's Vade Mecum" and takes as the pattern of his own conduct.[36] In his enthusiastic appraisal of the work of the Florentine, he asks, "Was the value of the political system presented in *The Prince* confined to the time when the book was written, and therefore necessarily limited and transitory, or does it remain of universal and contemporary application—particularly contemporary application?" His answer is perhaps one to which all integral nationalists would subscribe: "I affirm that the teaching of

[34] Mussolini, *loc. cit.,* p. 15.

[35] Rocco, *loc. cit.,* pp. 19-20.

[36] In 1924, Mussolini submitted a thesis to the University of Bologna for the doctor's degree entitled *A Commentary in the Year 1924 upon the Prince of Machiavelli.* His introduction, under the title, "Prelude to Machiavelli," was published in the *Living Age,* November 22, 1924, pp. 420-423.

Machiavelli is valid today after the lapse of four centuries because, even though the external aspects of our life have changed radically, those changes do not imply fundamental modifications in the mind and character of individuals and peoples."[37] Politics, to Mussolini, is the art of governing men by "guiding, utilizing, and evoking their passions, their egoisms, their interests" in the service of "general ends." These general ends, as conceived by the Fascists, seem to lie principally in the field of international politics where a virile state's will-to-power can find scope.[38]

It is perhaps to be expected that Fascism should be frankly imperialistic in its outlook and its objectives. The wide gap between Italian resources and the needs of a large and rapidly growing population has been pointed out. A conceivable alternative to a policy of territorial expansion in Italy's case would be a policy designed to adjust the population to the given standing room and resources, in part by encouraging emigration to foreign countries, but principally by discouraging large families. No state in the past, however, has shown a disposition to seek a solution of its "over-population" problem by such a policy, and it is farthest from the thoughts of the Fascists.[39] On the contrary, Mussolini and his followers have had as one of their preoccupations the acceleration of the growth of the population. The government has placed taxes on bachelors (which, however, may have a fiscal motive), has resorted to subsidizing honeymoons, has extolled, honored, and rewarded the fathers of large families, and has in other ways sought to stimulate the birthrate. For "the real wealth of Italy," says a Fascist spokesman,[40] "is man power," that "greatest of all raw

[37] "Prelude to Machiavelli," *loc. cit.*, p. 420.

[38] Mussolini seems to regard people in the mass, for all important purposes, as so much raw material. "Can you imagine," he asks, "a war declared by referendum? A referendum serves very well for choosing the best site for a village fountain, but when the supreme interests of a nation are at stake even the most democratic governments take good care not to leave them to the decision of the masses." (*Living Age*, November 22, 1924, p. 422.) Rocco, however, appears to think the Italian masses, at any rate, are most dependable in moments of crisis: ". . . among peoples with a great history and with noble traditions, even the lowest elements of society possess an instinctive discernment of what is necessary for the welfare of the race, which in moments of great historical crises reveals itself to be almost infallible. It is therefore as wise to afford to this instinct the means of declaring itself as it is judicious to entrust the normal control of the commonwealth to a selected élite." (*Loc. cit.*, p. 21.)

[39] Cippico, *op. cit.*, p. 42.

[40] Beniamino de Ritis, "Aims and Policies of the Fascist Régime in Italy," *International Conciliation* (Jan., 1935), No. 306, p. 19.

materials." This raw material in larger quantity is a real need, according to Mussolini: "An unintelligent person says: 'we are too numerous. Intelligent persons will reply, 'We are too few.' . . Let us speak plainly. What are 40 million Italians beside 90 million Germans and 200 million Slavs? Let us turn westward. What are 40 million Italians beside 40 million French people and their 90 million colonial inhabitants; or beside 46 million English people and the 450 millions in their colonies? Gentlemen, Italy in order to count for something must present itself on the threshold of the second half of this century with a population of not less than 60 million inhabitants." [41]

The tendency of Fascist writers and orators to dwell on the theme of empire and to insist at the same time that Italy must have a larger population, has occasioned considerable nervousness among certain European nations. And the frank and outspoken demands Fascists have at one time or another made for additional territories, coupled with the threat that they will one day take them by force if the colonially satiated Powers do not see the light and make concessions, have increased the uneasiness in certain quarters. Mussolini and some of his supporters, however, have on occasion been at pains to point out that "empire" has various meanings and that when one uses the term he is not necessarily thinking of territorial expansion. Thus: "According to Fascism, government is not so much a thing to be expressed in territorial or military terms as in terms of morality and the spirit. It must be thought of as an empire—that is to say, a nation which directly or indirectly rules other nations, without the need for conquering a single square yard of territory. For Fascism, the growth of empire, that is to say the expansion of the nation, is an essential manifestation of vitality, and its opposition a sign of decadence. Peoples which are rising, or rising again after a period of decadence, are always imperialist; any renunciation is a sign of decay and of death." [42] "Renunciation" may doubtless take many forms, and *Il Duce* does not specify at this point what they may be. It is clear, however, that he and his followers

[41] Benito Mussolini, *Discorsi del 1927* (Milan, 1928), pp. 78–79.

[42] Mussolini, "The Political and Social Doctrine of Fascism," *International Conciliation* (Jan., 1935), No. 306, p. 16, published by the Carnegie Endowment for International Peace. This view was expressed in substance by Mussolini in 1919 when he declared: "Imperialism is the eternal and immutable law of life. At bottom it is but the need, the desire, and the will for expansion which every living, healthy individual or people has in itself." Quotation taken from Schneider, *op. cit.*, p. 273.

would regard restriction of the birthrate in Italy and willingness to see Italian emigrants "lost to the flag" as an evidence of renunciation. Territorial expansion, therefore, either through the graceful acquiescence of other peoples, or by means of war, would seem to be one of the forms which Fascists intend Italian imperialism to take.[43]

The Fascists have no compunctions about resorting to war if it is necessary to employ it in order to reach the desired objectives. In fact the chief concern of Mussolini has been to prepare and discipline the Italian nation and endow the youth with a "warrior mind" so that Italy will be "respected and feared" and in a position to employ war when its adversaries in the struggle for existence do not yield gracefully. In 1927 he declared: "We must be ready at a moment's notice to mobilize five million men [44] and be able to arm them; we must strengthen our navy; and it is necessary that our air force, in which I have increasing confidence, be so numerous and so powerful that the roar of its motors can drown out every other noise on the peninsula and the surface of its wings obscure the sun. Then between 1935 and 1940, when we shall be at a point which I would call crucial for European history, we shall finally be able to make our voice heard and see our rights recognized." [45] The latest decree (September 18, 1934) relating to military training is most sweeping and comprehensive. It is based on the assumption, so widely held in military and even diplomatic circles in the decade prior to the World War, that war must come sooner or later. Italian boys as young as six years are compulsorily enlisted by the state for two years in the pre-Balilla in order, at

[43] For a Fascist view of imperialism see Enrico Corradini, "Italian Imperialist Doctrine," *Living Age*, March 1, 1924, pp. 403-405. The article originally appeared in *Gerachia*, December, 1923, Milan Fascist monthly of which Mussolini was Editor-in-chief.

[44] After his imitators, the German Nazis, evinced a determination to annex Austria, Mussolini raised the figure to eight million, according to an interview with H. R. Knickerbocker, published in the *San Francisco Examiner*, September 30, 1934.

[45] Benito Mussolini, *Discorsi del 1927* (Milan, 1928), pp. 147-148. Interestingly enough, the year 1935 saw Mussolini's first determined effort to carve out a large imperial domain in Africa at the expense of Ethiopia, in spite of the fact that the latter country is a member of the League of Nations and, as such, entitled to have the other members of the League respect its territorial integrity and political independence. Mussolini's troops are now (November, 1935) waging war against Ethiopia, and the Italian dictator continues to defy the efforts of the League to restrain him. In the meantime he threatens to have Italy withdraw from the League, should the latter go too far in its attempt to compel him to abandon his African enterprise.

the earliest moment, to enlist their interest in the life of the soldier. From the age of eight until they are fourteen, they are placed in the Balilla organization whose program is designed to continue and deepen that interest "by means of frequent contacts with the armed forces of the nation, whose glories and traditions will be taught to them." From fourteen to eighteen, the training is carried a stage farther in the Avanguardisti organizations. At the age of eighteen the Italian boy becomes a soldier and serves in the Fascist militia until he is twenty-one. At twenty-one years of age he is drafted and begins two years of compulsory army service. For the following ten years he receives post-military training designed "to preserve in former soldiers the military spirit and *esprit de corps* and to maintain in readiness a reserve of specialists skilled in their respective military functions and well acquainted with the newest materials and most recent developments in the arts of war." Occasional training continues up to the age of fifty-five years. In addition to the direct military training received by all Italian boys, they are required to take "military culture" courses from the time they leave the elementary schools until their formal education is over.[46]

Although Fascist spokesmen, doubtless "for reasons of expediency," often declare that Fascist Italy "desires" peace even though it may be "compelled" to wage war, they feel no scruples about using violence to achieve political ends, whether against domestic or foreign enemies, whenever in their judgment such "surgery" is necessary.[47] Moreover, war receives the highest endorsement on ethical and spiritual grounds, and one gathers that men would lose something very precious for which no satisfactory substitute could be found if war were ever to disappear, and the "sheep's paradise" of pacifism should become a reality. Mussolini undoubtedly states the Fascist viewpoint—which, incidentally, is in substance that of von Treitschke, Bernhardi, and many other writers of the nineteenth century—[48] in the following considered judgment: "And above all, Fascism, the more it considers and observes the future and the development of humanity quite apart from political considerations of the moment, believes neither in the possibility nor

[46] See article by Arnaldo Cortesi in *New York Times,* September 19, 1934. This militarization of Italy Mussolini contends "is the highest form of moral education of the people. It is a school of heroism and sacrifice. National consciousness is not conceivable without military consciousness." From interview published in the *San Francisco Examiner,* September 30, 1934.

[47] Coker, *op. cit.,* pp. 479-481.

[48] *Supra,* Ch. XII.

the utility of perpetual peace. It thus repudiates the doctrine of Pacifism—born of a renunciation of the struggle and an act of cowardice in the face of sacrifice. War alone brings up to its highest tension all human energy and puts the stamp of nobility upon the peoples who have the courage to meet it. All other trials are substitutes, which never really put men into the position where they have to make the great decision—the alternative of life or death. Thus a doctrine which is founded upon this harmful postulate of peace is hostile to Fascism. And thus hostile to the spirit of Fascism, though accepted for what use they can be in dealing with particular political situations, are all the international leagues and societies which, as history will show, can be scattered to the winds when once strong national feeling is aroused. . ." [49]

The Fascist attitude toward the League of Nations is intelligible in the light of the doctrines and objectives that have been outlined. When the Fascists came into power, the League was an accomplished fact and a going concern. Germany, the late enemy, was not a member, and Soviet Russia, whose social ends were radically different from those of Fascist Italy, was likewise outside the League circle. On the other hand, the other great European powers were League members and its chief support. Italy, as a Great Power, already occupied a permanent seat along with them on the Council of the League, and was therefore in a position, as far as the League organization might afford the opportunity, to help dictate affairs in Europe. In so far, then, as the League might be a medium for the prosecution of Italian interests and the furtherance of Fascist designs in collaboration with other Great Powers, it could certainly not be ignored by Rome. And in any event Italy would gain more by shrewd utilization of such opportunities for the advancement of national interests, as membership on the Council might furnish, than by a policy of hostility.[50] On the other hand, it is obvious

[49] Benito Mussolini, "The Political and Social Doctrine of Fascism," *loc. cit.*, pp. 7-8. In the light of this doctrine the following remarks of *Il Duce* are very suggestive: "The last century was the century of our dependence; this century must be that of our power . . . every one of you must consider himself a soldier, a molecule, feeling and pulsating with the entire organism." *The Nation*, Vol. CXXI (Nov. 11, 1925), No. 3149.

[50] This point of view is expressed in substance by Cesare Salvati in *Critica Fascista*, September 15, 1926. See Frank H. Simonds and Brooks Emeny, *The Great Powers in World Politics* (New York, 1935), p. 273 ff., for Fascist attitude toward the League as interpreted by two American writers.

that unless the League were to be merely an instrument of the Great Powers for making and carrying out decisions in their own interests, a government imbued with Fascist doctrine could hardly be expected to welcome it. And certainly a League following the Wilsonian conception would be not only distasteful in theory but also embarrassing in practice. Designed to stabilize European relations in accordance with a territorial settlement unsatisfactory from the Italian standpoint, it clearly ran athwart the dynamic concept of political relationships held by the Fascists. Having as a primary aim the immediate discouragement and ultimate extinction of war, it stood as an obstacle to the realization by war of the aims of men who did not desire to see the old time-honored method of self-help denied to a "rising" nation, and who professed to believe that war, from time to time, was a necessary cleansing and purifying agent. Finally, by taking small states into its membership on a plane of equality with the Great Powers, and by attempting to apply the methods and work in the spirit of republican and parliamentary institutions, the League represented a denial in the sphere of international relations of the aristocratic and authoritarian concepts of the Fascists, and once more an obstacle to a state that preferred to "live dangerously" and rely upon power and guile rather than persuasion to achieve its ends. Within the state Fascism deliberately circumscribes the freedom of the individual in many ways in order to make a strong, unified, and powerful state able to inspire respect and fear abroad. But the "sphere of anarchy" of individual states, on the other hand, it would not contract; and to the extent that the League in practice may limit a state's freedom of action it is not congenial to Fascism.[51]

The first favorable opportunity for an open attack on the League came in 1933 when two intransigent members, Japan and Germany,

[51] This was shown at the time of the Corfu incident in 1923, when Italy, in advance of the culpability of another member of the League having been established in connection with the murder of an Italian officer on Greek soil, resorted to violence against a fellow League member, denied the competence of the League, and attempted to flout its authority. Pressure exerted through the Council and Assembly of the League of Nations was probably responsible for Italy's withdrawal from the island of Corfu which she had bombarded and seized. The Fascists criticized the League on this occasion as having the serious defect of allowing small nations to discuss and dictate the affairs of the Great Powers. Felix Morley, *The Society of Nations* (Washington, 1932), p. 428; William Rappard, *International Relations as Viewed from Geneva* (London, 1925), pp. 197-198; Benns, *op. cit.*, pp. 233-235.

gave notice of their intention to withdraw from membership.[52] In April, the Fascist Grand Council hinted that Italy might withdraw from the League if the Disarmament Conference failed to achieve results. In the meantime, Mussolini proposed a Four-Power Pact which was designed, apparently, to replace the equalitarian League by a directorship of four Great Powers—Great Britain, France, Germany, and Italy. These Powers in reality were apparently to make the decisions on all important issues of international policy for the period of ten years during which the treaty was to be in operation, although the formal League organization would remain. The attack on the League continued, however, Mussolini declaring in November, 1933, that "the League of Nations has lost all that would be able to give it a political significance and a historical import. . ." In the following month the Fascist Grand Council issued a statement that "the further story of Italy in the League is conditioned upon a radical reform of that organization, to be effected in the shortest space of time and which must touch the League of Nations in its constitution, its working, and its object."[53] Most of the League members, however, have rallied against any drastic tampering with the Covenant. Russia has joined the organization and added to its prestige; Nazi Germany has by her Austrian policy, caused Italy to draw closer to France and the other staunch supporters of the League, so that at the moment it is seemingly not propitious for Mussolini to continue his offensive against it.

In general, conditions similar to those which led to Fascism in Italy were responsible for the victory of national socialism and the setting up of a totalitarian régime in Germany. Not only was the latter politically, socially, and economically demoralized by the War, but she lost part of her territory and resources in Europe, was stripped of her mercantile marine and her colonies, disarmed, and saddled with a staggering bill of reparations, not to mention other handicaps that were imposed upon her. In the trying years prior to 1924, culminating in the occupation of the Ruhr and the disastrous policy of inflation, the middle

[52] Japan gave notice in March, after the League Assembly had condemned her action in Manchuria. Germany gave notice in April, ostensibly because the League's Disarmament Conference failed to meet Germany's demand for equality.

[53] George Kidd, "Changes in the League, Past and Proposed," *Geneva Special Studies*, Vol. V, (1934), Nos. 7-8, pp. 26-27. The Fascists appear to be chiefly interested, if the League must continue, in divorcing it from the peace treaties, facilitating treaty revision, and converting the organization into an instrument of the Great Powers.

class was almost wiped out of existence and her position became desperate. In the following years, marked by a more liberal attitude toward her by her former enemies, by a policy of stabilization and fulfillment under Stresemann, and by the rationalization of her industry, Germany appeared to be on the road to recovery. In 1929, however, on the eve of the world-wide depression, her situation again began to grow desperate. Foreign bankers, from whom she had been securing loans for financing trade and industry as well as for meeting a large part of her indebtedness, were no longer in a position to extend her extensive credits. High tariffs against her goods restricted the growth of her export trade which was vital to her ultimate recovery. Her industry began to decline, unemployment rapidly increased, and additional burdens to care for those who could secure no work had to be assumed. Internal demands by the more conservative groups and business elements for financial and fiscal reforms, involving the curtailment of public works and decreases in the amount spent for social insurance, met with resistance from the Social Democrats. In the following years, prior to the victory of the National Socialists, various governments of the republican régime attempted to secure agreement on a program and avert complete collapse. They failed, however, and Germany after 1930 came to be governed more and more by presidential emergency decrees. In the meantime, as conditions grew worse the National Socialists under Adolph Hitler, deriving their inspiration in part from the Italian Fascists and copying the methods of the latter in their appeals to the German masses against the dangers of communism and the hostility of the outside world, exploited the situation skillfully and perfected their organization so that when their leader was appointed Chancellor in January, 1933, they were prepared to establish a dictatorship and move swiftly toward the realization of their ideal, the totalitarian state.[54]

The Nazi notions of the state and of international relations are, in most essentials, the same as those of the Italian Fascists and integral nationalists generally. Democratic and parliamentary institutions are derided and condemned because of their inefficiency and for their weakening effect on the national will. Individual liberty, including freedom

[54] For a fuller account than can be given here of conditions in Germany, after the War and prior to the taking over of the government by the National Socialists, see Benns, *op. cit.*, pp. 383-429.

of speech, publication, assembly, association, etc., must give way before the necessity of creating a united and militant nation, different from and superior to all others by virtue of its God-given racial qualities.[55] As in the case of Italian Fascism, German Nazism is also anti-intellectual. Feeling is exalted above thinking, for the masses at any rate, and instinct is regarded as truer than reason.[56] Thought and direction come from the top. Adolph Hitler, *Der Führer,* is not responsible to the electorate. The electorate is responsible to him and to the élite whom he selects to govern with him, for according to Nazi doctrine authority starts at the top and proceeds downward to the masses while responsibility starts at the bottom and ascends upward. Each individual is responsible to the one who is "destined" to stand above him in the Nazi hierarchy. All are answerable to *Der Führer,* and he is answerable, as were the divine-right monarchs, to God.[57]

In National Socialist doctrine one also observes the same attitude of contempt for pacifism and internationalism that is so frequently encountered across the Alps, but it is based in part on a peculiar racial dogma that Hitler and some of his followers have developed to explain Germany's present unhappy situation. The arch-enemy of Germany and, indeed, of civilization is the Jew. It was he who must be held accountable for the "stab in the back" that caused Germany to collapse before her adversaries in 1918, and for the misfortunes she has since endured under the "Jew Republic" established in 1919. The selection of the Jew as the scapegoat for all these misfortunes, and race purification as the solution for German ills, was due in part to a certain anti-Jewish fixation that Hitler and some of his followers had acquired in the post-war period, but also, apparently, to the realization of the propaganda-value of a single enemy.[58] Although Hitler may not have

[55] The Italian Fascists, however, did not make race a fetish and draw their inspiration from the Gobineaus and Chamberlains as the Nazis were to do.

[56] Frederick L. Schuman, "The Political Theory of German Fascism," *American Political Science Review,* Vol. XXVIII (April, 1934), No. 2, p. 211.

[57] *Ibid.,* pp. 226-227. Hitler and his lieutenants, like the Fascists in Italy, claim to be the true interpreters of the aspirations of an awakened and disillusioned people and, in that sense, to have a popular mandate, but elections and majorities do not seem to be necessary from the point of view of the National Socialists.

[58] Hitler, in *Mein Kampf* (Munich, 1934 printing), p. 129, says in substance that a great leader will make several enemies appear as one so that the masses will harbor no doubts, and the unity of the nation will not be weakened by an attitude of objectivity on the part of the people. The Nazis believe in "the nationalization of truth" along with everything else.

directly derived his inspiration for the racial dogma he has preached for a number of years from such racialists as Gobineau and Chamberlain, it may be observed, nevertheless, that at bottom there seems to be a close affinity between these nineteenth century racialists and the present-day Nazi theorists. Gobineau, the Frenchman, in his famous *Essai sur l'Inégalité des Races Humaines* (Paris, 1884), advanced the thesis of the innate superiority of the Aryan branch of the white peoples, and declared that the Teutons were the purest modern representatives of the Aryan family, a tenet strongly held by the Nazis. He also traced the decline of civilizations to race degeneracy brought about by the admixture of blood of superior and inferior stocks, also an article of faith of the National Socialists.[59] Chamberlain, the Englishman who became a naturalized German citizen and who was also obsessed with the genius of the Teutons, regarded race mixture as fatal to superior breeds, and the future of civilization as dependent upon the ability of the Teutons to restore their racial purity which was being undermined by Jews and other alien elements. This is essentially the thesis of the National Socialists today.[60]

The particular Nazi contribution to race as the master key to history consists in a variant of an ingenious theory of a great world conspiracy engineered by Jewry against the "white" race.[61] The Jew, ac-

[59] Nazi exhortations for a return to the simplicity and ways of life of the early Germans in which at times the old German pagan gods are extolled remind one that Gobineau also encouraged the cult of ancestor worship as a device for the preservation of racial purity.

[60] See Chamberlain's *Foundations of the Nineteenth Century,* 2 vols. (London and New York, 1911), a translation by John Lees (1910) of *Die Grundlagen des Neunzehnten Jahrhunderts,* 2 vols. (Munich, 1899). It is interesting to note that according to a recent German writer, Chamberlain wrote a letter of adulation to Hitler as early as October, 1923, in which he said he saw in him the great leader who was arousing the German soul from sleep and enabling him, Houston Stewart Chamberlain, to enjoy the first deep refreshing sleep he had had since the fateful August day of 1914. That Germany, in her hour of greatest need had produced for herself a Hitler was proof of her vitality. In this letter Chamberlain also said that the parliamentary régime must go before the Fatherland will have any chance of rejuvenation. He also rejoiced that Hitler recognized that Judaism was destroying the life of the German nation and proposed to remedy the situation. In 1924, on the occasion of Hitler's birthday, Chamberlain delivered another panegyric, and mentioned that Hitler had called on him, and that he had met the deliverer twice. See purported texts of the letters and of Chamberlain's eulogy on the occasion of Hitler's birthday in *Chamberlain der Seher des Dritten Reiches,* by Georg Schott (Munich, 1934), pp. 11-13, 15-18.

[61] The conspiracy idea antedates the Nazis. In 1905, the Protocols of the elders of Zion was published in Russia. The Protocols were said to have been stolen from the inner circle of Jewish conspirators who were plotting to bring the world

cording to the usual version, has been careful to keep his own race "pure" by marriage within the tribe, but has diabolically defiled the blood of superior peoples by miscegenation, and has lived for centuries as a parasite among them. His weapons in the fight to dominate the world have been lies, calumny, poison, and decomposition. He has worked through the liberal press, parliamentary democracy, international finance, pacifism, and finally Bolshevism in order to accomplish his fell purpose. Already he has attained complete domination in Russia. He now seeks the conquest of the entire world through Bolshevism. If Germany is to have a renaissance and regain her position in the world, she must therefore eliminate the Jewish poison.[62] Various measures to that end have been taken by the National Socialist government. Decrees of the government have debarred Jews to a great extent from practicing law or medicine, and Jewish educators and professors in the universities, however great their eminence, have been progressively dismissed. Jewish writers, journalists, artists, musicians, scientists, and business men in large numbers have also been driven from their customary employment, and many have fled abroad to escape persecution and starvation. And, of course, decrees have been promulgated making intermarriage of Jews and "Aryans" (Germans) a penal offense, for Nazis who proudly boast that "we think with our blood" cannot afford to have that blood polluted. By these and other devices designed to make Germany unhealthy for the Jew and all "un-German" influences, the Nazis hope to rejuvenate Germany.[63]

In their international outlook, the National Socialists, like the Italian Fascists, apparently place their chief reliance for a "rising" state

under the dominion of the Jews. They were later proven to be forgeries, but contributed to anti-Semitism in the United States as well as in Europe. See article on Anti-Semitism, *Encyclopedia of the Social Sciences,* II, 119-125. The Nazi version of the world conspiracy of Jewry is based on an interpretation of recent history as well as upon the discredited Protocols.

[62] Adolph Hitler, *op. cit.*, pp. 123, 357-358, 372, 750-752. See also Schuman, *loc. cit.*, pp. 215-216, whose discussion of Nazi theory is based on an examination of a number of additional sources that have not been available to me.

[63] Many German university professors of history, economics, political science, and philosophy, etc., other than Jews, have likewise been dismissed because their views did not conform to Nazi specifications. Public libraries have been overhauled and purified of "un-German" books. A book-burning day was decreed, and the books of some 160 writers were publicly burned in various university centers. (Benns, *op. cit.*, p. 437.) See also, for these and more recent measures to ban unorthodox writers and literature and to promote an orthodox literature, art, and science with a Nazi philosophy, Frederick Schuman, *The Nazi Dictatorship* (New York, 1935), pp. 347-386.

on "blood-and-iron" solutions. The Stresemann-Briand policy of conciliation, which won for Germany several concessions from her former enemies and which many Liberals think might have resulted in a complete rapprochement had it been continued, the Nazis regard with contempt. The republican policy of weakness must be replaced with a policy of strength. Then Germany will demand the things to which she feels she is entitled, and will use the sword whenever necessary to force compliance with her wishes. Both Mussolini and Hitler have stressed the importance of work as a means of solving the economic difficulties of their peoples, but they have also shown a coldness and contempt for the slow processes of negotiation, which are the only means of avoiding war in matters of importance in international affairs, have bent their energies toward preparing their countries for war, and have expressed both their contempt for pacifism and their conviction that Gordian Knots can only be cut with the sword.

When the various statesmen at the Disarmament Conference in 1933 were seeking a formula that would enable them to reach an agreement which Germany could accept, the National Socialist government suddenly recalled the German delegates from the Conference and shortly announced Germany's intention to withdraw from the League. In the meantime, the Nazis by unilateral action denounced the disarmament clauses of the Treaty of Versailles and began to arm. The foreign policies of the Third Reich, as a whole, whatever justification they may have in German eyes in view of various injustices in the peace treaties, have seemed sufficiently aggressive and intransigent to alienate the other Powers (except Poland?), including Germany's former friend, Italy.[64]

That Germany's neighbors have been uneasy since the advent to power of the National Socialists is due not only to the foreign policy that has been pursued but also to the implications of the Nazi doctrines. Some Nazi spokesmen have taken the position that their racial objective will not be realized until all Germans in Europe are under the sovereignty of the German state. States having German minorities wonder whether this means a revival of the pre-war dreams of the Pan-Germanists. Hitler, in *Mein Kampf,* speaks frankly of the necessity of expansion for economic reasons. Germany's population is too large

[64] Henri Lichtenberger, "Les Répercussions Internationales du Hitlerisme," *L'Esprit International,* VII (Oct., 1933), 590-607.

for the land and resources which she possesses. Like Mussolini, he rejects the proposal for the restriction of numbers, arguing that such a policy will lead to the survival of the weak and unfit and eventually to conquest by a stronger race. Moreover, no final solution can be expected by means of increasing the productiveness of the soil. The only satisfactory solution is for the strong to reach out and seize what is necessary for their existence. Rather than perish, a great nation has a duty as well as a right to take what it needs. Mankind has grown through eternal struggle; in eternal peace it will perish. Applying this reasoning to the German situation, he contends that Germany should look to the east rather than to the south and west, or overseas, for the lands she requires. And she must expand there and become a world power or cease to exist altogether. Fate, he thinks, has pointed the way, for Russia has been delivered up to Bolshevism by the Jews and is ripe for collapse. Before the War, it had survived and become powerful because of the genius and efficiency of the Germanic elements within it. But the Jews have no organizing genius and cannot continue to dominate such a powerful empire. When they lose their hold, however, Russia will also cease to be a state. The German sword will then prepare the way for the German plow.[65]

Reviewing the doctrines and policies of both Fascist Italy and Nazi Germany from the point of view of international relations, it seems reasonably clear that the leaders of both assume and act upon the assumption that the strong, irresponsible, regimented, and autocratically governed state, ever "living dangerously" in an anarchical struggle for existence, is the state of the future.[66] Those with the will-to-power will overcome the weaker and give the blessings of their rule to the lesser breeds. Under such a conception the battle is to the strong both within and between states, and the law is the law of the jungle.[67] The political

[65] Hitler, *op. cit.*, pp. 144-146, 154, 740-743.

[66] It is true, however, that many of Hitler's utterances on foreign relations since he has been in power, and perhaps especially since Germany's rearming has tended to bring about her political isolation, have emphasized Germany's desire for a peaceful solution of all international problems. See approved English translation of the speech he delivered in the Reichstag, May 21, 1935 (Berlin, 1935).

[67] "A political doctrine based on the omnipotence and glorification of the state as an end in itself will naturally result, and has usually resulted, in the negation of the law of nations as a body of rules which, both in its binding force and in its creation is independent of the will of the state." H. Lauterpacht, "Spinoza and International Law," *The British Year Book of International Law, 1927* (London, 1927), p. 91.

philosophy of the integral nationalists in general is spiritually akin to that of Machiavelli, Hobbes, Bacon, and Spinoza.

REFERENCES

Barnes, J. S., *The Universal Aspects of Fascism* (London, 1928).

Bartels, A., *Rasse und Volkstum* (Weimar, 1920).

Benoist, C., "L'Esprit de Machiavel et les Méthodes Politiques," *Revue des Deux Mondes,* XXXV (Sept., 1926), 375-400.

Chamberlain, H. S., *Foundations of the Nineteenth Century,* 2 vols. (London and New York, 1911).

Cippico, A., *Italy, the Central Problem of the Mediterranean* (New Haven, Conn., 1926).

Coker, F. W., *Recent Political Thought* (New York, 1934), Chs. XVI, XVII.

Crespi, A., *Contemporary Thought of Italy* (London, 1926).

De Ritis, B., "Aims and Policies of the Fascist Régime in Italy," *International Conciliation* (Jan., 1935), No. 306.

Elliott, W. Y., *The Pragmatic Revolt in Politics* (New York, 1928).

Feder, G., *Der Deutsche Staat* (Munich, 1933).

Gentile, G., "The Philosophic Basis of Fascism," *Foreign Affairs,* Vol. VI (Jan., 1928), No. 2, pp. 290-304.

Gobineau, J. A., Comte de, *Essai sur l'Inégalité des Races Humaines* (Paris, 1884).

Grandi, D., "The Foreign Policy of the Duce," *Foreign Affairs,* Vol. XII (July, 1934), No. 4, pp. 553-566.

Günther, H., *Der Nordische Gedanke unter den Deutschen: Rassenkunde Europas, Rassenkunde des Deutschen Volkes, Rassenkunde des Jüdischen Volkes* (Munich, 1924).

Haider, C., "The Meaning and Significance of German Fascism," *Political Science Quarterly,* Vol. XLVIII (Dec., 1933), No. 4, pp. 556-564.

Hayes, C. J. H., *Historical Evolution of Modern Nationalism* (New York, 1931), Chs. VI, VII.

Hitler, A., *Mein Kampf* (Munich, 1932).

Holborn, H., "National Socialism in Germany," *International Affairs,* Vol. XIII (Jan.-Feb., 1934), No. 1, pp. 93-101.

Kracht, G. V., "The Fundamental Issue between Nationalism and Internationalism," *International Journal of Ethics,* XXX (April, 1920), 241-266.

Lasswell, H. D., "The Psychology of Hitlerism," *Political Quarterly,* IV (1933), 373-384.

Lichtenberger, H., "Les Répercussions Internationales du Hitlérisme," *L'Esprit International,* VII (Oct., 1933), 590-607.

Mitchell, M., "Emile Durkheim and the Philosophy of Nationalism," *Political Science Quarterly,* Vol. XLVI (March, 1931), No. 1, pp. 87-106.

Munro, I. S., *Through Fascism to World Power* (London, 1933), Pt. II.

Mussolini, B., *My Autobiography* (New York, 1928).

——————, "The Political and Social Doctrine of Fascism," *International Conciliation* (Jan., 1935), No. 306.

Nitti, F. S., *Bolshevism, Fascism and Democracy* (New York, 1927).

Norlin, G., "Hitlerism: Why and Whither," *University of Colorado Bulletin,* Vol. XXXIV, No. 7, pp. 3-16. (General Series No. 343.)

Orth, S. P., "Law and Force in International Affairs," *International Journal of Ethics,* XXVI (April, 1916), 339-346.

Parmelee, M., *Bolshevism, Fascism and the Liberal-democratic State* (New York, 1934).

Rocco, A., "The Political Doctrine of Fascism," *International Conciliation* (Oct., 1926), No. 223, pp. 389-415.

Rosenberg, A., *Die Entwicklung der Deutschen Freiheitsbewegung* (Munich, 1933).

——————, *Der Mythos des 20. Jahrhunderts; Eine Wertung der Seelisch-geistigen Gestaltenkämpfe Unserer Zeit* (Munich, 1930).

——————, "Le Mouvement National Socialiste," *L'Esprit International,* Vol. VIII (Jan., 1934), No. 29, pp. 26-40.

Schneider, H. W., *Making the Fascist State* (New York, 1928), Ch. I and Appendix, Pts. II and V.

Schott, G., *Chamberlain, der Seher des Dritten Reiches* (Munich, 1934).

Schuman, F. L., *The Nazi Dictatorship* (New York, 1935).

——————, "The Political Theory of German Fascism," *American Political Science Review,* Vol. XXVIII (April, 1934), No. 2, pp. 210-232.

Simonds, F., and Emeny, B., *The Great Powers in World Politics* (New York, 1935).

Soltau, R. H., *French Political Thought in the Nineteenth Century* (New Haven, Conn., 1931), Ch. XII.

Spengler, O., *The Hour of Decision,* tr. by Charles Francis Atkinson (New York, 1934).

——————, *Jahre der Entscheidungen* (Munich, 1933).

Stewart, W. K., "The Mentors of Mussolini," *American Political Science Review,* Vol. XXII (Nov., 1928), No. 4, pp. 843-869.

CHAPTER XXII

SOCIALISM AND COMMUNISM

Not only has Wilsonian internationalism as embodied in the League system had to contend with the mining and sapping of the integral nationalists, but its fundamental postulates have been challenged by the Marxian socialists who regard the League as an expression of the hated capitalistic system. It is not necessary or possible to go into the intricacies of the economic theory of the Marxians in order to explain their outlook on world affairs.[1] An understanding of Marx's philosophy of history, however, and more particularly the theory of class struggle developed by him and, to some extent by Friedrich Engels, is essential. Karl Marx (1818-1883) was a brilliant German Jew educated at the universities of Berlin, Bonn, and Jena, and inclined in his earlier years toward middle-class liberalism. Liberal opinion, however, was not tolerated by the Prussian government of his day, and when the youthful doctor of philosophy applied for a lectureship at the University of Bonn, his unorthodox views insured his rejection by the Prussian authorities. Marx then turned toward journalism, but his vigorous assault on old dogmas soon earned the ill-will of the government and he had to transfer his activities to Paris where he came into contact with French socialism and communism. This led him to explore socialist literature, which he studied assiduously, and helped pave the way for his conversion shortly to Socialism.[2] Several years later, at a time when revolutionary uprisings on the continent were expressing nationalist rather than class aspirations, Marx, with the collaboration of Engels, issued the famous *Communist Manifesto* which

[1] A careful exposition and analysis of Marxian "scientific" socialism, as well as a good discussion of socialistic thought in general may be found in Coker, *op. cit.*, Chs. I-IX. For an excellent historical treatment, see Harry W. Laidler, *A History of Socialist Thought* (New York, 1927). See also Appendix for important excerpts from the *Communist Manifesto* of Marx and Engels, which outlines the Communist philosophy.

[2] Laidler, *op. cit.*, pp. 149-154.

embodied a philosophy different from, and in a large measure incompatible with, that of the racialists and nationalists.

The theory of class struggle outlined in this pamphlet and later elaborated by Marx[3] is essentially an attempt to explain human progress in terms of the struggle of economic or class groups. Race and nationality lose their significance in the light of this interpretation. From the Marxian point of view, they are mere incidents or effects occurring at a certain stage in the evolution of mankind and disappearing in due course. There are no "superior" and "inferior" races, and no Chosen Peoples, therefore, whom nature selects in different epochs as the carriers of the world's culture. All peoples have the inherent capacity for growth and development, and in the course of time all separate national cultures will be merged in a higher universal human culture. The true key to human history, on the other hand, is to be found in the class struggles that have been waged from the beginning of the era of private property, and that will continue until the downfall of the present capitalist class throughout the world prepares the way for a classless world society. This ceaseless struggle goes on not only as between the upper (exploiting) and lower (exploited) classes of society but among the upper classes themselves. Each strives to wield political power, impose its particular economy on the political community, and subordinate the interests of the other classes. Classes themselves change in character as the industrial organization of society changes, but always and everywhere may be observed the basic antagonisms of exploiters and exploited. The process will go on as long as private property is the foundation of the social-economic order. After its abolition and the cessation of class warfare by the final victory of the proletariat, human progress will be effected by other and more peaceful means.[4] Thus, according to Marx and his disciples, war was not to be a permanent institution in the life of mankind. Class war as well as capitalist war would disappear with the demise of capitalism. Marx and his followers were not content merely to theorize and predict. The new day whose dawning they foresaw as a part of the "historic process" was to be hastened by purposive action. The *Communist*

[3] See especially his monumental work, *Das Kapital,* 3 vols. (Hamburg, 1890-1894). English translation by Samuel Moore and E. B. Aveling (Chicago, 1906-1909).

[4] Louis B. Boudin, *Socialism and War* (New York, 1916), pp. 216-234; N. Bukharin, *Imperialism and World Economy* (London, 1917), pp. 110-112.

Manifesto was a ringing militant appeal to the workers of the world in effect to substitute class consciousness for national consciousness and to unite against the common enemy, the capitalist exploiters.[5]

The Marxian explanation of imperialism is based on the theory of the class struggle together with that of surplus value. Under the existing capitalist system, it is argued, goods and commodities are produced for profit. Capitalists, on account of their ownership of the great instruments of production, secure these profits at the expense of the working class whose labor they exploit. The workers are paid subsistence wages, or even less where possible, and the surplus value which they create in the productive process accrues to the capitalists. As a result of the anarchical competition of capitalist entrepreneurs in an organized economic society and the desire of each to add to his profits, there is constant business expansion. Overproduction inevitably results. The workers are unable to purchase the goods which they have produced, and the capitalists have surpluses over and above what they can expend for the satisfaction of their own wants and which they cannot profitably invest in view of the glutted market. Under these circumstances, there is constant pressure for new markets. At the same time, industrialization leads to protective tariffs in the various capitalistic states, so that the home market may be monopolized by domestic producers. The result is that foreign markets tend to shrink rather than expand. This leads to a struggle between the capitalists of all industrial nations to capture unprotected markets. It also drives them to seek colonies and spheres of influence not only as markets but also as sources of the raw materials which they demand in ever increasing quantity. All of this, according to the orthodox Marxians, is an inevitable development under capitalism and has the effect of prolonging its life. Eventually, however, the remedy itself contributes to the downfall of the system it was designed to bolster up. Expansion into new non-capitalist regions results in converting them to a capitalist industrial economy. But the consequence of their industrialization is that they become new competitors for markets and a new means of pauperizing the labor of the advanced countries where higher labor standards prevail.[6] Wars and militarism are also inevitable accompaniments of

[5] See Appendix for parts of the text of the *Manifesto* selected to illustrate especially the Marxian view of class and national struggles.

[6] B. J. Hovde, "Socialistic Theories of Imperialism Prior to the Great War," *Journal of Political Economy*, Vol. XXXVI (Oct., 1928), No. 5, pp. 569-591;

the whole expansionist process. Capitalists, however, invoke patriotism, and concoct racial and national myths to make it appear that the masses are fighting in their own interests and on behalf of progress, whereas they are the dupes and victims of the capitalists who have the additional motive of diverting their attention to imperialistic enterprises so that they may not feel so acutely their misery at home.[7]

The basic Marxian ideas concerning the nature and inevitability of imperialism were elaborated a few years before the War by the Austrian socialist, Rudolf Hilferding,[8] and during it by the Russian, Nikolai Lenin.[9] The thesis of the latter, who was to father the Russian Revolution of November, 1917, and become the acknowledged successor of Marx, definitely restricts the term "imperialism" to the last phase of capitalism, beginning at about the opening of the twentieth century. Prior to this, capitalism had been able to spread in comparative peace over large areas of unoccupied lands and countries not yet drawn into the capitalistic vortex. This is the stage of capitalism characterized by free competition. In time, however, this gives way as a result of the elimination of small industries and the creation of larger and still larger establishments, and eventually the formation of great trusts and monopolies international in extent and ruled by the power of finance capital. We then have imperialism which, according to Lenin, is "the monopoly stage of capitalism." This stage is distinguished by "the concentration of production and capital, developed so highly that it creates monopolies which play a decisive rôle in economic life"; by the "fusion of banking capital with industrial capital and the creation, on the basis of this financial capital, of a financial oligarchy"; by "the export of capital, which has become extremely important, as distinguished from the export of commodities"; by "the formation of international capitalist monopolies which share out the world amongst themselves"; and by

E. M. Winslow, "Marxian, Liberal, and Sociological Theories of Imperialism," *Journal of Political Economy,* Vol. XXXIX (Dec., 1931), No. 6, pp. 713-758. See also Karl Kautsky, *The Class Struggle,* tr. by E. Bohn (Chicago, 1910), pp. 57-87, for the analysis of one of the Marxist theoreticians.

[7] Bukharin, *op. cit.*, pp. 110-112; Hovde, *loc. cit.*, p. 572.

[8] *Das Finanzkapital* (Vienna, 1910).

[9] *Der Imperialismus als Jüngste Etappe des Kapitalismus* (Zurich, 1916). English translation, *Imperialism; and the State and Revolution* (New York, 1929). See also his introduction to N. Bukharin's *Imperialism and World Economy* (London, 1915).

"the territorial division of the whole earth completed by the greatest capitalist powers."[10]

Imperialism, therefore, is not merely the tendency of great industrial nations to reach out for undeveloped regions, as some of the socialist writers contended,[11] but an inevitable struggle, in a period when most of the world has already been partitioned, for highly-industrialized regions as well; and with the idea not only of direct advantage but also the purpose of securing bases for operations against rivals. Will this development, however, continue until a single great world trust—"ultra-imperialism"—emerges and absorbs all existing antagonisms? Lenin is positive that there are too many contradictions in capitalism to allow of such a consummation. "There is no doubt," he says, "that the development is going *in the direction* of a single world trust that will swallow up all enterprises and all states without exception. But the development in this direction is proceeding under such stress, with such a tempo, with such contradictions, conflicts, and convulsions—not only economical, but also political, national, etc., etc.—that before a single world trust will be reached, before the respective national finance capitals will have formed a world union of 'ultra-imperialism,' imperialism will inevitably explode. . ."[12]

Bukharin, whose analysis is in general of a similar nature, looked for the explosion of the World War to have repercussions in the form of an uprising of the disillusioned proletariat. The workers in the stronger imperialist states, he pointed out, had for the moment benefited to some extent by receiving higher wages due to industrial prosperity brought about, however, by the cruel exploitation of helpless backward peoples. The World War, bringing suffering to all of them far greater than any momentary benefits, would, in Bukharin's opinion, open their eyes to the true nature of imperialism and cause proletarians in the ranks to turn their arms against the real enemy.[13]

[10] *Imperialism; and The State and Revolution,* pp. 71-72.

[11] Rosa Luxemburg and Karl Kautsky among others. See Winslow, *loc. cit.,* pp. 723, 730; also Lenin, *op. cit., passim,* for quotations from Kautsky and refutations of the latter's position; and references to relevant works of these two writers at end of chapter.

[12] Introduction to Nikolai Bukharin, *op. cit.,* p. 14. For a denial by a non-communist that imperialism has any connection with capitalism, see Joseph Schumpeter, *Zur Soziologie der Imperialismen* (Tubingen, 1919).

[13] *Ibid.,* pp. 164-170.

The evolutionary and revisionist groups of socialists take a somewhat different attitude toward imperialism. In the first place, they do not accept the Marxian position that capitalism is the sole cause, and that capitalists are driven inevitably by the nature of the system to imperialistic policies. If a policy of expansion is adopted, it is or may be a matter of choice—the desire better to serve the needs of an advancing society. The position of many of the moderate socialists in fact can hardly be distinguished from that of liberals of the persuasion of J. A. Hobson.[14] They contend that the expansion of advanced nations into backward areas may, and should, under proper safeguards enlarge the area of civilization rather than serve exclusively the selfish interests of particular economic groups or classes. Semi-civilized peoples should not be exploited, but on the other hand should not be allowed to retard the advance of civilization. This demands a positive policy involving tutelage of backward peoples affected and safeguards against their exploitation. Even under socialism, it is argued, the products of colonial areas would be needed. A particular argument was advanced in the years before the World War by Eduard Bernstein, the German socialist, who believed that socialism would gradually win its way over the world state by state. In such a case, socialist states should not have to depend upon hostile capitalist countries for the necessary raw materials, but must have colonies of their own.[15] Addressing himself particularly to German socialists in 1899, Bernstein declared: "However speedy socialists may imagine the course of development in Germany toward themselves to be, yet we cannot be blind to the fact that it will need a considerable time before a whole series of other countries are converted to Socialism." On the matter of principle, he said: "It is neither necessary that the occupation of tropical lands by Europeans should injure the natives in their enjoyment of life, nor has it hitherto usually been the case. Moreover, only a conditional right of savages to the land occupied by them can be recognized. The higher civilization ultimately can claim a higher right. Not the conquest, but the cultivation of the land gives the historical legal title to its use."[16]

[14] *Supra*, pp. 273-278.

[15] Hovde, *loc. cit.*, pp. 578-581, for good general discussion of this point of view as held by Jean Jaurès of France, Émile Vandervelde of Belgium, and others.

[16] *Evolutionary Socialism* (New York, 1909), pp. 178-179. This is a translation by Edith C. Harvey of Bernstein's *Die Voraussetzungen des Sozialismus und die Aufgaben der Sozialdemokratie* (Stuttgart, 1909). Bernstein also defended the acquisition of the lease of Kiaochow by Germany on the ground that it constituted

The position of socialists on the subject of war, as revealed prior to 1914, is not as clear as the class-struggle theory might indicate. To the revolutionary or orthodox Marxian socialists in general, the only war that may be theoretically justified is the class war in which the exploited class rises against the exploiters and dispossesses them. International war is regarded by them as essentially a struggle between competing capitalists to serve their own interests at the expense of the masses who fight and pay the bills, rather than a product of human nature or of unwise policies. It would therefore appear that Marxians as well as evolutionary socialists would find themselves on common ground with bourgeois pacifists and humanitarians in their opposition to international war in principle, even though differing on the question of the fundamental basis; and in general this has been true. Moreover, socialists have shown the same tendency that the less extreme pacifists reveal—to admit, perhaps reluctantly, that a nation is justified in engaging in war under certain circumstances. Socialists, for example, usually approve the French revolutionary wars and the American Civil War as wars of liberation and as instruments of human progress. Marx looked upon the Crimean War with favor and even urged English intervention because he regarded Russia as an obstacle in the way of the democratic reorganization of Europe and an outstanding enemy of the interests of the working class. In fact, humanitarians are more likely to oppose war in general, because of its repulsiveness and the human suffering it causes, than are thoroughgoing Marxians, at any rate. The latter are more likely to approach the question in an objective fashion, judging each war on its merits from the point of view of their belief as to its effect on human progress toward the socialist goal.[17] They differ also, therefore, from the pacifist school of Novicow, which holds that all war retards progress.[18] If a particular war is regarded as serving the interests of the working class, Marxians will favor it as a step toward the goal; if it is, in their opinion, an "imperialistic" war, they will resist it as far as possible or utilize it when it comes for the purpose of fomenting revolution in the states involved.

The World War presented the socialists of Europe with a test case

"a pledge for the safeguarding of the future interests of Germany in China," by countering the encirclement policy of Russia—an unusual position for a socialist to take. (*Op. cit.*, pp. 172-174.)

[17] Boudin, *op. cit.*, pp. 183-192.

[18] *Supra*, pp. 247-250.

of unusual complexity, and confronted many of them with a dilemma. Many years prior to its outbreak, the question of the proper socialist attitude in war crises had been debated in socialist associations and congresses.[19] Moreover, certain machinery was set up to make socialist action more effective on such occasions. In 1906, for example, an Inter-Parliamentary Committee of the Second International, which gave a great deal of attention to the question of militarism, was appointed. Its purpose was "to keep the Socialist and Labour Parliamentary groups in European Parliaments in touch with each other, to afford an intimate means of discussing international affairs, and especially to be prepared to take action in the event of disputes or threatenings of war rising between the Governments of any of the nations." [20] In the following year, at the Stuttgart Congress, a debate on the attitude socialists should take in the event of a threatened war revealed widely different opinions among the delegates. Jean Jaurès and the majority of the French socialists at the gathering asked the Congress to take the position that "militarism is to be viewed exclusively as the arming of the state in order to keep the working classes in political and economic subjection to the capitalist class," and to call upon the International Socialist Bureau and the International Parliamentary Conference "to form the necessary institutions in order to be able to take suitable action" whenever war threatens. Its prevention "is to be brought about by national and international socialist action of the working class by all means, from parliamentary intervention to public agitation and the general strike and insurrection." [21] This position was opposed by a minority of the French delegation and by August Bebel and the remainder of his German comrades. The latter were willing to refuse to vote money for the army, navy, and colonies; but they contended, among other things, that the employment of the general strike and insurrection would militate against the socialists' winning converts to their cause and thus being in a position finally to eliminate war alto-

[19] A. W. Humphrey, *International Socialism and the War* (London, 1915), pp. 7-19. W. E. Walling, *The Socialists and the War* (New York, 1915), Chs. IV-V.

[20] Humphrey, *op. cit.*, p. 16. Meetings of the Bureau were held at Zurich at the time of the Morocco crisis in 1911, and in 1912 in connection with the Balkan War. In the former instance, no action was necessary, for the crisis passed. In the latter case, a resolution was adopted, calling upon the International to oppose annexations of Balkan territory by the Powers. This was followed by demonstrations in a number of European capitals against war.

[21] Walling, *op. cit.*, p. 27.

gether. The opposition was led by Bebel, who declared that socialists should not adopt an attitude of negation, but should condition their support of a war on its character.[22] In the case of a defensive war, they should rally to the support of their fatherland, but if their country starts a war of aggression, socialists should refuse to lend their support.[23] In the meantime they should carry on a campaign of education against militarism for, although a European war would further the socialist cause more than ten years of agitation, it would be too dreadful a means to contemplate for the attainment of the goal.

The resolution eventually adopted by the Stuttgart Congress, although avoiding a definite stand as to the specific tactics which socialists in all countries must employ in the event of war or a threat of war, did pledge them to a course of action against it under all circumstances in cooperation with the International Socialist Bureau. The position taken by the Stuttgart Congress was stated clearly in the following paragraphs of the resolution: "If war ever threatens to break out, the working classes and their representatives in parliament in the countries affected should, with the assistance of the International Bureau, strive to take every step possible in order to avoid the occurrence of war. They must use every effort which in their view, according to the political situation and the opposing class interests, will best contribute to the maintenance of peace.

"If, however, despite all efforts, war breaks out, then it becomes their primary duty to bring about its conclusion as quickly as possible, and thereafter to make the most of the opportunities offered by the economic and political crises which are sure to follow the war, in stirring up public opinion and hastening forward the abolition of capitalist class rule." [24]

[22] *Ibid.*, pp. 28-36.

[23] Boudin, *op. cit.*, p. 199. Contrary to Bebel, Karl Kautsky denied that it would be possible for socialists easily to distinguish between a war of aggression and a defensive war, for governments could so maneuver as to make an aggressive war appear defensive. (Boudin, *op. cit.*, p. 199.) Bebel, himself, in the heat of debate went further and declared that if Germany attacked Russia he would be the first to shoulder a rifle because the war would serve the purpose of liberating the oppressed Russian masses and would at the same time weaken the forces of reaction in Germany. H. N. Brailsford, *The War of Steel and Gold* (10th ed., London, 1918), p. 188. The conclusion to which this led was that a war, whether aggressive or not, might be supported if it advanced the cause of the workers.

[24] Walling, *op. cit.*, pp. 48-49, for part of text of the resolution. It is of interest to note that Nikolai Lenin was one of the authors of the last paragraph. (*Ibid.*, p. 39.) See also Lewis L. Lorwin, *Labor and Internationalism* (New York, 1929), p. 92.

In the next Socialist Congress, held at Copenhagen in 1910, the British delegates added their support to the idea of an international general strike, but the matter was finally postponed for consideration by the Congress which was to have met at Vienna on August 23, 1914. Only two weeks before the World War, the French socialists, at a special Congress, reiterated their stand on the general strike as an anti-war measure. On July 29, an emergency session of the International Bureau was called to mobilize the socialists against the war which was now imminent. It was unanimously agreed that the French and German workers should immediately bring all possible pressure to bear on their respective governments to take measures to moderate the attitude of their respective allies. German socialists should seek to have their government restrain Austria, and French socialists should work to have France secure an undertaking from Russia that the latter would keep out of the conflict. The workers in Great Britain and Italy should likewise bring all their influence to the side of peace. Finally, the Bureau adopted a resolution congratulating the workers of Russia "on their revolutionary attitude," and invited them "to continue their heroic efforts against Czardom as being one of the most effective guarantees against the threatened world war." [25] Finally, on July 30, after Russia had started mobilization, the Bureau participated in a great demonstration against the war in which Hugo Haase spoke for the German socialists and Jean Jaurès for the workers of France. Haase denounced Austria's ultimatum to Serbia, accused her of desiring war, and declared that German socialists were against Germany's espousal of the Austrian cause even though Russia should intervene on behalf of Serbia. Jaurès declared that should Russia refuse to follow the French government's counsels of prudence and patience, she should be told: "We know but one treaty, that which binds us to the human race." In the meantime, the German government made its decision and on August 1 declared war on Russia. The previous day the French socialist leader, Jaurès, was assassinated by a fanatic, and the attempts of the socialists of Germany and France to come to an agreement to refrain from voting war credits for their governments were unsuccessful.[26] This virtually

[25] Lorwin, *op. cit.*, p. 136; Walling, *op. cit.*, 125-126.

[26] A representative of the German Social Democratic Party, Hermann Mueller, was sent to Paris to seek concerted action on the part of the German and French socialists. Although he expressed the conviction that the German socialists would not vote war credits, the executive committee of the party had not as yet defined

ended any hope the socialists may have had of stopping, or even of localizing, the war.

The failure of the socialists, theoretically committed to the view that the class struggle was the only form of "war" which the workers of the world should normally support, to agree on a universal program of action to be pursued by them in their several parliaments in the event of a threatened war contributed to the futility of their efforts in August, 1914. This failure, in turn, was perhaps chiefly due to the fact that however strongly socialists were imbued with the class struggle doctrine and with the belief that international war was a capitalistic enterprise fraught with suffering for the masses, they lived and worked and had intimate ties within their several fatherlands and, with few exceptions, were subtly but powerfully influenced by the fears, prejudices, emotions, and ambitions generated in the particularistic atmosphere of the modern national state. Moreover, socialism had made unequal progress in different states. In Germany, under the Hohenzollerns, it had made great advances in the years before the War. At the same time that "capitalism" was developing and expanding the German state, the social legislation of the capitalistic régime was ameliorating the lot of the German workers. Strict Marxians might still speak in terms of the solidarity of a world proletariat and of the necessity of a united front under all circumstances against the common enemy, capitalism, but evolutionary socialists began to compare their lot quite favorably with that of the oppressed Russian masses and to look forward to constantly improved conditions and their eventual complete triumph by the evolutionary process. Under these circumstances, it is not altogether surprising that Bebel, the German socialist leader, in 1907 could declare his willingness to shoulder a musket and march to war against Tsarist Russia, and not at all strange that German socialists declined to "leave the fatherland in the lurch" by refusing to vote war credits after Russia had begun general mobilization in 1914. What would happen to the German workers, they asked, if Russian Tsardom should overwhelm Germany?

Thus, with the exception of Karl Kautsky, Hugo Haase, Karl Liebknecht, Rosa Luxemburg, and a few others, the German socialists de-

its attitude. Under the circumstances, and fearful of invasion by the German armies, the French socialists did not feel that they could pledge themselves not to vote for war credits. (Lorwin, *op. cit.*, pp. 136-137.)

cided to vote for the war credits on August 4th. In Belgium and France, it was inevitable that the socialists should almost unanimously support their governments. The French government appeared to the socialists to be doing everything possible to avert war, withdrawing French troops six miles from the frontier, and indicating a conciliatory attitude. Germany's violation of Belgium territory, however, and the drive toward Paris decided the socialists of Belgium and France that they must take up arms "for the defense of their country, of civilization, and of the freedom of the peoples of Europe." Moreover, in both countries, socialists took governmental posts and thus played their part in the prosecution of the War. In England, as late as August 2nd, the socialists, who had all along been opposed to the alliance with autocratic Russia, held anti-war meetings, but after the invasion of Belgium split into two groups. The Labour Party and Right Wing elements supported the government's decision to enter the war and fight for democracy and the freedom of small nations, but the Independent Labour Party and Left Wing groups denounced it. In Russia, the socialists, with the exception of the Bolsheviki, supported the government. The fourteen members of this group in the Duma, however, declared their solidarity "with the European proletariat" and walked out.[27]

In Austria, the socialists, although declaring at the outset that the government could have obtained redress from Serbia by peaceful means and must bear responsibility for the war, completely capitulated and became quite bourgeois in their sentiments once the war had begun. The official party organ, the Vienna *Arbeiter Zeitung,* declared on August 23 that since the war had come in spite of all their efforts, "the proletariat in all countries, which formerly did its international duty, now does its duty as sons of its people, who risk everything in order that the people shall not be conquered, in order that its soil will not be delivered to the horrors of a defeat. We all suffer wrong; we all do right to protect ourselves against it. . . But even in this tragic moment we do not forget that we are International Social Democrats. Our heart bleeds because of the frightful necessity of this conflict, but we give to our people and to the state what belongs to the people and the state."[28]

In Italy, the socialists refrained from action before the outbreak of

[27] Lorwin, *op. cit.,* Ch. VI.
[28] Quotation from Walling, *op. cit.,* p. 148.

the War because the Italian people were opposed to participation at the time and they did not desire to disturb this attitude. However, they shared the anti-Austrian and anti-German feeling of non-socialist groups. They declared for neutrality, in the words of the moderate socialist Turati, not only because they were opposed to war on principle, but also "in consideration of the principle of nationality, basely reviled and menaced by the aggressiveness" of Austria and Germany.[29] Before the end of 1914, however, Mussolini, editor-in-chief of the Socialist *Avanti,* changed his position and began to advocate the entry of Italy into the War against Germany and Austria. In the following year, many of the socialists and syndicalists were converted, but the party as a whole continued to stand out against war even after the government had brought the country into it, and remained in a position to advocate socialist efforts to bring it to an end.

During the War the only concerted unofficial efforts of importance on behalf of its termination were made by groups of socialists in belligerent as well as neutral countries who though engulfed in, or largely paralyzed in their activities by, the War, sought occasions to bring about a negotiated peace. In January, 1915, for example, the Socialist parties of Norway, Sweden, Denmark, and Holland met at Copenhagen to discuss peace terms upon which socialists of all countries might be brought to unite. As the War went on, however, the minds of the less orthodox socialists in the belligerent countries took on a more nationalistic set and efforts for peace became more difficult. In Germany, Philip Scheidemann and other leaders, now wholeheartedly supporting the government, scrapped the class struggle doctrine altogether for the time being and advised the German workers that their interests were identical with the interests of the German nation and that a German victory would advance the cause of the proletariat all over the world. In England, France, and Belgium, socialist leaders told their followers that the only hope for the sort of world to which they aspired lay in the defeat of the Central Powers.

On the other hand, Center and Left Wing elements among the socialists of all the belligerents labored to keep alive a proletarian consciousness so that the Socialist International, which had ceased to function, might be reconstituted at the end of the War. They also sought to have their respective governments state the terms upon which they would

[29] *Ibid.,* Ch. XVII; Humphrey, *op. cit.,* Ch. XIII.

be willing to terminate the conflict.[30] In September, 1915, on the initiative of the Italian Socialist Party, a socialist conference was convened at Zimmerwald, Switzerland. Official delegates attended from various socialist groups in Russia, Poland, Rumania, Sweden, and Norway. Unofficial delegates came from France and Germany. Delegates from the Independent Labour Party of England were prevented from attending on account of the English government's refusal to grant them passports. Lenin, who was a representative of the Bolsheviki faction of Russia, made drastic proposals designed at once to end the War and usher in the proletarian revolution in the belligerent countries. Socialists were called upon to refuse to vote war credits, to withdraw their representatives from bourgeois governments, to write, agitate, and organize demonstrations against their governments, carry their propaganda into the trenches, and in every way to foment civil war.[31] The conference as a whole was not willing to endorse these tactics, but it did adopt a manifesto placing the responsibility for the War on the capitalistic governments, the press, and the churches, and censuring the socialists in all countries who had failed to stand by their principles. Finally it called upon the workers of all countries to unite against an imperialistic peace: "No annexations, no indemnities. Across frontiers, battlefields, devastated cities, and countries—Workers Unite." [32]

By the latter part of 1916, there seemed to be some prospect that the efforts of the socialists to end the War might be successful. The masses in the various belligerent countries had had to endure such privations and bear such heavy burdens that a great war-weariness began to manifest itself. There were no glorious victories to tone up flagging national energies. With armies deadlocked on the eastern and western fronts in spite of tremendous efforts and staggering losses on both sides, a sense of the futility of the struggle grew. Under these conditions the minority groups of socialists in Germany, France, England, and Russia struggled with new vigor to gain a hearing for an early peace along democratic lines. Finally in the spring of 1917 conditions became unbearable in Russia. The government's prosecution of the War had been characterized by the most notorious corruption and inefficiency and the most heartless sacrifice of the lives of the soldiers. Hunger finally drove the people to rioting in the streets of Petro-

[30] Lorwin, *op. cit.*, pp. 151-153.
[31] Laidler, *op. cit.*, p. 519.
[32] Quoted in Lorwin, *op. cit.*, p. 155.

grad, and after that, revolution came swiftly, for the government was utterly unfit to cope with the situation. A republic was declared and a liberal government, including the socialist revolutionary, Kerensky, was set up. The Russian masses were war-weary, but the new government, composed of men not so much opposed to the War as to the way in which the Tsarist government had conducted it, determined to continue the struggle until the Central Powers were defeated. In the meantime, hope for peace on a liberal and secure basis was strengthened by the entry of the United States into the War, with its general aim to "make the world safe for democracy" and its specific Fourteen Point program of President Wilson.

Altogether, the time seemed propitious for the holding of a general international socialist conference which should include delegates from neutrals and belligerents alike who would make a determined effort for peace. Eventually the Socialist parties of Russia, Germany, France, Italy, and the United States agreed to accept a joint invitation of the International Socialist Bureau and certain European socialist groups to send delegations to a conference to be held at Stockholm toward the end of 1917. The government of the United States refused passports to the American delegates, however, and the governments of Great Britain, France, and Italy followed its lead. The Conference met with delegates from the Central Powers, Russia, and the neutral states in attendance, but the absence of the delegates from the other countries defeated its purpose.[33] This virtually ended the concerted effort of the socialists as such to bring about peace, although the ideas of a non-imperialistic peace which they shared with the liberal groups of all countries were to have an influence at the Peace Conference in 1919. In the meantime, Left Wing revolutionary socialists under the leadership of Nikolai Lenin were to seize power in Russia, make peace with Germany in order to entrench themselves in power, and confront the world for the first time with a state completely in the hands of a dictatorship of the proletariat dedicated to the realization of the aims of Karl Marx.

The directing genius of the revolutionary socialist movement who battered down all opposition and seized power from the mixed bourgeois and socialist government of Kerensky in November, 1917, was Vladimir Ilyitch Ulianov (1870-1924), known to the world as Nikolai Lenin.

[33] *Ibid.*, pp. 157-162.

Almost from the time of his expulsion from the University for revolutionary agitation, Lenin engaged in ceaseless activity against the Tsarist government. Exiled to Siberia for a time, he resumed his agitation in St. Petersburg on his return, organizing and leading strikes and inflaming the minds of the working class who, according to his conviction, were the only means of liberating Russia from the despotism of the Tsars. After the revolution of 1905, Lenin worked out a technique of revolution which might possibly be applied within Russia in the future when the time was ripe. In the first stage, the support of the peasants should be sought for the overthrow of the monarchy, the landlords, and other medieval survivals. This bourgeois stage should be followed by a proletarian revolution in which the industrial masses would rise against the bourgeoisie and establish a socialist régime. From 1906 to 1917 Lenin lived abroad, studying, writing, and carrying on revolutionary agitation. The World War, in the meantime, although paralyzing the effective efforts of socialists in all countries temporarily, furnished the conditions under which revolutionary outbreaks might have a chance of success, and from the beginning of the struggle Lenin urged socialists to exploit the War for their purposes. After the revolution of March, 1917, resulted in the overthrow of the old régime, the setting up of a bourgeois government, and the pardon of political offenders, he was able to return from his exile in Switzerland. This gave him and Leon Trotsky [34] an opportunity to work within Russia against the provisional government, and to realize the proletarian phase of the revolution in the *coup d'état* of November, 1917.

The success of the Bolsheviks under Lenin's leadership was due in great part to the fact that their program appealed to the war-weary and oppressed elements both in the cities and in the country. They proposed, among other things, that a general peace should be concluded immediately, that the landed estates in Russia should be confiscated at once without remuneration to the owners, that the workers should be given possession of the factories, that production and distribution should be placed under national control, and that soviets

[34] Leon Davidovich Bronstein (Leon Trotsky), a Russian middle-class Jew, had, like Lenin, early become imbued with Marxian doctrines and had also had the experience of a Siberian exile. He, too, returned to Russia after the overthrow of the Tsarist régime and became the outstanding collaborator of Lenin and organizer of the Red armies. Although a brilliant organizer as well as orator and pamphleteer, he did not possess the coolness and caution that characterized Lenin, and was not always in accord with the more realistic tactics of the latter.

of workers, peasants, and soldiers should replace the bourgeois political machinery and establish a dictatorship of the proletariat.[35] "Bread to the workers, land to the peasants, and peace to all"—such a slogan made a powerful appeal to the Russian masses in 1917.

Upon their assumption of power, Lenin and his associates not only were confronted with the problem of following a policy that would win the support of the Russian masses and enable them to consolidate their position, but were faced with nationalist movements within the Russian state. The empire of the Tsars extended over an immense area, and was inhabited by a great number of races and tribes presenting the greatest diversity in language, customs, religion, and traditions. In addition to the Great Russians who furnished the governing class, and who comprised about forty-seven per cent of the total population, there were nationally self-conscious Ukranians, Poles, Lithuanians, Finns and many others, held within the empire by force rather than by consent. The Russian government had pursued a policy of Russification of these diverse elements, attempting to stamp out their local languages and institutions and direct their life from the capital. The World War presented the first favorable opportunity for dissatisfied non-Slavic elements within the empire to demand consideration. When the provisional government took control, it abolished racial and religious discrimination but, except in the case of Poland, which was occupied by German and Austrian troops, it showed no disposition to accord satisfaction to the different nationalities who desired complete independence. The Bolshevik leaders, however, were committed in principle to the thesis that nationalities desiring to separate from the parent state should have their wish granted. As early as 1903 Lenin declared at a party conference for

[35] Laidler, *op. cit.*, pp. 456-459, 462-465; Benns, *op. cit.*, pp. 76-86. It should be mentioned that Stalin and other leaders were not in agreement at the beginning with Lenin's view of the establishment of a dictatorship of the proletariat and the creation of a soviet state. They were rather inclined to support a democratic republic as a necessary preliminary stage to be followed by socialism at a later and more propitious time. (M. T. Florinsky, *World Revolution and the U. S. S. R.* [New York, 1933], pp. 125-126). It should be pointed out also that while Lenin and his followers have contended that the transition from capitalism to socialism is absolutely impossible without compulsion and dictatorship, eventually with the dying out of classes the state, as the embodiment of class domination, will die and with it all forms of coercion. See Nikolai Lenin, *The Soviets at Work* (4th ed., New York, 1918), pp. 29-30. In the meantime iron dictatorship quite as thorough and ruthless as that in Italy or Germany continues in Russia. Recently (1935) there seems to be some disposition toward relaxation of the despotic control of Stalin and his associates, but it is by no means clear at the present time that there is any real trend toward the freedoms that characterize liberal régimes.

"the complete right of self-determination of all nations," and at a later congress in the same year, the following plank was adopted: "Right of self-determination of all nations included in any state."[36] Likewise during the World War this slogan was freely used by the Bolsheviks, as well as by other socialist and liberal groups. On their attainment of power in November, 1917, the Bolsheviks issued a Declaration of the Rights of the Peoples of Russia, signed by Lenin and Joseph Stalin, in which it was asserted that the council of the people's commissaries, in accordance with the will of the Congress of Soviets, held in October, would be guided in the question of nationalities by certain principles. These were: "1. The equality and sovereignty of the peoples of Russia. 2. The right of the peoples of Russia to dispose of their own fate, even to separation and the establishment of an independent state. 3. Abolition of all privileges and limitations, national or religious. 4. Free development of national minorities and ethnographic groups inhabiting Russian territory."[37]

"Self-determination," as understood and applied by the Bolsheviks, however, was something quite different from self-determination as conceived by Wilson and the liberals. Joseph Stalin, who was to exercise the greatest influence in determining Soviet policy toward the nationalities of Russia, indicated the later Bolshevik attitude as early as 1913. "A nation," he said, "has a right to determine its own fate as it wishes, provided it does not infringe upon the right of other nations." A nation not only has the right of autonomy; it has the right to secede. But, he added, "this does not mean that it may take this step under any conditions or that autonomy or secession everywhere and always shall be a profit for the nation, that is, for its majority, i.e., its working masses."[38] The test of the validity of secession or even autonomy, therefore, in Stalin's opinion, seems to be the effect on the working class, and it is for the social democracy to "interfere and firmly influence the will of the nation" in order that the decision shall reflect the will and interests of the masses. After the November revolution, Lenin, Bukharin, Stalin, and other Bolshevik leaders defined their position in similar terms but with even more precision. Bukharin, for example, in a pamphlet issued in July 1918, entitled *Program of Com-*

[36] W. R. Batsell, *Soviet Rule in Russia* (New York, 1929), p. 105.
[37] See M. W. Graham, *New Governments of Eastern Europe* (New York, 1927), pp. 594-595, for complete text.
[38] Batsell, *op. cit.*, pp. 120-121.

munists,[39] made it clear that the decision as to separation lay only with the working classes. ". . . the Russian workman who has the power, says to the workmen of other peoples living in Russia: 'Comrades, if you do not care to become members of our Soviet Republic, if you desire to form your own Soviet Republic, do so. We give you the full right to do so. We do not wish to hold you by force a single minute.'" Even more explicitly Bukharin defined the Soviet position in the following words: "We do not speak of the right of self-determination of nations (i.e., of their bourgeoisie and their workmen), but only of the right of the working classes. Therefore, the so-called 'will of the nation' is not sacred for us. Should we wish to learn the will of the nation," he went on to explain, "we would be forced to call a Constituent Assembly of the nation. . . During the dictatorship of the proletariat, not the will of the Constituent Assembly, but the will of the Soviets of the working people decides the question. And if at the same time, in two different parts of Russia two assemblies should be called, a Constituent Assembly and a Congress of Soviets, and the former should against the will of the latter proclaim a 'separation,' we will defend the latter with all means, using armed force if necessary." [40]

It is to be observed, however, that the Russian Communists have adopted a different attitude toward national movements in other states. Although, ideally, separatist movements should have a working class character and result in the establishment of proletarian dictatorships in the seceding communities, as a matter of tactics in the struggle against imperialism, separatist movements, whether bourgeois or proletarian, have received the blessing of the Communists. As Laski has pointed out, the Communists have been inclined to regard national self-determination as "a stage in the development of international working-class solidarity." Eventually the workers will come to see that their struggle against national oppression is "only a form of the struggle against capitalist oppression," and will then rise and throw off the yoke.[41]

[39] English text may be found in Cooke and Stickney, *Readings in European International Relations since 1879,* pp. 852-854.

[40] Cf. also following remarks of Trotsky: "But wherever the fiction of self-determination becomes, in the hands of the bourgeoisie, a weapon directed against the proletarian revolution (as in the case of Georgia), we have no occasion to treat the fiction differently from the other 'democratic principles' perverted by capitalism." Quoted in H. J. Laski, *Communism* (New York, 1927). Georgia was overrun by the Bolsheviks, it may be noted, because it was Menshevik rather than Bolshevik.

[41] Laski, *op. cit.,* pp. 218, 220; Batsell, *op. cit.,* p. 115.

After their accession to power the Communists were forced to deal with secessionist movements in the Ukraine and in the Baltic states. The policies they then adopted were in part in accordance with the theory of working-class self-determination, and in part dictated by political and economic expediency, and necessity. It was a foregone conclusion that they could not look with complete complacency upon national movements that would cause the loss to Soviet Russia, and therefore to Communism, of large and rich areas. Economic considerations as well as reasons of defense of the Soviet régime forbade an attitude of indifference. With evident reluctance, they were compelled, however, to recognize the independence of the bourgeois Baltic states whose claims for independence were supported by England and France as a part of their offensive against the Soviet régime.[42] In the case of the rich Ukraine, however, in which a strong independence movement grew up, Lenin is reported to have declared that "only the Ukrainian workers and peasants in their all-Russian Congress of Soviets may and shall decide the question as to whether the Ukraine shall be united with Russia, or whether she shall remain independent, and, in the latter case, what *federal* relation shall be established between this republic and Russia."[43] In so far as the Bolsheviks could control matters, this policy, as outlined by Lenin with respect to the Ukraine, was followed in other cases.

In their treatment of national minorities, the Russian Communists have again been guided in part by reasons of expediency as well as by considerations of sound Communist doctrine. To engage upon a policy of Russification after the fashion of the Tsars would identify them, in the minds of the Ukrainians and other non-Russian peoples within the R.S.F.S.R., with the old régime. It would also lead to rebellion and give the enemies of Bolshevism an opportunity to capitalize the situation and weaken the Communist front. On the other hand, they were not disposed to see the empire melt away before their eyes. By

[42] The treaty of peace of February 2, 1920, between the Bolshevik government and Estonia, read: "Article 2. On the basis of the right of all peoples freely to decide their own destinies, and even to separate completely from the state of which they form a part, a right proclaimed by the R.S.F.S.R., Russia recognizes unreservedly the independence and autonomy of the state of Estonia and renounces voluntarily and forever all rights of sovereignty formerly held by Russia over the Estonian people and territory by virtue of the former legal situation and by virtue of international treaties which, in respect of such rights, shall henceforth be invalid." (*League of Nations Treaty Series*, Vol. XI, No. 289, p. 30.)

[43] As quoted in Batsell, *op. cit.*, p. 104.

1921, the Bolsheviks had succeeded in beating back all attacks and "bourgeois" secession movements, consolidating their power on all fronts and setting up regional Soviets throughout the vast area under their control. In the same year, Stalin outlined the practical necessity and advantages of an organized union of the parts as follows: "The isolated existence of separate soviet republics is by no means stable because of the danger of destruction by the capitalistic states. Common interests of defense of the soviet republics on the one hand, the reconstruction of the productive forces destroyed during the war, on the other, and the necessary assistance by supplies of food to the soviet republics on the part of those which are prosperous, insistently dictate a union of separate soviet republics as the only means to safety from imperialistic slavery and national oppression." [44] In 1922, the various sovietized republics were transformed by treaty, voluntarily entered into by the various republics, into the Union of Socialist Soviet Republics.[45] Under the terms of the Union and in order to form "a firm bulwark against world capitalism," the conduct of foreign affairs, military and commercial policy, and authority over transportation and communication were reserved to the Union government, directed from Moscow.[46]

The nationalities question was given careful attention. Joseph Stalin, who was made commissar of nationalities, made a plea before the Twelfth Congress of the Communist Party in 1923 for action designed to allay the discontent of the sixty-five millions of non-Russians and solve the nationality problem. He advocated the creation "at Moscow of a supreme organ, made up of the representatives of these nationalities." "This organ," he explained, "must reflect not only the general interests of the proletariat, but also the particular interests of each specific nationality." [47] In the same year, a Soviet of Nationalities was created to carry out Stalin's idea, kill the opposition of nationalities with kindness and consideration, and perhaps show other nationalities under capitalist rule the way to solve their own problem. Nor was this merely a paper concession. The Soviet of Nationalities has been invested not

[44] As quoted in Batsell, *op. cit.*, pp. 121-122.

[45] At present (1935) there are seven federated Soviet Republics, each of which is theoretically and constitutionally entitled to secede from the Union. Actually, it may be doubted whether this would not meet with resistance.

[46] For a good discussion of other matters within the sphere of action of the Union and a clear statement of the character of the union, see M. W. Graham, *op. cit.*, pp. 153-157. For text of the Treaty of Union, see pp. 608-617.

[47] As quoted in Graham, *op. cit.*, p. 158.

only with a share in the determination of the policies of the Union, but with the responsibility for the scientific study of the problems presented in a political federation containing 185 ethnic groups speaking 147 languages, and the safeguarding and encouragement of national cultures. Actually, the policy has been followed, in general, of allowing every nationality to have its own language in the schools, courts, and in the transaction of public business, and to accord protection to minority enclaves within areas of larger nationalities.[48] In fact, the Soviet has encouraged racial minorities to develop their own languages. In the Ukraine, particularly, a process of Ukrainization has been carried on by the ruling Communist Party resulting in the "nationalization" of the public services, a decline in the use of the Russian language, and a general growth of Ukrainian self-consciousness.[49] Doubtless these measures have been shrewdly designed for the purpose of taking the wind out of the sails of anti-Bolshevik separatist agitators and making the various republics safe for Bolshevism, but in any case they present a sharp contrast to the methods of solving the nationality problem used in other countries. It remains to be said, however, that the freedom granted to nationalities does not extend to the point of allowing them to dissent from Communist doctrine and establish bourgeois régimes. Their political and economic institutions must conform to Bolshevik patterns. They must maintain the "proletarian" outlook and, in practice, look to Moscow for light and leading on matters of Communist doctrine. So long as they do this and maintain the rule of the proletariat, they may be as "national" as they please.

In 1917, when they came into power, Trotsky, Zinoviev, and other Bolshevik leaders seem to have been convinced that the November revolution must and would be followed by proletariat uprisings throughout the world. When they entered into peace negotiations with Germany at Brest-Litovsk, they sought to use the occasion for the spread of revolutionary propaganda among the peoples of the central empires.[50] Contrary to the more cautious tactics advocated by Lenin, the Left Wing communists advocated a holy war against the capitalists of all countries. Trotsky succeeded in winning the Council of People's Commissars over to his view that they should adopt the formula, "No war,

[48] W. H. Chamberlin, *Soviet Russia* (Boston, 1930), p. 218.

[49] *Ibid.*, pp. 220-221. See also C. A. Macartney, *National States and National Minorities* (London, 1934).

[50] M T. Florinsky, *op. cit.*, p. 33.

no peace," demobilize the Russian army, declare the War at an end, but make no actual peace with Germany. These tactics were based on the belief that they would have great propaganda value with the German soldiers and that the German government would not dare to order an advance into Russia. Bukharin, one of the most influential of the Left Wingers, asserted that "the Russian revolution will either expand, or will be crushed by world imperialism," and that the world revolution should be promoted even if it should result in the overthrow of Communism in Russia. Lenin, on the other hand, advocated making peace with Germany in order to afford a breathing spell for the consolidation of the Bolshevik régime, fearing that otherwise the cause would be lost both in Russia and in other countries. His view was adopted after the Germans had started their advance toward Petrograd, and the drastic peace of Brest-Litovsk was signed.

There remained, however, the policy of promoting revolutions in other countries. This was good Marxian tactics, but it was also regarded as dictated by the needs of self-defense. During the first three years, the Bolshevik régime had to meet not only counter-revolutionary attempts from within but attacks from without as well. The Allied countries regarded Russia as a "traitor" for signing a separate peace with Germany. Moreover, a state founded on the subversive doctrines of Karl Marx was naturally viewed with alarm, and the Bolshevik's repudiation of the financial obligations of the Tsarist régime aroused further resentment. For these, as well as for military reasons, the Allies and the United States sent expeditionary forces to Murmansk, Archangel, and Vladivostok in 1918. After the Armistice, Allied governments gave support to "White" counter-revolutionary generals who organized armies and attacked the Soviet forces at various points. These attacks were met directly by the organization and resistance of a Red army. Indirectly, they were fought by spreading communist propaganda among the peoples of the Allied countries who were tired of war, and by building a back-fire among the subject peoples to whom the Allied countries had not granted "self determination." In January, 1919, the Central Committee of the Russian Communist Party invited communists from all countries to attend a world conference in Moscow. The meeting was held in March. It was attended chiefly by communists from neighboring countries, was dominated by the Russians, and resulted in the formation of the Third International, or Comintern. Unlike the

Second International, which the Bolsheviks regarded as a discredited tool of the bourgeoisie on account of its weak policy before and during the World War, the Comintern, created and directed by the Russian communists, frankly threw down the gauntlet to capitalism. It regarded the latter as impotent before the forces it had itself generated —a socialized war economy, a revolutionary-minded working class, and a passion for freedom among the small nationalities. In the meantime, events were occurring in various parts of Europe which seemed to presage a fulfillment of their hopes. In January, 1919, the Spartacists staged an uprising in Berlin. A few months later, Bela Kun seized Hungary and set up a communist dictatorship. Uprisings followed in various parts of Germany and in Italy. Although these efforts eventually failed, they were regarded as the precursors to a general movement of the workers that would be successful. In the meantime the Red armies beat back all of the attacks of the White generals, advanced toward Warsaw in 1920, and aroused hopes among the communists that they might continue to Berlin and arouse the proletariat throughout Europe to revolt. In this optimistic atmosphere the Second Congress of the Third International met at Moscow in the latter part of 1920, and was attended by delegates from Left groups all over the world. The delegates were advised that the critical hour had struck, that they must return to their respective countries and do all in their power to accelerate the coming revolution, and were instructed as to the precise manner in which the dictatorship of the proletariat might be applied in different countries.[51]

The attitude of the communists toward the League of Nations and the International Labor Organization may readily be understood in the light of their theory of class warfare. Anticipating the formation of the League, they denounced it in advance as "the Holy Alliance of the bourgeoisie for the suppression of the proletarian revolution." They were, of course, not invited to participate in the making of the Covenant, and from their point of view it was a device to bolster up capitalism and to fight communism. And they could cite high authority for their contention. President Wilson is reported to have spoken of the League to Lloyd George in March 1919 as "an alternative to Bolshevism." [52]

[51] Lorwin, *op. cit.*, pp. 171-172, 211-216.

[52] H. W. V. Temperley, *A History of the Peace Conference of Paris;* 6 vols. (London, 1920-24), VI, 500.

In so far, therefore, as it might serve as a rallying point and instrument of cohesion for the forces of capitalism against Bolshevism, it represented a distinct and dangerous menace from the communist point of view, and elicited both fear and ridicule. The fact that the two nations—Great Britain and France—most active in the policy of intervention against Soviet Russia were also the chief supporters of the League from the time of its formation, tended to confirm the views of the communists as to its character. And when France aided Poland during the latter's war with Russia in 1920-1921, Lenin indulged in a bitter and derisive tirade against "this Plague of Nations" which he accused, among other things, of "blockading, starving and fighting openly and secretly the peasants and workers of Soviet Russia." [53]

The attitude of the communists toward the International Labor Organization was likewise one of contempt and distrust. They were well aware that one of the reasons for its establishment was the bourgeois fear of the spread of communism in 1919 and the desire to give some international recognition to labor elements in the different countries so that they would not be attracted to Bolshevism. The Labor Charter upon which the Organization was founded, however, fell short of the desires even of the less radical International Federation of Trade Unions, which accepted it with some reluctance.[54] It owed its origin in large part to Samuel Gompers, the conservative President of the American Federation of Labor. Under the provisions for the International Labor Organization itself, there was little if any chance for the more radical labor elements to secure representation or have any influence on policy.[55] It was inevitable, therefore, that the communists should regard it as an "abominable masquerade to trick the proletariat," and that the Soviet government should, in the first years of its existence, refuse to cooperate in any way with it.[56] At the Second Congress of

[53] Nikolai Lenin, "Against the Plague of Nations: An Address to Thinking People on the Polish Question." Quotation is from the text as given in Cooke and Stickney, *op. cit.*, p. 849. For the views of an American communist, on the eve of the establishment of the League, see Scott Nearing, *Labor and the League of Nations* (New York, 1919). He regarded the League as the last stand of capitalism and the last obstacle to the emancipation of labor. It would be impotent to prevent war, however, because of the nature of the peace concluded, and above all because it ignored the causes of modern war which are economic. Nearing believed in the imperative need of a league, but to be effective it must be a socialist League of Nations.

[54] Lorwin, *op. cit.*, p. 194.

[55] See Appendix.

[56] Kathryn W. Davis, "The Soviet Union and the League of Nations, 1919-1933," *Geneva Special Studies,* Vol. V (1934), No. 1, p. 10.

the Third International, one of the conditions laid down for admission of any group to the Communist International was that it should carry on a stubborn struggle against the International Labor Organization.[57]

On the other hand, the attitude of the evolutionary and reformist socialists toward the League of Nations system was from the beginning more favorable. Gradualists in general saw in it much imperfection, but regarded it as a forward step which opponents of war and unrestrained imperialism and advocates of democracy should support. As a matter of fact, socialists were in part responsible for its formation, and seem to have had some influence on the form which it took. As early as February, 1915, an Allied Socialist Conference adopted a resolution on war aims which included the aspiration for "a peaceful federation of the United States of Europe and the world" after the War.[58] In February, 1918, an Inter-Allied Labor and Socialist Conference, meeting in London, made the establishment of a League of Nations the central part of its program for the reconstruction of the world at the end of the War. "Whoever triumphs," it was declared, "the peoples will have lost unless an international system is established which will prevent war. It would mean nothing to declare the right of peoples to self-determination if this right were left at the mercy of new violations, and was not protected by a super-national authority. That authority can be no other than the League of Nations, which not only all the present belligerents, but every other independent State, should be pressed to join." [59] Finally, a combined Labor and Socialist Conference meeting at Berne, Switzerland, in February 1919, had endorsed President Wilson's Fourteen Points and had called for the establishment of a universal League of Nations made up of representation from parliaments rather than from governments.[60]

Since 1923, when the Labor and Socialist International was organized to represent the various socialist groups opposed to the policies of the Communist Third International, an approach to a unified program of socialist internationalism has been made. In general, the view has been adopted that it is necessary to work toward socialism within the capitalistic system, and that socialists can beneficially work within

[57] Lorwin, *op. cit.*, p. 217.

[58] J. T. Shotwell, *The Origins of the International Labor Organization*, 2 vols. (New York, 1934), II, 4, for text of resolution.

[59] *Ibid.*, pp. 58-59. Complete text of war aims, pp. 57-69.

[60] Lorwin, *op. cit.*, p. 168.

existing international institutions such as the League of Nations for the improvement of international relationships and for the maintenance of peace. Like the liberals, the socialists of various states have taken government posts within their several countries and occupied positions in the League at one time or another in order to advance the movement towards disarmament, compulsory arbitration, and other matters which the League has attempted to further. Although many profess to regard it as a tool of capitalism, for the most part socialists look upon the League as "the first effective international organization in history, the germ of the future juridical organization of the world, and a possible instrument for transforming the international 'bourgeois state' of today into the International Socialist State of tomorrow." They would like to see it become universal in its membership; they advocate larger powers for the assembly in relation to the council; and would have it representative of parliaments rather than representative of governments as it is at present. Above all, perhaps, they would increase the League's authority in the economic sphere. Recognizing the part played by economic maladjustments in causing friction and war in the modern world, they would have the League set up an International Economic Council, in which labor would have representation "to deal with monetary policy, production and consumption, facilities of communication, distribution of raw materials, the unification of economic legislation, and the liberalization of commercial policies."[61]

During the eighteen years that the communists have held power in Russia the impact of events has caused them not only to shift their policies but also to modify or reinterpret certain of the doctrines of Marx and Engels. The latter, for example, declared that it was quite out of the question to expect socialism to succeed in a single country. The development of large scale industry and the growth of a world market had created a situation which, in Engels' opinion, would make it impossible. On the other hand, on account of the growth and mutual antagonism of the bourgeoisie and the proletariat as the chief social classes, Engels looked forward to the simultaneous outbreak of communist revolutions, at least in the principal industrial countries. These would later spread to the entire world. History, however, refused to accommodate itself to this thesis. The revolutionary outbreaks toward the end of, and shortly after, the World War had not led to communist

[61] *Ibid.*, pp. 433-435.

régimes, and in many countries there were no revolutions at all. In one of them, Italy, the revolution that succeeded was anti-communist and bourgeois. In the meantime, communism did succeed in Russia, and eventually the attacks upon this proletarian citadel had lessened and practically ceased. As the Russian leaders then began to look inward with the idea of building up Russia as a center of communism rather than to concentrate on the overthrow of capitalism in other countries, the attitude of Stalin and the majority of the other leaders changed, and they reread and quoted Marx and Lenin [62] to show that socialism in one country could succeed. And although they did not discard the Marxian belief that imperialistic wars are inevitable under capitalism, they did come to desire to postpone rather than to welcome them until, at any rate, the Soviet Union should have consolidated its position. Russia, said Zinoviev in 1923, must try to avoid war. "We need peace. So does our country. It is essential to the proletarian revolution that Russia should, economically, get upon her feet." [63] This view was attacked by Trotsky and other Left Wingers, but the position of Stalin was sustained, and Trotsky, who proved obdurate, was finally exiled.

In the meantime, the Stalinsts have proceeded with a vast industrial program designed to create a new Russia. To succeed in this, they have needed foreign capital, foreign technical experts, and foreign trade. To secure these, they have had to modify their policies, if not their anti-capitalist slogans. They have also needed peace and security, and this, too, has caused them finally to recede from their original position of undisguised suspicion and hostility toward capitalism and all its works, and to collaborate more and more with capitalist countries and institutions. Until recently, however, the Soviets have sought security by means of bilateral non-aggression treaties pledging the parties not to attack or commit acts of aggression or enter into coalitions against each other, and to submit their differences to some form of peaceful settlement. It is to be observed that these regional treaties likewise provided that, should one of the parties become involved in war, the other would remain neutral. By this means the Soviets sought to enhance their security without entering into any system of collective security with capitalist states such as was envisaged in the League of Nations

[62] Lenin, in the meantime, had died (1924), but was recognized by all communists as the successor of Marx, and his writings ranked along with those of Marx as their gospel.

[63] Quoted in Florinsky, *op. cit.*, p. 119.

Covenant.[64] Soviet Russia was anxious to have peace but it was not ready actively to collaborate with the capitalist world. This was also shown in connection with efforts at disarmament. Prior to the meeting of the Disarmament Conference in 1932, the Soviet government as has been observed proposed total disarmament,[65] was scathing in its criticism of other less sweeping plans, but evinced no disposition to enter into any cooperative plan to secure peace.

Since 1932, however, certain events have swept the Soviet government on to the stage of active political collaboration with western capitalist nations. In 1932, Japan's drive for the control of Manchuria leading to the creation under Japanese auspices of the "state" of Manchoukuo, her aggressive policy toward China, and her refusal to sign a non-aggression treaty offered by Russia, alarmed the Soviets, who were fearful of an attack on their Far Eastern provinces. In 1933, the National Socialists of Germany, the avowed enemies of communism, under the leadership of a man who had frankly stated that Germany must expand at the expense of Russia, came into power in the Reich, and immediately began a drive to free Germany from the disarmament restrictions of the Treaty of Versailles. The League attempted to restrain Japanese imperialism, and Japan gave notice that she would withdraw from the Geneva organization. The League's Disarmament Conference sought to reach a compromise with Germany on the matter of armament, but Germany withdrew from the Conference and, like Japan, turned her back upon the League. Soviet Russia was thus exposed to attack front and rear by two nations that had thrown off the restraints of the Covenant and seemed bent on a career of aggression. Under these circumstances, the communists had to decide whether they should remain outside the Geneva security system and risk a war which they would probably have to fight alone, or whether they would stray further from the doctrines of Marx by joining and collaborating with a group of capitalist nations whose peace was also threatened by the policies of Japan and Germany. The decision of Soviet Russia to join the League apparently marks the abandonment of the policy of aloofness and her definite acceptance of the principle of cooperation, for certain definite ends, with capitalist states, even through a "bourgeois" agency.

[64] In this connection see M. W. Graham, "The Soviet Security System," *International Conciliation* (Sept., 1929), No. 252.

[65] *Supra,* pp. 436-437.

It also seems to indicate that the present rulers of Russia think peace is possible under capitalism, although this is contrary to the traditional communist position.[66]

The decision of the Russian communists to build "socialism in a single country" has meant the abandonment, for the time being at any rate, of the cause of Marxian international socialism and the substitution of a form of national communism in its stead. Soviet Russia has become more and more absorbed in her internal development. The communist leaders at the party congresses still use the language of Marx and the phrases of the *Communist Manifesto,* but they exhort the workers of other lands as well as those of Russia to protect Soviet Russia, "the fatherland of the proletariat," against capitalism, and they extol the achievements that Red Russia has to her credit. The Red Army of Russia, though theoretically organized in behalf of the cause of the proletariat of the world, is actually the creation of a national state and is for the purpose of defending the land and people of a particular country. In the field of education, the trend is toward the inculcation of a national viewpoint as well as the imposition of communist dogma, and the foreign policy of the Soviet government touching trade and economic matters has placed an emphasis on national self-sufficiency not altogether distinguishable from the policies of national bourgeois states. Recent danger of attack from without has tended to stimulate a strong national rather than purely proletarian spirit. For example, recent developments in Germany inspired an editorial in *Pravda,* organ of the Communist Party, entitled "Soviet Patriotism," in which the note of class-consciousness is almost drowned out by the following patriotic panegyric: "Never anywhere did the heroism of the struggle for one's country rise to such heights as here. All the enchanting history of the revolutionary movement in Russia, all the history of the Soviet Union showed and is showing what the workers are able to do when the fate of their country is involved. . . The Soviet Union is the spring of humanity. The name of Moscow sounds for all workers and peasants, all honest and cultured people of the whole globe, a militant summons and hope for a bright future and victory over Facist barbarism."[67] To

[66] See Appendix for extract from *Report on the Work of the Central Committee of the Communist Party of the Soviet Union,* by Joseph Stalin. It deals at length with the Soviet attitude and position as regards relations with other states.

[67] Quotation of United Press correspondent in the *Berkeley Gazette,* March 19. 1935.

Trotsky and other Left Wing communists this is doubtless more evidence of the bourgeoisification of the communist state.

REFERENCES

Angell, N., "Russia and the International Organization of Defence," *Time and Tide,* June 2, 1934, *Foreign Affairs Supplement.*

Batsell, W. R., *Soviet Rule in Russia* (New York, 1929), Chs. III, X, XIII.

————, "The Soviets' Treatment of National Minorities," *Current History,* Vol. XXVIII (Sept., 1928), No. 6, pp. 922-926.

Bernstein, E., *Evolutionary Socialism,* tr. by Edith C. Harvey (New York, 1909).

Boudin, L. B., *Socialism and War* (New York, 1916).

Brailsford, H. N., *The War of Steel and Gold* (10th ed. rev., London, 1918).

Bukharin, N. I., *Imperialism and World Economy* (London, 1917).

Chamberlin, W. H., *Soviet Russia* (Boston, 1930), Chs. IX, XVI.

Davis, K. W., "The Soviet Union and the League of Nations, 1919-1933," *Geneva Special Studies,* Vol. V (1934), No. 1, pp. 3-23.

Dutt, R. P., *Fascism and Social Revolution* (New York, 1934).

Fischer, L., *The Soviets in World Affairs,* 2 vols. (London and New York, 1930).

Florinsky, M. T., *World Revolution and the U.S.S.R.* (New York, 1933).

Foreman, C., *The New Internationalism* (New York, 1934), Ch. III.

Harper, S. N., "The Soviet Union—National or International?" *Annals of the American Academy of Political and Social Science,* CLXXV (Sept., 1934), 51-59.

Hervé, G., *L'Internationalisme* (Paris, 1910).

Hilferding, R., *Das Finanzkapital* (Vienna, 1910).

Hovde, B. J., "Socialistic Theories of Imperialism Prior to the Great War," *Journal of Political Economy,* Vol. XXXVI (Oct., 1928), No. 5, pp. 569-591.

Humphrey, A. W., *International Socialism and the War* (London, 1915).

Hyndman, H. M., *The Future of Democracy* (London, 1915).

Kautsky, K., *The Class Struggle,* tr. by E. Bohn (Chicago, 1910).

————, *Sozialismus und Kolonialpolitik* (Berlin, 1907).

Kohn, H., *Nationalism in the Soviet Union* (New York, 1933).

Laidler, H. W., *A History of Socialist Thought* (New York, 1927).

Laski, H. J., *Communism* (London, 1927).

Lenin, N., *Der Imperialismus als Jüngste Etappe des Kapitalismus* (Zurich, 1916). English translation, *Imperialism;* and *The State and Revolution* (New York, 1929).

Liebknecht, K., *Militarism* (Toronto, 1917).

Lorwin, L. L., *Labor and Internationalism* (New York, 1929).

Luxemburg, R., *Die Akkumulation des Kapitals* (Berlin, 1913).

Macartney, C. A., *National States and National Minorities* (London, 1934), pp. 450-464.

Nearing, S., *The American Empire* (2nd ed., New York, 1921).

——————, *Labor and The League of Nations* (New York, 1919).

Oneal, J., *American Communism* (New York, 1927), Ch. II.

Parmelee, M., *Bolshevism, Fascism and the Liberal Democratic State* (New York, 1934), Pt. 1.

Pavlovitch, M., *The Foundations of Imperialist Policy* (London, 1922).

Radek, K., "The Bases of Soviet Foreign Policy," *Foreign Affairs,* Jan., 1934, pp. 193-206.

Russell, B., *The Practice and Theory of Bolshevism* (London, 1920), Pt. II.

Shotwell, J. T., ed., *The Origins of the International Labor Organization,* 2 vols. (New York, 1934).

Stalin, J., "The Political and Social Doctrine of Communism; Report on the Work of the Central Committee of the Communist Part of the Soviet Union," *International Conciliation* (Dec., 1934), No. 305, pp. 383-451.

Strachey, J., *The Coming Struggle for Power* (New York, 1933), Chs. IV, XII, XIX.

Taracouzio, T. A., *The Soviet Union and International Law* (New York, 1935).

Thomas, N., *America's Way Out: A Program for Democracy* (New York, 1931), Chs. III, VII, XIV.

Trotsky, L., *The Bolsheviki and World Peace* (New York, 1918).

Walling, W. E., *The Socialists and the War* (New York, 1915).

Winslow, E. M., "Marxian, Liberal and Sociological Theories of Imperialism," *Journal of Political Economy,* Vol. XXXIX (Dec., 1931), No. 6, pp. 713-758.

Yarmolinsky, A., *The Jews and Other Minor Nationalities under the Soviets* (New York, 1928).

CHAPTER XXIII

LAISSEZ-FAIRE VS. INTERNATIONAL ORGANIZATION

At the conclusion of a survey of the development of international thought, one is likely, if he concentrates his gaze on certain facts and foibles to be observed in the international society of the present moment, to come to the conclusion that the philosopher who defined human history as "a brief and discreditable episode in the life history of one of the meaner planets," was not far wrong. Four hundred years of that "episode" have been added to the record of *homo sapiens* since Machiavelli's *Prince* laid down the rules whereby "stern men with empires in their brains," as some writer has expressed it, might reach their goals. In the meantime, the energy, curiosity, and ingenuity of man have put the world through such a shrinking process that continents separated by seas and deserts are, as far as communication is concerned, nearer to one another today than were neighboring countries when the Florentine wrote his manual of statecraft. Travel and trade have increased enormously, and national states have become, to a very great extent, economically, and even politically, interdependent. The tariff and other trade policies of states, though regarded as strictly "domestic," have economic and political consequences reaching far beyond the national frontiers. Political upheavals and economic dislocations in any important state, at any rate, are likely to have repercussions in others that may set in motion forces of the utmost consequence eventually for the entire international community. The power of states to injure one another in war has also, in view of modern inventions, increased enormously, and its evil consequences are not confined to the combatants. Some countries managed to avoid being swept into the World War, but no civilized state was able to insulate itself from its demoralizing effects. And no state has altogether escaped the Great Depression, which has been prolonged and aggravated, incidentally, by the fact that most of them have sought exclusively "national" solutions of their economic difficulties, some by way of formulas of autarchy and self-containment, others by naked imperialistic enterprises designed to secure a monopoly of markets and exclusive or preferential access to raw materials.

In this new interdependent world of the twentieth century a theory of sovereignty developed in its absolute form in the sixteenth century, at a time when national monarchs were seeking completely to unify their kingdoms within and to throw off the last vestiges of control from outside, still bars the way to the realization of a system of international law superior to the will of the individual states composing the international community. For, according to the theory of absolute sovereignty, still widely accepted, the state is possesed of absolute and unlimited legal power and enjoys complete freedom of action in international relations except as it may elect to accept limitations. If it accepts restraints or agrees to restrictions on its freedom of action, it does so voluntarily; and its own will likewise determines how long and under what circumstances such restrictions or limitations are to be accepted. Each state, therefore, in legal theory has an unfettered will which may be exercised without regard to the wills of other states. The framers of the Covenant of the League of Nations, as we have seen, were careful not to challenge this sacred dogma. In fact, it was acknowledged at least by implication in several places in the Covenant. On the other hand, states were asked voluntarily to accept and exhaust the remedies of a system curtailing their liberty of action in certain matters regarded as affecting the welfare of the international community. States were henceforth to respect one another's frontiers and political independence, and agree to help one another in preserving them against external aggression from any quarter. They were likewise asked to agree that they would seek through the League of Nations, or through other agencies of peaceful settlement, the adjustment of their disputes rather than resort to the expensive and haphazard remedy of war. Time has demonstrated, however, that members of the League, as well as states outside, have not modified their conceptions of national sovereignty and are not disposed to surrender the precarious freedom that is necessarily associated with an "anarchy of sovereignties." The debates that have taken place in League Commissions and in international conferences on disarmament, minorities, mandates, sanctions, and other matters reveal that up to the present the farthest that many, perhaps most, states are willing to go is to confer regularly on all matters regarded as having an international interest, and seek unanimous consent of the sovereign states for demonstrably necessary international action.

At the present moment, and for several years past, the prestige of the League of Nations has suffered because of its impotence in the face of the flouting of the obligations of the Covenant by one or another member impatient with, or contemptuous of, the slow processes of international negotiation and adjustment, or indisposed to accept even the principle of international adjudication of questions involving other members of the League and of the international community. In many quarters the obligations laid down in the Covenant are regarded as embodying an idealistic conception of international relationships impossible of realization in a nationalistic age. One prominent American nationalist not only declares that such misguided idealism was bound to fail, but suggests that it deserved to fail: "Another revolution, therefore, has failed. It had to fail. It could not escape the living past. It did not weigh sufficiently the inertia of human nature, it underestimated the strength of those ancient prejudices and fears, as well as those ancient faiths and beliefs, the intellectual and moral paths over which men and women have trodden for centuries. The fight against nationalism has lost. It was bound to lose. It was a fight against the strongest and noblest passion, outside of those which spring from man's relation to his God, that moves or controls the impulses of the human heart. Without it civilization would wane and utterly decay. Men would sink to the level of savages. Individuality in persons is the product of the most persistent and universal law of nature. It is woven of millions of subtle and tireless forces. No power can change this law or frustrate its operation. This is equally true of nations. Internationalism, if it means anything more than the friendly cooperation between separate, distinct, and wholly independent nations, rests upon a false foundation. And when undertaken, it will fail as in the name of progress and humanity it should fail." [1]

The views of Senator Borah are inspired by one who loves liberty and who sees in a *laissez-faire* individualism in the international sphere as well as within nations the best means of its preservation. Within nations, the liberty of the individual is best preserved by maintaining

[1] Excerpt from address of Senator William E. Borah on "American Foreign Policy in a Nationalistic World" before the Council on Foreign Relations in New York City on January 8, 1934. Reprinted as Supplement to *Foreign Affairs*, Vol. XII (Jan., 1934), No. 2.

a large "sphere of anarchy" within which he is free from governmental restrictions and control. In the international field, national states are the individuals who properly have been, and will continue to be, opposed to endowing any international agency with authority to control or coerce them or infringe upon their complete freedom to determine their course of action in all matters affecting their individual interests or welfare.

If the régime of *laissez-faire* in international relations were the necessary condition for the maintenance of the freedom of the states composing the international community and the welfare of their citizens, there would probably be few internationalists who would advocate its abandonment. For internationalists in general emphasize the importance of preserving human freedom. Their insistence upon the necessity of extending law and organization into the international field is in large part based upon their conviction that the freedom of *laissez-faire* is the freedom of the strong to violate the freedom of the weak. This is well understood by the small states, which have been the most loyal supporters of the League of Nations and the most anxious to see its authority sustained and its influence strengthened. Far from desiring to see the experiment abandoned, or the League shorn of any of its powers, they have consistently demanded that is should be armed with the necessary additional authority to insure peace and justice in the international community.

It seems clear that individualism in international relations as advocated by extreme nationalists—and even by those of the cast of thought of Senator Borah, who doubtless would not admit the adjective—not only does not result in freedom for the weak, but, in so far as it makes for national exclusiveness and leads to armed rivalry and recurring war involving the strong, results in regimentation and the deprivation of the populations of Great Powers as well as those of small states of freedom of inquiry, discussion, and criticism of governmental policies. For liberty does not, and cannot, flourish in wartime. Nor can liberty and justice long survive in states enjoying the freedom of warring and being warred on, and therefore under the compulsion of preoccupying themselves in time of peace with preparations for "the next war." Thus, peace today would seem to be necessary for the realization, among other goods, of liberty and justice. On the other hand, if one emphasizes human welfare, and seeks a system whereby individual human beings throughout the earth may enjoy the most favorable conditions possible for living the good life, he will concentrate not only upon peace but also upon the conditions that make for human unhappiness and dissatisfaction, and the best means of remedying them. As a prominent American philosopher and pacifist has expressed it, "Peace . . . is itself not an ideal at all; it is a state attendant upon the achievement of an ideal. The ideal itself is human liberty, justice and honorable conduct of an orderly and humane society. Given this, a durable peace follows naturally as a matter of course. Without this, there is no peace, but only a rule of force until liberty and justice revolt against it in search of peace." [2]

It is hardly to be denied, however, that such liberty and justice as have been realized within states have been attained as a result of the development of legal and political institutions upon which individuals might rely for the adjustment of their claims, the redress of their grievances, and the carrying out of policies designed to safeguard their security and promote the general welfare. As such institutions were developed, self-help could be dispensed with and fortuitous justice replaced by community justice in which, in principle, might could only vindicate its claims on the basis of legal right. This development, of course, has not meant that law is found always to be synonymous with justice, but it has made the conditions of human existence so much more tolerable and the lives of the individuals within these communities so much more secure that no one proposes that the restrictions on individual liberty that are involved should be removed and the "liberty" of self-help restored. In the opinion of an increasing number of students of international relations, an analogous development, already taking rudimentary form in the League of Nations system, must replace the system of self-help and *laissez-faire* in international relations before liberty, justice, and security for the organized peoples of the world can reasonably be expected and thus the conditions necessary for international peace be realized.

Although the League of Nations has been in existence and has developed a jurisprudence of pacific settlement over a period of fifteen years, as well as performing other useful services on behalf of the international community, it has not furnished the security to its mem-

[2] Nicholas Murray Butler, *The Path of Peace* (New York and London, 1930) pp. 202-203.

bers for which the framers of the Covenant hoped. In the opinion of many who are not opposed to the League in principle, as are the integral nationalists and the communists, its weakness is due fundamentally to the unwillingness of nations, jealous of their sovereignty, to endow it with the necessary powers, or even to accept the implications or latent possibilities of certain articles of the Covenant. Far from accepting a doctrine of implicit powers, they have at times asserted a doctrine of implied powerlessness to go beyond the strict letter of the Covenant. In addition, many regard the Covenant as defective on account of its strong emphasis on the maintenance of the political and territorial *status quo* established by the victors in 1919 and its assertedly inadequate provisions for peacefully changing the *status quo,* as it is shown to be unjust or not to correspond to the ascertained needs of the populations concerned and the welfare of the international community.[3] It should be obvious that in a dynamic world in which change is the one sure constant among innumerable variables, no treaties involving the distribution of territories and power can be regarded as answering for all time the needs or reflecting the legitimate aspirations of the populations affected by them. Any imposed peace rigidly maintained by superior force, regardless of considerations of justice or of the laws of growth and change, will lead to discontents and hardships that will be endured only as long as those imposing such a peace are able to command the bigger battalions. And, in the meantime, a healthy progress will be impeded. Peace is perhaps the greatest need of the world today, for without it liberty and security for the people of the world as a whole cannot be realized. But it should not be conceived in static terms. That way lies stagnation, tempered by violent upheavals from time to time which bring fresh suffering and new injustices in their train. It should rather be conceived as a dynamic condition in which changes and re-adjustments continuously take place under circumstances in which reason rather than passion, and a "decent respect to the opinions of mankind" rather than a regard only for national power, are the deciding factors.

If peace and justice are measurably to be realized in the international sphere, and the requisite conditions for men and women to live the good life within states attained, it would seem that states must

[3] Compare, for example, Articles X and XVI of the Covenant, with Articles XI and XIX.

abandon the notion that the ultimate in political authority is and must continue to be the national state, and that they must accept a much greater degree of international government than they have as yet been willing to tolerate. It would seem to be neither possible nor desirable that this development should take the form of a unitary world state; but the progressive organization of the world community on the federal principle, with due regard for regional needs and interests, in which as much local freedom will be preserved as is compatible with the welfare and safety of the whole, would seem to be imperative. In principle, the area of political control should correspond to the area of relationships and common interests. "All matters of joint concern between nations must be matters of joint decision." This means that the authority and powers of the League of Nations, if it is to be accepted as the instrument of the international community, must be strengthened, especially in the economic field. At the present time, even though action may be clearly necessary for the welfare of the society of states, and a large majority of states may favor it, the unanimity rule, requiring that such action cannot be taken if any state refuses to give its consent, can be utilized to paralyze and frustrate the will of the entire community. Obviously, this closely guarded bulwark of sovereignty must give way before any great progress can be made toward organizing the world for peace and security. To remove this and other legal notions that serve as obstructions in the path of international progress the brilliant political scientist, H. J. Laski, goes so far as to suggest the necessity of a new philosophy of international law in which national states will be legally subordinated to the society of states. "We must begin by postulating the society of States, the *civitas maxima* in which all have their being, as the source from which the competence of all individual States is derived. The law, then, of this society is binding upon its individual members. Despite differences of territory and wealth and power, each can have equal claims with its fellows because each is equally subject to the law." Likewise in the political realm this writer holds that "it is important to postulate the non-sovereign character of the State as the condition of the *civitas maxima*" in order that "the hinterland between states" may be adequately organized. Moreover, as the purpose of all government is to protect and provide for the happiness of individual men and women, "the right of the world community to have direct access to its citizens independently of its access to them through individual States is clearly paramount." Thus if an individual state fails to furnish the "conditions without which no man can hope to realize the potentialities of his nature," he will be able to appeal directly to the appropriate institution of the international community for protection and redress.[4]

Whether one is prepared to go the whole distance with Laski on the matter of the essential legal and political relationship between national states and the international community, he must realize, if he accepts the proposition that states exist for the purpose of providing security and the best possible conditions for the happiness of their individual citizens, that under twentieth century conditions international government of a less nebulous character, and of a far greater sweep than exists at present, is indispensable. It is at least doubtful whether any state on earth, no matter how great its resources or how much money it may be able to expend on armament, can, under conditions of modern war, by its own strength secure its citizens against war and war's disastrous consequences. In any event, war on any considerable scale cannot but adversely affect the welfare, if it does not jeopardize the safety, of the citizens of all states in the stream of civilized intercourse. Cooperative or pooled security seems to be the only answer to present-day needs. It is equally patent that in the economic sphere, few states, if any, are capable, through reliance on themselves alone or through policies of economic nationalism, of furnishing the conditions under which their citizens can enjoy economic security and well-being.[5] Individual "protective" tariffs demoralize international trade and react disastrously on the citizens of states imposing them by ruining markets, depressing industry, aggravating unemployment, and leading to lower standards of living. Here is a "domestic question" that cannot be dealt with satisfactorily by separate national action or ultimately even by isolated bilateral agreements. Likewise, the attempts of nations to strive for unilateral solutions of the monetary problem, rather than face the facts and recognize that the operations of international trade and investment require international action, are only intelligible on the

[4] "The Theory of an International Society," *Problems of Peace, Sixth Series* (London, 1932), pp. 195, 199-201. For a criticism of the position of those who advocate the complete supersession of national sovereignty, see Ramsay Muir, *The Interdependent World and Its Problems* (Boston, 1933), pp. 114-120.

[5] This point of view is challenged, as far as the United States is concerned, in C. A. Beard, *The Open Door at Home* (New York, 1934).

assumption that national states are or can be made into water-tight economic units above the necessity of international trade or intercourse. Beyond these lie other questions which as yet states have been unwilling to allow the League or any international agency to deal with in general, although they are the very questions which breed international animosity and war, against which the League is expected to form a barrier. States suffering from population pressure, having an insufficiency of raw materials, and denied outlets for their surplus numbers by immigration restrictions of other countries that are, perhaps, underpopulated and at the same time favored by nature with an abundance of natural resources, are likely to try to blast their way to a place in the sun, regardless of commitments to respect the *status quo* if the League is powerless to afford them any relief.[6] In the near future, probably, the Society of States will have to decide whether the liberty of individual decision in these and like matters, involving the perpetuation of war and the rule of jungle justice, is worth the increasingly heavy cost and whether in any event it can continue without the complete breakdown of civilization.

If an ordered Cosmos is to replace the present Chaos in international relations, it seems obvious that one of the first tasks is to organize a system of collective security which will create sufficient confidence that states will not fear to reduce, and eventually dispense with, their expensive and fear-breeding armed establishments. In the case of most nations, it is probably safe to say that it is fear rather than pride and ambition that causes them to insist on keeping their powder dry and keeping plenty of it. Others are rightly or wrongly dissatisfied with their position in the world and want to be strong enough to change it, if necessary, by armed force. But if there can be developed a dynamic international political system capable not only of maintaining the *status quo* against violent change, but also of modifying it or effecting adjustments in international conditions whenever justice and equity demand them, no legitimate reason remains for such nations to maintain large armed establishments. It is idle, however, to expect that nations will disarm unless the international community is prepared to defend their frontiers and their legitimate interests. And it is naïve to expect that international agreements will always be respected by all states, even

[6] The Lytton Report exemplifies the spirit and suggests the possibilities of the internationalist approach.

assuming a system providing for orderly change, without an international policeman somewhere in the background. There is no reason for believing that we can skip the policeman stage in international government and rely exclusively upon public opinion when public opinion does not even yet suffice against law-breakers within the state. If every effort is made to see that law corresponds as nearly as possible with justice and is kept abreast of changing needs, there will doubtless be few occasions to employ coercive sanctions; but there should also be no objection to international government being equipped with them. In the final analysis, international government, if it is to afford security and a happier environment for human beings, must be capable of enforcing the law of the community, when it is challenged by force of arms or a negative refusal to respect it, as well as endowed with the power to remedy patent injustices.

Another *sine qua non* of effective international government is the full participation and loyal collaboration on the basis of equality before the law, of all of the civilized members of the Society of States, large as well as small. This, in turn, implies a general consensus concerning the nature of the state and interstatal relationships that, as preceding chapters have indicated, is unhappily lacking at the present time. Formal membership in the League of Nations in itself means little. Members regarding it purely from the point of view of how it may serve their exclusive national interests, and refusing to take their commitments seriously whenever it is inconvenient to do so, tend to discredit and weaken international government. At the present moment, the Society of States has in its membership states under iron dictatorships as well as those adhering to parliamentary democracy. The former, accepting and accustomed to employ violence as a normal means of internal social control, can hardly be expected to adjust their thinking to a democratic procedure in the field of international relations, and brook the restraints that effective international government requires.[7] On the other hand, states theoretically sympathetic with the League of Nations, in so far as it seeks to prevent war and promote the common welfare, but unwilling to pledge themselves in advance to participate in any collective effort to restrain a treaty-breaking state bent on con-

[7] Japan and Germany have withdrawn from the League of Nations, and Italy threatens to do so if the League makes a serious effort to restrain her from coercing Ethiopia.

quest, are hindrances in their own way to the development of international government. Any Great Power such as the United States, which refuses to participate in a collective system and insists on preserving its complete freedom to stand aside and remain neutral when multilateral treaties are violated, judging each case for itself as it arises and then determining its policy, will contribute powerfully toward the maintenance of international anarchy. Altogether, the obstacles to the realization of an international system that shall fulfill the high hopes of the framers of the Covenant are great, and no useful purpose is served by glossing them over. A new outlook and the formation of the appropriate consensus are needed.

REFERENCES

Armstrong, H. F., "Power Politics and the Peace Machinery," *Foreign Affairs,* Vol. XIV (Oct., 1935), No. 1, pp. 1-11.

Avenol, J., "The Future of the League of Nations," *International Affairs,* Vol. XIII (March-April, 1934), No. 2, pp. 143-158.

Beard, C. A., *The Open Door at Home* (New York, 1934).

Borah, W. E., "American Foreign Policy in a Nationalistic World," *Foreign Affairs,* Vol. XII (January, 1934), No. 2, Special Supplement.

Bosanquet, B., *Social and International Ideals* (London, 1917).

Brailsford, H. N., *If We Want Peace* (London, 1932).

————, *Property or Peace* (New York, 1934).

Brown, P. M., *International Society: Its Nature and Interests* (New York, 1923).

Buell, R. L., and Dewey, John, "Are Sanctions Necessary to International Organization?," *Foreign Policy Association Pamphlets* (New York), 1931-32 Series, Nos. 82-83.

Butler, N. M., *The Path to Peace* (New York, 1930).

Carr-Saunders, A. M., "Biology and War," *Foreign Affairs,* Vol. VII (April, 1929), No. 3, pp. 427-438.

Catlin, G. E. G., *A Study of the Principles of Politics* (London, 1930), pp. 206-219.

Cole, G. D. H., *A Guide through World Chaos* (New York, 1932).

Davies, D., *The Problem of the Twentieth Century* (London, 1934).

Dickinson, E. D., "The Law of Change in International Relations," *Proceedings of the Institute of World Affairs,* XI (1933), 173-182.

Dorfman, J., "Two Unpublished Papers of Thorstein Veblen on the Nature of Peace," *Political Science Quarterly,* XLVII (June, 1932), 185-203.

Eagleton, C., "La Révision des Traités, Est-Elle Nécessaire?," *L'Esprit International,* January, 1931, pp. 61-76.

Ferrero, G., *Peace and War* (London, 1933).

Foreman, C., *The New Internationalism* (New York, 1934).

Foster, H. P., "International Sanctions: Two Old Views and a New One," *Political Science Quarterly,* Vol. XLIX (Sept., 1934), No. 3, pp. 372-385.

Garner, J. W., "Limitations on National Sovereignty in International Relations," *American Political Science Review,* Vol. XIX (Feb., 1925), No. 1, pp. 1-24.

Hindmarsh, A. E., *Force in Peace* (Cambridge, Mass., 1933).

Hocking, W. E., *The Spirit of World Politics* (New York, 1932), Chs. XXVII-XXXI.

Holland, T. H., "The International Relationship of Minerals," and "International Movement of Mineral Products in Peace and War," *International Conciliation* (Jan., 1931), No. 266.

Howard, Esme, Lord of Penrith, *The Prevention of War by Collective Action* (London, 1933).

Kunz, J. L., "The Law of Nations; Static and Dynamic," *American Journal of International Law,* Vol. XXVII (Oct., 1933), No. 4, pp. 630-650.

Lane, Ralph (Norman Angell, pseud.), *The Fruits of Victory* (London, 1921).

La Pradelle, A. de, "Les Nouvelles Tendances du Droit International," *L'Esprit International,* Vol. I (July, 1927), No. 3, pp. 342-349.

Lauterpacht, H., *The Function of Law in the International Community* (Oxford, 1933).

——————, *The Development of International Law by the Permanent Court of International Justice* (London, 1934), Ch. V.

MacIver, R. M., *The Modern State* (Oxford, 1926), Book II, Chs. VII-VIII.

Mitrany, David, *The Progress of International Government* (New Haven, Conn., 1933).

Muir, R., *The Interdependent World and Its Problems* (Boston, 1933).

Murray, G., *The Ordeal of This Generation* (New York and London, 1929).

Politis, Nicolas, *Les Nouvelles Tendances du Droit International* (Paris, 1927).

Problems of Peace, Sixth Series (London, 1922), Lectures delivered at the Geneva Institute of International Relations, August, 1931.

Rappard, W. E., "Nationalism and the League Today," *American Political Science Review,* XXVII (Oct., 1933), 721-737.

Riegel, O. W., *Mobilizing for Chaos* (New Haven, Conn., 1934).

Ritter, W. E., *War, Science, and Civilization* (Boston, 1915).

Rockow, Lewis, *Contemporary Political Thought in England* (London, 1925), Ch. X.

Salter, Sir Arthur, "The Future of Economic Nationalism," *Foreign Affairs,* Vol. XI (Oct., 1932), No. 1, pp. 8-20.

Scelle, Georges, "Essai sur la Crise de la Société des Nations," *L'Esprit International,* April, 1934, pp. 163-182.

Schuman, F. L., "The Ethics and Politics of International Peace," *International Journal of Ethics,* Vol. XLII (Jan., 1932), No. 2, pp. 148-162.

————, *International Politics* (New York, 1933), Chs. XIII, XIX.

Seronya, H., *Le Problème Philosophique de la Guerre et de la Paix* (Paris, 1932).

Simonds, Frank H. and Emeny, Brooks, *The Great Powers in World Politics* (New York, 1935).

Stratton, G. M., *International Delusions* (London, 1935).

————, *Social Psychology of International Conduct* (New York and London, 1929), Part III.

Temple, W., *The State in its External Relations* (London, 1932).

Wild, Payson S., *Sanctions and Treaty Enforcement* (Cambridge, Mass., 1934).

Williams, John Fischer, "Treaty Revision and the Future of the League," *International Affairs,* Vol. X (May, 1931), No. 3, pp. 326-351.

Wright, Q., "The Future of Neutrality," *International Conciliation* (Sept., 1928), No. 242.

Zimmern, A., "The Right Road to World Order," *Fortnightly Review,* CXL (July, 1933), 110.

APPENDIX I

A

COVENANT OF THE LEAGUE OF NATIONS *

THE HIGH CONTRACTING PARTIES,

In order to promote international co-operation and to achieve international peace and security

by the acceptance of obligations not to resort to war,

by the prescription of open, just and honourable relations between nations,

by the firm establishment of the understandings of international law as the actual rule of conduct among Governments, and

by the maintenance of justice and a scrupulous respect for all treaty obligations in the dealings of organised peoples with one another,

Agree to this Covenant of the League of Nations.

ARTICLE I

1. The original Members of the League of Nations shall be those of the Signatories which are named in the Annex to this Covenant and also such of those other States named in the Annex as shall accede without reservation to this Covenant. Such accession shall be effected by a Declaration deposited with the Secretariat within two months of the coming into force of the Covenant. Notice thereof shall be sent to all other Members of the League.

2. Any fully self-governing State, Dominion or Colony not named in the Annex may become a Member of the League if its admission is agreed to by two-thirds of the Assembly, provided that it shall give effective guarantees of its sincere intention to observe its international obligations, and shall accept such regulations as may be prescribed by the League in regard to its military, naval and air forces and armaments.

3. Any Member of the League may, after two years' notice of its inten-

* As amended down to December, 1933. The parts of the text printed in italics indicate the amendments that have been adopted. League of Nations, Information Section, *Essential Facts about the League of Nations* (4th ed. rev., 1935), pp. 235-250.

tion so to do, withdraw from the League, provided that all its international obligations and all its obligations under this Covenant shall have been fulfilled at the time of its withdrawal.

Article II

The action of the League under this Covenant shall be effected through the instrumentality of an Assembly and of a Council, with a permanent Secretariat.

Article III

1. The Assembly shall consist of Representatives of the Members of the League.

2. The Assembly shall meet at stated intervals and from time to time as occasion may require at the Seat of the League or at such other place as may be decided upon.

3. The Assembly may deal at its meetings with any matter within the sphere of action of the League or affecting the peace of the world.

4. At meetings of the Assembly, each Member of the League shall have one vote, and may have not more than three Representatives.

Article IV

1. The Council shall consist of Representatives of the Principal Allied and Associated Powers, together with Representatives of four other Members of the League. These four Members of the League shall be selected by the Assembly from time to time in its discretion. Until the appointment of the Representatives of the four Members of the League first selected by the Assembly, Representatives of Belgium, Brazil, Spain and Greece shall be members of the Council.

2. With the approval of the majority of the Assembly, the Council may name additional Members of the League whose Representatives shall always be Members of the Council; the Council with like approval may increase the number of Members of the League to be selected by the Assembly for representation on the Council.

2bis. *The Assembly shall fix by a two-thirds majority the rules dealing with the election of the non-permanent Members of the Council, and particularly such regulations as relate to their term of office and the conditions of re-eligibility.*

3. The Council shall meet from time to time as occasion may require, and at least once a year, at the Seat of the League, or at such other place as may be decided upon.

4. The Council may deal at its meetings with any matter within the sphere of action of the League or affecting the peace of the world.

5. Any Member of the League not represented on the Council shall be invited to send a Representative to sit as a member at any meeting of the Council during the consideration of matters specially affecting the interests of that Member of the League.

6. At meetings of the Council, each Member of the League represented on the Council shall have one vote, and may have not more than one Representative.

Article V

1. Except where otherwise expressly provided in this Covenant or by the terms of the present Treaty, decisions at any meeting of the Assembly or of the Council shall require the agreement of all the Members of the League represented at the meeting.

2. All matters of procedure at meetings of the Assembly or of the Council, including the appointment of Committees to investigate particular matters, shall be regulated by the Assembly or by the Council and may be decided by a majority of the Members of the League represented at the meeting.

3. The first meeting of the Assembly and the first meeting of the Council shall be summoned by the President of the United States of America.

Article VI

1. The permanent Secretariat shall be established at the Seat of the League. The Secretariat shall comprise a Secretary-General and such secretaries and staff as may be required.

2. The first Secretary-General shall be the person named in the Annex; thereafter the Secretary-General shall be appointed by the Council with the approval of the majority of the Assembly.

3. The secretaries and staff of the Secretariat shall be appointed by the Secretary-General with the approval of the Council.

4. The Secretary-General shall act in that capacity at all meetings of the Assembly and of the Council.

5. *The expenses of the League shall be borne by the Members of the League in the proportion decided by the Assembly.*

Article VII

1. The Seat of the League is established at Geneva.

2. The Council may at any time decide that the Seat of the League shall be established elsewhere.

3. All positions under or in connection with the League, including the Secretariat, shall be open equally to men and women.

4. Representatives of the Members of the League and officials of the League when engaged on the business of the League shall enjoy diplomatic privileges and immunities.

5. The buildings and other property occupied by the League or its officials or by Representatives attending its meetings shall be inviolable.

Article VIII

1. The Members of the League recognise that the maintenance of peace requires the reduction of national armaments to the lowest point consistent with national safety and the enforcement by common action of international obligations.

2. The Council, taking account of the geographical situation and circumstances of each State, shall formulate plans for such reduction for the consideration and action of the several Governments.

3. Such plans shall be subject to reconsideration and revision at least every ten years.

4. After these plans shall have been adopted by the several Governments, the limits of armaments therein fixed shall not be exceeded without the concurrence of the Council.

5. The Members of the League agree that the manufacture by private enterprise of munitions and implements of war is open to grave objections. The Council shall advise how the evil effects attendant upon such manufacture can be prevented, due regard being had to the necessities of those Members of the League which are not able to manufacture the munitions and implements of war necessary for their safety.

6. The Members of the League undertake to interchange full and frank information as to the scale of their armaments, their military, naval and air programmes and the condition of such of their industries as are adaptable to warlike purposes.

Article IX

A Permanent Commission shall be constituted to advise the Council on the execution of the provisions of Articles I and VIII and on military, naval and air questions generally.

Article X

The Members of the League undertake to respect and preserve as against external aggression the territorial integrity and existing political independence of all Members of the League. In case of any such aggression or in case of any threat or danger of such aggression the Council shall advise upon the means by which this obligation shall be fulfilled.

Article XI

1. Any war or threat of war, whether immediately affecting any of the Members of the League or not, is hereby declared a matter of concern to the whole League, and the League shall take any action that may be deemed wise and effectual to safeguard the peace of nations. In case any such emergency should arise the Secretary-General shall on the request of any Member of the League forthwith summon a meeting of the Council.

2. It is also declared to be the friendly right of each Member of the League to bring to the attention of the Assembly or of the Council any circumstance whatever affecting international relations which threatens to disturb international peace or the good understanding between nations upon which peace depends.

Article XII

1. The Members of the League agree that if there should arise between them any dispute likely to lead to a rupture they will submit the matter either to arbitration *or judicial settlement* or to enquiry by the Council, and they agree in no case to resort to war until three months after the award by the arbitrators *or the judicial decision* or the report by the Council.

2. In any case under this Article the award of the arbitrators *or the judicial decision* shall be made within a reasonable time, and the report of the Council shall be made within six months after the submission of the dispute.

Article XIII

1. The Members of the League agree that whenever any dispute shall arise between them which they recognise to be suitable for submission to arbitration *or judicial settlement,* and which cannot be satisfactorily settled by diplomacy, they will submit the whole subject-matter to arbitration *or judicial settlement.*

2. Disputes as to the interpretation of a treaty, as to any question of international law, as to the existence of any fact which, if established, would constitute a breach of any international obligation, or as to the extent and nature of the reparation to be made for any such breach, are declared to be among those which are generally suitable for submission to arbitration *or judicial settlement.*

3. *For the consideration of any such dispute, the court to which the case is referred shall be the Permanent Court of International Justice, established in accordance with Article XIV, or any tribunal agreed on by the parties to the dispute or stipulated in any convention existing between them.*

4. The Members of the League agree that they will carry out in full good faith any award *or decision* that may be rendered, and that they will not

resort to war against a Member of the League which complies therewith. In the event of any failure to carry out such an award *or decision,* the Council shall propose what steps should be taken to give effect thereto.

Article XIV

The Council shall formulate and submit to the Members of the League for adoption plans for the establishment of a Permanent Court of International Justice. The Court shall be competent to hear and determine any dispute of an international character which the parties thereto submit to it. The Court may also give an advisory opinion upon any dispute or question referred to it by the Council or by the Assembly.

Article XV

1. If there should arise between Members of the League any dispute likely to lead to a rupture, which is not submitted to arbitration *or judicial settlement* in accordance with Article XIII, the Members of the League agree that they will submit the matter to the Council. Any party to the dispute may effect such submission by giving notice of the existence of the dispute to the Secretary-General, who will make all necessary arrangements for a full investigation and consideration thereof.

2. For this purpose the parties to the dispute will communicate to the Secretary-General, as promptly as possible, statements of their case with all the relevant facts and papers, and the Council may forthwith direct the publication thereof.

3. The Council shall endeavour to effect a settlement of the dispute, and if such efforts are successful, a statement shall be made public giving such facts and explanations regarding the dispute and the terms of settlement thereof as the Council may deem appropriate.

4. If the dispute is not thus settled, the Council either unanimously or by a majority vote shall make and publish a report containing a statement of the facts of the dispute and the recommendations which are deemed just and proper in regard thereto.

5. Any Member of the League represented on the Council may make public a statement of the facts of the dispute and of its conclusions regarding the same.

6. If a report by the Council is unanimously agreed to by the members thereof other than the Representatives of one or more of the parties to the dispute, the Members of the League agree that they will not go to war with any party to the dispute which complies with the recommendations of the report.

7. If the Council fails to reach a report which is unanimously agreed

to by the members thereof, other than the Representatives of one or more of the parties to the dispute, the Members of the League reserve to themselves the right to take such action as they shall consider necessary for the maintenance of right and justice.

8. If the dispute between the parties is claimed by one of them, and is found by the Council, to arise out of a matter which by international law is solely within the domestic jurisdiction of that party, the Council shall so report, and shall make no recommendation as to its settlement.

9. The Council may in any case under this Article refer the dispute to the Assembly. The dispute shall be so referred at the request of either party to the dispute provided that such request be made within fourteen days after the submission of the dispute to the Council.

10. In any case referred to the Assembly, all the provisions of this Article and of Article XII relating to the action and powers of the Council shall apply to the action and powers of the Assembly, provided that a report made by the Assembly, if concurred in by the Representatives of those Members of the League represented on the Council and of a majority of the other Members of the League, exclusive in each case of the Representatives of the parties to the dispute, shall have the same force as a report by the Council concurred in by all the members thereof other than the Representatives of one or more of the parties to the dispute.

Article XVI

1. Should any Member of the League resort to war in disregard of its covenants under Articles XII, XIII or XV, it shall *ipso facto* be deemed to have committed an act of war against all other Members of the League, which hereby undertake immediately to subject it to the severance of all trade or financial relations, the prohibition of all intercourse between their nationals and the nationals of the covenant-breaking State, and the prevention of all financial, commercial, or personal intercourse between the nationals of the covenant-breaking State and the nationals of any other State, whether a Member of the League or not.

2. It shall be the duty of the Council in such a case to recommend to the several Governments concerned what effective military, naval or air force the Members of the League shall severally contribute to the armed forces to be used to protect the covenants of the League.

3. The Members of the League agree, further, that they will mutually support one another in the financial and economic measures which are taken under this Article, in order to minimise the loss and inconvenience resulting from the above measures, and that they will mutually support one another in resisting any special measures aimed at one of their number by

the covenant-breaking State, and that they will take the necessary steps to afford passage through their territory to the forces of any of the Members of the League which are co-operating to protect the covenants of the League.

4. Any Member of the League which has violated any covenant of the League may be declared to be no longer a Member of the League by a vote of the Council concurred in by the Representatives of all the other Members of the League represented thereon.

Article XVII

1. In the event of a dispute between a Member of the League and a State which is not a Member of the League, or between States not Members of the League, the State or States not Members of the League shall be invited to accept the obligations of membership in the League for the purposes of such dispute, upon such conditions as the Council may deem just. If such invitation is accepted the provisions of Articles XII to XVI inclusive shall be applied with such modifications as may be deemed necessary by the Council.

2. Upon such invitation being given the Council shall immediately institute an inquiry into the circumstances of the dispute and recommend such action as may seem best and most effectual in the circumstances.

3. If a State so invited shall refuse to accept the obligations of membership in the League for the purposes of such dispute, and shall resort to war against a Member of the League, the provisions of Article XVI shall be applicable as against the State taking such action.

4. If both parties to the dispute when so invited refuse to accept the obligations of membership in the League for the purposes of such dispute, the Council may take such measures and make such recommendations as will prevent hostilities and will result in the settlement of the dispute.

Article XVIII

Every treaty or international engagement entered into hereafter by any Member of the League shall be forthwith registered with the Secretariat and shall as soon as possible be published by it. No such treaty or international engagement shall be binding until so registered.

Article XIX

The Assembly may from time to time advise the reconsideration by Members of the League of treaties which have become inapplicable and the consideration of international conditions whose continuance might endanger the peace of the world.

Article XX

1. The Members of the League severally agree that this Covenant is accepted as abrogating all obligations or understandings *inter se* which are inconsistent with the terms thereof, and solemnly undertake that they will not hereafter enter into any engagements inconsistent with the terms thereof.

2. In case any Member of the League shall, before becoming a Member of the League, have undertaken any obligations inconsistent with the terms of this Covenant, it shall be the duty of such Member to take immediate steps to procure its release from such obligations.

Article XXI

Nothing in this Covenant shall be deemed to affect the validity of international engagements, such as treaties of arbitration or regional understandings like the Monroe doctrine, for securing the maintenance of peace.

Article XXII

1. To those colonies and territories which as a consequence of the late war have ceased to be under the sovereignty of the States which formerly governed them and which are inhabited by peoples not yet able to stand by themselves under the strenuous conditions of the modern world, there should be applied the principle that the well-being and development of such peoples form a sacred trust of civilisation and that securities for the performance of this trust should be embodied in this Covenant.

2. The best method of giving practical effect to this principle is that the tutelage of such peoples should be entrusted to advanced nations who by reason of their resources, their experience or their geographical position can best undertake this responsibility, and who are willing to accept it, and that this tutelage should be exercised by them as Mandatories on behalf of the League.

3. The character of the mandate must differ according to the stage of the development of the people, the geographical situation of the territory, its economic conditions and other similar circumstances.

4. Certain communities formerly belonging to the Turkish Empire have reached a stage of development where their existence as independent nations can be provisionally recognised subject to the rendering of administrative advice and assistance by a Mandatory until such time as they are able to stand alone. The wishes of these communities must be a principal consideration in the selection of the Mandatory.

5. Other peoples, especially those of Central Africa, are at such a stage that the Mandatory must be responsible for the administration of the territory under conditions which will guarantee freedom of conscience and relig-

ion, subject only to the maintenance of public order and morals, the prohibition of abuses such as the slave trade, the arms traffic and the liquor traffic, and the prevention of the establishment of fortifications or military and naval bases and of the military training of the natives for other than police purposes and the defence of territory, and will also secure equal opportunities for the trade and commerce of other Members of the League.

6. There are territories, such as South-West Africa and certain of the South Pacific Islands, which, owing to the sparseness of their population, or their small size, or their remoteness from the centres of civilisation, or their geographical contiguity of the territory of the Mandatory, and other circumstances, can be best administered under the laws of the Mandatory as integral portions of its territory, subject to the safeguards above mentioned in the interests of the indigenous population.

7. In every case of mandate, the Mandatory shall render to the Council an annual report in reference to the territory committed to its charge.

8. The degree of authority, control, or administraion to be exercised by the Mandatory shall, if not previously agreed upon by the Members of the League, be explicitly defined in each case by the Council.

9. A permanent Commission shall be constituted to receive and examine the annual reports of the Mandatories and to advise the Council on all matters relating to the observance of the mandates.

Article XXIII

Subject to and in accordance with the provisions of international conventions existing or hereafter to be agreed upon, the Members of the League:

(a) will endeavour to secure and maintain fair and humane conditions of labour for men, women and children, both in their own countries and in all countries to which their commercial and industrial relations extend, and for that purpose will establish and maintain the necessary international organisations;

(b) undertake to secure just treatment of the native inhabitants of territories under their control;

(c) will entrust the League with the general supervision over the execution of agreements with regard to the traffic in women and children, and the traffic in opium and other dangerous drugs;

(d) will entrust the League with the general supervision of the trade in arms and ammunition with the countries in which the control of this traffic is necessary in the common interest;

(e) will make provision to secure and maintain freedom of communications and of transit and equitable treatment for the commerce of all Members of the League. In this connection, the special necessities of the regions devastated during the war of 1914-1918 shall be borne in mind.

(f) will endeavour to take steps in matters of international concern for the prevention and control of disease.

Article XXIV

1. There shall be placed under the direction of the League all international bureaux already established by general treaties if the parties to such treaties consent. All such international bureaux and all commissions for the regulation of matters of international interest hereafter constituted shall be placed under the direction of the League.

2. In all matters of international interest which are regulated by general conventions but which are not placed under the control of international bureaux or commissions, the Secretariat of the League shall, subject to the consent of the Council and if desired by the parties, collect and distribute all relevant information and shall render any other assistance which may be necessary or desirable.

3. The Council may include as part of the expenses of the Secretariat the expenses of any bureau or commission which is placed under the direction of the League.

Article XXV

The Members of the League agree to encourage and promote the establishment and co-operation of duly authorised voluntary national Red Cross organisations having as purposes the improvement of health, the prevention of disease and the mitigation of suffering throughout the world.

Article XXVI

1. Amendments to this Covenant will take effect when ratified by the Members of the League whose Representatives compose the Council and by a majority of the Members of the League whose Representatives compose the Assembly.

2. No such amendments shall bind any Member of the League which signifies its dissent therefrom, but in that case it shall cease to be a Member of the League.

APPENDIX I

B

STATUTE FOR THE PERMANENT COURT OF INTERNATIONAL JUSTICE* PROVIDED FOR BY ARTICLE 14 OF THE COVENANT OF THE LEAGUE OF NATIONS

Article 1

A Permanent Court of International Justice is hereby established, in accordance with Article 14 of the Covenant of the League of Nations. This Court shall be in addition to the Court of Arbitration organised by the Conventions of The Hague of 1899 and 1907, and to the special Tribunals of Arbitration to which States are always at liberty to submit their disputes for settlement.

CHAPTER I

ORGANISATION OF THE COURT

Article 2

The Permanent Court of International Justice shall be composed of a body of independent judges, elected regardless of their nationality from amongst persons of high moral character, who possess the qualifications required in their respective countries for appointment to the highest judicial offices, or are jurisconsults of recognised competence in international law.

Article 3

The Court shall consist of fifteen members: eleven judges and four deputy-judges. The number of judges and deputy-judges may hereafter be increased by the Assembly, upon the proposal of the Council of the League of Nations, to a total of fifteen judges and six deputy-judges.

Article 4

The members of the Court shall be elected by the Assembly and by the Council from a list of persons nominated by the national groups in the Court of Arbitration, in accordance with the following provisions.

* Text is taken from League of Nations *Treaty Series,* VI (1921), pp. 391-411. Several amendments to the Court Statute were proposed in the Revision Protocol of September 14, 1929, but are not yet (July, 1935) in force. They may be found in J. E. Harley, *Documentary Textbook on International Relations* (Los Angeles, Cal., 1934), pp. 181-188.

In the case of Members of the League of Nations not represented in the Permanent Court of Arbitration, the lists of candidates shall be drawn up by national groups appointed for this purpose by their Governments under the same conditions as those prescribed for members of the Permanent Court of Arbitration by Article 44 of the Convention of The Hague of 1907 for the pacific settlement of international disputes.

ARTICLE 5

At least three months before the date of the election, the Secretary-General of the League of Nations shall address a written request to the members of the Court of Arbitration belonging to the States mentioned in the Annex to the Covenant or to the States which join the League subsequently, and to the persons appointed under Paragraph 2 of Article 4, inviting them to undertake, within a given time, by national groups, the nomination of persons in a position to accept the duties of a member of the Court.

No group may nominate more than four persons, not more than two of whom shall be of their own nationality. In no case must the number of candidates nominated be more than double the number of seats to be filled.

ARTICLE 6

Before making these nominations, each national group is recommended to consult its Highest Court of Justice, its Legal Faculties and Schools of Law, and its National Academies and national sections of International Academies devoted to the study of Law.

ARTICLE 7

The Secretary-General of the League of Nations shall prepare a list in alphabetical order of all the persons thus nominated. Save as provided in Article 12, Paragraph 2, these shall be the only persons eligible for appointment.

The Secretary-General shall submit this list to the Assembly and to the Council.

ARTICLE 8

The Assembly and the Council shall proceed independently of one another to elect, firstly the judges, then the deputy-judges.

ARTICLE 9

At every election, the electors shall bear in mind that not only should all the persons appointed as members of the Court possess the qualifications required, but the whole body also should represent the main forms of civilisation and the principal legal systems of the world.

ARTICLE 10

Those candidates who obtain an absolute majority of votes in the Assembly and in the Council shall be considered as elected.

In the event of more than one national of the same Member of the League being elected by the votes of both the Assembly and the Council, the eldest of these only shall be considered as elected.

ARTICLE 11

If, after the first meeting held for the purpose of the election, one or more seats remain to be filled, a second and, if necessary, a third meeting shall take place.

ARTICLE 12

If, after the third meeting, one or more seats still remain unfilled, a joint conference consisting of six members, three appointed by the Assembly and three by the Council may be formed, at any time, at the request of either the Assembly or the Council, for the purpose of choosing one name for each seat still vacant, to submit to the Assembly and the Council for their respective acceptance.

If the Conference is unanimously agreed upon any person who fulfils the required conditions, he may be included in its list, even though he was not included in the list of nominations referred to in Articles 4 and 5.

If the joint Conference is satisfied that it will not be successful in procuring an election, those members of the Court who have already been appointed shall, within a period to be fixed by the Council, proceed to fill the vacant seats by selection from amongst those candidates who have obtained votes either in the Assembly or in the Council.

In the event of an equality of votes amongst the judges, the eldest judge shall have a casting vote.

ARTICLE 13

The members of the Court shall be elected for nine years.

They may be re-elected.

They shall continue to discharge their duties until their places have been filled. Though replaced, they shall finish any cases which they may have begun.

ARTICLE 14

Vacancies which may occur shall be filled by the same method as that laid down for the first election. A member of the Court elected to replace a member whose period of appointment had not expired will hold the appointment for the remainder of his predecessor's term.

ARTICLE 15

Deputy-judges shall be called upon to sit in the order laid down in a list.

This list shall be prepared by the Court and shall have regard firstly to priority of election and secondly to age.

ARTICLE 16

The ordinary members of the Court may not exercise any political or administrative function. This provision does not apply to the deputy-judges, except when performing their duties on the Court.

Any doubt on this point is settled by the decision of the Court.

ARTICLE 17

No member of the Court can act as agent, counsel or advocate in any case of an international nature. This provision only applies to the deputy-judges as regards cases in which they are called upon to exercise their functions on the Court.

No member may participate in the decision of any case in which he has previously taken an active part, as agent, counsel or advocate for one of the contesting parties, or as a member of a national or international Court, or of a commission of enquiry, or in any other capacity.

Any doubt on this point is settled by the decision of the Court.

ARTICLE 18

A member of the Court cannot be dismissed unless, in the unanimous opinion of the other members, he has ceased to fulfil the required conditions.

Formal notification thereof shall be made to the Secretary-General of the League of Nations, by the Registrar.

This notification makes the place vacant.

ARTICLE 19

The members of the Court, when engaged on the business of the Court, shall enjoy diplomatic privileges and immunities.

ARTICLE 20

Every member of the Court shall, before taking up his duties, make a solemn declaration in open Court that he will exercise his powers impartially and conscientiously.

ARTICLE 21

The Court shall elect its President and Vice-President for three years; they may be re-elected.

It shall appoint its Registrar.

The duties of Registrar of the Court shall not be deemed incompatible with those of Secretary-General of the Permanent Court of Arbitration.

Article 22

The seat of the Court shall be established at The Hague.

The President and Registrar shall reside at the seat of the Court.

Article 23

A session of the Court shall be held every year.

Unless otherwise provided by rules of Court, this session shall begin on the 15th of June, and shall continue for so long as may be deemed necessary to finish the cases on the list.

The President may summon an extraordinary session of the Court whenever necessary.

Article 24

If, for some special reason, a member of the Court considers that he should not take part in the decision of a particular case, he shall so inform the President.

If the President considers that for some special reason one of the members of the Court should not sit on a particular case, he shall give him notice accordingly.

If in any such case the member of the Court and the President disagree, the matter shall be settled by the decision of the Court.

Article 25

The full Court shall sit except when it is expressly provided otherwise.

If eleven judges cannot be present, the number shall be made up by calling on deputy-judges to sit.

If, however, eleven judges are not available, a quorum of nine judges shall suffice to constitute the Court.

Article 26

Labour cases, particularly cases referred to in Part XIII (Labour) of the Treaty of Versailles and the corresponding portions of the other Treaties of Peace, shall be heard and determined by the Court under the following conditions:

The Court will appoint every three years a special chamber of five judges, selected so far as possible with due regard to the provisions of Article 9. In addition, two judges shall be selected for the purpose of replacing a judge who finds it impossible to sit. If the parties so demand, cases will be heard and determined by this chamber. In the absence of any such demand, the Court will sit with the number of judges provided for in Article 25. On all occasions the judges will be assisted by four technical assessors sitting with them, but without the right to vote, and chosen with a view to ensuring a just representation of the ccmpeting interests.

If there is a national of one only of the parties sitting as a judge in the chamber referred to in the preceding paragraph, the President will invite one of the other judges to retire in favour of a judge chosen by the other party in accordance with Article 31.

The technical assessors shall be chosen for each particular case in accordance with rules of procedure under Article 30 from a list of "Assessors for Labour cases" composed of two persons nominated by each Member of the League of Nations and an equivalent number nominated by the Governing Body of the Labour Office. The Governing Body will nominate as to one-half, representatives of the workers, and as to one-half, representatives of employers from the list referred to in Article 412 of the Treaty of Versailles and the corresponding Articles of the other Treaties of Peace.

In Labour cases the International Labour Office shall be at liberty to furnish the Court with all relevant information, and for this purpose the Director of that Office shall receive copies of all the written proceedings.

Article 27

Cases relating to transit and communications, particularly cases referred to in Part XII (Ports, Waterways and Railways) of the Treaty of Versailles and the corresponding portions of the other Treaties of Peace, shall be heard and determined by the Court under the following conditions:

The Court will appoint every three years a special chamber of five judges, selected so far as possible with due regard to the provisions of Article 9. In addition, two judges shall be selected for the purpose of replacing a judge who finds it impossible to sit. If the parties so demand, cases will be heard and determined by this chamber. In the absence of any such demand, the Court will sit with the number of judges provided for in Article 25. When desired by the parties or decided by the Court, the judges will be assisted by four technical assessors sitting with them, but without the right to vote.

If there is a national of one only of the parties sitting as a judge in the chamber referred to in the preceding paragraph, the President will invite one of the other judges to retire in favour of a judge chosen by the other party in accordance with Article 31.

The technical assessors shall be chosen for each particular case in accordance with rules of procedure under Article 30 from a list of "Assessors for

Transit and Communications cases" composed of two persons nominated by each Member of the League of Nations.

ARTICLE 28

The special chambers provided for in Articles 26 and 27 may, with the consent of the parties to the dispute, sit elsewhere than at The Hague.

ARTICLE 29

With a view to the speedy despatch of business, the Court shall form annually a chamber composed of three judges who, at the request of the contesting parties, may hear and determine cases by summary procedure.

ARTICLE 30

The Court shall frame rules for regulating its procedure. In particular, it shall lay down rules for summary procedure.

ARTICLE 31

Judges of the nationality of each contesting party shall retain their right to sit in the case before the Court.

If the Court includes upon the Bench a judge of the nationality of one of the parties only, the other party may select from among the deputy-judges a judge of its nationality, if there be one. If there should not be one, the party may choose a judge, preferably from among those persons who have been nominated as candidates as provided in Articles 4 and 5.

If the Court includes upon the Bench no judge of the nationality of the contesting parties, each of these may proceed to select or choose a judge as provided in the preceding paragraph.

Should there be several parties in the same interest, they shall, for the purpose of the preceding provisions, be reckoned as one party only. Any doubt upon this point is settled by the decision of the Court.

Judges selected or chosen as laid down in Paragraphs 2 and 3 of this Article shall fulfil the conditions required by Articles 2, 16, 17, 20, 24 of this Statute. They shall take part in the decision on an equal footing with their colleagues.

ARTICLE 32

The judges shall receive an annual indemnity to be determined by the Assembly of the League of Nations upon the proposal of the Council. This indemnity must not be decreased during the period of a judge's appointment.

The President shall receive a special grant for his period of office, to be fixed in the same way.

The Vice-President, judges and deputy-judges shall receive a grant for the actual performance of their duties, to be fixed in the same way.

Travelling expenses incurred in the performance of their duties shall be refunded to judges and deputy-judges who do not reside at the seat of the Court.

Grants due to judges selected or chosen as provided in Article 31 shall be determined in the same way.

The salary of the Registrar shall be decided by the Council upon the proposal of the Court.

The Assembly of the League of Nations shall lay down, on the proposal of the Council, a special regulation fixing the conditions under which retiring pensions may be given to the personnel of the Court.

Article 33

The expenses of the Court shall be borne by the League of Nations, in such a manner as shall be decided by the Assembly upon the proposal of the Council.

CHAPTER II

COMPETENCE OF THE COURT

Article 34

Only States or Members of the League of Nations can be parties in cases before the Court.

Article 35

The Court shall be open to the Members of the League and also to States mentioned in the Annex to the Covenant.

The conditions under which the Court shall be open to other States shall, subject to the special provisions contained in treaties in force, be laid down by the Council, but in no case shall such provisions place the parties in a position of inequality before the Court.

When a State which is not a Member of the League of Nations is a party to a dispute, the Court will fix the amount which that party is to contribute towards the expenses of the Court.

Article 36

The jurisdiction of the Court comprises all cases which the parties refer to it and all matters specially provided for in Treaties and Conventions in force.

The Members of the League of Nations and the States mentioned in the Annex to the Covenant may, either when signing or ratifying the protocol to which the present Statute is adjoined, or at a later moment, declare that they recognise as compulsory *ipso facto* and without special agreement, in relation to any other Member or State accepting the same obligation, the jurisdiction of the Court in all or any of the classes of legal disputes concerning:

(a) The interpretation of a Treaty;

(b) Any question of International Law;

(c) The existence of any fact which, if established, would constitute a breach of an international obligation;

(d) The nature or extent of the reparation to be made for the breach of an international obligation.

The declaration referred to above may be made unconditionally or on condition of reciprocity on the part of several or certain Members or States, or for a certain time.

In the event of a dispute as to whether the Court has jurisdiction, the matter shall be settled by the decision of the Court.

Article 37

When a treaty or convention in force provides for the reference of a matter to a tribunal to be instituted by the League of Nations, the Court will be such tribunal.

Article 38

The Court shall apply:

(1) International conventions, whether general or particular, establishing rules expressly recognised by the contesting States;

(2) International custom, as evidence of a general practice accepted as law;

(3) The general principles of law recognised by civilised nations;

(4) Subject to the provisions of Article 59, judicial decisions and the teachings of the most highly qualified publicists of the various nations, as subsidiary means for the determination of rules of law.

This provision shall not prejudice the power of the Court to decide a case *ex aequo et bono,* if the parties agree thereto.

CHAPTER III

PROCEDURE

Article 39

The official languages of the Court shall be French and English. If the parties agree that the case shall be conducted in French, the judgment will be delivered in French. If the parties agree that the case shall be conducted in English, the judgment will be delivered in English.

In the absence of an agreement as to which language shall be employed, each party may, in the pleadings, use the language which it prefers;

the decision of the Court will be given in French and English. In this case the Court will at the same time determine which of the two texts shall be considered as authoritative.

The Court may, at the request of the parties, authorize a language other than French or English to be used.

Article 40

Cases are brought before the Court, as the case may be, either by the notification of the special agreement, or by a written application addressed to the Registrar. In either case the subject of the dispute and the contesting parties must be indicated.

The Registrar shall forthwith communicate the application to all concerned.

He shall also notify the Members of the League of Nations through the Secretary-General.

Article 41

The Court shall have the power to indicate, if it considers that circumstances so require, any provisional measures which ought to be taken to reserve the respective rights of either party.

Pending the final decision, notice of the measures suggested shall forthwith be given to the parties and the Council.

Article 42

The parties shall be represented by agents.

They may have the assistance of Counsel or Advocates before the Court.

Article 43

The procedure shall consist of two parts: written and oral.

The written proceedings shall consist of the communication to the judges and to the parties of cases, counter-cases and, if necessary, replies; also all papers and documents in support.

These communications shall be made through the Registrar, in the order and within the time fixed by the Court.

A certified copy of every document produced by one party shall be communicated to the other party.

The oral proceedings shall consist of the hearing by the Court of witnesses, experts, agents, counsel and advocates.

Article 44

For the service of all notices upon persons other than the agents, counsel and advocates, the Court shall apply direct to the Government of the State upon whose territory the notice has to be served.

The same provision shall apply whenever steps are to be taken to procure evidence on the spot.

ARTICLE 45

The hearing shall be under the control of the President or, in his absence, of the Vice-President; if both are absent, the senior judge shall preside.

ARTICLE 46

The hearing in Court shall be public, unless the Court shall decide otherwise, or unless the parties demand that the public be not admitted.

ARTICLE 47

Minutes shall be made at each hearing, and signed by the Registrar and the President.

These minutes shall be the only authentic record.

ARTICLE 48

The Court shall make orders for the conduct of the case, shall decide the form and time in which each party must conclude its arguments, and make all arrangements connected with the taking of evidence.

ARTICLE 49

The Court may, even before the hearing begins, call upon the agents to produce any document, or to supply any explanations. Formal note shall be taken of any refusal.

ARTICLE 50

The Court may, at any time, entrust any individual, body, bureau, commission, or other organisation that it may select, with the task of carrying out an enquiry or giving an expert opinion.

ARTICLE 51

During the hearing, any relevant questions are to be put to the witness and experts under the conditions laid down by the Court in the rules of procedure referred to in Article 30.

ARTICLE 52

After the Court has received the proofs and evidence within the time specified for the purpose, it may refuse to accept any further oral or written evidence that one party may desire to present unless the other side consents.

ARTICLE 53

Whenever one of the parties shall not appear before the Court, or shall fail to defend his case, the other party may call upon the Court to decide in favour of his claim.

The Court must, before doing so, satisfy itself, not only that it has jurisdiction in accordance with Articles 36 and 37, but also that the claim is well founded in fact and law.

ARTICLE 54

When, subject to the control of the Court, the agents, advocates and counsel have completed their presentation of the case, the President shall declare the hearing closed.

The Court shall withdraw to consider the judgment.

The deliberations of the Court shall take place in private and remain secret.

ARTICLE 55

All questions shall be decided by a majority of the judges present at the hearing.

In the event of an equality of votes, the President or his deputy shall have a casting vote.

ARTICLE 56

The judgment shall state the reasons on which it is based.

It shall contain the names of the judges who have taken part in the decision.

ARTICLE 57

If the judgment does not represent in whole or in part unanimous opinion of the judges, dissenting judges are entitled to deliver a separate opinion.

ARTICLE 58

The judgment shall be signed by the President and by the Registrar. It shall be read in open Court, due notice having been given to the agents.

ARTICLE 59

The decision of the Court has no binding force except between the parties and in respect of that particular case.

ARTICLE 60

The judgment is final and without appeal. In the event of dispute as to the meaning or scope of the judgment, the Court shall construe it upon the request of any party.

ARTICLE 61

An application for revision of a judgment can be made only when it is based upon the discovery of some fact of such a nature as to be a decisive factor, which fact was, when the judgment was given, unknown to the Court and also to the party claiming revision, always provided that such ignorance was not due to negligence.

The proceedings for revision will be opened by a judgment of the Court expressly recording the existence of the new fact, recognising that it has such a character as to lay the case open to revision, and declaring the application admissible on this ground.

The Court may require previous compliance with the terms of the judgment before it admits proceedings in revision.

The application for revision must be made at latest within six months of the discovery of the new fact.

No application for revision may be made after the lapse of ten years from the date of the sentence.

Article 62

Should a State consider that it has an interest of a legal nature which may be affected by the decision in the case, it may submit a request to the Court to be permitted to intervene as a third party.

It will be for the Court to decide upon this request.

Article 63

Whenever the construction of a convention to which States other than those concerned in the case are parties is in question, the Registrar shall notify all such States forthwith.

Every State so notified has the right to intervene in the proceedings: but if it uses this right, the construction given by the judgment will be equally binding upon it.

Article 64

Unless otherwise decided by the Court, each party shall bear its own costs.

APPENDIX I

C

TREATY OF VERSAILLES, PART XIII *: LABOUR

Section I. ORGANISATION OF LABOUR

Whereas the League of Nations has for its object the establishment of universal peace, and such a peace can be established only if it is based upon social justice;

And whereas conditions of labour exist involving such injustice, hardship and privation to large numbers of people as to produce unrest so great that the peace and harmony of the world are imperilled; as, for example, by the regulation of the hours of work, including the establishment of a maximum working day and week, the regulation of the labour supply, the prevention of unemployment, the provision of an adequate living wage, the protection of the worker against sickness, disease and injury arising out of his employment, the protection of children, young persons and women, provision for old age and injury, protection of the interests of workers when employed in countries other than their own, recognition of the principle of freedom of association, the organisation of vocational and technical education and other measures;

Whereas also the failure of any nation to adopt humane conditions of labour is an obstacle in the way of other nations which desire to improve the conditions in their own countries;

The HIGH CONTRACTING PARTIES, moved by sentiments of justice and humanity as well as by the desire to secure the permanent peace of the world, agree to the following:

CHAPTER I

ORGANISATION

ARTICLE 387

A permanent organisation is hereby established for the promotion of the objects set forth in the Preamble.

* Taken from *The Treaty of Peace between the Allied and Associated Powers and Germany* (London, His Majesty's Stationery Office, 1919), pp. 193-203. The following extract includes the section of the Treaty, setting up the International Labour Organisation, with the exception of the transitory provisions.

The original Members of the League of Nations shall be the original Members of this organisation, and hereafter membership of the League of Nations shall carry with it membership of the said organisation.

Article 388

The permanent organisation shall consist of:

(1) a General Conference of Representatives of the Members and,

(2) an International Labour Office controlled by the Governing Body described in Article 393.

Article 389

The meetings of the General Conference of Representatives of the Members shall be held from time to time as occasion may require, and at least once in every year. It shall be composed of four Representatives of each of the Members, of whom two shall be Government Delegates and the two others shall be Delegates representing respectively the employers and the workpeople of each of the Members.

Each Delegate may be accompanied by advisers, who shall not exceed two in number for each item on the agenda of the meeting. When questions specially affecting women are to be considered by the Conference, one at least of the advisers should be a woman.

The Members undertake to nominate non-Government Delegates and advisers chosen in agreement with the industrial organisations, if such organisations exist, which are most representative of employers or workpeople, as the case may be, in their respective countries.

Advisers shall not speak except on a request made by the delegate whom they accompany and by the special authorization of the President of the Conference, and may not vote.

A Delegate may by notice in writing addressed to the President appoint one of his advisers to act as his deputy, and the adviser, while so acting, shall be allowed to speak and vote.

The names of the Delegates and their advisers will be communicated to the International Labour Office by the Government of each of the Members.

The credentials of Delegates and their advisers shall be subject to scrutiny by the Conference, which may, by two-thirds of the votes cast by the Delegates present, refuse to admit any Delegate or adviser whom it deems not to have been nominated in accordance with this Article.

Article 390

Every Delegate shall be entitled to vote individually on all matters which are taken into consideration by the Conference.

If one of the Members fails to nominate one of the non-Government Delegates whom it is entitled to nominate, the other non-Government Delegate shall be allowed to sit and speak at the Conference, but not to vote.

If in accordance with Article 389 the Conference refuses admission to a Delegate of one of the Members, the provisions of the present Article shall apply as if that Delegate had not been nominated.

ARTICLE 391

The meetings of the Conference shall be held at the seat of the League of Nations, or at such other place as may be decided by the Conference at a previous meeting by two-thirds of the votes cast by the Delegates present.

ARTICLE 392

The International Labour Office shall be established at the seat of the League of Nations as part of the organisation of the League.

ARTICLE 393

The International Labour Office shall be under the control of a Governing Body consisting of twenty-four persons, appointed in accordance with the following provisions:

The Governing Body of the International Labour Office shall be constituted as follows:

Twelve persons representing the Governments;

Six persons elected by the Delegates to the Conference representing the employers;

Six persons elected by the Delegates to the Conference representing the workers.

Of the twelve persons representing the Governments eight shall be nominated by the Members which are of the chief industrial importance, and four shall be nominated by the Members selected for the purpose by the Government Delegates to the Conference, excluding the Delegates of the eight Members mentioned above.

Any questions as to which are the Members of the chief industrial importance shall be decided by the Council of the League of Nations.

The period of office of the Members of the Governing Body will be three years. The method of filling vacancies and other similar questions may be determined by the Governing Body subject to the approval of the Conference.

The Governing Body shall, from time to time, elect one of its members to act as its Chairman, shall regulate its own procedure and shall fix its own times of meeting. A special meeting shall be held if a written request to that effect is made by at least ten members of the Governing Body.

ARTICLE 394

There shall be a Director of the International Labour Office, who shall be appointed by the Governing Body, and, subject to the instructions of the Governing Body, shall be responsible for the efficient conduct of the International Labour Office and for such other duties as may be assigned to him.

The Director or his deputy shall attend all meetings of the Governing Body.

ARTICLE 395

The staff of the International Labour Office shall be appointed by the Director, who shall, so far as is possible with due regard to the efficiency of the work of the Office, select persons of different nationalities. A certain number of these persons shall be women.

ARTICLE 396

The functions of the International Labour Office shall include the collection and distribution of information on all subjects relating to the international adjustment of conditions of industrial life and labour, and particularly the examination of subjects which it is proposed to bring before the Conference with a view to the conclusion of international conventions, and the conduct of such special investigations as may be ordered by the Conference.

It will prepare the agenda for the meetings of the Conference.

It will carry out the duties required of it by the provisions of this Part of the present Treaty in connection with international disputes.

It will edit and publish in French and English, and in such other languages as the Governing Body may think desirable, a periodical paper dealing with problems of industry and employment of international interest.

Generally, in addition to the functions set out in this Article, it shall have such other powers and duties as may be assigned to it by the Conference.

ARTICLE 397

The Government Departments of any of the Members which deal with questions of industry and employment may communicate directly with the Director through the Representative of their Government on the Governing Body of the International Labour Office, or failing any such Representative, through such other qualified official as the Government may nominate for the purpose.

ARTICLE 398

The International Labour Office shall be entitled to the assistance of the Secretary-General of the League of Nations in any matter in which it can be given.

ARTICLE 399

Each of the Members will pay the travelling and subsistence expenses of its Delegates and their advisers and of its Representatives attending the meeetings of the Conference or Governing Body, as the case may be.

All the other expenses of the International Labour Office and of the meetings of the Conference or Governing Body shall be paid to the Director by the Secretary-General of the League of Nations out of the general funds of the League.

The Director shall be responsible to the Secretary-General of the League for the proper expenditure of all moneys paid to him in pursuance of this Article.

CHAPTER II

PROCEDURE

ARTICLE 400

The agenda for all meetings of the Conference will be settled by the Governing Body, who shall consider any suggestion as to the agenda that may be made by the Government of any of the Members or by any representative organisation recognized for the purpose of Article 389.

ARTICLE 401

The Director shall act as the Secretary of the Conference, and shall transmit the agenda so as to reach the Members four months before the meeting of the Conference, and, through them, the non-Government Delegates when appointed.

ARTICLE 402

Any of the Governments of the Members may formally object to the inclusion of any item or items in the agenda. The grounds for such objection shall be set forth in a reasoned statement addressed to the Director, who shall circulate it to all the Members of the Permanent Organisation.

Items to which such objection has been made shall not, however, be excluded from the agenda, if at the Conference a majority of two-thirds of the votes cast by the Delegates present is in favour of considering them.

If the Conference decides (otherwise than under the preceding paragraph) by two-thirds of the votes cast by the Delegates present that any subject shall be considered by the Conference, that subject shall be included in the agenda for the following meeting.

ARTICLE 403

The Conference shall regulate its own procedure, shall elect its own President, and may appoint committees to consider and report on any matter.

Except as otherwise expressly provided in this Part of the present Treaty, all matters shall be decided by a simple majority of the votes cast by the Delegates present.

The voting is void unless the total number of votes cast is equal to half the number of the Delegates attending the Conference.

ARTICLE 404

The Conference may add to any committees which it appoints technical experts, who shall be assessors without power to vote.

ARTICLE 405

When the Conference has decided on the adoption of proposals with regard to an item in the agenda, it will rest with the Conference to determine whether these proposals shall take the form: (a) of a recommendation to be submitted to the Members for consideration with a view to effect being given to it by national legislation or otherwise, or (b) of a draft international convention for ratification by the Members.

In either case a majority of two-thirds of the votes cast by the Delegates present shall be necessary on the final vote for the adoption of the recommendation or draft convention, as the case may be, by the conference.

In framing any recommendation or draft convention of general application the Conference shall have due regard to those countries in which climatic conditions, the imperfect development of industrial organisation or other special circumstances make the industrial conditions substantially different and shall suggest the modifications, if any, which it considers may be required to meet the case of such countries.

A copy of the recommendation or draft convention shall be authenticated by the signature of the President of the Conference and of the Director and shall be deposited with the Secretary-General of the League of Nations. The Secretary-General will communicate a certified copy of the recommendation or draft convention to each of the Members.

Each of the Members undertakes that it will, within the period of one year at most from the closing of the session of the Conference, or if it is impossible owing to exceptional circumstances to do so within the period of one year, then at the earliest practicable moment and in no case later than eighteen months from the closing of the session of the Conference, bring the recommendation or draft convention to each of the Members.

Each of the Members undertakes that it will, within the period of one year at most from the closing of the session of the Conference, or if it is impossible owing to exceptional circumstances to do so within the period of one year, then at the earliest practicable moment and in no case later than eighteen months from the closing of the session of the Conference, bring the recommendation or draft convention before the authority or authorities within whose competence the matter lies, for the enactment of legislation or other action.

In the case of a recommendation, the Members will inform the Secretary-General of the action taken.

In the case of a draft convention, the Member will, if it obtains the consent of the authority or authorities within whose competence the matter lies, communicate the formal ratification of the convention to the Secretary-General and will take such action as may be necessary to make effective the provisions of such convention.

If on a recommendation no legislative or other action is taken to make a recommendation effective, or if the draft convention fails to obtain the consent of the authority or authorities within whose competence the matter lies, no further obligation shall rest upon the Member.

In the case of a federal State, the power of which to enter into conventions on labour matters is subject to limitations, it shall be in the discretion of that Government to treat a draft convention to which such limitations apply as a recommendation only, and the provisions of this Article with respect to recommendations shall apply in such case.

The above Article shall be interpreted in accordance with the following principle:

In no case shall any Member be asked or required, as a result of the adoption of any recommendation or draft convention by the Conference, to lessen the protection afforded by its existing legislation to the workers concerned.

Article 406

Any convention so ratified shall be registered by the Secretary-General of the League of Nations, but shall only be binding upon the Members which ratify it.

Article 407

If any convention coming before the Conference for final consideration fails to secure the support of two-thirds of the votes cast by the Delegates present, it shall nevertheless be within the right of any of the Members of the Permanent Organisation to agree to such convention among themselves.

Any convention so agreed to shall be communicated by the Governments concerned to the Secretary-General of the League of Nations, who shall register it.

Article 408

Each of the Members agrees to make an annual report to the International Labour Office on the measures which it has taken to give effect to the provisions of conventions to which it is a party. These reports shall be made in such form and shall contain such particulars as the Governing Body may request. The Director shall lay a summary of these reports before the next meeting of the Conference.

Article 409

In the event of any representation being made to the International Labour Office by an industrial association of employers or of workers that any of the Members has failed to secure in any respect the effective observance within its jurisdiction of any convention to which it is a party, the Governing Body may communicate this representation to the Government against which it is made and may invite that Government to make such statement on the subject as it may think fit.

Article 410

If no statement is received within a reasonable time from the Government in question, or if the statement when received is not deemed to be satisfactory by the Governing Body, the latter shall have the right to publish the representation and the statement, if any, made in reply to it.

Article 411

Any of the Members shall have the right to file a complaint with the International Labour Office if it is not satisfied that any other Member is securing the effective observance of any convention which both have ratified in accordance with the foregoing Articles.

The Governing Body may, if it thinks fit, before referring such a complaint to a Commission of Enquiry, as hereinafter provided for, communicate with the Government in question in the manner described in Article 409.

If the Governing Body does not think it necessary to communicate the complaint to the Government in question, or if, when they have made such communication, no statement in reply has been received within a reasonable time which the Governing Body considers to be satisfactory, the Governing Body may apply for the appointment of a Commission of Enquiry to consider the complaint and to report thereon.

The Governing Body may adopt the same procedure either of its own motion or on receipt of a complaint from a Delegate to the Conference.

When any matter arising out of Articles 410 or 411 is being considered by the Governing Body, the Government in question shall, if not already represented thereon, be entitled to send a representative to take part in the proceedings of the Governing Body while the matter is under consideration.

Adequate notice of the date on which the matter will be considered shall be given to the Government in question.

ARTICLE 412

The Commission of Enquiry shall be constituted in accordance with the following provisions:

Each of the Members agrees to nominate within six months of the date on which the present Treaty comes into force three persons of industrial experience, of whom one shall be a representative of employers, one a representative of workers, and one a person of independent standing, who shall together form a panel from which the Members of the Commission of Enquiry shall be drawn.

The qualifications of the persons so nominated shall be subject to scrutiny by the Governing Body, which may by two-thirds of the votes cast by the representatives present refuse to accept the nomination of any person whose qualifications do not in its opinion comply with the requirements of the present Article.

Upon the application of the Governing Body, the Secretary-General of the League of Nations shall nominate three persons, one from each section of this panel, to constitute the Commission of Enquiry, and shall designate one of them as the President of the Commission. None of these three persons shall be a person nominated to the panel by any Member directly concerned in the complaint.

ARTICLE 413

The Members agree that, in the event of the reference of a complaint to a Commission of Enquiry under Article 411, they will each, whether directly concerned in the complaint or not, place at the disposal of the Commission all the information in their possession which bears upon the subject-matter of the complaint.

ARTICLE 414

When the Commission of Enquiry has fully considered the complaint, it shall prepare a report embodying its findings on all questions of fact relevant to determining the issue between the parties and containing such recommendations as it may think proper as to the steps which should be taken to meet the complaint and the time within which they should be taken.

It shall also indicate in this report the measures, if any, of an economic character against a defaulting Government which it considers to be appropriate, and which it considers other Governments would be justified in adopting.

ARTICLE 415

The Secretary-General of the League of Nations shall communicate the report of the Commission of Enquiry to each of the Governments concerned in the complaint, and shall cause it to be published.

Each of these Governments shall within one month inform the Secretary-General of the League of Nations whether or not it accepts the recommendations contained in the report of the Commission; and if not, whether it proposes to refer the complaint to the Permanent Court of International Justice of the League of Nations.

ARTICLE 416

In the event of any Member failing to take the action required by Article 405, with regard to a recommendation or draft Convention, any other Member shall be entitled to refer the matter to the Permanent Court of International Justice.

ARTICLE 417

The decision of the Permanent Court of International Justice in regard to a complaint or matter which has been referred to it in pursuance of Article 415 or Article 416 shall be final.

ARTICLE 418

The Permanent Court of International Justice may affirm, vary or reverse any of the findings or recommendations of the Commission of Enquiry, if any, and shall in its decision indicate the measures, if any, of an economic character which it considers to be appropriate, and which other Governments would be justified in adopting against a defaulting Government.

ARTICLE 419

In the event of any Member failing to carry out within the time specified the recommendations, if any, contained in the report of the Commission of Enquiry, or in the decision of the Permanent Court of International Justice, as the case may be, any other Member may take against that Member the measures of an economic character indicated in the report of the Commission or in the decision of the Court as appropriate to the case.

ARTICLE 420

The defaulting Government may at any time inform the Governing Body that it has taken the steps necessary to comply with the recommendations of the Commission of Enquiry or with those in the decision of the Permanent Court of International Justice, as the case may be, and may request it to apply to the Secretary-General of the League to constitute a Commission of Enquiry to verify its contention. In this case the provisions of Articles 412, 413, 414, 415, 417 and 418 shall apply, and if the report of the Commission of Enquiry or the decision of the Permanent Court of International Justice is in favour of the defaulting Government, the other Governments shall forthwith discontinue the measures of an economic character that they have taken against the defaulting Government.

CHAPTER III

GENERAL

Article 421

The Members engage to apply conventions which they have ratified in accordance with the provisions of this Part of the present Treaty to their colonies, protectorates and possessions which are not fully self-governing:

(1) Except where owing to the local conditions the convention is inapplicable, or,

(2) Subject to such modifications as may be necessary to adapt the convention to local conditions.

And each of the Members shall notify to the International Labour Office the action taken in respect of each of its colonies, protectorates and possessions which are not fully self-governing.

Article 422

Amendments to this Part of the present Treaty which are adopted by the Conference by a majority of two-thirds of the votes cast by the Delegates present shall take effect when ratified by the States whose representatives compose the Council of the League of Nations and by three-fourths of the Members.

Article 423

Any question or dispute relating to the interpretation of this Part of the present Treaty or of any subsequent convention concluded by the Members in pursuance of the provisions of this Part of the present Treaty shall be referred for decision to the Permanent Court of International Justice.

* * * * *

APPENDIX I

D

PROTOCOL *
FOR THE
PACIFIC SETTLEMENT OF INTERNATIONAL DISPUTES

Adopted by the Fifth Assembly
of the League of Nations on October 2, 1924

Animated by the firm desire to ensure the maintenance of general peace and the security of nations whose existence, independence or territories may be threatened:

Recognising the solidarity of the members of the international community;

Asserting that a war of aggression constitutes a violation of this solidarity and an international crime;

Desirous of facilitating the complete application of the system provided in the Covenant of the League of Nations for the pacific settlement of disputes between States and of ensuring the repression of international crimes; and

For the purpose of realising as contemplated by Article 8 of the Covenant, the reduction of national armaments to the lowest point consistent with national safety and the enforcement by common action of international obligations;

The Undersigned, duly authorised to that effect, agree as follows:

Article 1

The signatory States undertake to make every effort in their power to secure the introduction into the Covenant of amendments on the lines of the provisions contained in the following articles.

They agree that, as between themselves, these provisions shall be binding as from the coming into force of the present Protocol and that, so far as they are concerned, the Assembly and the Council of the League of Nations shall thenceforth have power to exercise all the rights and perform all the duties conferred upon them by the Protocol.

* **Original text from League of Nations, IX. Disarmament. 1924 (C.606.M.211.).**

Article 2

The signatory States agree in no case to resort to war either with one another or against a State which, if the occasion arises, accepts all the obligations hereinafter set out, except in case of resistance to acts of aggression or when acting in agreement with the Council or the Assembly of the League of Nations in accordance with the provisions of the Covenant and of the present Protocol.

Article 3

The signatory States undertake to recognise as compulsory, *ipso facto* and without special agreement, the jurisdiction of the Permanent Court of International Justice in the cases covered by paragraph 2 of Article 36 of the Statute of the Court, but without prejudice to the right of any State, when acceding to the special protocol provided for in the said Article and opened for signature on December 16th, 1920, to make reservations compatible with the said clause.

Accession to this special protocol, opened for signature on December 16th, 1920, must be given within the month following the coming into force of the present Protocol.

States which accede to the present Protocol after its coming into force must carry out the above obligation within the month following their accession.

Article 4

With a view to render more complete the provisions of paragraphs 4, 5, 6, and 7 of Article 15 of the Covenant, the signatory States agree to comply with the following procedure:

1. If the dispute submitted to the Council is not settled by it as provided in paragraph 3 of the said Article 15, the Council shall endeavour to persuade the parties to submit the dispute to judicial settlement or arbitration.

2. (a) If the parties cannot agree to do so, there shall, at the request of at least one of the parties, be constituted a Committee of Arbitrators. The Committee shall so far as possible be constituted by agreement between the parties.

(b) If within the period fixed by the Council the parties have failed to agree, in whole or in part, upon the number, the names and the powers of the arbitrators and upon the procedure, the Council shall settle the points remaining in suspense. It shall with the utmost possible despatch select in consultation with the parties the arbitrators and their President from among persons who by their nationality, their personal character and their experience, appear to it to furnish the highest guarantees of competence and impartiality.

(c) After the claims of the parties have been formulated, the Committee of Arbitrators, on the request of any party, shall through the medium of the Council request an advisory opinion upon any points of law in dispute from the Permanent Court of International Justice, which in such case shall meet with the utmost possible despatch.

3. If none of the parties asks for arbitration, the Council shall again take the dispute under consideration. If the Council reaches a report which is unanimously agreed to by the members thereof other than the representatives of any of the parties to the dispute, the signatory States agree to comply with the recommendations therein.

4. If the Council fails to reach a report which is concurred in by all its members, other than the representatives of any of the parties to the dispute, it shall submit the dispute to arbitration. It shall itself determine the composition, the powers and the procedure of the Committee of Arbitrators and, in the choice of the arbitrators, shall bear in mind the guarantees of competence and impartiality referred to in paragraph 2 (b) above.

5. In no case may a solution, upon which there has already been a unanimous recommendation of the Council accepted by one of the parties concerned, be again called in question.

6. The signatory States undertake that they will carry out in full good faith any judicial sentence or arbitral award that may be rendered and that they will comply, as provided in paragraph 3 above, with the solutions recommended by the Council. In the event of a State failing to carry out the above undertakings, the Council shall exert all its influence to secure compliance therewith. If it fails therein, it shall propose what steps should be taken to give effect thereto, in accordance with the provision contained at the end of Article 13 of the Covenant. Should a State in disregard of the above undertakings resort to war, the sanctions provided for by Article 16 of the Covenant, interpreted in the manner indicated in the present Protocol, shall immediately become applicable to it.

7. The provisions of the present article do not apply to the settlement of disputes which arise as the result of measures of war taken by one or more signatory States in agreement with the Council or the Assembly.

Article 5

The provisions of paragraph 8 of Article 15 of the Covenant shall continue to apply in proceedings before the Council.

If in the course of an arbitration, such as is contemplated in Article 4 above, one of the parties claims that the dispute, or part thereof, arises out of a matter which by international law is solely within the domestic jurisdiction of that party, the arbitrators shall on this point take the advice of the Permanent Court of International Justice through the medium of the Council. The opinion of the Court shall be binding upon the arbitrators, who, if the opinion is affirmative, shall confine themselves to so declaring in their award.

If the question is held by the Court or by the Council to be a matter solely within the domestic jurisdiction of the State, this decision shall not prevent consideration of the situation by the Council or by the Assembly under Article 11 of the Covenant.

Article 6

If in accordance with paragraph 9 of Article 15 of the Covenant a dispute is referred to the Assembly, that body shall have for the settlement of the dispute all the powers conferred upon the Council as to endeavouring to reconcile the parties in the manner laid down in paragraphs 1, 2 and 3 of Article 15 of the Covenant and in paragraph 1 of Article 4 above.

Should the Assembly fail to achieve an amicable settlement:

If one of the parties asks for arbitration, the Council shall proceed to constitute the Committee of Arbitrators in the manner provided in subparagraphs (a), (b) and (c) of paragraph 2 of Article 4 above.

If no party asks for arbitration, the Assembly shall again take the dispute under consideration and shall have in this connection the same powers as the Council. Recommendations embodied in a report of the Assembly, provided that it secures the measure of support stipulated at the end of paragraph 10 of Article 15 of the Covenant, shall have the same value and effect, as regards all matters dealt with in the present Protocol, as recommendations embodied in a report of the Council adopted as provided in paragraph 3 of Article 4 above.

If the necessary majority cannot be obtained, the dispute shall be submitted to arbitration and the Council shall determine the composition, the powers and the procedure of the Committee of Arbitrators as laid down in paragraph 4 of Article 4 above.

Article 7

In the event of a dispute arising between two or more signatory States, these States agree that they will not, either before the dispute is submitted to proceedings for pacific settlement or during such proceedings, make any increase of their armaments or effectives which might modify the position established by the Conference for the Reduction of Armaments provided for by Article 17 of the present Protocol, nor will they take any measure of military, naval, air, industrial or economic mobilisation, nor, in general, any action of a nature likely to extend the dispute or render it more acute.

It shall be the duty of the Council, in accordance with the provisions of Article 11 of the Covenant, to take under consideration any complaint as to infraction of the above undertakings which is made to it by one or more of the States parties to the dispute. Should the Council be of opinion that the complaint requires investigation, it shall, if it deems it expedient, arrange for enquiries and investigations in one or more of the countries concerned. Such enquiries and investigations shall be carried out with the utmost possible despatch and the signatory States undertake to afford every facility for carrying them out.

The sole object of measures taken by the Council as above provided is to facilitate the pacific settlement of disputes and they shall in no way prejudge the actual settlement.

If the result of such enquiries and investigations is to establish an infraction of the provisions of the first paragraph of the present Article, it shall be the duty of the Council to summon the State or States guilty of the infraction to put an end thereto. Should the State or States in question fail to comply with such summons, the Council shall declare them to be guilty of a violation of the Covenant or of the present Protocol, and shall decide upon the measures to be taken with a view to end as soon as possible a situation of a nature to threaten the peace of the world.

For the purposes of the present Article decisions of the Council may be taken by a two-thirds majority.

Article 8

The signatory States undertake to abstain from any act which might constitute a threat of aggression against another State.

If one of the signatory States is of opinion that another State is making preparations for war, it shall have the right to bring the matter to the notice of the Council.

The Council, if it ascertains that the facts are as alleged, shall proceed as provided in paragraphs 2, 4, and 5 of Article 7.

Article 9

The existence of demilitarised zones being calculated to prevent aggression and to facilitate a definite finding of the nature provided for in Article 10 below, the establishment of such zones between States mutually consenting thereto is recommended as a means of avoiding violations of the present Protocol.

The demilitarised zones already existing under the terms of certain treaties or conventions, or which may be established in future between States mutually consenting thereto, may at the request and at the expense of one or more of the conterminous States, be placed under a temporary or permanent system of supervision to be organised by the Council.

ARTICLE 10

Every State which resorts to war in violation of the undertakings contained in the Covenant or in the present Protocol is an aggressor. Violation of the rules laid down for a demilitarised zone shall be held equivalent to resort to war.

In the event of hostilities having broken out, any State shall be presumed to be an aggressor, unless a decision of the Council, which must be taken unanimously, shall otherwise declare:

1. If it has refused to submit the dispute to the procedure of pacific settlement provided by Articles 13 and 15 of the Covenant as amplified by the present Protocol, or to comply with a judicial sentence or arbitral award or with a unanimous recommendation of the Council, or has disregarded a unanimous report of the Council, a judicial sentence or an arbitral award recognising that the dispute between it and the other belligerent State arises out of a matter which by international law is solely within the domestic jurisdiction of the latter State; nevertheless, in the last case the State shall only be presumed to be an aggressor if it has not previously submitted the question to the Council or the Assembly, in accordance with Article 11 of the Covenant.

2. If it has violated provisional measures enjoined by the Council for the period while the proceedings are in progress as contemplated by Article 7 of the present Protocol.

Apart from the cases dealt with in paragraphs 1 and 2 of the present Article, if the Council does not at once succeed in determining the aggressor, it shall be bound to enjoin upon the belligerents an armistice, and shall fix the terms, acting, if need be, by a two-thirds majority and shall supervise its execution.

Any belligerent which has refused to accept the armistice or has violated its terms shall be deemed an aggressor.

The Council shall call upon the signatory States to apply forthwith against the aggressor the sanctions provided by Article 11 of the present Protocol, and any signatory State thus called upon shall thereupon be entitled to exercise the rights of a belligerent.

ARTICLE 11

As soon as the Council has called upon the signatory States to apply sanctions, as provided in the last paragraph of Article 10 of the present Protocol, the obligations of the said States, in regard to the sanctions of all kinds mentioned in paragraphs 1 and 2 of Article 16 of the Covenant, will immediately become operative in order that such sanctions may forthwith be employed against the aggressor.

Those obligations shall be interpreted as obliging each of the signatory States to cooperate loyally and effectively in support of the Covenant of the League of Nations, and in resistance to any act of aggression, in the degree which its geographical position and its particular situation as regards armaments allow.

In accordance with paragraph 3 of Article 16 of the Covenant the signatory States give a joint and several undertaking to come to the assistance of the State attacked or threatened, and to give each other mutual support by means of facilities and reciprocal exchanges as regards the provision of raw materials and supplies of every kind, openings of credits, transport and transit, and for this purpose to take all measures in their power to preserve the safety of communications by land and by sea of the attacked or threatened State.

If both parties to the dispute are aggressors within the meaning of Article 10, the economic and financial sanctions shall be applied to both of them.

Article 12

In view of the complexity of the conditions in which the Council may be called upon to exercise the functions mentioned in Article 11 of the present Protocol concerning economic and financial sanctions, and in order to determine more exactly the guarantees afforded by the present Protocol to the signatory States, the Council shall forthwith invite the economic and financial organisations of the League of Nations to consider and report as to the nature of the steps to be taken to give effect to the financial and economic sanctions and measures of cooperation contemplated in Article 16 of the Covenant and in Article 11 of this Protocol.

When in possession of this information, the Council shall draw up through its competent organs:

1. Plans of action for the application of the economic and financial sanctions against an aggressor State;

2. Plans of economic and financial co-operation between a State attacked and the different States assisting it; and shall communicate these plans to the Members of the League and to the other signatory States.

Article 13

In view of the contingent military, naval and air sanctions provided for by Article 16 of the Covenant and by Article 11 of the present Protocol, the Council shall be entitled to receive undertakings from States determining in advance the military, naval and air forces which they would be able to bring into action immediately to ensure the fulfilment of the obligations in regard to sanctions which result from the Covenant and the present Protocol.

Furthermore, as soon as the Council has called upon the signatory States to apply sanctions, as provided in the last paragraph of Article 10 above, the said States may, in accordance with any agreements which they may previously have concluded, bring to the assistance of a particular State, which is the victim of aggression, their military, naval and air forces.

The agreements mentioned in the preceding paragraph shall be registered and published by the Secretariat of the League of Nations. They shall remain open to all States Members of the League which may desire to accede thereto.

Article 14

The Council shall alone be competent to declare that the application of sanctions shall cease and normal conditions be re-established.

Article 15

In conformity with the spirit of the present Protocol, the signatory States agree that the whole cost of any military, naval or air operations undertaken for the repression of an aggression under the terms of the Protocol, and reparation for all losses suffered by individuals, whether civilians or combatants, and for all material damage caused by the operations of both sides, shall be borne by the aggressor State up to the extreme limit of its capacity.

Nevertheless, in view of Article 10 of the Covenant, neither the territorial integrity nor the political independence of the aggressor State shall in any case be affected as the result of the application of the sanctions mentioned in the present Protocol.

Article 16

The signatory States agree that in the event of a dispute between one or more of them and one or more States which have not signed the present Protocol and are not Members of the League of Nations, such non-Member States shall be invited, on the conditions contemplated in Article 17 of the Covenant, to submit, for the purpose of a pacific settlement, to the obligations accepted by the States signatories of the present Protocol.

If the State so invited, having refused to accept the said conditions and obligations, resorts to war against a signatory State, the provisions of Article 16 of the Covenant, as defined by the present Protocol, shall be applicable against it.

Article 17

The signatory States undertake to participate in an International Conference for the Reduction of Armaments which shall be convened by the Council and shall meet at Geneva on Monday, June 15th, 1925. All other States, whether Members of the League or not, shall be invited to this Conference.

In preparation for the convening of the Conference, the Council shall draw up with due regard to the undertakings contained in Articles 11 and 13 of the present Protocol, a general programme for the reduction and limitation of armaments, which shall be laid before the Conference and which shall be communicated to the Governments at the earliest possible date, and at the latest three months before the Conference meets.

If by May 1st, 1925, ratifications have not been deposited by at least a majority of the permanent Members of the Council and ten other Members of the League, the Secretary-General of the League shall immediately consult the Council as to whether he shall cancel the invitations or merely adjourn the Conference to a subsequent date to be fixed by the Council so as to permit the necessary number of ratifications to be obtained.

Article 18

Wherever mention is made in Article 10, or in any other provision of the present Protocol, of a decision of the Council, this shall be understood in the sense of Article 15 of the Covenant, namely, that the votes of the representatives of the parties to the dispute shall not be counted when reckoning unanimity or the necessary majority.

Article 19

Except as expressly provided by its terms, the present Protocol shall not affect in any way the rights and obligations of Members of the League as determined by the Covenant.

Article 20

Any dispute as to the interpretation of the present Protocol shall be submitted to the Permanent Court of International Justice.

Article 21

The present Protocol, of which the French and English texts are both authentic, shall be ratified.

The deposit of ratifications shall be made at the Secretariat of the League of Nations as soon as possible.

States of which the seat of government is outside Europe will be entitled merely to inform the Secretariat of the League of Nations that their ratification has been given; in that case, they must transmit the instrument of ratification as soon as possible.

So soon as the majority of the permanent Members of the Council and ten other Members of the League have deposited or have effected their ratifications, a *procès-verbal* to that effect shall be drawn up by the Secretariat.

After the said *procès-verbal* has been drawn up, the Protocol shall come into force as soon as the plan for the reduction of armaments has been adopted by the Conference provided for in Article 17.

If within such period after the adoption of the plan for the reduction of armaments as shall be fixed by the said Conference, the plan has not been carried out, the Council shall make a declaration to that effect; this declaration shall render the present Protocol null and void.

The grounds on which the Council may declare that the plan drawn up by the International Conference for the Reduction of Armaments has not been carried out, and that in consequence the present Protocol has been rendered null and void, shall be laid down by the Conference itself.

A signatory State which, after the expiration of the period fixed by the Conference, fails to comply with the plan adopted by the Conference, shall not be admitted to benefit by the provisions of the present Protocol.

In faith whereof the Undersigned, duly authorised for this purpose, have signed the present Protocol.

Done at Geneva, on the second day of October, nineteen hundred and twenty-four, in a single copy, which will be kept in the archives of the Secretariat of the League and registered by it on the date of its coming into force.

F. S. Noli (*Albanie—Albania*)
Afranio de Mello-Franco (*Brésil—Brazil*)
Ch. Kalfoff (*Bulgarie—Bulgaria*)
E. Villegas (*Chili—Chile*)
General F. Laidoner (*Estonie—Estonia*)
Ari. Briand (*France*)
Politis (*Grèce—Greece*)
S. Seja (*Lettonie—Latvia*)
Al. Skrzyński (*Pologne—Poland*)
João Chagas (*Portugal*)
Dr. Kosta Koumanoudi (*Royaume des Serbes, Croates et Slovènes-Kingdom of the Serbs, Croates and Slovenes*)
Dr. Edvard Beneš (*Tchécoslovaquie—Czechoslovakia*)

APPENDIX I

E

PACIFIC SETTLEMENT OF INTERNATIONAL DISPUTES, NON-AGGRESSION, AND MUTUAL ASSISTANCE: GENERAL ACT *

CHAPTER I—CONCILIATION

ARTICLE 1

Disputes of every kind between two or more Parties to the present General Act which it has not been possible to settle by diplomacy shall, subject to such reservations as may be made under Article 39, be submitted, under the conditions laid down in the present Chapter, to the procedure of conciliation.

ARTICLE 2

The disputes referred to in the preceding article shall be submitted to a permanent or special Conciliation Commission constituted by the parties to the dispute.

ARTICLE 3

On a request to that effect being made by one of the Contracting Parties to another Party, a permanent Conciliation Commission shall be constituted within a period of six months.

ARTICLE 4

Unless the parties concerned agree otherwise, the Conciliation Commission shall be constituted as follows:

1. The Commission shall be composed of five members. The parties shall each nominate one commissioner, who may be chosen from among their respective nationals. The three other commissioners shall be appointed by agreement from among the nationals of third Powers. These three commissioners must be of different nationalities and must not be habitually resident in the territory nor be in the service of the parties. The parties shall appoint the President of the Commission from among them.

2. The commissioners shall be appointed for three years. They shall be re-eligible. The commissioners appointed jointly may be replaced during

* Original text from League of Nations, IX. Disarmament. 1928. 13. (C.536.M. 164.), pp. 10-15.

the course of their mandate by agreement between the parties. Either party may, however, at any time replace a commissioner whom it has appointed. Even if replaced, the commissioners shall continue to exercise their functions until the termination of the work in hand.

3. Vacancies which may occur as a result of death, resignation or any other cause shall be filled within the shortest possible time in the manner fixed for the nominations.

ARTICLE 5

If, when a dispute arises, no permanent Conciliation Commission appointed by the parties is in existence, a special commission shall be constituted for the examination of the dispute within a period of three months from the date at which a request to that effect is made by one of the parties to the other party. The necessary appointments shall be made in the manner laid down in the preceding article, unless the parties decide otherwise.

ARTICLE 6

1. If the appointment of the commissioners to be designated jointly is not made within the periods provided for in Articles 3 and 5, the making of the necessary appointments shall be entrusted to a third Power, chosen by agreement between the parties, or on request of the parties, to the Acting President of the Council of the League of Nations.

2. If no agreement is reached on either of these procedures, each party shall designate a different Power, and the appointment shall be made in concert by the Powers thus chosen.

3. If, within a period of three months, the two Powers have been unable to reach an agreement, each of them shall submit a number of candidates equal to the number of members to be appointed. It shall then be decided by lot which of the candidates thus designated shall be appointed.

ARTICLE 7

1. Disputes shall be brought before the Conciliation Commission by means of an application addressed to the President by the two parties acting in agreement, or in default thereof by one or other of the parties.

2. The application, after giving a summary account of the subject of the dispute, shall contain the invitation to the Commission to take all necessary measures with a view to arriving at an amicable solution.

3. If the application emanates from only one of the parties, the other party shall, without delay, be notified by it.

ARTICLE 8

1. Within fifteen days from the date on which a dispute has been brought by one of the parties before a permanent Conciliation Commission, either

party may replace its own commissioner, for the examination of the particular dispute, by a person possessing special competence in the matter.

2. The party making use of this right shall immediately notify the other party; the latter shall, in such case, be entitled to take similar action within fifteen days from the date on which it received the notification.

ARTICLE 9

1. In the absence of agreement to the contrary between the parties, the Conciliation Commission shall meet at the seat of the League of Nations, or at some other place selected by its President.

2. The Commission may in all circumstances request the Secretary-General of the League of Nations to afford it his assistance.

ARTICLE 10

The work of the Conciliation Commission shall not be conducted in public unless a decision to that effect is taken by the Commission with the consent of the parties.

ARTICLE 11

1. In the absence of agreement to the contrary between the parties, the Conciliation Commission shall lay down its own procedure, which in any case must provide for both parties being heard. In regard to enquiries, the Commission, unless it decides unanimously to the contrary, shall act in accordance with the provisions of Part III of the Hague Convention of October 18th, 1907, for the Pacific Settlement of International Disputes.

2. The parties shall be represented before the Conciliation Commission by agents, whose duty shall be to act as intermediaries between them and the Commission; they may, moreover, be assisted by counsel and experts appointed by them for that purpose and may request that all persons whose evidence appears to them desirable shall be heard.

3. The Commission, for its part, shall be entitled to request oral explanations from the agents, counsel and experts of both parties, as well as from all persons it may think desirable to summon with the consent of their Governments.

ARTICLE 12

In the absence of agreement to the contrary between the parties, the decisions of the Conciliation Commission shall be taken by a majority vote, and the Commission may only take decisions on the substance of the dispute if all its members are present.

ARTICLE 13

The parties undertake to facilitate the work of the Conciliation Commission, and particularly to supply it to the greatest possible extent with all relevant documents and information, as well as to use the means at their disposal to allow it to proceed in their territory, and in accordance with their law, to the summoning and hearing of witnesses or experts and to visit the localities in question.

ARTICLE 14

1. During the proceedings of the Commission, each of the commissioners shall receive emoluments the amount of which shall be fixed by agreement between the parties, each of which shall contribute an equal share.

2. The general expenses arising out of the working of the Commission shall be divided in the same manner.

ARTICLE 15

1. The task of the Conciliation Commission shall be to elucidate the questions in dispute, to collect with that object all necessary information by means of enquiry or otherwise, and to endeavour to bring the parties to an agreement. It may, after the case has been examined, inform the parties of the terms of settlement which seem suitable to it, and lay down the period within which they are to make their decision.

2. At the close of its proceedings, the Commission shall draw up a *procès-verbal* stating, as the case may be, either that the parties have come to an agreement and, if need arise, the terms of the agreement, or that it has been impossible to effect a settlement. No mention shall be made in the *procès-verbal* of whether the Commission's decisions were taken unanimously or by a majority vote.

3. The proceedings of the Commission must, unless the parties otherwise agree, be terminated within six months from the date on which the Commission shall have been given cognisance of the dispute.

ARTICLE 16

The Commission's *procès-verbal* shall be communicated without delay to the parties. The parties shall decide whether it shall be published.

CHAPTER II—JUDICIAL SETTLEMENT

ARTICLE 17

All disputes with regard to which the parties are in conflict as to their respective rights shall, subject to any reservations which may be made under Article 39, be submitted for decision to the Permanent Court of International Justice, unless the parties agree, in the manner hereinafter provided, to have resort to an arbitral tribunal.

It is understood that the disputes referred to above include in particular those mentioned in Article 36 of the Statute of the Permanent Court of International Justice.

ARTICLE 18

If the parties agree to submit the disputes mentioned in the preceding article to an arbitral tribunal, they shall draw up a special agreement in which they shall specify the subject of the dispute, the arbitrators selected, and the procedure to be followed. In the absence of sufficient particulars in the special agreement, the provisions of The Hague Convention of October 18th, 1907, for the Pacific Settlement of International Disputes shall apply so far as is necessary. If nothing is laid down in the special agreement as to the rules regarding the substance of the dispute to be followed by the arbitrators, the tribunal shall apply the substantive rules enumerated in Article 38 of the Statute of the Permanent Court of International Justice.

ARTICLE 19

If the parties fail to agree concerning the special agreement referred to in the preceding article, or fail to appoint arbitrators, either party shall be at liberty, after giving three months' notice, to bring the dispute by an application direct before the Permanent Court of International Justice.

ARTICLE 20

1. Notwithstanding the provisions of Article 1, disputes of the kind referred to in Article 17 arising between parties who have acceded to the obligations contained in the present chapter shall only be subject to the procedure of conciliation if the parties so agree.

2. The obligation to resort to the procedure of conciliation remains applicable to disputes which are excluded from judicial settlement only by the operation of reservations under the provisions of Article 39.

3. In the event of recourse to and failure of conciliation, neither party may bring the dispute before the Permanent Court of International Justice or call for the constitution of the arbitral tribunal referred to in Article 18 before the expiration of one month from the termination of the proceedings of the Conciliation Commission.

CHAPTER III—ARBITRATION

ARTICLE 21

Any dispute not of the kind referred to in Article 17 which does not, within the month following the termination of the work of the Conciliation Commission provided for in Chapter 1, form the object of an agreement between the parties, may, subject to such reservations as may be made under Article 39, be brought before an arbitral tribunal which, unless the parties otherwise agree, shall be constituted in the manner set out below.

ARTICLE 22

The Arbitral Tribunal shall consist of five members. The parties shall each nominate one member, who may be chosen from among their respective nationals. The two other arbitrators and the Chairman shall be chosen by common agreement from among the nationals of third Powers. They must be of different nationalities and must not be habitually resident in the territory nor be in the service of the parties.

ARTICLE 23

1. If the appointment of the members of the Arbitral Tribunal is not made within a period of three months from the date on which one of the parties requested the other party to constitute an arbitral tribunal, a third Power, chosen by agreement between the parties, shall be requested to make the necessary appointments.

2. If no agreement is reached on this point, each party shall designate a different Power, and the appointments shall be made in concert by the Powers thus chosen.

3. If, within a period of three months, the two Powers so chosen have been unable to reach an agreement, the necessary appointments shall be made by the President of the Permanent Court of International Justice. If the latter is prevented from acting or is a subject of one of the parties, the nomination shall be made by the Vice-President. If the latter is prevented from acting or is a subject of one of the parties, the appointments shall be made by the oldest member of the Court who is not a subject of either party.

ARTICLE 24

Vacancies which may occur as a result of death, resignation or any other cause shall be filled within the shortest possible time in the manner fixed for the nominations.

ARTICLE 25

The parties shall draw up a special agreement determining the subject of the disputes and the details of procedure.

ARTICLE 26

In the absence of sufficient particulars in the special agreement regarding the matters referred to in the preceding article, the provisions of The Hague Convention of October 18th, 1907, for the Pacific Settlement of International Disputes shall apply so far as is necessary.

Article 27

Failing the conclusion of a special agreement within a period of three months from the date on which the Tribunal was constituted, the dispute may be brought before the Tribunal by an application by one or other party.

Article 28

If nothing is laid down in the special agreement or no special agreement has been made, the Tribunal shall apply the rules in regard to the substance of the dispute enumerated in Article 38 of the Statute of the Permanent Court of International Justice. In so far as there exists no such rule applicable to the dispute, the Tribunal shall decide *ex aequo et bono*.

Chapter IV—GENERAL PROVISIONS

Article 29

1. Disputes for the settlement of which a special procedure is laid down in other conventions in force between the parties to the dispute shall be settled in conformity with the provisions of those conventions.

2. The present General Act shall not affect any agreements in force by which conciliation procedure is established between the Parties or they are bound by obligations to resort to arbitration or judicial settlement which ensure the settlement of the dispute. If, however, these agreements provide only for a procedure of conciliation, after such procedure has been followed without result, the provisions of the present General Act concerning judicial settlement or arbitration shall be applied in so far as the parties have acceded thereto.

Article 30

If a party brings before a Conciliation Commission a dispute which the other party, relying on conventions in force between the parties, has submitted to the Permanent Court of International Justice or an Arbitral Tribunal has pronounced upon the conflict of competence. The same rule shall apply if the Court or the Tribunal is seized of the case by one of the parties during the conciliation proceedings.

Article 31

1. In the case of a dispute the occasion of which, according to the municipal law of one of the parties, falls within the competence of its judicial or administrative authorities, the party in question may object to the matter in dispute being submitted for settlement by the different methods laid down in the present General Act until a decision with final effect has been pronounced, within a reasonable time, by the competent authority.

2. In such a case, the party which desires to resort to the procedures laid down in the present General Act must notify the other party of its intention within a period of one year from the date of the aforementioned decision.

ARTICLE 32

If, in a judicial sentence or arbitral award, it is declared that a judgment, or a measure enjoined by a court of law or other authority of one of the parties to the dispute, is wholly or in part contrary to international law, and if the constitutional law of that party does not permit or only partially permits the consequences of the judgment or measure in question to be annulled, the parties agree that the judicial sentence or arbitral award shall grant the injured party equitable satisfaction.

ARTICLE 33

1. In all cases where a dispute forms the object of arbitration or judicial proceedings, and particularly if the question on which the parties differ arises out of acts already committed or on the point of being committed, the Permanent Court of International Justice, acting in accordance with Article 41 of its Statute, or the Arbitral Tribunal, shall lay down within the shortest possible time the provisional measures to be adopted. The parties to the dispute shall be bound to accept such measures.

2. If the dispute is brought before a Conciliation Commission, the latter may recommend to the parties the adoption of such provisional measures as it considers suitable.

3. The parties undertake to abstain from all measures likely to react prejudicially upon the execution of the judicial or arbitral decision or upon the arrangements proposed by the Conciliation Commission and, in general, to abstain from any sort of action whatsoever which may aggravate or extend the dispute.

ARTICLE 34

Should a dispute arise between more than two Parties to the present General Act, the following rules shall be observed for the application of the forms of procedure described in the foregoing provisions:

(a) In the case of conciliation procedure a special commission shall invariably be constituted. The composition of such commission shall differ according as the parties all have separate interests or as two or more of their number act together.

In the former case, the parties shall each appoint one commissioner and shall jointly appoint commissioners nationals of third Powers not parties to the dispute, whose number shall always exceed by one the number of commissioners appointed separately by the parties.

In the second case, the parties who act together shall appoint their commissioner jointly by agreement between themselves and shall combine with the other party or parties in appointing third commissioners.

In either event, the parties, unless they agree otherwise, shall apply Article 5 and the following articles of the present Act, so far as they are compatible with the provisions of the present article.

(b) In the case of judicial procedure, the Statute of the Permanent Court of International Justice shall apply.

(c) In the case of arbitral procedure, if agreement is not secured as to the composition of the tribunal, in the case of the disputes mentioned in Article 17 each party shall have the right, by means of an application, to submit the dispute to the Permanent Court of International Justice; in the case of the disputes mentioned in Article 21, the above Article 22 and following articles shall apply, but each party having separate interests shall appoint one arbitrator and the number of arbitrators separately appointed by the parties to the dispute shall always be one less than that of the other arbitrators.

ARTICLE 35

1. The present General Act shall be applicable as between the Parties thereto, even though a third Power, whether a party to the Act or not, has an interest in the dispute.

2. In conciliation procedure, the parties may agree to invite such third Power to intervene.

ARTICLE 36

1. In judicial or arbitral procedure, if a third Power should consider that it has an interest of a legal nature which may be affected by the decision in the case, it may submit to the Permanent Court of International Justice or to the arbitral tribunal a request to intervene as a third Party.

2. It will be for the Court or the tribunal to decide upon this request.

ARTICLE 37

1. Whenever the construction of a convention to which States other than those concerned in the case are parties is in question, the Registrar of the Permanent Court of International Justice or the arbitral tribunal shall notify all such States forthwith.

2. Every State so notified has the right to intervene in the proceedings; but, if it uses this right, the construction given by the decision will be binding upon it.

ARTICLE 38

Accessions to the present General Act may extend:

A. Either to all the provisions of the Act (Chapters I, II, III, and IV);

B. Or to those provisions only which relate to conciliation and judicial settlement (Chapters I and II), together with the general provisions dealing with these procedures (Chapter IV);

C. Or to those provisions only which relate to conciliation (Chapter I), together with the general provisions concerning that procedure (Chapter IV).

The Contracting Parties may benefit by the accessions of other Parties only in so far as they have themselves assumed the same obligations.

Article 39

1. In addition to the power given in the preceding article, a Party, in acceding to the present General Act, may make his acceptance conditional upon the reservations exhaustively enumerated in the following paragraph. These reservations must be indicated at the time of accession.

2. These reservations may be such as to exclude from the procedure described in the present Act:

(a) Disputes arising out of facts prior to the accession either of the Party making the reservation or of any other Party with whom the said Party may have a dispute;

(b) Disputes concerning questions which by international law are solely within the domestic jurisdiction of States;

(c) Disputes concerning particular cases or clearly specified subject-matters, such as territorial status, or disputes falling within clearly defined categories.

3. If one of the parties to a dispute has made a reservation, the other parties may enforce the same reservation in regard to that party.

4. In the case of Parties who have acceded to the provisions of the present General Act relating to judicial settlement or to arbitration, such reservations as they may have made shall, unless otherwise expressly stated, be deemed not to apply to the procedure of conciliation.

Article 40

A Party whose accession has been only partial, or was made subject to reservation, may at any moment, by means of a simple declaration, either extend the scope of his accession or abandon all or part of his reservations.

Article 41

Disputes relating to the interpretation or application of the present General Act, including those concerning the classification of disputes and the scope of reservations, shall be submitted to the Permanent Court of International Justice.

ARTICLE 42

The present General Act, of which the French and English texts shall both be authentic, shall bear the date of the 26th of September, 1928.

ARTICLE 43

1. The present General Act shall be open to accession by all the Heads of States or other competent authorities of the Members of the League of Nations and the non-Member States to which the Council of the League of Nations has communicated a copy for this purpose.

2. The instruments of accession and the additional declarations provided for by Article 40 shall be transmitted to the Secretary-General of the League of Nations, who shall notify their receipt to all the Members of the League and to the non-Member States referred to in the preceding paragraph.

3. The Secretary-General of the League of Nations shall draw up three lists, denominated respectively by the letters A, B and C, corresponding to the three forms of accession to the present Act provided for in Article 38, in which shall be shown the accessions and additional declarations of the Contracting Parties. These lists, which shall be continually kept up to date, shall be published in the annual report presented to the Assembly of the League of Nations by the Secretary-General.

ARTICLE 44

1. The present General Act shall come into force on the ninetieth day following the receipt by the Secretary-General of the League of Nations of the accession of not less than two Contracting Parties.

2. Accessions received after the entry into force of the Act, in accordance with the previous paragraph, shall become effective as from the ninetieth day following the date of receipt by the Secretary-General of the League of Nations. The same rule shall apply to the additional declarations provided for by Article 40.

ARTICLE 45

1. The present General Act shall be concluded for a period of five years, dating from its entry into force.

2. It shall remain in force for further successive periods of five years in the case of Contracting Parties which do not denounce it at least six months before the expiration of the current period.

3. Denunciation shall be effected by a written notification addressed to the Secretary-General of the League of Nations, who shall inform all the Members of the League and the non-Member States referred to in Article 43.

4. A denunciation may be partial only, or may consist in notification of reservations not previously made.

5. Notwithstanding denunciation by one of the Contracting Parties concerned in a dispute, all proceedings pending at the expiration of the current period of the General Act shall be duly completed.

ARTICLE 46

A copy of the present General Act, signed by the President of the Assembly and by the Secretary-General of the League of Nations, shall be deposited in the archives of the Secretariat; a certified true copy shall be delivered by the Secretary-General to all the Members of the League of Nations and to the non-Member States indicated by the Council of the League of Nations.

ARTICLE 47

The present General Act shall be registered by the Secretary-General of the League of Nations on the date of its entry into force.

The President of the ninth ordinary session of the
Assembly of the League of Nations:
(Signed) HERLUF ZAHLE.

The Secretary-General:
(Signed) ERIC DRUMMOND.

APPENDIX II

TEXT OF THE GENERAL PACT FOR THE RENUNCIATION OF WAR

Signed in Paris, August 27, 1928 *

THE PRESIDENT OF THE GERMAN REICH, THE PRESIDENT OF THE UNITED STATES OF AMERICA, HIS MAJESTY THE KING OF THE BELGIANS, THE PRESIDENT OF THE FRENCH REPUBLIC, HIS MAJESTY THE KING OF GREAT BRITAIN, IRELAND AND THE BRITISH DOMINIONS BEYOND THE SEAS, EMPEROR OF INDIA, HIS MAJESTY THE KING OF ITALY, HIS MAJESTY THE EMPEROR OF JAPAN, THE PRESIDENT OF THE REPUBLIC OF POLAND, THE PRESIDENT OF THE CZECHOSLOVAK REPUBLIC.

Deeply sensible of their solemn duty to promote the welfare of mankind;

Persuaded that the time has come when a frank renunciation of war as an instrument of national policy should be made to the end that the peaceful and friendly relations now existing between their peoples may be perpetuated;

Convinced that all changes in their relations with one another should be sought only by pacific means and be the result of a peaceful and orderly process, and that any signatory Power which shall hereafter seek to promote its national interests by resort to war should be denied the benefits furnished by this Treaty;

Hopeful that, encouraged by their example, all the other nations of the world will join in this humane endeavor and by adhering to the present Treaty as soon as it comes into force bring their peoples within the scope of its beneficent provisions, thus uniting the civilized nations of the world in a common renunciation of war as an instrument of their national policy;

Have decided to conclude a Treaty and for that purpose have appointed as their respective Plenipotentiaries:

THE PRESIDENT OF THE GERMAN REICH:

Dr. Gustav Stresemann, Minister for Foreign Affairs;

THE PRESIDENT OF THE UNITED STATES OF AMERICA:

The Honorable Frank B. Kellogg, Secretary of State;

* Reprinted from State Department Publication, Washington, D. C.

HIS MAJESTY THE KING OF THE BELGIANS:

Mr. Paul Hymans, Minister for Foreign Affairs, Minister of State;

THE PRESIDENT OF THE FRENCH REPUBLIC:

Mr. Aristide Briand, Minister for Foreign Affairs;

HIS MAJESTY THE KING OF GREAT BRITAIN, IRELAND AND THE BRITISH DOMINIONS BEYOND THE SEAS, EMPEROR OF INDIA:

For Great Britain and Northern Ireland and all parts of the British Empire which are not separate Members of the League of Nations:

The Right Honourable Lord Cushendun, Chancellor of the Duchy of Lancaster, Acting Secretary of State for Foreign Affairs;

For the DOMINION OF CANADA:

The Right Honourable William Lyon Mackenzie King, Prime Minister and Minister for External Affairs;

For the COMMONWEALTH OF AUSTRALIA:

The Honourable Alexander John McLachlan, Member of the Executive Federal Council;

For the DOMINION OF NEW ZEALAND:

The Honourable Sir Christopher James Parr, High Commissioner for New Zealand in Great Britain;

For the UNION OF SOUTH AFRICA:

The Honourable Jacobus Stephanus Smit, High Commissioner for the Union of South Africa in Great Britain;

For the IRISH FREE STATE:

Mr. William Thomas Cosgrave, President of the Executive Council;

For INDIA:

The Right Honourable Lord Cushendun, Chancellor of the Duchy of Lancaster, Acting Secretary of State for Foreign Affairs;

HIS MAJESTY THE KING OF ITALY:

Count Gaetano Manzoni, His Ambassador Extraordinary and Plenipotentiary at Paris;

HIS MAJESTY THE EMPEROR OF JAPAN:

Count Uchida, Privy Councillor;

THE PRESIDENT OF THE REPUBLIC OF POLAND:

Mr. A. Zaleski, Minister for Foreign Affairs;

THE PRESIDENT OF THE CZECHOSLOVAK REPUBLIC:

Dr. Eduard Benes, Minister of Foreign Affairs;

who, having communicated to one another their full powers found in good and due form have agreed upon the following articles:

Article I

The High Contracting Parties solemnly declare in the names of their respective peoples that they condemn recourse to war for the solution of international controversies, and renounce it as an instrument of national policy in their relations with one another.

Article II

The High Contracting Parties agree that the settlement or solution of all disputes or conflicts of whatever nature or of whatever origin they may be, which may arise among them, shall never be sought except by pacific means.

Article III

The present Treaty shall be ratified by the High Contracting Parties named in the Preamble in accordance with their respective constitutional requirements, and shall take effect as between them as soon as all their several instruments of ratification shall have been deposited at Washington.

This Treaty shall, when it has come into effect as prescribed in the preceding paragraph, remain open as long as may be necessary for adherence by all the other Powers of the world. Every instrument evidencing the adherence of a Power shall be deposited at Washington and the Treaty shall immediately upon such deposit become effective as between the Power thus adhering and the other Powers parties hereto.

It shall be the duty of the Government of the United States to furnish each Government named in the Preamble and every Government subsequently adhering to this Treaty with a certified copy of the Treaty and of every instrument of ratification or adherence. It shall also be the duty of the Government of the United States telegraphically to notify such Governments immediately upon the deposit with it of each instrument of ratification or adherence.

IN FAITH WHEREOF the respective Plenipotentiaries have signed this Treaty in the French and English languages both texts having equal force, and hereunto affix their seals.

DONE at Paris the twenty-seventh day of August in the year one thousand nine hundred and twenty-eight.

(Seal) Gustav Stresemann
(Seal) Frank B. Kellogg
(Seal) Paul Hymans
(Seal) Ari. Briand
(Seal) Cushendun
(Seal) W. L. Mackenzie King
(Seal) A. J. McLachlan
(Seal) C. J. Parr
(Seal) J. S. Smit
(Seal) Liam T. MacCosgair
(Seal) Cushendun
(Seal) G. Manzoni
(Seal) Uchida
(Seal) August Zaleski
(Seal) Dr. Eduard Beneš

APPENDIX III

MEMORANDUM ON THE ORGANIZATION OF A RÉGIME OF EUROPEAN FEDERAL UNION *

(Translation †)

In the course of a first meeting held on September 9, 1929, at Geneva, on the request of the Representative of France, the authorized Representatives of the twenty-seven European States, members of the League of Nations, were requested to consider the desirability of an understanding between the Governments concerned with a view to the institution, among European peoples, of a kind of federal bond establishing among them a régime of constant solidarity, and permitting them, in all cases when it might be necessary, to enter into immediate contact for the study, the discusion, and the solution of the problems susceptible of concerning them in common.

Unanimous in recognizing the necessity of an effort in this direction, the Representatives consulted all undertook to recommend to their respective Governments the study of the question which was submitted directly to them by the Representative of France and which the latter had already had occasion, on September 5, to raise before the Tenth Assembly of the League of Nations.

In order better to prove such unanimity which already sanctioned the principle of a European moral union, they believed that they ought to decide, without delay, on the procedure which appeared to them the best adapted to facilitate the study proposed they entrusted to the Representative of France the task of defining in a memorandum to the Governments concerned the essential points with which their study should deal; of collecting and of registering their opinions; of drawing the conclusions from such broad consultation, and of making it the subject of a report to be submitted to the deliberations of a European Conference which might be held at Geneva at the time of the next Assembly of the League of Nations.

At the moment of discharging the mission which was entrusted to it, the Government of the Republic desires to recall the general preoccupation and the essential reservations which have not ceased to dominate the thought

* *International Conciliation,* June, 1930, Special Bulletin, pp. 327-353.

† Translation made in the Department of State, Washington, D. C.

of all the Representatives assembled at Geneva on the 9th of September, last. The proposal taken under consideration by twenty-seven European Governments found its justification in the very definite sentiment of a collective responsibility in face of the danger which threatens European peace, from the political as well as from the economic and social point of view, because of the lack of coordination which still prevails in the general economy of Europe. The necessity of establishing a permanent régime of conventional solidarity for the rational organization of Europe arises, in fact, from the very conditions of the security and the well-being of the peoples which their geographical situation compels, in this part of the world to participate in a *de facto* solidarity.

No one doubts today that the lack of cohesion in the grouping of the material and moral forces of Europe constitutes, practically, the most serious obstacle to the development and efficiency of all political or juridical institutions on which it is the tendency to base the first attempts for a universal organization of peace. This scattering of forces limits, no less seriously, the possibilities of enlargement of the economic market, the attempts to intensify and improve industrial production, and for that very reason all guarantees against labor crises which are sources of political as well as social instability. Now, the danger of such division is still more increased by the circumstance of the extent of the new frontiers (more than 20,000 kilometers of customs barriers) which the treaties of peace had to create in order to do justice, in Europe, to national aspirations.

The very action of the League of Nations, the responsibilities of which are the greater because it is universal, might be exposed in Europe to serious obstacles if such breaking up of territory were not offset, as soon as possible, by a bond of solidarity permitting European nations to at last become conscious of European geographical unity and to effect, within the framework of the League, one of those regional understandings which the Covenant formally recommended.

* * * * *

This means that the search for a formula of European cooperation in connection with the League of Nations, far from weakening the authority of this latter must and can tend only to strengthen it, for it is closely connected with its aims.

It is not at all a question of constituting a European group outside of the League of Nations, but on the contrary of harmonizing European interests under the control (contrôle) and in the spirit of the League of Nations by incorporating in its universal system a limited system all the more effective. The realization of a federative organization of Europe would always be attributed to the League of Nations as an element of progress to its credit from which extra European nations themselves might benefit.

Such a conception can leave no room for doubt, any more than that which gave rise, within still more restricted regional limits, to the collective negotiations of the Locarno Agreements which inaugurated the real policy of European cooperation.

In fact, certain questions concern Europe particularly for which European States may feel the need of an action of their own, more immediate and more direct in the very interest of peace and for which furthermore they enjoy a special competence arising from their ethnical affinities and their community of civilization. The League of Nations itself in the general exercise of its activities, has had more than once to take account of the fact of this geographical unity which Europe presents and which may call for common solutions, the application of which could not be applied to the whole world. Preparing and facilitating the coordination of the strictly European activities of the League of Nations would be precisely one of the tasks of the association contemplated.

Far from constituting a new contentious jurisdiction for the settlement of disputes, the European Association, which could not be called on in such matters to exercise its good offices except in a purely advisory capacity would be without authority to treat thoroughly special problems, the adjustment of which has been entrusted by the Pact or by the Treaties to a special procedure of the League of Nations or to any other procedure expressly defined. But in the very cases in which it might be a question of an essential task reserved to the League of Nations, the federal bond between European States would still play a very useful rôle in preparing a favorable atmosphere for the pacific adjustments of the League or facilitating in practice the execution of its decisions.

Therefore the Representative of France took care from the beginning to avoid any ambiguity when taking the initiative for the first European meeting. He believed that it ought to include only the Representatives of States members of the League of Nations and be held at Geneva itself on the occasion of the first Assembly, that is to say, in the atmosphere and within the framework of the League of Nations.

* * * * *

The European organization contemplated could not oppose any ethnic group, on other continents or in Europe itself, outside of the League of Nations, any more than it could oppose the League of Nations.

The work of European coordination answers to necessities sufficiently immediate and sufficiently vital to seek its end in itself in a labor truly constructive and which it is out of the question to direct or ever to allow to be directed against anyone. Quite on the contrary, this work should be pursued in full friendly confidence and often even in collaboration with all other States or groups of States which are interested with sufficient sincerity in the universal organization of peace to recognize the desirability of a greater homogeneity of Europe, and which understand, furthermore, with sufficient clearness the modern laws of international economics to seek, in the best organization of a simplified Europe, and for that very reason, a Europe removed from the constant menace of conflicts, the condition of stability indispensable to the development of their own economic exchanges.

The policy of European union to which the search for a first bond of solidarity between European Governments ought to tend, implies in fact, a conception absolutely contrary to that which may have determined formerly, in Europe, the formation of customs unions tending to abolish internal customs houses in order to erect on the boundaries of the community a more rigorous barrier, that is to say, to constitute in fact an instrument of struggle against States situated outside of those unions.

Such a conception would be incompatible with the principles of the League of Nations, which is deeply attached to the idea of universality which remains its object and its end even when it pursues or favors partial realizations.

* * * * *

It is important, finally, to place the proposed inquiry under the general conception that in no case and in no degree can the institution of the federal bond sought for between European Governments affect in any manner the sovereign rights of the States, members of such a *de facto* association.

It is on the basis of absolute sovereignty and of entire political independence that the understanding between European Nations ought to be effected. Furthermore, it would be impossible to imagine the least thought of political domination in an organization deliberately placed under the control (contrôle) of the League of Nations, the two fundamental principles of which are precisely, the sovereignty of States and the equality of rights. And with the rights of sovereignty, is it not the very genius of every nation which can find in its individual cooperation in the collective work the means of affirming itself still more consciously under a régime of federal union fully compatible with the respect of the traditions and characteristics special to each people?

APPENDIX IV

A

EXTRACTS FROM THE COMMUNIST MANIFESTO *

BOURGEOIS AND PROLETARIANS †

The history of all hitherto existing society ‡ is the history of class struggles.

Freeman and slave, patrician and plebeian, lord and serf, guild-master § and journeyman, in a word, oppressor and oppressed, stood in constant opposition to one another, carried on an uninterrupted, now hidden, now open fight, a fight that each time ended, either in a revolutionary re-constitution of society at large, or in the common ruin of the contending classes.

In the earlier epochs of history, we find almost everywhere a complicated arrangement of society into various orders, a manifold graduation of social rank. In ancient Rome we have patricians, knights, plebeians, slaves; in the middle ages, feudal lords, vassals, guild-masters, journeymen, apprentices, serfs; in almost all of these classes, again, subordinate gradations.

The modern bourgeois society that has sprouted from the ruins of feudal society, has not done away with class antagonisms. It has but estab-

* The following excerpts are taken from the translation of Mr. Samuel Moore, edited and annotated by Frederick Engels, and published by Chas. H. Kerr & Company, Chicago.

† By "bourgeoisie" is meant the class of modern capitalists, owners of the means of social production and employers of wage-labor. By "proletariat," the class of modern wage-laborers who, having no means of production of their own, are reduced to selling their labor-power in order to live.

‡ That is, all written history. In 1847, the pre-history of society, the social organization existing previous to recorded history, was all but unknown. Since then, Haxthausen discovered common ownership of land in Russia, Maurer proved it to be the social foundation from which all Teutonic races started in history, and by and by village communities were found to be, or to have been, the primitive form of society everywhere from India to Ireland. The inner organization of this primitive Communistic society was laid bare, in its typical form, by Morgan's crowning discovery of the true nature of the gens and its relation to the tribe. With the dissolution of these primeval communities society begins to be differentiated into separate and finally antagonistic classes. I have attempted to retrace this process of dissolution in "The Origin of the Family, Private Property and the State" (Chicago, Charles H. Kerr & Co.).

§ Guild-master, that is a full member of a guild, a master within, not a head of, a guild.

lished new classes, new conditions of oppression, new forms of struggle in place of the old ones.

Our epoch, the epoch of the bourgeoisie, possesses, however, this distinctive feature; it has simplified the class antagonisms. Society as a whole is more and more splitting up into two great hostile camps, into two great classes directly facing each other: Bourgeoisie and Proletariat.

From the serfs of the middle ages sprang the chartered burghers of the earliest towns. From these burgesses the first elements of the bourgeoisie were developed.

The discovery of America, the rounding of the Cape, opened up fresh ground for the rising bourgeoisie. The East-Indian and Chinese markets, the colonization of America, trade with the colonies, the increase in the means of exchange and in commodities generally, gave to commerce, to navigation, to industry, an impulse never before known, and thereby, to the revolutionary element in the tottering feudal society, a rapid development.

The feudal system of industry, under which industrial production was monopolized by close guilds, now no longer sufficed for the growing wants of the new markets. The manufacturing system took its place. The guild-masters were pushed on one side by the manufacturing middle-class; division of labor between the different corporate guilds vanished in the face of division of labor in each single work-shop.

Meantime the markets kept ever growing, the demand, ever rising. Even manufacture no longer sufficed. Thereupon, steam and machinery revolutionized industrial production. The place of manufacture was taken by the giant, Modern Industry, the place of the industrial middle-class, by industrial millionaires, the leaders of whole industrial armies, the modern bourgeois.

Modern industry has established the world-market, for which the discovery of America paved the way. This market has given an immense development to commerce, to navigation, to communication by land. This development has, in its turn, reacted on the extension of industry; and in proportion as industry, commerce, navigation, railways extended, in the same proportion the bourgeoisie developed, increased its capital, and pushed into the background every class handed down from the Middle Ages.

We see, therefore, how the modern bourgeoisie is itself the product of a long course of development, of a series of revolutions in the modes of production and of exchange.

Each step in the development of the bourgeoisie was accompanied by a corresponding political advance of that class. An oppressed class under the sway of the feudal nobility, an armed and self-governing association in the mediaeval commune,* here independent urban republic (as in Italy and

* "Commune" was the name taken, in France, by the nascent towns even before

Germany), there taxable "third estate" of the monarchy (as in France), afterwards, in the period of manufacture proper, serving either the semi-feudal or the absolute monarchy as a counterpoise against the nobility, and, in fact, corner stone of the great monarchies in general, the bourgeoisie has at last, since the establishment of Modern Industry and of the world-market, conquered for itself, in the modern representative State, exclusive political sway. The executive of the modern State is but a committee for managing the common affairs of the whole bourgeoisie.

The bourgeoisie, historically, has played a most revolutionary part.

The bourgeoisie, wherever it has got the upper hand, has put an end to all feudal, patriarchal, idyllic relations. It has pitilessly torn asunder the motely feudal ties that bound man to his "natural superiors," and has left remaining no other nexus between man and man than naked self-interest, than callous "cash payment." It has drowned the most heavenly ecstasies of religious fervor, of chivalrous enthusiasm, of philistine sentimentalism, in the icy water of egotistical calculation. It has resolved personal worth into exchange value, and in place of the numberless indefeasible chartered freedoms, has set up that single, unconscionable freedom—Free Trade. In one word, for exploitation, veiled by religious and political illusions, it has substituted naked, shameless, direct, brutal exploitation.

The bourgeoisie has stripped of its halo every occupation hitherto honored and looked up to with reverent awe. It has converted the physician, the lawyer, the priest, the poet, the man of science, into its paid wage-laborers.

The bourgeoisie has torn away from the family its sentimental veil, and has reduced the family relation to a mere money relation.

The bourgeoisie has disclosed how it came to pass that the brutal display of vigor in the Middle Ages, which Reactionists so much admire, found its fitting complement in the most slothful indolence. It has been the first to show what man's activity can bring about. It has accomplished wonders far surpassing Egyptian pyramids, Roman aqueducts, and Gothic cathedrals; it has conducted expeditions that put in the shade all former Exoduses of nations and crusades.

The bourgeoisie cannot exist without constantly revolutionizing the instruments of production, and thereby the relations of production, and with them the whole relations of society. Conservation of the old modes of production in unaltered form, was, on the contrary, the first condition of existence for all earlier industrial classes. Constant revolutionizing of pro-

they had conquered from their feudal lords and masters, local self-government and political rights as "the Third Estate." Generally speaking, for the economic development of the bourgeoisie, England is here taken as the typical country, for its political development, France.

duction, uninterrupted disturbance of all social conditions, everlasting uncertainty and agitation distinguish the bourgeois epoch from all earlier ones. All fixed, fast-frozen relations, with their train of ancient and venerable prejudices and opinions, are swept away, all new-formed ones become antiquated before they can ossify. All that is solid melts into air, all that is holy is profaned, and man is at last compelled to face with sober senses, his real conditions of life, and his relations with his kind.

The need of a constantly expanding market for its products chases the bourgeoisie over the whole surface of the globe. It must nestle everywhere, settle everywhere, establish connections everywhere.

The bourgeoisie has through its exploitation of the world-market given a cosmopolitan character to production and consumption in every country. To the great chagrin of Reactionists, it has drawn from under the feet of industry the national ground on which it stood. All old-established national industries have been destroyed or are daily being destroyed. They are dislodged by new industries, whose introduction becomes a life and death question for all civilized nations, by industries that no longer work up indigenous raw material, but raw material drawn from the remotest zones; industries whose products are consumed, not only at home, but in every quarter of the globe. In place of the old wants, satisfied by the productions of the country, we find new wants, requiring for their satisfaction the products of distant lands and climes. In place of the old local and national seclusion and self-sufficiency, we have intercourse in every direction, universal interdependence of nations. And as in material, so also in intellectual production. The intellectual creations of individual nations become common property. National one-sidedness and narrow-mindedness become more and more impossible, and from the numerous national and local literatures there arises a world-literature.

The bourgeoisie, by the rapid improvement of all instruments of production, by the immensely facilitated means of communication, draws all, even the most barbarian, nations into civilization. The cheap prices of its commodities are the heavy artillery with which it batters down all Chinese walls, with which it forces the barbarians' intensely obstinate hatred of foreigners to capitulate. It compels all nations, on pain of extinction, to adopt the bourgeois mode of production; it compels them to introduce what it calls civilization into their midst, i.e., to become bourgeois themselves. In a word, it creates a world after its own image.

The bourgeoisie has subjected the country to the rule of the towns. It has created enormous cities, has greatly increased the urban population as compared with the rural, and has thus rescued a considerable part of the population from the idiocy of rural life. Just as it has made the country dependent on the towns, so it has made barbarian and semi-barbarian countries dependent on the civilized ones, nations of peasants on nations of bourgeois, the East on the West.

The bourgeoisie keeps more and more doing away with the scattered state of the population, of the means of production, and of property. It has agglomerated population, centralized means of production, and has concentrated property in a few hands. The necessary consequence of this was political centralization. Independent, or but loosely connected provinces, with separate interests, laws, governments and systems of taxation, became lumped together in one nation, with one government, one code of laws, one national class-interest, one frontier and one customs-tariff.

The bourgeoisie, during its rule of scarce one hundred years, has created more massive and more colossal productive forces than have all preceding generations together. Subjection of Nature's forces to man, machinery, application of chemistry to industry and agriculture, steam-navigation, railways, electric telegraphs, clearing of whole continents for cultivation, canalization of rivers, whole populations conjured out of the ground—what earlier century had even a presentiment that such productive forces slumbered in the lap of social labor?

We see then: the means of production and of exchange on whose foundation the bourgeoisie built itself up, were generated in feudal society. At a certain stage in the development of these means of production and of exchange, the conditions under which feudal society produced and exchanged, the feudal organization of agriculture and manufacturing industry, in one word, the feudal relations of property became no longer compatible with the already developed productive forces; they became so many fetters. They had to burst asunder; they were burst asunder.

Into their places stepped free competition, accompanied by a social and political constitution adapted to it, and by the economic and political sway of the bourgeois class.

A similar movement is going on before our own eyes. Modern bourgeois society with its relations of production, of exchange and of property, a society that has conjured up such gigantic means of production and of exchange, is like the sorcerer, who is no longer able to control the powers of the nether world whom he has called up by his spells. For many a decade past the history of industry and commerce is but the history of the revolt of modern productive forces against modern conditions of production, against the property relations that are the conditions for existence of the bourgeoisie and of its rule. It is enough to mention the commercial crises that by their periodical return put on its trial, each time more threateningly, the existence of the entire bourgeois society. In these crises a great part not only of the existing products, but also of the previously created productive forces, are periodically destroyed. In these crises there breaks out an epidemic that, in all earlier epochs, would have seemed an absurdity—the epidemic of over-production. Society suddenly finds itself put back into a state of momentary barbarism; it appears as if a famine, a universal war of devastation had cut off the supply of every means of subsistence; industry and commerce seem to be destroyed; and why? Because there is too much civilization, too much means of subsistence, too much industry, too much commerce. The productive forces at the disposal of society no longer tend to further the development of the conditions of bourgeois property; on the contrary, they have become too powerful for these conditions, by which they are fettered, and so soon as they overcome these fetters, they bring disorder into the whole of bourgeois society, endanger the existence of bourgeois property. The conditions of bourgeois society are too narrow to comprise the wealth created by them. And how does the bourgeoisie get over these crises? On the one hand by enforced destruction of a mass of productive forces; on the other, by the conquest of new markets, and by the more thorough exploitation of the old ones. That is to say, by paving the way for more extensive and more destructive crises, and by diminishing the means whereby crises are prevented.

The weapons with which the bourgeoisie felled feudalism to the ground are now turned against the bourgeoisie itself.

But not only has the bourgeoisie forged the weapons that bring death to itself; it has also called into existence the men who are to wield those weapons—the modern working-class—the proletarians.

In proportion as the bourgeoisie, i.e., capital, is developed, in the same proportion is the proletariat, the modern working-class, developed, a class of laborers, who live only so long as they find work, and who find work only so long as their labor increases capital. These laborers, who must sell themselves piecemeal, are a commodity, like every other article of commerce, and all consequently exposed to all the vicissitudes of competition, to all the fluctuations of the market.

* * * * *

The proletariat goes through various stages of development. With its birth begins its struggle with the bourgeoisie. At first the contest is carried on by individual laborers, then by the workpeople of a factory, then by the operatives of one trade, in one locality, against the individual bourgeois who directly exploits them. They direct their attacks not against the bourgeois conditions of production, but against the instruments of production themselves; they destroy imported wares that compete with their labor, they smash to pieces machinery, they set factories ablaze, they seek to restore by force the vanished status of the workman of the Middle Ages.

At this stage the laborers still form an incoherent mass scattered over the whole country, and broken up by their mutual competition. If anywhere they unite to form more compact bodies, this is not yet the consequence of their own active union, but of the union of the bourgeoisie, which class, in order to attain its own political ends, is compelled to set the whole proletariat in motion, and is moreover, yet for a time, able to do so. At this stage, therefore, the proletarians do not fight their enemies, but the enemies of their enemies, the remnants of absolute monarchy, the landowners, the non-industrial bourgeois, the petty bourgeoisie. Thus the whole historical movement is concentrated in the hands of the bourgeoisie; every victory so obtained is a victory for the bourgeoisie.

But with the development of industry the proletariat not only increases in number, it becomes concentrated in greater masses, its strength grows, and it feels that strength more. The various interests and conditions of life within the ranks of the proletariat are more and more equalized, in proportion as machinery obliterates all distinctions of labor, and nearly everywhere reduces wages to the same low level. The growing competition among the bourgeois, and the resulting commercial crises, make the wages of the workers ever more fluctuating. The unceasing improvement of machinery, ever more rapidly developing, makes their livelihood more and more precarious; the collisions between individual workmen and individual bourgeois take more and more the character of collisions between two classes. Thereupon the workers begin to form combinations (Trades' Unions) against the bourgeois; they club together in order to keep up the rate of wages; they found permanent associations in order to make provision beforehand for these occasional revolts. Here and there the contest breaks out into riots.

Now and then the workers are victorious, but only for a time. The real fruit of their battles lies, not in the immediate result, but in the ever expanding union of the workers. This union is helped on by the improved means of communication that are created by modern industry, and that place the workers of different localities in contact with one another. It was just this contact that was needed to centralize the numerous local struggles, all of the same character, into one national struggle between classes. But every class struggle is a political struggle. And that union, to attain which the burghers of the Middle Ages, with their miserable highways, required centuries, the modern proletarians, thanks to railways, achieve in a few years.

This organization of the proletarians into a class, and consequently into a political party, is continually being upset again by the competition between the workers themselves. But it ever rises up again, stronger, firmer, mightier. It compels legislative recognition of particular interests of the workers, by taking advantage of the divisions among the bourgeoisie itself. Thus the ten-hour bill in England was carried.

Altogether collisions between the classes of the old society further, in many ways, the course of development of the proletariat. The bourgeoisie finds itself involved in a constant battle. At first with the aristocracy; later on, with those portions of the bourgeoisie itself, whose interests have become antagonistic to the progress of industry; at all times, with the bourgeoisie of foreign countries. In all these battles it sees itself compelled to appeal to the proletariat, to ask for its help, and thus, to drag it into the political arena. The bourgeoisie itself, therefore, supplies the proletariat with its own elements of political and general education, in other words, it furnishes the proletariat with weapons for fighting the bourgeoisie.

Further, as we have already seen, entire sections of the ruling classes are, by the advance of industry, precipitated into the proletariat, or are at least threatened in their conditions of existence. These also supply the proletariat with fresh elements of enlightenment and progress.

Finally, in times when the class-struggle nears the decisive hour, the process of dissolution going on within the ruling class, in fact, within the whole range of old society, assumes such a violent, glaring character, that a small section of the ruling class cuts itself adrift, and joins the revolutionary class, the class that holds the future in its hands. Just as, therefore, at an earlier period, a section of the nobility went over to the bourgeoisie, so now a portion of the bourgeoisie goes over to the proletariat, and in particular, a portion of the bourgeois ideologists, who have raised themselves to the level of comprehending theoretically the historical movements as a whole.

Of all the classes that stand face to face with the bourgeoisie today, the proletariat alone is a really revolutionary class. The other classes decay and finally disappear in the face of modern industry; the proletariat is its special and essential product.

* * * * *

The Communists are further reproached with desiring to abolish countries and nationalities.

The working men have no country. We cannot take from them what they have not got. Since the proletariat must first of all acquire political supremacy, must rise to be the leading class of the nation, must constitute itself the nation, it is, so far, itself national, though not in the bourgeois sense of the word.

National differences, and antagonisms between peoples, are daily more and more vanishing, owing to the development of the bourgeoisie, to freedom of commerce, to the world-market, to uniformity in the mode of production and in the conditions of life corresponding thereto.

The supremacy of the proletariat will cause them to vanish still faster. United action, of the leading civilized countries at least, is one of the first conditions for the emancipation of the proletariat.

In proportion as the exploitation of one individual by another is put an end to, the exploitation of one nation by another will also be put an end to. In proportion as the antagonism between classes within the nation vanishes, the hostility of one nation to another will come to an end.

* * * * *

APPENDIX IV

B

EXTRACT FROM *REPORT ON THE WORK OF THE CENTRAL COMMITTEE OF THE COMMUNIST PARTY OF THE SOVIET UNION*

By Joseph Stalin, Secretary General of the Communist Party, to the Seventeenth All-Union Communist Party Congress held in Moscow, January 26 to February 10, 1934 *

. . .

Capitalism has succeeded in somewhat easing the position of industry at the expense of the workers—increasing their exploitation by increasing the intensity of their labor; at the expense of the farmers—by pursuing a policy of paying the lowest prices for the product of their labor, for foodstuffs and partly for raw materials; at the expense of the peasants in the colonies and in the economically weak countries—by still further forcing down the prices of the products of their labor, principally of raw material, and also of foodstuffs.

Does this mean that we are witnessing a transition from a crisis to an ordinary depression which brings in its train a new boom and flourishing industry? No, it does not mean that. At all events at the present time there are no data, direct or indirect, that indicate the approach of an industrial boom in capitalist countries. More than that, judging by all things, there cannot be such data, at least in the near future. There cannot be, because all the unfavorable conditions which prevent industry in the capitalist countries from rising to any serious extent still continue to operate. I have in mind the continuing general crisis of capitalism in the midst of which the economic crisis is proceeding, the chronic working of the enterprises under capacity, the chronic mass unemployment, the interweaving of the industrial crisis with the agricultural crisis, the absence of tendencies towards any serious renewal of basic capital which usually heralds the approach of a boom, etc., etc.

Apparently, what we are witnessing is the transition from the lowest point of decline of industry, from the lowest depth of the industrial crisis to a depression, not an ordinary depression, but to a depression of a special

* Taken from *International Conciliation* (December, 1934), No. 305, pp. 383-399, published by the Carnegie Endowment for International Peace.

kind which does not lead to a new boom and flourishing industry, but which, on the other hand, does not force industry back to the lowest point of decline.

2. THE GROWING ACUTENESS OF THE POLITICAL SITUATION IN CAPITALIST COUNTRIES

A result of the protracted economic crisis was the hitherto unprecedented acuteness of the political situation in capitalist countries, both within the respective countries as well as between them.

The intensified struggle for foreign markets, the abolition of the last vestiges of free trade, prohibitive tariffs, trade war, currency war, dumping and many other analogous measures which demonstrate extreme nationalism in economic policy, have caused the relations between the countries to become extremely acute, have created the soil for military conflicts and have brought war to the front as a means for a new redistribution of the world and spheres of influence in favor of the strongest States.

Japan's war against China, the occupation of Manchuria, Japan's withdrawal from the League of Nations and her advance in North China have served to make the situation still more acute. The intensified struggle for the Pacific and the growth of the naval armaments of Japan, the United States, England, and France, represent the results of this increased acuteness.

Germany's withdrawal from the League of Nations and the spectre of *revanche* have given a fresh impetus to the acuteness of the situation and to the growth of armaments in Europe.

It is not surprising that bourgeois pacifism is now dragging out a miserable existence, and that idle talk about disarmament is being replaced by "business-like" talk about arming and re-arming.

Again as in 1914 the parties of bellicose imperialism, the parties of war and *revanche* are coming into the foreground.

Quite clearly things are moving towards a new war.

In view of the operation of these same factors the internal situation of the capitalist countries is becoming still more acute. Four years of industrial crisis have exhausted the working class and reduced it to despair. Four years of agricultural crisis have finally ruined the poorer strata of the peasantry, not only in the principal capitalist countries but also—and particularly—in the dependent and colonial countries. It is a fact that notwithstanding all the attempts to manipulate statistics in order to show a diminution in the number of unemployed, the number of unemployed according to the official returns of bourgeois institutions reaches 3,000,000 in England, 5,000,000 in Germany and 10,000,000 in the United States, not to speak of other countries in Europe. Add to this the number of workers employed part-time, which exceeds ten million, add the millions of ruined peasants—and you will get an approximate picture of the poverty and despair of the toiling masses. The masses of the people have not yet reached the stage when they are ready to storm the citadel of capitalism, but the idea of storming it is maturing in the minds of the masses—there can hardly be any doubt about that. This is eloquently testified to by such facts as, say, the Spanish revolution which overthrew the fascist régime, and the expansion of the Soviet regions in China which the united counter-revolution of the Chinese and foreign bourgeoisie is unable to stop.

This, as a matter of fact, explains the fact that the ruling classes in the capitalist countries are zealously destroying, or nullifying, the last vestiges of parliamentarism and bourgeois democracy which might be used by the working class in its struggle against the oppressors, the fact that they are driving the Communist Parties underground and resorting to open terrorist methods in order to maintain their dictatorship.

Chauvinism and preparation for war as the main elements of foreign policy, bridling the working class and terror in the sphere of home policy as a necessary means for strengthening the rear of future war fronts—this is what is particularly engaging the minds of contemporary imperialist politicians.

It is not surprising that fascism has now become the most fashionable commodity among bellicose bourgeois politicians. I do not mean fascism in general, I mean, primarily, fascism of the German type, which is incorrectly called National-Socialism, for the most searching examination will fail to reveal even an atom of socialism in it.

In this connection the victory of fascism in Germany must be regarded not only as a symptom of the weakness of the working class and as a result of the betrayal of the working class by Social-Democracy, which paved the way for fascism; it must also be regarded as a symptom of the weakness of the bourgeoisie, as a symptom of the fact that the bourgeoisie is already unable to rule by the old methods of parliamentarism and bourgeois democracy, and, as a consequence, is compelled in its home policy to resort to terroristic methods of administration—it must be taken as a symptom of the fact that it is no longer able to find a way out of the present situation on the basis of a peaceful foreign policy, as a consequence of which it is compelled to resort to a policy of war.

That is the position.

Thus, you see that things are moving towards a new imperialist war as a way out of the present situation.

Of course there are no grounds for assuming that the war can provide a real way out. On the contrary, it must confuse the situation still more. More than that, it will certainly unleash revolution and put in question the very existence of capitalism in a number of countries, as was the case in the course of the first imperialist war. And if, notwithstanding the experience of the first imperialist war, the bourgeois politicians clutch at war as a drowning man clutches at a straw, it shows that they have become utterly confused, have reached an impassé, and are ready to rush headlong over the precipice.

It will not be amiss, therefore, briefly to examine the plans for the organization of war which are now being hatched in the circles of bourgeois politicians.

Some think that war must be organized against one of the Great Powers. They think of imposing a crushing defeat upon it and of improving their own affairs at its expense. Let us assume that they organize such a war. What can come of it? As is well known, during the first imperialist war it was intended to destroy one of the Great Powers, viz., Germany, and to profit at her expense. And what came of it? They did not destroy Germany, but in Germany they sowed such a hatred for the victors and created such a rich soil for *revanche* that they have not been able to clear up the revolting mess they have made even to this day, and will not, perhaps, be able to do so for some time. But instead, they got the smash-up of capitalism in Russia, the victory of the proletarian revolution in Russia and—of course—the Soviet Union. What guarantee is there that the second imperialist war will produce "better" results for them than the first? Would it not be more correct to assume that the opposite will be the case?

Others think that war should be organized against a country that is militarily weak, but which represents an extensive market—for example, against China, which moreover, they have discovered, cannot be described as a State in the strict sense of the word, but which merely represents "unorganized territory" which needs to be seized by strong States. Apparently, they want to divide it up completely and improve their affairs at its expense. Let us assume that they organize such a war. What will come of it? It is well known that in the beginning of the nineteenth century the same opinion was held in regard to Italy and Germany as is now held in regard to China, viz., they were regarded as "unorganized territories" and not States, and they were enslaved. But what came of it? As is well known, it resulted in wars of independence waged by Germany and Italy and their unification into independent States. It resulted in increased hatred in the hearts of the peoples of these countries for the oppressors, the results of which have not been liquidated to this day and will not, perhaps, be liquidated for some time. The question arises: what guarantee is there that the same thing will not happen as a result of an imperialist war against China?

Still others think that war should be organized by a "superior race," say, the German "race" against an "inferior race," primarily against the Slavs, that only such a war can provide a way out of the situation because it is the mission of the "superior race" to fertilize the "inferior race" and rule over it. Let us assume that this queer theory, which is as far removed from science as heaven is from earth, let us assume that this queer theory is put into practice. What will come of it? It is well known that ancient Rome regarded the ancestors of the present-day Germans and French in the same way as the representatives of the "superior race" now regard the Slavonic tribes. It is well known that ancient Rome treated them as an "inferior race," as "barbarians" whose destiny it was to be eternally subordinated to the "superior race," to "great Rome," and, between ourselves let it be said, ancient Rome had some grounds for this which cannot be said about the representatives of the present "superior race." But what came of it? The result was that the non-Romans, i.e., all the "Barbarians" united against the common enemy, hurled themselves against Rome and overthrew it. The question arises: what guarantee is there that the claims of the representatives of the present "superior race" will not lead to the same deplorable results? What guarantee is there that the fascist-literary politicians in Berlin will be more fortunate than the ancient and experienced conquerors in Rome? Would it not be more correct to assume that the opposite will be the case?

Still others, again, think that war should be organized against the U.S.S.R. Their plan is to smash the U.S.S.R., divide up its territory and profit at its expense. It would be a mistake to believe that it is only certain military circles in Japan who think in this way. We know that similar plans are being hatched in the circles of political leaders of certain States of Europe. Let us assume that these gentlemen pass from words to deeds. What can come of it? There can hardly be any doubt that such a war would be a very dangerous war for the bourgeoisie. It would be a very dangerous war, not only because the peoples of the U.S.S.R. would fight to the very death to preserve the gains of the revolution; it would be a very dangerous war for the bourgeoisie also because such a war will be waged not only at the fronts but also in the rear of the enemy. The bourgeoisie need have no doubt that the numerous friends of the working class of the U.S.S.R. in Europe and in Asia will be sure to strike a blow in the rear at their oppressors who commenced a criminal war against the fatherland of the working class of all countries. And let not Messieurs the bourgeoisie blame us if on the morrow of the outbreak of such a war they will miss certain of the governments that are near and dear to them and who are today happily ruling "by the grace of God." One such war against the U.S.S.R. has been waged, already, if you remember, fifteen years ago. As is well known, the universally esteemed Churchill clothed this war in a poetic formula—"the invasion of fourteen States." You remember of course that this war rallied the toilers of our country in a single camp of heroic warriors who defended their workers' and peasants' homeland against the foreign foe tooth and nail. You know how it ended. It ended with the invaders being driven from our country and the establishment of revolutionary Councils of Action in Europe. It can hardly be doubted that a second war against the U.S.S.R. will lead to the complete defeat of the aggressors, to revolution in a number of countries in Europe and in Asia, and to the overthrow of the bourgeois-landlord governments in these countries.

Such are the war plans of the perplexed bourgeois politicians.

As you see they are not distinguished either for their brilliance or valor.

But if the bourgeoisie chooses the path of war, then the working class in the capitalist countries who have been reduced to despair by four years of crisis and unemployment takes the path of revolution. That means that a revolutionary crisis is maturing and will continue to mature. And the more the bourgeoisie becomes entangled in its war combinations, the more frequently it resorts to terroristic methods in the struggle against the working class and the toiling peasantry, the sooner will the revolutionary crisis mature.

Some comrades think that as soon as a revolutionary crisis occurs the bourgeoisie must drop into a hopeless position, that its end is predetermined, that the victory of the revolution is assured, and that all they have to do is to wait for the bourgeoisie to fall, and to draw up victorious resolutions. This is a profound mistake. The victory of revolution never comes by itself. It has to be prepared for and won. And only a strong proletarian revolutionary party can prepare for and win victory. Moments occur when the situation is revolutionary, when the rule of the bourgeoisie is shaken to its very foundations, and yet the victory of the revolution does not come, because there is no revolutionary party of the proletariat sufficiently strong and authoritative to lead the masses and take power. It would be unwise to believe that such "cases" cannot occur.

In this connection, it will not be amiss to recall Lenin's prophetic words on a revolutionary crisis, uttered at the Second Congress of the Communist International:

We have now come to the question of the revolutionary crisis as the basis of our revolutionary action. And here we must first of all note two widespread errors. On the one hand, the bourgeois economists depict this crisis simply as "unrest," to use the elegant expression of the English. On the other hand, revolutionaries sometimes try to prove that there is absolutely no way out of the crisis. That is a mistake. There is no such thing as absolutely hopeless positions. The bourgeoisie behaves like an arrogant brigand who has lost his head, it commits blunder after blunder, thus making the position more acute and hastening its own doom. All this is true. But it cannot be "proved" that there are absolutely no possibilities whatever for it to lull a certain minority of the exploited with certain concessions, for it to suppress a certain movement or uprising of a certain section of the oppressed and exploited. To try to "prove" beforehand that a position is "absolutely" hopeless would be sheer pedantry or playing with concepts and catchwords. Practice alone can serve as real "proof" in this and similar questions. The bourgeois system all over the world is experiencing a great revolutionary crisis. And the revolutionary parties must now "prove" by their practice that they are sufficiently intelligent and organized, have contacts with the exploited masses, are sufficiently determined and skilful to utilize this crisis for a successful and victorious revolution. (Lenin, *Collected Works,* Vol. XXV, 1920.)

3. THE RELATION BETWEEN THE U.S.S.R. AND THE CAPITALIST STATES

It is quite easy to understand how difficult it has been for the U.S.S.R. to pursue its peace policy in this atmosphere poisoned with the miasma of war combinations.

In the midst of this eve-of-the-war hullabaloo which is going on in a number of countries, the U.S.S.R. during these years has stood firmly and indomitably by its position of peace, fighting against the menace of war, fighting to preserve peace, going out to meet those countries which in one way or another stand for the preservation of peace, exposing and tearing the masks from those who are preparing for and provoking war.

What did the U.S.S.R. rely on in this difficult and complex struggle for peace?

(a) On its growing economic and political might.

(b) On the moral support of millions of the working class in every country who are vitally interested in the preservation of peace.

(c) On the common sense of those countries which for this or that motive are not interested in disturbing the peace, and which want to develop commercial relations with such a punctual client as the U.S.S.R.

(d) Finally—on our glorious army, which is ready to defend our country against attack from without.

On this basis arose our campaign for the conclusion of pacts of non-aggression and of pacts defining the aggressor with our neighboring States.

You know that this campaign has been successful. As is known, pacts of non-aggression have been concluded not only with the majority of our neighbors in the West and in the South, including Finland and Poland, but also with such countries as France and Italy; and pacts defining the aggressor have been concluded with these same neighboring States, including the Little Entente.

On this basis also the friendship between the U.S.S.R. and Turkey was consolidated, relations between the U.S.S.R. and Italy have improved and have become indisputably satisfactory, relations with France, Poland, and other Baltic States have improved, relations have been restored with the U.S.A., China, etc.

Of the facts reflecting the successes of the peace policy of the U.S.S.R. two facts of indisputably serious significance should be noted and singled out.

(1) I have in mind, first, the change for the better that has taken place recently in the relations between the U.S.S.R. and Poland, between the U.S.S.R. and France. As is well known, our relations with Poland in the past were not at all good. Representatives of our State were assassinated in Poland. Poland regarded herself as the barrier of the Western States against the U.S.S.R. All and sundry imperialists looked upon Poland as the vanguard in the event of a military attack upon the U.S.S.R. The relations between the U.S.S.R. and France were not much better. It is sufficient to recall the facts in the history of the trial of the Ramzin wreckers' group in Moscow in order to restore in one's mind the picture of the relations between the U.S.S.R. and France. But now these undesirable relations are gradually beginning to disappear. They are being replaced by other relations, which cannot be otherwise described than relations of rapprochement. It is not only that we have concluded pacts of non-aggression with these countries, although these pacts in themselves are of very serious importance. The most important thing first of all is that the atmosphere charged with mutual distrust is beginning to be dissipated. This does not mean, of course, that the incipient process of rapprochement can be regarded as sufficiently stable and as guaranteeing ultimate success. Surprises and zigzags in policy, for example in Poland, where anti-Soviet moods are still strong, cannot be regarded as being excluded by a long way. But a change for the better in our relations irrespective of its results in the future, is a fact worthy of being noted and put in the forefront as a factor in the advancement of the cause of peace.

What is the cause of this change? What stimulates it?

First of all, the growth of the strength and might of the U.S.S.R. In our times it is not the custom to give any consideration to the weak—consideration is only given to the strong. Then there have been certain changes in the policy of Germany which reflect the growth of *revanche*-ist and imperialist moods in Germany.

In this connection certain German politicians say that now the U.S.S.R. has taken an orientation towards France and Poland, that from being an opponent of the Versailles Treaty it has become a supporter of it and that this change is to be explained by the establishment of a fascist régime in Germany. This is not true. Of course, we are far from being enthusiastic about the fascist régime in Germany. But fascism is not the issue here, if only for the reason that fascism, for example in Italy, did not prevent the U.S.S.R. establishing very good relations with that country. Nor are the alleged changes in our attitude towards the Versailles Treaty the point of issue. It is not for us, who have experienced the shame of the Brest-Litovsk Peace, to sing the praises of the Versailles Treaty. We merely do not agree to the world being flung into the throes of a new war for sake of this treaty. The same thing must be said in regard to the alleged orientation taken by the U.S.S.R. We never had any orientation towards Germany nor have we any orientation towards Poland and France. Our orientation in the past and our orientation at the present time is towards the U.S.S.R. and towards the U.S.S.R. alone. And if the interests of the U.S.S.R. demand rapprochement with this or that country which is not interested in disturbing peace, we shall take this step without hesitation.

No, that is not the point. The point is that the policy of Germany has changed. The point is that even before the present German politicians came into power, and particularly after they came into power, a fight between two political lines broke out in Germany, between the old policy which found expression in the well-known treaties between the U.S.S.R. and Germany and the "new" policy which in the main recalls the policy of the ex-Kaiser of Germany who at one time occupied the Ukraine, undertook a march against Leningrad and transformed the Baltic countries into a *place d'armes* for this march and this "new" policy is obviously gaining the upper hand over the old policy. The fact that the supporters of the "new" policy are gaining supremacy in all things while the supporters of the old policy are in disgrace cannot be regarded as an accident. Nor can the well-known action of Hugenberg in London, nor the equally well-known declarations of Rosenberg, the director of the foreign policy of the ruling party in Germany, be regarded as accidents. That is the point, comrades.

(2) Secondly, I have in mind the restoration of normal relations between the U.S.S.R. and the United States. There cannot be any doubt that this act has very serious significance for the whole system of international relations. It is not only that it improves the chances of preserving peace,

that it improves the relations between the two countries, strengthens commercial intercourse between them and creates a base for mutual cooperation; it is a landmark between the old, when the United States in various countries was regarded as the bulwark for all sorts of anti-Soviet tendencies, and the new, when this bulwark was voluntarily removed, to the mutual advantage of both countries.

Such are the two main facts which reflect the successes of the Soviet peace policy.

It would be wrong, however, to think that every thing went smoothly in the period under review. No, not everything went smoothly by a long way.

Recall, say, the pressure that was brought to bear upon us by England, the embargo on our exports, the attempt to interfere in our internal affairs and to put out feelers to test our power of resistance. It is true that nothing came of this attempt and that later the embargo was removed, but the aftermath of these attacks is still felt in all things that affect the relations between England and the U.S.S.R., including the negotiations for a commercial treaty. And these attacks upon the U.S.S.R. must not be regarded as accidental. It is well known that one section of the English conservatives cannot live without such attacks. And precisely because they are not accidental we must bear in mind that attacks on the U.S.S.R. will be made in the future, that all sorts of menaces will be created, attempts to damage it will be made, etc.

Nor can we lose sight of the relations between the U.S.S.R. and Japan which stand in need of very considerable improvement. Japan's refusal to conclude a pact of non-aggression, of which Japan stands in need no less than the U.S.S.R., once again emphasizes the fact that all is not well in the sphere of our relations. The same thing must be said in regard to the rupture of negotiations concerning the Chinese-Eastern Railway due to no fault of the U.S.S.R., and also in regard to the outrageous deeds the Japanese agents are committing on the C.E.R., the illegal arrests of Soviet employees on the C.E.R., etc. This is quite apart from the fact that one section of the military men in Japan are openly advocating in the press the necessity for a war against the U.S.S.R. and the seizure of the Maritime Province with the avowed approval of another section of the military, while the government of Japan, instead of calling these instigators of war to order, is pretending that this is not a matter that concerns it. It is not difficult to understand that such circumstances cannot but create an atmosphere of uneasiness and uncertainty. Of course, we will continue persistently to pursue the policy of peace and strive for an improvement in our relations with Japan because we want to improve these relations. But it does not entirely depend upon us. That is why we must at the same time adopt all measures for the purpose of guarding our country against surprises and be prepared to defend it in the event of attack.

As you see, besides successes in our peace policy we also have a number of negative phenomena.

Such are the foreign relations of the U.S.S.R.

Our foreign policy is clear. It is a policy of preserving peace and strengthening commercial relations with all countries. The U.S.S.R. does not think of threatening anybody—let alone of attacking anybody. We stand for peace and champion the cause of peace. But we are not afraid of threats and are prepared to answer blow for blow against the instigators of war. Those who want peace and are striving for business intercourse with us will always receive our support. And those who try to attack our country—will receive a stunning rebuff to teach them not to poke their pig's snout into our Soviet garden again.

Such is our foreign policy.

The task is to continue to pursue this policy with all persistence and consistency.

. . .

INDEX

A

B

C

M

T

U

V

W

Z

1.25